Lecture Notes in Computer Science

Commenced Publication in 1973
Founding and Former Series Editors:
Gerhard Goos, Juris Hartmanis, and Jan van Leeuwen

Dimitra Giannakopoulou
Dominique Méry (Eds.)

FM 2012:
Formal Methods

18th International Symposium
Paris, France, August 27-31, 2012
Proceedings

 Springer

Volume Editors

Dimitra Giannakopoulou
NASA Ames Research Center
Mail Stop 269-2
Moffett Field, CA 94035, USA
E-mail: dimitra.giannakopoulou@nasa.gov

Dominique Méry
Université de Lorraine, LORIA
Campus Scientifique, BP 239
54506 Vandoeuvre-lès-Nancy, France
E-mail: dominique.mery@loria.fr

ISSN 0302-9743   e-ISSN 1611-3349
ISBN 978-3-642-32758-2   e-ISBN 978-3-642-32759-9
DOI 10.1007/978-3-642-32759-9
Springer Heidelberg Dordrecht London New York

Library of Congress Control Number: 2012944269

CR Subject Classification (1998): D.2.4-5, F.4, D.2, F.3, J.2, J.3, K.6, F.1.1, F.2.2

LNCS Sublibrary: SL 2 – Programming and Software Engineering

Typesetting: Camera-ready by author, data conversion by Scientific Publishing Services, Chennai, India

Printed on acid-free paper

Springer is part of Springer Science+Business Media (www.springer.com)

Preface

FM 2012 was the 18th in a series of symposia organized by Formal Methods Europe, an independent association whose aim is to stimulate the use of, and research on, formal methods for software development. The symposia have been notably successful in bringing together innovators and practitioners in precise mathematical methods for software and systems development, industrial users, as well as researchers. In August 2012, the *Conservatoire National des Arts et Métiers* (Le Cnam Paris) hosted FM 2012 in Paris (France).

The special theme of FM 2012 was "Interdisciplinary Formal Methods," with the goal of highlighting the development and application of formal methods in connection with a variety of disciplines including medicine, biology, human cognitive modeling, human automation interactions, and aeronautics. We were honored to have three invited speakers whose talks emphasized the special theme.

Martin Abadi, with his talk titled "Software Security – A Formal Perspective," discussed software security with an emphasis on low-level attacks and defenses and on their formal aspects. Asaf Degani gave a talk titled "Formal Methods in the Wild: Trains, Planes, and Automobiles." Through this talk, Dr. Degani drew upon his experience with aerospace and automotive applications to provide a perspective on how formal methods could improve the design of such applications. Finally, Alan Wassyng, in his talk titled "Who Are We, and What Are We Doing Here?," stressed the importance of viewing formal methods from a rigorous software engineering perspective, and discussed his experiences with the certification of software-intensive systems. All three talks raised the awareness of the community to the fact that formal methods live in the intersection of disciplines; research in this domain must also consider how to increase the industrial impact of formal methods.

FM 2012 welcomed submissions in the following areas, among others:

- Interdisciplinary formal methods: techniques, tools and experiences demonstrating formal methods in interdisciplinary frameworks, such as formal methods related to maintenance, human automation interaction, human in the loop, system engineering, medicine and biology
- Formal methods in practice: industrial applications of formal methods, experience with introducing formal methods in industry, tool usage reports, experiments with challenge problems
- Tools for formal methods: advances in automated verification and model-checking, integration of tools, environments for formal methods, experimental validation of tools
- Role of formal methods in software and systems engineering: development processes with formal methods, usage guidelines for formal methods, method integration
- Theoretical foundations: all aspects of theory related to specification, verification, refinement, and static and dynamic analysis

— Teaching formal methods: insight, evaluations and suggestions for courses
of action regarding the teaching of formal methods, including teaching experiences, educational resources, the integration of formal methods into the
curriculum, the definition of a formal methods body of knowledge, etc

We solicited two types of contributions: research papers and tool demon-
stration papers. We received submissions from 39 countries around the world:
162 abstracts followed by 132 full submissions. The selection process was rigorous. Each paper received at least four reviews. We obtained external reviews
for papers that lacked expertise within the Program Committee. The Program
Committee, after long and very careful discussions of the submitted papers, decided to accept only 28 full papers and seven tool papers, which corresponds to
an overall acceptance rate of approximately 26%. Some of the accepted papers
were additionally shepherded by expert members of the Program Committee to
ensure the quality of their final version. The accepted papers made a scientif-
ically strong and exciting program, which triggered interesting discussions and
exchange of ideas among the FM participants. The accepted papers cover several
aspects of formal methods, including verification, synthesis, runtime monitoring,
testing and controller synthesis, as well as novel applications of formal methods in interesting domains such as satellites, autonomous vehicles, and disease
dynamics.

We would like to thank all authors who submitted their work to FM 2012.
Without their excellent contributions we would not have managed to prepare a
strong program. We are grateful to the Program Committee members and external reviewers for their high-quality reviews and dedication. Finally, we wish to
thank the Steering Committee members for their excellent support. The logistics
of our job as Program Chairs were facilitated by the EasyChair system.

June 2012

Dimitra Giannakopoulou
Dominique Méry

Symposium Organization

We are grateful to Formal Methods Europe (FME) and the Conservatoire National des Arts et Métiers (Le Cnam Paris) for organizing FM 2012. Our special thanks to the faculty, students, and staff of Mefosyloma Research Group, who volunteered their time in the Organizing Committee.

General Chairs

Kamel Barkaoui	Cedric, CNAM, France
Béatrice Bérard	LIP6, UPMC, France

Program Chairs

Dimitra Giannakopoulou	NASA Ames, USA
Dominique Méry	Université de Lorraine, France

Workshop Chairs

Nihal Pekergin	LACL, University Paris-Est Créteil
Laure Petrucci	LIPN, University Paris-Nord
Tayssir Touili	LIAFA, University Paris Diderot - Paris 7

Tutorials Chairs

Serge Haddad	LSV, ENS Cachan
Fabrice Kordon	LIP6, University Pierre et Marie Curie

Industry Day Chairs

Karim Djouani	LISSI, University Paris-Est Créteil
Thierry Lecomte	ClearSy R&D, Aix en Provence
Bruno Monsuez	LEI, Ensta ParisTech
Isabelle Perseil	LTCI, Telecom ParisTech

Doctoral Chairs

Christine Choppy	LIPN, University Paris-Nord
David Delahaye	Cedric, CNAM
Kais Klai	LIPN, University Paris-Nord
Franck Pommereau	IBISC, University of Évry

Publicity Chairs

Hanna Klaudel   IBISC, University of Évry
Frédéric Lemoine   Computer Science Department, CNAM
Franck Pommereau   IBISC, University of Évry
Olivier Pons   Cedric, CNAM

Sponsors

We are thankful for the organizational support from FME (Formal Methods Europe) and CNAM (Conservatoire National des Arts et Métiers). We gratefully acknowledge sponsorships from the following orgnanizations: Digiteo, Ada-Core, SNCF, LEI, ENSTA ParisTech, Mefosyloma Research Group: CEDRIC (CNAM), LACL (UPEC Créteil), LIP6 (Université Pierre et Marie Curie), LIPN (Université Paris-Nord), LSV (ENS Cachan), IBISC (Univ. Evry), LTCI (Télécom ParisTech).

le cnam

Program Committee

Yamine Ait Ameur   IRIT/ENSEIHT, France
Keijiro Araki   Kyushu University, Japan
Jos Baeten   TUE, The Netherlands
Howard Barringer   The University of Manchester, UK
Saddek Bensalem   VERIMAG, France
Bruno Blanchet   INRIA, France
Ahmed Bouajjani   LIAFA, University of Paris 7 (Paris Diderot),
                           France
Patricia Bouyer   LSV, CNRS and ENS Cachan, France
Victor Braberman   Universidad de Buenos Aires, Argentina
Michael Butler   University of Southampton, UK
Andrew Butterfield   Trinity College Dublin, Ireland
Ana Cavalcanti   University of York, UK

Krishnendu Chatterjee   Institute of Science and Technology (IST),
                                 Austria
Marsha Chechik   University of Toronto, Canada
Yu-Fang Chen   Academia Sinica, Taiwan
Leonardo De Moura   Microsoft Research, USA
Dino Distefano   Queen Mary, University of London, UK
Matt Dwyer   University of Nebraska, USA
Bernd Finkbeiner   Saarland University, Germany
J.S. Fitzgerald   Newcastle University, UK
Dimitra Giannakopoulou   NASA Ames Research Center, USA
Stefania Gnesi   ISTI-CNR, Italy
Patrice Godefroid   Microsoft Research, USA
Ganesh Gopalakrishnan   University of Utah, USA
Kim Guldstrand Larsen   Aalborg University, Denmark
Klaus Havelund   Jet Propulsion Laboratory, California Institute
                                 of Technology, USA
Ian J. Hayes   University of Queensland, Australia
Matthew Hennessy   Trinity College Dublin, Ireland
Jane Hillston   University of Edinburgh, UK
Bart Jacobs   Institute for Computing and Information
                                 Sciences (ICIS), Radboud University
                                 Nijmegen, The Netherlands
Claude Jard   ENS Cachan Bretagne, France
Panagiotis Katsaros   Aristotle University of Thessaloniki, Greece
Sarfraz Khurshid   The University of Texas at Austin, USA
Daniel Kroening   Oxford University, UK
Marta Kwiatkowska   Oxford University, UK
Pascale Le Gall   Université d'Evry, France
Rustan Leino   Microsoft Research, USA
Michael Leuschel   University of Düsseldorf, Germany
Zhiming Liu   United Nations University - International
                                 Institute for Software Technology, Macau
Tom Maibaum   McMaster University, Canada
Rupak Majumdar   Max Planck Institute, Germany
Annabelle Mciver   Macquarie University, Australia
Dominique Méry   Université de Lorraine, LORIA, France
Cesar Munoz   National Aeronautics and Space
                                 Administration, USA
Fernando Orejas   UPC, Spain
Isabelle Perseil   INSERM, France
Andre Platzer   Carnegie Mellon University, USA
Shengchao Qin   Teesside University, UK
S. Ramesh   General Motors R&D, India
Jean-Francois Raskin   ULB, Belgium
Neha Rungta   NASA Ames Research Center, USA
Augusto Sampaio   Federal University of Pernambuco, Brazil

Bernhard Schaetz	TU München, Germany
Wolfram Schulte	Microsoft Research, USA
Kaisa Sere	Abo Akademi University, Finland
Bernhard Steffen	University of Dortmund, Germany
Kenji Taguchi	AIST, Japan
Francois Vernadat	LAAS-CNRS INSA, France
Willem Visser	Stellenbosch University, South Africa
Michael Whalen	University of Minnesota, USA

Additional Reviewers

Aananthakrishnan, Sriram
Aguirre, Nazareno
Aiguier, Marc
Akshay, S.
Albarghouthi, Aws
Alves, Vander
Andrews, Zoe
Axel, Legay
Ballarini, Paolo
Banach, Richard
Bartocci, Ezio
Batina, Lejla
Batista, Thais
Bauer, Sebastian
Becker, Klaus
Bernardi, Giovanni
Beyer, Dirk
Blech, Jan Olaf
Bortolussi, Luca
Bosnacki, Dragan
Boström, Pontus
Boyer, Benoit
Bozga, Marius
Brain, Martin
Bryans, Jeremy W.
Cassez, Franck
Castro, Pablo
Cerny, Pavol
Chawdhary, Aziem
Chen, Taolue
Chen, Zhenbang
Cheng, Chih-Hong
Cheng, Chihong

Chiang, Wei-Fan
Cirstea, Horatiu
Clark, Allan
Cohen, Cyril
Colley, John
Craciun, Florin
Danos, Vincent
David, Alexandre
David, Cristina
de Halleux, Jonathan
De Vink, Erik
de Vries, Edsko
Decker, Normann
Degerlund, Fredrik
Diciolla, Marco
Dimitrova, Rayna
D'ippolito, Nicolas
Dixit, Manoj
Dobrikov, Ivo
Dongol, Brijesh
Draeger, Klaus
Dragoi, Cezara
Du, Dehui
Edmunds, Andrew
Ehlers, Rüdiger
Enea, Constantin
Faber, Johannes
Falcone, Ylies
Fantechi, Alessandro
Faymonville, Peter
Feng, Lu
Ferrari, Alessio
Florian, Mihai

Fontaine, Pascal
Funes, Diego
Galpin, Vashti
Gao, Sicun
Gaston, Christophe
Gherghina, Cristian
Gilmore, Stephen
Gopinath, Divya
Gorogiannis, Nikos
Grigore, Radu
Gulwani, Sumit
Haar, Stefan
Han, Tingting
Hasuo, Ichiro
Hawblitzel, Chris
He, Guanhua
Heljanko, Keijo
Hladik, Pierre-Emmanuel
Holik, Lukas
Hou, Ping
Howar, Falk
Huang, Yanhong
Ingram, Claire
Isberner, Malte
Ishikawa, Fuyuki
Jacobs, Bart
Jastram, Michael
Jonker, Hugo
Kaiser, Alexander
Kong, Weiqiang
Koutavas, Vasileios
Krebbers, Robbert
Kupriyanov, Andrey
Kusakabe, Shigeru
Ladenberger, Lukas
Laibinis, Linas
Larsen, Peter Gorm
Latella, Diego
Lawford, Mark
Le Botlan, Didier
Lerner, Benjamin
Leroux, Jerome
Lewis, Matt
Li, Chun
Li, Guodong

Li, Xiaoshan
Loos, Sarah
Loreti, Michele
Maamria, Issam
Maddalon, Jeff
Martins, João G.
Massoni, Tiago
Mateescu, Maria-Emanuela-Canini
Melgratti, Hernan
Mercer, Eric
Mereacre, Alexandru
Merz, Stephan
Mikučionis, Marius
Mochio, Hiroshi
Mohalik, Swarup
Morgan, Carroll
Moser, Heinrich
Moskal, Michał
Mou, Dongyue
Mounier, Laurent
Møller, Mikael H.
Nadales Agut, Damian
Narkawicz, Anthony
Naujokat, Stefan
Navarro-Lopez, Eva
Ndukwu, Ukachukwu
Neovius, Mats
Nimal, Vincent
Nokhbeh Zaeem, Razieh
Nyman, Ulrik
Oliveira, Marcel
Oliveras, Albert
Omori, Yoichi
Parker, David
Patcas, Lucian
Pavese, Esteban
Person, Suzette
Peter, Hans-Jörg
Petre, Luigia
Plagge, Daniel
Qamar, Nafees
Quesel, Jan-David
Quilbeuf, Jean
Rabe, Markus
Radhakrishna, Arjun

Raman, Vishwanath
Rathke, Julian
Rayadurgam, Sanjai
Reger, Giles
Renshaw, David
Rezine, Ahmed
Rocha, Camilo
Roveri, Marco
Ruemmer, Philipp
Ruething, Oliver
Rusinowitch, Michael
Rydeheard, David
Rüthing, Oliver
Salay, Rick
Salehi Fathabadi, Asieh
Sampath, Prahladavaradan
Sanders, Jeff
Satpathy, M
Satpathy, Manoranjan
Schäf, Martin
Servais, Frédéric
Serwe, Wendelin
Sezgin, Ali
Sharma, Subodh
Siddiqui, Junaid Haroon
Sighireanu, Mihaela
Siminiceanu, Radu
Singh, Neeraj Kumar
Smans, Jan
Snook, Colin
Solin, Kim
Srba, Jiri
Strazny, Tim
Sun, Jun

Tarasyuk, Anton
Tautschnig, Michael
Tesnim, Abdellatif
Thoma, Daniel
Tiezzi, Francesco
Tkachuk, Oksana
Trachtenherz, David
Traonouez, Louis-Marie
Tribastone, Mirco
Troya, Javier
Tsay, Yih-Kuen
Tsiopoulos, Leonidas
Uchitel, Sebastian
Vafeiadis, Viktor
Vain, Juri
Varacca, Daniele
Venet, Arnaud
Verdejo, Alberto
Verhoef, Marcel
Villard, Jules
Vojnar, Tomas
Wang, Bow-Yaw
Wassyng, Alan
Winter, Kirsten
Wright, Stephen
Yamagata, Yoriyuki
Yang, Guowei
Yeganefard, Sanaz
Zantema, Hans
Zhang, Chenyi
Zhang, Lingming
Zhu, Ping
Zubkova, Nadya
Zufferey, Damien

Table of Contents

Software Security: A Formal Perspective
(Notes for a Talk)

Martín Abadi[1,2]

[1] Microsoft Research Silicon Valley
[2] University of California, Santa Cruz

Abstract. Weaknesses in software security have been numerous, sometimes startling, and often serious. Many of them stem from apparently small low-level errors (e.g., buffer overflows). Ideally, those errors should be avoided by design, or at least fixed after the fact. In practice, on the other hand, we may have to tolerate some vulnerabilities, with appropriate models, architectures, and tools.

This short paper is intended to accompany a talk at the 18th International Symposium on Formal Methods (FM 2012). The talk will discuss software security with an emphasis on low-level attacks and defenses and on their formal aspects. It will focus on systematic mitigations (specifically, techniques for layout randomization and control-flow integrity) that aim to be effective in the presence of buggy software and powerful attackers.

1 The Problem

Security depends not only on the properties of security models and designs but also on implementation details. Flaws, at any level, can result in vulnerabilities that attackers may be able to exploit. In the domain of software, those vulnerabilities often stem from small but catastrophic programming errors. For instance, buffer overflows remain frequent, and they can have serious consequences. An unchecked buffer overflow in a mundane parser can lead to the complete compromise of an operating system.

Although this short paper emphasizes low-level phenomena such as buffer overflows, similar considerations often apply for higher-level software. Indeed, attacks at all levels present common themes. For instance, attacks of various sorts often exploit errors in parsing and in sanitizing inputs in order to inject code into a target system.

Many errors may be fixed or avoided altogether by the use of suitable programming methods and tools. In particular, strong type systems may prevent the occurrence of many frequent flaws. The application of formal methods may further provide evidence of finer properties of software systems, or may establish essential properties of those system components that rely on low-level languages. For example, in this spirit, recent work [20] combines type safety and verification to obtain correctness guarantees for a research operating system.

However, to date, those methods and tools frequently fall short, in at least two respects:

D. Giannakopoulou and D. Méry (Eds.): FM 2012, LNCS 7436, pp. 1–5, 2012.

- Much code is still written in C, C++, and other low-level languages, often for performance or compatibility reasons. Full verification remains rare. Current tools for static and dynamic code analysis for those languages are remarkably effective, but still imperfect.
- Even code written in modern languages, and even verified code, should be treated with a healthy degree of caution. While type-safe programming languages like Java may well improve security, their implementations may not provide all the expected properties [1]. They have been the target of significant, successful attacks. For example, in 2012, malicious software called Flashback exploits a vulnerability in Java systems in order to install itself on Mac computers.

Moreover, implementation details, right or wrong, ultimately should be understood and judged in the context of security requirements. Programming methods and tools typically do not address how those requirements should be formulated. That is the role of security models (e.g., [12]). These models define precise security goals, with abstract concepts (such as principal and object) and properties (such as non-interference). Even though here we discuss them only briefly, these models are arguably crucial to software security. With the guidance of models, there is at least some hope that security measures are applied consistently and pervasively—they often are not.

We may ask, then, what is our fall-back position? Articulating and developing a tenable "Plan B" may be the best we can do, and quite useful.

2   Some Approaches

Despite their many flaws, software systems should guarantee at least some basic security properties, at least most of the time. Ideally, these guarantees should be obtained even in the absence of complete, precise security definitions and requirements, and even if many aspects of the systems are designed without security in mind. Although usually implicit, and perhaps still too optimistic, this point of view has motivated much recent work on architectures and tools.

In particular, the development of robust architectures may help confine the effects of dangerous errors. A system can sometimes be structured in such a way that a local compromise in one component does not immediately endanger the security of the entire system. This idea is not new. It appears, in particular, in classic work on mandatory access control, which aims to guarantee security even in the presence of Trojan horses [8].

Furthermore, the effects of flaws may be mitigated at run-time [6]. For instance, with the use of stack canaries, attacks that rely on buffer overflows can sometimes be detected and stopped before they take control of a target system [4]. These mitigations are often imperfect, and seldom enforce well-defined security properties. Nevertheless, these mitigations are based on useful insights on the goals and mechanisms of attacks. Their deployment has led attackers to shift their targets or to develop more elaborate techniques (e.g., [6,16,18]), in particular techniques that rely somewhat less bluntly on code injection.

Some advanced attacks include accessing data (e.g., communication buffers) or running code (e.g., library functions) that are present in the target system at predictable locations. One popular approach to thwarting such attacks consists in randomizing the placement of that data and code in memory (e.g., [5,15]); other types of randomization may also play a role (e.g., [7,14]). Recent research [3,9,17] shows that—at least in theory and in simple settings—randomization can yield precise guarantees comparable to those offered by the use of language-level abstractions.

More broadly, many attacks include unexpected accesses to data and unexpected control transfers. Run-time techniques for enforcing policies on data accesses and on control transfers can thwart such attacks (e.g., [2,10,11,13,19,21]). Recent research on these techniques has leveraged formal ideas and methods, defining models of machines, programs, run-time guards, and their objectives (which are typically safety properties), and then proving that those objectives are met.

Suppose, for example, that a piece of trusted code contains the computed-jump instruction jmp ecx, which transfers control to the address contained in register ecx. Let us assume that a programming mistake allows an attacker to corrupt or even to choose the contents of ecx. If the attacker knows the address A of another piece of code, and arranges that this address be placed in ecx, then it can cause that code to be executed. In the worst case, the code at address A could then give complete control to the attacker.

Since the attack has several hypotheses and steps, several possible countermeasures may be considered. These include:

1. We may identify and fix the mistake so that the attacker cannot tamper with ecx.
2. We may make the value A unguessable, by randomizing the layout of code in memory.
3. We may preface the instruction jmp ecx by a sequence of instructions that, dynamically, will check that ecx contains one of a set of expected values considered safe. (This set of expected values would be defined by a policy, perhaps inferred from source code.)

The first strategy is principled, but it may not always seem viable. Although the second and the third strategies also present non-trivial requirements, they are realistic and attractive in many low-level systems. Each strategy leads to different guarantees. For instance, with the third strategy, we obtain probabilistic properties at best.

Many variants and combinations of protection techniques are under consideration, often still with only preliminary analyses and prototype implementations. Further research may address the traditional goals of these techniques (e.g., proving isolation properties) and more delicate aspects of the subject (e.g., permitting controlled sharing). In this context, the application of formal ideas and methods will not lead to absolute proofs of security, but it can nevertheless be fruitful.

References

1. Abadi, M.: Protection in Programming-Language Translations. In: Larsen, K.G., Skyum, S., Winskel, G. (eds.) ICALP 1998. LNCS, vol. 1443, pp. 868–883. Springer, Heidelberg (1998)
2. Abadi, M., Budiu, M., Erlingsson, Ú., Ligatti, J.: Control-Flow Integrity: Principles, Implementations, and Applications. ACM Transactions on Information and System Security 13(1), 1–40 (2009)
3. Abadi, M., Plotkin, G.D.: On Protection by Layout Randomization. ACM Transactions on Information and System Security (to appear, 2012); The talk at FM 2012 will also cover an unpublished variant, joint work with Jérémy Planul
4. Cowan, C., Pu, C., Maier, D., Hinton, H., Walpole, J., Bakke, P., Beattie, S., Grier, A., Wagle, P., Zhang, Q.: StackGuard: Automatic Adaptive Detection and Prevention of Buffer-Overflow Attacks. In: Proceedings of the 7th Usenix Security Symposium, pp. 63–78 (1998)
5. Druschel, P., Peterson, L.L.: High-Performance Cross-Domain Data Transfer. Technical Report TR 92-11, Department of Computer Science, The University of Arizona (March 1992)
6. Erlingsson, Ú.: Low-Level Software Security: Attacks and Defenses. In: Aldini, A., Gorrieri, R. (eds.) FOSAD 2007. LNCS, vol. 4677, pp. 92–134. Springer, Heidelberg (2007)
7. Forrest, S., Somayaji, A., Ackley, D.H.: Building Diverse Computer Systems. In: 6th Workshop on Hot Topics in Operating Systems, pp. 67–72 (1997)
8. Gasser, M.: Building a Secure Computer System. Van Nostrand Reinhold, New York (1988)
9. Jagadeesan, R., Pitcher, C., Rathke, J., Riely, J.: Local Memory Via Layout Randomization. In: Proceedings of the 24th IEEE Computer Security Foundations Symposium, pp. 161–174 (2011)
10. Kiriansky, V., Bruening, D., Amarasinghe, S.: Secure Execution Via Program Shepherding. In: Proceedings of the 11th Usenix Security Symposium, pp. 191–206 (2002)
11. McCamant, S., Morrisett, G.: Evaluating SFI for a CISC Architecture. In: Proceedings of the 15th USENIX Security Symposium, pp. 15–15 (2006)
12. McLean, J.: Security Models. In: Marciniak, J. (ed.) Encyclopedia of Software Engineering. Wiley & Sons (1994)
13. Morrisett, G., Tan, G., Tassarotti, J., Tristan, J.-B., Gan, E.: RockSalt: Better, Faster, Stronger SFI for the x86. In: 33rd ACM SIGPLAN Conference on Programming Language Design and Implementation (to appear, 2012)
14. Pappas, V., Polychronakis, M., Keromytis, A.D.: Smashing the Gadgets: Hindering Return-Oriented Programming Using in-Place Code Randomization. In: IEEE Symposium on Security and Privacy, pp. 601–615 (2012)
15. PaX Project. The PaX project (2004), http://pax.grsecurity.net/
16. Pincus, J., Baker, B.: Beyond Stack Smashing: Recent Advances in Exploiting Buffer Overruns. IEEE Security and Privacy 2(4), 20–27 (2004)
17. Pucella, R., Schneider, F.B.: Independence from Obfuscation: A Semantic Framework for Diversity. In: 19th IEEE Computer Security Foundations Workshop, pp. 230–241 (2006)
18. Sotirov, A., Dowd, M.: Bypassing Browser Memory Protections: Setting Back Browser Security by 10 Years (2008), http://www.blackhat.com/presentations/bh-usa-08/Sotirov_Dowd/bh08-sotirov-dowd.pdf

19. Wahbe, R., Lucco, S., Anderson, T.E., Graham, S.L.: Efficient Software-Based Fault Isolation. ACM SIGOPS Operating Systems Review 27(5), 203–216 (1993)
20. Yang, J., Hawblitzel, C.: Safe to the Last Instruction: Automated Verification of a Type-Safe Operating System. Communications of the ACM 54(12), 123–131 (2011)
21. Yee, B., Sehr, D., Dardyk, G., Bradley Chen, J., Muth, R., Ormandy, T., Okasaka, S., Narula, N., Fullagar, N.: Native Client: a Sandbox for Portable, Untrusted x86 Native Code. Communications of the ACM 53(1), 91–99 (2010)

Formal Methods in the Wild:
Trains, Planes, & Automobile

Asaf Degani

General Motors
asaf.degani@gmail.com

Abstract. Why is it that carefully researched and well-formulated theoretical and methodological constructs don't make their way into
industrial applications? This keynote speech takes a look at my personal
experiences in both the aviation and automotive fields to suggest what
can be done about it. I will first try to explain why engineers (and even
industry scientists) tend not to use the kind of methods and tools that
emerge from academic settings while working on actual products, and
then show some of the consequences of not using such methods. I will
end with a few vignettes from my own trials and tribulations in applying
formal methods in engineering design processes as well as some of the
future prospects, for both academia and industry, as human-automation
systems become more demanding and complex.

D. Giannakopoulou and D. Méry (Eds.): FM 2012, LNCS 7436, p. 6, 2012.

Who Are We, and What Are We Doing Here?

Alan Wassyng

McMaster Centre for Software Certification, Department of Computing and Software,
McMaster University, Hamilton, Ontario, Canada
wassyng@mcmaster.ca

Abstract. Many Formal Methods researchers and practitioners seem to treat Formal Methods more as a religion than as an approach to rigorous software engineering. This fervour has a few side-effects: i) There have been spectacular advances in a few areas in Formal Methods; ii) There are a significant number of highly effective Formal Methods advocates - and practitioners; iii) The Formal Methods community at large seems to be condescendingly dismissive of any protestation of disbelief; and iv) Different methods and approaches seem to be judged on a belief basis rather than through evidence based analysis. The essential fact remains though, that after decades of research, Formal Methods are not used much in industrial software development. It is time that we, the Formal Methods community, question the basis of our existence. I argue that we exist to further the use of mathematics and rigorous analysis in the development of software applications, in the same way that electrical engineers, mechanical engineers, civil engineers, chemical engineers further the safe and effective development of a multitude of devices, buildings, manufacturing processes etc. This is clearly not a new thought. It does, however, suggest that we need to examine the link between Formal Methods and Software Engineering more carefully than is currently the case. A definition of engineering from the Academic Press Dictionary of Science and Technology is *"the application of scientific knowledge about matter and energy for practical human uses such as construction, machinery, products, or systems"*. Engineers use science as the basis for their work. This is not a one-way street. Feedback from engineering as to what are the important scientific problems to be solved is an important driver in scientific endeavours. Engineering work, in turn, forms a basis for the work done by technicians in our everyday lives. Again, feedback is an essential driver for the engineering community. In the modern digital world, Software Engineers should assume the role of the engineer. If we are truly serious about Software Engineering as an engineering profession, we need to consider the roles of Computer Scientists and Software Developers in this context. To be consistent with other domains, Software Engineers should use scientific knowledge as the basis of their work. This knowledge includes the growing domain of knowledge generated by Computer Science, and in particular, the specialized forms of mathematics that are applicable in the digital domain. In addition to Computer Scientists and Software Engineers, we also have Software Developers the technicians of our domain. This is a nice and neat correlation with other engineering fields unfortunately it is not, at this time, an accurate description of the

D. Giannakopoulou and D. Méry (Eds.): FM 2012, LNCS 7436, pp. 7–9, 2012.
© Springer-Verlag Berlin Heidelberg 2012

situation. In most countries, the difference between Computer Science and Software Engineering is decidedly blurry. Even when the difference should be obvious (for example, Canada insists that to call yourself an *"engineer"* you must be recognized as such by a professional engineering accreditation body), it is commonplace to find Computer Scientists playing the role of both engineer and technician. What does this mean for Formal Methods? Are Formal Methods people Computer Scientists, Software Engineers, Software Developers all of the above any of the above? If you look back at what I said about our *raison d'etre*, and if you agreed with what I said, perhaps you agreed too quickly!

Lately, my interests have been focused on the certification of software intensive systems: methods for building software intensive systems so that they can be certified; and methods for certifying such systems. This has made me rethink why, in spite of some amazing advances, Formal Methods are not used more often in everyday practice. I strongly believe that it is both possible and necessary to define *engineering methods* for the development of high integrity software applications, that these engineering methods must be based on mathematics, science, and well-founded heuristics, that "approved" methods should be significantly more prescriptive/objective than current software development techniques, and that these methods have to be supported by high quality tool chains. I also believe that the development of these methods is the task, primarily, of Software Engineers. What is the implication of this for the Formal Methods community? I think the answer is simple but not yet widely palatable. I think there is not enough focus on Software Engineering as opposed to Computer Science. It seems to me that the feedback from the engineering domain to the science domain is haphazard at best - non-existent a lot of the time! Over the past twenty years we have seen papers on myths of Formal Methods, Challenges of Formal Methods, the Ten Commandments of Formal Methods, experience of Formal Methods in industry, rethinking Formal Methods and the list goes on. So, why another talk on what seems to be a talked-out subject? Arrogance, of course! And, I hope, some new observations that may help us define our future path. I did not come to these conclusions all on my own. I have been extremely fortunate in my career, both in industry and in academia, to work with incredibly smart and dedicated colleagues, and I am indebted to them for teaching me so much about a very complex subject.

From a Software Engineering perspective, there are a number of fundamental principles that need to guide our design of Formal Methods: integration of the Formal Methods aspects with the rest of the software development life cycle; integration of the life cycle phases; comprehensive tool chains integrated into the methods; completeness criteria; ability to handle real-world aspects; scalability; the methods and tools must be understandable and usable by average, educated, practitioners (technicians); prescriptive/objective guidance; experimental validation of resulting methods and tools; and development with certification as a goal. In this talk I will use a running example to illustrate and discuss these principles. I hope this talk will be viewed as an exhortation to great technical successes, and even greater success in producing powerful methods and tools that software developers will want to use.

Acknowledgements. The opinions expressed in this talk are mine, but I have been incredibly fortunate to work with many extremely knowledgeable and capable software professionals over the past twenty years, both in academia and in industry. There are too many to mention all of them, but I do need to acknowledge my gratitude to: Mark Lawford, Tom Maibaum, Paul Joannou, and Dave Parnas for the hours of discussion (not to mention arguments) and collaboration, especially over the past ten years. Also, my colleagues Rick Hohendorf, Glenn Archinoff, Dominic Chan, David Lau, Greg Moum, Mike Viola, Jeff McDougall, David Tremaine, Peter Froebel and Alanna Wong, showed me how to approach software engineering as a true engineering discipline. Thanks to all of you!

Automata Learning through Counterexample Guided Abstraction Refinement*

Fides Aarts[1], Faranak Heidarian[1,**], Harco Kuppens[1],
Petur Olsen[2], and Frits Vaandrager[1]

[1] Institute for Computing and Information Sciences, Radboud University Nijmegen
P.O. Box 9010, 6500 GL Nijmegen, The Netherlands
[2] Department of Computer Science, Aalborg University, Aalborg, Denmark

Abstract. Abstraction is the key when learning behavioral models of realistic systems. Hence, in most practical applications where automata learning is used to construct models of software components, researchers manually define abstractions which, depending on the history, map a large set of concrete events to a small set of abstract events that can be handled by automata learning tools. In this article, we show how such abstractions can be constructed fully automatically for a restricted class of extended finite state machines in which one can test for equality of data parameters, but no operations on data are allowed. Our approach uses counterexample-guided abstraction refinement: whenever the current abstraction is too coarse and induces nondeterministic behavior, the abstraction is refined automatically. Using Tomte, a prototype tool implementing our algorithm, we have succeeded to learn – fully automatically – models of several realistic software components, including the biometric passport and the SIP protocol.

1 Introduction

The problem to build a state machine model of a system by providing inputs to it and observing the resulting outputs, often referred to as black box system identification, is both fundamental and of clear practical interest. A major challenge is to let computers perform this task in a rigorous manner for systems with large numbers of states. Many techniques for constructing models from observation of component behavior have been proposed, for instance in [3,20,10]. The most efficient such techniques use the setup of *active learning*, where a model of a system is learned by actively performing experiments on that system. LearnLib [20,11,17], for instance, the winner of the 2010 Zulu competition on regular inference, is currently able to learn state machines with at most 10,000 states. During the last few years important developments have taken place on the borderline

---

* Supported by STW project 11763 Integrating Testing And Learning of Interface Automata (ITALIA) and EU FP7 grant no 214755 (QUASIMODO).
** Supported by NWO/EW project 612.064.610 Abstraction Refinement for Timed Systems (ARTS).

D. Giannakopoulou and D. Méry (Eds.): FM 2012, LNCS 7436, pp. 10–27, 2012.

of verification, model-based testing and automata learning, see e.g. [4,15,20]. There are many reasons to expect that by combining ideas from these three areas it will become possible to learn models of realistic software components with state-spaces that are many orders of magnitude larger than what tools can currently handle. Tools that are able to infer state machine models automatically by systematically "pushing buttons" and recording outputs have numerous applications in different domains. For instance, they support understanding and analyzing legacy software, regression testing of software components [13], protocol conformance testing based on reference implementations, reverse engineering of proprietary/classified protocols, fuzz testing of protocol implementations [8], and inference of botnet protocols [6].

Abstraction turns out to be the key for scaling existing automata learning methods to realistic applications. Dawn Song et al [6], for instance, succeeded to infer models of realistic botnet command and control protocols by placing an emulator between botnet servers and the learning software, which concretizes the alphabet symbols into valid network messages and sends them to botnet servers. When responses are received, the emulator does the opposite — it abstracts the reponse messages into the output alphabet and passes them on to the learning software. The idea of an intermediate component that takes care of abstraction is very natural and is used, implicitly or explicitly, in many case studies on automata learning. Aarts, Jonsson and Uijen [1] formalized the concept of such an intermediate abstraction component. Inspired by ideas from predicate abstraction [16], they defined the notion of a *mapper* $\mathcal{A}$, which is placed in between the teacher $\mathcal{M}$ and the learner, and transforms the interface of the teacher by an abstraction that maps (in a history dependent manner) the large set of actions of the teacher into a small set of abstract actions. By combining the abstract machine $\mathcal{H}$ learned in this way with information about the mapper $\mathcal{A}$, they can effectively learn a (symbolically represented) state machine that is equivalent to $\mathcal{M}$. Aarts et al [1] demonstrated the feasibility of their approach by learning models of (fragments of) realistic protocols such as SIP and TCP [1], and of the new biometric passport [2]. The learned SIP model is an extended finite state machine with 29 states, 3741 transitions, and 17 state variables with various types (booleans, enumerated types, (long) integers, character strings,..). This corresponds to a state machine with an astronomical number of states and transitions, thus far fully out of reach of automata learning techniques.

In this article, we present an algorithm that is able to compute appropriate abstractions for a restricted class of system models. We also report on a prototype implementation of our algorithm named Tomte, after the creature that shrank Nils Holgersson into a gnome and (after numerous adventures) changed him back to his normal size again. Using Tomte, we have succeeded to learn *fully automatically* models of several realistic software components, including the biometric passport and the SIP protocol.

Nondeterminism arises naturally when we apply abstraction: it may occur that the behavior of a teacher or system-under-test (SUT) is fully deterministic but that due to the mapper (which, for instance, abstracts from the value of certain input parameters), the SUT appears to behave nondeterministically from the perspective of the learner. We use LearnLib as our basic learning tool and therefore the abstraction of the SUT may not exhibit any nondeterminism: if it does then LearnLib crashes and we have to refine the abstraction. This is exactly what has been done repeatedly during the manual construction of the abstraction mappings in the case studies of [1]. We formalize this procedure and describe the construction of the mapper in terms of a counterexample guided abstraction refinement (CEGAR) procedure, similar to the approach developed by Clarke et al [7] in the context of model checking. The idea to use CEGAR for learning state machines has been explored recently by Howar at al [12], who developed and implemented a CEGAR procedure for the special case in which the abstraction is static and does not depend on the execution history. Our approach is applicable to a much richer class of systems, which for instance includes the SIP protocol and the various components of the Alternating Bit Protocol.

Our algorithm applies to a class of extended finite state machines, which we call scalarset Mealy machines, in which one can test for equality of data parameters, but no operations on data are allowed. The notion of a scalarset data type originates from model checking, where it has been used for symmetry reduction [14]. Scalarsets also motivated the recent work of [5], which establishes a canonical form for a variation of our scalarset automata. Currently, Tomte can learn SUTs that may only remember the last and first occurrence of a parameter. We expect that it will be relatively easy to dispose of this restriction. We also expect that our CEGAR based approach can be further extended to systems that may apply simple or known operations on data, using technology for automatic detection of likely invariants, such as Daikon [9].

Even though the class of systems to which our approach currently applies is limited, the fact that we are able to learn models of systems with data fully automatically is a major step towards a practically useful technology for automatic learning of models of software components. The Tomte tool and all models that we used in our experiments are available via www.italia.cs.ru.nl/tools. A full version of this article including proofs is available via http://www.italia.cs.ru.nl/publications/

2   Mealy Machines

We will use *Mealy machines* to model SUTs. A *(nondeterministic) Mealy machine (MM)* is a tuple $\mathcal{M} = \langle I, O, Q, q_0, \rightarrow \rangle$, where I, O, and Q are nonempty sets of input symbols, output symbols, and states, respectively, $q_0 \in Q$ is the initial state, and $\rightarrow \subseteq Q \times I \times O \times Q$ is the *transition relation*. We write $q \xrightarrow{i/o} q'$ if $(q, i, o, q') \in \rightarrow$, and $q \xrightarrow{i/o}$ if there exists a q' such that $q \xrightarrow{i/o} q'$. Mealy machines are assumed to be *input enabled*: for each state q and input i, there exists an output o such that $q \xrightarrow{i/o}$. A Mealy machine is *deterministic* if for each state q and input symbol i there is exactly one output symbol o and exactly one state q'

such that $q \xrightarrow{i/o} q'$. We say that a Mealy machine is *finite* if the set Q of states and the set I of inputs are finite.

Intuitively, at any point in time, a Mealy machine is in some state $q \in Q$. It is possible to give inputs to the machine by supplying an input symbol $i \in I$. The machine then (nondeterministically) selects a transition $q \xrightarrow{i/o} q'$, produces output symbol o, and transforms itself to the new state q'.

Example 1. Figure 1 depicts a Mealy machine $\mathcal{M} = \langle I, O, Q, q_0, \rightarrow \rangle$ that we will use as a running example in the article. $\mathcal{M}$ describes a simple login procedure in which a user may choose a login name and password once, and then may use these values for subsequent logins. Let $L = \{\mathsf{INIT}, \mathsf{OUT}, \mathsf{IN}\}$ be the

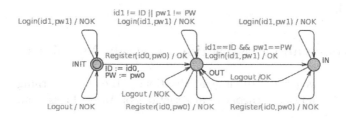

Fig. 1. Mealy machine

set of location names used in the diagram. Then the set of states is given by $Q = L \times \mathbb{N} \times \mathbb{N}$, the initial state is $q_0 = (\mathsf{INIT}, 0, 0)$, the set of inputs is $I = \{\mathsf{Register}(i, p), \mathsf{Login}(i, p), \mathsf{Logout} \mid i, p \in \mathbb{N}\}$ and the set of outputs is $O = \{\mathsf{OK}, \mathsf{NOK}\}$. In Section 4, we will formally define the symbolic representation used in Figure 1 and its translation to Mealy machines, but the reader will have no difficulty to associate a transition relation $\rightarrow$ to the diagram of Figure 1, assuming that in a state (l, i, p), i records the value of variable ID, and p records the value of variable PW.

The transition relation of a Mealy machine is extended to sequences by defining $\overset{u/s}{\Rightarrow}$ to be the least relation that satisfies, for $q, q', q'' \in Q$, $u \in I^*$, $s \in O^*$, $i \in I$, and $o \in O$,

- $q \overset{\epsilon/\epsilon}{\Rightarrow} q$, and
- if $q \xrightarrow{i/o} q'$ and $q' \overset{u/s}{\Rightarrow} q''$ then $q \overset{i\,u/o\,s}{\Rightarrow} q''$.

Here we use ϵ to denote the empty sequence. Observe that $q \overset{u/s}{\Rightarrow} q'$ implies $|u| = |s|$. A state $q \in Q$ is called *reachable* if $q_0 \overset{u/s}{\Rightarrow} q$, for some u and s.

An *observation* over input symbols I and output symbols O is a pair $(u, s) \in I^* \times O^*$ such that sequences u and s have the same length. For $q \in Q$, we define $obs_{\mathcal{M}}(q)$, the set of observations of $\mathcal{M}$ from state q, by

$$obs_{\mathcal{M}}(q) = \{(u, s) \in I^* \times O^* \mid \exists q' : q \overset{u/s}{\Rightarrow} q'\}.$$

We write $obs_{\mathcal{M}}$ as a shorthand for $obs_{\mathcal{M}}(q_0)$. Note that, since Mealy machines are input enabled, $obs_{\mathcal{M}}(q)$ contains at least one pair (u, s), for each input sequence $u \in I^*$. We call $\mathcal{M}$ *behavior deterministic* if $obs_{\mathcal{M}}$ contains exactly one pair (u, s), for each $u \in I^*$. It is easy to see that a deterministic Mealy machine is also behavior deterministic.

Two states $q, q' \in Q$ are *observation equivalent*, denoted $q \approx q'$, if $obs_{\mathcal{M}}(q) = obs_{\mathcal{M}}(q')$. Two Mealy machines $\mathcal{M}_1$ and $\mathcal{M}_2$ with the same sets of input symbols I are *observation equivalent*, notation $\mathcal{M}_1 \approx \mathcal{M}_2$, if $obs_{\mathcal{M}_1} = obs_{\mathcal{M}_2}$. We say that $\mathcal{M}_1 \leq \mathcal{M}_2$ if $obs_{\mathcal{M}_1} \subseteq obs_{\mathcal{M}_2}$.

Lemma 1. *If $\mathcal{M}_1 \leq \mathcal{M}_2$ and $\mathcal{M}_2$ is behavior deterministic then $\mathcal{M}_1 \approx \mathcal{M}_2$.*

We say that a Mealy machine is *finitary* if it is observation equivalent to a finite Mealy machine.

3   Inference and Abstraction of Mealy Machines

In this section, we present slight generalizations of the active learning framework of Angluin [3] and of the theory of abstractions of Aarts, Jonsson and Uijen [1].

3.1   Inference of Mealy Machines

We assume there is a *teacher*, who knows a behavior deterministic Mealy machine $\mathcal{M} = \langle I, O, Q, q_0, \rightarrow \rangle$, and a *learner*, who initially has no knowledge about $\mathcal{M}$, except for its sets I and O of input and output symbols. The teacher maintains the current state of $\mathcal{M}$ using a state variable of type Q, which at the beginning is set to q_0. The learner can ask three types of queries to the teacher:

- An *output query* $i \in I$.

  Upon receiving output query i, the teacher picks a transition $q \xrightarrow{i/o} q'$, where q is the current state, returns output $o \in O$ as answer to the learner, and updates its current state to q'.
- A *reset query*.

  Upon receiving a reset query the teacher resets its current state to q_0.
- An *inclusion query* $\mathcal{H}$, where $\mathcal{H}$ is a Mealy machine.

  Upon receiving inclusion query $\mathcal{H}$, the teacher will answer *yes* if the hypothesized Mealy machine $\mathcal{H}$ is correct, that is, $\mathcal{M} \leq \mathcal{H}$, or else supply a *counterexample*, which is an observation $(u, s) \in obs_{\mathcal{M}} - obs_{\mathcal{H}}$.

Note that *inclusion queries* are more general than the *equivalence queries* used by Angluin [3]. However, if $\mathcal{M} \leq \mathcal{H}$ and $\mathcal{H}$ is behavior deterministic then $\mathcal{M} \approx \mathcal{H}$ by Lemma 1. Hence, for behavior deterministic Mealy machines, a hypothesis is correct in our setting iff it is correct in the settings of Angluin. The reason for our generalization will be discussed in Section 3.2. The typical behavior of a learner is to start by asking sequences of output queries (alternated with resets) until a "stable" hypothesis $\mathcal{H}$ can be built from the answers. After that an inclusion query is made to find out whether $\mathcal{H}$ is correct. If the answer is *yes* then the learner has succeeded. Otherwise the returned counterexample is used to perform subsequent output queries until converging to a new hypothesized automaton, which is supplied in an inclusion query, etc.

For finitary, behavior deterministic Mealy machines, the above problem is well understood. The L^* algorithm, which has been adapted to Mealy machines by Niese [18], generates finite, deterministic hypotheses $\mathcal{H}$ that are the minimal Mealy machines that agree with a performed set of output queries. Since in practice a SUT cannot answer equivalence or inclusion queries, LearnLib "approximates" such queries by generating a long test sequence that is computed using standard methods such as random walk or the W-method. The algorithms have been implemented in the LearnLib tool [19], developed at the Technical University Dortmund.

3.2   Inference Using Abstraction

Existing implementations of inference algorithms only proved effective when applied to machines with small alphabets (sets of input and output symbols). Practical systems, however, typically have large alphabets, e.g. inputs and outputs with data parameters of type integer or string. In order to infer large or infinite-state MMs, we divide the concrete input domain into a small number of abstract equivalence classes in a state-dependent manner. We place a mapper in between the teacher and the learner, which translates the concrete symbols in I and O to abstract symbols in X and Y, and vice versa. The task of the learner is then reduced to infering a "small" MM with alphabet X and Y.

3.3   Mappers

The behavior of the intermediate component is fully determined by the notion of a *mapper*. A mapper encompasses both concrete and abstract sets of input and output symbols, a set of states and a transition function that tells us how the occurrence of a concrete symbol affects the state, and an abstraction function which, depending on the state, maps concrete to abstract symbols.

Definition 1 (Mapper). *A mapper for a set of inputs I and a set of outputs O is a tuple $\mathcal{A} = \langle I, O, R, r_0, \delta, X, Y, abstr \rangle$, where*

- *I and O are disjoint sets of concrete input and output symbols,*
- *R is a set of mapper states,*
- *$r_0 \in R$ is an initial mapper state,*
- *$\delta : R \times (I \cup O) \to R$ is a transition function; we write $r \xrightarrow{a} r'$ if $\delta(r, a) = r'$,*
- *X and Y are finite sets of abstract input and output symbols, and*
- *$abstr : R \times (I \cup O) \to (X \cup Y)$ is an abstraction function that preserves inputs and outputs, that is, for all $a \in I \cup O$ and $r \in R$, $a \in I \Leftrightarrow abstr(r, a) \in X$.*

We say that mapper $\mathcal{A}$ is output-predicting if, for all $o, o' \in O$, $abstr(r, o) = abstr(r, o') \Rightarrow o = o'$, that is, abstr is injective on outputs for fixed r.

Example 2. We define a mapper $\mathcal{A} = \langle I, O, R, r_0, \delta, X, Y, abstr \rangle$ for the Mealy machine $\mathcal{M}$ of Example 1. The sets I and O of the mapper are the same as for $\mathcal{M}$. The mapper records the login name and password selected by the user: $R = (\mathbb{N} \cup \{\bot\}) \times (\mathbb{N} \cup \{\bot\})$. Initially, no login name and password have been selected: $r_0 = (\bot, \bot)$. The state of the mapper only changes when a Register input occurs in the initial state:

$$\delta((i,p), a) = \begin{cases} (i', p') \text{ if } (i,p) = (\bot, \bot) \wedge a = \textsf{Register}(i', p') \\ (i, p) \text{ if } (i,p) \neq (\bot, \bot) \vee a \notin \{\textsf{Register}(i', p') \mid i', p' \in \mathbb{N}\}. \end{cases}$$

The abstraction forgets the parameters of the input actions, and only records whether a login is correct or wrong: $X = \{\textsf{Register}, \textsf{CLogin}, \textsf{WLogin}, \textsf{Logout}\}$ and $Y = O$. The abstraction function *abstr* is defined in the obvious way, the only interesting case is the Login input:

$$abstr((i,p), \textsf{Login}(i', p')) = \begin{cases} \textsf{CLogin} \text{ if } (i,p) = (i', p') \\ \textsf{WLogin} \text{ otherwise} \end{cases}$$

Mapper $\mathcal{A}$ is output predicting since *abstr* acts as the identity function on outputs.

A mapper allows us to abstract a Mealy machine with concrete symbols in I and O into a Mealy machine with abstract symbols in X and Y, and, conversely, to concretize a Mealy machine with symbols in X and Y into a Mealy machine with symbols in I and O. Basically, the abstraction of Mealy machine $\mathcal{M}$ via mapper $\mathcal{A}$ is the Cartesian product of the underlying transition systems, in which the abstraction function is used to convert concrete symbols into abstract ones.

Definition 2 (Abstraction). *Let $\mathcal{M} = \langle I, O, Q, q_0, \rightarrow \rangle$ be a Mealy machine and let $\mathcal{A} = \langle I, O, R, r_0, \delta, X, Y, abstr \rangle$ be a mapper. Then $\alpha_{\mathcal{A}}(\mathcal{M})$, the abstraction of $\mathcal{M}$ via $\mathcal{A}$, is the Mealy machine $\langle X, Y \cup \{\bot\}, Q \times R, (q_0, r_0), \rightarrow' \rangle$, where $\rightarrow'$ is given by the rules*

$$\frac{q \xrightarrow{i/o} q', \; r \xrightarrow{i} r' \xrightarrow{o} r'', \; abstr(r, i) = x, \; abstr(r', o) = y}{(q, r) \xrightarrow{x/y}{}' (q', r'')} \qquad \frac{\nexists i \in I : abstr(r, i) = x}{(q, r) \xrightarrow{x/\bot}{}' (q, r)}$$

The second rule is required to ensure that $\alpha_{\mathcal{A}}(\mathcal{M})$ is input enabled. Given some state of the mapper, it may occur that for some abstract input action x there is no corresponding concrete input action i. In this case, an input x triggers a special "undefined" output $\bot$ and leads the state unchanged.

Example 3. Consider the abstraction of the Mealy machine $\mathcal{M}$ of Example 1 via the mapper $\mathcal{A}$ of Example 2. States of the abstract Mealy machine $\alpha_{\mathcal{A}}(\mathcal{M})$ have the form $((l, i, p), (i', p'))$ with $l \in L$ and $i, p, i', p' \in \mathbb{N}$. It is easy to see that, for any reachable state, if $l = \textsf{INIT}$ then $(i, p) = (0, 0) \wedge (i', p') = (\bot, \bot)$ else $(i, p) = (i', p')$. In fact, $\alpha_{\mathcal{A}}(\mathcal{M})$ is observation equivalent to the deterministic Mealy machine $\mathcal{H}$ of Figure 2. Hence $\alpha_{\mathcal{A}}(\mathcal{M})$ is behavior deterministic. Note that, by the second rule in Definition 2, an abstract input CLogin in the initial state triggers an output $\bot$, since in this state there exists no concrete input action that abstracts to CLogin.

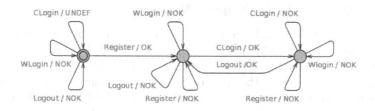

Fig. 2. Abstract Mealy machine for login procedure

We now define the *concretization operator*, which is the dual of the abstraction operator. For a given mapper $\mathcal{A}$, the corresponding concretization operator turns any abstract MM with symbols in X and Y into a concrete MM with symbols in I and O. The concretization of MM $\mathcal{H}$ via mapper $\mathcal{A}$ is the Cartesian product of the underlying transition systems, in which the abstraction function is used to convert abstract symbols into concrete ones.

Definition 3 (Concretization). *Let $\mathcal{H} = \langle X, Y \cup \{\bot\}, H, h_0, \rightarrow \rangle$ be a Mealy machine and let $\mathcal{A} = \langle I, O, R, r_0, \delta, X, Y, abstr \rangle$ be a mapper for I and O. Then $\gamma_{\mathcal{A}}(\mathcal{H})$, the concretization of $\mathcal{H}$ via $\mathcal{A}$, is the Mealy machine $\langle I, O \cup \{\bot\}, R \times H, (r_0, h_0), \rightarrow'' \rangle$, where $\rightarrow''$ is given by the rules*

$$\frac{r \xrightarrow{i} r' \xrightarrow{o} r'', \ abstr(r, i) = x, \ abstr(r', o) = y, \ h \xrightarrow{x/y} h'}{(r, h) \xrightarrow{i/o}{}'' (r'', h')}$$

$$\frac{r \xrightarrow{i} r', \ abstr(r, i) = x, \ h \xrightarrow{x/y} h', \ \nexists o \in O : abstr(r', o) = y}{(r, h) \xrightarrow{i/\bot}{}'' (r, h)}$$

The second rule is required to ensure the concretization $\gamma_{\mathcal{A}}(\mathcal{H})$ is input enabled and indeed a Mealy machine.

Example 4. If we take the abstract MM $\mathcal{H}$ for the login procedure displayed in Figure 2 and apply the concretization induced by mapper $\mathcal{A}$ of Example 2, the resulting Mealy machine $\gamma_{\mathcal{A}}(\mathcal{H})$ is observation equivalent to the concrete MM $\mathcal{M}$ displayed in Figure 1. Note that the transitions with output $\bot$ in $\mathcal{H}$ play no role in $\gamma_{\mathcal{A}}(\mathcal{H})$ since there exists no concrete output that is abstracted to $\bot$. Also note that in this specific example the second rule of Definition 3 does not play a role, since *abstr* acts as the identity function on outputs.

The next lemma is a direct consequence of the definitions.

Lemma 2. *Suppose $\mathcal{H}$ is a deterministic Mealy machine and $\mathcal{A}$ is an output-predicting mapper. Then $\gamma_{\mathcal{A}}(\mathcal{H})$ is deterministic.*

The following key result estabishes the duality of the concretization and abstraction operators.

Theorem 1. *Suppose $\alpha_{\mathcal{A}}(\mathcal{M}) \leq \mathcal{H}$. Then $\mathcal{M} \leq \gamma_{\mathcal{A}}(\mathcal{H})$.*

3.4   The Behavior of the Mapper Module

We are now prepared to establish that, by using an intermediate mapper component, a learner can indeed learn a correct model of the behavior of the teacher. To begin with, we describe how a mapper $\mathcal{A} = \langle I, O, R, r_0, \delta, X, Y, abstr \rangle$ fully determines the behavior of the intermediate mapper component. The mapper component for $\mathcal{A}$ maintains a state variable of type R, which initially is set to r_0. The behavior of the mapper component is defined as follows:

- Whenever the mapper is in a state r and receives an output query $x \in X$ from the learner, it nondeterministically picks a concrete input symbol $i \in I$ such that $abstr(r, i) = x$, forwards i as an output query to the teacher, and jumps to state $r' = \delta(r, i)$. If there exists no i such that $abstr(r, i) = x$ then the mapper returns output $\bot$ to the learner.
- Whenever the mapper is in state r' and receives a concrete answer o from the teacher, it forwards the abstract version $abstr(r', o)$ to the learner and jumps to state $r'' = \delta(r', o)$.
- Whenever the mapper receives a reset query from the learner, it changes its current state to r_0, and forwards a reset query to the teacher.
- Whenever the mapper receives an inclusion query $\mathcal{H}$ from the learner, it answers yes if $\alpha_{\mathcal{A}}(\mathcal{M}) \leq \mathcal{H}$, or else answers no and supplies a counterexample $(u, s) \in obs_{\alpha_{\mathcal{A}}(\mathcal{M})} - obs_{\mathcal{H}}$.

From the perspective of a learner, a teacher for $\mathcal{M}$ and a mapper component for $\mathcal{A}$ together behave exactly like a teacher for $\alpha_{\mathcal{A}}(\mathcal{M})$. Hence, if $\alpha_{\mathcal{A}}(\mathcal{M})$ is finitary and behavior deterministic, LearnLib may be used to infer a deterministic Mealy machine $\mathcal{H}$ that is equivalent to $\alpha_{\mathcal{A}}(\mathcal{M})$. Our mapper uses randomization to select concrete input symbols for the abstract input symbols contained in LearnLib equivalence queries for $\mathcal{H}$. More research will be required to find out whether this provides a good approach for testing $\alpha_{\mathcal{A}}(\mathcal{M}) \leq \mathcal{H}$. Whenever $\mathcal{H}$ is correct for $\alpha_{\mathcal{A}}(\mathcal{M})$, then it follows by Theorem 1 that $\gamma_{\mathcal{A}}(\mathcal{H})$ is correct for $\mathcal{M}$. In general, $\gamma_{\mathcal{A}}(\mathcal{H})$ will not be deterministic: it provides an over-approximation of the behavior of $\mathcal{M}$. However, according to Lemma 2, if $\mathcal{H}$ is deterministic and $\mathcal{A}$ is output-predicting, then $\gamma_{\mathcal{A}}(\mathcal{H})$ is also deterministic. Lemma 1 then implies $\mathcal{M} \approx \gamma_{\mathcal{A}}(\mathcal{H})$.

4   The World of Tomte

Our general approach for using abstraction in automata learning is phrased most naturally at the semantic level. However, if we want to devise effective algorithms and implement them, we must restrict attention to a class of automata and mappers that can be finitely represented. In this section, we describe the class of SUTs that our tool can learn, as well as the classes of mappers that it uses.

    Below we define *scalarset Mealy machines*. The scalarset datatype was introduced by Ip and Dill [14] as part of their work on symmetry reduction in verification. Operations on scalarsets are restricted so that states are guaranteed to have the same future behaviors, up to permutation of the elements of the scalarsets. On scalarsets no operations are allowed except for constants, and the only predicate symbol that may be used is equality.

We assume a universe $\mathcal{V}$ of *variables*. Each variable $v \in \mathcal{V}$ has a domain $\mathsf{type}(v) \subseteq \mathbb{N} \cup \{\bot\}$, where $\mathbb{N}$ is the set of natural numbers and $\bot$ denotes the undefined value. A *valuation* for a set $V \subseteq \mathcal{V}$ of variables is a function ξ that maps each variable in V to an element of its domain. We write $\mathsf{Val}(V)$ for the set of all valuations for V. We also assume a finite set C of *constants* and a function $\gamma : C \to \mathbb{N}$ that assigns a value to each constant. If $c \in C$ is a constant then we define $\mathsf{type}(c) = \{\gamma(c)\}$. A *term* over V is either a variable or a constant, that is, an element of $C \cup V$. We write $\mathcal{T}$ for the set of terms over $\mathcal{V}$. If t is a term over V and ξ is a valuation for V then we write $[\![t]\!]_{\xi}$ for the value to which t evaluates: if $t \in V$ then $[\![t]\!] = \xi(t)$ and if $t \in C$ then $[\![t]\!] = \gamma(t)$. A *formula* φ over V is a Boolean combination of expressions of the form $t = t'$, where t and t' are terms over V. We write $\mathcal{G}$ for the set of all formulas over $\mathcal{V}$. If ξ is a valuation for V and φ is a formula over V, then we write $\xi \models \varphi$ to denote that ξ satisfies φ. We assume a set E of *event primitives* and for each event primitive ε an arity $\mathsf{arity}(\varepsilon) \in \mathbb{N}$. An *event term* for $\varepsilon \in E$ is an expression $\varepsilon(t_1, \ldots, t_n)$ where $t_1, \ldots, t_n$ are terms and $n = \mathsf{arity}(\varepsilon)$. We write $\mathcal{ET}$ for the set of event terms. An *event signature* Σ is a pair $\langle T_I, T_O \rangle$, where T_I and T_O are finite sets of event terms such that $T_I \cap T_O = \emptyset$ and each term in $T_I \cup T_O$ is of the form $\varepsilon(p_1, \ldots, p_n)$ with $p_1, \ldots, p_n$ pairwise different variables with $\mathsf{type}(p_i) \subseteq \mathbb{N}$, for each i. We require that the event primitives as well as the variables of different event terms in $T_I \cup T_O$ are distinct. We refer to the variables occurring in an event signature as *parameters*.

Definition 4. *A scalarset Mealy machine (SMM) is a tuple* $\mathcal{S} = \langle \Sigma, V, L, l_0, \Gamma \rangle$, *where*

- $\Sigma = \langle T_I, T_O \rangle$ *is an event signature,*
- $V \subseteq \mathcal{V}$ *is a finite set of state variables, with* $\bot \in \mathsf{type}(v)$, *for each* $v \in V$; *we require that variables from* V *do not occur as parameters in* Σ,
- L *is a finite set of locations,*
- $l_0 \in L$ *is the initial location,*
- $\Gamma \subseteq L \times T_I \times \mathcal{G} \times (V \to \mathcal{T}) \times \mathcal{ET} \times L$ *is a finite set of transitions. For each transition* $\langle l, \varepsilon_I(p_1, \ldots, p_k), g, \varrho, \varepsilon_O(u_1, \ldots, u_l), l' \rangle \in \Gamma$, *we refer to* l *as the source,* g *as the* guard, ϱ *as the* update, *and* l' *as the* target. *We require that* g *is a formula over* $V \cup \{p_1, \ldots, p_k\}$, *for each* v, $\varrho(v) \in V \cup C \cup \{p_1, \ldots, p_k\}$ *and* $\mathsf{type}(\varrho(v)) \subseteq \mathsf{type}(v)$, *and there exists an event term* $\varepsilon_O(q_1, \ldots, q_l) \in T_O$ *such that, for each* i, u_i *is a term over* V *with* $\mathsf{type}(u_i) \subseteq \mathsf{type}(q_i) \cup \{\bot\}$,

We say $\mathcal{S}$ *is* deterministic *if, for all distinct transitions* $\tau_1 = \langle l_1, e_1^I, g_1, \varrho_1, e_1^O, l_1' \rangle$ *and* $\tau_2 = \langle l_2, e_2^I, g_2, \varrho_2, e_2^O, l_2' \rangle$ *in* Γ, $l_1 = l_2$ *and* $e_1^I = e_2^I$ *implies* $g_1 \wedge g_2 \equiv \mathsf{false}$.

To each SMM $\mathcal{S}$ we associate a Mealy machine $[\![\mathcal{S}]\!]$ in the obvious way. The states of $[\![\mathcal{S}]\!]$ are pairs of a location l and a valuation ξ of the state variables. A transition may fire if its guard, which may contain both state variables and parameters of the input action, evaluates to true. Then a new valuation of the state variables is computed using the update part of the transition. This new valuation also determines the values of the parameters of the output action.

Definition 5 (Semantics SMM). *The semantics of an event term $\varepsilon(p_1, \ldots, p_k)$ is the set $[\![\varepsilon(p_1, \ldots, p_k)]\!] = \{\varepsilon(d_1, \cdots, d_k) \mid d_i \in type(p_i), 1 \le i \le k\}$. The semantics of a set T of event terms is defined by pointwise extension: $[\![T]\!] = \bigcup_{e \in T} [\![e]\!]$.*
Let $\mathcal{S} = \langle \Sigma, V, L, l_0, \Gamma \rangle$ be a SMM with $\Sigma = \langle T_I, T_O \rangle$. The semantics of $\mathcal{S}$, denoted $[\![\mathcal{S}]\!]$, is the Mealy machine $\langle I, O, Q, q^0, \to \rangle$, where $I = [\![T_I]\!]$, $O = [\![T_O]\!]$, $Q = L \times Val(V)$, $q^0 = (l_0, \xi_0)$, with $\xi_0(v) = \bot$, for $v \in V$, and $\to \subseteq Q \times I \times O \times Q$ is given by the rule

$$\frac{\langle l, \varepsilon_I(p_1, \ldots, p_k), g, \varrho, \varepsilon_O(u_1, \ldots, u_\ell), l' \rangle \in \Gamma \\ \forall i \le k, \iota(p_i) = d_i \quad \xi \cup \iota \models g \\ \xi' = (\xi \cup \gamma \cup \iota) \circ \varrho \\ \forall i \le \ell, [\![u_i]\!]_{\xi'} = d'_i}{(l, \xi) \xrightarrow{\varepsilon_I(d_1, \ldots, d_k)/\varepsilon_O(d'_1, \ldots, d'_\ell)} (l', \xi')}$$

Our tool can infer models of SUTs that can be defined using deterministic SMMs that only record the first and the last occurrence of an input parameter.

Definition 6 (Restricted SMMs). *Let $\mathcal{S} = \langle \Sigma, V, L, l_0, \Gamma \rangle$ be a SMM. Variable v records the last occurrence of input parameter p if for each transition $\langle l, \varepsilon_I(p_1, \ldots, p_k), g, \varrho, e, l' \rangle \in \Gamma$, if $p \in \{p_1, \ldots, p_k\}$ then $\varrho(v) = p$ else $\varrho(v) = v$. Moreover, $\varrho(w) = v$ implies $w = v$. Variable v records the first occurrence of input parameter p if for each transition $\langle l, \varepsilon_I(p_1, \ldots, p_k), g, \varrho, e, l' \rangle \in \Gamma$, if $p \in \{p_1, \ldots, p_k\}$ and $g \Rightarrow v = \bot$ holds then $\varrho(v) = p$ else $\varrho(v) = v$. Moreover, $\varrho(w) = v$ implies $w = v$. We say that $\mathcal{S}$ only records the first and last occurrence of parameters if, whenever $\varrho(v) = p$ in some transition, v either records the first or the last occurrence of p.*

For each event signature, we introduce a family of symbolic abstractions, parametrized by what we call an *abstraction table*. For each parameter p, an abstraction table contains a list of variables and constants. If v occurs in the list for p then, intuitively, this means that for the future behavior of the SUT it may be relevant whether p equals v or not.

Definition 7 (Abstraction Table). *Let $\Sigma = \langle T_I, T_O \rangle$ be an event signature and let P and U be the sets of parameters that occur in T_I and T_O, respectively. For each $p \in P$, let v_p^f and v_p^l be fresh variables with $type(v_p^f) = type(v_p^l) = type(p) \cup \{\bot\}$, and let $V^f = \{v_p^f \mid p \in P\}$ and $V^l = \{v_p^l \mid p \in P\}$. An abstraction table for Σ is a function $F : P \cup U \to (V^f \cup V^l \cup C)^*$, such that, for each $p \in P \cup U$, all elements of sequence $F(p)$ are distinct, and, for each $p \in U$, $F(p)$ lists all the elements of $V^f \cup V^l \cup C$.*

Each abstraction table F induces a mapper. This mapper records, for each parameter p, the first and last value of this parameter in a run, using variables v_p^f

and v_p^l, respectively. In order to compute the abstract value for a given concrete value d for a parameter p, the mapper checks for the first variable or constant in sequence $F(p)$ with value d. If there is such a variable or constant, the mapper returns the index in $F(p)$, otherwise it returns $\bot$.

Definition 8 (Mapper Induced by Abstraction Table). *Let $\Sigma = \langle T_I, T_O \rangle$ be a signature and let F be an abstraction table for Σ. Let P be the set of parameters in T_I and let U be the set of parameters in T_O. Let, for $p \in P \cup U$, p' be a fresh variable with $\mathsf{type}(p') = \{0, \ldots, |F(p)| - 1\} \cup \{\bot\}$. Let $T_X = \{\varepsilon(p_1', \ldots, p_k') \mid \varepsilon(p_1, \ldots, p_k) \in T_I\}$ and $T_Y = \{\varepsilon(p_1', \ldots, p_l') \mid \varepsilon(p_1, \ldots, p_l) \in T_O\}$. Then the mapper $\mathcal{A}_\Sigma^F = \langle I, O, R, r^0, \delta, X, Y, abstr \rangle$ is defined as follows:*

- *$I = [\![T_I]\!]$, $O = [\![T_O]\!]$, $X = [\![T_X]\!]$, and $Y = [\![T_Y]\!]$.*
- *$R = \mathsf{Val}(V^f \cup V^l)$ and $r^0(v) = \bot$, for all $v \in V^f \cup V^l$.*
- *$\to$ and $abstr$ are defined as follows, for all $r \in R$,*
  1. *Let $o = \varepsilon_O(d_1, \ldots, d_k)$ and let $\varepsilon_O(q_1, \ldots, q_k) \in T_O$. Then $r \xrightarrow{o} r$ and $abstr(r, o) = \varepsilon_O(first([\![F(q_1)]\!]_r, d_1), \ldots, first([\![F(q_k)]\!]_r, d_k))$, where for a sequence of values σ and a value d, $first(\sigma, d)$ equals $\bot$ if d does not occur in σ, and equals the smallest index m with $\sigma_m = d$ otherwise, and for a sequence of terms $\rho = t_1 \cdots t_n$ and valuation ξ, $[\![\rho]\!]_\xi = [\![t_1]\!]_\xi \cdots [\![t_n]\!]_\xi$.*
  2. *Let $i = \varepsilon_I(d_1, \ldots, d_k)$, $\varepsilon_I(p_1, \ldots, p_k) \in T_I$, $r_0 = r$ and, for $1 \le j \le k$,*

$$r_j = \begin{cases} r_{j-1}[d_j/v_{p_j}^f][d_j/v_{p_j}^l] & \text{if } r_{j-1}(v_{p_j}^f) = \bot \\ r_{j-1}[d_j/v_{p_j}^l] & \text{otherwise} \end{cases} \tag{1}$$

Then $r \xrightarrow{i} r_k$ and $abstr(r, i) = \varepsilon_I(d_1', \ldots, d_k')$, where, for $1 \le j \le k$, $d_j' = first([\![F(p_j)]\!]_{r_j-1}, d_j)$.

Strictly speaking, the mappers $\mathcal{A}_\Sigma^F$ introduced above are not output-predicting: in each state r of the mapper there are infinitely many concrete outputs that are mapped to the abstract output $\bot$. However, in SUTs whose behavior can be described by scalarset Mealy machines, the only possible values for output parameters are constants and values of previously received inputs. As a result, the mapper will never send an abstract output with a parameter $\bot$ to the learner. This in turn implies that in the deterministic hypothesis $\mathcal{H}$ generated by the learner, $\bot$ will not occur as an output parameter. (Hypotheses in LearnLib only contain outputs actions that have been observed in some experiment.) Since $\mathcal{A}_\Sigma^F$ is output-predicting for all the other outputs, it follows by Lemma 2 that the concretization $\gamma_{\mathcal{A}_\Sigma^F}(\mathcal{H})$ is deterministic.

The two theorems below solve (at least in theory) the problem of learning a deterministic symbolic Mealy machine $\mathcal{S}$ that only records the first and last occurrence of parameters. By Theorems 2 and 3, we know that $\mathcal{M} = \alpha_{\mathcal{A}_\Sigma^{\mathsf{Full}(\Sigma)}}([\![\mathcal{S}]\!])$ is finitary and behavior deterministic. Thus we may apply the approach described in Section 3.4 with mapper $\mathcal{A}_\Sigma^{\mathsf{Full}(\Sigma)}$ in combination with any tool that is able to learn finite deterministic Mealy machines. The only problem is that in practice the state-space of $\mathcal{M}$ is too large, and beyond what state-of-the-art learning tools can handle. The proofs of Theorems 2 and 3 exploit the symmetry that is present in SMMs: using constant preserving automorphisms [14] we exhibit a finite bisimulation quotient and behavior determinacy.

Theorem 2. *Let* $S = \langle \Sigma, V, L, l_0, \Gamma \rangle$ *be a SMM that only records the first and last occurrence of parameters. Let F be an abstraction table for Σ. Then* $\alpha_{\mathcal{A}_\Sigma^F}([\![S]\!])$ *is finitary.*

Theorem 3. *Let* $S = \langle \Sigma, V, L, l_0, \Gamma \rangle$ *be a deterministic SMM that only records the first and last occurrence of parameters. Then* $\alpha_{\mathcal{A}_\Sigma^{Full(\Sigma)}}([\![S]\!])$ *is behavior deterministic.*

Example 5. Consider our running example of a login procedure. The mapper induced by the full abstraction table has 8 state variables, which record the first and last values of 4 parameters. This means that for each parameter there are 9 abstract values. Hence, for each of the event primitives Login and Register, we need 81 abstract input actions. Altogether we need 164 abstract inputs. The performance of LearnLib degrades severely if the number of inputs exceeds 20, and learning models with 164 inputs typically is not possible. Example 2 presented an optimal abstraction with just 4 inputs. In the next section, we present a CEGAR approach that allows us to infer an abstraction with 7 inputs.

5   Counterexample-Guided Abstraction Refinement

In order to avoid the practical problems that arise with the abstraction table $Full(\Sigma)$, we take an approach based on counterexample-guided abstraction. We start with the simplest mapper, which is induced by the abstraction table F with $F(p) = \epsilon$, for all $p \in P$, and only refine the abstraction (i.e., add an element to the table) when we have to. For any table F, $\alpha_{\mathcal{A}_\Sigma^F}([\![S]\!])$ is finitary by Theorem 2. If, moreover, $\alpha_{\mathcal{A}_\Sigma^F}([\![S]\!])$ is behavior deterministic then LearnLib can find a correct hypothesis and we are done. Otherwise, we refine the abstraction by adding an entry to our table. Since there are only finitely many possible abstractions and the abstraction that corresponds to the full table is behavior deterministic, by Theorem 3, our CEGAR approach will always terminate.

During the construction of a hypothesis we will not observe nondeterministic behavior, even when table F is not full: in Tomte the mapper always chooses a fresh concrete value whenever it receives an abstract action with parameter value $\bot$, i.e. the mapper induced by F will behave exactly as the mapper induced by $Full(\Sigma)$, except that the set of abstract actions is smaller. In contrast, during the testing phase Tomte selects random values from a small domain. In this way, we ensure that the full concretization $\gamma_{\mathcal{A}}(\mathcal{H})$ is explored. If the teacher responds with a counterexample (u, s), with $u = i_1, \ldots, i_n$ and $s = o_1, \ldots, o_n$, we may face a problem: the counterexample may be due to the fact that $\mathcal{H}$ is incorrect, but it may also be due to the fact that $\alpha_{\mathcal{A}_\Sigma^F}([\![S]\!])$ is not behavior-deterministic. In order to figure out the nature of the counterexample, we first construct the unique execution of $\mathcal{A}_\Sigma^F$ with trace $i_1 o_1 i_2 o_2 \cdots i_n o_n$. Then we assign a color to each occurrence of a parameter value in this execution:

Definition 9. *Let* $r \xrightarrow{i} r'$ *be a transition of* $\mathcal{A}_\Sigma^F$ *with* $i = \varepsilon_I(d_1, \ldots, d_k)$ *and let* $\varepsilon_I(p_1, \ldots, p_k) \in T_I$. *Let* $abstr(r, i) = \varepsilon_I(d_1', \ldots, d_k')$. *Then we say that the occurrence of value* d_j *is* green *if* $d_j' \neq \bot$. *Occurrence of value* d_j *is* black *if* $d_j' = \bot$ *and* d_j *equals the value of some constant or occurs in the codomain of state* r_{j-1} *(where* r_{j-1} *is defined as in equation (1) above). Occurrence of value* d_j *is* red *if it is neither green nor black.*

Intuitively, an occurrence of a value of an input parameter p is green if it equals a value of a previous parameter or constant that is listed in the abstraction table, an occurrence is black if it equals a previous value that is not listed in the abstraction table, and an occurrence is red if it is fresh. The mapper now does a new experiment on the SUT in which all the black occurrences of input parameters in the trace are converted into fresh "red" occurrences. If, after abstraction, the trace of the original counterexample and the outcome of the new experiment are the same, then hypothesis $\mathcal{H}$ is incorrect and we forward the abstract counterexample to the learner. But if they are different then we may conclude that $\alpha_{\mathcal{A}_\Sigma^F}(\mathcal{S})$ is not behavior-deterministic and the current abstraction is too coarse. In this case, the original counterexample contains at least one black occurrence, which determines a new entry that we need to add to the abstraction table.

Algorithm 1. Abstraction refinement

Input: Counterexample $c = i_1 \cdots i_n$
Output: Pair (p, v) with v new entry for $F(p)$ in abstraction table
1: **while** abstraction not found **do**
2:     Pick a black value b from c
3:     $c' := c$, where b is set to a fresh value
4:     **if** output from running c' on SUT is different from output of c **then**
5:         $c'' := c$, where $\mathsf{source}(b)$ is set to a fresh value
6:         **if** output from running c'' on SUT is different from output of c **then**
7:             **return** $(\mathsf{param}(b), \mathsf{variable}(\mathsf{source}(b)))$
8:         **else** $c := c''$
9:         **end if**
10:     **else** $c := c'$
11:     **end if**
12: **end while**

The procedure for finding this new abstraction is outlined in Algorithm 1. Here, for an occurrence b, $\mathsf{param}(b)$ gives the corresponding formal parameter, $\mathsf{source}(b)$ gives the previous occurrence b' which, according to the execution of $\mathcal{A}_\Sigma^F$, is the source of the value of b, and $\mathsf{variable}(b)$ gives the variable in which the value of b is stored in the execution of $\mathcal{A}_\Sigma^F$. To keep the presentation simple, we assume here that the set of constants is empty. If changing some black value b into a fresh value changes the observable output of the SUT, and also a change of $\mathsf{source}(b)$ into a fresh value leads to a change of the observable output, then this strongly suggests that it is relevant for the behavior of the SUT whether or not b and source(b) are equal, and we obtain a new entry for the abstraction table. If changing the value of either b or source(b) does not change the output, we obtain a counterexample with fewer black values. If b is the only black value then, due to the inherent symmetry of SMMs, changing b or source(b) to a fresh value in both cases leads to a change of observable output. When the new abstraction entry has been added to the abstraction table, the learner is restarted with the new abstract alphabet.

6　Experiments

We illustrate the operation of Tomte by means of the Session Initiation Protocol (SIP) as presented in [1]. Initially, no abstraction for the input is defined in the learner, which means all parameter values are $\perp$. As a result every parameter in every input action is treated in the same way and the mapper selects a fresh concrete value, e.g. the abstract input trace $IINVITE(\perp, \perp, \perp)$, $IACK(\perp, \perp, \perp)$, $IPRACK(\perp, \perp, \perp)$, $IPRACK(\perp, \perp, \perp)$ is translated to the concrete trace $IINVITE(1, 2, 3)$, $IACK(4, 5, 6)$, $IPRACK(7, 8, 9)$, $IPRACK(10, 11, 12)$. In the learning phase queries with distinct parameter values are sent to the SUT, so that the learner constructs the abstract Mealy machine shown in Figure 3. In

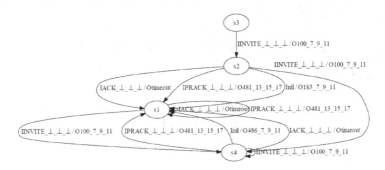

Fig. 3. Hypothesis of SIP protocol

the testing phase parameter values may be duplicated, which may lead to non-deterministic behavior. The test trace $IINVITE, IACK, IPRACK, IPRACK$ in Figure 4 leads to an $O200$ output that is not foreseen by the hypothesis, which produces an $O481$.

Rerunning the trace with distinct values as before leads to an $O481$ output. Thus, to resolve this problem, we need to refine the input abstraction. Therefore, we identify the green and black values in the trace and try to remove black values. The algorithm first successfully removes black value 1 by replacing the nine in the $IPRACK$ input with a fresh value and observing the same output as before. However, removing black value 2 changes the final outcome of the trace to an $O481$ output. Also replacing the first 16 with a fresh value gives an $O481$ output. As a result, we need to refine the input abstraction by adding an

IINVITE			O100			IACK			timeout / IPRACK			O481			IPRACK			O200		
p1	p2	p3	o1	o2	o3	q1	q2	q3	r1	r2	r3	t1	t2	t3	r1	r2	r3	u1	u2	u3
⊥	⊥	⊥	7	9	11	⊥	⊥	⊥	⊥	⊥	⊥	13	15	17	⊥	⊥	⊥	13	15	17
16	17	9	16	17	9	4	10	25	9	3	22	9	3	22	16	15	21	16	15	21

1   2

Fig. 4. Non-determinism in SIP protocol

Table 1. Learning statistics

System under test	Constants/ Parameters	Input refine- ments	Learning/ Testing queries	States	Learning/ Testing time
Alternating Bit Protocol Sender	2/2	1	193/4	7	0.6s/0.1s
Alternating Bit Protocol Receiver	2/2	2	145/3	4	0.4s/0.2s
Alternating Bit Protocol Channel	0/2	0	31/0	2	0.1s/0.0s
Biometric Passport [2]	3/1	3	2199/2607	5	3.9s/32.0s
Session Initiation Protocol [1]	0/3	2	1153/101	14	3.0s/0.9s
Login procedure (Example 1)	0/4	2	283/40	4	0.5s/0.7s
Farmer-Wolf-Goat-Cabbage	4/1	4	610/1279	9	1.7s/16.2s
Palindrome/Repdigit Checker	0/16	9	1941/126	1	2.4s/3.3s

equality check between the first parameter of the last *IINVITE* message and the first parameter of an *IPRACK* message to every *IPRACK* input. Apart from refining the input alphabet, every concrete output parameter value is abstracted to either a constant or a previous occurrence of a parameter. The abstract value is the index of the corresponding entry in the abstraction table. After every input abstraction refinement, the learning process needs to be restarted. We proceed until the learner finishes the inference process without getting interrupted by a non-deterministic output.

Table 1 gives an overview of the systems we learned with the numbers of constant and action parameters used in the models, the number of input refinement steps, total numbers of learning and testing queries, number of states of the learned abstract model, and the time needed for learning and testing (in seconds). These numbers and times do not include the last equivalence query, in which no counterexample has been found. In all our experiments, correctness of hypotheses was tested using random walk testing. The outcomes depend on the return value of function variable(b) in case b is the first occurrence of a parameter p: v_p^f or v_p^l. Table 1 is based on the optimal choice, which equals v_p^f for SIP and the Login Procedure, and v_p^l for all the other benchmarks. The Biometric Passport case study [2] has also been learned fully automatically by [12]. All other benchmarks require history dependent abstractions, and Tomte is the first tool that has been able to learn these models fully automatically. We have checked that all models inferred are observation equivalent to the corresponding SUT. For this purpose we combined the learned model with the abstraction and used the CADP tool set, http://www.inrialpes.fr/vasy/cadp/, for equivalence checking. Our tool and all models can be found at http://www.italia.cs.ru.nl/tools.

Acknowledgement. Gábor Angyal helped with the Tomte tool.

References

1. Aarts, F., Jonsson, B., Uijen, J.: Generating Models of Infinite-State Communication Protocols Using Regular Inference with Abstraction. In: Petrenko, A., Simão, A., Maldonado, J.C. (eds.) ICTSS 2010. LNCS, vol. 6435, pp. 188–204. Springer, Heidelberg (2010)
2. Aarts, F., Schmaltz, J., Vaandrager, F.W.: Inference and Abstraction of the Biometric Passport. In: Margaria, T., Steffen, B. (eds.) ISoLA 2010. LNCS, vol. 6415, pp. 673–686. Springer, Heidelberg (2010)
3. Angluin, D.: Learning regular sets from queries and counterexamples. Inf. Comput. 75(2), 87–106 (1987)
4. Berg, T., Grinchtein, O., Jonsson, B., Leucker, M., Raffelt, H., Steffen, B.: On the Correspondence Between Conformance Testing and Regular Inference. In: Cerioli, M. (ed.) FASE 2005. LNCS, vol. 3442, pp. 175–189. Springer, Heidelberg (2005)
5. Cassel, S., Howar, F., Jonsson, B., Merten, M., Steffen, B.: A Succinct Canonical Register Automaton Model. In: Bultan, T., Hsiung, P.-A. (eds.) ATVA 2011. LNCS, vol. 6996, pp. 366–380. Springer, Heidelberg (2011)
6. Cho, C.Y., Babic, D., Shin, E.C.R., Song, D.: Inference and analysis of formal models of botnet command and control protocols. In: Conference on Computer and Communications Security, pp. 426–439. ACM (2010)
7. Clarke, E.M., Grumberg, O., Jha, S., Lu, Y., Veith, H.: Counterexample-guided abstraction refinement for symbolic model checking. J. ACM 50(5), 752–794 (2003)
8. Comparetti, P.M., Wondracek, G., Krügel, C., Kirda, E.: Prospex: Protocol specification extraction. In: IEEE Symposium on Security and Privacy, pp. 110–125. IEEE CS (2009)
9. Ernst, M.D., Perkins, J.H., Guo, P.J., McCamant, S., Pacheco, C., Tschantz, M.S., Xiao, C.: The Daikon system for dynamic detection of likely invariants. SCP 69(1-3), 35–45 (2007)
10. de la Higuera, C.: Grammatical Inference: Learning Automata and Grammars. Cambridge University Press (April 2010)
11. Howar, F., Steffen, B., Merten, M.: From ZULU to RERS. In: Margaria, T., Steffen, B. (eds.) ISoLA 2010. LNCS, vol. 6415, pp. 687–704. Springer, Heidelberg (2010)
12. Howar, F., Steffen, B., Merten, M.: Automata learning with automated alphabet abstraction refinement. In: Jhala, R., Schmidt, D. (eds.) VMCAI 2011. LNCS, vol. 6538, pp. 263–277. Springer, Heidelberg (2011)
13. Hungar, H., Niese, O., Steffen, B.: Domain-Specific Optimization in Automata Learning. In: Hunt Jr., W.A., Somenzi, F. (eds.) CAV 2003. LNCS, vol. 2725, pp. 315–327. Springer, Heidelberg (2003)
14. Ip, C.N., Dill, D.L.: Better verification through symmetry. FMSD 9(1/2), 41–75 (1996)
15. Leucker, M.: Learning Meets Verification. In: de Boer, F.S., Bonsangue, M.M., Graf, S., de Roever, W.-P. (eds.) FMCO 2006. LNCS, vol. 4709, pp. 127–151. Springer, Heidelberg (2007)
16. Loiseaux, C., Graf, S., Sifakis, J., Boujjani, A., Bensalem, S.: Property preserving abstractions for the verification of concurrent systems. FMSD 6(1), 11–44 (1995)

17. Merten, M., Steffen, B., Howar, F., Margaria, T.: Next Generation LearnLib. In: Abdulla, P.A., Leino, K.R.M. (eds.) TACAS 2011. LNCS, vol. 6605, pp. 220–223. Springer, Heidelberg (2011)
18. Niese, O.: An Integrated Approach to Testing Complex Systems. PhD thesis, University of Dortmund (2003)
19. Raffelt, H., Steffen, B., Berg, T.: Learnlib: a library for automata learning and experimentation. In: FMICS 2005, pp. 62–71. ACM Press, New York (2005)
20. Raffelt, H., Steffen, B., Berg, T., Margaria, T.: Learnlib: a framework for extrapolating behavioral models. STTT 11(5), 393–407 (2009)

JULIENNE: A Trace Slicer for Conditional Rewrite Theories⋆

María Alpuente[1], Demis Ballis[2], Francisco Frechina[1], and Daniel Romero[1]

[1] DSIC-ELP, Universitat Politècnica de València,
Camino de Vera s/n, Apdo 22012, 46071 Valencia, Spain
{alpuente,ffrechina,dromero}@dsic.upv.es
[2] DIMI, Università degli Studi di Udine,
Via delle Scienze 206, 33100 Udine, Italy
demis.ballis@uniud.it

Abstract. Trace slicing is a transformation technique that reduces the size of execution traces for the purpose of program analysis and debugging. Based on the appropriate use of antecedents, trace slicing tracks back reverse dependences and causality along execution traces and then cuts off irrelevant information that does not influence the data observed from the trace. In this paper, we describe the first slicing tool for conditional rewrite theories that can be used to drastically reduce complex, textually-large system computations w.r.t. a user-defined slicing criterion that selects those data that we want to track back from a given point.

1 Introduction

Software systems commonly generate large and complex execution traces, whose analysis (or even simple inspection) is extremely time-consuming and, in some cases, is not feasible to perform by hand. Trace slicing is a technique that simplifies execution traces by focusing on selected execution aspects, which makes it well suited to program analysis, debugging, and monitoring [6].

Rewriting Logic (RWL) is a very general *logical* and *semantic framework* that is particularly suitable for formalizing highly concurrent, complex systems (e.g., biological systems [5] and Web systems [1,4]). RWL is efficiently implemented in the high-performance system Maude [7]. Rewriting logic-based tools, like the Maude-NPA protocol analyzer, Maude LTLR model checker, and the Java PathExplorer runtime verification tool (just to mention a few [11]), are used in the analysis and verification of programs and protocols wherein the states are represented as algebraic entities that use equational logic and the transitions are represented using conditional rewrite rules. These transitions are performed *modulo* conditional equational theories that may also contain algebraic axioms

⋆ This work has been partially supported by the EU (FEDER) and the Spanish MEC TIN2010-21062-C02-02 project, by Generalitat Valenciana, ref. PROMETEO2011/052. Also, D. Romero is supported by FPI-MEC grant BES-2008-004860 and F. Frechina is supported by FPU-ME grant AP2010-5681.

D. Giannakopoulou and D. Méry (Eds.): FM 2012, LNCS 7436, pp. 28–32, 2012.

such as commutativity and associativity. The execution traces produced by such tools are usually very complex and are therefore not amenable to manual inspection. However, not all the information that is in the trace is needed for analyzing a given piece of information in a given state of the trace. For instance, consider the following rules [1] that define (a part of) the standard semantics of a simple imperative language: 1) `crl <while B do I, St> => <skip, St>` if `<B, St> => false /\ isCommand(I)`, 2) `rl <skip, St> => St`, and 3) `rl <false, St> => false`. Then, in the execution trace `<while false do X := X + 1, {}> → <skip, {}> → {}`, we can observe that the statement `X := X + 1` is not relevant to compute the output `{}`. Therefore, the trace could be simplified by replacing `X := X + 1` with a special variable • and by enforcing the compatibility condition `isCommand(•)`. This condition guarantees the correctness of the simplified trace [3]. In other words, any concretization of the simplified trace (which instantiates the variable • and meets the compatibility condition) is a valid trace that still generates the target data that we are observing (in this case, the output `{}`).

The JULIENNE slicing tool is based on the conditional slicing technique described in [3] that slices an input execution trace with regard to a set of *target symbols* (which occur in a selected state of the trace), by propagating them backwards through the trace so that all pieces of information that are not an antecedent of the target symbols are simply discarded. Unlike standard backward tracing approaches, which are based on a costly, dynamic labeling procedure [2,10], in [3], the relevant data are traced back by means of a less expensive, incremental technique of matching refinement. JULIENNE generalizes and supersedes a previous unconditional slicer mentioned in [2]. The system copes with the extremely rich variety of conditions that occur in Maude theories (i.e., equational conditions $s = t$, matching conditions $p := t$, and rewrite expressions $t \Rightarrow p$) by taking into account the precise way in which Maude mechanizes the conditional rewriting process so that all those rewrite steps are revisited backwards in an instrumented, fine-grained way. In order to formally guarantee the strong correctness of the generated trace slice, the instantiated conditions of the equations and rules are recursively processed, which may imply slicing a number of (originally internal) execution traces, and a Boolean compatibility condition is carried, which ensures the executability of the sliced rewrite steps.

2   The Slicing Tool JULIENNE

The slicing tool JULIENNE is written in Maude and consists of about 170 Maude function definitions (approximately 1K lines of source code). It is a stand-alone application (which can be invoked as a Full Maude trace slicing command or used online through a Java Web service) that correctly handles general rewrite theories that may contain (conditional) rules and equations, built-in operators, and algebraic axioms. JULIENNE also comes with an intuitive Web user interface

---

[1]   We use Maude notation (c)rl to introduce (conditional) rewrite rules.

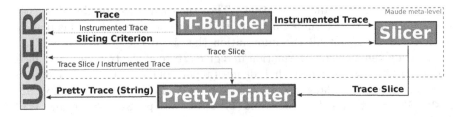

Fig. 1. JULIENNE architecture

that is based on the AJAX technology, which allows the slicing engine to be used through the WWW. It is publicly available at [9].

The architecture of JULIENNE, which is depicted in Figure 1, consists of three system modules named **IT-Builder**, **Slicer**, and **Pretty-Printer**.

IT-Builder. The Instrumented **Trace Builder** module is a pre-processor that provides an expanded instrumented version of the original trace in which all reduction steps are explicitly represented, including equational simplification steps and applications of the *matching modulo* algorithm. Showing all rewrites is not only required to successfully apply our methodology, but it can also be extremely useful for debugging purposes because it allows the user to inspect the equational simplification subcomputations that occur in a given trace.

Slicer. This module implements the trace slicing method of [3] by using Maude reflection and meta-level functionality. Specifically, it defines a new meta-level command called `back-sl` (*backward-slicing*) that takes as input an instrumented trace $t \to^* s$ (given as a Maude term of sort `Trace`) and a slicing criterion that represents the target symbols of the state s to be observed. It then delivers (i) a trace slice in which the data that are not relevant w.r.t. the chosen criterion are replaced by special •-variables and (ii) a compatibility condition that ensures the correctness of the generated trace slice. This module is also endowed with a simple pattern-matching filtering language that helps to select the target symbols in s without the encumbrance of having to refer to them by their addressing positions.

Pretty-Printer. This module implements the command `prettyPrint`, which provides a human-readable, nicely structured view of the generated trace slice where the carried compatibility condition can be displayed or hidden, depending on the interest of the user. Specifically, it delivers a pretty representation of the trace as a term of sort String that is aimed to favor better inspection and debugging activities within the Maude environment.

3   Experimental Evaluation and Conclusion

JULIENNE is the first slicing tool that can be used to analyze execution traces of RWL-based programs and tools. JULIENNE greatly reduces the size of the execution traces thus making their analysis feasible even in the case of complex, real-size problems. We have experimentally evaluated our tool in several case studies that are available at the JULIENNE Web site [9] and within the distribution package, which also contains a user guide, the source files of the slicer, and related literature.

We have tested JULIENNE on rather large execution traces, such as the counterexample traces delivered by the Maude LTLR model-checker [8]. We have used JULIENNE to slice execution traces of a real-size Webmail application in order to isolate critical data such as the navigation of a malicious user and the messages exchanged by a specific Web browser with the Webmail server. Typical traces for this application consist of sequences of 100 -1000 states, each of which contains more than 5K characters. In all the experiments, the trace slices that we obtained show impressive reduction rates (up to $\sim 98\%$). Other benchmark programs we have considered include the specification of a fault-tolerant communication protocol, a banking system, and the automated verifier WEB-TLR developed on top of Maude's model-checker itself. In most cases, the delivered trace slices were cleansed enough to be easily inspected by hand. It is very important to note that the slicer does not remove any information that is relevant, independently of the skills of the user.

With regard to the time required to perform the analyses, our implementation is extremely time efficient; the elapsed times are small even for very complex traces and scale linearly. For example, running the slicer for a 20Kb trace w.r.t. a Maude specification with about 150 rules and equations –with AC rewrites– took less than 1 second (480.000 rewrites per second on standard hardware, 2.26GHz Intel Core 2 Duo with 4Gb of RAM memory).

References

1. Alpuente, M., Ballis, D., Espert, J., Romero, D.: Model-Checking Web Applications with WEB-TLR. In: Bouajjani, A., Chin, W.-N. (eds.) ATVA 2010. LNCS, vol. 6252, pp. 341–346. Springer, Heidelberg (2010)
2. Alpuente, M., Ballis, D., Espert, J., Romero, D.: Backward Trace Slicing for Rewriting Logic Theories. In: Bjørner, N., Sofronie-Stokkermans, V. (eds.) CADE 2011. LNCS, vol. 6803, pp. 34–48. Springer, Heidelberg (2011)
3. Alpuente, M., Ballis, D., Frechina, F., Romero, D.: Backward Trace Slicing for Conditional Rewrite Theories. In: Bjørner, N., Voronkov, A. (eds.) LPAR-18 2012. LNCS, vol. 7180, pp. 62–76. Springer, Heidelberg (2012)
4. Alpuente, M., Ballis, D., Romero, D.: Specification and Verification of Web Applications in Rewriting Logic. In: Cavalcanti, A., Dams, D.R. (eds.) FM 2009. LNCS, vol. 5850, pp. 790–805. Springer, Heidelberg (2009)
5. Baggi, M., Ballis, D., Falaschi, M.: Quantitative Pathway Logic for Computational Biology. In: Degano, P., Gorrieri, R. (eds.) CMSB 2009. LNCS, vol. 5688, pp. 68–82. Springer, Heidelberg (2009)
6. Chen, F., Roşu, G.: Parametric Trace Slicing and Monitoring. In: Kowalewski, S., Philippou, A. (eds.) TACAS 2009. LNCS, vol. 5505, pp. 246–261. Springer, Heidelberg (2009)
7. Clavel, M., Durán, F., Eker, S., Lincoln, P., Martí-Oliet, N., Meseguer, J., Talcott, C.: Maude Manual (Version 2.6): Tech. rep., SRI,
   http://maude.cs.uiuc.edu/maude2-manual/

8. Clavel, M., Durán, F., Hendrix, J., Lucas, S., Meseguer, J., Ölveczky, P.C.: The Maude Formal Tool Environment. In: Mossakowski, T., Montanari, U., Haveraaen, M. (eds.) CALCO 2007. LNCS, vol. 4624, pp. 173–178. Springer, Heidelberg (2007)
9. The JULIENNE Web site (2012),
   http://users.dsic.upv.es/grupos/elp/soft.html
10. TeReSe (ed.): Term Rewriting Systems. Cambridge University Press, Cambridge, UK (2003)
11. Martí-Oliet, N., Palomino, M., Verdejo, A.: Rewriting logic bibliography by topic: 1990-2011. Journal of Logic and Algebraic Programming (to appear, 2012)

IMITATOR 2.5: A Tool for Analyzing Robustness in Scheduling Problems

Étienne André[1], Laurent Fribourg[2], Ulrich Kühne[3], and Romain Soulat[2]

[1] LIPN, CNRS UMR 7030, Université Paris 13, France
[2] LSV – ENS Cachan & CNRS
[3] Universität Bremen, Germany

Abstract. The tool IMITATOR implements the *Inverse Method (IM)* for Timed Automata (TAs). Given a TA $\mathcal{A}$ and a tuple π_0 of reference valuations for timings, *IM* synthesizes a constraint around π_0 where $\mathcal{A}$ behaves in the same discrete manner. This provides us with a quantitative measure of robustness of the behavior of $\mathcal{A}$ around π_0. The new version IMITATOR 2.5 integrates the new features of stopwatches (in addition to standard clocks) and updates (in addition to standard clock resets), as well as powerful algorithmic improvements for state space reduction. These new features make the tool well-suited to analyze the robustness of solutions in several classes of preemptive scheduling problems.

Keywords: Real-Time Systems, Parametric Timed Automata, Stopwatches.

1 Motivation

IMITATOR 2.5 (for *Inverse Method for Inferring Time AbstracT behaviOR*) is a tool for parameter synthesis in the framework of real-time systems based on the inverse method *IM* for Parametric Timed Automata (PTAs). Different from CEGAR-based methods, this algorithm for parameter synthesis makes use of a "good" parameter valuation π_0 instead of a set of "bad" states [4]. IMITATOR takes as input a network of PTAs with stopwatches and a reference valuation π_0; it synthesizes a constraint K on the parameters such that (1) $\pi_0 \models K$ and (2) for all parameter valuation π satisfying K, the trace set (i.e., the discrete behavior) of $\mathcal{A}$ under π is the same as for $\mathcal{A}$ under π_0. This provides the system with a criterion of *robustness* (see, e.g., [14]) around π_0.

Fig. 1. Functional view of IMITATOR

D. Giannakopoulou and D. Méry (Eds.): FM 2012, LNCS 7436, pp. 33–36, 2012.

History and New Features. A basic implementation named IMITATOR has first been proposed, under the form of a Python script calling HYTECH [11]. The tool has then been entirely rewritten in IMITATOR II [3], under the form of a standalone OCaml program. A number of case studies containing up to 60 timing parameters could be efficiently verified in the purely timed framework.

Since [3], we extended the input formalism to PTAs equipped with *stop-watches*: clocks can now be stopped for some time while others keep growing. Also, we added clock updates: clocks can now be set to arbitrary linear combinations of other clocks, parameters and discrete variables. These extensions, together with powerful algorithmic improvements for state space reduction, allow us to consider larger classes of case studies, such as scheduling problems.

2   Architecture and Features

The core of IMITATOR (available in [1] under the GNU GPL license) is written in OCaml, and interacts with the Parma Polyhedra Library (PPL) [6]. Exact arithmetics with unbounded precision is used. IMITATOR takes as input a network of PTAs with stopwatches. The input syntax allows the use of clocks (or stopwatches), rational-valued discrete variables, and parameters (i.e., unknown constants) to be used altogether in linear terms, within guards, invariants and updates. A constraint is output in text format; furthermore, the set of traces computed by the analysis can be output under a graphical form (using Graphviz) for case studies with reasonable size (up to a few thousands reachable states).

IMITATOR implements in particular the following algorithms:

Full reachability analysis. Given a PTA, it computes the reachability graph.
Inverse method. Given a PTA and a reference parameter valuation π_0, it computes a constraint K on the parameter guaranteeing the same time-abstract behavior as under π_0 (see Figure 1).

IMITATOR 2.5 makes use of several algorithmic optimizations. In particular, we implemented a technique that merges any two states sharing the same discrete part and such that the union of their constraint on the clocks and parameters is convex [5]. This optimization preserves the correctness of all our algorithms; better, the output constraint is then always weaker or equal, i.e., covers a set of parameter valuations larger or equal. It behaves particularly well in the framework of scheduling problems, where the state space is drastically reduced. Actually, most of the scheduling examples we consider run out of memory without this merging technique.

3   Application to Robustness Analysis in Scheduling

Due to the aforementioned state space reduction and the use of stopwatches, IMITATOR 2.5 becomes an interesting tool for synthesizing robust conditions for scheduling problems. Let us illustrate this on a preemptive jobshop example given in [2]. The jobshop scheduling problem is a generic resource allocation problem in which common resources ("machines") are required at various time points (and for given duration) by different tasks. For instance, one needs to use a machine m_1 for d_1 time units, machine m_2 for d_2 time units, and so on. The goal is to find a way ("schedule") to allocate the resources such that all tasks terminate as early as possible ("minimal makespan"). Let us consider the jobshop problem $\{J_1, J_2\}$ for 2 jobs and 3 machines with: $J_1 = (m_1, d_1), (m_2, d_2), (m_3, d_3)$ and $J_2 = (m_2, d'_2)$ with $d_1 = 3, d_2 = 2, d_3 = 4, d'_2 = 5$. There are many possible schedules. In [2], this problem is modeled as a product $\mathcal{A}$ of TAs with stopwatches, each TA modeling a job. Each schedule corresponds to a branch in the reachability tree of $\mathcal{A}$. The makespan value corresponds to the duration of the shortest branch, here 9.

Let us explain how to analyze the robustness of the valuation π_0 : $\{d_2 = 2, d'_2 = 5\}$ with respect to the makespan value 9. We first consider a parametric version of $\mathcal{A}$ where d_2 and d'_2 become parameters. In the same spirit as in [9], we add an observer $\mathcal{O}$, which is a TA synchronized with $\mathcal{A}$, that fires a transition labeled *DEADLINE* as soon as a schedule spends more than 9 time units. We then use IMITATOR (instead of a CEGAR-like method as in [9]) with $\mathcal{A} \parallel \mathcal{O}$ as a model input and π_0 as a valuation input. This yields the constraint K: $7 > d'_2 \wedge 3 > d_2 \wedge d'_2 + d_2 \geq 7$. By the *IM* principle, the set of traces (i.e., discrete runs) of $\mathcal{A} \parallel \mathcal{O}$ is always the same, for any point (d_2, d'_2) of K. Since the makespan for π_0 is 9, we know that some branches of the tree do not contain any *DEADLINE* label. This holds for each point (d_2, d'_2) of K. The makespan of the system is thus always at most 9 in K. (In particular, we can increase d_2 from 2 to 3, or increase d'_2 from 5 to 7 while keeping the makespan less than or equal to 9.)

All case studies and experiments are described in a research report [15], and available in [1].

4 Comparison with Related Work

The use of models such as PTAs and parametric Time Petri Nets (TPNs) for solving scheduling problems has received attention in the past few years. For example, Roméo [13] performs model checking for parametric TPNs with stopwatches, and synthesizes parameter valuations satisfying TCTL formulæ. An extension of UPPAAL allows parametric model checking [7], although the model itself remains non-parametric. The approach most related to IMITATOR 2.5 is [9,12], where the authors infer parametric constraints guaranteeing the feasibility of a schedule, using PTAs with stopwatches. The main difference between [9,12] and IMITATOR relies in our choice of the inverse method, rather than a CEGAR-based method. First results obtained on the same case studies are incomparable (although similar in form), which seems to indicate that the two methods are complementary. The problem of finding the schedulability region was attacked in analytic terms in [8]; the size of our examples is rather modest compared to those treated using such analytic methods. However, in many schedulability problems, no analytic solution exists (see, e.g., [16]), and exhaustive simulation is exponential in the number of jobs. In such cases, symbolic methods as ours and those of [9,12] are useful to treat critical real-life examples of small size. We are thus involved in a project [10] with an industrial partner with first interesting results.

References

1. http://www.lsv.ens-cachan.fr/Software/imitator/
2. Abdeddaïm, Y., Maler, O.: Preemptive Job-Shop Scheduling Using Stopwatch Automata. In: Katoen, J.-P., Stevens, P. (eds.) TACAS 2002. LNCS, vol. 2280, pp. 113–126. Springer, Heidelberg (2002)
3. André, É.: IMITATOR II: A tool for solving the good parameters problem in timed automata. In: INFINITY. EPTCS, vol. 39, pp. 91–99 (2010)
4. André, É., Chatain, T., Encrenaz, E., Fribourg, L.: An inverse method for parametric timed automata. International Journal of Foundations of Computer Science 20(5), 819–836 (2009)
5. André, É., Fribourg, L., Soulat, R.: Enhancing the Inverse Method with State Merging. In: Goodloe, A.E., Person, S. (eds.) NFM 2012. LNCS, vol. 7226, pp. 100–105. Springer, Heidelberg (2012)
6. Bagnara, R., Hill, P.M., Zaffanella, E.: The Parma Polyhedra Library: Toward a complete set of numerical abstractions for the analysis and verification of hardware and software systems. Science of Computer Programming 72(1–2), 3–21 (2008)
7. Behrmann, G., Larsen, K.G., Rasmussen, J.I.: Beyond Liveness: Efficient Parameter Synthesis for Time Bounded Liveness. In: Pettersson, P., Yi, W. (eds.) FORMATS 2005. LNCS, vol. 3829, pp. 81–94. Springer, Heidelberg (2005)
8. Bini, E., Buttazzo, G.C.: Schedulability analysis of periodic fixed priority systems. IEEE Trans. Computers 53(11), 1462–1473 (2004)
9. Cimatti, A., Palopoli, L., Ramadian, Y.: Symbolic computation of schedulability regions using parametric timed automata. In: RTSS, pp. 80–89. IEEE Computer Society, Washington, DC (2008)
10. Fribourg, L., Lesens, D.: Projet ROSCOV: Robuste ordonnancement de systèmes de contrôle de vol. Project report (December 2011)(in French), http://www.farman.ens-cachan.fr/ROSCOV.pdf
11. Henzinger, T.A., Ho, P.H., Wong-Toi, H.: Hytech: A model checker for hybrid systems. Software Tools for Technology Transfer 1, 460–463 (1997)
12. Le, T., Palopoli, L., Passerone, R., Ramadian, Y., Cimatti, A.: Parametric analysis of distributed firm real-time systems: A case study. In: ETFA, pp. 1–8 (2010)
13. Lime, D., Roux, O.H., Seidner, C., Traonouez, L.-M.: Romeo: A Parametric Model-Checker for Petri Nets with Stopwatches. In: Kowalewski, S., Philippou, A. (eds.) TACAS 2009. LNCS, vol. 5505, pp. 54–57. Springer, Heidelberg (2009)
14. Markey, N.: Robustness in real-time systems. In: SIES, pp. 28–34. IEEE (2011)
15. Soulat, R.: Scheduling with IMITATOR: Some case studies. Research Report LSV-12-05, Laboratoire Spécification et Vérification, France (March 2012), http://www.lsv.ens-cachan.fr/Publis/ RAPPORTS_LSV/PDF/rr-lsv-2012-05.pdf
16. Sun, J., Gardner, M.K., Liu, J.W.S.: Bounding completion times of jobs with arbitrary release times, variable execution times, and resource sharing. IEEE Trans. Softw. Eng. 23, 603–615 (1997)

Maximal and Compositional Pattern-Based Loop Invariants

Virginia Aponte[1], Pierre Courtieu[1], Yannick Moy[2], and Marc Sango[2]

[1] CNAM, 292 rue Saint-Martin F-75141 Paris Cedex 03 - France
{maria-virginia.aponte_garcia,pierre.courtieu}@cnam.fr
[2] AdaCore, 46 rue d'Amsterdam, F-75009 Paris France
{moy,sango}@adacore.com

Abstract. We present a novel approach for the automatic generation of inductive loop invariants over non nested loops manipulating arrays. Unlike most existing approaches, it generates invariants containing disjunctions and quantifiers, which are rich enough for proving functional properties over programs which manipulate arrays. Our approach does not require the user to provide initial assertions or postconditions. It proceeds first, by translating body loops into an intermediate representation of parallel assignments, and second, by recognizing through static analysis code patterns that respect stability properties on accessed locations. We associate with each pattern a formula that we prove to be a so-called local invariant, and we give conditions for local invariants to compose an inductive invariant of the complete loop. We also give conditions over invariants to be locally maximal, and we show that some of our pattern invariants are indeed maximal.

Keywords: Loop invariants, compositional reasoning, automatic invariant generation.

1 Introduction

Thanks to the increased capabilities of automatic provers, deductive program verification emerges as a realistic verification technique in industry, with commercially supported toolsets [11,30], and new certification standards recognizing its use [27]. In deductive program verification, users first annotate their programs with logical specifications; then a tool generates Verification Conditions (VCs), *i.e.* formulas encoding that the program respects its specifications; finally a tool is called to automatically prove those VCs. The problem is that, in many cases, in particular during development, not all VCs are proved automatically. Dealing with those VCs is a non-trivial task. Three cases are possible: (1) the program does not implement the specification; (2) the specification is not provable inductively; (3) the automatic prover does not find the proof. The solution to (1) is to correct the program or the specification. The solution to (3) is to use a better automatic prover. The solution to (2) is certainly the most challenging for the user. The problem occurs when, for a given loop, the user should supply

D. Giannakopoulou and D. Méry (Eds.): FM 2012, LNCS 7436, pp. 37–51, 2012.
© Springer-Verlag Berlin Heidelberg 2012

an inductive loop invariant: this invariant should hold when entering the loop; it should be provable for the $n+1^{th}$ iteration by assuming only that it holds at the nth iteration; it should be sufficient to prove subsequent properties of interest after the loop. In practice, the user has to strengthen the loop invariant with additional properties until it can be proved inductively. In general, this requires understanding the details of the generation of VCs and the underlying mathematical theory, which is not typical engineering knowledge.

Generation of loop invariants is a well researched area, for which there exists a rich set of techniques and tools. Most of these techniques focus on the discovery of predicates that express rich arithmetic properties with a simple Boolean structure (typically, linear or non-linear constraints over program variables). In our experience with supporting industrial users of the SPARK [2] technology, these are seldom the problematic loop invariants. Indeed, users are well aware of the arithmetic properties that should be maintained through loops, and thus have no difficulty manually annotating loops with the desired arithmetic invariants. Instead, users very often have difficulties annotating loops with invariants stating *additional* properties, that that they do not recognize as required for inductive reasoning. These properties typically have a complex Boolean structure, with disjunctions and quantifiers, for expressing both the effects of past iterations and the locations not being modified by past iterations. In this paper, we focus on the automatic generation of these richer loop invariants.[1]

We present a novel technique for generating rich inductive loop invariants, possibly containing disjunctions and quantifiers (universal and existential) over loops manipulating scalar and array variables. Our method is compositional, which differentiates it from previous approaches working on entire loops: we consider a loop as a composition of smaller pieces (called reduced loops), on which we can reason separately to generate local invariants, which are then aggregated to generate an invariant of the complete loop. The same technique can be applied both to unannotated loops and to loops already annotated, in which case it uses the existing loop invariant.

Local invariants are generated based on an extensible collection of patterns, corresponding to simple but frequently used loops over scalar and array variables. As our technique relies on pattern matching to infer invariants, the choice and the variety of patterns is crucial. We have identified five categories of patterns, for search, scalar update, scalar integration, array mapping and array exchange, comprising a total of 16 patterns. For each pattern we define, we provide a local invariant, and prove it to be local, and for some of them maximal. An invariant is *local* when it refers only to variables modified locally in the reduced loop, and when it can strengthen an inductive invariant over the complete loop. We give conditions for invariants to be local. A local invariant is *maximal* when it is at least as strong as any invariant on the reduced loop. To our knowledge, this is the first work dealing with compositional reasoning on loop invariants, defining modularity and maximality criteria. We also extend the notion of stable variables introduced by Kovács and Voronkov[19].

---

[1] For the sake of simplicity we omit array bound constraints in generated invariants.

Our technique, applied to a loop L that iterates over the loop index i, can be summarized as follows:

1. We translate L into an intermediate language of parallel assignments, which facilitates both defining patterns and reasoning on local invariants. The translation consists in transforming a sequence of assignments guarded by conditions (if-statements) into a set of parallel assignments of guarded values (if-expressions). This can be done using techniques for efficient computing of static single assignment variables as described in [7,26]. Due to lack of space, details of the translation are omitted.
2. Using a simple syntactic static analysis, we detect stable [19] scalar and array variables occurring in L. A scalar variable is stable if it is never modified. An array variable is stable on the range $a..b$ if the value of the array between indexes a and b is not modified in the first i iterations (where a and b may refer to the current value of i). We define a *preexisting* invariant over L, denoted $\wp_L$, to express these stability properties.
3. We match our patterns against the intermediate representation of L. We require stability conditions on matched code, which are resolved based on $\wp_L$. For each match involving pattern P_k, we instantiate the corresponding local invariant ϕ_k with variables and expressions occurring in L.
4. We combine all generated local invariants $\phi_1 \dots \phi_n$ with $\wp_L$ to obtain an inductive invariant on the complete L given by $\wp_L \wedge \phi_1 \wedge \dots \wedge \phi_n$.

This article is organized as follows. In the rest of this section we survey related work and introduce a running example. Section 2 presents the intermediate language. In Section 3, we introduce reduced loops and local invariants. In Section 4, we define loop patterns as particular instances of reduced loops restricted to some stable expressions. We present four examples of concrete patterns and we provide their corresponding local invariants. In Section 5, we present sufficient criteria for a local invariant to be maximal, and we state maximality results on two concrete pattern invariants. We finally conclude and discuss perspectives in Section 6. Due to lack of space, proofs are omitted but are available in [1].

1.1   Related Work

Most existing techniques generate loop invariants in the form of conjunctions of (in)equalities between polynomials in the program variables, whether by abstract interpretation [6,24], predicate abstraction [12], Craig's interpolation [22,23] or algebraic techniques [5,28,18]. Various works have defined disjunctive abstract domains on top of the base abstract domains [20,15,29].

A few works have targeted the generation of loop invariants with a richer Boolean structure and quantifiers, based on techniques for quantifier-free invariants. Halbwachs and Péron [14] describe an abstract domain to reason about array contents over *simple programs* that they describe as *"one-dimensional arrays, traversed by simple for loops"*. They are able to represent facts like $(\forall i)(2 \leq i \leq n \Rightarrow A[i] \geq A[i-1]$, in which a point-wise relation is established between elements of array slices, where this relation is supported by a quantifier-free base abstract domain. Gulwani *et al.* [13] describe a general lifting procedure that creates a quantified disjunctive abstract domain from quantifier-free domains. They are able to represent facts like $(\forall i)(0 \leq i < n \Rightarrow a[i] = 0)$, in which the formula is universally quantified over an implication between quantifier-free formulas of the base domains. McMillan [21] describes an instrumentation of a resolution-based prover that generates quantified invariants describing facts over simple loops manipulating arrays. Using a similar technique, Kovács and Voronkov [19] generate invariants containing quantifier alternation. Our technique may find a weaker invariant than the previous approaches in some cases (like insertion sort) and a stronger invariant in other cases. The main benefit of our technique is its simplicity and its extensibility: once the loop is converted to a special form of parallel assignment, the technique consists simply in pattern matching on the loop statements, and patterns can be added easily to adapt the technique to new code bases, much like in [8].

1.2   Running Example

We will use the program of Fig. 1 as a running example throughout the paper. A simpler version of this program appears in previous works [3,19].

The program fills an array B with the negative values of a source array A, an array C with the positive values of A, and it erases the corresponding elements from A. It stops at the first null value found in A. As pointed out in [19], there are many properties relating the values of A, B and C before and after the loop, that one may want to generate automatically for this program. In this paper, we show how the different steps of our technique apply to this loop.

```
b := 1; c := 1; erased := 0;
for i in 1..10 while A[i] ≠ 0 do
  if A[i] < 0 then
      B[b] := A[i]; b := b+1;
  else
      C[c] := A[i]; c := c+1;
  end if
  A[i]:=erased;
end
```

Fig. 1. Array partitioning

2   A Language of Parallel Assignments

In this section we introduce the intermediate language $\mathcal{L}$ and its formal semantics. $\mathcal{L}$ is a refinement of the language introduced in [19] that allows us to group all the assignements performed on the same location in a single syntactic unit.

Fig. 2.(a) presents the syntax of $\mathcal{L}$. In this language, programs are restricted to a single non nested for-like loop (possibly having an extra exit condition) over scalar and one-dimensional array variables. Assignments in $\mathcal{L}$ are performed in parallel. Note that location expressions (e_l) can be either scalar variables or array cells, and that all statements (s_l) of a group ($\mathcal{G}$) assign to the same variable: either the group (only) contains guarded statements $g_k \rightarrow x := e_k$ assigning to

$\mathcal{L} ::= \textbf{loop } i \textbf{ in } \alpha \mathbin{..} \omega \textbf{ exit } e_b$ $\qquad \textbf{do } B \textbf{ end}$	loop	$\textbf{loop } i \textbf{ in } 1..10 \textbf{ exit } A[\,i\,] = 0 \textbf{ do}$ $\quad \{ \quad A[\,i\,] < 0 \quad \rightarrow B[b] := A[\,i\,]\}$
$\mathcal{B} ::= \textbf{skip} \mid \mathcal{G}(\|\ \mathcal{G})^*$	body	$\|\ \{ \quad A[\,i\,] < 0 \quad \rightarrow b \ := b{+}1 \}$
$\mathcal{G} ::= \{s_l(;\, s_l)^*\}$	group	$\|\ \{ \ \neg(A[\,i\,] < 0) \rightarrow C[c] := A[\,i\,]\}$
$s_l ::= e_b \rightarrow e_l := e_a$	assignment	$\|\ \{ \ \neg(A[\,i\,] < 0) \rightarrow c \ := c{+}1 \}$
$e_l ::= x \mid A[e_a]$	location expr	$\|\ \{ \quad \textbf{true} \rightarrow A[\,i\,] := \text{erased} \}$
$e_a \in \textbf{Aexp}, \ e_b \in \textbf{Bexp}$		$\textbf{end}$

Fig. 2. (a) Formal syntax of loop programs (b) Running example translation (Fig. 1)

some scalar variable x; or it contains statements $g_p \rightarrow A[a_p] := e_p$ assigning to the possibly different cells $A[a_1], A[a_2] \dots$ of some array variable A. A loop body ($\mathcal{B}$) is an unordered collection of groups for different variables.

Running example. [Step 1: Translation into the intermediate language] The translation of the running example loop (Fig. 1) into $\mathcal{L}$ is given in Fig. 2.(b).

Expressions and Variables. n, k stand for (non negative) constants of the language; lower case letters x, a are scalar variables; upper-case letters A, C are array variables; v is any variable; e_a is an arithmetic expression; ϵ, e_b, g are Boolean expressions; e is any expression. Subscripted variables x_0 and A_0 denote respectively the initial value of variables x and A.

Informal Semantics. Groups are executed *simultaneously*: expressions and guards are evaluated *before* assignments are executed. We assume groups and bodies to be *write-disjoint*, and loops to be *well-formed*. A group G is write-disjoint if all its assignments update the same variable, and if for any two different guards g_1, g_2 in G, $g_1 \wedge g_2$ is unsatisfiable. A loop body $B = G_1 \| \dots \| G_n$ is write-disjoint if all G_k update different variables and if they are all write-disjoint. A loop L is well-formed if its body is write-disjoint. Thus, on each iteration, at most one assignment is performed for each variable. Conditions on guarded assignments are essentially the same as in the work of Kovacs and Voronkov [19], with a slightly different formalism. For simplicity, we require here unsatisfiability of $g_1 \wedge g_2$ for two guards within a group assigning to array A, even in the case where the updated cells for those guards are actually different.

Loop Conventions. L denotes a loop, B a body, and i is always the loop index. The loop index is not a variable, so it cannot be assigned. For simplicity, we assume that i is increased (and not decreased) after each run through the loop, from its initial value α to its final value ω. We use $\ell_{(\alpha,\omega,\epsilon)}\{B\}$ to abbreviate **loop** i **in** $\alpha..\omega$ **exit** ϵ **do** B **end**, and $\ell_{(\alpha,\omega)}\{B\}$ when $\epsilon = $ *false*. $\vec{G}$ denotes a body $G_1 \| \dots \| G_n$ (for some n), while $\vec{G} \| B$, is the parallel composition of groups $G_1, \dots G_n$ from G with all groups from B. $\{\overrightarrow{g_k \rightarrow l_k := e_k}\}$ denotes a group made of the guarded assignments $\{g_1 \rightarrow l_1 := e_1; \dots; g_n \rightarrow l_n := e_n\}$. $\mathcal{G}(B)$ denotes the set of groups occurring in B.

Loop Variables. $V(L)$ is the set of variables occurring in L (note that $i \notin V(L)$). $V_w(L)$ is the set of variables assigned in L, referred to as local (to L). $V_{nw}(L)$ is the set of variables occuring in L but not assigned in L, referred to as external (to L): $V_{nw}(L) = V(L) - V_w(L)$. Given a set of variables V, the *initialisation predicate* ι_V is defined as $\iota_V = \bigwedge_{v \in V} v = v_0$ asserting that all variables $v \in V$ have as initial (abstract) value v_0. Sets and formulas defined on the loop L are similarly defined on the loop body B.

Quantifications, Substitutions and Fresh Variables. ϕ, ψ, ι and $\wp$ denote formulas. The loop index i may occur in the formula ϕ or in the expression e, respectively denoted $\phi(i)$ or $e(i)$, but it can be omitted when not relevant. Except for logical assertions (*i.e.* invariants, Hoare triples), formulas are implicitly universally quantified on the set of all their free variables, including i. To improve readability, these quantifications are often kept implicit. We denote by $\exists V.\phi$ the formula $\exists v_1 \ldots v_n.\phi$ for all $v_i \in V$, and by $[V_1 \leftarrow V_2]$ the substitution of each variable of the set V_1 by the corresponding variable of the set V_2. Given a set of variables V, V' denotes the set containing a fresh variable v' for each variable $v \in V$. Given an expression e, we denote $e'^V = e[V \leftarrow V']$ and $\phi'^V = \phi[V \leftarrow V']$.

2.1   Strongest Postcondition Semantics

The predicate transformer sp introduced by Dijkstra [9,10] computes the strongest postcondition holding after the execution of a given statement. We shall use it to obtain the strongest postcondition holding after the execution of an arbitrary iteration of the loop body, which will be useful when comparing loop invariants according to maximality criteria (see Section 5). Thus, we express the semantics of the intermediate language $\mathcal{L}$ through the formal definition of sp. As our goal is the generation of loop invariants, and not the generation of loop postconditions, we only need to describe sp for loop bodies, instead of giving it for entire loops in $\mathcal{L}$. Note that Definition 1 requires replacing a variable v assigned in the loop body with a fresh logical variable v', standing for the value of v prior to the assignment.

Definition 1 (Predicate Transformer sp). *Let ϕ be a formula, $\overrightarrow{G_k}$ a loop body, and $V = V_w(\overrightarrow{G_k})$. We define $\mathrm{sp}(\overrightarrow{G_k}, \phi)$ as:*

$$\mathrm{sp}(\boldsymbol{skip}, \phi) = \phi \qquad\qquad \mathrm{sp}(\overrightarrow{G_k}, \phi) = \exists V'. \left(\phi'^V \wedge \bigwedge_k \mathrm{Psp}(G_k, V) \right)$$

$$\mathrm{Psp}(\{\overrightarrow{g_k \rightarrow x := e_k}\}, V) = \bigwedge_k (g_k'^V \Rightarrow x = e_k'^V) \wedge \left(\left(\bigwedge_k \neg g_k'^V \right) \Rightarrow x = x' \right)$$

$$\mathrm{Psp}(\{\overrightarrow{g_k \rightarrow A[a_k] := e_k}\}, V) = \bigwedge_k (g_k'^V \Rightarrow A[a_k'^V] = e_k'^V)$$

$$\wedge \forall j. \left(\bigwedge_k \neg(g_k'^V \wedge j = a_k'^V) \right) \Rightarrow A[j] = A'[j].$$

3   Reduced Loops and Local Invariants

Remember that we seek to infer local properties over code pieces occurring in a loop L. In this section, we introduce *reduced loops*, which are loops built on groups taken from a loop L, and *local loop invariants*, which are inductive properties holding *locally* on reduced loops. We state a compositionality result for locally inferred invariants allowing us to compose them into an inductive invariant that holds on the entire loop. Our notion of local invariant is generic: it is not limited to the stability properties used by patterns in Section 4.

3.1   (Inductive) ι_L-Loop Invariants

To define inductive loop invariants, we rely on the classical relation $\vDash_{\mathrm{par}}$ of satisfaction under partial correctness for Hoare triples [17,25]. Invariants are defined relative to a given initialisation predicate ι_L providing initial values to loop variables. We define $\iota_L = \iota_V$, where V is the set of all variables occurring in L. An ι_L-loop invariant is an inductive loop invariant under ι_L initial conditions. Also, we say that ι_L *covers* ϕ when $V(\phi) \subseteq V(\iota_L)$. In the following, we assume that the initialisation predicate ι_L covers all properties stated on L.

Definition 2 ((Inductive) ι_L-Loop Invariant). *Assume ι_L covers a formula ϕ. ϕ is an ι_L-loop invariant on the loop $L = \ell_{(\alpha,\omega,\epsilon)}\{B\}$, iff*
(a) $(i = \alpha \wedge \iota_L) \Rightarrow \phi$; *and*   *(b)* $\vDash_{\mathrm{par}} \{\alpha \leq i \leq \omega \wedge \neg\epsilon \wedge \phi\} B; \ i := i + 1 \{\phi\}$.

3.2   Local (Reduced) Loop Invariants

A *reduced loop* from a loop $L = \ell_{(\alpha,\omega,\epsilon)}\{B\}$, is a loop with the same index range as L but whose body B_r is a collection of groups occuring within B (*i.e.* $\mathcal{G}(B_r) \subseteq \mathcal{G}(B)$). These loops either take the form $L_r = \ell_{(\alpha,\omega,\epsilon)}\{B_r\}$ or $L_r = \ell_{(\alpha,\omega)}\{B_r\}$. Remember that each group brings together all assignements of a unique variable. Quite naturally, we seek inferring properties restricted to the locally modified variables of reduced loops. Thus, we distinguish between variables updated within reduced loops, called *local*, and variables appearing without being assigned within them, called *external*.

   To deduce properties holding locally on L_r, we assume given an inductive loop invariant $\wp_L$ holding on the entire loop, that states properties over variables external to L_r. Thus, we use a global pre-established property on external variables in order to deduce local properties over local variables. The notion of relative-inductive invariants, borrowed from [4], captures this style of reasoning: ϕ is inductive relative to another formula $\wp_L$, when the inductive step of the proof of ϕ holds under the assumption of $\wp_L$ (see Example 1 below).

Definition 3 (Relative Inductive Invariant). *Assume ι_L covers a formula ϕ. ϕ is $\wp_L$-inductive on loop L, if*
(1) $(i = \alpha \wedge \iota_L) \Rightarrow \phi$; *(2)* $\mathrm{sp}(B, \alpha \leq i \leq \omega \wedge \neg\epsilon \wedge \wp_L(i) \wedge \phi(i)) \Rightarrow \phi(i + 1)$.

a := 0; b := 0;
loop i **in** 1..10 **do**
   b := a+1;
   a :=i;
end
	init: $\iota_L = (a = 0 \wedge b = 0)$
	previous: $\wp_L = (a = i - 1)$
	loop i **in** 1..10 **do**
	   { **true** $\rightarrow$ a :=i }
	‖ { **true** $\rightarrow$ b := a+1 }
	end
		$L_r =$ **loop** i **in** 1..10 **do**
		   { **true** $\rightarrow$ b := a+1 }
		end
		
		local: $\boxed{\phi_r = (b = i - 1)}$
		
		final global inv: $\boxed{\wp_L \wedge \phi_r}$

Fig. 3. (a) Loop L   (b) Init, previous, translation (c) Reduced loop L_r, local prop

ϕ is a $\wp_L$-*local loop invariant* on loop L_r, if ϕ only refers to variables locally modified in L_r, and if ϕ holds inductively on L_r relatively to the property $\wp_L$.

Definition 4 ($\wp_L$-Local Loop Invariant). *ϕ is a $\wp_L$-local loop invariant for loop L_r if (a) $V(\phi) \subseteq V_w(L_r)$; and   (b) ϕ is $\wp_L$-inductive on L_r.*

Example 1 (A $\wp_L$-local loop invariant). Fig. 3.(a) shows a loop L, whose translation and initialisation ι_L are given in 3.(b). The reduced loop L_r in 3.(c) is built on the group that assigns to b. There are two variables in L_r: a is external, while b is local to it. We take $\wp_L$ shown in 3.(b) as previously known property (over variables external to L_r). Clearly, $\wp_L$ does not hold on the reduced loop L_r, but is does hold as ι_L-loop invariant on the entire loop L. The local property $\phi_r(i)$ from 3.(c) does not hold (inductively) by itself on the reduced loop, yet $\wp_L \wedge \phi_r(i)$ holds as inductive invariant of L_r. Therefore, $\phi_r(i)$ is $\wp_L$-inductive on L_r. Moreover, as $\phi_r(i)$ only contains variables local to L_r, it follows that $\phi_r(i)$ is $\wp_L$-local on L_r. Finally, as $\wp_L$ holds inductively on the entire loop, according to the Theorem 1 below, the composed invariant $\wp_L \wedge \phi_r$ is indeed an ι_L-invariant on the whole loop L.

Informally, the Theorem 1 says that whenever a property $\wp_L$, used to deduce that a local property ϕ holds on a reduced loop, is itself an inductive invariant on the entire loop, then $\wp_L \wedge \phi$ is an inductive invariant of the entire loop.

Theorem 1 (Compositionality of $\wp_L$-Local Invariants). *Assume that loops $L = \ell_{(\alpha,\omega,\epsilon)}\{\overrightarrow{G} \parallel B\}$ and $L_r = \ell_{(\alpha,\omega,\epsilon)}\{B\}$ are well-formed. Assume that (h_1) ϕ_r is a $\wp_L$-local loop invariant on L_r; (h_2) $\wp_L$ is an ι_L-invariant on L. Then, $\wp_L \wedge \phi_r$ is an ι_L-invariant on L.*

4   Stable Loop Patterns

In this section, we introduce the stability property for expressions, and we give sufficient conditions for this property to hold. Stability over expressions generalizes the notion of stablity on variables introduced in [19] (see 4.2). We define $\wp_L$-stable loop patterns, as a particular instance of reduced loops restricted to stable expressions[2]. As examples, we present four concrete patterns and we provide their corresponding local invariants.

4.1 Stability on Variables and Expressions

Given an initialisation ι_L , we define the *initial value* of an expression $e(i)$, denoted $e_0(i)$, as the result of replacing any occurrence of a variable x in e, *except* i^3, by its initial value x_0 according to the initialisation ι_L. Informally, an expression e occurring in a loop L, is stable, if on any run through the loop, e is equal to its initial value e_0. Here, we are interested in being able to prove that $e = e_0$ under the assumption of a preexisting inductive loop invariant $\wp_L$.

Definition 5 (Stable Expressions). *An expression $e(i)$ is said to be $\wp_L$-stable in loop L, denoted $\wp_L$-s, if there exists an ι_L-loop invariant $\wp_L$ on L such that:*

$$\wp_L(i) \Rightarrow (e(i) = e_0(i)).$$

The rationale behind stability is that, given a preexisting inductive loop invariant $\wp_L$, a $\wp_L$-stable expression e can be replaced by its initial value e_0 when reasoning on the loop body using the predicate transformer sp.

4.2 Sufficient Conditions for Stability

In this section we generalize the notion of stability over variables introduced in [19], in order to express the following properties:

1. a scalar variable x keeps its initial value x_0 throughout the loop;
2. there exist a constant offset from i, denoted $p(i)$, that corresponds to a valid index for array A, such that every cell value in the array slice $A[p(i)\dots n]$ is equal to its initial value.

For array A and loop L, these properties are formally expressed by:

$$\beth_x \equiv \quad x = x_0 \qquad\qquad\qquad\qquad \text{Scalar stability}$$
$$\triangle_{A,p} \equiv \quad \forall j.(j \geq p(i) \Rightarrow A[j] = A_0[j]) \qquad \text{Array } p-\text{stability}$$

If $\triangle_{A,p}$ holds, we say that A is p-stable. When $p(i) = \alpha$ this property is equivalent to $A = A_0$. To increase readability, the latter notation is preferred.

A sufficient condition for a variable to be stable is when this variable is not updated at all in the loop. An array B in this case verifies the property $\triangle_{B,\alpha}$. Finding p-stability on some array A can be done by examining all updates to cells $A[p_k(i)]$ and choosing $p(i)$ as $p(i) = max(\overrightarrow{p_k(i)})$. Assume now that array A is known to be p-stable, and that $A[a]$ occurs in some expression e. If $A[a]$ corresponds to an access in the stable slice of A, then e is stable, which can be verified by checking that $a \geq p$ is a loop invariant.

---

[2] More precisely, to expressions whose location expressions defined over external variables are stable.

[3] And except occurrences at array index positions.

Running example. [Step 2: Extracting a preexisting global invariant] The variable erased is never assigned in this loop, so it is stable. Array A is updated only in cell $A[i]$, entailing i-stability for A. Thus, we can extract the following inductive invariant expressing stability properties for our loop: $\wp_L = \dashv_{\mathsf{erased}} \wedge \triangle_{A,i}$.

4.3 $\wp_L$-Loop Patterns

Given a preexisting inductive loop invariant $\wp_L$, we define loop patterns relative to $\wp_L$, or $\wp_L$-*loop patterns*, as triples $P_n = (L_n, C_n, \phi_n)$, where: L_n is a loop scheme given by a valid loop construction in our intermediate language $\mathcal{L}$; C_n is a list of constraints requiring the $\wp_L$-s property on generic sub-expressions $e_1, e_2 \dots$ of L_n; ϕ_n is an invariant scheme referring only to variables local to L_n.

Fig. 4 presents examples of three concrete loop patterns. For each of them, the corresponding loop scheme is given in the upper-left entry, the constraints in the upper-right entry, and the invariant scheme in the bottom entry. To identify the pattern P_n within the source loop L, L_n must match actual constructions occurring in L, and the pattern constraints must be satisfied. In that case, we generate the corresponding local invariant by instantiating ϕ_n with matched constructions from L.

Theorem 2 establishes that each invariant scheme ϕ_n from Fig. 4 is indeed a $\wp_L$-local invariant on its corresponding loop scheme L_n. By the compositional result of Theorem 1, each generated local invariant can be composed with the preexisting ι_L-invariant to obtain a richer ι_L-invariant holding on the entire loop.

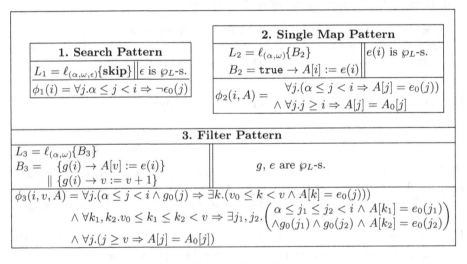

Fig. 4. Three $\wp_L$-Loop Patterns

Theorem 2 (Search, Map and Filter Invariant Schemes are $\wp_L$-local).
For $n \in [1, 2, 3]$ assume that $P_n = (L_n, C_n, \phi_n)$ corresponds to the patterns given in Fig. 4. Assume having three pairs $(\iota_{L_n}, \wp_{L_n})$ satifying each the constraints C_n for pattern P_n. Then, each ϕ_n is a $\wp_{L_n}$-local loop invariant on the loop L_n.

Running example. [Step 3: Discovering patterns, generating local properties] We take $\wp_L \equiv \dashv_{\mathsf{erased}} \wedge \triangle_{A,i}$ (see Step 2) as preexisting inductive invariant. By pattern-matching, we can recognize three patterns in L: the Search pattern on line 1; the Single Map pattern on line 6; the Filter pattern, once on lines 2-3, and once again on lines 4-5. We must check that all pattern constraints are respected. First note that $\wp_L$ entails i-stability for A, and therefore the location expression $A[i]$ (occurring in both instances of the Filter pattern) is $\wp_L$-s, as well as expressions $A[i] = 0$ in the Search pattern, and $A[i] < 0$ in the Filter pattern. Finally, $\wp_L$ entails stability of erased in the Map pattern. We instantiate the corresponding invariant schemes and obtain the local invariants shown below. Note that $\phi_3(i, b, B)$ and $\phi_3(i, c, C)$ correspond to different instances of the Filter pattern. We unfold only one of them here:

$$\phi_1(i) = \forall j. \alpha \leq j < i \Rightarrow \neg(A_0[i] = 0)$$

$$\phi_2(i, A) = \forall j.(\alpha \leq j < i \Rightarrow A[j] = \mathsf{erased}_0) \wedge \forall j.(j \geq i) \Rightarrow A[j] = A_0[j]$$

$$\phi_3(i, c, C) = \ldots$$

$$\phi_3(i, b, B) = \forall j.(\alpha \leq j < i \wedge A_0[j] < 0 \Rightarrow \exists k.(b_0 \leq k < b \wedge B[k] = A_0[j]))$$

$$\wedge \; \forall k_1, k_2. b_0 \leq k_1 \leq k_2 < b \Rightarrow \exists j_1, j_2. \left(\begin{array}{l} \alpha \leq j_1 \leq j_2 \leq i \\ \wedge \; A_0[j_2] < 0 \wedge B[k_1] = A_0[j_1] \\ \wedge \; A_0[j_2] < 0 \wedge B[k_2] = A_0[j_2] \end{array} \right)$$

$$\wedge \; \forall j.(j \geq b \Rightarrow B[j] = B_0[j])$$

Example 2 (A disjunctive/existential pattern example). Fig. 5 provides an example of pattern whose invariant contains disjunctions and existential quantifiers. This pattern typically corresponds to the inner loop in a sorting algorithm. The local invariant obtained for the loop from Fig. 5.(b) is:

$$((m = m_0) \wedge \forall j.(\alpha \leq j < i \Rightarrow \neg(A_0[j] < A_0[m_0])))$$
$$\vee \; (\exists j.(\alpha \leq j < i \wedge m = j) \wedge \forall k.(\alpha \leq k < i \Rightarrow \neg(A_0[k] < A_0[m])))$$

Min Index Pattern		for i in 1..n do
$L_4 = \ell_{(\alpha,\omega)}\{B_4\}$	$e(i)$ is $\wp_L$-s.	if A[i] < A[m]
$B_4 = \{e(i) < e(a) \rightarrow a := i\}$		then m := i;
$\phi_4(i, a) = ((a = a_0) \wedge \forall j.(\alpha \leq j < i \Rightarrow \neg(e_0(j) < e_0(a_0))))$		end if
$\vee \; (\exists j.(\alpha \leq j < i \wedge a = j \wedge \forall k.(\alpha \leq k < i \Rightarrow \neg(e_0(k) < e_0(a)))))$		end

Fig. 5. (a) A pattern with existentials and disjunctions   (b) A loop instance

Running example. [Step 4: Aggregating local invariants] We know that the preexisting invariant $\wp_L$ holds as ι_L-invariant on L. By Theorem 2, ϕ_1 is $\wp_L$-local on $L_1 = \ell_{(\alpha,\omega,\epsilon)}\{\mathsf{skip}\}$, and ϕ_2 and ϕ_3 are $\wp_L$-local on loops $L_k = \ell_{(\alpha,\omega)}\{B_k\}$ respectively for $k = 1, 2$. It is easy to obtain from these results, that ϕ_2 and ϕ_3 are $\wp_L$-local on loops $L_k = \ell_{(\alpha,\omega,\epsilon)}\{B_k\}$. Therefore, according to Theorem 1, we can compose all these invariants to obtain the following richer ι_L-invariant holding on L: $\wp_L \wedge \phi_1(i) \wedge \phi_2(i, A) \wedge \phi_3(i, b, B) \wedge \phi_3(i, c, C)$.

5   Maximal Loop Invariants

In this section, we present maximality criteria on loop invariants, whether inductive or not. A loop invariant is maximal when it is stronger than any invariant
holding on that loop. For consistency, we compare loop invariants only if they
are covered by the same initialisation predicate. We adapt this notion to reduced loops by defining *local invariant maximality*. These notions are rather
generic and apply to any loop language equipped with a strongest postcondition
semantics.

Definition 6 (Maximal ι_L-Loop Invariant). ϕ *is a maximal ι_L-loop invariant of loop L if (1) ϕ is an ι_L-loop invariant for L, and (2) for any other ι_L-loop
invariant ψ of L, $\phi \Rightarrow \psi$ is an ι_L-loop invariant of L.*

Theorem 3 (Loop Invariant Maximality). *Let $L = \ell_{(\alpha,\omega,\epsilon)}\{B\}$ and assume
that ϕ is some formula covered by ι_L. ϕ is a maximal ι_L-invariant of L if*

(a) $i = \alpha \wedge \iota_L \Leftrightarrow i = \alpha \wedge \phi(i)$
(b) $\mathrm{sp}(B, \alpha \leq i \leq \omega \wedge \neg \epsilon(i) \wedge \phi(i)) \Leftrightarrow \alpha \leq i \leq \omega \wedge \phi(i+1)$

As seen in Section 3, a local invariant ϕ_r refers only to variables locally modified
in the reduced loop L_r. Nevertheless, external variables may occur in L_r, for
which we are unable to locally infer properties. To ensure consistency when
comparing local invariants, we reason on the maximality of ϕ_r, strenghtened by
a formula $\beth$ stating that all variables external to L_r remain constant through
the execution of the reduced loop.

Definition 7 (Local Invariant Maximality). *Let $L = \ell_{(\alpha,\omega,\epsilon)}\{\vec{G} \parallel B\}$ be a
well-formed loop, and $L_r = \ell_{(\alpha,\omega,\epsilon)}\{B\}$. Let ι_r be an initialisation restricted to
variables occurring in L_r, and $\beth$ a formula asserting constant values $x = x_0$,
$A = A_0$ for all variables x, A external to L_r. We say that ϕ_r is locally maximal
on L_r when $\beth \wedge \phi_r$ is a maximal ι_r-loop invariant of L_r.*

In [1] we provide proofs for the Theorem 4 below. We show that the local loop
invariants schemes $\phi_1(i)$ for the Search Pattern, and $\phi_2(i)$ for the Single Map
Pattern, as stated in Fig. 4, are indeed locally maximal on their corresponding
reduced loop. Notice that $\phi_3(i)$ for the Filter Pattern is not maximal as stated
in Fig. 4. For example, it would be possible to state a stronger invariant for this
pattern by recursively defining a logic function for counting the number of array
elements satisfying the guard g_0 up to the ith element, and using this function
in the loop invariant to give the current value of the variable v.

Theorem 4 (Search and Single Map Invariants Local Maximality). *Let
ϕ_1, L_1, ϕ_2, L_2 as given in Fig. 4. ϕ_1 is locally maximal on the loop L_1, and ϕ_2
is locally maximal on the loop L_2.*

6   Conclusion and Further Work

We present a novel and compositional approach to generate loop invariants. Our approach complements previous approaches: instead of generating relatively weak invariants on any kind of loop, we focus on generating strong or even maximal invariants on particular loop patterns, in a modular way.

The central idea in our approach is to separately generate local loop invariants on reduced versions of the entire loop. This is supported by the introduction of a preexisting loop invariant, which states external properties (*i.e.* properties which do not necessarily hold locally) on the complete loop. This preexisting invariant is then strengthened by the local loop invariants. Since there is no constraint on the way the external invariant is found, our approach fits in smoothly with other automated invariant generation mechanisms.

We propose a specialized version of reduced loops, for which the external invariant is a stability property of some locally accessed variables. We give loop pattern schemes and syntactic criteria to generate invariants for any loop containing these patterns. Independently, we present conditions on arbitrary loop invariants to be maximal, and state results of local maximality for some of our loop patterns. When not maximal, our inferred invariants are essentially as expressive as those generated by previous approaches, but have the advantage of being pre-proven, and thus are well adapted to integration on full automatic invariant generation of industrial oriented frameworks.

Our method applies to programs in an intermediate language of guarded and parallel assignments, to which source programs should first be translated. We have designed such a translation from a subset of the SPARK language, based on an enriched version of static single assignment form [26]. The idea is to transform a sequence of assignments to variables guarded by conditions (if-statements) into a set of parallel assignments to SSA variables [7], where the value assigned has guard information (if-expressions). In the case of array variables, array index expressions that are literals or constant offsets from the loop index are treated specially, in order to generate array index expressions that can be matched to the patterns we define. This translation is exponential in the number of source code statements in the worst-case, but this does not occur on hand-written code.

We expect to implement the translation and the pattern-based loop invariant generation in the next generation of SPARK tools [16,30]. We believe that combining this technique with other ones (and with itself) will be very efficient.

Going further we could develop a broader repository of pattern-driven invariants, to address the more frequent and known loop patterns. As proof of patterns (correctness and optionally maximality) are tedious and error-prone, we plan to mechanize them in a proof assistant and design a repository of formally proven patterns. In particular, as the present technology seems perfectly applicable to non terminating loops, we plan to define new patterns for while loops.

The current approach does not handle nested loops, and the patterns we define do not apply to loops with a complex accumulation property, where the effect of the ith iteration depends in a complex way on the cumulative effect of previous iterations. So it does not apply for example to insertion sort, which can be treated by other approaches [14,13] based on complex abstract domains in abstract interpretation. We are interested in pursuing the approach to treat these more complex examples.

Acknowledgements. We would like to thank Laura Kovács for her feedback on an early version of this work, Benjamin Brosgol for his careful review of the manuscript and anonymous referees for their valuable comments.

References

1. Aponte, V., Courtieu, P., Moy, Y., Sango, M.: Maximal and Compositional Pattern-Based Loop Invariants - Definitions and Proofs. Technical Report CEDRIC-12-2555, CEDRIC laboratory, CNAM-Paris, France (2011), http://cedric.cnam.fr/fichiers/art_2555.pdf
2. Barnes, J.: High Integrity Software: The SPARK Approach to Safety and Security. Addison-Wesley Longman Publishing Co., Inc., Boston (2003)
3. Beyer, D., Henzinger, T.A., Majumdar, R., Rybalchenko, A.: Path invariants. In: Proceedings of the 2007 ACM SIGPLAN Conference on Programming language Design and Implementation, PLDI 2007, pp. 300–309. ACM, New York (2007)
4. Bradley, A., Manna, Z.: Property-directed incremental invariant generation. Formal Aspects of Computing 20, 379–405 (2008), doi:10.1007/s00165-008-0080-9
5. Colón, M.A., Sankaranarayanan, S., Sipma, H.B.: Linear Invariant Generation Using Non-linear Constraint Solving. In: Hunt Jr., W.A., Somenzi, F. (eds.) CAV 2003. LNCS, vol. 2725, pp. 420–432. Springer, Heidelberg (2003)
6. Cousot, P., Halbwachs, N.: Automatic discovery of linear restraints among variables of a program. In: Proceedings of the 5th ACM SIGACT-SIGPLAN Symposium on Principles of Programming Languages, POPL 1978, pp. 84–96. ACM, New York (1978)
7. Cytron, R., Ferrante, J., Rosen, B.K., Wegman, M.N., Zadeck, F.K.: Efficiently computing static single assignment form and the control dependence graph. ACM Trans. Program. Lang. Syst. 13(4), 451–490 (1991)
8. Denney, E., Fischer, B.: A generic annotation inference algorithm for the safety certification of automatically generated code. In: Proceedings of the 5th International Conference on Generative Programming and Component Engineering, GPCE 2006, pp. 121–130. ACM, New York (2006)
9. Dijkstra, E.W.: Guarded commands, non-determinacy and formal derivation of programs. Comm. ACM 18(8), 453–457 (1975)
10. Dijkstra, E.W., Scholten, C.S.: Predicate calculus and program semantics. Springer (1990)
11. Verifier, E.C.: http://www.eschertech.com/products/ecv.php (2012)
12. Graf, S., Saïdi, H.: Construction of Abstract State Graphs with PVS. In: Grumberg, O. (ed.) CAV 1997. LNCS, vol. 1254, pp. 72–83. Springer, Heidelberg (1997)
13. Gulwani, S., McCloskey, B., Tiwari, A.: Lifting abstract interpreters to quantified logical domains. In: Proceedings of the 35th Annual ACM SIGPLAN-SIGACT Symposium on Principles of Programming Languages, POPL 2008, pp. 235–246. ACM, New York (2008)
14. Halbwachs, N., Péron, M.: Discovering properties about arrays in simple programs. In: Proceedings of the 2008 ACM SIGPLAN Conference on Programming Language Design and Implementation, PLDI 2008, pp. 339–348. ACM, New York (2008)

15. Harris, W.R., Sankaranarayanan, S., Ivančić, F., Gupta, A.: Program analysis via satisfiability modulo path programs. In: Proceedings of the 37th Annual ACM SIGPLAN-SIGACT Symposium on Principles of Programming Languages, POPL 2010, pp. 71–82. ACM, New York (2010)
16. Hi-Lite: Simplifying the use of formal methods, http://www.open-do.org/projects/hi-lite/
17. Hoare, C.A.R.: An axiomatic basis for computer programming. Commun. ACM 12, 576–580 (1969)
18. Kovács, L.: Invariant Generation for P-Solvable Loops with Assignments. In: Hirsch, E.A., Razborov, A.A., Semenov, A., Slissenko, A. (eds.) CSR 2008. LNCS, vol. 5010, pp. 349–359. Springer, Heidelberg (2008)
19. Kovács, L., Voronkov, A.: Finding loop invariants for programs over arrays using a theorem prover. In: Proceedings of the 2009 11th International Symposium on Symbolic and Numeric Algorithms for Scientific Computing. SYNASC 2009, IEEE Computer Society, Washington, DC (2009)
20. Mauborgne, L., Rival, X.: Trace Partitioning in Abstract Interpretation Based Static Analyzers. In: Sagiv, M. (ed.) ESOP 2005. LNCS, vol. 3444, pp. 5–20. Springer, Heidelberg (2005)
21. McMillan, K.L.: Quantified Invariant Generation Using an Interpolating Saturation Prover. In: Ramakrishnan, C.R., Rehof, J. (eds.) TACAS 2008. LNCS, vol. 4963, pp. 413–427. Springer, Heidelberg (2008)
22. McMillan, K.L.: Interpolation and SAT-based model checking. In: Hunt Jr., W.A., Somenzi, F. (eds.) CAV 2003. LNCS, vol. 2725, pp. 1–13. Springer, Heidelberg (2003)
23. McMillan, K.L.: Lazy Abstraction with Interpolants. In: Ball, T., Jones, R.B. (eds.) CAV 2006. LNCS, vol. 4144, pp. 123–136. Springer, Heidelberg (2006)
24. Miné, A.: The octagon abstract domain. Higher Order Symbol. Comput. 19, 31–100 (2006)
25. Nielson, H.R., Nielson, F.: Semantics with Applications: a formal introduction. John Wiley & Sons, Inc., New York (1992)
26. Ottenstein, K.J., Ballance, R.A., MacCabe, A.B.: The program dependence web: a representation supporting control-, data-, and demand-driven interpretation of imperative languages. In: Proceedings of the ACM SIGPLAN 1990 Conference on Programming Language Design and Implementation, PLDI 1990, pp. 257–271. ACM, New York (1990)
27. RTCA. Formal methods supplement to DO-178C and DO-278A. Document RTCA DO-333, RTCA (December 2011)
28. Sankaranarayanan, S., Sipma, H.B., Manna, Z.: Non-linear loop invariant generation using Gröbner bases. In: Proceedings of the 31st ACM SIGPLAN-SIGACT Symposium on Principles of Programming Languages, POPL 2004, pp. 318–329. ACM, New York (2004)
29. Sharma, R., Dillig, I., Dillig, T., Aiken, A.: Simplifying Loop Invariant Generation Using Splitter Predicates. In: Gopalakrishnan, G., Qadeer, S. (eds.) CAV 2011. LNCS, vol. 6806, pp. 703–719. ACM, New York (2011)
30. SPARK Pro (2012), http://www.adacore.com/home/products/sparkpro/

A Formal Approach to Autonomous Vehicle Coordination

Mikael Asplund, Atif Manzoor, Mélanie Bouroche,
Siobhàn Clarke, and Vinny Cahill

Lero - The Irish Software Engineering Research Centre
Distributed Systems Group
School of Computer Science and Statistics
Trinity College Dublin
{asplunda,atif.manzoor,melanie.bouroche,
siobhan.clarke,vinny.cahill}@scss.tcd.ie

Abstract. Increasing demands on safety and energy efficiency will require higher levels of automation in transportation systems. This involves dealing with safety-critical distributed coordination. In this paper we demonstrate how a Satisfiability Modulo Theories (SMT) solver can be used to prove correctness of a vehicular coordination problem. We formalise a recent distributed coordination protocol and validate our approach using an intersection collision avoidance (ICA) case study. The system model captures continuous time and space, and an unbounded number of vehicles and messages. The safety of the case study is automatically verified using the Z3 theorem prover.

1 Introduction

As the number of cars in the world crosses the 1 billion mark and the future travel needs of the world population keep increasing, we are paying an increasingly heavy price. Every year nearly 1.2 million people get killed in traffic [25], and as many die from urban pollution. Moreover, transportation stands for 23% of the total emissions of carbon dioxide in the European Union [11].

Better software allows us to make cars smarter, safer, and more efficient, thereby ameliorating some of the adverse effects of car-based transport. Modern cars are equipped with a wide range of sensors and driver assistance systems and there are already a number of self-driving cars that are being tested by the major automotive companies as well as Google. The fact that the state of Nevada passed legislation allowing driver-less vehicles to operate on public roads can be seen as a sign of the momentum in the industry at the moment. Previously unsolved problems such as accurate positioning and reliable object detection now have credible solutions. The next big challenge is to enable efficient *coordination* among smart vehicles to further increase the safety and efficiency of the traffic.

Collisions in intersections constitute 45% of all traffic personal car injury accidents [27], so there is a clear need for collision avoidance systems. Having a centralised authority for each intersection that directs the traffic can be a good

D. Giannakopoulou and D. Méry (Eds.): FM 2012, LNCS 7436, pp. 52–67, 2012.
© Springer-Verlag Berlin Heidelberg 2012

alternative to having traffic lights. However, the large majority intersections do not even have traffic lights today. It would not be cost effective to put a central manager to all these unmanaged crossings, a fully distributed solution will be needed. On the other hand, distributed coordination is a non-trivial problem. A dynamic environment where cars move at high speed and where communication is unreliable and subject to interference creates many challenges. Yet any solution to such a distributed coordination problem must be able to guarantee safety.

In this paper we propose to utilise the strengths of automated reasoning tools to tackle the problem of safe distributed coordination. We show how a coordination problem can be formalised in a constraint specification language called SMT-lib [3] and verified with the Z3 theorem prover [9]. The novelty of our approach lies in employing a fully automated theorem prover to a distributed coordination problem involving explicit message passing, continuous time and space as well as an unbounded number of cars. Our focus is not on new verification methods for hybrid systems, but rather on the application of formal methods to a coordination approach and how to verify safety of a collaborative vehicular application. Our longer term objective is to incorporate the basic building blocks introduced in this paper in a general tool for modelling and verifying vehicular applications. To evaluate the feasibility of our approach we model an intersection collision avoidance scenario, which is an instance of a distributed coordination problem. In summary, there are three main contributions of this paper.

- A formalisation of a distributed coordination protocol.
- A constraint-based modelling approach for collaborative vehicular applications.
- A simple but realistic case study demonstrating the usefulness of our approach.

The rest of this paper is organised as follows. Section 2 provides a formal description of the coordination problem and the CwoRIS protocol. The intersection collision avoidance case study is presented in Section 3 followed by Section 4, outlining the verification and proof strategies. Section 5 contains related work and finally, Section 6 concludes the paper.

2 Distributed Coordination as Constraint Verification

We now proceed to formalise the distributed coordination problem. We begin by giving an overview of our approach, then go on to describe how we model the communication channel before describing our formalisation of the CwoRIS coordination protocol.

2.1 Overview

Consider the problem of designing a software subsystem for a car (we use the more general notion of entity, or sometimes vehicle) that can affect the steering and speed of the entity and that takes its decision based on communication with surrounding vehicles. Examples of such systems are collaborative adaptive cruise

control, advanced collision avoidance
systems, and lane merging applications. Our aim is to prove such a system safe by proving that a specific
entity A will not collide with another
object.

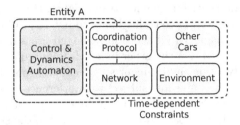

Fig. 1. System Model Overview

Figure 1 shows an overview of how
our system model is constructed. It is
composed of a "core" automaton and
a set of time-dependent constraints.
With core automaton, we refer to the state transitions involving variables specific to entity A. We now proceed to provide a more formal description of the
system model and how we represent it as a SMT problem. We model the system
as a tuple M as described below.

$$M = (\mathbf{E}, \mathbf{M}, \mathcal{S}, \mathcal{I}, T, \mathcal{F}, \mathcal{C})$$

$\mathbf{E}$ - a set of entities (i.e., the vehicles in the system)
$\mathbf{M}$ - a set of messages
$\mathcal{S}$ - a set of states
$\mathcal{I} \subset \mathcal{S}$ - set of initial states
$T : \mathcal{S} \times \mathcal{S} \to \mathbf{Bool}$ - A transition function
$\mathcal{F}$ - a finite set of uninterpreted functions
$\mathcal{C}$ - a finite set of constraints

Note that the sets $\mathbf{E}, \mathbf{M}, \mathcal{S}, \mathcal{I}$ can all be infinite, thereby allowing us to model an
unbounded number of cars and messages. The set of uninterpreted functions (or
predicates), $\mathcal{F}$, provides the semantics for the states. The allowed domains and
ranges of the functions are real numbers (time), integers, and any of the sets in
our model. An example of an uninterpreted function that we use in our model
is $x : \mathbf{E} \times \mathbb{R} \to \mathbb{R}$ which denotes the x position of an entity at some given time
point.

The constraints in $\mathcal{C}$ provide us with a way to describe the properties of
the environment and other assumptions that we need to make. The constraints
apply over the same domains as the uninterpreted functions, $\mathcal{F}$, and may also
contain quantifiers. An example of a constraint (which we do not use) could be
$\forall e \in \mathbf{E}, t \in \mathbb{R} : x(e, t) \leq 3.0$, which would require the x position of all entities to
be less than 3.0 at all times.

We let the states in $\mathcal{S}$ and the transition function T denote the state and
behaviour of the specific entity A. The behaviour of other entities in the system
is modelled using constraints in $\mathcal{C}$. This allows us to provide a more detailed
internal model of a single entity, and model other entities using assumptions on
their observable behaviour (including communication).

Finally, consider the transition function $T(i, j)$, where i and j are states,
which is used to characterise the behaviour of entity A. We encode the hybrid
automaton of A as a transition function that alternates between timed and non-
timed transitions. Let $\delta : \mathcal{S} \to Bool$ (we write δ^i) be an uninterpreted function,

Table 1. Communication Predicates

Predicate	Type	Description
$sent(m)$	**Bool**	message m was sent
$received(m, e)$	**Bool**	m was received by entity e at some point in time
$source(m)$	**E**	the sender of m
$sendtime(m)$	$\mathbb{R}$	the send time of m
$receivetime(m, e)$	$\mathbb{R}$	when m was received by entity e (if m is never received by e, this can have any value)
$isAck(m)$	**Bool**	True if message is an acknowledgement
$getReq(m)$	**M**	if m is an acknowledgement message, this denotes the message that m acknowledges

denoting whether the next transition should be a timed transition or not. Then we can define T as:

$$T(i,j) \equiv (T_D(i,j) \wedge \neg\delta^i \wedge \delta^j) \vee (T_C(i,j) \wedge \delta^i \wedge \neg\delta^j)$$

Where T_D is the transition function for non-timed (discrete) transitions and T_C for timed transitions (continuous).

2.2 Communication

We now proceed to introduce a subset of $\mathcal{F}$ relating to message passing. These are the basic concepts that we use to formally reason about communication in the system. Table 1 lists the predicates, the resulting type and a description of each. It might be worth pointing out a couple of things. First, the sent and received predicates do not have a time parameter. Thus, the semantics is that if a message m is sent at any time, then $sent(m)$ is true. To check whether a message had been sent at some given time t, this can be expressed as: $sent(m) \wedge (t \geq sendtime(m))$. Finally, messages can be either request messages or acknowledgements to requests. Thus the last two predicates are used to determine the message type and to identify the request associated with a given acknowledgement message.

We now describe the constraints relating to the basic communication properties. There are three constraints that have to be satisfied. First, any message that has been received by some entity must have been sent.

$$\forall m \in \mathbf{M}, e \in \mathbf{E} : received(m, e) \Rightarrow sent(m)$$

Second, the reception time of a message m at entity e must be strictly greater than the send time of the message.

$$\forall m \in \mathbf{M}, e \in \mathbf{E} : receivetime(m, e) > sendtime(m)$$

Finally, we need some consistency checks for when an acknowledgement can be sent. The following constraints states that for all acknowledgement that have been sent three conditions must be met, (1) it must correspond to a received message, (2), the received message cannot be an acknowledgement, and (3) the acknowledgement must have been sent after receiving the request.

$$\forall m \in \mathbf{M} : (sent(m) \wedge isAck(m)) \Rightarrow$$
$$(received(getReq(m), source(m))$$
$$\wedge \neg isAck(getReq(m))$$
$$\wedge\ receivetime(getReq(m), source(m)) \leq sendtime(m))$$

The above set of predicates and constraints provides some very basic elements of communication, which can easily be provided by any communication interface in a real application. However, in order to solve the coordination problem, we need to make an additional assumption on membership information. For this purpose we assume the existence of an *active area* in which entity A operates and that all entities within the active area are known to each other (i.e., essentially a perfect membership protocol). The membership information allows an entity to decide whether a message it has sent has reached all other entities in the area. While solving the membership problem using purely communication is recognised as a difficult problem [6], it can be solved in the vehicular domain with the aid of ranging sensors as shown by Slot and Cahill [23].

2.3   Distributed Coordination

We base our formalisation of distributed coordination on previous work by Bourouche [5] and Sin et al. [22]. The basic idea behind this model is that vehicles do not need to fully agree on a shared state in order to achieve safe co-ordination. Instead, the basic concept is that of *responsibility*. Each entity have a responsibility to ensure that certain safety criteria are met. If an entity is not able to ensure that its planned actions are compatible with those of other entities in the environment, it must adapt its behaviour accordingly (e.g. by stopping). The key aspect of this approach is that an entity does not need to agree on the behaviour of other entities in the system. While this might sound trivial, it is actually a step away from approaches where first all entities reach a distributed agreement on the course of actions to take, allowing greater flexibility.

In the CwoRIS protocol by Sin et al. [22], the responsibility requirement is implemented with the means of *resources*. A resource corresponds to a physical area of the road. An entity should not enter a resource without having made sure that it has exclusive access to the resource. While space does not allow a full description and explanation of the rationale of the CwoRIS protocol, we provide a brief intuition of how it works. Note that for the purpose of this formalisation we have made some simplifying assumptions compared to the original protocol. We allow only a single resource, requests are not allowed to be updated, and a sent request is assumed to be immediately received by the sender of the message, and no new entities enter the active area during the negotiation. These simplifications do not have a big impact on the core logic of the protocol, and we expect that removing these restrictions from the formalisation is a straightforward process. Table 2 describes the predicates that we use in the coordination mechanism.

Table 2. CwoRIS predicates

Predicate	Type	Description
$hasRequest(e, t)$	**Bool**	Entity e has an active request at time t
$c(e, t)$	**M**	Current request of entity e at time t
$start(m)$	$\mathbb{R}$	Resource request start time
$end(m)$	$\mathbb{R}$	Resource request end time
$prio(e)$	$\mathbb{Z}$	Priority of an entity
$valid(m)$	**Bool**	Message m is a valid request
$vtime(m)$	$\mathbb{R}$	Time when m was validated
$conflict(m, m')$	**Bool**	Requests m and m' are in conflict
$accepted(m, e)$	**Bool**	Message m is accepted by entity e
$hasResource(e, t)$	**Bool**	Entity e has the resource at time t

In essence the CwoRIS protocol works by entities sending out requests to access a shared resource, after which *hasRequest* becomes true for the sender entity, and the current request is referred to as $c(e, t)$. Each request has a *start* and *end* time and each entity has a unique priority[1]. If an entity has received an acknowledgement from all other entities in the area and not received any conflicting request from an entity with a higher priority, the request is considered to be *valid*. A *conflict* is said to occur between two requests if their request times overlap.

When sending out a new request, a node must make sure that the request it sends does not conflict with any previously received request that it has accepted. A message m is *accepted* by entity e if it is received by e, and one of three conditions hold

- e does not have a request when receiving m
- m does not conflict with the current request of e
- e has a strictly lower priority than the sender of m

Thus a message from a lower priority entity can be ignored by an entity with a higher priority. Note that two entities cannot ignore each others requests since both cannot have a higher priority than the other. Finally, node *hasResource* at time t if and only if it has a valid request for that resource and the time interval of the request covers t. We state this last constraint formally as it is the main interface to the other components in the system.

$$hasResource(e, t) \equiv hasRequest(e, t) \wedge valid(c(e, t)) \wedge vtime(c(e, t)) < t$$
$$\wedge\ start(c(e, t)) \leq t \leq end(c(e, t))$$

This concludes our description of the coordination protocol. Naturally, most of the above description is rather textual rather than formal. We refer to the full model[2] for the exact constraints.

---

[1] Uniqueness can be achieved through e.g. globally unique IPv6 addresses that are part of the future communication standard for vehicular applications, and should also take into account relative proximity to the intersection.

[2] Available at http://code.google.com/p/smtica/

3   Case Study

To demonstrate the applicability of our approach we have chosen a basic intersection scenario to model and validate. We first outline the general scenario and our assumptions, and then describe how the states and transition functions for the vehicle automaton are defined.

3.1   Scenario

We consider a four way intersection as depicted in Figure 2. The intersection is not equipped with a central traffic control mechanism such as a traffic light, so vehicles need to coordinate their actions to avoid collisions. The figure shows entity A approaching the intersection. For simplicity we have aligned the roads with the x and y axes respectively, and assumed that entity A will not turn. Thus, it will only need to travel in the x direction

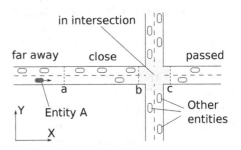

Fig. 2. Intersection Scenario

to cross the intersection. To tackle a wider range of road geometries one needs to transform coordinate system of the vehicle along the road (i.e., using longitudinal and lateral directions). Allowing the vehicle to turn can be easily incorporated in the model. There are four conceptual regions for this entity in relation to the intersection, "far away" when the x position is less than some specified value a, "close" when $a \leq x \leq b$, "in intersection", when $b \leq x \leq c$, and passed when $x \geq c$.

In our model, we have chosen to put as few restrictions on the allowed behaviour of the system as possible. However, some restrictions are necessary to prove the desired safety properties. Since the actual behaviour of a car is more restricted than our model of it, by proving that the wider envelope is safe, it follows that a restricted subset of the behaviour will also be safe.

We further assume that all entities use the CwoRIS resource reservation protocol to negotiate access to the intersection, and that if another entity is in the intersection then it must be in the active area given by the membership protocol. Apart from the assumption that entities keep in lane, the positions $x(e, t)$ of entities e other than entity A, are only restricted in the sense that if entity e is in the intersection, it must have the resource. For entity A this is not assumed, but proven to hold as explained in Section 4.2.

3.2   Core Automaton

We now proceed to describe the core automaton (the states $\mathcal{S}$, the initial states $\mathcal{I}$, and the transition function T) that encodes the behaviour of entity A. The

Table 3. State variables

Continuous state variables			Discrete state variables		
Predicate	**Type**	**Description**	**Predicate**	**Type**	**Description**
t^i	$\mathbb{R}$	time at state i	l^i	**L**	location
x^i	$\mathbb{R}$	x position in state i	v_t^i	$\mathbb{R}$	intended target speed
y^i	$\mathbb{R}$	y position in state i	P^i	**Bool**	will pass
v^i	$\mathbb{R}$	speed in state i			

logic of the vehicle is quite straightforward and roughly based on the intersection collision avoidance application described by Sin et al. [22].

Table 3 contains the continuous and discrete variables (that actually encode the discrete states), and Figure 3 shows a graphical representation of the discrete state transitions. The continuous state variables are time, x and y position and speed. The discrete variables are as follows. The location $l \in \mathbf{L} = \{farAway, close, inInter, passed\}$ denotes the logical location of the vehicles in relation to the intersection. The intended target speed v_t denotes the reference value to which the vehicle tries to adapts its speed. The Boolean variable P denotes an internal decision corresponding to whether the vehicle intends to pass the intersection in the near future.

Now consider Figure 3 which shows the discrete states and transitions of the core automaton (where all states have implicit self-loops). Initially, the vehicle is considered to be far away from the intersection, but when the x position of the vehicle passed the proximity point a, its state will change. There are two possibilities, either the entity has acquired the resource and will have it for a sufficiently long time to pass the intersection (we denote this *willHaveResource*), in which case it will set P (will pass) to true and prepare to cross the intersection. Otherwise, the vehicle must break (set target speed $v_t = 0$), and wait until a resource is acquired.

Once the entity has secured the resource it will need to maintain a minimum speed (v_{min}) while close to or in the intersection. When the entity passes $x = b$, it is considered to be in the intersection, until it passes point $x = c$, after which it sets its location to "passed".

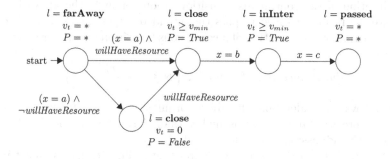

Fig. 3. Automaton for the behaviour of vehicle A

Having covered the logical control of the vehicle, we now turn to a simple model of its physical characteristics. This is defined by the continuous transition function $T_C(i, j)$ (where i and j are states), which is a conjunction of criteria on the allowed evolution (or flow) of the continuous variables.

$$T_C(i, j) \equiv move(i, j) \wedge speed(i, j) \wedge duration(i, j) \wedge$$
$$(t^i < t^j) \wedge consts(i, j) \wedge inv(i, j)$$

The allowed movement $(move(i, j))$ of the vehicle is defined below. This movement formula assumes that the average speed during the duration of the continuous transition is equal to the mean of the start and end speeds (v^i and v^j). This is true if for example the acceleration is constant during that time.

$$move(i, j) \equiv \left(x^j = x^i + \frac{v^i + v^j}{2}(t^j - t^i) \right)$$

The speed change during a continuous transition is controlled by the minimum absolute acceleration parameter a. In line with letting the behaviour of the car to be unrestricted unless required to prove the safety of the system we do not limit the maximum acceleration. Note that this does not mean that we assume vehicles to have unbounded acceleration, but rather that as long as the speed change is

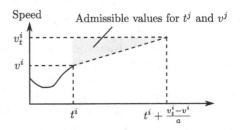

Fig. 4. Speed

within the envelope we are able to prove system safety. Formally, the allowed speed change is expressed as follows.

$$speed(i, j) \equiv \left((v^i_t = v^i) \wedge (v^j = v^i) \right) \vee$$
$$\left((v^i_t < v^i) \wedge (v^i_t \leq v^j \leq v^i - a(t^j - t^i)) \right) \vee$$
$$\left((v^i_t > v^i) \wedge (v^i + a(t^j - t^i) \leq v^j \leq v^i_t) \right)$$

If the duration of the continuous transition is long enough, the above formula will cause the resulting speed to pass the intended target speed. Therefore, we add a restriction on the duration of a continuous transition when there is a speed change:

$$duration(i, j) \equiv (v^i_t = v^i) \vee \left(t^j \leq t^i + \frac{|v^i_t - v^i|}{a} \right)$$

The easiest way to understand the above formulae is through figure 4. It shows the case where the target speed is higher than the increased speed. The grey area shows the admissible values for t^j and v^j.

The fourth criterion $(t^i < t^j)$ in T_C states that a timed transition must increment the clock, since otherwise it would be possible to have an infinite amount of transitions without any time passing. The $const(i, j)$ criterion simply requires all discrete variables to stay constant during the timed transition. Finally, with the invariant criterion inv, we introduce a restriction which is merely for sake of the reducing the search space. There is no algorithm for solving general non-linear arithmetic constraints, and with the model description so far Z3 returns *unknown* when asked for satisfiability. We were thus forced to restrict the search space by requiring that the speed variable v to be a multiple of $0.5m/s$. Each speed step can be seen as modelling a $0.5m/s$ wide range of the actual vehicle speed[3]. Note that this must be done with some care. Specifically, one must make sure that it does not lead to dead ends in the automaton from which there are no outgoing transitions, as we show in the next section.

4   Verification

Having described our model we now outline our efforts to verify safety properties of our model. Let $\mathcal{R} \subset \mathcal{S}$ be the set of states that are reachable from $\mathcal{I}$ with a finite sequence of transitions. Our objective is to show that all states in $\mathcal{R}$ fulfil some safety property $safe^i$. This predicate should exclude the possibility of vehicle A colliding with any other entity within the area, so we let $safe^i \equiv safeDist^i$, where:

$$safeDist^i \equiv \forall e \in \mathbf{E} : (e = A) \vee \neg inArea(e)$$
$$\vee \left(|x(A, t^i) - x(e, t^i)| > X_{min} \right) \qquad (1)$$
$$\vee \left(|y(A, t^i) - y(e, t^i)| > Y_{min} \right)$$

Note that we specify the minimum allowed distance individually for the x and y dimensions simply because the constraint solver we used could not cope with a proper euclidean distance constraint. We leave it to future work to find a way around this limitation. Moreover, we only include the vehicles in the active area to reduce the verification complexity. Having defined the safety predicate we now want to prove that all reachable states are safe: $M \models \forall i \in \mathcal{R} : safe^i$

Unfortunately, this formulation is not very suitable for automatic verification; we first have to transform the problem into a more tractable one. To do this we employ as basic variant of k-induction and manual invariant strengthening.

4.1   Safety by Induction

Proving safety using induction and a SAT solver was introduced by Sheeran et al. [21] and is naturally extended to SMT solvers. The basic idea is to prove safety of the system by induction, using paths of length K as the base case. By testing increasingly larger values for K, this method will eventually provide an answer for finite system representations. In the case of our model we use

---

[3] This can be seen as a discretisation of the speed variable, but does not restrict the possible values for the other continuous variables.

$K = 2$. Using only the first state as the base case is not enough since both a continuous and a discrete transition is needed to ensure that the next state is one that could reasonably occur for this system. Starting with the base case that all initial states and all successors to the initial states are safe:

$$M \models \forall i \in \mathcal{I}, j \in \mathcal{S} : safe^i \wedge (T(i, j) \Rightarrow safe^j)$$

We then formulate the inductive step, that if two successive states are safe, then the third successor must also be a safe state.

$$M \models \forall i, j, k \in \mathcal{S} : \left(safe^i \wedge safe^j \wedge T(i, j) \wedge T(j, k)\right) \Rightarrow safe^k$$

Recall that to prove these formulae we try to assert their negation in Z3. When the solver concludes that the negated formula is unsatisfiable, we know that the formula is a consequence of the model M, and that all reachable states are safe. If, on the other hand, the solver finds a solution to the constraint problem there are two possibilities. Either the system is not safe, in which case the variable assignment that satisfies the negation of what we want to prove provides us with an example of how the system can enter an unsafe state. This provides useful information for debugging the formulation of the model.

The other case is worse. The fact that the inductive step is false does not necessarily mean that the system is unsafe. If the solver finds a case where the safe states i and j lead to an unsafe state k, but i and j are not reachable states, the counterexample is of no use. In this case, the system might or might not be safe; we have no way of knowing. Increasing K does not help in our case since we do not enforce maximal progress of timed transitions. Moreover, the safe *safeDist* predicate only considers the positions of the vehicles. Thus, to prove safety we need to replace the safety criterion with a stronger invariant that also ensures proper speed and resource allocation.

4.2   Safety Invariants

The problem of finding invariants is often the key of automated theorem proving. Fortunately, in our case, the invariants are fairly straightforward to the problem at hand. Moreover, we do not consider it to be a problem that these need to be defined manually. When designing a system for automotive safety, there will be a large number of criteria in the system specification and these definitely fall within this range. Apart from the $safeDist^i$ property (equation (1)) we add two more invariants. The first *hasResInInter* requiring that if the entity is in the intersection, then it must (1) have acquired the resource (2) have this resource for a sufficient amount of time (3) have decided to pass the intersection and (4) have a minimum target speed v_{min}.

Finally, the predicate *safeSpeed* limits the maximum speed that the entity can have when being close to the intersection, but not having acquired the resource. Or, similar to the above, the entity has decided to pass, to have a minimum target speed. Figure 5 shows a graphical representation of the maximum speed before an intersection. When the vehicle is far away from the intersection, there is a

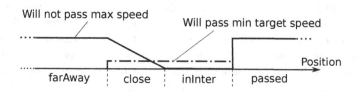

Fig. 5. SafeSpeed

fixed maximum speed. However, when the vehicle approaches the intersection, if it has not decided to pass, it must start to slow down. The final safety invariant is then defined as $safe^i \equiv safeDist^i \wedge hasResInInter^i \wedge safeSpeed^i$.

With these additions and the induction scheme outlined in the previous subsection we were able to prove the safety of all reachable states using the Z3 solver.

4.3 Deadlock Freedom

The final step in our verification process is to ensure that the model is sound in the sense that we have not made it overly restrictive. In particular, it should always be possible to transition to a new state. If the model is stuck, it means that we have made an error. One possible approach to show this is to use the same inductive reasoning as for proving safety.

$$M \models \forall i, j \in \mathcal{S} : T(i, j) \Rightarrow \exists k \in \mathcal{S} : T(j, k)$$

However, when feeding the negation of this formula to Z3 it returns "unknown". It turns out that one of the core reasons for this is that time must increase for a continuous transition $(t^j > t^i)$. Unfortunately we cannot not just remove this criterion, since it is required to prove safety. Instead we found another solution to this problem, based on *constructing* a successor to every state.

We introduced a successor function $succ : \mathcal{S} \rightarrow \mathcal{S}$ that for each state returns a new state to which there is a valid transition. The successor function can be derived without major effort from the definition of the transition function. Since *succ* is always guaranteed to give an output for every input state, we can prove freedom from deadlock by proving the following formula.

$$M \models \forall i, j : T(i, j) \Rightarrow T(j, succ(j))$$

The reason for having an antecedent $(T(i, j))$ is that this ensures that the state variables in state j are not in themselves contradictory.

4.4 Final Remarks

In addition to the above, we asserted basic properties such as that no two entities both believe that they had the resource and that there is a sequence of transitions in which A can pass the intersection. We did not formally prove progress of the model, but this would also be an important aspect for a model checking tool. We believe that our approach can be extended to handle this aspect provided stronger assumptions on the underlying communication system, this is currently work in progress. The entire model is composed of 825 lines of SMT-lib code (including comments), and the verification by Z3 took 14 seconds on a Dell optiplex 990 with a 3.4 GHz Intel Core i7 processor. According to the statistic outputs by Z3 109MB of memory was consumed and 965k equations were added by the constraint solver in the process.

5   Related Work

There is a rich field of research on verification of hybrid systems, see Alur [2] for a nice historic overview. Thanks to the foundational research on basic theories for hybrid automata and satisfiability [8,12], there are now a number of very powerful verification tools available. Our focus is on the application of such automatic formal verification tools on distributed coordination problems. Several works such as [14,24] use SMT solvers to verify real-time communication protocols but do not consider mobility and spatial safety constraints. The problem of how autonomous traffic agents (or robots) should avoid collisions has also been treated formally with manual proof strategies. For example, Damm et al. [7] present a proof rule for collision freedom of two vehicles. Such work is crucial for the understanding of the basic characteristics of the coordination problem, but can be difficult to directly translate in to a model which is machine verifiable.

Our approach to traffic management is based on a coordination scheme where a physical resource is allocated using a distributed coordination protocol. However, the collision avoidance can also be assured with the help of other abstractions. If a central authority can be deployed as in the case of the European Train Control System (ETCS), it is enough to verify that the agent does not go outside the boundary given by the manager [13,29]. Collision avoidance between two entities has also been studied in the context of air traffic management [26,15].

Another approach to ensuring collision freedom is to verify that the trajectories of the different entities do not intersect. Clearly, such an approach requires very sophisticated reasoning about the differential equations relating the vehicle movements. Althoff et al. [1] use reachability analysis to prove safety of evasive manoeuvres. Strong results can be shown with deductive methods as shown by Platzer [19]. This approach has been applied to platooning [16], air traffic management [20], and intersection collision avoidance [17]. While this method allows more powerful model of the vehicle dynamics than what was possible to verify in our model, verifying properties with a deductive approach often require manual interaction. For example, the safety of the intersection control application [17] required in total over 800 interactive steps to complete. Moreover, this study assumes the existence of a stop light, and does not explicitly model communication.

Autonomous intersection management has been extensively explored in the intelligent transportation community [10,22,28], though usually not with a focus on proving correctness. Naumann et al. [18] consider a formal model of the scenario, but it is based on a discrete set of locations for each car. The Comhordú coordination scheme on which the coordination approach presented here is based was formalised by Bhandal et al. [4] using a process algebraic approach.

6 Conclusions

In this paper we have presented a formalisation of the distributed coordination problem encountered by intelligent vehicles while contending for the same physical resource. We formalised a coordination protocol and an intersection collision avoidance case study in the SMT-lib language and proved system safety using the Z3 theorem prover.

We can draw two conclusions from this work. First, the responsibility approach to distributed coordination is a suitable abstraction for formal reasoning on system safety. The core of this approach is that every entity is responsible for making sure that it does not enter an unsafe state with respect to any other entity. This can be contrasted with the other approaches where consensus is required between all nodes, decisions are made by a central manager, or where each pair of nodes negotiates independently, all of which seem problematic from a scalability point of view.

The second conclusion is that automatic verification of collaborative vehicular applications with the help of SMT solvers is at least plausible. We have encountered some cases where the model could not be verified, and increasing the detail and scale of the model would certainly enlarge this problem. However, there are certainly domain-specific approximations that can be made to alleviate some of these problems. Our next step is to generalise our specific case study to construct a tool that allows high level models of applications for smart vehicles to be automatically verified using an underlying formal reasoning engine. This includes dealing with more general physical environment models (e.g., multiple intersections). Another interesting direction is to explore more detailed formal models of the membership protocol.

Acknowledgement. This work was supported, in part, by Science Foundation Ireland grant 10/CE/I1855 to Lero - the Irish Software Engineering Research Centre (www.lero.ie).

References

1. Althoff, M., Althoff, D., Wollherr, D., Buss, M.: Safety verification of autonomous vehicles for coordinated evasive maneuvers. In: IEEE Intelligent Vehicles Symposium, IV (2010), doi:10.1109/IVS.2010.5548121
2. Alur, R.: Formal verification of hybrid systems. In: Proceedings of the Ninth ACM International Conference on Embedded Software, EMSOFT. ACM (2011), doi:10.1145/2038642.2038685

3. Barrett, C., Stump, A., Tinelli, C.: The Satisfiability Modulo Theories Library (SMT-LIB) (2010), http://www.SMT-LIB.org

4. Bhandal, C., Bouroche, M., Hughes, A.: A process algebraic description of a temporal wireless network protocol. In: Proceedings of the Fourth International Workshop on Formal Methods for Interactive Systems (2011)

5. Bouroche, M.: Real-Time Coordination of Mobile Autonomous Entities. PhD thesis, Dept. of Computer Science, Trinity College Dublin (2007)

6. Chandra, T.D., Hadzilacos, V., Toueg, S., Charron-Bost, B.: On the impossibility of group membership. In: Fifteenth Annual ACM Symposium on Principles of Distributed Computing (PODC). ACM Press (1996), doi:10.1145/248052.248120

7. Damm, W., Hungar, H., Olderog, E.-R.: Verification of cooperating traffic agents. International Journal of Control 79(5) (2006), doi:10.1080/00207170600587531

8. De Moura, L., Bjørner, N.: Satisfiability modulo theories: introduction and applications. Commun. ACM 54 (2011), doi:
http://doi.acm.org/10.1145/1995376.1995394

9. de Moura, L., Bjørner, N.: Z3: An efficient SMT solver. In: Ramakrishnan, C.R., Rehof, J. (eds.) TACAS 2008. LNCS, vol. 4963, pp. 337–340. Springer, Heidelberg (2008)

10. Dresner, K., Stone, P.: A multiagent approach to autonomous intersection management. J. Artif. Int. Res. 31(1), 591–656 (2008)

11. European Commission. Eu energy and transport in figures (2010),
http://ec.europa.eu/energy/publications/statistics/statistics_en.htm
(accessed January 2012)

12. Henzinger, T.: The theory of hybrid automata. In: Proceedings. Eleventh Annual IEEE Symposium on Logics in Computer Science, LICS 1966 (1996), doi:10.1109/LICS.1996.561342

13. Herde, C., Eggers, A., Franzle, M., Teige, T.: Analysis of hybrid systems using hysat. In: Third International Conference on Systems, ICONS (2008), doi:10.1109/ICONS.2008.17

14. Huang, J., Blech, J., Raabe, A., Buckl, C., Knoll, A.: Static scheduling of a time-triggered network-on-chip based on SMT solving. In: Design, Automation Test in Europe Conference Exhibition (DATE), pp. 509–514 (2012)

15. Livadas, C., Lygeros, J., Lynch, N.: High-level modeling and analysis of the traffic alert and collision avoidance system (tcas). Proceedings of the IEEE 88(7) (2000), doi:10.1109/5.871302

16. Loos, S., Platzer, A., Nistor, L.: Adaptive Cruise Control: Hybrid, Distributed, and Now Formally Verified. In: Butler, M., Schulte, W. (eds.) FM 2011. LNCS, vol. 6664, pp. 42–56. Springer, Heidelberg (2011)

17. Loos, S.M., Platzer, A.: Safe intersections: At the crossing of hybrid systems and verification. In: 14th International IEEE Conference on Intelligent Transportation Systems, ITSC (2011), doi:10.1109/ITSC.2011.6083138

18. Naumann, R., Rasche, R., Tacken, J., Tahedi, C.: Validation and simulation of a decentralized intersection collision avoidance algorithm. In: IEEE Conference on Intelligent Transportation System, ITSC (1997), doi:10.1109/ITSC.1997.660579

19. Platzer, A.: Differential dynamic logic for hybrid systems. J. Autom. Reas. 41(2) (2008), doi:10.1007/s10817-008-9103-8

20. Platzer, A., Clarke, E.M.: Formal Verification of Curved Flight Collision Avoidance Maneuvers: A Case Study. In: Cavalcanti, A., Dams, D.R. (eds.) FM 2009. LNCS, vol. 5850, pp. 547–562. Springer, Heidelberg (2009)

21. Sheeran, M., Singh, S., Stålmarck, G.: Checking Safety Properties Using Induction and a SAT-Solver. In: Hunt Jr., W.A., Johnson, S.D. (eds.) FMCAD 2000. LNCS, vol. 1954, pp. 108–125. Springer, Heidelberg (2000)

22. Sin, M.L., Bouroche, M., Cahill, V.: Scheduling of dynamic participants in real-time distributed systems. In: 30th IEEE Symposium on Reliable Distributed Systems, SRDS (2011), doi:10.1109/SRDS.2011.37

23. Slot, M., Cahill, V.: A reliable membership service for vehicular safety applications. In: IEEE Intelligent Vehicles Symposium, IV (2011), doi:10.1109/IVS.2011.5940487

24. Steiner, W., Dutertre, B.: SMT-Based Formal Verification of a *TTEthernet* Synchronization Function. In: Kowalewski, S., Roveri, M. (eds.) FMICS 2010. LNCS, vol. 6371, pp. 148–163. Springer, Heidelberg (2010)

25. The World Bank. Road safety (2011),
    http://www.worldbank.org/transport/roads/safety.htm
    (accessed December 2011)

26. Tomlin, C., Pappas, G., Sastry, S.: Conflict resolution for air traffic management: a study in multiagent hybrid systems. IEEE Transactions on Automatic Control 43(4) (1998), doi:10.1109/9.664154

27. Traffic Accident Causation in Europe (TRACE) FP6-2004-IST-4. Deliverable 1.3 road users and accident causation (2009)

28. Verma, R., Vecchio, D.: Semiautonomous multivehicle safety. IEEE Robotics Automation Magazine 18(3) (2011), doi:10.1109/MRA.2011.942114

29. Zimmermann, A., Hommel, G.: A train control system case study in model-based real time system design. In: Proceedings. International ' (2003), doi:10.1109/IPDPS.2003.1213234

Quantified Event Automata:
Towards Expressive and Efficient Runtime Monitors

Howard Barringer[1], Yliès Falcone[2], Klaus Havelund[3,*],
Giles Reger[1,**], and David Rydeheard[1]

[1] University of Manchester, UK
[2] Laboratoire d'Informatique de Grenoble, UJF Université Grenoble I, France
[3] Jet Propulsion Laboratory, California Inst. of Technology, USA

Abstract. Runtime verification is the process of checking a property on a trace of events produced by the execution of a computational system. Runtime verification techniques have recently focused on parametric specifications where events take data values as parameters. These techniques exist on a spectrum inhabited by both efficient and expressive techniques. These characteristics are usually shown to be conflicting - in state-of-the-art solutions, efficiency is obtained at the cost of loss of expressiveness and vice-versa. To seek a solution to this conflict we explore a new point on the spectrum by defining an alternative runtime verification approach. We introduce a new formalism for concisely capturing expressive specifications with parameters. Our technique is more expressive than the currently most efficient techniques while at the same time allowing for optimizations.

1   Introduction

Runtime Verification [1–5, 7, 9–12] is the process of checking a property on a trace of events produced by the execution of a computational system. Over the last decade, a number of different formalisms were proposed for specifying such properties and mechanisms for checking traces. Early work focused on *propositional* events but recently there has been a growing interest in so-called *parametric* properties where events carry data values. Challenges that arise when designing a runtime verification framework incorporating parametric properties are twofold. The first lies in the (parametric) specification formalism used to specify the property; usually one seeks expressiveness. The second lies in the efficiency of monitoring algorithms associated with the formalism.

A spectrum of runtime verification. Specification formalisms differ in their level of expressiveness and usability and, monitoring algorithms differ in efficiency. In developing monitoring frameworks, one can distinguish between systems such as JAVAMOP [11] and TRACEMATCHES [1], which focus on efficiency rather than expressiveness, and systems such as EAGLE [2], RULER [2, 5], LOGSCOPE [3] and TRACECONTRACT [4],

---

* Part of the research described in this publication was carried out at Jet Propulsion Laboratory, California Institute of Technology, under a contract with the National Aeronautics and Space Administration.

** The work of this author was supported by the Engineering and Physical Sciences Research Council [grant number EP/P505208/1].

D. Giannakopoulou and D. Méry (Eds.): FM 2012, LNCS 7436, pp. 68–84, 2012.

which focus on expressiveness rather than efficiency. The development in this paper arose from our attempt to understand, reformulate and generalise parametric trace slicing (as adopted by JAVAMOP [7]), and more generally from our attempt to explore the spectrum between JAVAMOP and more expressive systems such as EAGLE, RULER, LOGSCOPE and TRACECONTRACT.

Contributions. This paper contributes to the general effort to understand the spectrum of monitoring techniques for parametric properties. We propose Quantified Event Automata (QEA) as a formalism for defining parametric properties that is more expressive than the formalisms behind the current most efficient frameworks such as JAVAMOP and TRACEMATCHES. This formalism is as expressive as the formalisms behind the most expressive frameworks, such as RULER, but is, in our opinion, more intuitive and allows for optimisation. Additionally we include guards and assignments in our new formalism. We present both a big-step semantics, operating on full finite traces, and a small-step semantics, operating on the trace step-by-step. The small-step semantics acts as a basis from which monitoring algorithms can be derived.

Paper Organization. Section 2 motivates our approach by exhibiting the limitations of parametric trace slicing and overviews how we overcome them. We introduce QEA in Sec. 4 by first defining Event Automata (EA) in Sec. 3. An EA defines a property over a set of parametric events, and QEA generalise these by quantifying over some variables in the EA. As we separate quantifications from the definition of the property we could replace Event Automata with some other formalism, such as context-free grammars, in the future. Sections 3 and 4 are concerned with the a big-step semantics of our formalism, whereas Sec. 5 presents a small-step semantics, along with a notion of acceptance in a four-valued verdict domain. Finally, we discuss related work in Sec. 6 and draw conclusions in Sec. 7.

2   Background

Runtime monitoring is the process of checking a property on a trace (finite sequence) of events. In this context, an event records some action or snapshot from the monitored system. A property defines a language over events and a monitor is a decision procedure for the property. An event is said to be *propositional* if it consists of a simple name, e.g., open, and *parametric* if it contains data values, e.g., open('file42'). We name properties and monitors in a similar way: propositional and parametric monitors, respectively.

A previous approach to parametric runtime monitoring is called parametric trace slicing [7] (an approach taken by JAVAMOP [11]). Here a parametric monitor, from a theoretical point of view, works by slicing its parametric input trace to a set of propositional traces that are then processed by separate propositional monitors. Let us illustrate this approach with a simple example. Consider the parametric property stating that for any file f, open(f) and close(f) events for that file f should alternate. This property can be formalised as the parametric regular expression $(\text{open}(f).\text{close}(f))^*$. Consider now the parametric trace open(1).close(2).close(1). In this parametric trace there are two different instantiations of f, namely $f=1$ and $f=2$. In this case slicing produces the following configuration consisting of two bindings associated with propositional traces:

$$[f \mapsto 1] : \texttt{open.close} \qquad [f \mapsto 2] : \texttt{close}$$

Each of these traces are then monitored by the monitor corresponding to the propositional property $(\texttt{open.close})^*$. It is clear that for $[f \mapsto 2]$ the property does not hold.

For practical purposes, instead of mapping each binding to a propositional trace as above, a configuration instead maps the binding to a propositional monitor state, the state the monitor will be in after observing that propositional trace. When a monitor receives an event it combines the event's parameters with the variables associated with that event to construct a binding (a map from variables to concrete values), and looks up the appropriate propositional monitor state for that binding, and then applies the propositional event in that monitor state to obtain a new state. For example, given the above trace, the first event $\texttt{open}(1)$ would be used to construct the binding $[f \mapsto 1]$. However, note that the binding constructed from an event does not necessarily match exactly any of the bindings in the configuration. Instead, a monitor state is updated if it is mapped to by any binding that *includes* the binding produced by the event. Looking up monitor states directly from events makes a slicing approach efficient.

The following definition defines for a given trace and a given binding what propositional trace this binding is mapped to, namely the slice corresponding to that binding.

Definition 1 (Parametric Trace Slicing). *Given a trace of parameterised events τ and a binding θ, the θ-slice of τ, written $\tau \downarrow_\theta$, is the propositional trace defined by:*

$$\epsilon \downarrow_\theta = \epsilon \qquad\qquad e(\theta').\tau \downarrow_\theta = \begin{cases} e.(\tau \downarrow_\theta) & \text{if } \theta' \sqsubseteq \theta \\ \tau \downarrow_\theta & \text{otherwise} \end{cases}$$

where ϵ is the empty trace, each parameterised event $e(\theta')$ consists of an event name e and a binding θ', and $\sqsubseteq$ is the submap relation on bindings.

However, as we shall see, parametric trace slicing has two main shortcomings. First, it is not possible to write a property where an event name is associated with two different lists of variables, for example $\texttt{open}(f)$ and $\texttt{open}(g)$, as when observing an event, such as $\texttt{open}(1)$, it must be possible to construct a unique binding, such as $[f \mapsto 1]$, hence relying on only one unique variable associated with $\texttt{open}$ (in this case f). Second, the theory assumes that all variables take part in slicing - forcing their values to remain fixed w.r.t. a monitor. Third, the theory implicitly assumes universal quantification on all parameters, hence forbidding alternation with existential quantification. Below are some properties that are not expressible in this parametric trace slicing setting:

Talking Philosophers. Any two philosophers may not speak at the same time - if one starts talking another cannot start until the first stops. Given any philosophers x and y, the property must therefore differentiate between events $\texttt{start}(x)$ and $\texttt{start}(y)$.

Auction Bidding. Amounts bid for an item should be strictly increasing. If bidding is captured by the event $\texttt{bid}(item, amount)$ the value given to $item$ should be fixed w.r.t. a monitor, but the value given to $amount$ should be allowed to vary.

Candidate Selection. For every voter there must exist a party that the voter is a member of, and the voter must rank all candidates for that party.

Our more general formalism allows us to express these and other properties with additional new features. We first introduce Event Automata (EA) to describe a property with parametric events containing both values and variables. An event name can occur with different (lists of) parameters, for example start(1), start(x) and start(y). We then introduce Quantified Event Automata (QEA), which generalise EA by quantifying over some of the variables, making them bound. Variables that are not quantified over, hence free, can be rebound as a trace is analysed. This is useful for specification purposes as we shall see. As we will always instantiate Event Automata before using them we can treat all variables as free variables and rebind them where necessary. In theory, trace acceptance can be decided using a set of instantiated EA generated using the QEA as a template and replacing quantified variables with values from their domain. In practice this approach is inefficient and we present an alternative that allows for optimisation.

3   Event Automata

An Event Automaton is a non-deterministic finite-state automaton whose alphabet consists of parametric events and whose transitions may be labelled with guards and assignments. These are generalised in the next section by quantifying over zero or more variables appearing in parametric events. Here we assume the Event Automaton has been instantiated and all quantified variables replaced with values.

We begin by formalising the structure of Event Automata, then give a transition semantics and define an Event Automaton's language, finishing with three examples.

We use $\bar{s}$ to denote a tuple $\langle s_0, \dots, s_k \rangle$. We use $X \to Y$ and $X \rightharpoonup Y$ to denote sets of total and partial functions between X and Y, respectively. We write maps (partial functions) as $[x_0 \mapsto v_0, \dots, x_i \mapsto v_i]$ and the empty map as $[\,]$. Given two maps A and B, the map override operator is defined as:

$$(A \dagger B)(x) = \begin{cases} B(x) & \text{if } x \in \underline{dom}(B), \\ A(x) & \text{if } x \notin \underline{dom}(B) \text{ and } x \in \underline{dom}(A), \\ \text{undefined otherwise.} \end{cases}$$

3.1 Syntax

We build the syntax from a set of propositional event names Σ, a set of values Val^1, and a set of variables Var (disjoint from Val) as follows.

Definition 2 (Symbols, Events, Alphabets and Traces). *Let $Sym = Val \cup Var$ be the set of all symbols (variables or values). An event is a pair $\langle e, \bar{s} \rangle \in \Sigma \times Sym^*$, written $e(\bar{s})$. An event $e(\bar{s})$ is ground if $\bar{s} \in Val^*$. Let $Event$ be the set of all events and $GEvent$ be the set of all ground events. A trace is a finite sequence of ground events. Let $Trace = GEvent^*$ be the set of all traces.*

---

[1] For example, integers, strings or objects from an object-oriented programming language.

We use x, y to refer to variables, s to refer to symbols, a to refer to ground events , b to refer to events which are not necessarily ground, and σ, τ to refer to traces. Note that we focus on finite traces. A continuously evolving system could be monitored through snapshots of finite traces - the trace seen so far.

Bindings are maps from variables to values, i.e., elements of $Bind = Var \rightharpoonup Val$. There is a partial order $\sqsubseteq$ on bindings such that $\theta_1 \sqsubseteq \theta_2$ iff θ_1 is a submap of θ_2. Guards are predicates on bindings, i.e., total functions in $Guard = Bind \rightarrow \mathbb{B}$. We use θ and φ to denote bindings and g to denote guards. A binding can be applied to a symbol as a substitution – replacing the symbol if it is defined in the binding. This can be lifted to events and used to give a definition of a ground event and an event matching:

Definition 3 (Substitution). *The binding* $\theta = [x_0 \mapsto v_0, \ldots, x_i \mapsto v_i]$ *can be applied to a symbol* s *and to an event* $e(\overline{s})$ *as follows:*

$$s(\theta) = \begin{cases} \theta(s) \; if \; s \in \underline{dom}(\theta) \\ s \quad otherwise \end{cases} \qquad e\langle s_0, \ldots, s_j \rangle(\theta) = e\langle s_0(\theta), \ldots, s_j(\theta) \rangle$$

Definition 4 (Matching). *Given a ground event* a *and event* b, *the predicate* $\mathtt{matches}(a, b)$ *holds iff there exists a binding* θ *s.t.* $b(\theta) = a$. *Moreover, let* $\mathtt{match}(a, b)$ *denote the smallest such binding w.r.t* $\sqsubseteq$ *if it exists (and is undefined otherwise).*

Assignments are total functions on bindings, i.e., elements of $Assign = Bind \rightarrow Bind$. We use γ to denote assignments. Guards and assignments may be described in suitable languages. We do not need to specify particular languages, but will use standard programming language notation in examples and assume that assignments maintain values they do not explicitly update. Now we are in a position to define Event Automata (EA).

Definition 5 (Event Automaton). *An EA* $\langle Q, \mathcal{A}, \delta, q_0, F \rangle$ *is a tuple where* Q *is a finite set of states,* $\mathcal{A} \subseteq Event$ *is a finite alphabet,* $\delta \in (Q \times \mathcal{A} \times Guard \times Assign \times Q)$ *is a finite set of transitions,* $q_0 \in Q$ *is an initial state, and* $F \subseteq Q$ *is a set of final states.*

3.2   Semantics

We give the semantics of EA within the context of an EA $\mathsf{E} = \langle Q, \mathcal{A}, \delta, q_0, F \rangle$.

Definition 6 (Configurations and Transition Relation). *We define configurations as elements of the set* $Config = Q \times Bind$. *Let* $\rightarrow \subseteq Config \times GEvent \times Config$ *be a relation on configurations s.t. configurations* $\langle q, \varphi \rangle$ *and* $\langle q', \varphi' \rangle$ *are related by the ground event* a, *written* $\langle q, \varphi \rangle \xrightarrow{a} \langle q', \varphi' \rangle$, *if and only if*

$$\exists b \in \mathcal{A}, \exists g \in Guard, \exists \gamma \in Assign : (q, b, g, \gamma, q') \in \delta \wedge$$
$$\mathtt{matches}(a, b) \wedge g(\varphi \dagger \mathtt{match}(a, b)) \wedge \varphi' = \gamma(\varphi \dagger \mathtt{match}(a, b)).$$

Let the transition relation $\rightarrow_\mathsf{E}$ *be the smallest relation containing* $\rightarrow$ *such that for any event* a *and configuration* c *if* $\nexists c : c \xrightarrow{a} c'$ *then* $c \xrightarrow{a}_\mathsf{E} c$. *The relation* $\rightarrow_\mathsf{E}$ *is lifted to traces. For any two configurations* c *and* c', $c \xrightarrow{\epsilon}_\mathsf{E} c$ *holds, and* $c \xrightarrow{a.\tau}_\mathsf{E} c'$ *holds iff there exists a configuration* c' *s.t.* $c \xrightarrow{a}_\mathsf{E} c''$ *and* $c'' \xrightarrow{\tau}_\mathsf{E} c'$.

In an EA, a configuration contains the values bound to the variables. These bindings are local to each EA – notably there is no shared global state. A ground event a can take $\langle q, \varphi \rangle$ into $\langle q', \varphi' \rangle$ if there exists a transition in δ starting in q, s.t. the events match, the guard is satisfied, and the new configuration contains the binding given by the assignment and state q'. Note that EA are non-deterministic.

Note. When we encounter an event for which there is no matching transition in the automaton we wait in the current state. There are alternative accounts, which are equivalent in the sense that we can translate automata between the different semantics. We have made this choice as our initial experience is that this makes writing specifications more straightforward as, when defining a property, we do not need to write transitions for events with no role in the specification.

Let us now define the language of an EA. An event denotes a set of ground events – for example, the event $\mathtt{start}(x)$ denotes the set $\{\mathtt{start}(v) \mid v \in Val\}$ and a ground event denotes the singleton set containing itself. We use this notion to define the *ground alphabet* of an EA. Let the ground alphabet of the EA E be

$$\mathtt{ground}(\mathsf{E}) = \{\mathsf{a} \in GEvent \mid \exists \mathsf{b} \in \mathcal{A} : \mathtt{matches}(\mathsf{a}, \mathsf{b})\}.$$

We say that there is a run on τ reaching a configuration c iff $\langle q_0, [\,] \rangle \xrightarrow{\tau}_\mathsf{E} c$. An EA accepts a trace if there is a run on that trace reaching a configuration in a final state.

Definition 7 (Event Automaton Language). *The language of the Event Automaton E is noted and defined as*

$$\mathcal{L}(\mathsf{E}) = \{\tau \in \mathtt{ground}(\mathsf{E})^* \mid \exists \langle \mathsf{q}, \varphi \rangle \in Config : \langle \mathsf{q}_0, [\,] \rangle \xrightarrow{\tau}_\mathsf{E} \langle \mathsf{q}, \varphi \rangle \wedge \mathsf{q} \in F\}.$$

3.3 Examples

To illustrate Event Automata and their languages, consider the three examples in Sec. 2, Talking Philosophers, Auction Bidding and Candidate Selection. Recall that all variables occuring in an EA are unquantified (free).

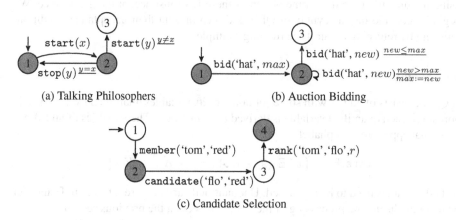

(a) Talking Philosophers   (b) Auction Bidding

(c) Candidate Selection

Fig. 1. Three EAs. We use shaded states to indicate final states and the notation $\frac{guard}{assignment}$ for writing guards and assignments on transitions.

Talking Philosophers. The EA Phil in Fig. 1a captures the property that no two philosophers can be talking at the same time. The philosopher currently talking is recorded in variable x, which can only be rebound after that philosopher stops talking. If a different philosopher starts talking before this happens this is an error. Consider the trace $\tau_1 = \texttt{start}(1).\texttt{stop}(1).\texttt{start}(2)$. This is in $\mathcal{L}(\textsf{Phil})$ as the run $\langle 1, [\ ] \rangle \xrightarrow{\texttt{start}(1)}$ $\langle 2, [x \mapsto 1] \rangle \xrightarrow{\texttt{stop}(1)} \langle 1, [x \mapsto 1, y \mapsto 1] \rangle \xrightarrow{\texttt{start}(2)} \langle 2, [x \mapsto 2, y \mapsto 1] \rangle$ ends in a final state. However, the trace $\tau_2 = \texttt{start}(1).\texttt{start}(2)$ is not in $\mathcal{L}(\textsf{Phil})$ as the run $\langle 1, [\ ] \rangle \xrightarrow{\texttt{start}(1)} \langle 2, [x \mapsto 1] \rangle \xrightarrow{\texttt{start}(2)} \langle 3, [x \mapsto 1, y \mapsto 2] \rangle$ does not end in a final state.

Auction Bidding. The EA Hat in Fig. 1b captures the property that bids on item 'hat' must be strictly increasing. Consider the trace $\tau_3 = \texttt{bid}(\text{'hat'}, 1).\texttt{bid}(\text{'hat'}, 10).$ $\texttt{bid}(\text{'hat'}, 5)$. The only run on τ_3 is $\langle 1, [\ ] \rangle \xrightarrow{\texttt{bid}(\text{'hat'},1)} \langle 2, [max \mapsto 1] \rangle \xrightarrow{\texttt{bid}(\text{'hat'},10)}$ $\langle 2, [max \mapsto 10, new \mapsto 10] \rangle \xrightarrow{\texttt{bid}(\text{'hat'},5)} \langle 3, [max \mapsto 10, new \mapsto 5] \rangle$. As state 3 is non-final, $\tau_3 \notin \mathcal{L}(\textsf{Hat})$. In this example, a guard is used to capture the failing behaviour out of state 2 and an assignment is used to keep track of the maximum bid.

Candidate Selection. The EA Candi in Fig. 1c captures the property that voter tom is a member of the red party, candidate flo is a candidate for the red party and voter tom ranks flo in position r - a variable. State 2 is accepting as tom only needs to rank flo if she is a candidate for the red party. The more general case is dealt with in the next section by replacing values 'tom', 'flo', and 'red' by quantified variables.

4   Quantified Event Automata

We now define Quantified Event Automata (QEA), which generalise EA by quantifying over zero or more of the variables used in an EA. Acceptance is decided by replacing these quantified variables by each value in their domain to generate a set of EA and then using the quantifiers to determine which of these EA must accept the given trace. We begin by considering the syntax of QEA and then present their acceptance condition, finishing by returning to our three running examples.

4.1   Syntax

A QEA consists of an EA with some (or none) of its variables quantified by $\forall$ or $\exists$. The domain of each quantified variable is derived from the trace. The variables of an EA are those that appear in its alphabet:

$$\texttt{vars}(\mathsf{E}) = \{x \mid \exists e(\bar{s}) \in \mathsf{E}.\mathcal{A} : x \in \bar{s} \wedge x \in \mathit{Var}\}.$$

Not all variables need to be quantified. Unquantified variables are left free in E and can be rebound during the processing of the trace - as seen in the previous section.

Definition 8 (Quantified Event Automaton). *A QEA is a pair* $\langle \Lambda, \mathsf{E} \rangle$ *where* E *is an EA and* $\Lambda \in (\{\forall, \exists\} \times \mathtt{vars}(\mathsf{E}) \times Guard)^*$ *is a list of quantified variables with guards.*

A QEA is well-formed if Λ contains each variable in $\mathtt{vars}(\mathsf{E})$ at most once. In the following, we consider a QEA $\mathsf{Q} = \langle \Lambda, \mathsf{E} \rangle$.

4.2 Acceptance

In Sec. 3 we defined the language of an EA. The intuitive idea here is to use the EA E in QEA Q as a template for generating a set of EA and then check if the trace is in the language of each generated EA. To do this, quantified variables in E are replaced by the values taken from the domain of these quantified variables. First we introduce the concept of EA instantiation to replace variables in E with values.

Definition 9 (Event Automaton Instantiation). *Given a binding* θ, *let* $\mathsf{E}(\theta) = \langle Q, \mathcal{A}(\theta), \delta(\theta), q_0, F \rangle$ *be the* θ-*instantiation of* E *where*

$$\mathcal{A}(\theta) = \{\mathbf{b}(\theta) \mid \mathbf{b} \in \mathcal{A}\}$$
$$(q, \mathbf{b}(\theta), g', \gamma', q') \in \delta(\theta) \ \textit{iff} \ (q, \mathbf{b}, g, \gamma, q') \in \delta \ \textit{and} \ g'(\varphi) = g(\theta \dagger \varphi)$$
$$\textit{and} \ \gamma'(\varphi) = \gamma(\theta \dagger \varphi).$$

The domain of each quantified variable is derived from the values in the trace. The intuition here is that the events $\mathtt{start}(x)$ and $\mathtt{stop}(x)$ allow us to identify the values that the quantified variable x can take. Therefore, the domain for x is computed by finding all values bound to x when matching any event in the trace with any event in the alphabet of the EA that uses x.

Definition 10 (Derived Domain). *The derived domain of a trace* τ *is a map from variables quantified in* Λ *to sets of values:*

$$Dom(\tau)(x) = \{\mathtt{match}(\mathbf{a}, \mathbf{b})(x) \mid \mathbf{b} = e(..., x, ...) \in \mathcal{A} \wedge \mathbf{a} \in \tau \wedge \mathtt{matches}(\mathbf{a}, \mathbf{b})\}.$$

Each instantiation of E is concerned only with the behaviour of a small set of values (or the events using those values) but a trace can contain other values - that is for binding θ a trace can contain events not in $\mathtt{ground}(\mathsf{E}(\theta))$. We need to restrict the trace so that we can test whether it is in the language of $\mathsf{E}(\theta)$. We do this by filtering out any event not in $\mathtt{ground}(\mathsf{E}(\theta))$. Note that our notion of projection is w.r.t. a set of parametric events (captured by an EA), which differs from the projection in parametric trace slicing (Definition 1) done w.r.t. a binding. Therefore, we are able to deal with event names which are associated with multiple different variable lists.

Definition 11 (Projection). *The projection of* $\tau \in Trace$ *w.r.t.* E *is defined as:*

$$\epsilon \downarrow_{\mathsf{E}} = \epsilon \qquad\qquad \mathbf{a}.\tau \downarrow_{\mathsf{E}} = \begin{cases} \mathbf{a}.(\tau \downarrow_{\mathsf{E}}) & \textit{if} \ \mathbf{a} \in \mathtt{ground}(\mathsf{E}), \\ (\tau \downarrow_{\mathsf{E}}) & \textit{otherwise.} \end{cases}$$

A trace τ satisfies the property w.r.t. a binding θ iff $\tau \downarrow_{\mathsf{E}(\theta)} \in \mathcal{L}(\mathsf{E}(\theta))$. Note that we could use a different formalism to define such a language, or alter the semantics of EA, and this notion of satisfaction would remain unchanged. Finally, the quantifiers use the derived domain to inductively generate bindings and dictates which of these bindings the trace must satisfy the property with respect to.

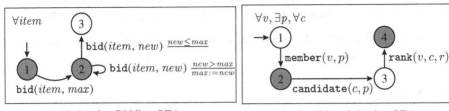

(a) Auction Bidding QEA   (b) Candidate Selection QEA

Fig. 2. Two QEAs

Definition 12 (Acceptance). Q *accepts a ground trace τ if $\tau \models_{[\,]} \Lambda.E$ where $\models_\theta$ is defined as*

$\tau \models_\theta (\forall x : g)\Lambda'.E$ *iff for all d in $Dom(\tau)(x)$ if $g(\theta \dagger [x \mapsto d])$ then $\tau \models_{\theta\dagger[x\mapsto d]} \Lambda'.E$*
$\tau \models_\theta (\exists x : g)\Lambda'.E$ *iff for some d in $Dom(\tau)(x)$ $g(\theta \dagger [x \mapsto d])$ and $\tau \models_{\theta\dagger[x\mapsto d]} \Lambda'.E$*
$\tau \models_\theta \epsilon.E$ *iff $\tau \downarrow_{E(\theta)} \in \mathcal{L}(E(\theta))$*

Universal (resp. existential) quantification means that a trace must satisfy the property w.r.t. all (resp. at least one) generated bindings.

4.3   Examples

We revisit the examples introduced in Sec. 2 and used in Sec. 3.

Talking Philosophers. The EA in Fig. 1a can be treated directly as a QEA with no quantifications - in this case a single global value (x) is used to record the currently talking philosopher and we are not concerned with the behaviour of individual philosophers in isolation.

Auction Bidding. The QEA Bid in Fig. 2a captures the general Auction Bidding property. The quantifications indicate that only the *item* variable should be instantiated, thus leaving the *max* and *new* variables free to be rebound whilst processing the trace.

Candidate Selection. The QEA Select in Fig 2b captures the general Candidate Selection property that for every voter there is a party that the voter is a member of, and the voter ranks all candidates for that party. Let us consider the following trace τ_4

```
member('tom','red').member('ali','blue').candidate('jim','red').candidate('flo','red').
candidate('don','blue').rank('tom','jim',1).rank('ali','don',1).
```

In this trace ali ranks all candidates for the blue party but tom only ranks one of the candidates for the red party. The derived domain is $Dom(\tau_4) = [v \mapsto \{\text{'tom', 'ali'}\}, p \mapsto \{\text{'red', 'blue'}\}, c \mapsto \{\text{'jim', 'flo', 'don'}\}]$ leading to 12 possible bindings. For space reasons we do not enumerate these bindings here, but leave it to the reader to verify that for five of these bindings the instantiated EA accepts the trace, and that adding the event rank('tom','flo',2) to the trace would make the trace accepting.

5   Step-Wise Evaluation of QEA

In the previous section, we presented an acceptance condition to decide whether a trace satisfies the property represented by a QEA. This first built up the derived domain by inspecting the trace, then used bindings generated from this domain to generate a set of instantiated EA, checked whether the trace was in the language of each instantiated EA and finally used this information, along with quantifiers, to decide whether the trace was accepted. This requires us to pass over the trace at least twice - first to generate the bindings and then to check the EAs instantiated with them.

For runtime verification purposes, we need to combine these two passes into one – passing over the trace as it is produced. To do this we process each event when it arrives by building the derived domain and keeping track of the status of each instantiated EA on the fly. To decide the acceptance of the trace received up to a certain point we need to compute the information required by Def. 12. This can be split into two concerns

1. *Building the Derived Domain.* When a new event is received the values it contains must be recorded. These values are obtained by matching (as per Def. 4) the received event with the events in the alphabet of the given EA.
2. *Tracking the status of Instantiated EAs.* The relevant bindings for Def. 12 are those that can be generated from the derived domain and that bind all quantified variables - we call such bindings *total*. We need to track the status of the EA instantiated with each such total binding.

For efficiency reasons, we capture the derived domain in the bindings that can be built from it, instead of storing this separately. The status of each instantiated EA can be captured by the configurations reachable by the trace received so far projected with respect to that instantiated EA. In the following we break this down into three steps:

1. Generating bindings and associating with them the relevant projected traces
2. Adapting this approach to generate configurations rather than projected traces
3. Showing how acceptance can be decided based on these configurations

When considering runtime verification, efficiency is obviously a major concern. We do not present an optimised algorithm here, but keep optimisation in mind when discussing design decisions. The approach presented here can be optimised in a number of ways - note that the main structure of the approach is similar to that taken by JAVAMOP, and therefore many optimisations applied in this tool would be applicable here.

We illustrate how to monitor a trace in a step-wise fashion by discussing the Candidate Selection example. We consider how the data structures relevant for monitoring are built up for the QEA Select in Fig 2b and the trace τ_4 given on page 76.

5.1   Generating Projections

In this section we show how to use a trace and a QEA to construct a *monitoring state*, which associates bindings with projected traces:

$$MonitoringState = Binding \rightharpoonup Trace$$

Table 1. The monitor state generated by monitoring τ_4 for Select. Event names have been truncated to three letters and parameter values to their first letter.

Partial bindings	Total bindings
$[\,] \quad\quad\quad\quad\quad \mapsto \epsilon$	$[v \mapsto \mathsf{t}, p \mapsto \mathsf{r}, c \mapsto \mathsf{j}] \quad \mapsto \mathsf{mem(t,r).can(j,r).ran(t,j,1)}$
$[v \mapsto \mathsf{t}, p \mapsto \mathsf{r}] \mapsto \mathsf{mem(t,r)}$	$[v \mapsto \mathsf{t}, p \mapsto \mathsf{r}, c \mapsto \mathsf{f}] \quad \mapsto \mathsf{mem(t,r).can(f,r)}$
$[v \mapsto \mathsf{a}, p \mapsto \mathsf{b}] \mapsto \mathsf{mem(a,r)}$	$[v \mapsto \mathsf{t}, p \mapsto \mathsf{r}, c \mapsto \mathsf{d}] \quad \mapsto \mathsf{mem(t,r)}$
$[p \mapsto \mathsf{r}, c \mapsto \mathsf{j}] \quad \mapsto \mathsf{can(j,r)}$	$[v \mapsto \mathsf{t}, p \mapsto \mathsf{b}, c \mapsto \mathsf{d}] \quad \mapsto \mathsf{can(d,b)}$
$[p \mapsto \mathsf{r}, c \mapsto \mathsf{f}] \quad \mapsto \mathsf{can(f,r)}$	$[v \mapsto \mathsf{a}, p \mapsto \mathsf{r}, c \mapsto \mathsf{j}] \quad \mapsto \mathsf{can(j,r)}$
$[p \mapsto \mathsf{b}, c \mapsto \mathsf{d}] \mapsto \mathsf{can(d,b)}$	$[v \mapsto \mathsf{a}, p \mapsto \mathsf{r}, c \mapsto \mathsf{f}] \quad \mapsto \mathsf{can(f,r)}$
	$[v \mapsto \mathsf{a}, p \mapsto \mathsf{b}, c \mapsto \mathsf{j}] \quad \mapsto \mathsf{mem(a,b)}$
	$[v \mapsto \mathsf{a}, p \mapsto \mathsf{b}, c \mapsto \mathsf{f}] \quad \mapsto \mathsf{mem(a,b)}$
	$[v \mapsto \mathsf{a}, p \mapsto \mathsf{b}, c \mapsto \mathsf{d}] \mapsto \mathsf{mem(a,b).can(d,b).ran(a,d,1)}$

The monitoring state for our example is given in Table 1. Note that the bindings contain quantified variables only. Let us consider how this monitoring state was built starting with the empty monitoring state $[\,] \mapsto \epsilon$. We first examine the QEA Select and note that its alphabet is $\{\mathtt{member}(v, p), \mathtt{candidate}(c, p), \mathtt{rank}(v, c, r)\}$.

On observing τ_4's first event, $\mathtt{member}(\text{'tom'}, \text{'red'})$, we construct the binding $[v \mapsto$ 'tom', $p \mapsto$ 'red'] by matching with $\mathtt{member}(v,p)$. This binding is added to the monitoring state, along with the associated projected trace. We process τ_4's second event in a similar way to add:

$$[v \mapsto \text{'tom'}, p \mapsto \text{'red'}] \mapsto \mathtt{member}(\text{'tom'}, \text{'red'})$$
$$[v \mapsto \text{'ali'}, p \mapsto \text{'blue'}] \mapsto \mathtt{member}(\text{'ali'}, \text{'blue'})$$

We did not add single bindings such as $[v \mapsto$ 'tom'] as the projected traces associated with these bindings would be empty, and therefore recording them would be redundant. We only record bindings for which the projected trace is non-empty. On observing τ_4's third event, $\mathtt{candidate}(\text{'jim'}, \text{'red'})$, we construct the binding $[p \mapsto$ 'red', $c \mapsto$ 'jim'] by matching with $\mathtt{candidate}(c,p)$ and add this to the monitoring state:

$$[p \mapsto \text{'red'}, c \mapsto \text{'jim'}] \mapsto \mathtt{candidate}(\text{'jim'}, \text{'red'})$$

We then combine this binding with the existing binding $[v \mapsto$ 'tom', $p \mapsto$ 'red'] to get the binding $[v \mapsto$ 'tom', $c \mapsto$ 'jim', $p \mapsto$ 'red']. The projected trace for this new binding is the trace associated with the original binding extended with the current event.

$$[v \mapsto \text{'tom'}, p \mapsto \text{'red'}, c \mapsto \text{'jim'}] \mapsto \mathtt{member}(\text{'tom'}, \text{'red'}).\mathtt{candidate}(\text{'jim'}, \text{'red'})$$

To see why we do this recall that the submap relation $\sqsubseteq$ gives a partial order on bindings – illustrated in Fig.3. By definition, the projected trace for a new binding will include all the projected traces for existing bindings it subsumes w.r.t. $\sqsubseteq$, and when it is created all such events are captured by the *largest* such existing binding. Like JAVAMOP we call this notion *maximality*. Therefore, the projected trace mapped to by a new binding must extend the projected trace mapped to by the maximal existing binding.

As noted earlier, we must record any binding that can be built from the derived domain that has a non-empty projection. We can build two such bindings by combining submaps of $[v \mapsto$ 'tom', $p \mapsto$ 'red'] with existing bindings as follows:

$$[v \mapsto \text{'ali'}, p \mapsto \text{'red'}, c \mapsto \text{'jim'}] \mapsto \mathtt{candidate}(\text{'jim'}, \text{'red'})$$
$$[v \mapsto \text{'ali'}, p \mapsto \text{'blue'}, c \mapsto \text{'jim'}] \mapsto \mathtt{member}(\text{'ali'}, \text{'blue'})$$

$$[v \mapsto \text{`tom'}, c \mapsto \text{`jim'}, p \mapsto \text{`red'}] \qquad\qquad [v \mapsto \text{`tom'}, c \mapsto \text{`flo'}, p \mapsto \text{`red'}]$$

$$[c \mapsto \text{`jim'}, p \mapsto \text{`red'}]\ [v \mapsto \text{`tom'}, p \mapsto \text{`red'}]\ [c \mapsto \text{`flo'}, p \mapsto \text{`red'}]$$

$$[\,]$$

Fig. 3. A subset of bindings from Table 1 ordered by the submap relation

We now formalise how these bindings and projected traces are generated. We will need to select the quantified part of a binding, hence, for an assumed quantifier list Λ, let $\texttt{quantified}(\theta) = [(x \mapsto v) \in \theta \mid x \in \texttt{vars}(\Lambda)]$ where $\texttt{vars}(\Lambda) = \{x \in Var \mid (\_, x, \_) \in \Lambda\}$. A binding θ is *total* if $\underline{dom}(\theta) = \texttt{vars}(\Lambda)$ and *partial* otherwise.

An event is added to the projection for a binding θ if it matches with an event in $\mathsf{E}(\theta).\mathcal{A}$ and the resulting binding does not contain quantified variables - this second part is necessary as θ may be partial. For example, $\texttt{member}(\text{`tom'}, \text{`red'})$ is not added to the projection for $[\,]$ as the binding that makes it match with $\texttt{member}(c, p)$ binds c and p.

Definition 13 (Event Relevance). *A ground event a is* relevant *to a binding θ iff*

$$\exists \mathbf{b} \in \mathcal{A}(\theta) : \texttt{matches}(\mathbf{a}, \mathbf{b}) \wedge \texttt{quantified}(\texttt{match}(\mathbf{a}, \mathbf{b})) = [\,]$$

To extend a binding θ we first find all bindings that match the received event with an event in $\mathsf{E}(\theta).\mathcal{A}$, and then compute all possible extensions to θ based on these bindings. If the received event is relevant to a generated new binding we add this event to the previous trace, otherwise the previous trace is just copied.

Definition 14 (Extending a Binding). *Let $direct(\theta, \mathbf{a})$ be the bindings that directly extend θ given $\mathbf{a}$, defined in terms of those bindings that can be built from $\mathbf{a}$.*

$$from(\theta, \mathbf{a}) = \{\texttt{quantified}(\texttt{match}(\mathbf{a}, \mathbf{b})) \mid \mathbf{b} \in \mathcal{A}(\theta)\}$$
$$direct(\theta, \mathbf{a}) = \{\theta \dagger \theta' \mid \exists \theta'' \in from(\theta, \mathbf{a}) : \theta' \sqsubseteq \theta'' \wedge \theta' \neq [\,]\}$$

Let $all(\theta, \mathbf{a})$ be the smallest superset of $direct(\theta, \mathbf{a})$ containing $\theta_1 \dagger \theta_2$ for all compatible θ_1 and θ_2 in $direct(\theta, \mathbf{a})$. The required extensions $\texttt{extend}(\mathbf{a}, \theta, \sigma)$ are given by

$$(\theta' \mapsto \sigma') \in \texttt{extend}(\mathbf{a}, \theta, \sigma) \textit{ iff } \theta' \in all(\theta, \mathbf{a}) \wedge \sigma' = \begin{cases} \sigma.\mathbf{a} & \textit{if } \exists \theta'' \in from(\theta, \mathbf{a}) : \theta'' \sqsubseteq \theta' \\ \sigma & \textit{otherwise} \end{cases}$$

On receiving a new event the next monitoring state is built by iterating through the current monitoring state and, for each binding, adding the event to its associated projected trace if it is relevant and adding new extending bindings as described above. To ensure that new bindings extend the maximal existing binding we iterate through bindings in the reverse order defined by $\sqsubseteq$ and only add bindings that do not already exist. This ensures that the maximal existing binding for a new binding will always be encountered first. By adding all bindings that extend existing bindings we ensure that the derived domain is correctly recorded and that all necessary total bindings will be created.

Definition 15 (Single Step Monitoring Construction). *Given ground event $\mathbf{a}$ and monitoring state M. Let $\theta_1, \ldots, \theta_m$ be a linearisation of the domain of M i.e. if $\theta_j \sqsubset \theta_k$*

then $j > k$ and every element in the domain of M is present once in the sequence, hence $m = |M|$. We define $(\mathbf{a} * M) = N_m \in MonitoringState$ where N_m is iteratively defined as follows for $i \in [1, m]$.

$$N_0 = [\,] \qquad N_i = N_{i-1} \dagger \mathrm{Add}_i \dagger \begin{cases} [\theta_i \mapsto M(\theta_i).\mathbf{a}] & \textit{if } \mathbf{a} \textit{ is relevant to } \theta_i \\ [\theta_i \mapsto M(\theta_i)] & \textit{otherwise} \end{cases}$$

where $\mathrm{Add}_i = [(\theta' \mapsto \sigma') \in \mathtt{extend}(\mathbf{a}, \theta_i, M(\theta_i)) \mid \theta' \notin \underline{dom}(N_{i-1})]$

Finally, for the input trace the construction of Def. 15 is applied to each event, starting with an initial monitoring state - the empty binding with the empty projection.

Definition 16 (Stepwise Monitoring). *For a trace $\tau = a_0.a_1 \ldots a_n$ we define the final monitoring state M_τ as $a_n * (\ldots * (a_0 * [\,[\,] \mapsto \epsilon\,]) \ldots)$.*

The final monitoring state M_τ contains the information required to decide whether the trace τ is accepted (as specified in Def. 12) (discussed in Sec. 5.3).

5.2 Generating Configurations

In the previous section we associated bindings with projected traces. However, using projected traces directly would not be efficient, especially as we would need to run through each projected trace to decide the status of acceptance on each step. Instead, we record the configurations reachable by those projections. To do this we define a new structure:

$MonitorLookup = Binding \rightarrow \mathcal{P}(Config)$

The monitor lookup for our example is given in Table 2. We adapt the construction in the previous section to build a monitor lookup by defining a function in Algorithm 1 that computes the

Algorithm 1. Finding the next configurations when adding an event to a projection

---

function NEXT(θ : Binding, $\mathbf{a}$: GEvent,
$\qquad\qquad\qquad$ C : Set[Config]) :Set[Config]
$\quad$ next $\leftarrow \emptyset$
$\quad$ **for** $\langle q, \varphi \rangle$ in C **do**
$\qquad$ **for** $(q_1, \mathbf{b}, g, \gamma, q_2) \in \mathrm{E}.\delta$ **do**
$\qquad\quad$ **if** $q_1{=}q \land \mathtt{matches}(\mathbf{a}, \mathbf{b}(\theta))$ **then**
$\qquad\qquad$ $\varphi' \leftarrow \varphi \dagger \mathtt{match}(\mathbf{a}, \mathbf{b}(\theta))$
$\qquad\qquad$ **if** $\mathtt{quantified}(\varphi'){=}[\,]$ and
$\qquad\qquad\quad$ $g(\mathtt{unquantified}(\varphi'))$ **then**
$\qquad\qquad\qquad$ next $\leftarrow$ next $+ \langle q_2,$
$\qquad\qquad\qquad\qquad \gamma(\mathtt{unquantified}(\varphi'))\rangle$
$\quad$ **if** no transitions are taken **then**
$\qquad$ next $\leftarrow$ next $\cup \langle q, \varphi \rangle$
$\quad$ **return** next

---

next configurations for a binding given a received event. Let $\mathtt{unquantified}(\theta) = \theta \backslash \mathtt{quantified}(\theta)$. We can modify Def. 15 to produce a monitoring lookup instead of a monitoring state by replacing the inductive definition of N_i with

$$N_i = N_{i-1} \dagger \mathrm{Add}_i \dagger [\theta_i \mapsto \mathrm{NEXT}(\theta_i, \mathbf{a}, M(\theta_i))]$$

where $\mathrm{Add}_i = [\theta \mapsto \mathrm{NEXT}(\theta, \mathbf{a}, M(\theta_i)) \mid \theta \in all(\theta_i, \mathbf{a})]$. This processes the projected trace for a binding as it is produced as $\mathrm{NEXT}(\theta, \mathbf{a}, C)$ gives all configurations reachable by event $\mathbf{a}$ from configurations in C on $\mathrm{E}(\theta)$, staying in the same configuration if no transition can be taken. Because of this last point no changes are made if the event is not relevant to the binding. The check that $\mathtt{quantified}(\varphi') = [\,]$ ensures that no new quantified variables are bound when taking a transition. Note that this function relies on the wait semantics of EA and could not necessarily be used without modification if we were to replace EA with an alternative formalism - the previous construction only assumes an alphabet of events to construct projected traces.

Table 2. The monitor lookup generated by monitoring τ_4 for Select. Parameter values have been truncated to their first letter.

$[\,] \mapsto \langle 1, [\,]\rangle$	$[p \mapsto \mathsf{b}, c \mapsto \mathsf{d}] \mapsto \langle 1, [\,]\rangle$	$[v \mapsto \mathsf{t}, p \mapsto \mathsf{b}, c \mapsto \mathsf{d}] \mapsto \langle 1, [\,]\rangle$
$[p \mapsto \mathsf{r}, c \mapsto \mathsf{j}] \mapsto \langle 1, [\,]\rangle$	$[v \mapsto \mathsf{a}, p \mapsto \mathsf{b}, c \mapsto \mathsf{d}] \mapsto \langle 4, [r \mapsto 1]\rangle$	$[v \mapsto \mathsf{a}, p \mapsto \mathsf{r}, c \mapsto \mathsf{j}] \mapsto \langle 1, [\,]\rangle$
$[v \mapsto \mathsf{t}, p \mapsto \mathsf{r}] \mapsto \langle 2, [\,]\rangle$	$[v \mapsto \mathsf{t}, p \mapsto \mathsf{r}, c \mapsto \mathsf{j}] \mapsto \langle 4, [r \mapsto 1]\rangle$	$[v \mapsto \mathsf{a}, p \mapsto \mathsf{r}, c \mapsto \mathsf{f}] \mapsto \langle 1, [\,]\rangle$
$[p \mapsto \mathsf{r}, c \mapsto \mathsf{f}] \mapsto \langle 1, [\,]\rangle$	$[v \mapsto \mathsf{t}, p \mapsto \mathsf{r}, c \mapsto \mathsf{f}] \mapsto \langle 3, [\,]\rangle$	$[v \mapsto \mathsf{a}, p \mapsto \mathsf{b}, c \mapsto \mathsf{j}] \mapsto \langle 2, [\,]\rangle$
$[v \mapsto \mathsf{a}, p \mapsto \mathsf{b}] \mapsto \langle 2, [\,]\rangle$	$[v \mapsto \mathsf{t}, p \mapsto \mathsf{r}, c \mapsto \mathsf{d}] \mapsto \langle 2, [\,]\rangle$	$[v \mapsto \mathsf{a}, p \mapsto \mathsf{b}, c \mapsto \mathsf{f}] \mapsto \langle 2, [\,]\rangle$

5.3 Acceptance

Here we consider when a monitor lookup is accepted. We adapt the notion of acceptance given in Def. 12 to detect success or failure as soon as it is possible. We define a four valued verdict domain containing the classifications *Strong Success*, *Weak Success*, *Strong Failure* and *Weak Failure*. The strong versions of success and failure indicate that no extensions of the trace can alter the verdict. For example, τ_3 is strongly failing for the QEA in Fig. 2a as no extensions will be accepted. We first identify the special states of E such that all extensions of trace τ reaching that state will be in $\mathcal{L}(\mathsf{E})$ iff τ is.

Definition 17 (Strong Success and Failure States). *Let* $\mathtt{reach}(q)$ *be the set of reachable states of* $q \in Q$. *Let* $\mathtt{strongS} = \{q \in F \mid \mathtt{reach}(q) \subseteq F\}$ *be the strong success states. Let* $\mathtt{strongF} = \{q \in Q \backslash F \mid \mathtt{reach}(q) \cap F = \emptyset\}$ *be the strong failure states. Note that it is not necessarily the case that* $(\mathtt{strongS} \cup \mathtt{strongF}) = Q$.

If all quantifiers are universal then all total bindings must reach successful configurations, and if one cannot (i.e., is in a strongly failing state) a strong failure can be reported, similarly if all quantifiers are existential then a single total binding reaching a configuration in a strongly successful state means that strong success can be reported. Strong success or failure cannot be reported where we have a mix of existential and universal quantification.

Definition 18 (Monitor Lookup Classification). *We define the function* $\mathtt{Check}(L, \mathsf{Q})$ *to decide whether a monitor lookup* L *satisfies a QEA* Q. *Let* $\mathtt{uni}$ *be true if all quantifiers in* $\mathsf{Q}.\Lambda$ *are universal,* $\mathtt{exi}$ *be true if they are all existential and* G *be the combination of all guards in* $\mathsf{Q}.\Lambda$, *i.e,* $G(\theta)$ *iff* $\forall(\_, \_, g) \in \Lambda : g(\theta)$.

$$\mathtt{Check}(L, \mathsf{Q}) = \begin{cases} StrongSuccess & \textit{iff } \mathtt{exi} \wedge \exists \theta \in \underline{dom}(L) : G(\theta) \\ & \wedge \exists \langle q, \varphi \rangle \in L(\theta) : q \in \mathtt{StrongS} \\ StrongFailure & \textit{iff } \mathtt{uni} \wedge \exists \theta \in \underline{dom}(L) : G(\theta) \\ & \wedge \forall \langle q, \varphi \rangle \in L(\theta) : q \in \mathtt{StrongF} \\ WeakSuccess & \textit{iff } \textit{not a strong result and } L \models_{[\,]} \mathsf{Q}.\Lambda \\ WeakFailure & \textit{iff } \textit{not a strong result and } L \not\models_{[\,]} \mathsf{Q}.\Lambda \end{cases}$$

for $L \models_\theta \Lambda$, *defined as*

$L \models_\theta (\forall x : g)\Lambda'$ *iff for all* d *in* $D_L(x)$ *if* $g(\theta \dagger [x \mapsto d])$ *then* $L \models_{\theta \dagger [x \mapsto d]} \Lambda'$

$L \models_\theta (\exists x : g)\Lambda'$ *iff for some* d *in* $D_L(x)$ $g(\theta \dagger [x \mapsto d])$ *and* $L \models_{\theta \dagger [x \mapsto d]} \Lambda'$

$L \models_\theta \epsilon$ *iff* $\begin{cases} \exists \langle q, \varphi \rangle \in L(\theta) : q \in \mathsf{E}.F & \textit{if } \theta \in \underline{dom}(L) \\ q_0 \in F & \textit{otherwise} \end{cases}$

where $D_L(x) = \{\theta(x) \mid \theta \in \underline{dom}(L) \wedge x \in \underline{dom}(\theta)\}$

Note that if $\theta \notin \underline{dom}(L)$ then there were no events relevant to θ in the trace and therefore the projected trace for θ is empty. An efficient algorithm for computing Check (L, Q) would keep track of the current status and update this whenever a relevant change is made to the monitor lookup, rather than recomputing it on each step.

The monitor lookup in Table. 2 is weakly failing. The monitor lookup for the trace τ_4.rank('tom', 'flo', 2) is weakly successful as this changes the configuration associated with $[c \mapsto \mathrm{t}, p \mapsto \mathrm{r}, c \mapsto f]$ to $\langle 4, [r \mapsto 2] \rangle$ and then tom ranks all candidates for the red party and ali ranks all candidates for the blue party. Observe that it is important that state 2 is accepting – as voters only need to rank candidates for the given party.

6   Related Work

QEA extends the parametric trace slicing approach [7] taken by JAVAMOP [11] by allowing event names to be associated with multiple different variable lists, by allowing non-quantified variables to vary during monitoring, and by allowing existential quantification in addition to universal quantification. This results in a strictly more expressive logic. JAVAMOP can be considered as a framework supporting parameterization for any propositional logic, provided as a plugin. QEA is similarly composed of quantification added to event automata, which can be replaced with other forms of logic. Parametric trace slicing can be seen as a special case of our notion of projection used to define whether a trace is in the language of a monitor for some binding.

TRACEMATCHES [1] is an extension of AspectJ where specifications are given as regular expressions over pointcuts. Parametric properties are monitored rather efficiently, but TRACEMATCHES, like JAVAMOP, suffers from the the limitation that each event name is associated with a unique list of variables.

A number of expressive techniques supporting data parameterization are based on rewriting. EAGLE [2] is based on rewriting of temporal logic formulas. For each new event, a formula is rewritten into a new formula that has to hold in the next step. RULER [2, 5] supports a specification language based on explicit rewrite-rules. Parameterized state machines are supported by LOGSCOPE [3] and TRACECONTRACT [4]. TRACECONTRACT is defined as an internal DSL in Scala (an API), re-using Scala's language constructs, including for example pattern matching. In both cases, states are explicitly parameterized with data, similar to how for example functions in a programming language are parameterized. A variant of LOGSCOPE has been created (not described in [3]) where the notion of maximality can be encoded by allowing transitions to refer to the presence (or non-presence) of other states with specific bindings as guards.

JLO [14] is a parameterized LTL, from which monitors are generated. A formula is rewritten into a new formula for each new event, as in EAGLE. JLO events are defined by pointcuts inspired by aspect-oriented programming, and monitors are generated as AspectJ aspects. An embedding of LTL in Haskell is described in [15]. It is similar to TRACECONTRACT, but whereas TRACECONTRACT handles data parameterization by re-using Scala's built-in notion of partial functions and pattern matching, [15] introduces a concept called *formula templates* instantiated for all possible permutations of propositions. Stolz introduced temporal assertions with parametrized propositions [13] with a similar aim of adding free variables and quantification to a runtime monitoring formalism (next-free LTL). The main distinction wrt. this work is the treatment of quantification - in [13] the domain of quantification is based on the current state only.

In Sec. 5 we use a four-valued verdict domain, which has been previously studied in the context of runtime monitoring e.g., in [6, 8]. RULER also uses a four-valued logic.

7 Conclusion and Future Work

We have introduced a new formalism for parametric runtime monitoring that is more expressive than the current most efficient techniques. We have presented both big-step and small-step semantics for our new formalism. Although not described in this paper, we have used these small-step semantics to implement a basic runtime monitoring algorithm in `Scala` and carried out initial testing.

We plan to explore four main areas of future work. Firstly, we intend to explore further the language theoretic properties of QEA. Secondly, we wish to explore different efficient runtime monitoring implementations. As our approach generalises the parametric trace slicing approach we may adapt optimisations implemented in JAVAMOP. Our stepwise construction also allows for alternative optimisations. Thirdly, we wish to consider the utility of QEA as a specification language. So far we have structured the development to separate EA, which define properties of specific sets of values, and QEA which generalise these. We may exploit this separation to replace EA with different formalisms, such as regular or context-free grammars, leading to a more general framework for specifying properties. These replacements would be to increase the usability rather than expressiveness of the framework. Finally, whilst developed in the context of runtime verification, the ideas in this paper appear to be relevant to specification mining (attempting to derive specifications by examining patterns in traces) and we intend to explore this link further.

References

1. Allan, C., Avgustinov, P., Christensen, A.S., Hendren, L., Kuzins, S., Lhoták, O., de Moor, O., Sereni, D., Sittampalam, G., Tibble, J.: Adding trace matching with free variables to AspectJ. SIGPLAN Not. 40, 345–364 (2005)
2. Barringer, H., Goldberg, A., Havelund, K., Sen, K.: Rule-Based Runtime Verification. In: Steffen, B., Levi, G. (eds.) VMCAI 2004. LNCS, vol. 2937, pp. 44–57. Springer, Heidelberg (2004)
3. Barringer, H., Groce, A., Havelund, K., Smith, M.: Formal analysis of log files. Journal of Aerospace Computing, Information, and Communication (2010)
4. Barringer, H., Havelund, K.: TRACECONTRACT: A Scala DSL for Trace Analysis. In: Butler, M., Schulte, W. (eds.) FM 2011. LNCS, vol. 6664, pp. 57–72. Springer, Heidelberg (2011)
5. Barringer, H., Rydeheard, D., Havelund, K.: Rule systems for run-time monitoring: from EAGLE to RuleR. J. Logic Computation 20(3), 675–706 (2010)
6. Bauer, A., Leucker, M., Schallhart, C.: The Good, the Bad, and the Ugly, But How Ugly Is Ugly? In: Sokolsky, O., Taşıran, S. (eds.) RV 2007. LNCS, vol. 4839, pp. 126–138. Springer, Heidelberg (2007)

7. Chen, F., Roşu, G.: Parametric Trace Slicing and Monitoring. In: Kowalewski, S., Philippou, A. (eds.) TACAS 2009. LNCS, vol. 5505, pp. 246–261. Springer, Heidelberg (2009)

8. Falcone, Y., Fernandez, J.-C., Mounier, L.: What can you verify and enforce at runtime? STTT 14(3), 349–382 (2012)

9. Havelund, K., Goldberg, A.: Verify Your Runs. In: Meyer, B., Woodcock, J. (eds.) VSTTE 2005. LNCS, vol. 4171, pp. 374–383. Springer, Heidelberg (2008)

10. Leucker, M., Schallhart, C.: A brief account of runtime verification. Journal of Logic and Algebraic Programming 78(5), 293–303 (2008)

11. Meredith, P., Jin, D., Griffith, D., Chen, F., Roşu, G.: An overview of the MOP runtime verification framework. J. Software Tools for Technology Transfer, 1–41 (2011)

12. Runtime Verification, http://www.runtime-verification.org (2001-2011)

13. Stolz, V.: Temporal assertions with parametrized propositions*. J. Log. and Comput. 20, 743–757 (2010)

14. Stolz, V., Bodden, E.: Temporal assertions using AspectJ. In: Proc. of the 5th Int. Workshop on Runtime Verification (RV 2005). ENTCS, vol. 144(4), pp. 109–124. Elsevier (2006)

15. Stolz, V., Huch, F.: Runtime verification of concurrent Haskell programs. In: Proc. of the 4th Int. Workshop on Runtime Verification (RV 2004). ENTCS, vol. 113, pp. 201–216. Elsevier (2005)

Decentralised LTL Monitoring

Andreas Bauer[1] and Yliès Falcone[2],*

[1] NICTA Software Systems Research Group** and Australian National University
[2] Laboratoire d'Informatique de Grenoble, UJF Université Grenoble I, France

Abstract. Users wanting to monitor distributed or component-based systems often perceive them as monolithic systems which, seen from the outside, exhibit a uniform behaviour as opposed to many components displaying many local behaviours that together constitute the system's global behaviour. This level of abstraction is often reasonable, hiding implementation details from users who may want to specify the system's global behaviour in terms of an LTL formula. However, the problem that arises then is how such a specification can actually be monitored in a distributed system that has no central data collection point, where all the components' local behaviours are observable. In this case, the LTL specification needs to be decomposed into sub-formulae which, in turn, need to be distributed amongst the components' locally attached monitors, each of which sees only a distinct part of the global behaviour.

The main contribution of this paper is an algorithm for distributing and monitoring LTL formulae, such that satisfaction or violation of specifications can be detected by local monitors alone. We present an implementation and show that our algorithm introduces only a minimum delay in detecting satisfaction/violation of a specification. Moreover, our practical results show that the communication overhead introduced by the local monitors is generally lower than the number of messages that would need to be sent to a central data collection point.

1 Introduction

Much work has been done on monitoring systems w.r.t. formal specifications such as linear-time temporal logic (LTL [1]) formulae. For this purpose, a system is thought of more or less as a "black box", and some (automatically generated) monitor observes its outside visible behaviour in order to determine whether or not the runtime behaviour satisfies an LTL formula. Applications include monitoring programs written in Java or C (cf. [2,3]) or abstract Web services (cf. [4]) to name just a few.

From a system designer's point of view, who defines the overall behaviour that a system has to adhere to, this "black box" view is perfectly reasonable. For example, most modern cars have the ability to issue a warning if a passenger (including the driver) is not wearing a seat belt after the vehicle has reached a certain speed. One could imagine

---

* This author was supported by an Inria Grant to visit NICTA Canberra where part of this work has been carried out.
** NICTA is funded by the Australian Government as represented by the Department of Broadband, Communications and the Digital Economy and the Australian Research Council through the ICT Centre of Excellence program.

D. Giannakopoulou and D. Méry (Eds.): FM 2012, LNCS 7436, pp. 85–100, 2012.
© Springer-Verlag Berlin Heidelberg 2012

using a monitor to help issue this warning based on the following LTL formalisation, which captures this abstract requirement:

$$\varphi = \mathbf{G}\big(speed\_low \vee ((pressure\_sensor\_1\_high \Rightarrow seat\_belt\_1\_on)$$
$$\wedge \ldots \wedge (pressure\_sensor\_n\_high \Rightarrow seat\_belt\_n\_on)))$$

The formula φ asserts that, at all times, when the car has reached a certain speed, and the pressure sensor in a seat $i \in [1, n]$ detects that a person is sitting in it ($pressure\_sensor\_i$ $\_high$), it has to be the case that the corresponding seat belt is fastened ($seat\_belt\_i\_on$). Moreover, one can build a monitor for φ, which receives the respective sensor values and is able to assert whether or not these values constitute a violation—*but*, only if some central component exists in the car's network of components, which collects these sensor values and consecutively sends them to the monitor as input! In many real-world scenarios, such as the automotive one, this is an unrealistic assumption mainly for economic reasons, but also because the communication on a car's bus network has to be kept minimal. Therefore one cannot continuously send unnecessary sensor information on a bus that is shared by critical applications where low latency is paramount (cf. [5,6]). In other words, in these scenarios, one has to monitor such a requirement not based on a single behavioural trace, assumed to be collected by some global sensor, but based on the many *partial* behavioural traces of the components which make up the actual system. We refer to this as *decentralised LTL monitoring* when the requirement is given in terms of an LTL formula.

The main constraint that decentralised LTL monitoring addresses is the lack of a global sensor and a central decision making point asserting whether the system's behaviour has violated or satisfied a specification. We already pointed out that, from a practical point of view, a central decision making point (i.e., global sensor) would require all the individual components to continuously send events over the network, and thereby negatively affecting response time for other potentially critical applications on the network. Moreover from a theoretical point of view, a central observer (resp. global sensor) basically resembles classical LTL monitoring, where the decentralised nature of the system under scrutiny does not play a role. Arguably, there exist many real-world component-based applications, where the monitoring of an LTL formula can be realised via global sensors or central decision making points, e.g., when network latency and criticality do not play an important role. However, here we want to focus on those cases where there exists no global trace, no central decision making point, and where the goal is to keep the communication, required for monitoring the LTL formula, minimal.

In the decentralised setting, we assume that the system under scrutiny consists of a set of components $\mathcal{C} = \{C_1, C_2, \ldots, C_n\}$, communicating on a synchronous bus acting as global clock. Each component emits events synchronously and has a local monitor attached to it. The set of all events is $\Sigma = \Sigma_1 \cup \Sigma_2 \cup \ldots \cup \Sigma_n$, where Σ_i is the set of events visible to the monitor at component C_i. The global LTL formula, on the other hand, is specified over a set of propositions, AP, such that $\Sigma = 2^{AP}$. Moreover, we demand for all $i, j \leq n$ with $i \neq j$ that $\Sigma_i \cap \Sigma_j = \emptyset$ holds, i.e., events are local w.r.t. the components where they are monitored.

At first, the synchronous bus may seem an overly stringent constraint imposed by our setting. However, it is by no means unrealistic, since in many real-world systems, especially critical ones, communication occurs synchronously. For example, the FlexRay bus protocol, used for safety-critical systems in the automotive domain, allows synchronous communication (cf. [7,5,8]). What is more, experts predict "that the data volume on FlexRay buses will increase significantly in the future" [6, Sec. 2], promoting techniques to minimise the number of used communication slots. Hence, one could argue that synchronous distributed systems such as FlexRay, in fact, motivate the proposed decentralised monitoring approach. (Although, one should stress that the results in this paper do not directly target FlexRay or any other specific bus system.)

Let as before φ be an LTL formula formalising a requirement over the system's global behaviour. Then every local monitor, M_i, will at any time, t, monitor its own LTL formula, φ_i^t, w.r.t. a partial behavioural trace, u_i. Let us use $u_i(m)$ to denote the $(m+1)$-th event in a trace u_i, and $\mathbf{u} = (u_1, u_2, \ldots, u_n)$ for the *global trace*, obtained by pair-wise parallel composition of the partial traces, each of which at time t is of length $t+1$ (i.e., $\mathbf{u} = u_1(0) \cup \ldots \cup u_n(0) \cdot u_1(1) \cup \ldots \cup u_n(1) \cdots u_1(t) \cup \ldots \cup u_n(t)$, a sequence of union sets). Note that from this point forward we will use $\mathbf{u}$ only when, in a given context, it is important to consider a global trace. However, when the particular type of trace (i.e., partial or global) is irrelevant, we will simply use u, u_i, etc. We also shall refer to partial traces as local traces due to their locality to a particular monitor in the system.

The decentralised monitoring algorithm evaluates the global trace $\mathbf{u}$ by considering the locally observed traces u_i, $i \in [1, n]$, in separation. In particular, it exhibits the following properties.

- If a local monitor yields $\varphi_i^t = \bot$ (resp. $\varphi_i^t = \top$) on some component C_i by observing u_i, it implies that $\mathbf{u}\Sigma^\omega \subseteq \Sigma^\omega \setminus \mathcal{L}(\varphi)$ (resp. $\mathbf{u}\Sigma^\omega \subseteq \mathcal{L}(\varphi)$) holds where $\mathcal{L}(\varphi)$ is the set of infinite sequences in Σ^ω described by φ. That is, a locally observed violation (resp. satisfaction) is, in fact, a global violation (resp. satisfaction). Or, in other words, $\mathbf{u}$ is a bad (resp. good) prefix for φ.
- If the monitored trace $\mathbf{u}$ is such that $\mathbf{u}\Sigma^\omega \subseteq \Sigma^\omega \setminus \mathcal{L}(\varphi)$ (resp. $\mathbf{u}\Sigma^\omega \subseteq \mathcal{L}(\varphi)$), one of the local monitors on some component C_i yields $\varphi_i^{t'} = \bot$ (resp. $\varphi_i^{t'} = \top$), $t' \geq t$, for an observation u_i', an extension of u_i, the local observation of $\mathbf{u}$ on C_i, because of some latency induced by decentralised monitoring, as we shall see.

However, in order to allow for the local detection of global violations (and satisfactions), monitors must be able to communicate, since their traces are only partial w.r.t. the global behaviour of the system. Therefore, our second objective is to monitor with *minimal communication overhead* (in comparison with a centralised solution where at any time, t, all n monitors send the observed events to a central decision making point).

Outline. Preliminaries are in Sec. 2. LTL monitoring via formula rewriting (progression), a central concept to our paper, is discussed in Sec. 3. In Sec. 4, we lift it to the decentralised setting. The semantics induced by decentralised LTL monitoring is outlined in Sec. 5, whereas Sec. 6 details on how the local monitors operate in this setting and gives a concrete algorithm. Experimental results are presented in Sec. 7. Section 8 concludes and gives pointers to related work. Formal proofs are available in an extended version of this paper, available as technical report [9].

2 Preliminaries

Each component of the system emits events at discrete time instances. An event σ is a set of *actions* denoted by some atomic propositions from the set AP, i.e., $\sigma \in 2^{AP}$. We denote 2^{AP} by Σ and call it the *alphabet* (of system events).

As our system operates under the *perfect synchrony hypothesis* (cf. [10]), we assume that its components communicate with each other in terms of sending and receiving messages (which, for the purpose of easier presentation, can also be encoded by actions) at *discrete* instances of time, which are represented using identifier $t \in \mathbb{N}^{\geq 0}$. Under this hypothesis, it is assumed that neither computation nor communication take time. In other words, at each time t, a component may receive up to $n - 1$ messages and dispatch up to 1 message, which in the latter case will always be available at the respective recipient of the messages at time $t + 1$. Note that these assumptions extend to the components' monitors, which operate and communicate on the same synchronous bus. The hypothesis of perfect synchrony essentially abstracts away implementation details of how long it takes for components or monitors to generate, send, or receive messages. As indicated in the introduction, this is a common hypothesis for certain types of systems, which can be designed and configured (e.g., by choosing an appropriate duration between time t and $t + 1$) to not violate this hypothesis (cf. [10]).

We use a projection function Π_i to restrict atomic propositions or events to the local view of monitor M_i, which can only observe those of component C_i. For atomic propositions, $\Pi_i : 2^{AP} \to 2^{AP}$ and we denote $AP_i = \Pi_i(AP)$ for $i \in [1, n]$. For events, $\Pi_i : 2^{\Sigma} \to 2^{\Sigma}$ and we denote $\Sigma_i = \Pi_i(\Sigma)$ for $i \in [1, n]$. We also assume $\forall i, j \leq n.\ i \neq j \Rightarrow AP_i \cap AP_j = \emptyset$ and consequently $\forall i, j \leq n.\ i \neq j \Rightarrow \Sigma_i \cap \Sigma_j = \emptyset$. Seen over time, each component C_i produces a *trace* of events, also called its *behaviour*, which for t time steps is encoded as $u_i = u_i(0) \cdot u_i(1) \cdots u_i(t - 1)$ with $\forall t' < t.\ u_i(t') \in \Sigma_i$. Finite traces over an alphabet Σ are elements of the set Σ^* and are typically encoded by $u, u', \ldots$, whereas infinite traces over Σ are elements of the set Σ^{ω} and are typically encoded by $w, w', \ldots$ The set of all traces is given by the set $\Sigma^{\infty} = \Sigma^* \cup \Sigma^{\omega}$. The set $\Sigma^* \setminus \{\epsilon\}$ is noted Σ^+. The finite or infinite sequence w^t is the *suffix* of the trace $w \in \Sigma^{\infty}$, starting at time t, i.e., $w^t = w(t) \cdot w(t + 1) \cdots$. The system's global behaviour, $\mathbf{u} = (u_1, u_2, \ldots, u_n)$ can now be described as a sequence of pair-wise union of the local events in component's traces, each of which at time t is of length $t + 1$ i.e., $\mathbf{u} = u(0) \cdots u(t)$.

Moreover since we use LTL to specify system behaviour, we also assume that the reader is familiar with the standard definition of LTL (cf. [1,9]) and the usual syntactic "sugar". We refer to the syntactically correct set of LTL formulae over a finite set of atomic propositions, AP, by $\text{LTL}(AP)$. When AP does not matter or is clear from the context, we also refer to this set simply by LTL. Finally, for some $\varphi \in \text{LTL}(AP)$, $\mathcal{L}(\varphi) \subseteq \Sigma^{\omega}$ denotes the individual models of φ (i.e., set of traces). A set $L \subseteq \Sigma^{\omega}$ is also called a *language* (over Σ).

3 Monitoring LTL Formulae by Progression

Central to our monitoring algorithm is the notion of *good and bad prefixes* for an LTL formula or, to be more precise, for the language it describes:

Definition 1. *Let* $L \subseteq \Sigma^\omega$ *be a language. The set of all* good prefixes *(resp.* bad prefixes*) of* L *is given by* $\mathrm{good}(L)$ *(resp.* $\mathrm{bad}(L)$*) and defined as follows:*

$$\mathrm{good}(L) = \{u \in \Sigma^* \mid u \cdot \Sigma^\omega \subseteq L\}, \qquad \mathrm{bad}(L) = \{u \in \Sigma^* \mid u \cdot \Sigma^\omega \subseteq \Sigma^\omega \setminus L\}.$$

We will shorten $\mathrm{good}(\mathcal{L}(\varphi))$ (resp. $\mathrm{bad}(\mathcal{L}(\varphi))$) to $\mathrm{good}(\varphi)$ (resp. $\mathrm{bad}(\varphi)$).

Although there exist a myriad of different approaches to monitoring LTL formulae, based on various finite-trace semantics (cf. [11]), one valid way of looking at the monitoring problem for some formula $\varphi \in$ LTL is the following: The monitoring problem of $\varphi \in$ LTL is to devise an efficient monitoring algorithm which, in a stepwise manner, receives events from a system under scrutiny and states whether or not the trace observed so far constitutes a good or a bad prefix of $\mathcal{L}(\varphi)$. One monitoring approach along those lines is described in [12]. We review an alternative monitoring procedure based on formula rewriting, which is also known as formula progression, or just *progression* in the domain of planning with temporally extended goals (cf. [13]).

Progression splits a formula into a formula expressing what needs to be satisfied by the current observation and a new formula (referred to as a *future goal* or *obligation*), which has to be satisfied by the trace in the future. As progression plays a crucial role in decentralised LTL monitoring, we recall its definition for the full set of LTL operators.

Definition 2. *Let* $\varphi, \varphi_1, \varphi_2 \in$ LTL, *and* $\sigma \in \Sigma$ *be an event. Then, the* progression *function* $P : LTL \times \Sigma \to LTL$ *is inductively defined as follows:*

$$
\begin{aligned}
P(p \in AP, \sigma) &= \top, \; \textit{if } p \in \sigma, \bot \textit{ otherwise} \\
P(\varphi_1 \vee \varphi_2, \sigma) &= P(\varphi_1, \sigma) \vee P(\varphi_2, \sigma) \\
P(\varphi_1 \mathbf{U} \varphi_2, \sigma) &= P(\varphi_2, \sigma) \vee P(\varphi_1, \sigma) \wedge \varphi_1 \mathbf{U} \varphi_2 \\
P(\mathbf{G}\varphi, \sigma) &= P(\varphi, \sigma) \wedge \mathbf{G}(\varphi) \\
P(\mathbf{F}\varphi, \sigma) &= P(\varphi, \sigma) \vee \mathbf{F}(\varphi)
\end{aligned}
\qquad
\begin{aligned}
P(\top, \sigma) &= \top \\
P(\bot, \sigma) &= \bot \\
P(\neg\varphi, \sigma) &= \neg P(\varphi, \sigma) \\
P(\mathbf{X}\varphi, \sigma) &= \varphi
\end{aligned}
$$

Note that monitoring using rewriting with similar rules as above has been described, for example, in [14,15], although not necessarily with the same finite-trace semantics in mind that we are discussing in this paper. Informally, the progression function "mimics" the LTL semantics on an event σ, as it is stated by the following lemmas.

Lemma 1. *Let* φ *be an* LTL *formula,* σ *an event and* w *an infinite trace, we have* $\sigma \cdot w \models \varphi \Leftrightarrow w \models P(\varphi, \sigma)$.

Lemma 2. *If* $P(\varphi, \sigma) = \top$, *then* $\sigma \in \mathrm{good}(\varphi)$, *if* $P(\varphi, \sigma) = \bot$, *then* $\sigma \in \mathrm{bad}(\varphi)$.

Moreover it follows that if $P(\varphi, \sigma) \notin \{\top, \bot\}$, then there exist traces $w, w' \in \Sigma^\omega$, such that $\sigma \cdot w \models \varphi$ and $\sigma \cdot w' \not\models \varphi$ hold. Let us now get back to [12], which introduces a finite-trace semantics for LTL monitoring called LTL$_3$. It is captured by the following definition.

Definition 3. *Let* $u \in \Sigma^*$, *the satisfaction relation of* LTL$_3$, $\models_3 : \Sigma^* \times$ LTL $\to \mathbb{B}_3$, *with* $\mathbb{B}_3 = \{\top, \bot, ?\}$, *is defined as*

$$
u \models_3 \varphi = \begin{cases}
\top & \textit{if } u \in \mathrm{good}(\varphi), \\
\bot & \textit{if } u \in \mathrm{bad}(\varphi), \\
? & \textit{otherwise.}
\end{cases}
$$

Based on this definition, it now becomes obvious how progression *could* serve as a monitoring algorithm for LTL_3.

Theorem 1. *Let $u = u(0) \cdots u(t) \in \Sigma^+$ be a trace, and $v \in \text{LTL}$ be the verdict, obtained by $t + 1$ consecutive applications of the progression function of φ on u, i.e., $v = P(\ldots(P(\varphi, u(0)), \ldots, u(t))))$. The following cases arise: If $v = \top$, then $u \models_3 \varphi = \top$ holds. If $v = \bot$, then $u \models_3 \varphi = \bot$ holds. Otherwise, $u \models_3 \varphi = ?$ holds.*

Note that in comparison with the monitoring procedure for LTL_3, described in [12], our algorithm, implied by this theorem, has the disadvantage that the formula, which is being progressed, may grow in size relative to the number of events. However, in practice, the addition of some practical simplification rules to the progression function usually prevents this problem from occurring.

4   Decentralised Progression

Conceptually, a monitor, M_i, attached to component C_i, which observes events over $\Sigma_i \subseteq \Sigma$, is a rewriting engine that accepts as input an event $\sigma \in \Sigma_i$, and an LTL formula φ, and then applies LTL progression rules. Additionally at each time t, in our n-component architecture, a monitor can send a message and receive up to $n - 1$ messages in order to communicate with the other monitors in the system, using the same synchronous bus that the system's components communicate on. The purpose of these messages is to send future or even past obligations to other monitors, encoded as LTL formulae. In a nutshell, a formula is sent by some monitor M_i, whenever the most urgent outstanding obligation imposed by M_i's current formula at time t, φ_i^t, cannot be checked using events from Σ_i alone. Intuitively, the urgency of an obligation is defined by the occurrences (or lack of) certain temporal operators in it. For example, in order to satisfy $p \wedge \mathbf{X}q$, a trace needs to start with p, followed by a q. Hence, the obligation imposed by the subformula p can be thought of as "more urgent" than the one imposed by $\mathbf{X}q$. A more formal definition is given later in this section.

When progressing an LTL formula, e.g., in the domain of planning to rewrite a temporally extended LTL goal during plan search, the rewriting engine, which implements the progression rules, will progress a state formula $p \in AP$, with an event σ such that $p \notin \sigma$, to $\bot$, i.e., $P(p, \emptyset) = \bot$ (see Definition 2). However, doing this in the decentralised setting, could lead to wrong results. In other words, we need to make a distinction as to why $p \notin \sigma$ holds locally, and then to progress accordingly. Consequently, the progression rule for atomic propositions is simply adapted by parameterising it with a local set of atomic propositions AP_i:

$$P(p, \sigma, AP_i) = \begin{cases} \top & \text{if } p \in \sigma, \\ \bot & \text{if } p \notin \sigma \wedge p \in AP_i, \\ \overline{\mathbf{X}}p & \text{otherwise,} \end{cases} \tag{1}$$

where for every $w \in \Sigma^\omega$ and $j > 0$, we have $w^j \models \overline{\mathbf{X}}\varphi$ if and only if $w^{j-1} \models \varphi$. In other words, $\overline{\mathbf{X}}$ is the dual to the $\mathbf{X}$-operator, sometimes referred to as the "previously-operator" in past-time LTL (cf. [16]). To ease presentation, the formula $\overline{\mathbf{X}}^m \varphi$ is a short for $\underbrace{\overline{\mathbf{X}}\,\overline{\mathbf{X}}\ldots\overline{\mathbf{X}}}_{m}\,\varphi$. Our operator is somewhat different to the standard use of $\overline{\mathbf{X}}$: it can only precede an atomic proposition or an atomic proposition which is preceded by further $\overline{\mathbf{X}}$-operators. Hence, the restricted use of the $\overline{\mathbf{X}}$-operator does not give us the full flexibility (or succinctness gains [17]) of past-time LTL. Using the $\overline{\mathbf{X}}$-operator, let us now formally define the *urgency* of a formula φ using a pattern matching as follows:

Definition 4. *Let φ be an LTL formula, and $\Upsilon : \text{LTL} \to \mathbb{N}^{\geq 0}$ be an inductively defined function assigning a level of* urgency *to an LTL formula as follows.*

$$\Upsilon(\varphi) = \text{match } \varphi \text{ with } \varphi_1 \vee \varphi_2 \mid \varphi_1 \wedge \varphi_2 \to \max(\Upsilon(\varphi_1), \Upsilon(\varphi_2))$$
$$\mid \overline{\mathbf{X}}\varphi' \qquad\qquad\quad \to 1 + \Upsilon(\varphi')$$
$$\mid - \qquad\qquad\qquad\quad\ \to 0.$$

A formula φ is said to be more urgent *than formula ψ, if and only if $\Upsilon(\varphi) > \Upsilon(\psi)$ holds. A formula φ where $\Upsilon(\varphi) = 0$ holds is said to be not urgent.*

Moreover, the above modification to the progression rules has obviously the desired effect: If $p \in \sigma$, then nothing changes, otherwise if $p \notin \sigma$, we return $\overline{\mathbf{X}}p$ in case that the monitor M_i cannot observe p at all, i.e., in case that $p \notin AP_i$ holds. This effectively means, that M_i cannot decide whether or not p occurred, and will therefore turn the state formula p into an obligation for some other monitor to evaluate rather than produce a truth-value. Of course, the downside of rewriting future goals into past goals that have to be processed further, is that violations or satisfactions of a global goal will usually be detected *after* they have occurred. However, since there is no central observer which records all events at the same time, the monitors *need* to communicate their respective results to other monitors, which, on a synchronous bus, occupies one or more time steps, depending on how often a result needs to be passed on until it reaches a monitor which is able to actually state a verdict. We shall later give an upper bound on these communication times, and show that our decentralised monitoring framework does not introduce any additional delay under the given assumptions (see Theorem 2).

Example 1. Let us assume we have a decentralised system consisting of components A, B, C, s.t. $AP_A = \{a\}$, $AP_B = \{b\}$, and $AP_C = \{c\}$, and that a formula $\varphi = \mathbf{F}(a \wedge b \wedge c)$ needs to be monitored in a decentralised manner. Let us further assume that, initially, $\varphi_A^0 = \varphi_B^0 = \varphi_C^0 = \varphi$. Let $\sigma = \{a, b\}$ be the system event at time 0; that is, M_A observes $\Pi_A(\sigma) = \{a\}$ (resp. $\Pi_B(\sigma) = \{b\}$, $\Pi_C(\sigma) = \emptyset$ for M_B and M_C) when σ occurs. The rewriting that takes place in all three monitors to generate the next local goal formula, using the modified set of rules, and triggered by σ, is as follows:

$$\varphi_A^1 = P(\varphi, \{a\}, \{a\}) = P(a, \{a\}, \{a\}) \wedge P(b, \{a\}, \{a\}) \wedge P(c, \{a\}, \{a\}) \vee \varphi$$
$$= \overline{\mathbf{X}}b \wedge \overline{\mathbf{X}}c \vee \varphi$$
$$\varphi_B^1 = P(\varphi, \{b\}, \{b\}) = P(a, \{b\}, \{b\}) \wedge P(b, \{b\}, \{b\}) \wedge P(c, \{b\}, \{b\}) \vee \varphi$$
$$= \overline{\mathbf{X}}a \wedge \overline{\mathbf{X}}c \vee \varphi$$
$$\varphi_C^1 = P(\varphi, \emptyset, \{c\}) \quad = P(a, \emptyset, \{c\}) \wedge P(b, \emptyset, \{c\}) \wedge P(c, \emptyset, \{c\}) \vee \varphi$$
$$= \overline{\mathbf{X}}a \wedge \overline{\mathbf{X}}b \wedge \perp \vee \varphi = \varphi$$

But we have yet to define progression for past goals: For this purpose, each monitor has local storage to keep a *bounded* number of past events. The event that occurred at time $t - k$ is referred as $\sigma(-k)$. On a monitor observing Σ_i, the progression of a past goal $\overline{\mathbf{X}}^m \varphi$, at time $t \geq m$, is defined as follows:

$$P(\overline{\mathbf{X}}^m \varphi, \sigma, AP_i) = \begin{cases} \top & \text{if } \varphi = p \text{ for some } p \in AP_i \cap \Pi_i(\sigma(-m)), \\ \bot & \text{if } \varphi = p \text{ for some } p \in AP_i \setminus \Pi_i(\sigma(-m)), \\ \overline{\mathbf{X}}^{m+1} \varphi & \text{otherwise,} \end{cases} \quad (2)$$

where, for $i \in [1, n]$, Π_i is the projection function associated to each monitor M_i, respectively. Note that since we do not allow $\overline{\mathbf{X}}$ for the specification of a global system monitoring property, our definitions will ensure that the local monitoring goals, φ_i^t, will never be of the form $\overline{\mathbf{X}}\mathbf{X}\mathbf{X}p$, which is equivalent to a future obligation, despite the initial $\overline{\mathbf{X}}$. In fact, our rules ensure that a formula preceded by the $\overline{\mathbf{X}}$-operator is either an atomic proposition, or an atomic proposition which is preceded by one or many $\overline{\mathbf{X}}$-operators. Hence, in rule (2), we do not need to consider any other cases for φ.

5   Semantics

In the previous example, we can clearly see that monitors M_A and M_B cannot determine whether or not σ, if interpreted as a trace of length 1, is a good prefix for the global goal formula φ.[1] Monitor M_C on the other hand did not observe an action c and, therefore, is the only monitor after time 0, which knows that σ is not a good prefix and that, as before, after time 1, φ is the goal that needs to be satisfied by the system under scrutiny. Intuitively, the other two monitors know that if their respective past goals were satisfied, then σ would be a good prefix, but in order to determine this, they need to send and receive messages to and from each other, containing LTL obligations.

Before we outline how this is done in our setting, let us discuss the semantics, obtained from this decentralised application of progression. We already said that monitors detect good and bad prefixes for a global formula; that is, if a monitor's progression yields $\top$ (resp. $\bot$), then the trace seen so far is a good (resp. bad) prefix, and if neither monitor yields a Boolean truth-value as verdict, we keep monitoring. The latter case indicates that, so far, the trace is neither a good nor a bad prefix for the global formula.

Definition 5. *Let $\mathcal{C} = \{C_1, \ldots, C_n\}$ be the set of system components, $\varphi \in$ LTL be a global goal, and $\mathcal{M} = \{M_1, \ldots, M_n\}$ be the set of component monitors. Further, let $\mathbf{u} = u_1(0) \cup \ldots \cup u_n(0) \cdot u_1(1) \cup \ldots \cup u_n(1) \cdots u_1(t) \cup \ldots \cup u_n(t)$ be the global behavioural trace, at time $t \in \mathbb{N}^{\geq 0}$. If for some component C_i, with $i \leq n$, containing a local obligation φ_i^t, M_i reports $P(\varphi_i^t, u_i(t), AP_i) = \top$ (resp. $\bot$), then $\mathbf{u} \models_D \varphi = \top$ (resp. $\bot$). Otherwise, $\mathbf{u} \models_D \varphi = ?$.*

By $\models_D$ we denote the satisfaction relation on finite traces in the decentralised setting to differentiate it from LTL$_3$ as well as standard LTL which is defined on infinite traces. Obviously, $\models_3$ and $\models_D$ both yield values from the same truth-domain. However, the semantics are not equivalent, since the modified progression function used in the above definition sometimes rewrites a state formula into an obligation concerning the past rather than returning a verdict. On the other hand, in the case of a one-component system (i.e., all propositions of a formula can be observed by a single monitor), the definition of $\models_D$ matches Theorem 1, in particular because our progression rule (1) is then equivalent to the standard case. Monitoring LTL$_3$ with progression becomes a special case of decentralised monitoring, in the following sense:

---

[1] Note that $\mathcal{L}(\varphi)$, being a *liveness* language, does not have any bad prefixes.

Corollary 1. *If* $|\mathcal{M}| = 1$, *then* $\forall u \in \Sigma^*.\; \forall \varphi \in$ LTL. $u \models_3 \varphi = u \models_D \varphi$.

6   Communication and Decision Making

Let us now describe the communication mechanism that enables local monitors to determine whether a trace is a good or a bad prefix. Recall that each monitor only sees a projection of an event to its locally observable set of actions, encoded as a set of atomic propositions, respectively.

Generally, at time t, when receiving an event σ, a monitor, M_i, will progress its current obligation, φ_i^t, into $P(\varphi_i^t, \sigma, AP_i)$, and send the result to another monitor, $M_{j \neq i}$, whenever the most urgent obligation, $\psi \in \mathrm{sus}(P(\varphi_i^t, \sigma, AP_i))$, is such that $\mathrm{Prop}(\psi) \subseteq (AP_j)$ holds, where $\mathrm{sus}(\varphi)$ is the *set of urgent subformulae* of φ and $\mathrm{Prop}: \mathrm{LTL} \to 2^{AP}$ yields the set of occurring propositions of an LTL formula.

Definition 6. *The function* $\mathrm{sus}: \mathrm{LTL} \to 2^{\mathrm{LTL}}$ *is inductively defined as follows:*

$$\mathrm{sus}(\varphi) = match\ \varphi\ with \quad \begin{aligned} &\varphi_1 \vee \varphi_2 \mid \varphi_1 \wedge \varphi_2 \to \mathrm{sus}(\varphi_1) \cup \mathrm{sus}(\varphi_2) \\ &\mid \neg\varphi' \qquad\qquad\quad\ \to \mathrm{sus}(\varphi') \\ &\mid \overline{\mathbf{X}}\varphi' \qquad\qquad\quad\ \to \{\overline{\mathbf{X}}\varphi'\} \\ &\mid \_ \qquad\qquad\qquad\ \to \emptyset \end{aligned}$$

The set $\mathrm{sus}(\varphi)$ contains the past sub-formulae of φ, i.e., sub-formulae starting with a future temporal operator are discarded. It uses the fact that, in decentralised progression, $\overline{\mathbf{X}}$-operators are only introduced in front of atomic propositions. Thus, only the cases mentioned explicitly in the pattern matching need to be considered. Moreover, for formulae of the form $\overline{\mathbf{X}}\varphi'$, i.e., starting with an $\overline{\mathbf{X}}$-operator, it is not needed to apply sus to φ' because φ' is necessarily of the form $\overline{\mathbf{X}}^d p$ with $d \geq 0$ and $p \in AP$, and does not contain more urgent formulae than $\overline{\mathbf{X}}\varphi'$. Note that, if there are several equally urgent obligations for distinct monitors, then M_i sends the formula to only one of the corresponding monitors according to a priority order between monitors. This order ensures that the delay induced by evaluating the global system specification in a decentralised fashion is bounded, as we shall see in Theorem 2. For simplicity in the following, for a set of component monitors $\mathcal{M} = \{M_1, \dots, M_n\}$, the sending order is the natural order on the interval $[1, n]$. This choice of the local monitor to send the obligation is encoded through the function $\mathrm{Mon}: \mathcal{M} \times 2^{AP} \to \mathcal{M}$. For a monitor $M_i \in \mathcal{M}$ and a set of atomic propositions $AP' \in 2^{AP}$, $\mathrm{Mon}(M_i, AP')$ is the monitor $M_{j_{\min}}$ s.t. $j_{\min}$ is the smallest integer in $[1, n]$ s.t. there is a monitor for an atomic proposition in AP'. Formally: $\mathrm{Mon}(M_i, AP') = j_{\min} = \min\{j \in [1, n] \setminus \{i\} \mid AP' \cap AP_j \neq \emptyset\}$.

Once M_i has sent $P(\varphi_i^t, \sigma, AP_i)$, it sets $\varphi_i^{t+1} = \#$, where $\# \notin AP$ is a special symbol for which we define progression by

$$P(\#, \sigma, AP_i) = \#, \tag{3}$$

and $\forall \varphi \in$ LTL. $\varphi \wedge \# = \varphi$. On the other hand, whenever M_i receives a formula, $\varphi_{j \neq i}$, sent from a monitor M_j, it will add the new formula to its existing obligation, i.e., its current obligation φ_i^t will be replaced by the conjunction $\varphi_i^t \wedge \varphi_{j \neq i}$. Should M_i receive further obligations from other monitors but j, it will add each new obligation as an additional conjunct in the same manner.

Let us now summarise the above steps in the form of an explicit algorithm that describes how the local monitors operate and make decisions.

Algorithm L (*Local Monitor*).   Let φ be a global system specification, and $\mathcal{M} = \{M_1, \ldots, M_n\}$ be the set of component monitors. The algorithm Local Monitor, executed on each M_i, returns $\top$ (resp. $\bot$), if $\sigma \models_D \varphi_i^t$ (resp. $\sigma \not\models_D \varphi_i^t$) holds, where $\sigma \in \Sigma_i$ is the projection of an event to the observable set of actions of the respective monitor, and φ_i^t the monitor's current local obligation.

L1. [Next goal.] Let $t \in \mathbb{N}^{\geq 0}$ denote the current time step and φ_i^t be the monitor's current local obligation. If $t = 0$, then set $\varphi_i^t := \varphi$.

L2. [Receive event.] Read next σ.

L3. [Receive messages.] Let $\{\varphi_j\}_{j \in [1,n], j \neq i}$ be the set of received obligations at time t from other monitors. Set $\varphi_i^t := \varphi_i^t \wedge \bigwedge_{j \in [1,n], j \neq i} \varphi_j$.

L4. [Progress.] Determine $P(\varphi_i^t, \sigma, AP_i)$ and store the result in φ_i^{t+1}.

L5. [Evaluate and return.] If $\varphi_i^{t+1} = \top$ return $\top$, if $\varphi_i^{t+1} = \bot$ return $\bot$.

L6. [Communicate.] Let $\Psi \subseteq \mathrm{sus}(\varphi_i^{t+1})$ be the set of most urgent obligations of φ_i^{t+1}. Send φ_i^{t+1} to monitor $\mathrm{Mon}(M_i, \cup_{\psi \in \Psi} \mathrm{Prop}(\psi))$.

L7. [Replace goal.] If in step L6 a message was sent at all, set $\varphi_i^{t+1} := \#$. Then go back to step L1.   □

The input to the algorithm, σ, will usually resemble the latest observation in a consecutively growing trace, $u_i = u_i(0) \cdots u_i(t)$, i.e., $\sigma = u_i(t)$. We then have that $\sigma \models_D \varphi_i^t$ (i.e., the algorithm returns $\top$) implies that $u \models_D \varphi$ holds (resp. for $\sigma \not\models_D \varphi_i^t$).

Example 2. To see how this algorithm works, let us continue the decentralised monitoring process initiated in Example 1. Table 1 shows how the situation evolves for all three monitors, when the global LTL specification in question is $\mathbf{F}(a \wedge b \wedge c)$ and the ordering between components is $A < B < C$. An evolution of M_A's local obligation, encoded as $P(\varphi_B^1 \wedge \#, \sigma, AP_A)$ (see cell M_A at $t = 1$) indicates that communication between the monitors has occurred: M_B (resp. M_A) sent its obligation to M_A (resp. to another monitor), at the end of step 0. Likewise for the other obligations and monitors. The interesting situations are marked in grey: In particular at $t = 0$, M_C is the only monitor who knows for sure that, so far, no good nor bad prefix occurred (see grey cell at $t = 0$). At $t = 1$, we have the desired situation $\sigma = \{a, b, c\}$, but because none of the

Table 1. Decentralised progression of $\varphi = \mathbf{F}(a \wedge b \wedge c)$ in a 3-component system

t:	0	1	2	3
σ:	$\{a,b\}$	$\{a,b,c\}$	$\emptyset$	$\emptyset$
M_A:	$\varphi_A^1 = P(\varphi, \sigma, AP_A)$ $= \overline{\mathbf{X}}b \wedge \overline{\mathbf{X}}c \vee \varphi$	$\varphi_A^2 = P(\varphi_B^1 \wedge \#, \sigma, AP_A)$ $= \overline{\mathbf{X}}^2 c \vee (\overline{\mathbf{X}}b \wedge \overline{\mathbf{X}}c \vee \varphi)$	$\varphi_A^3 = P(\varphi_C^2 \wedge \#, \sigma, AP_A)$ $= \overline{\mathbf{X}}^2 b \vee (\overline{\mathbf{X}}b \wedge \overline{\mathbf{X}}c \vee \varphi)$	$\varphi_A^4 = P(\varphi_C^3 \wedge \#, \sigma, AP_A)$ $= \overline{\mathbf{X}}^3 b \vee (\overline{\mathbf{X}}b \wedge \overline{\mathbf{X}}c \vee \varphi)$
M_B:	$\varphi_B^1 = P(\varphi, \sigma, AP_B)$ $= \overline{\mathbf{X}}a \wedge \overline{\mathbf{X}}c \vee \varphi$	$\varphi_B^2 = P(\varphi_A^1 \wedge \#, \sigma, AP_B)$ $= \overline{\mathbf{X}}^2 c \vee (\overline{\mathbf{X}}a \wedge \overline{\mathbf{X}}c \vee \varphi)$	$\varphi_B^3 = P(\#, \sigma, AP_B)$ $= \#$	$\varphi_B^4 = P(\varphi_A^3 \wedge \#, \sigma, AP_B)$ $= \top$
M_C:	$\varphi_C^1 = P(\varphi, \sigma, AP_C)$ $= \varphi$	$\varphi_C^2 = P(\varphi, \sigma, AP_C)$ $= \overline{\mathbf{X}}a \wedge \overline{\mathbf{X}}b \vee \varphi$	$\varphi_C^3 = P(\varphi_A^2 \wedge \varphi_B^2 \wedge \#, \sigma, AP_C)$ $= \overline{\mathbf{X}}^2 a \wedge \overline{\mathbf{X}}^2 b \vee \varphi$	$\varphi_C^4 = P(\#, \sigma, AP_C)$ $= \#$

monitors can see the other monitors' events, it takes another two rounds of communication until both M_A and M_B detect that, indeed, the global obligation had been satisfied at $t = 1$ (see grey cell at $t = 3$).

This example highlights a worst case *delay* between the occurrence and the detection of a good (resp. bad) trace by a good (resp. bad) prefix, caused by the time it takes for the monitors to communicate obligations to each other. This delay depends on the number of monitors in the system, and is also the upper bound for the number of past events each monitor needs to store locally to be able to progress all occurring past obligations:

Theorem 2. *Let, for any $p \in AP$, $\overline{\mathbf{X}}^m p$ be a local obligation obtained by Algorithm L executed on some monitor $M_i \in \mathcal{M}$. At any time $t \in \mathbb{N}^{\geq 0}$, $m \leq \min(|\mathcal{M}|, t + 1)$.*

Proof. For a full proof cf. [9]. Here, we only provide a sketch, explaining the intuition behind the theorem. Recall that $\overline{\mathbf{X}}$-operators are only introduced directly in front of atomic propositions according to rule (1) when M_i rewrites a propositional formula p with $p \notin AP_i$. Further $\overline{\mathbf{X}}$-operators can only be added according to rule (2) when M_i is unable to evaluate an obligation of the form $\overline{\mathbf{X}}^h p$. The interesting situation occurs when a monitor M_i maintains a set of urgent obligations of the form $\{\overline{\mathbf{X}}^h p_1, \ldots, \overline{\mathbf{X}}^j p_l\}$ with $h, j \in \mathbb{N}^{\geq 0}$, then, according to step L6 of Algorithm L, M_i will transmit the obligations to one monitor only thereby adding one additional $\overline{\mathbf{X}}$-operator to the remaining obligations: $\{\overline{\mathbf{X}}^{h+1} p_2, \ldots, \overline{\mathbf{X}}^{j+1} p_l\}$. Obviously, a single monitor cannot have more than $|\mathcal{M}| - 1$ outstanding obligations that need to be sent to the other monitors at any time t. So, the worst case delay is initiated during monitoring, if at some time *all* outstanding obligations of each monitor M_i, $i \in [1, |\mathcal{M}|]$, are of the form $\{\overline{\mathbf{X}} p_1, \ldots, \overline{\mathbf{X}} p_l\}$ with $p_1, \ldots, p_l \notin AP_i$ (i.e., the obligations are all equally urgent), in which case it takes $|\mathcal{M}| - 1$ time steps until the last one has been chosen to be sent to its respective monitor M_j. Using an ordering between components ensures here that each set of obligations will decrease in size after being transmitted once. Finally, a last monitor, M_j will receive an obligation of the form $\overline{\mathbf{X}}^{|\mathcal{M}|} p_k$ with $1 \leq k \leq l$ and $p_k \in AP_j$.   □

Consequently, the monitors only need to memorise a *bounded history* of the trace read so far, i.e., the last $|\mathcal{M}|$ events.

Example 2 also illustrates the relationship to the LTL$_3$ semantics discussed earlier in Sec. 3. This relationship is formalised by the two following theorems stating the soundness and completeness of the algorithm.

Theorem 3. *Let $\varphi \in$ LTL and $u \in \Sigma^*$, then $u \models_D \varphi = \top/\bot \Rightarrow u \models_3 \varphi = \top/\bot$, and $u \models_3 \varphi = ? \Rightarrow u \models_D \varphi = ?$.*

In particular, the example shows how the other direction of the theorem does not necessarily hold. Consider the trace $u = \{a, b\} \cdot \{a, b, c\}$: clearly, $u \models_3 \mathbf{F}(a \wedge b \wedge c) = \top$, but we have $u \models_D \mathbf{F}(a \wedge b \wedge c) = ?$ in our example. Again, this is a direct consequence of the delay introduced in our setting. However, Algorithm L detects all verdicts for a specification as if the system was not distributed.

Theorem 4. *Let $\varphi \in$ LTL and $u \in \Sigma^*$, then $u \models_3 \varphi = \top/\bot \Rightarrow \exists u' \in \Sigma^*. |u'| \leq n \wedge u \cdot u' \models_D \varphi = \top/\bot$, where n is the number of components in the system.*

7   Experimental Results

DECENTMON is an implementation, simulating the above distributed LTL monitoring algorithm in 1,800 LLOC, written in the functional programming language OCaml. It can be freely downloaded and run from [18]. The system takes as input multiple traces (that can be automatically generated), corresponding to the behaviour of a distributed system, and an LTL formula. Then the formula is monitored against the traces in two different modes: a) by merging the traces to a single, global trace and then using a "central monitor" for the formula (i.e., all local monitors send their respective events to the central monitor who makes the decisions regarding the trace), and b) by using the decentralised approach introduced in this paper (i.e., each trace is read by a separate monitor). We have evaluated the two different monitoring approaches (i.e., centralised vs. decentralised) using two different set-ups described in the remainder of this section.

Evaluation using randomly generated formulae. DECENTMON randomly generated 1,000 LTL formulae of various sizes in the architecture described in Example 1.

How both monitoring approaches compared on these formulae can be seen in Table 2. The first column shows the size of the monitored LTL formulae. Note, our system measures formula size in terms of the operator entailment[2] inside it (state formulae excluded), e.g., $G(a \wedge b) \vee Fc$ is of size 2. The entry |trace| denotes the average length of the traces needed to reach a verdict. For example, the last line in Table 2 says that we monitored 1,000 randomly gen-

Table 2. Benchmarks for random formulae

	centralised		decentralised		*diff. ratio*	
$|\varphi|$	|trace|	#msg.	|trace|	#msg.	|trace|	#msg.
1	1.369	4.107	1.634	0.982	1.1935	0.2391
2	2.095	6.285	2.461	1.647	1.1747	0.262
3	3.518	10.554	4.011	2.749	1.1401	0.2604
4	5.889	17.667	6.4	4.61	1.0867	0.2609
5	9.375	28.125	9.935	7.879	1.0597	0.2801
6	11.808	35.424	12.366	9.912	1.0472	0.2798

erated LTL formulae of size 6. On average, traces were of length 11.808 when the central monitor came to a verdict, and of length 12.366 when one of the local monitors came to a verdict. The difference ratio, given in the second last column, then shows the average delay; that is, on average the traces were 1.0472 times longer in the decentralised setting. The number of messages, #msg., in the centralised setting, corresponds to the number of events sent by the local monitors to the central monitor (i.e., the length of the trace times the number of components) and in the decentralised setting to the number of obligations transmitted between local monitors. What is striking here is that the amount of communication needed in the decentralised setting is ca. only 25% of the communication overhead induced by central monitoring, where local monitors need to send each event to a central monitor.

Evaluation Using Specification Patterns. In order to evaluate our approach also at the hand of realistic LTL specifications, we conducted benchmarks using LTL formulae following the well-known LTL specification patterns ([19], whereas the actual formulae underlying the patterns are available at this site [20] and recalled in [18]). In this

---

[2] Our experiments show that this way of measuring the size of a formula is more representative of how difficult it is to progress it in a decentralised manner. Formulae of size above 6 are not realistic in practice.

context, to randomly generate formulae, we proceeded as follows. For a given specification pattern, we randomly select one of the formulae associated to it. Such a formula is "parametrised" by some atomic propositions. To obtain the randomly generated formula, using the distributed alphabet, we randomly instantiate the atomic propositions.

The results of this test are reported in Table 3: for each kind of pattern (absence, existence, bounded existence, universal, precedence, response, precedence chain, response chain, constrained chain), we generated again 1,000 formulae, monitored over the same architecture as used in Example 1.

Discussion. Both benchmarks substantiate the claim that decentralised monitoring of an LTL formula can induce a much lower communication overhead compared to a centralised solution. In fact, when considering the more realistic benchmark using the specification patterns, the communication overhead was significantly lower compared to monitoring randomly generated formulae. The same holds true for the delay: in case of monitoring LTL formulae corresponding to specification patterns, the delay is almost negligible; that is, the local monitors detect violation/satisfaction of a monitored formula at almost the same time as a global monitor with access to all observations.

Besides the above, we conducted further experiments to determine which are the parameters that make decentralised monitoring (less) effective w.r.t. a centralised solution, and whether or not the user can control them or at least estimate them prior to monitoring. To this end, we first considered a policy change for sending messages: Under the new policy, components send messages to the central observer only when the truth values have changed w.r.t. a previous event. The experimental results generally vary with the size of the formulae, but the decentralised case induced only around half the number messages under this policy. Moreover, the advantage remains in favour of decentralised monitoring as the size of the local alphabets was increased. We then extended this setting by considering specific *probability distributions* for the occurrence of local propositions. As one would expect, the performance of decentralised monitoring deteriorates when the occurrence of a local proposition has a very high or a very low probability since it induces a low probability for a change of the truth value of a local

Table 3. Benchmarks for LTL specification patterns

	centralised		decentralised		*diff. ratio*	
pattern	|trace|	#msg.	|trace|	#msg.	|trace|	#msg.
absence	156.17	468.51	156.72	37.94	1.0035	0.0809
existence	189.90	569.72	190.42	44.41	1.0027	0.0779
bounded existence	171.72	515.16	172.30	68.72	1.0033	0.1334
universal	97.03	291.09	97.66	11.05	1.0065	0.0379
precedence	224.11	672.33	224.72	53.703	1.0027	0.0798
response	636.28	1,908.86	636.54	360.33	1.0004	0.1887
precedence chain	200.23	600.69	200.76	62.08	1.0026	0.1033
response chain	581.20	1,743.60	581.54	377.64	1.0005	0.2165
constrained chain	409.12	1,227.35	409.62	222.84	1.0012	0.1815

proposition to occur. Similar to the first setting, as the size of local alphabets grows, the performance of decentralised monitoring improves again.

Clearly, further experiments are needed to determine the conditions under which the decentralised case unambiguously outperforms alternatives, but the above gives first indications. The detailed results are available and continuously updated at [18].

8   Conclusions and Related Work

This work is by no means the first to introduce an approach to monitoring the behaviour of distributed systems. For example, the *diagnosis (of discrete-event systems)* has a similar objective (i.e., detect the occurrence of a fault after a finite number of discrete steps) (cf. [21,22,23]). In diagnosis, however, one tries to isolate root causes for failure (i.e., identify the component in a system which is responsible for a fault). A key concept is that of *diagnosability*: a system model is diagnosable if it is always the case that the occurrence of a fault can be detected after a finite number of discrete steps. In other words, in diagnosis the model of a system, which usually contains both faulty and nominal behaviour, is assumed to be part of the problem input, whereas we consider systems more or less as a "black box". Diagnosability does not transfer to our setting, because we need to assume that the local monitors always have sufficient information to detect violation (resp. satisfaction) of a specification. Also, it is common in diagnosis of distributed systems to assert a central decision making point, even if that reflects merely a Boolean function connecting the local diagnosers' verdicts, while in our setting the local monitors directly communicate without a central decision making point.

A natural counterpart of diagnosability is that of *observability* as defined in decentralised observation [24]: a distributed system is said to be x-observable, where x ranges over different parameters such as whether local observers have finite or infinite memory available to store a trace (i.e., jointly unbounded-memory, jointly bounded-memory, locally unbounded-memory, locally finite-memory), if there exists a total function, always able to combine the local observers' states after reading some trace to a truthful verdict w.r.t. the monitored property. Again, the main difference here is that we take observability for granted, in that we assume that the system can always be monitored w.r.t. a given property, because detailed system topology or architectural information is not part of our problem input. Moreover, unlike in our setting, even in the locally-observable cases, there is still a central decision making point involved, combining the local verdicts. Note also that, to the best of our knowledge, both observation and diagnosis do not concern themselves with minimising the communication overhead needed for observing/diagnosing a distributed system.

A specific temporal logic, MTTL, for expressing properties of asynchronous multi-threaded systems has been presented in [25]. Its monitoring procedure takes as input a *safety* formula and a partially ordered execution of a parallel asynchronous system. It then establishes whether or not there exist runs in the execution that violate the MTTL formula. While the synchronous case can be interpreted as a special case of the asynchronous one, there are some noteworthy differences between [25] and our work. Firstly, we take LTL "off-the-shelf"; that is, we do not add modalities to express properties concerning the distributed/multi-threaded nature of the system under scrutiny.

On the contrary, our motivation is to enable users to conceive a possibly distributed system as a single, monolithic system by enabling them to specify properties over the outside visible behaviour only—independent of implementation specific-details, such as the number of threads or components—and to automatically "distribute the monitoring" process for such properties for them. Secondly, we address the fact that in some distributed systems it may not be possible to collect a global trace or insert a global decision making point, thereby forcing the automatically distributed monitors to communicate. But at the same time we try and keep communication at a minimum. This aspect, on the other hand, does not play a role in [25] where the implementation was tried on parallel (Java) programs which are not executed on physically separated CPUs, and where one can collect a set of global behaviours to then reason about. Finally, our setting is not restricted to *safety* formulae, i.e., we can monitor any LTL formula as long as its set of good (resp. bad) prefixes is not empty. However, we have not investigated whether or not the restriction of safety formulae is inherent to [25] or made by choice. Other recent works like [26] target physically distributed systems, but do not focus on the communication overhead that may be induced by their monitoring. Similarly, this work also mainly addresses the problem of monitoring systems which produce partially ordered traces (à la Diekert and Gastin), and introduces abstractions to deal with the combinational explosion of these traces.

To the best of our knowledge, our work is the first to address the problem of automatically distributing LTL monitors, and to introduce a decentralised monitoring approach that not only avoids a global point of observation or any form of central trace collection, but also tries to keep the number of communicated messages between monitors at a minimum. What is more, our experimental results show that this approach does not only "work on paper", but that it is feasible to be implemented. Indeed, even the expected savings in communication overhead could be observed for the set of chosen LTL formulae and the automatically generated traces, when compared to a centralised solution in which the local monitors transmit all observed events to a global monitor.

References

1. Pnueli, A.: The temporal logic of programs. In: Foundations of Computer Science (FOCS), pp. 46–57. IEEE (1977)
2. Seyster, J., Dixit, K., Huang, X., Grosu, R., Havelund, K., Smolka, S.A., Stoller, S.D., Zadok, E.: Aspect-oriented instrumentation with GCC. In: Barringer, et al. (eds.) [27], pp. 405–420
3. Meredith, P.O., Rosu, G.: Runtime verification with the RV System. In: Barringer, et al. (eds.) [27], pp. 136–152
4. Hallé, S., Villemaire, R.: Runtime verification for the web-a tutorial introduction to interface contracts in web applications. In: Barringer, et al. (eds.) [27], pp. 106–121
5. Gunzert, M., Nägele, A.: Component-based development and verification of safety critical software for a brake-by-wire system with synchronous software components. In: Intl. Symp. on SE for Parallel and Distributed Systems (PDSE), pp. 134–145. IEEE (1999)
6. Lukasiewycz, M., Glaß, M., Teich, J., Milbredt, P.: FlexRay schedule optimization of the static segment. In: 7th IEEE ACM Intl. Conf. on Hardware Software Codesign and System Synthesis (CODES+ISSS), pp. 363–372. ACM (2009)
7. Pop, T., Pop, P., Eles, P., Peng, Z., Andrei, A.: Timing analysis of the FlexRay communication protocol. Real-Time Syst. 39, 205–235 (2008)

8. Miller, S.P., Whalen, M.W., Cofer, D.D.: Software model checking takes off. Commun. ACM 53, 58–64 (2010)
9. Bauer, A., Falcone, Y.: Decentralised LTL monitoring. arXiv:1111.5133 (2011)
10. Jantsch, A.: Modeling Embedded Systems and SoC's: Concurrency and Time in Models of Computation. Morgan Kaufmann (2003)
11. Bauer, A., Leucker, M., Schallhart, C.: Comparing LTL semantics for runtime verification. Logic and Computation 20(3), 651–674 (2010)
12. Bauer, A., Leucker, M., Schallhart, C.: Runtime verification for LTL and TLTL. ACM Trans. Softw. Eng. Methodol. (TOSEM) 20(4), 14 (2011)
13. Bacchus, F., Kabanza, F.: Planning for temporally extended goals. Annals of Mathematics and Artificial Intelligence 22, 5–27 (1998)
14. Roşu, G., Havelund, K.: Rewriting-based techniques for runtime verification. Automated Software Engineering 12(2), 151–197 (2005)
15. Barringer, H., Rydeheard, D.E., Havelund, K.: Rule systems for run-time monitoring: from Eagle to RuleR. J. Log. Comput. 20(3), 675–706 (2010)
16. Lichtenstein, O., Pnueli, A., Zuck, L.D.: The glory of the past. In: Logic of Programs 1979, pp. 196–218. Springer (1985)
17. Markey, N.: Temporal logic with past is exponentially more succinct, concurrency column. Bulletin of the EATCS 79, 122–128 (2003)
18. DecentMon Website, http://decentmonitor.forge.imag.fr
19. Dwyer, M.B., Avrunin, G.S., Corbett, J.C.: Patterns in property specifications for finite-state verification. In: Intl. Conf. on Software Engineering (ICSE), pp. 411–420. ACM (1999)
20. Specification Patterns Website, http://patterns.projects.cis.ksu.edu/
21. Wang, Y., Yoo, T.-S., Lafortune, S.: New results on decentralized diagnosis of discrete event systems. In: Proc. 42nd Ann. Allerton Conf. on Communication, Control, and Computing (October 2004)
22. Wang, Y., Yoo, T.-S., Lafortune, S.: Diagnosis of discrete event systems using decentralized architectures. Discrete Event Dynamic Systems 17, 233–263 (2007)
23. Cassez, F.: The Complexity of Codiagnosability for Discrete Event and Timed Systems. In: Bouajjani, A., Chin, W.-N. (eds.) ATVA 2010. LNCS, vol. 6252, pp. 82–96. Springer, Heidelberg (2010)
24. Tripakis, S.: Decentralized observation problems. In: 44th IEEE Conf. Decision and Control (CDC-ECC), pp. 6–11. IEEE (2005)
25. Sen, K., Vardhan, A., Agha, G., Rosu, G.: Decentralized runtime analysis of multithreaded applications. In: 20th Parallel and Distributed Processing Symposium (IPDPS). IEEE (2006)
26. Genon, A., Massart, T., Meuter, C.: Monitoring Distributed Controllers: When an Efficient LTL Algorithm on Sequences Is Needed to Model-Check Traces. In: Misra, J., Nipkow, T., Karakostas, G. (eds.) FM 2006. LNCS, vol. 4085, pp. 557–572. Springer, Heidelberg (2006)
27. Barringer, H., Falcone, Y., Finkbeiner, B., Havelund, K., Lee, I., Pace, G., Roşu, G., Sokolsky, O., Tillmann, N. (eds.): RV 2010. LNCS, vol. 6418. Springer, Heidelberg (2010)

Measles Epidemics and PEPA: An Exploration of Historic Disease Dynamics Using Process Algebra

Soufiene Benkirane, Rachel Norman, Erin Scott, and Carron Shankland

University of Stirling, Stirling UK
ces@cs.stir.ac.uk
http://www.cs.stir.ac.uk/SystemDynamics/

Abstract. We demonstrate the use of the process algebra PEPA for realistic models of epidemiology. The results of stochastic simulation of the model are shown, and ease of modelling is compared to that of Bio-PEPA. PEPA is shown to be capable of capturing the complex disease dynamics of the historic data for measles epidemics in the UK from 1944–1964, including persistent fluctuations due to seasonal effects.

1 Introduction

According to the World Health Organization [26], in 2002, about 19.1% of worldwide deaths, and 52.7% of deaths in Africa were caused by infectious and parasitic diseases. Understanding a given disease, to prevent, cure or reduce its impact, is inherently a multidisciplinary endeavour, involving medicine, geography, sociology and biology, but also, through modelling, mathematics and computer science. Most epidemiological modelling has been mathematical; for example, using Ordinary Differential Equations (ODEs) [1]. Formal methods, traditionally used for computer science, are beginning to be more widely used to construct computational models of disease [3,17,18,7]. Process algebras are designed to describe a system of interacting autonomous agents and allow study of emerging collective dynamics (the epidemic). This is in contrast to the typical mathematical biology approach which is forced to make assumptions about how interaction leads to population-level effects. Using process algebra, those effects are generated by the underlying semantics of interaction.

We present a novel case study in using PEPA (Performance Evaluation Process Algebra) [14] for epidemiology. The discussion of general principles of modelling disease spread is focussed through application to the specific example of measles dynamics in England and Wales between 1944 and 1964. The emergent behaviour of measles is complex, involving recurrent outbreaks in small populations and cyclic outbreaks in larger populations [4]. Adequate modelling requires a number of features common to other diseases, including transmission, population growth, seasonality and immigration. Moreover, a large data set is freely available of the number of reported cases of measles in England and Wales over more than 20 years. This allows the model to be validated.

D. Giannakopoulou and D. Méry (Eds.): FM 2012, LNCS 7436, pp. 101–115, 2012.

Our group has long experience of applying process algebra to epidemiology. Initially WSCCS [24], a CCS inspired process algebra, was used by Norman and Shankland [21] to model basic transmission mechanisms. Further work with Mc-Caig incorporated the essential features of population growth [18] and showed the advantages of the approach over traditional styles of epidemiological modelling [17]. PEPA has also been used by our group [3]. Few other groups have made extensive study of epidemiology using process algebra beyond simple examples. A notable exception is the study of contact network structure and avian influenza by Ciocchetta and Hillston [7] using Bio-PEPA [6]. Their models are on a closed population, and do not include seasonal behaviour.

This paper is organised as follows. A brief introduction to PEPA is given in Section 2 and to measles at the start of Section 3. Modelling of measles dynamics raises generic issues for modelling epidemiology: these are discussed in the context of PEPA in Section 3. The complete model appears at the end of that section. No new language features are introduced: our contribution is to test the expressivity of PEPA for realistic models of epidemiology. Stochastic simulations of the model are compared in Section 3.2 with data available on the University of Cambridge website [25]. Since Bio-PEPA has features especially designed for biology, Section 3.3 gives details of how to model measles dynamics in Bio-PEPA and a comparison with PEPA. Conclusions are drawn in Section 4 regarding the benefits and limitations of PEPA as a modelling tool for epidemiology.

2   PEPA

PEPA [14] has been used to study the performance of a wide variety of systems [15]. PEPA has a small set of combinators, allowing system descriptions to be built up as the concurrent execution and interaction of simple sequential components which undertake actions. We informally introduce the syntax required for the model of Section 3 below. More detail can be found in [14].

Prefix: $(\alpha, r).P$ carries out action α at rate r, behaving subsequently as P. In PEPA actions have a duration, or delay. Thus the expression $(\alpha, r).P$ denotes a component which can undertake an α action, at rate r defining an exponential distribution (where rate is 1/delay) to evolve into a component P.

Choice: $P + Q$ represents a system which may behave either as P or as Q.

Constant: $X \stackrel{def}{=} E$ assigns the name X to the pattern of behaviour E.

Cooperation: $P \bowtie_L Q$ denotes cooperation between P and Q over L. The *cooperation set* L determines those activities on which the *cooperands* are forced to synchronise. For action types not in L, the components proceed independently and concurrently with their enabled activities. $P \parallel Q$ abbreviates $P \bowtie_{\{\}} Q$.

Unlike some other stochastic process algebras, PEPA assumes *bounded capacity*: a component cannot be made to perform an activity faster by cooperation, so the rate of a shared activity is the minimum of the rates of the activity in the cooperating components. In some cases, when an activity is known to be carried out in cooperation with another component, a component may be *passive* with respect to that activity. This means that the rate of the activity is left unspecified (denoted ⊤) and is determined upon cooperation by the rate of the activity in the other component. All passive actions must be synchronised.

3   Modelling Measles Dynamics in PEPA

Despite the worldwide efforts to vaccinate children against it, measles is still the vaccine-preventable disease of childhood that causes the most deaths [9]. Without vaccination, measles infects 95-98% of children before they turn eighteen [22], and an infectious person will infect 75%-90% of susceptible household contacts. The incubation period lasts for six to nine days [4], then measles symptoms begin with increasing fever, cough, coryza and conjunctivitis [22]. This is when the infectivity is highest. A rash then appears on the face and the neck, and may spread to the rest of the body. Usually, the individual recovers after six to seven days and then has lifelong immunity to the disease.

Measles has been extensively studied, giving an opportunity to show that formal methods can perform as well as long-established techniques of mathematical biology. A detailed set of data is freely available for measles in England and Wales between 1944 and 1964[1] giving an excellent opportunity to validate results from modelling. Certain key features are required to model disease transmission in general. We demonstrate that PEPA can be used to capture these, specifically in relation to the benchmark disease measles, despite not being designed for this purpose. Benkirane's thesis [2] identified the following key characteristics of measles epidemics:

Transmission of Disease. McCaig [19, page 137-138] showed in his work on epidemiology and WSCCS that in process algebra all forms of transmission can be reduced to either *direct* or *indirect* transmission. Direct transmission indicates that the disease is passed through host-to-host contact, as in measles. Indirect transmission uses an intermediary (e.g. air, surface, or via a vector). For human diseases it is common to assume the number of contacts an individual makes is constant and independent of population size. In ODE models this is known as frequency dependent transmission.

Births and Deaths. For anything other than a short timescale epidemic, the population must have births and deaths, immigration and emigration. In the case of measles, if these are not included the model shows a single initial epidemic, after which the whole population becomes resistant to the disease and there are no further outbreaks, in contradiction with observed behaviour.

Timed Events. Timed events are essential in many biological and epidemiological systems, whether these are one-off events (e.g. control measures such as

---

[1] In 1944, national notification of measles patients was made mandatory in England and Wales [11]. This provides the number and location of measles cases, with a reporting rate of over 50% [4]. Mass vaccination was introduced in 1968 [23], changing the landscape of the disease entirely. We use an earlier cut-off for data, due to some changes in administrative regions.

vaccination), or recurring events (e.g. circadian clock and seasonality). Seasonality is an essential feature of measles epidemics: disease dynamics are strongly dependent on transmission rate, which is in turn influenced by the aggregation of children at school [4]. In addition, immigration provides new infectious individuals to a city where the disease had faded out, especially in the case of small and isolated cities.

Structured Populations. The capacity to allocate the population to different categories can be essential in describing certain diseases. The structuring category can be diverse: age, social, hobbies, space, etc., depending on which feature has an important influence on the behaviour of the disease. In the case of measles dynamics, the spatial location of cities and their degree of connection impacts the overall behaviour of the disease. Smaller cities usually experience fade-outs of the disease, but still experience regular outbreaks, often within weeks of those in neighbouring cities.

Benkirane shows it is possible to code all of these features using PEPA [2], but due to limited space, only the first three will be illustrated here. The model presented is a representation of the city of Leeds from 1944 to 1964. The city initially has a population of 508,010, ten of whom are assumed to be infectious. The model is based on Bjørnstad et al. [4], apart from the immigration mechanism and parameters, which are inspired by Finkenstädt et al. [12]. In the following sections, modelling of the elements above will be discussed in turn.

3.1   Presentation of the Model

Transmission of Disease. The classic mathematical model of disease transmission is the SIR model, first described by Kermack and McKendrick [16] in 1927. SIR corresponds to *Susceptible, Infectious* and *Recovered* as follows:

Susceptibles represent the people that never had the disease, and may acquire it after exposure to the infection.

Infectious are the people who carry the disease, and may pass it (directly or indirectly) to *susceptible* individuals.

Recovered (or Removed) are immune to the disease. This might be because they have been infectious and recovered from it, because they have been vaccinated, or because they are naturally immune to the disease.

Additional classes may be necessary for particular diseases. For example, measles requires an *Exposed* class:

Exposed are infected *susceptibles* who are not yet infectious, i.e. they are undergoing an incubation period.

This general model of disease spread has been successfully applied to a wide range of different diseases. It is straightforward to encode these behaviours as separate process algebra agents: see the model of Figure 1, where the agents S, E, I and R respectively represent the *Susceptible, Exposed, Infectious* and

$$S \stackrel{def}{=} (contact, \top).E$$
$$E \stackrel{def}{=} (infected, ir).I$$
$$I \stackrel{def}{=} (contact, \top).I + (recover, rr).R$$
$$R \stackrel{def}{=} (contact, \top).R + (lose\_immunity, li).S$$

$$I' = (contact, cr).I' + (recover, \top).Rest;$$
$$Rest = (infected, \top).I';$$

$$(S[990] \parallel I[10]) \underset{\{infected, contact, recover\}}{\bowtie} (I'[10] \parallel Rest[990])$$

Fig. 1. Simple direct transmission in PEPA

Recovered individuals. Activities occur at rates controlled by the exponential variables ir (incubation), rr (recovery), li (loss of immunity), and cr (contact). Exponential rates are highly suitable for the first three, since these take place at a constant rate, and provide a reasonable approximation for contact behaviour.

The additional agents I' and $Rest$ are required to implement direct transmission[2]. With standard PEPA syntax it is possible to have all I agents communicate with all S agents, or none, but not a single I communicating with a single S. One solution would be to introduce new operators capturing the desired behaviour. Instead, we wish to operate within the constraints of standard PEPA. To achieve direct transmission, it is necessary to have a main population of S and I who do not communicate directly with each other ($\parallel$) but who can communicate one-to-one with the "mirror group" of I' and $Rest$. The addition of the mirror group splits the *Infectious* functionality between two agents. On one hand, agent I, the infectious individual who can be passively contacted, or recover. On the other hand, agent I', the infectious individual actively contacting other individuals to pass on infection. This idea of where the driver of functionality lies is reflected in the choice to make *contact* passive in I but not in I'. To guarantee that the model remains consistent, the number of I and their mirror I' must be equal at all times. The mirror $Rest$ agents have been added so that the mirror I' group can grow and shrink with the I population correctly. Note that $Rest$ does not have to model all the behaviour of agents S, E and R: it only has to capture the movement from exposed to infectious. A more detailed discussion of direct transmission and the mirror group may be found in Benkirane's thesis [2].

Births and Deaths. PEPA is limited when expressing births and deaths because agents cannot be created or deleted: a more inventive approach must be adopted. Three different approaches to births and deaths are considered in Benkirane's thesis [2]: only the one adopted for his measles model is described here.

---

[2] Indirect transmission is straightforward. To agents S, E, I and R of Figure 1 add agents for the environment and a suitable system equation describing interaction [3].

A method to describe births and deaths arises naturally from the introduction of a reserve pool of *dormant* agents, as shown in this simple example:

$$Active \overset{def}{=} (death, death\_rate).Dormant$$
$$Dormant \overset{def}{=} (birth, birth\_rate).Active$$

The pool corresponds to available agents, ready to be activated when needed. Also, when an individual dies, it returns to the pool. The initial size of the pool has to be chosen carefully: too many means longer processing times for the model, too few and the pool might run out and the number of births will be blocked as long as it is empty, leading to unexpected behaviour.

In the complete measles model of Figure 2 a similar *Dormant* population is used, while the *Active* agents correspond to the S, *Exp*, *Inf* and R agents. All agents S, *Exp*, *Inf* and R can give birth and die naturally. Newborns are susceptible. This new behaviour is added to the mirror group via the *DS* agents.

Although not done for this reason here, the introduction of *Dormant* also gives a way to regulate population size. If the birth and death rate are roughly constant, the number of agents initially in *Dormant* can be chosen such that *Dormant* + *Active* = K with K the carrying capacity of the population. This way, the population can never increase past the carrying capacity, and the overall number of births naturally decreases with the number dormant. Although in general this solution is biologically unrealistic, it may be useful for cases where the population does not fluctuate much. This is true for measles dynamics: the disease is not usually deadly, and the number of immigrants over the period is low compared to the total population. The number of *Dormant* here is selected to ensure that as many births or immigrations as required can take place.

Timed Events. Infectious immigrants to the city can start a new outbreak, if the timing is right[3]. Immigration is represented by a subgroup formed by a single component type, *Immigration*. The action *immigration* fires every $1/imrate$ time step and one agent in *Dormant* moves to the *Inf* state. This models the arrival of one infectious immigrant in the city. Note the asymmetry between births and immigration. Births are driven from the main group, while immigration is driven from its own subgroup. In PEPA, given $P = (\alpha, r).Q$ the rate r follows the cumulative distribution function of the exponential distribution $F_\alpha(t) = 1 - e^{-rt}$. That is, on average, α will be fired after $1/r$ time steps. The actual moment at which the intervention takes place varies. This is very suitable for immigration: the timing of immigration is not precise. It is not suitable for seasonality, where more control over the timing of events is required.

Still considering $P = (\alpha, r).Q$, an action firing at rate 1 has actually only a 38% probability of happening between 0.5 and 1.5 time steps. In order to reduce this variability, one solution is to split the action into several steps. In other

---

[3] Susceptible or recovered immigrants and emigrants do not influence the dynamics of the disease and are not modelled here. Similarly, infectious or exposed emigrants do not have any influence on the dynamics of the disease in the studied city, and their number is sufficiently low to have a negligible impact on population size.

words, an expression $(\alpha, r).Q$ is replaced by $(\alpha', r \times n).(\alpha', r \times n).....(\alpha', r \times n).Q$ with n the number of steps, that we will denote $(\alpha', r \times n)^n.Q$ for readability purposes. The distribution of the resulting chain of actions can be calculated using the following theorem [10]:

Theorem 1. *If $X_1, X_2, ... X_n$ are independent following an exponential distribution $Exp(\alpha)$ then $\sum\limits_{i=1}^{n} X_i$ follows a Gamma distribution $Gamma(n, 1/\alpha)$*

As the rate of each of the activities is actually rn, the resulting probability density function is:

$$f_{n,r}(x) = \frac{x^{n-1}.e^{-rnx}.(rn)^n}{(n-1)!} \tag{1}$$

The cumulative density function can be simplified, in the special case where $n \in \mathbb{N}$ to the following expression:

$$F_{n,r}(x) = \sum_{i=n}^{\infty} \frac{(rnx)^i}{i!} e^{-rnx} \tag{2}$$

This formula allows us to estimate the probability of an event happening between time $t = a$ and $t = b$ (with $b > a$) as:

$$F_{n,r}(b) - F_{n,r}(a) = \sum_{i=n}^{\infty} \frac{(rnb)^i}{i!} e^{-rnb} - \sum_{i=n}^{\infty} \frac{(rna)^i}{i!} e^{-rna} \tag{3}$$

Thus, the number of steps n can be chosen to provide the modeller with what she deems an acceptable probability of an action occurring within the desired time. We use this technique to model seasonality using the following agent:

$$Summer \overset{def}{=} (go\_winter, n/summer\_duration)^n.Winter + (insummer, big).Summer$$
$$Winter \overset{def}{=} (go\_summer, n/winter\_duration)^n.Summer + (inwinter, big).Winter$$

The season agent has two roles: performing the chain of actions leading to a change in season (go_winter and go_summer), or broadcasting the current season ($inwinter$ or $insummer$) to all agents for the whole season. The rate big is introduced as a practical proxy for $\top$ in simulations.

Seasonality affects measles dynamics through a varying contact rate. The average age of the infected individual according to data is low [20, Table II]: the disease is very infectious, and getting infected grants lifelong immunity. The average number of contacts a child makes change significantly depending on season, as more contacts are made when children go to school (in winter). The two seasons only affect Inf', the mirror component of Inf, which has been divided into Inf'_s for the summer, and Inf'_w for the winter. The difference between the two is contact rate (crs and crw). The model is composed of two seasons: a four month summer, and an eight month winter.

To explain the seasonality mechanism further, for example, once the season changes from $Summer$ to $Winter$, $Winter$ cooperates with the agents in Inf'_s (of

Figure 2) over the action *inwinter*, in order for them all to move to Inf'_w (also of Figure 2). The rate at which the cooperation is performed has to be very large compared to the other parameters of the model in order for the process to be considered instantaneous. In this model, this rate is at least $big/crs \approx 1.66 \times 10^8$ times bigger than any other rate in the model. The number of infectious individuals is always under 1000, so the whole operation takes less than $1000/big \approx 10^{-6}$ time step to be performed. Note that any immigrating individuals move to Inf'_s initially, but if the season is winter they will move almost instantaneously to Inf'_w. After the action *go_summer* has been fired n times, the agent describing the season moves from *Winter* to *Summer*, and the agents in Inf'_w are forced to move to Inf'_s. The choice of the value of n depends on the precision required by the modeller, as well as the processing time of the model.

Complete Model and Parameters. The measles model is presented in Figure 2, and the parameters used presented in Figure 3 (taken from the literature [4,12,25] except n, srs, srw) . In the final measles model of Figure 2 there are agents for *S*, *Exp*, *Inf*, *R* and *Dormant*, as above. There is not a direct mapping between agents in the main group and and the mirror group (S', Inf'_s, Inf'_w and DS). In particular, DS only models movement of births and $DS \neq Dormant$. Other *Dormant* behaviour is captured in S'. The model obeys two invariants concerning agent numbers: $Inf = Inf'_s + Inf'_w$, and $S + Exp + R + Dormant + Immi = S' + DS$.

$$Summer \stackrel{def}{=} (go\_winter, srs)^n.Winter + (insummer, big).Summer$$
$$Winter \stackrel{def}{=} (go\_summer, srw)^n.Summer + (inwinter, big).Winter$$
$$S \stackrel{def}{=} (contact, \top).Exp + (birth, br).S + (die, dr).Dormant$$
$$Exp \stackrel{def}{=} (contact, \top).Exp + (incubation, ir).Inf + (die, dr).Dormant + (birth, br).Exp$$
$$Inf \stackrel{def}{=} (contact, \top).Inf + (recover, rr).R + (dieI, dr).Dormant + (birth, br).Inf$$
$$R \stackrel{def}{=} (contact, \top).R + (birth, br).R + (die, dr).Dormant$$
$$Dormant \stackrel{def}{=} (born, big).S + (immigration, \top).Immi$$
$$Immi \stackrel{def}{=} (gotoInf, big).Inf$$
$$S' \stackrel{def}{=} (incubation, \top).Inf'_s + (birth, \top).DS + (gotoInf, \top).Inf'_s$$
$$Inf'_s \stackrel{def}{=} (contact, crs).Inf'_s + (recover, \top).S' + (inwinter, \top).Inf'_w + (dieI, \top).S'$$
$$Inf'_w \stackrel{def}{=} (contact, crw).Inf'_w + (recover, \top).S' + (insummer, \top).Inf'_s + (dieI, \top).S'$$
$$DS \stackrel{def}{=} (born, \top).S' + (timeout, 100.0).S'$$
$$Immigration \stackrel{def}{=} (immigration, imrate).Immigration$$

$$((S[508000] \parallel Inf[10] \parallel Dormant[100000] \underset{\{born,birth,incubation,recover,contact,dieI,gotoInf\}}{\bowtie}$$
$$S'[608000] \parallel Inf'_w[10]) \underset{\{immigration\}}{\bowtie} Immigration) \underset{\{insummer,inwinter\}}{\bowtie} Winter$$

Fig. 2. PEPA measles model for Leeds

According to Bjørnstad et al. [4, p. 171], the critical community size, in order for the virus not to go extinct, lies between $300,000$ and $500,000$ in England and Wales. For this reason, the city of Leeds has been chosen to test this model: its

Parameter	Rate (per day)	Description
popn	508010	Total population size [25]
big	999999999	The fast rate used for immigration and seasonality
ir	1/7.5	Incubation rate is 1/incubation period [4]
rr	1/6.5	Recovery rate is 1/infectious period [4]
crw	39.1/6.5	Winter contact rate [4]
crs	19.8/6.5	Summer contact rate [4]
br, dr	0.017/360	Birth rate and Death rate [4]
imrate	$0.02 * \sqrt{popn}/360$	Immigration rate of infectious individuals [12]
n	96	Number of iterations of the change of season action
srw	$1/(8 \times 30) \times n$	Rate of one iteration of change season (winter)
srs	$1/(4 \times 30) \times n$	Rate of one iteration of change season (summer)

Fig. 3. The parameters used in the model in Figure 2

population in 1944 was about $508,000$ inhabitants. The model starts with 100% susceptible individuals, and evolves naturally towards its steady state susceptible proportion of between 3.5 and 9%. This number of susceptibles is consistent with biological studies [4, p. 180]. The model displays transient behaviour while establishing the susceptible population. This has been empirically determined to correspond to the first thousand steps, and has been removed from the results shown in Figure 4 as it does not relate to the observed behaviour of measles.

Finkenstädt et al [12, p. 755] give immigration of infectious individuals as:

$$\text{average number of imports per year} = 0.02\sqrt{\text{population size}}$$

In the case of our model, it results in $0.02\sqrt{508000} = 14.25$ infectious imports per year. This results in a total of 285 immigrants across the twenty-one years studied, who increase the overall population by 0.056%. The birth and death rates are assumed to be constant by taking average figures for the period. While this was not the case in reality (the maximum number of births recorded was 10821 in 1947, and the minimum was 7584 in 1954), the difference can be considered negligible for the scope of this analysis.

The contact rate has been chosen based on the value of R_0 given in the paper by Bjørnstad et al. [4, p. 180]. R_0 is the number of successful contacts an infectious individual would make in an entirely susceptible population. According to that paper, its maximum value is 39.1 in December, and its minimum value is 19.8 in August. In the absence of an average value over the course of a season, or a monthly value, these values are used for the winter and summer season respectively. The daily number of contacts are derived in a standard way from R_0 by dividing it by the infectious period.

Finally, the parameters related to the seasons are *srw*, *srs* and *n*. Seasonality has been simplified by assuming that a month lasts 30 days, and a year 360 days. Winter has been assumed to last eight months. The choice of the value of *n* lies in the hands of the modeller: it must be chosen in order to give an acceptable variability in the season length, while not increasing the length of the simulations too much. With $n = 96$, and using equation (3), the probability that the winter lasts between 7 and 9 months, and that the summer lasts between 3.5 and 4.5 months, is 78%, which is deemed sufficient for the scope of this study.

3.2   Results

Analysis of the model is performed through a series of single stochastic simulations. Due to variability in the timing of season change, stochastic simulations cannot be meaningfully averaged. Moreover, the analysis will only be performed on semi-quantitative factors, such as the length of the cycle between two consecutive outbreaks and the average size of the peak of each epidemic. Although Benkirane developed a tool to derive ODEs from PEPA models [2], this cannot be used here as the hypothesis behind the derivation, that the number of agents is large, is not met by the subgroups for seasonality and immigration (one instance each). Their effect of the main group would not be correctly captured in the derived ODEs. A benefit of process algebra (not explored here) is that additional analyses are possible via the PEPA plugin [13].

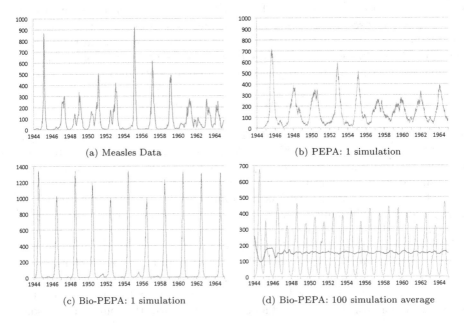

Fig. 4. Graphical results for Measles epidemics in Leeds between 1944 and 1964. The horizontal axis is year, and the vertical axis is number of infectious individuals.

Comparing the model with measured data is not straightforward: this is one of the problems of carrying out a realistic case study. The data to which the model is compared (city of Leeds only) is available from University of Cambridge [25]. The data must be normalised to match the format of the simulated data. The simulated data reports number of infected individuals every day, while the field data is reported every 14 days. Each data point in the original data has been divided by 14 (to get the number of reported infectious individuals per day) and multiplied by 6.5 (to reflect the average infectious period of 6.5 days). Bjørnstad et al. [4, p. 172] mention a reporting rate across England and Wales of just over 50%. We assume every individual is infected at some point in her life, therefore, the number of births should correspond to the number of cases. For Leeds between 1944 and 1964 (inclusive), 181,539 births were recorded, while 109,730 cases of measles were reported. Assuming the birth rate was constant (as above) gives an average reporting rate of 60.4%. A constant reporting rate will be assumed. The number of infectious individuals at each data point are corrected by multiplying the reported number of cases by (number of births / reported cases). Figure 4(a) shows the corrected data.

A sample simulation of the model of Figure 2 is shown in Figure 4(b). It corresponds to 8560 days of simulations, where the first 1000 days have been removed, as described previously. The two graphs exhibit comparable behaviour. In both cases, measles outbreaks occur on a regular cycle. The length of the cycle varies between the collected data and the stochastic simulation. In the case of the data, the cycle lasts exactly two years, with very little variation over the length of the studied period, apart from a single one year cycle between the 1963 and the 1964 epidemics. The simulation on the other hand, has biennial cycles most of the time, but sometimes exhibits 2.5 year cycles. Across the studied period, the collected data experiences 11 outbreaks, for 9 in the simulation. As detailed by Bjørnstad et al. [4], the cycles are a consequence of the addition of seasonality to the model. The presence of a summer season where the contact rate is lower allows more time for the pool of susceptibles to increase in size, until the contact rate increases again in the winter. The number of infectious individuals at the peak of infection in both cases can vary a lot, between 260 and 920 in the case of the collected data, and 260 and 710 in the simulation. The average of the number of individuals at the peak of each outbreak confirms this difference: 479 infecteds in the case of the collected data, for 424 in the case of the simulations.

3.3   Comparison with Bio-PEPA

It can be seen from the discussion above that some epidemiological features, while they can be modelled in PEPA, are not naturally expressed. For example, neither direct transmission, nor births and deaths, are very elegantly expressed in PEPA. An obvious question arises: are these features better modelled in Bio-PEPA, which was designed for biological systems? Brief details of repeating the modelling exercise with Bio-PEPA are given here. The model was based on a combination of standard mathematical biology techniques [1,11] and the model of Figure 2. The Bio-PEPA model is shown in Figure 5. The syntax used here is the syntax of the Bio-PEPA tool [8]. Parameter values are as in Figure 3.

Transmission of Disease. Control is given to the modeller via the kinetic laws: any rate expressed via arithmetic and trigonometric functions can be

$endWinter \stackrel{def}{=} 4;\ startWinter \stackrel{def}{=} 9;\ month \stackrel{def}{=} floor(time/30);$

$season\_time \stackrel{def}{=} H(((month - 12 * floor(month/12)) - endWinter)$
$* (startWinter - (month - 12 * floor(month/12))));$

$kineticLawOf\ birth$: $br * (S + Exp + Inf + R);$

$kineticLawOf\ dieS$: $dr * S;$

$kineticLawOf\ dieExp$: $dr * Exp;$

$kineticLawOf\ dieInf$: $dr * Inf;$

$kineticLawOf\ dieR$: $dr * R;$

$kineticLawOf\ contact$: $((crw * S * Inf)/(S + Exp + Inf + R)) * (1 - season\_time) +$
$((crs * S * Inf)/(S + Exp + Inf + R)) * (season\_time);$

$kineticLawOf\ incubation$: $ir * Exp;$

$kineticLawOf\ recover$: $rr * Inf;$

$kineticLawOf\ immigration$: $imrate;$

$$S = (contact, 1) \ll +(birth, 1) \gg +(dieS, 1) \ll;$$
$$Exp = (contact, 1) \gg +(incubation, 1) \ll +(dieExp, 1) \ll +(birth, 1)(.);$$
$$Inf = (contact, 1)(.) + (incubation, 1) \gg +(dieInf, 1) \ll +(birth, 1)(.)$$
$$+(recover, 1) \ll +immigration \gg;$$
$$R = (recover, 1) \gg +(birth, 1)(.) + (dieR, 1) \ll;$$

$$Inf[10] < * > S[508000] < * > Exp[0] < * > R[0]$$

Fig. 5. Bio-PEPA measles model for Leeds

given. This is rather similar to the way in which mathematical biologists choose terms in their ODE models: the link with interacting processes is decreased. Thus incorporating direct transmission is no longer about designing the right sort of interaction, it is simply a matter of writing the commonly used term for frequency-dependent direct transmission in the kinetic law for *contact*.

Births and Deaths. In Bio-PEPA the style is to describe change to species numbers, where species are similar to agents in PEPA. In Figure 5 the species are S, Exp, Inf and R. For example, increasing population through birth is described by the event $(birth, 1) \gg$ and decreasing population through death by the event $(dieS, 1) \ll$ (increase or decrease being indicated by the direction of the arrows). The 1 in these events describes the change to the number of susceptibles, but not the rate. The rate is described by the appropriate kinetic laws for *birth* and *death*.

Timed Events. Time can be used explicitly in the model through the variable *time*, and thus can influence variables and hence kinetic laws. In Figure 5 the variable *season_time* switches between 0 and 1 (with the use of the built-in Heaviside function H) to indicate winter or summer respectively. This is then used in the kinetic law for *contact*.

Bio-PEPA, like PEPA, gives access to a range of analysis techniques through a tool: the Bio-PEPA plugin [8], which offers, for example, stochastic simulations, interpretation as ODEs, translation to SBML, invariant inference and model-checking. The result of a single simulation of the Bio-PEPA model is given in Figure 4(c): the pattern of outbreaks is similar to the collected data of 1944–1964, although the peaks are significantly higher. In Bio-PEPA the switch between seasons happens on the same day every year, in every simulation. For interest, Figure 4(d) shows the average of one hundred simulations for both the seasonally switching contact rate (lighter line) and a fixed (crw) contact rate (heavier line). For the former, the average tends to peak lower, and annually: the period between epidemics varies from one to three years. For the latter, the long-term pattern shows a more steady rate of infection of around 150 individuals. Both of these simulations are shown starting after 1720 steps: the Bio-PEPA simulation takes slightly longer to stabilise than the PEPA simulations.

Bio-PEPA overcomes some of the feature-capturing problems of PEPA. Arguably the model of Figure 5 is simpler and more elegant: the species are no longer confused with modelling artefacts to handle one-to-one communication. Bio-PEPA also has limitations. The formulation of kinetic laws means rates no longer depend on interaction and semantics: they come from implicit assumptions the modeller has made about population-level dynamics. This is therefore rather similar to the standard mathematical biology approach.

4   Conclusions

PEPA and Bio-PEPA models have been constructed to reflect cyclic epidemics of measles, and their output compared to collected data. While PEPA is not ideally suited to capturing all features of disease progression, suitable approximations can be made. An important feature is that the population dynamics emerge from the specified individual behaviour. In contrast, the Bio-PEPA model may be simpler, but required high-level assumptions to be made about population dynamics. In both cases, existing well-developed tools [13,8] were used for analysis. The results are promising: the simulated results for both PEPA and Bio-PEPA are comparable to the collected data and would allow meaningful exploration of patterns of epidemics under different parameter regimes. The PEPA results are closer to the collected results than the Bio-PEPA results, which demonstrate too much regularity. Differences between our results and the data may be associated with the granularity of modelling. For example, birth and death rates have the same value throughout the simulation. Seasonality has been approximated by splitting the year into two seasons each with a single contact rate which does not change throughout the season. The value used by Bjørnstad et al. [4, Fig. 7, p. 178] varies noticeably within each season. The models presented here could be altered to reflect these changes, with varying degrees of difficulty.

One of the difficulties encountered in this study, and encountered in any realistic modelling exercise, is the problem of parameter values. For example, the main source for this model was Bjørnstad et al. [4] who give incubation rate and infectious period as 7.5 and 6.5 days respectively. As shown in Section 3.2 this gives a good match to the measured data. Our models have also been tested with data from Bolker et al. [5] who propose an incubation period of ten days, and infectious period of 3.7 days. This gives fewer disease outbreaks than shown by the data (3-4 years between outbreaks, with peaks between 600-1500 cases). The beauty of modelling is that the parameter choices can be easily explored. A further difficulty of dealing with collected data for measles is estimating the reporting rate. The approximation used might impact the number of infectious individuals at a given time, but would not influence cycle duration.

Due to lack of space, the influence of the nearby cities have been completely ignored in this study. Benkirane [2] has developed a novel extension to PEPA to allow structured populations to be easily expressed, and demonstrates its use through a more complex model of measles in the linked cities of Cardiff, Newport, Bristol and Bath. Similarly, Bio-PEPA has compartments which allow spatial elements of epidemiology to be modelled.

Process algebra has been shown here to be useful in modelling quite complex infectious disease systems. Determining which approach is suitable for a given problem depends on which questions we wish to answer about that problem; that is, the sort of analysis we wish to carry out. An advantage of process algebra over traditional mathematical biology is the range of automated analyses available.

Acknowledgments. This work was carried out under the EPSRC award *System Dynamics from Individual Interactions: A process algebra approach to epidemiology* (EP/E006280/1, 2007-2010), in consultation with Mike Begon, School of Biology and Biological Sciences, University of Liverpool. The authors thank the PEPA and Bio-PEPA Plug-in development team at the University of Edinburgh, for help, particularly Mirco Tribastone, Adam Duguid and Allan Clark. Finally, we thank the anonymous reviewers for their helpful comments.

References

1. Anderson, R.M., May, R.M.: The population-dynamics of micro-parasites and their invertebrate hosts. Philosophical Transactions of the Royal Society of London Series B 291, 451–524 (1981)
2. Benkirane, S.: Process algebra for epidemiology: evaluating and enhancing the ability of PEPA to describe biological systems. Ph.D. thesis, University of Stirling (2011), http://hdl.handle.net/1893/3603
3. Benkirane, S., Hillston, J., McCaig, C., Norman, R., Shankland, C.: Improved Continuous Approximation of PEPA Models through Epidemiological Examples. In: From Biology to Concurrency and Back, FBTC 2008. ENTCS, vol. 229, pp. 59–74. Elsevier (2008)
4. Bjørnstad, O.N., Finkenstädt, B.F., Grenfell, B.T.: Dynamics of measles epidemics: estimating scaling of transmission rates using a time series SIR model. Ecological Monographs 72(2), 169–184 (2002)
5. Bolker, B., Grenfell, B.: Space, persistence and dynamics of measles epidemics. Philosophical Transactions of the Royal Society of London - Series B: Biological Sciences 348(1325), 309–320 (1995)
6. Ciocchetta, F., Hillston, J.: Bio-PEPA: A framework for the modelling and analysis of biological systems. Theor. Comput. Sci. 410(33-34), 3065–3084 (2009)

7. Ciocchetta, F., Hillston, J.: Bio-PEPA for epidemiological models. Electronic Notes in Theoretical Computer Science 261, 43–69 (2010); Proceedings of Practical Application of Stochastic Modelling (PASM 2009)

8. Duguid, A., Gilmore, S., Guerriero, M.L., Hillston, J., Loewe, L.: Design and development of software tools for Bio-PEPA. In: Proc. of Winter Simulation Conference 2009, pp. 956–967 (2009)

9. Duke, T., Mgone, C.S.: Measles: not just another viral exanthem. The Lancet 361, 763–773 (2003)

10. Durrett, R.: Probability: Theory and Examples. Cambridge Series in Statistical and Probabilistic Mathematics (2010)

11. Fine, P.E., Clarkson, J.A.: Measles in England and Wales–I: An analysis of factors underlying seasonal patterns. Int. Journal of Epidemiology 11(1), 5–14 (1982)

12. Finkenstädt, B.F., Keeling, M., Grenfell, B.T.: Patterns of density dependence in measles dynamics. Proceedings of the Royal Society B 265, 753–762 (1998)

13. Gilmore, S., Tribastone, M., Duguid, A., Clark, A.: PEPA plug-in for eclipse (2008), homepages.inf.ed.ac.uk/mtribast/plugin/

14. Hillston, J.: A Compositional Approach to Performance Modelling. Cambridge University Press (1996)

15. Hillston, J.: Tuning systems: From composition to performance. The Computer Journal 48(4), 385–400 (2005); The Needham Lecture Paper

16. Kermack, W.O., McKendrick, A.G.: Contributions to the mathematical theory of epidemics. Proceedings of the Royal Society of London A 115, 700–721 (1927)

17. McCaig, C., Begon, M., Norman, R., Shankland, C.: A rigorous approach to investigating common assumptions about disease transmission: Process algebra as an emerging modelling methodology for epidemiology. Theory in Biosciences 130, 19–29 (2011); special issue on emerging modelling methodologies

18. McCaig, C., Norman, R., Shankland, C.: From individuals to populations: A symbolic process algebra approach to epidemiology. Mathematics in Computer Science 2(3), 139–155 (2009)

19. McCaig, C.: From individuals to populations: changing scale in process algebra models of biological systems. Ph.D. thesis, University of Stirling (2008), http://hdl.handle.net/1893/398

20. Miller, D.L.: Frequency of complications of measles, 1963. British Medical Journal 2, 75–78 (1964)

21. Norman, R., Shankland, C.: Developing the Use of Process Algebra in the Derivation and Analysis of Mathematical Models of Infectious Disease. In: Moreno-Díaz Jr., R., Pichler, F. (eds.) EUROCAST 2003. LNCS, vol. 2809, pp. 404–414. Springer, Heidelberg (2003)

22. Perry, R., Halsey, N.: The clinical significance of measles: A review. Journal of Infectious Diseases 189(1), S4–S16 (2004)

23. The Medical News: Measles history, http://www.news-medical.net/health/Measles-History.aspx

24. Tofts, C.: Processes with probabilities, priority and time. Formal Aspects of Computing 6, 536–564 (1994)

25. University of Cambridge: Pathogen population dynamics (2002), http://www.zoo.cam.ac.uk/zoostaff/grenfell/measles.htm

26. World Health Organization: The world health report 2004 (2004), http://www.who.int/whr/2004/annex/topic/en/annex_2_en.pdf

A Certified Constraint Solver
over Finite Domains

Matthieu Carlier[1], Catherine Dubois[1,2], and Arnaud Gotlieb[3,4]

[1] ENSIIE, Évry, France
{carlier,dubois}@ensiie.fr
[2] INRIA Paris Rocquencourt, Paris, France
[3] Certus V&V Center, SIMULA RESEARCH LAB., Lysaker, Norway
arnaud@simula.no
[4] INRIA Rennes Bretagne-Atlantique, Rennes, France

Abstract. Constraint programs such as those written in modern Constraint Programming languages and platforms aim at solving problems coming from optimization, scheduling, planning, etc. Recently CP programs have been used in business-critical or safety-critical areas as well, e.g., e-Commerce, air-traffic control applications, or software verification. This implies a more skeptical regard on the implementation of constraint solvers, especially when the result is that a constraint problem has no solution, i.e., unsatisfiability. For example, in software model checking, using an unsafe constraint solver may result in a dramatic wrong answer saying that a safety property is satisfied while there exist counterexamples. In this paper, we present a Coq formalisation of a constraint filtering algorithm — AC3 and one of its variant AC2001 — and a simple labeling procedure. The proof of their soundness and completeness has been completed using Coq. As a result, a formally certified constraint solver written in OCaml has been automatically extracted from the Coq specification of the filtering and labeling algorithms. The solver, yet not as efficient as specialized existing (unsafe) implementations, can be used to formally certify that a constraint system is unsatisfiable.

1 Introduction

Context. Automated software verification relies on constraint resolution [23], either to prove functional properties over programs or to generate automatically test inputs [13]. For example, formal verification involves showing that a formula embedding the negation of a property is *unsatisfiable*, i.e., the formula has no model or solution. While most verification techniques are based on SAT and SMT (Satisfiability Modulo Theory), tools built over *Constraint Programming over Finite Domains*, noted CP(FD) [14], become more and more competitive e.g., CPBPV [11], or OSMOSE [5,4]. In this context, *finite domains* mean finite sets of labels or possible values associated to each variable of the program. Existing results show that CP(FD) is a complementary approach to SMT for certain classes of verification problems [5,3].

D. Giannakopoulou and D. Méry (Eds.): FM 2012, LNCS 7436, pp. 116–131, 2012.

Problem. Effective constraint-based verification involves using efficient constraint solvers. However, efficiency comes at the price of complexity in the design of these solvers. And even if developing CP(FD) solvers is the craft of a few great specialists, it is nearly impossible to guarantee by manual effort that their results are error-free. A constraint solver declaring a formula being unsatisfiable while it is not the case, can entail dramatic consequences for a safety-critical software system. Thus, an emerging trend in software verification is to equip code with correctness proofs, called *certificates* [12], that can be checked by third-party certifiers [20,8,1,7]. As soon as these certificates involve finite domains constraint systems, external constraint solvers are used without any guarantee on their results.

Contribution. Following the research direction opened up by CompCert [17] that offered us a formally certified compiler for a subset of C, the work presented in this paper is part of a bigger project aiming at building a certified testing environment for functional programs based on finite domains constraint solving. A significant first step has been reached by formally certifying the test case generation method [9], provided that a correct constraint solver is available. This paper specifically tackles this second step of the project by building a certified CP(FD) solver. We developed a sound and complete CP(FD) solver able to provide correct answers, relying on the Coq interactive proof assistant. The constraints are restricted to binary normalized constraints, i.e., distinct relations over two variables [10], but are not necessarily represented as set of binary tuples. The language of constraints is in fact a parameter of our formalisation. Our certified CP(FD) solver implements a classical filtering algorithm, AC3 [19] and one of its extension AC2001 [10], thus focuses on arc-consistency. By *filtering algorithm*, we mean a fixpoint computation that applies domain filtering operators to the finite domains of variables. The Coq formalisation is around 8500 lines long. The main difficulties have been to discover or re-discover implicit assumptions and classical knowledge about these algorithms.

Following the Coq proof extraction mechanism, the executable code of the solver in OCaml has been automatically derived from its formal development, and used to solve some constraint systems. The solver, yet not as efficient as specialized existing but unsafe implementations, can be used to formally certify that a constraint system is unsatisfiable or satisfiable. According to our knowledge, this is the first time a constraint solver over finite domains is formally certified. The Coq code and the OCaml extracted files are available on the web at www.ensiie.fr/~dubois/CoqsolverFD .

Outline. The rest is organized as follows: Sec. 2 introduces the notations and the definitions of the notions of consistency, solution, solving procedure used in our formalisation. Sec. 3 presents the filtering algorithm AC3 and an implementation of the local consistency property called REVISE. It also presents an optimized version of the filtering algorithm called AC2001. Sec. 4 describes the formalisation of the search heuristics. Sec. 5 presents our first experimental results and discusses related work. Finally, sec. 6 concludes the paper.

2 Formalisation of a Constraint Solving Problem

A *Constraint Satisfaction Problem* (csp for short) or network of constraints [19] is a triple (X, D, C) where X is a set of ordered variables, C is a set of binary normalized constraints over X and D is a partial function that associates a finite domain $D(x)$ to each variable x in X. In our setting, the values of a finite domain belong to a set $\mathcal{V}$ equipped with a decidable equality. The set C is composed of *binary* and *normalized constraints*, meaning respectively that constraints hold over 2 variables, and that two distinct constraints cannot hold over exactly the same variables. The function *get_vars* retrieves the ordered pair of variables of a constraint c. For example, $get\_vars(c)$ returns (x_1, x_2) iff x_1 is smaller than x_2, (x_2, x_1) otherwise. Note that this ordering is introduced for convenience, but does not limit the generality of the purpose. We also suppose that each variable of X appears at least once in a constraint of C. Restricting to binary normalized constraints does not weaken the contribution as constraints over finite domains with higher arity can always be rewritten into binary constraints [2], and it is always possible to merge two constraints holding over the same two variables into a single one. Omitting unary constraints is not a restriction either since unary constraints are semantically equivalent to domain constraints, that are captured by D in our formal settings

Fig.1 shows the Coq formalisation of constraint network where types of constraints, variables and values are made abstract. To define constraints, we only require the definition of 2 functions *get_vars* and an interpretation function *interp*. We expect the following meaning: if $get\_vars(c) = (x, y)$, then *interp c u v* = *true* iff c is satisfied by substituting x by u and y by v, noted $c(u, v)$ or (*consistent_value c x u y v*) in Coq code. In the following, Coq excerpts are not true Coq code in the sense that mathematical notations are used when they ease the reading, e.g. $\in$ denotes list or set membership, whereas prefixe notation *In* is kept for membership in domain tables. The formalisation of domains *Doms* is

```
Parameter constraint : Set.
Parameter interp : constraint → value → value → bool.
Parameter get_vars : constraint → variable × variable.
Parameter get_vars_spec : ∀ c x1 x2, get_vars c = (x1, x2) → x1 < x2.
Record network : Type := Make_csp {
CVars : list variable ; Doms : mapdomain ; Csts : list constraint }.
```

Fig. 1. Coq formalisation of constraint network

captured by lists without replicates and saved in a table (of type *mapdomain*) indexed by the variables[1].

The Coq record *network_inv csp* that captures well-formedness properties of a constraint network *csp*, is given in Fig2. The first proj. *Dwf* specifies that

---

[1] The Coq module *Fmap* is used to keep these tables, and the AVL implementation from the Coq's standard library is used in the extracted code.

the network variables (and only those), have an associated domain in the table embedded in *csp*. The second proj. *Cwf1* specifies that the variables of a constraint are indeed variables of the network *csp*. The third proj. *Cwf2* specifies that each variable appears at least once in the network. Finally, *norm* specifies that two constraints sharing the same variables must be identical.

Record *network_inv csp* : **Prop** := *Make_csp_inv* {
    Dwf : $\forall$ *x, In x* (*Doms csp*) $\leftrightarrow$ *In x* (*CVars csp*) ;
    Cwf1 : $\forall$ (*c:constraint*) (*x1 x2* : *variable*),
           c $\in$ (*Csts csp*) $\rightarrow$ *get_vars c* = (*x1, x2*) $\rightarrow$
             x1 $\in$ (*CVars csp*) $\wedge$ *x2* $\in$ (*CVars csp*) ;
    Cwf2 : $\forall$ *x, x* $\in$ (*CVars csp*) $\rightarrow$ $\exists$ *c,*
           c $\in$ (*Csts csp*) $\wedge$ (*fst* (*get_vars c*) = *x* $\vee$ *snd* (*get_vars c*) = *x*);
    Norm : $\forall$ *c c', c* $\in$ (*Csts csp*) $\rightarrow$ *c'* $\in$ (*Csts csp*) $\rightarrow$
        get_vars c = *get_vars c'* $\rightarrow$ *c* = *c'* }.

Fig. 2. Well-formedness properties of a constraint network in Coq

2.1   Assignment - Solution

Following the definitions given in [6], an *assignment* is a partial map of some variables of the constraint network to values[2], a *valid assignment* is an assignment of some variables to a value from their domain, a *locally consistent assignment* is a valid assignment of some variables that satisfy the constraints that hold over them (and only those), and finally a *solution* is a locally consistent assignment of all the variables of the constraint network. We formalized these notions but do not expose their Coq specification very close to the previous informal definitions.

An important lemma about solutions, named *no_sol* given below, is involved in the completeness proof of the CP(FD) solver. It establishes that as soon as a domain in the constraint network *csp* becomes empty, then *csp* is shown be *unsatisfiable*, i.e., it has no solution. The lemma states that, in this case, any assignment defined over the set of variables of *csp* cannot be a solution. It uses the *find* function defined on tables such that *find x a* returns the value *v* associated to *x* in the instantiation *a* (encoded as *Some v*), fails otherwise (*None* is returned).

Lemma *no_sol* : $\forall$ *csp,*
($\exists$ *v, find v* (*Doms csp*) = *Some* []) $\rightarrow$ $\forall$ *a* , $\neg$ (*solution a csp*).

2.2   Arc-Consistency

The main idea of constraint filtering algorithms such as those used in CP(FD) solvers is to repeatedly filter inconsistent values from the domains. Thus, they reduce the search space while maintaining solutions. Several local consistency properties have been proposed to characterize the pruned domains [14,6], but

---

[2] Implemented in Coq by using the *Fmap* module, as variable-indexed table.

we focus here on the former and widely used *arc-consistency* property. Roughly speaking, a binary constraint $c(x, y)$ is arc-consistent w.r.t (X, D, C) iff for any value u in the domain of x (i.e., $u \in D(x)$), there exists a value v in the domain of y such as $c(u, v)$ is consistent, and conversely for any value $v \in D(y)$, there exists a value $u \in D(x)$ such as $c(u, v)$ is consistent. A constraint network (X, D, C) is arc-consistent iff any of its constraints c in C is arc-consistent. It is worth noticing that a constraint network can be arc-consistent, while it has no solution [6]. If a constraint network is arc-consistent and all of its domains are singletons, then it has a single solution.

In the original presentation of arc-consistency, a constraint network is represented with an undirected graph where nodes are associated to the variables, and edges are used to capture the constraints [19]. An edge between node x and node y exists iff there is a constraint c containing variables x and y ($c(x,y)$) in the constraint network. However, by considering that constraints are undirected relations, this representation is implicitly ambiguous as it does not distinguish constraint $c(x, y)$ from $c(y, x)$. In our Coq formalisation, we tackled this problem by considering an order over the variables, and specified arc-consistency by distinguishing two arcs, denoted (x, c, y) and (y, c, x). Reconsidering the definition of arc-consistency given above, we say that (x, c, y) is arc-consistent if for each value v of the domain of x, there exists a value t in the domain of y, such that c is satisfied. The value t is usually called the *support* of v for c. Note that nothing is required regarding to the values from the domain of y. Our Coq formalisation is given in Fig.3, where d is the table of domains and *compat_var_const* is the predicate that associates a constraint and its variables.

Definition *arc_consistent* x y c d :=
compat_var_const x y c →
$\forall$ dx dy, *find* x d = *Some* dx → *find* y d = *Some* dy →
$\forall$ v, $v \in dx$ → $\exists$ t, $t \in dy$ $\wedge$ *consistent_value* c x v y t.

Fig. 3. Our Coq formalisation of arc-consistency

3   Formalisation and Verification of a Filtering Algorithm

In a CP(FD) solver, local consistency property, such as arc-consistency, is repeatedly applied over each constraint in a fixpoint computation algorithm, i.e., a filtering algorithm. Several distinct filtering algorithms exist, but the most well-known is AC3 [19,6]. At the heart of AC3 is a function that prunes the domain of a variable according to a constraint, commonly named REVISE.

Unlike existing pseudo-code presentations of AC3, we introduce in this section a Coq functional programming code of both algorithms REVISE and AC3.

3.1   Formalisation and Verification of Algo. REVISE

In our Coq formalisation shown in Fig.4, the function *revise* takes as arguments c, x, y, dx and dy where x and y are the variables of constraint c, with resp. domain dx and dy. Function *revise* returns a new domain d' for x and a boolean *bool_rev*. If dx has been revised, i.e., dx has been pruned to d' where d' is strictly included in dx, then *bool_rev* is true. Otherwise, *bool_rev* is false. A lot of

```
Fixpoint revise c x y dx dy {struct dx} :=
    match dx with
        nil ⇒ (false, dx)
      | v::r ⇒ let (b, d) := revise c x y r dy in
                if List.existsb (fun t ⇒ consistent_value c x v y t) dy
                then (b, v::d)
                else (true, d)
    end.
```

Fig. 4. Coq formalisation of Algo REVISE (function *revise*)

theorems about *revise* are required in the following, but we present only a selection of them in Fig.5. Many of these properties are demonstrated with the help of a functional induction on *revise* which is a tailored induction schema that follows carefully the different paths of the function. Part a. contains theorems showing the conformity of the functional text with respect to the informal specification. Part b. presents 2 theorems: the first one establishes that once a domain dx has been revised to d', then its associated arc (x, c, y) is arc-consistent with d'. And the second one: when dx is not revised, it means that arc (x, c, y) was already locally consistent. Part c. contains a formal explanation of puzzling elements of $AC3$, it is concerned with the relationship between arc (x, c, y) and (y, c, x) w.r.t. arc-consistency. Roughly speaking, it means the modification of the domain of x does not affect the arc-consistency of y. Finally, theorems in part d. state that *revise* preserves the solutions of a *csp*, and, equally important, does not add extra solutions.

3.2 Formalisation of Algorithm AC3

The main idea behind AC3 consists to revise the domains of all the variables in order to make all arcs arc-consistent. When this is done for arc (x, c, y), we remove only values from the domain of x. Hence, other arcs whose target is also x may not be consistent anymore, and they have to be revisited. AC3 maintains a queue containing all the arcs to be visited or revisited. When the queue is empty, AC3 has reached a fixpoint which is a state on which no more pruning is possible. During this fixpoint computation, if a domain becomes empty, then the constraint system is shown to be unsatisfiable.

The corresponding $AC3$ function shown in Fig.6 takes as arguments the set of constraints of the network and a pair, composed of an initial map of variables to domains and a queue, containing arcs to be made arc-consistent. It results either in the pruned domains (of type *option mapdomain*), or *None* if the network has no solution or if the network is not well-formed. To add arcs in the queue, we use the function $\oplus$ that appends two lists without repetition.

a. Conformity of *revise*

Lemma *revise_true_sublist* : ∀ *c x y dx dy newdx,*
  compat_var_const x y c →
  revise c x y dx dy = (*true, newdx*) →
    newdx ⊂ *dx.*

Lemma *revise_false_eq* : ∀ *c x y dx dy newdx,*
  revise c x y dx dy = (*false, newdx*) → *newdx* = *dx.*

b. *revise* **and arc-consistency**

Lemma *revise_arc_consistent* : ∀ *csp c x y* ,
  c ∈ (*Csts csp*) → *compat_var_const x y c* →
  ∀ *dx dy dx' b,*
    find x (*Doms csp*) = *Some dx* → *find y* (*Doms csp*) = *Some dy* →
    revise c x y dx dy = (*b, dx'*) →
      arc_consistent x y c (*add x dx'* (*Doms csp*)).

Lemma *revise_false_consistent* : ∀ *csp c x y dx dy,*
  c ∈ (*Csts csp*) → *compat_var_const x y c* →
  find x (*Doms csp*) = *Some dx* → *find y* (*Doms csp*) = *Some dy* →
  ∀ *newdx, revise c x y dx dy* = (*false, newdx*) →
    arc_consistent x y c (*Doms csp*).

c. Relations on arcs (x, y, c) **and** (z, x, c) **w.r.t. arc-consistency**

Lemma *revise_x_y_consistent_y_x* : ∀ *csp c x y dx dy* ,
  c ∈ (*Csts csp*) → *compat_var_const x y c* →
  find x (*Doms csp*) = *Some dx* → *find y* (*Doms csp*) = *Some dy* →
  ∀ *newdx, revise c x y dx dy* = (*true, newdx*) →
    arc_consistent y x c (*Doms csp*) →
      arc_consistent y x c (*add x newdx* (*Doms csp*)).

Lemma *revise_x_y_consistent_x_z* : ∀ *d x y dx dy c newdx,*
  compat_var_const x y c →
  find x d = *Some dx* → *find y d* = *Some dy* →
  revise c x y dx dy = (*true, newdx*) →
  ∀ *z c0, compat_var_const x z c0* →
    arc_consistent x z c0 d →
      arc_consistent x z c0 (*add x newdx d*).

d. Completeness of *revise*

Theorem *revise_complete* : ∀ *csp c x y dx dy* (*a* : *assign*) ,
  network_inv csp →
  c ∈ (*Csts csp*) → *compat_var_const x y c* →
  find x (*Doms csp*) = *Some dx* → *find y* (*Doms csp*) = *Some dy* →
  solution a csp →
    ∀ *newdx, revise c x y dx dy* = (*true, newdx*) →
      solution a (*set_domain x newdx csp*).

Theorem *revise_strict_solution* : ∀ *csp c x y dx dy* ,
  network_inv csp →
  c ∈ (*Csts csp*) → *compat_var_const x y c* →
  find x (*Doms csp*) = *Some dx* → *find y* (*Doms csp*) = *Some dy* →
  ∀ *a newdx, solution a* (*set_domain x newdx csp*) →
    revise c x y dx dy = (*true, newdx*) →
      solution a csp.

Fig. 5. Properties of *revise*

Function AC3 (csts : list constraint)
        (d_q : mapdomain × list arc) {wf AC3_wf d_q} : option mapdomain :=
    let *(doms, qu) := d_q* **in**
    match *qu* **with**
    | *nil* ⇒ *Some (doms)*
    | *(x, c, y)::r* ⇒
        match *find x doms, find y doms* **with**
        | *Some dx, Some dy* ⇒
            let *(bool_red, newdx) := revise c x y dx dy* **in**
                if *bool_red* **then**
                    if *is_empty newdx*
                    then *None*
                    else *AC3 csts (add x newdx doms, r ⊕ (to_be_revised x y csts))*
                else *AC3 csts (doms, r)*
        | _, _ ⇒ *None*
    end   **end.**

Definition *measure_map (d: mapdomain) :=*
*fold (**fun** x ⇒ **fun** l ⇒ **fun** sum ⇒ (length l) + sum) d 0.*

Fig. 6. Formalisation of *AC3*

In this function, *to_be_revised x y c* computes the set of arcs (z, c', x) where $z \neq y$, that is the arcs that may have become inconsistent. Arc (y, c, x) and arcs having x as a source are discarded because the domain of x after revision is necessarily included in the previous domain of x, and arc-consistency asks for a support for y for each value of the domain of x. In our settings, we proved the above assertions (as captured by theorems *revise_x_y_consistent_y_x* and *revise_x_y_consistent_x_z*) which are required to establish soundness of *AC3*.

AC3 is defined as a general recursive function with the Coq construction *Function* which allows us to write the function as in any functional programming language. The overhead includes the definition of a well-founded order and the proof of decrease in the arguments in the recursive calls. For that, a lexicographic ordering, *AC3_wf*, defined on pairs (d, q) was built from two measures. The measure of a queue was introduced as its number of elements. For maps, the measure *measure_map* was introduced as the sum of the lengths of the domains, as shown in Fig.6.[3] The proof of the decrease of the arguments required, in the case of the first recursive call, tedious manipulations of maps and lists and application of the lemma *revise_true_sublist* (see Fig.5, part a).

3.3   Correction of AC3

Soundness. The main soundness theorem, *AC3_sound*, shown in Fig.7 states that *AC3* reduces the domains in order to achieve arc-consistency for each constraint at the end of the computation. In our formalisation, *complete_graph* computes the graph associated with the constraints, as a list of arcs. Soundness is

---

[3] Implemented with the map iterator *fold* defined in the module *Fmap*.

proved using a functional induction on $AC3$ and the invariant PNC (for Potentially Non arc-Consistent), given in Fig.7. If l is a list of arcs from the constraint network csp, PNC csp d l holds iff each arc (x, c, y) not arc_consistent w.r.t. the table of domains d are in l. The main idea is to verify that at each step of the computation all the arcs that may be non arc-consistent are in the queue. The corresponding lemmas are given in Fig.7. Difficulties in these proofs have been to discover the invariant and the properties on which correctness relies. As often when formalizing existing algorithms, implicit hypotheses are to be made explicit and it can be hard work.

a. Soundness theorem

> **Theorem** $AC3\_sound$: $\forall$ csp d',
> $network\_inv$ csp $\rightarrow$
> $AC3$ $(Csts$ $csp)$ $(Doms$ $csp,$ $complete\_graph$ $(Csts$ $csp)) = Some$ d' $\rightarrow$
> $\forall$ x y $c,$ $(x, c, y) \in (complete\_graph$ $(Csts$ $csp)) \rightarrow$
> $arc\_consistent$ x y c d'.

b. Invariant

> **Definition** PNC $csts$ $(d : mapdomain)$ $(l : list$ $arc)$: **Prop** := $\forall$ x y $c,$
> $(x, c, y) \in (complete\_graph$ $csts) \rightarrow \neg(arc\_consistent$ x y c $d) \rightarrow$
> $(x, c, y) \in l.$

> **Lemma** $PNC\_invariant\_to\_be\_revised$: $\forall$ csp c x y dx dy r $newdx,$
> $network\_inv$ $csp \rightarrow (x, c, y) \in (complete\_graph$ $(Csts$ $csp)) \rightarrow$
> $find$ x $(Doms$ $csp) = Some$ $dx \rightarrow find$ y $(Doms$ $csp) = Some$ $dy \rightarrow$
> $revise$ c x y dx $dy = (true, newdx) \rightarrow$
> PNC $(Csts$ $csp)$ $(Doms$ $csp)$ $((x, c, y)::r) \rightarrow$
> PNC $(Csts$ $(set\_domain$ x $newdx$ $csp))$ $(add$ x $newdx$ $(Doms$ $csp))$
> $r \oplus (to\_be\_revised$ x y $(Csts$ $csp))).$

> **Lemma** $PNC\_invariant\_tail$: $\forall$ csp d x y c $r,$
> $(x, c, y) \in (complete\_graph$ $(Csts$ $csp)) \rightarrow arc\_consistent$ x y c $d \rightarrow$
> PNC $(Csts$ $csp)$ d $((x, c, y)::r) \rightarrow$
> PNC $(Csts$ $csp)$ d $r.$

c. Completeness

> **Theorem** $AC3\_complete$: $\forall$ csp $(a : assign)$ $d',$
> $network\_inv$ $csp \rightarrow solution$ a $csp \rightarrow$
> $AC3$ $(Csts$ $csp)$ $(Doms$ $csp,$ $(complete\_graph$ $(Csts$ $csp))) = Some$ $(d') \rightarrow$
> $solution$ a $(set\_domains$ d' $csp).$

Fig. 7. Correction of AC3

Completeness. Completeness means that $AC3$ preserves the set of solutions. If a is a solution of a constraint network, then filtering with $AC3$ will preserve it. In the formal settings of Fig.7 part c, the constraint networks before and after filtering only differ by their map of domains. In addition, a more general theorem where an arbitrary queue q is introduced under the hypothesis that it is included in $(complete\_graph$ $(Csts$ $csp))$, has been proved by functional induction on $AC3$, relying mainly on *revise* completeness. We have also proved that $AC3$ does not add any supplementary solution. The statement and proof of this theorem relies on the analogous property for *revise*. Those theorems are not given here to save space in the paper, but they are all available on our webpage.

3.4   An Optimization: AC2001

AC2001 is an improvement of AC3 published in [10] which achieves optimal time complexity of arc-consistency. When a support has to be found for a value, AC3 starts to search in the entire domain for the support, without remembering what happened in a previous step of filtering. AC2001 improves searching of a support by maintaining a structure named **last** which records, for each arc (x, c, y) and value $v \in D(x)$, the smallest value $t \in D(y)$ such that $c(v, t)$ holds. So AC2001 requires a set of ordered values, while it is not the case for AC3. Hence, each time an arc is enforced to arc-consistency, the algorithm checks for each value v in $D(x)$ whether the value t recorded in **last** still belongs to $D(y)$. When it is not the case, AC2001 looks for a new value by enumerating all values in $D(y)$ greater than t. AC2001 shares all the AC3 formalisation items, but the *revise* function. Let us call this function *revise2001* for AC2001. It takes an extra argument, the **last** structure which we call a memory (of type *memory*) in our formalisation. The function returns also the new memory state, since it is modified when a revision takes place. A memory m is represented by a table from *variable * variable* to *list (value * value)*: if the variables of the constraint c are x and y (in this order), then for $(v, t) \in m(x, y)$, t is the smallest support found for v. It means that c is satisfied for these values ($c(v, t)$) and that c is not satisfied when assigning v to x and a value $w < t$ to y. Furthermore, for efficiency reasons, we require the list $m(x, y)$ to be ordered (on the first components of the pairs). All these properties are recorded in an invariant we call *memory_inv*. The core of *revise*2001 is the function formalized in Fig. 8 which acts directly on the list *last* defined as $m(x, y)$. Cases (1) and (2) are very similar but differ wrt the existence or not of a support for the value vx in *last*. The former happens when it is the first time the revision is done (*revise_exists c x y vx dy* tries to find a support for vx in the entire domain dy), the latter is the nominal case (*revise2001_a_value c x y vx vy dy* tries to find a support for vx in dy, starting from the old recorded support vy). Initial memory is the memory where each pair of variables is assigned the empty list. The final function *revise*2001 is just a wrapping embedding a memory m. All theorems that we proved for *revise* can be established for *revise*2001, in particular soundness and completeness. Of course, they are modified w.r.t. the input and output memories. We also demonstrated that *revise*2001 preserves the memory invariant.

The Coq model corresponding to Sec. 2 and Sec. 3 contains ≈ 6000 lines of code. A functor has been implemented in order to factorize the formalisation of AC3 and AC2001 allowing us to share around 1500 lines.

Fixpoint *revise2001_aux* (*c* : *constraint*) (*x y* : *variable*) *dx dy*
                    (***last_elem*** : ***list*** (***value*** × ***value***)) {struct *dx*}
                    : (*bool* × (*list value* × ***list*** (***value*** × ***value***))) :=
  match *dx* with
    nil ⇒ (*false*, (*dx*, *nil*))
  | *vx::dx* ⇒ let (*o_vy*, *last_elem*) := *last_elem_get vx last_elem* in
    let (*bool_red*, (*dx*, *last*)) := *revise2001_aux c x y dx dy last_elem* in
    match *o_vy* with
(1) | *None* ⇒   match *revise_exists c x y vx dy* with
              | *None* ⇒ (*true*, (*dx*, *last*))
              | *Some vy* ⇒ (*bool_red*, (*vx::dx*, (*vx*, *vy*)::*last*))
              end
(2) | *Some vy* ⇒ match *revise2001_a_value c x y vx vy dy* with
              | *None* ⇒ (*true*, *dx_last*)
              | *Some vy* ⇒ (*bool_red*, (*vx::dx*, (*vx*, *vy*) :: *last*))
              end
  end   end.

Fig. 8. Coq definition of AC2001

4   Labeling Search

Labeling implements a systematic search based on backtracking interleaved with local-consistency domain filtering. *Backtracking* incrementally attempts to extend an assignment toward a complete solution, by repeatedly choosing a value for an uninstantiated variable. Thus, the algorithm chooses a not yet assigned variable x and a value v in its domain following a given search heuristics, enforces the unary constraint $x = v$ (by assigning the domain to this unique value), re-establishes local consistency by applying the filtering algorithm (e.g., $AC3$) on each constraint. At this stage if filtering fails, it means there is no solution with v as a value for the variable x, then backtrack to another value for x or another variable, if possible. If filtering succeeds then go on with another variable if any. The labeling search procedure is *complete* if it can explore the overall search space. In our Coq formalisation, we implemented a complete search procedure with a simple heuristics, taking the first non assigned variable, with the first value met in the domain. Furthermore the labeling search procedure is independant from the filtering algorithm (e.g., $AC3$ or $AC2001$). In our settings, labeling is formalized in a module parameterized by the filtering algorithm and its required properties. Thus proofs about labeling are done only once, whatever be the filtering algorithm. Quantitatively, it means 1800 shared Coq lines vs 30 lines per instance. We adopted a style mixing computation and proof with the help of dependent types and the *Program Definition* construct, that eases a lot that style. The labeling function takes a well-formed constraint network and returns the first found solution if any, *None* otherwise. It uses an auxiliary function that takes as argument a list of constraints *csts*, a list of variables to be assigned *vars*, the map d of non empty domains for those variables satisfying arc-consistency. The type of the result is written as follows: {*ret*: *option domain*

| *result_ok ret csts vars d*}. The result is either *None* or *Some d'* and it must verify the expected soundness property, that is: if *None*, the csp (*vars, d, csts*) has no solution, if *Some d'*, then *d'* can be turned in a solution of (*vars, d, csts*): *d'* assigns a unique value to the variables of *vars*, and all the constraints are arc-consistent w.r.t. *d'*. *Program Definition* generates 28 proof obligations, e.g., each recursive call requires to receive arguments verifying the embedded pre-conditions. In particular, the proof relies on properties about *AC3* such as its soundness, and the fact that it reduces the domains. Some of these proof obligations concern the termination of the function, it relies again on a measure on maps of domains. We do not expose the code of the labeling function, as it just follows the informal description given above and encodes chronological backtracking in a recursive functional manner. All can be found on the webpage.

5 Evaluation

5.1 Extracting the Certified CP(FD) Solver

The extraction mechanism of Coq allows one to transform Coq proofs and functions into functional programs, erasing logical contents from them. Currently, we extract executable OCaml code only from Coq functions, as our proofs have no computational content. In a function defined with *Function*, such as *AC3*, or with *Program Definition*, such as labeling, proofs attached to proof obligations are just erased. So we can extract an operational certified CP(FD) solver for any language of binary constraints and arbitrary values. By *certified*, we mean a CP(FD) solver that returns provably-correct results in both cases, satisfiable and unsatisfiable formulas.

However the user still has to provide the constraint language, including (i) the OCaml type for the variables and the associated equality and ordering, (ii) the OCaml type for the variables and also the associated equality and ordering if AC2001 is used, and (iii) the OCaml type of constraints with the OCaml implementation of the *get_vars* and *interp* functions. It is worth noticing that the user still has to ensure the conformity of the *interp* function with the expected behaviour of the constraints. For our experiments, we introduce a language of binary constraints including operators $<, =, >$, the $\neq$ (e.g. $x > z$), conjunctions ($x > y \wedge x \bmod y = 0$) and disjunctions (e.g., $x \bmod y = 0 \vee x \bmod y = 2$) and the add/mult/sub/mod operators over 2 variables and a constant (e.g., $x = y+3$). We also implemented in OCaml a function translating addition constraints between 3 variables into binary constraints. Again the correctness of this preprocessing step, or more ambitious decomposition approaches, is not ensured by our formalisation and could be an extension. However, it seems that constraint decomposition requires source-to-source semantics preserving proofs which are less challenging than proving the correctness of filtering algorithms.

5.2 Experimental Results

The goal of our experiment was to evaluate the capabilities of the automatically extracted CP(FD) solver to solve classical benchmark programs of the

Constraints community. Of course, we did not expect our solver to compete with optimized (but unsafe) existing CP(FD) solvers, but we wanted to check whether our approach was feasible or not. We selected five well-known problems that may have interesting unsatisfiable instances, as we believe that a certified CP(FD) solver is much more interesting in this case. We selected a small puzzle (sport) (find a place to go to do sport with friends), the generic SEND+MORE=MONEY (smm) puzzle problem, the SUDOKU (sudoku) problem, the pigeon-hole problem (pigeon) and the Golomb rulers (golomb) problem. All problems but sport rely on a symbolic language of constraints whereas sport is defined via relations and tuples. Unlike the first four, the last one is a constraint optimization problem. Certifying unsatisfiability in this case is interesting for demonstrating that a given value for a cost objective function is actually a minimum value, i.e., any smaller value leads to the unsatisfiability of the problem. The Golomb rulers problem has various applications in fields such as Radio communications or X-Ray crystallography. A Golomb ruler is a set $x_1, .., x_m$ of m ordered marks such as all the distances $\{x_j - x_i \mid 1 \leq i < j \leq m\}$ between two marks are distinct. The goal of Golomb rulers problem is to find a ruler of order m with minimal length $(minimize\ x_m)$. For example, $[0, 2, 5, 6]$ is an optimal Golomb ruler with 4 marks. All our experiments[4] have been performed on a standard *3.06Ghz clocked Intel Core 2 Duo* with *4Gb 1067 MHz DDR3 SDRAM* and are reported in Tab.1. The results show that extracting a reasonably-efficient certified CP(FD) solver is feasible. The solver is powerful enough to handle some classical problems of the CP Community, and useful to certify unsatisfiability. For instance, certifying that there is no Golomb ruler with 6 marks of length less than 17 takes about 23 sec (i.e., the Golomb ruler found by our solver is $[0, 2, 7, 13, 16, 17]$).

Table 1. CPU Time required with our certified AC3-based CP(FD) solver

Examples	sport	smm	sudoku	p(6)	p(7)	p(8)	p(9)	p(10)	g(4)	g(5)	g(6)
in ms	0,02	117	253	6	17	158	1611	17541	7	350	23646

5.3   Related Work and Discussion

A first concretization of automated certifying processes lates back to the middle of the nineties with the work of Necula on proof-carrying code [21]. The idea was to join correctness proof evidence to mobile code in order to offer the receiver some guarantee over the code. Since then, several large initiatives have been undertaken to build certifying compilers [22] or certified compilers [17] But, it is only recently that the needs for certifying/certified constraint solvers, i.e. SMT solvers, emerged from formal verification [12,20]. For certifying a SMT solver, one can think of two distinct approaches. A first approach is to make the

---

[4] We have no specialized implementation for the global constraint ALLDIFF. It is translated into a list of binary difference constraints.

constraint solver produce an external trace of its computations in addition of its *sat/unsat* result. This external trace, sometimes called a *certificate* [12], can then be formally verified by a proof checker. Examples of such an approach include HOL Light used to certify results of the CVC Lite solver [20], or Isabelle/HOL to certify results of Harvey [12] and Z3 [8]. More recently, proof witnesses based on Type Theory in the proof assistant Coq have also been used to certify the results of decision procedures in SMT solvers [1,7]. A second approach, which is the one we picked up in our work even if it is considered harder than the first one, is 1) to develop the solver within the proof assistant, 2) to formally prove its correctness and 3) to extract automatically its code. For SAT/SMT solver, [18] is the only work we are aware of following this research direction. In this work, a Coq formalisation of an algorithm deciding the satisfiability of SAT formulas is proposed, and a fully reflexive tactic is automatically extracted to solve these formulas. According to our knowledge, the approach reported in this paper is the first attempt to certify a CP(FD) constraint solver. CP(FD) solving is currently outside the scope of arithmetic decision procedures, and SMT solvers rely on the BitVectors Theory to handle finitely-encoded integers [5]. We selected the second approach discussed above, to build our certified CP(FD) solver, because unsatisfiability in these solvers is not reported with certificates or proof trees. It means that using an external certified checker is not possible in that case. As a drawback, our approach cannot currently be used to certify directly the most advanced CP(FD) solvers such as Gecode or Zinc[5] that are used in industrial applications of CP. But, although our certified CP(FD) is not competitive with these hand-crafted solvers, it could be integrated as a back-end to certify a posteriori the unsatisfiable constraint systems detected by these solvers.

6   Conclusion

This paper describes a formally certified constraint solver over finite domains, i.e. CP(FD) with Coq[6]. Our formal model contains around 8500 lines ($\approx$ 110 definitions and 200 lemmas). The OCaml code of the solver has been automatically extracted. The solver implements either AC3 or AC2001 as a filtering algorithm, and can be used with any constraint language, provided that a constraint interpretation is given. According to our knowledge, this is the first time a CP(FD) solver can be used to formally certify the absence of solution, or guarantee that an assignment is actually a solution. Our main short-term future work involves the application of this certified solver to software verification. For that, we envision to integrate the solver within FocalTest our formally certified test case generator [9]. We will also parametrize the solver with another local consistency property, called bound-consistency [14], mainly used because it handles efficiently large sized finite domains. Other longer-term perspectives include the usage of our certified solver for solving constraint systems extracted from business or critical constraint models, e.g., in e-Commerce [15] or Air-Traffic Control.

---

[5] http://www.gecode.org/ and http://g12.research.nicta.com.au/
[6] Available at http://www.ensiie.fr/~dubois/CoqsolverFD

Thanks. We are very grateful to Benoit Robillard who helped us proving formally the termination of the *AC3* function. We also thank the anonymous referees.

References

1. Armand, M., Faure, G., Grégoire, B., Keller, C., Théry, L., Werner, B.: A modular integration of sat/smt solvers to coq through proof witnesses. In: Jouannaud, Shao (eds.) [16], pp. 135–150.
2. Bacchus, F., Chen, X., Beek, P., Walsh, T.: Binary vs. non-binary constraints. Artificial Intelligence 140(1-2), 1–37 (2002)
3. Bardin, S., Gotlieb, A.: FDCC: A Combined Approach for Solving Constraints over Finite Domains and Arrays. In: Beldiceanu, N., Jussien, N., Pinson, É. (eds.) CPAIOR 2012. LNCS, vol. 7298, pp. 17–33. Springer, Heidelberg (2012)
4. Bardin, S., Herrmann, P.: Osmose: Automatic structural testing of executables. Software Testing, Verification and Reliability (STVR) 21(1), 29–54 (2011)
5. Bardin, S., Herrmann, P., Perroud, F.: An Alternative to SAT-Based Approaches for Bit-Vectors. In: Esparza, J., Majumdar, R. (eds.) TACAS 2010. LNCS, vol. 6015, pp. 84–98. Springer, Heidelberg (2010)
6. Bessiere, C.: Constraint propagation. In: Handbook of Constraint Programming, ch. 3. Elsevier (2006)
7. Besson, F., Cornilleau, P.-E., Pichardie, D.: Modular smt proofs for fast reflexive checking inside coq. In: Jouannaud, Shao (eds.) [16]
8. Böhme, S., Fox, A., Sewell, T., Weber, T.: Reconstruction of z3's bit-vector proofs in hol4 and isabelle/hol. In: Shao, Jouannaud (eds.) [16]
9. Carlier, M., Dubois, C., Gotlieb, A.: A First Step in the Design of a Formally Verified Constraint-Based Testing Tool: FocalTest. In: Brucker, A.D., Julliand, J. (eds.) TAP 2012. LNCS, vol. 7305, pp. 35–50. Springer, Heidelberg (2012)
10. Bessiere, R.Y.C., Régin, J.-C., Zhang, Y.: An optimal coarse-grained arc consistency algorithm. Artificial Intelligence, pp. 165–185 (2005)
11. Collavizza, H., Rueher, M., Van Hentenryck, P.: Cpbpv: A constraint-programming framework for bounded program verification. Constraints Journal 15(2), 238–264 (2010)
12. Fontaine, P., Marion, J.-Y., Merz, S., Nieto, L.P., Tiu, A.F.: Expressiveness + Automation + Soundness: Towards Combining SMT Solvers and Interactive Proof Assistants. In: Hermanns, H. (ed.) TACAS 2006. LNCS, vol. 3920, pp. 167–181. Springer, Heidelberg (2006)
13. Godefroid, P., Klarlund, N.: Software Model Checking: Searching for Computations in the Abstract or the Concrete. In: Romijn, J.M.T., Smith, G.P., van de Pol, J. (eds.) IFM 2005. LNCS, vol. 3771, pp. 20–32. Springer, Heidelberg (2005)
14. Van Hentenryck, P., Saraswat, V., Deville, Y.: Design, implementation, and evaluation of the constraint language cc(fd). JLP 37, 139–164 (1998)
15. Holland, A., O'Sullivan, B.: Robust solutions for combinatorial auctions. In: Riedl, J., Kearns, M.J., Reiter, M.K. (eds.) ACM Conf. on Electronic Commerce (EC 2005), Vancouver, BC, Canada, pp. 183–192 (2005)
16. Jouannaud, J.-P., Shao, Z. (eds.): CPP 2011. LNCS, vol. 7086. Springer, Heidelberg (2011)
17. Leroy, X.: Formal verification of a realistic compiler. Communications of the ACM 52(7), 107–115 (2009)

18. Lescuyer, S., Conchon, S.: A Reflexive Formalization of a SAT Solver in Coq. In: Emerging Trends of the 21st Int. Conf. on Theorem Proving in Higher Order Logics, TPHOLs (2008)
19. Mackworth, A.: Consistency in networks of relations. Art. Intel. 8(1), 99–118 (1977)
20. McLaughlin, S., Barrett, C., Ge, Y.: Cooperating theorem provers: A case study combining hol-light and cvc lite. ENTCS, vol. 144(2) (January 2006)
21. Necula, G.C.: Proof-carrying code. In: POPL 1997, pp. 106–119 (1997)
22. Necula, G.C., Lee, P.: The design and implementation of a certifying compiler. In: PLDI 1998, pp. 333–344 (1998)
23. Rushby, J.: Verified software: Theories, tools, experiments. In: Automated Test Generation and Verified Software, pp. 161–172. Springer (2008)

Collaborative Verification and Testing with Explicit Assumptions

Maria Christakis, Peter Müller, and Valentin Wüstholz

ETH Zurich, Switzerland
{maria.christakis,peter.mueller,valentin.wuestholz}@inf.ethz.ch

Abstract. Many mainstream static code checkers make a number of compromises to improve automation, performance, and accuracy. These compromises include not checking certain program properties as well as making implicit, unsound assumptions. Consequently, the results of such static checkers do not provide definite guarantees about program correctness, which makes it unclear which properties remain to be tested. We propose a technique for collaborative verification and testing that makes compromises of static checkers explicit such that they can be compensated for by complementary checkers or testing. Our experiments suggest that our technique finds more errors and proves more properties than static checking alone, testing alone, and combinations that do not explicitly document the compromises made by static checkers. Our technique is also useful to obtain small test suites for partially-verified programs.

1 Introduction

Static program checkers are increasingly applied to detect defects in real-world programs. There is a wide variety of such checkers, ranging from relatively simple heuristic tools, over static program analyzers and software model checkers, to verifiers based on automatic theorem proving.

Although effective in detecting software bugs, many practical static checkers make compromises in order to increase automation, improve performance, and reduce both the number of false positives and the annotation overhead. These compromises include not checking certain properties and making implicit, unsound assumptions. For example, HAVOC [1] uses write effect specifications without checking them, Spec# [3] ignores arithmetic overflow and does not consider exceptional control flow, ESC/Java [16] unrolls loops a fixed number of times, and the Code Contracts static checker, Clousot [13], assumes that the arguments to a method call refer to disjoint memory regions, to name a few.

Due to these compromises, static checkers do not provide definite guarantees about the correctness of a program—as soon as a static checker makes a compromise, errors may be missed. This has three detrimental consequences: (1) Static checkers that make such compromises cannot ensure the absence of errors. (2) Even though one would expect static checking to reduce the test effort, it is unclear how to test exactly those properties that have not been soundly verified. In practice, programmers need to test their programs as if no static

D. Giannakopoulou and D. Méry (Eds.): FM 2012, LNCS 7436, pp. 132–146, 2012.

checking had been applied, which is inefficient. (3) Static checkers cannot be easily integrated to complement each other.

In this paper, we propose a technique that enables the combination of multiple, complementary static checkers and the reinforcement of static checking by automated, specification-based test case generation to check the program executions and properties that have not been soundly verified. Our technique handles sequential programs, properties that can be expressed by contract languages [12,20], and the typical compromises made by abstract interpreters and deductive verifiers. An extension to concurrent programs, more advanced properties (such as temporal properties), and the compromises made by model checkers (such as bounding the number of heap objects) are future work.

Our work is closely related to conditional model checking [6], which is an independently developed line of work. Both approaches make the results of static checking precise by tracking which properties have been verified, and under which assumptions. By documenting all compromises, a static checker becomes sound relatively to its compromises. However, accidental unsoundness, for instance due to bugs in the implementation of the checker, is neither handled nor prevented. Moreover, both approaches promote the collaboration of complementary static checkers and direct the static checking to the properties that have not been soundly verified. A detailed comparison of the two approaches is provided in Sect. 5. The three contributions made by our paper are:

1. It proposes a simple language extension for making many deliberate compromises of static checkers explicit and marking every program assertion as either fully verified, partially verified (that is, verified under certain assumptions), or not verified. This information is expressed via two new constructs whose semantics is defined in terms of assignments and assertions. They are, thus, easy to support by a wide range of static checkers. All assumptions are expressed at the program points where they are made. Therefore, *modular* static checkers may encode their verification results *locally* in the checked module (for instance, locally within a method). This is crucial to allow subsequent checkers to also operate modularly. Moreover, *local* assumptions and verification results are suitable to automatically generate *unit tests* for the module. We demonstrate the effectiveness of our language extension in encoding typical compromises of mainstream static checkers.

2. It presents a technique to automatically generate unit tests from the results of static checkers providing the user with a choice on how much effort to devote to static checking and how much to testing. For example, a user might run an automatic verifier without devoting any effort to making the verification succeed (for instance, without providing auxiliary specifications, such as loop invariants). The verifier may prove some properties correct, and our technique enables the effective testing of all others. Alternatively, a user might try to verify properties about critical components of a program and leave any remaining properties (e.g., about library components) for testing. Consequently, the degree of static checking is configurable and may range from zero to complete.

3. It enables a tool chain that directs the static checking and test case generation to the partially-verified or unverified properties. This leads to more targeted static checking and testing, in particular, smaller and more effective test suites. We implemented our tool chain based on an adaptation of the Dafny verifier [21] and the concolic testing tool Pex [24]. Our experiments suggest that our technique finds more errors and proves more properties than static checking alone, testing alone, and combined static checking and testing without our technique.

Outline. Sect. 2 gives a guided tour to our approach through an example. Sect. 3 explains how we encode the results and compromises of static checkers. We demonstrate the application of our technique to some typical verification scenarios in Sect. 4. We review related work in Sect. 5 and conclude in Sect. 6.

2 Guided Tour

This section gives a guided tour to collaborative verification and testing with explicit assumptions. Through a running example, we discuss the motivation behind the approach and the stages of the tool chain.

Running Example. Let us consider the C# program of Fig. 1 with .NET Code Contracts [12]. Method `foo` takes two `Cell` objects with non-zero values. The intention of the `if` statement is to guarantee that the two values have different signs and therefore, ensure that their product is negative. However, this program violates its postcondition in two cases: (1) The multiplications in the `if` and `return` statements (lines 16 and 20, respectively) might overflow and produce a positive result even if the integers have different signs. (2) In case parameters c and d reference the same object, the assignment on line 16 changes the sign of both `c.value` and `d.value` and the result is positive.

Checking this program with the Code Contracts static checker, Clousot, detects none of the errors because it ignores arithmetic overflow and uses a heap abstraction that assumes that method arguments are not aliased. A user who is not familiar with the tool's implicit assumptions does not know how to interpret the absence of warnings. Given that errors might be missed, the code has to be tested as if the checker had not run at all.

Running the Code Contracts testing tool, Pex, on method `foo` generates a test case that reveals the aliasing error, but misses the overflow error. Since no branch in the method's control flow depends on whether the multiplications in the `if` and `return` statements overflow, the tool does not generate a test case that exhibits this behavior. So, similarly to the static checker, the absence of errors provides no definite guarantee about program correctness.

Our technique enables collaborative verification and testing by making explicit which properties have been verified, and under which assumptions. The tool chain that we propose is presented in Fig. 2 and consists of two stages: static verification and testing.

```
1 public class Cell
2 {
3   public int value;
4
5   public static int foo(Cell c, Cell d)
6   {
7     Contract.Requires(c != null && d != null);
8     Contract.Requires(c.value != 0 && d.value != 0);
9     Contract.Ensures(Contract.Result<int>() < 0); // verified under a_na, a_ui0, a_ui1
10
11    // assumed c != d as a_na
12    if ((0 < c.value && 0 < d.value) || (c.value < 0 && d.value < 0))
13    {
14      // assumed new BigInteger(-1) * new BigInteger(c.value) ==
15      //         new BigInteger(-1 * c.value) as a_ui0
16      c.value = (-1) * c.value;
17    }
18    // assumed new BigInteger(c.value) * new BigInteger(d.value) ==
19    //         new BigInteger(c.value * d.value) as a_ui1
20    return c.value * d.value;
21  }
22 }
```

Fig. 1. Example program that illustrates the motivation for our technique. The method postcondition is violated if one of the multiplications overflows or if parameters c and d reference the same object. The comments document the compromises made by a checker that ignores arithmetic overflow and assumes that parameters are not aliased.

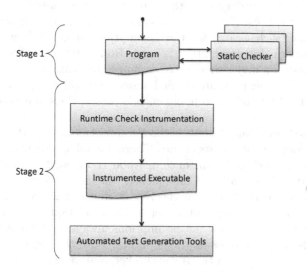

Fig. 2. The collaborative verification and testing tool chain. Tools are depicted by boxes and programs with specifications by flowchart document symbols.

Stage 1: Collaborative Verification. The static checking (or verification) stage allows the user to run an arbitrary number (possibly zero) of static checkers. Each checker reads the program, which contains the code, the specification, and the results of prior static checking attempts. More precisely, each assertion is marked to be either fully (that is, soundly) verified, partially verified under certain explicit assumptions, or not verified (that is, not attempted or failed to verify). A checker then attempts to prove the assertions that have not been fully verified by upstream tools. For this purpose, it may assume the properties that have already been fully verified. For partially-verified assertions, it is sufficient to show that the assumptions made by a prior checker hold or the assertions hold regardless of the assumptions, which simplifies the verification task. For instance, if the first checker verifies that all assertions hold assuming no arithmetic overflow occurs, then it is sufficient for a second (possibly specialized) checker to confirm this assumption. Each checker records its results in the program that serves as input to the next downstream tool.

The intermediate versions of the program precisely track which properties have been fully verified and which still need validation. This allows developers to stop the static verification cycle at any time, which is important in practice, where the effort that a developer can devote to static checking is limited. Any remaining unverified or partially-verified assertions may then be covered by the subsequent testing stage.

The comments in Fig. 1 illustrate the result of running the Code Contracts static checker on the example. The checker makes implicit assumptions in three places, for the non-aliasing of method arguments (line 11) and the unbounded integer arithmetic (lines 14 and 18). Since some assumptions depend on the current execution state, we document them at the place where they occur rather than where they are used to prove an assertion. We give each assumption a unique identifier (such as a_{na} for the assumption on line 11), which is used to document where this assumption is used. Running the checker verifies the method postcondition under these three assumptions, which we reflect by marking the postcondition as partially verified under assumptions a_{na}, a_{ui0}, and a_{ui1} (line 9). We will show how to formally encode assumptions and verification results in Sect. 3.

Note that the Code Contracts static checker works modularly, that is, it checks each method independently of its clients. Therefore, all assumptions are local to the method being checked; for instance, method foo is analyzed independently of any assumptions in its callers. Consequently, the method's verification results are suitable for subsequent modular checkers or unit test generation tools.

Since our example actually contains errors, any subsequent checker will neither be able to fully verify that the assumptions always hold nor that the postcondition holds in case the assumptions do not. Nevertheless, the assumptions document the precise result of the static checker, and we use this information to generate targeted test cases in the subsequent testing stage.

Stage 2: Testing. We apply dynamic symbolic execution [18,23], also called concolic testing [23], to automatically generate parameterized unit tests from the program code, the specification, and the results of static checking.

Concolic testing collects constraints describing the test data that will cause the program to take a particular branch in the execution or violate an assertion[1].

---

[1] An assertion is viewed as a conditional statement, where one branch throws an exception. A test case generation tool aiming for branch coverage will therefore attempt to generate test data that violates the assertion.

To use this mechanism, we instrument the program with assertions for those properties that have not been fully verified. That is, we assert all properties that have not been verified at all, and for partially-verified properties, we assert that the property holds in case the assumptions made by the static checker do not hold. This way, the properties that remain to be checked as well as the assumptions made by static checkers occur in the instrumented program, which causes the symbolic execution to generate the constraints and test data that exercise these properties.

In our example, the postcondition has been partially verified under three assumptions. The instrumentation therefore introduces an assertion for the property that all three assumptions hold or the original postcondition holds: $a_{na} \wedge a_{ui0} \wedge a_{ui1} \vee$ c.value * d.value < 0. Here, we use the assumption identifiers like boolean variables, which are assigned to when the assumption is made (see Sect. 3 for details), and we substitute the call to Contract.Result by the expression that method foo returns.

Running Pex on the instrumented version of the partially-verified program generates unit tests that reveal both errors, whereas without the instrumentation Pex finds only the aliasing error. A failing unit test is now also generated for the overflow error because the explicit assumptions on lines 14 and 18 of the program create additional branches in the method's control flow graph, thus enriching the constraints that are collected and solved by the testing tool.

In case the code must be fully verified, an alternative second stage of the tool chain could involve proving the remaining, precisely documented program properties with an interactive theorem prover. The intention then is to prove as many properties as possible automatically and to direct the manual effort towards proving the remaining properties. Yet another alternative is to use the explicit assumptions and partial verification results for targeted code reviews.

3   Verification Results with Explicit Assumptions

To make assumptions and (partially) verified properties explicit in the output of static checkers, we extend the programming and specification language with two new constructs: assumed statements and verified attributes for assertions. In this section, we present these extensions and define their semantics in terms of their weakest preconditions.

Extensions. An assumed statement of the form assumed P as a records that a checker assumed property P at a given point in the code. P is a predicate of the assertion language, and a is a unique *assumption identifier*, which can be used in verified attributes to express that a property has been verified using this assumption. assumed statements do not affect the semantics of the program, but they are used to define the semantics of verified attributes, as we discuss below. In particular, our assumed statements are different from the classical assume statements, which express properties that any static checker or testing tool may take for granted and need not check.

In our example of Fig. 1, the assumptions on lines 11, 14, and 18 will be formalized by adding **assumed** statements with the respective predicates. We also allow programmers, in addition to static checkers, to add **assumed** statements in their code, which is for instance useful when they want to verify the code only for certain cases and leave the other cases for testing.

In order to record (partial) verification results, we use assertions of the form **assert** V P, where P is a predicate of the assertion language and V is a set of **verified** attributes. A **verified** attribute has the form {**:verified** A}, where A is a set of assumption identifiers, each of which is declared in an **assumed** statement.

When a static checker verifies an assertion, it adds a **verified** attribute to the assertion that lists the assumptions used for its verification. Consequently, an assertion is unverified if it has no **verified** attributes, that is, V is empty (no static checker has verified the assertion). The assertion is fully verified if it has at least one **verified** attribute that has an empty assumption set A (at least one static checker has verified the assertion without making any assumptions). Otherwise, the assertion is partially verified.

Note that it is up to each individual verifier to determine which assumptions it used to verify an assertion. For instance, a verifier based on weakest preconditions could collect all assumptions that are on any path from the start of a method to the assertion; it could try to minimize the set of assumptions using techniques such as slicing to determine which assumptions actually influence the truth of the assertion. In our example, the assertion for the postcondition will be decorated with the attribute {**:verified** $\{a_{na}, a_{ui0}, a_{ui1}\}$} to indicate that the static checker used all three assumptions to verify the postcondition.

Semantics. The goal of collaborative verification and testing is to let static checkers and test case generation tools benefit from the (partial) verification results of earlier static checking attempts. This is achieved by defining a semantics for assertions that takes into account what has already been verified. For a fully-verified assertion, a static checker or test case generation tool later in the tool chain does not have to show anything. For partially-verified assertions, it is sufficient if a later tool shows that the assertion holds in case the assumptions made by earlier static checking attempts do not hold. We formalize this intuition as a weakest-precondition semantics.

In the semantics, we introduce a boolean *assumption variable* for each assumption identifier that occurs in an **assumed** statement; all assumption variables are initialized to true. For modular static checking, which checks each method individually, assumption variables are local variables of the method that contains the **assumed** statement. Assumptions of whole-program checking may be encoded via global variables. An **assumed** statement replaces the occurrence of an assumption variable by the assumed property:

$$wp(\textbf{assumed } P \textbf{ as } a, R) \equiv R[a := P]$$

where $R[a := P]$ denotes the substitution of a by P in R. This semantics ensures that an assumption is evaluated in the state in which it is made rather than the state in which it is used. Since each assumption variable is initialized to true, every occurrence of an assumption variable in a weakest-precondition computation will eventually be substituted either by the assumed property or by true in those execution paths that do not include an **assumed** statement for that assumption variable.

We define the semantics of assertions as follows:

$$wp(\texttt{assert V } P, R) \equiv \left(\left(\bigvee_{A \in V} CA(A) \right) \vee P \right) \wedge (P \Rightarrow R)$$

where $CA(A)$ denotes the conjunction of all assumptions in one **verified** attribute (all assumptions of one static checker). That is, $CA(A) \equiv \bigwedge_{a \in A} var(a)$, where $var(a)$ is the assumption variable for the assumption identifier a.

The first conjunct in the weakest precondition expresses that in order to fully verify the assertion, it is sufficient to show that all assumptions made by one of the checkers actually hold or that the asserted property P holds anyway. The disjunction weakens the assertions and therefore, lets tools benefit from the partial results of prior static checks. Note that in the special case that one of the **verified** attributes has an empty assumption set A, $CA(A)$ is true, and the first conjunct of the weakest precondition trivially holds (that is, the assertion has been fully verified and nothing remains to be checked). Since the first conjunct of the weakest precondition ensures that assertion P is verified, the second conjunct requires only that postcondition R is verified under the assumption that P holds.

In our example, the weakest precondition of the partially-verified postcondition is $a_{na} \wedge a_{ui0} \wedge a_{ui1} \vee \texttt{c.value * d.value < 0}$. As we explained in Sect. 2, we use this condition to instrument the program for the test case generation.

When multiple static checkers (partially) verify an assertion, we record each of their results in a separate **verified** attribute. However, these attributes are not a mere accumulation of the results of independent static checking attempts. Due to the above semantics, the property to be verified typically becomes weaker with each checking attempt. Therefore, many properties can eventually be fully verified, without making any further assumptions. The remaining ones can be tested or verified interactively.

4   Examples

For the evaluation of our tool chain and the underlying technique, we used the Dafny language and verifier, and the testing tool Pex. Dafny is an imperative, class-based programming language with built-in specification constructs to support sound static verification. For our purposes, we extended the Dafny language with the **assumed** statements and **verified** attributes of Sect. 3, and changed the Dafny verifier to simulate common compromises made by mainstream static checkers. For the instrumentation phase of the architecture, we extended the existing Dafny-to-C# compiler to generate runtime checks, expressed as Code Contracts, for program properties that have not been fully verified.

In this section, we demonstrate how common compromises may be encoded with our language extensions and subsequently tested. We apply our technique to three verification scenarios and show that it finds more errors than the architecture's constituent tools alone and achieves small, targeted test suites.

4.1   Encoding of Common Compromises

To simulate common compromises, we implemented three variants of the Dafny verifier: (1) ignoring arithmetic overflow, like e.g. Spec#, (2) unrolling loops a fixed number of times, like e.g. ESC/Java, and (3) using write effect specifications without checking them, like e.g. HAVOC.

Unbounded Integers. A common compromise of static checkers is to ignore overflow in bounded integer arithmetic, as in the case of ESC/Java and Spec#. To model this behavior in Dafny, which uses unbounded integers, we adapted the verifier to add explicit assumptions about unbounded integer arithmetic and modified the compiler to use bounded (32-bit) integers.

We use `BigInteger` to express that a static checker that ignores arithmetic overflow considers bounded integer expressions in the code to be equivalent to their mathematical counterparts. For instance, the assumption that the expression `c.value * d.value` from Fig. 1 does not lead to an overflow is expressed as:

```
assumed new BigInteger(c.value) * new BigInteger(d.value) ==
        new BigInteger(c.value * d.value) as $a_{ui1}$;
```

Loop Unrolling. To avoid the annotation overhead of loop invariants, some static checkers unroll loops a fixed number of times. For instance, ESC/Java unrolls loops 1.5 times by default: first, the condition of the loop is evaluated and in case it holds, the loop body is checked once; then, the loop condition is evaluated again after assuming its negation. As a result, the code following the loop is checked under the assumption that the loop iterates at most once.

This compromise cannot be modeled using explicit assumptions alone. For this reason, we implemented a variant of the Dafny verifier that transforms loops as shown in Fig. 3. After unrolling the loop once, an explicit assumption is added which states that the loop condition does not hold. Assertions following the `assumed` statement are verified under this assumption. Note that the loop is still part of the transformed program so that the original semantics is preserved for downstream static checkers, which might not make the same compromise, and testing tools.

Write Effects. Another compromise made by static tools, such as HAVOC and ESC/Java, involves assuming write effect specifications without checking them. We encode this compromise by simply leaving all the required checks unverified, that is, by not marking them with a `verified` attribute.

Original loop.   Transformed loop.

```
while (C) {                     if (C) {
  B                               B
}                               }
                                assumed ¬C as a;
                                while (C) {
                                  B
                                }
```

Fig. 3. Loop transformation and explicit assumption about loop unrolling. The loop is unrolled 1.5 times.

4.2   Improved Defect Detection

Having shown how `assumed` statements may be used to encode common compromises of static checkers, we will now discuss two scenarios in which Pex exploits explicit assumptions made by upstream static checkers to find more errors than any of these tools alone.

Scenario 1: Overflow Errors. The method of Fig. 4 computes the sum of squares $\sum_{i=\text{from}}^{\text{to}} i^2$, where `from` and `to` are input parameters. When we run the version of the Dafny verifier that ignores arithmetic overflow on this method, no verification errors are reported and the invariant is partially verified under explicit assumptions about unbounded integer arithmetic. For instance, an `assumed` statement with predicate

```
new BigInteger(i) + new BigInteger(1) == new BigInteger(i + 1)
```

is added before line 10. Running Pex on the original method, where the invariant has been translated into two Code Contracts assertions (one before the loop and one at the end of the loop body), generates five failing unit tests in all of which the invariant is violated before the loop due to an overflow. However, when we run Pex on the partially-verified program produced by the verifier, an additional failing unit test is generated revealing a new error: the invariant is not preserved by the loop due to an overflow in the loop body.

In analyzing these results, we notice that without the explicit assumptions Pex is not able to craft appropriate input values for the method parameters such that

```
0 static method SumOfSquares(from: int, to: int) returns (r: int)
1   requires from ≤ to;
2 {
3   r := from * from;
4   var i := from + 1;
5   while (i ≤ to)
6     invariant from * from ≤ r;
7     decreases to - i;
8   {
9     r := r + i * i;
10    i := i + 1;
11  }
12 }
```

Fig. 4. Method that computes the sum of squares $\sum_{i=\text{from}}^{\text{to}} i^2$. The loop invariant is violated in case an integer overflow occurs before the loop or in the loop body.

the invariant preservation error also be revealed. This is because after a bounded number of loop iterations the constraints imposed by the invariant become too complex for the underlying constraint solver to solve under certain time limits, if at all. However, the explicit assumptions added by the verifier create new branches in the method's control flow graph which Pex tries to explore. It is these branches that enrich the tool's path constraints and guide it in picking input values that reveal the remaining error.

Scenario 2: Aliasing Errors. In this scenario, we consider an object hierarchy in which class `Student` and interface `ITeacher` both inherit from interface `IAcademicPerson`, and class `TeachingAssistant` inherits both from class `Student` and interface `ITeacher`. Interface `IAcademicPerson` declares a method `Evaluate` for giving an evaluation grade to an academic person, and a method `Evaluations` for getting all the evaluation grades given to an academic person. Method `EvaluateTeacher` of Fig. 5 takes a student and a rating for the teacher that is associated with the student, and ensures that evaluating the teacher does not affect the student's evaluation grades. The postcondition may be violated when a teaching assistant that is their own teacher is passed to the method. Clousot misses this error because of its heap abstraction, which assumes that certain forms of aliasing do not occur. Pex is also unable to generate a failing unit test because no constraint forces it to generate an object structure that would reveal the error. However, with the explicit assumption shown on line 7 of Fig. 5, Pex does produce a unit test revealing this error.

```
1 public static void EvaluateTeacher(Student s, char rating)
2 {
3    Contract.Requires(s != null && s.Teacher() != null && "ABCDF".Contains(rating));
4    Contract.Ensures(s.Evaluations() ==              // verified under a_nse
5                     Contract.OldValue<string>(s.Evaluations()));
6
7    // assumed s.Teacher() != s as a_nse
8    s.Teacher().Evaluate(rating);
9 }
```

Fig. 5. Method for the evaluation of a student's teacher. The postcondition may be violated when a teaching assistant that is their own teacher is passed to the method.

4.3   Small Test Suites

In addition to finding more errors, our technique is also useful in obtaining small, targeted test suites for partially-verified programs as methods that are fully verified need not be tested. To illustrate this, we developed a `List` class with a number of common list operations: the constructor of the list and methods `Length`, `Equals`, `ContainsElement`, `Head`, `Tail`, `LastElement`, `Prepend`, `Append`, `Concatenate`, `Clone`, and `ReverseInPlace`[2]. This implementation is written in Dafny, consists of about 270 lines of code, and may be found at the URL http://www.pm.inf.ethz.ch/publications/FM12/List.dfy.

---

[2] `ReverseInPlace` is the only method that is implemented iteratively.

In order to simulate a realistic usage scenario of our tool chain, we decided to spend no more than two hours on attempting to soundly verify the code. By the end of that time frame, we had not managed to complete the proof of the `ReverseInPlace` method and were obliged to add `assumed` statements in methods `Equals` and `ContainsElement`.

To evaluate the effectiveness of our technique in achieving small test suites, we compared the size of the suite that was generated by running Pex alone on the list implementation to the number of unit tests that were produced with collaborative verification and testing. For the verification stage of the tool chain, we employed the following four variants of the Dafny verifier: sound verification (S), verification with unbounded integer arithmetic (UIA), verification with loop unrolling (LU), and verification with unbounded integer arithmetic and loop unrolling (UIA & LU). Table 1 shows the percentage by which the size of the test suite was reduced using our technique, and the methods that were still tested (that is, had not been fully verified) in each of the aforementioned verification attempts.

Table 1. Effectiveness of our technique in achieving small test suites

Verification	Test Reduction	Tested Methods
S	66%	Equals, ContainsElement, ReverseInPlace
UIA	58%	Length, Equals, ContainsElement, ReverseInPlace
LU	65%	Equals, ContainsElement, ReverseInPlace
UIA & LU	58%	Length, Equals, ContainsElement, ReverseInPlace

5 Related Work

Many automatic static checkers that target mainstream programming languages make compromises to improve performance and reduce the number of false positives and the annotation overhead. We already mentioned some of the compromises made by HAVOC, Spec#, ESC/Java, and the Code Contracts static checker. In addition to those, KeY [4] does not soundly support multi-object invariants, Krakatoa [14] does not handle class invariants and class initialization soundly, and Frama-C [7] uses plug-ins for various analyses with possibly conflicting assumptions. Our technique would allow these tools to collaborate and be effectively complemented by automatic test case generation.

Integration of Checkers. The work most closely related to ours is conditional model checking (CMC) [6], which combines complementary model checkers to improve performance and state-space coverage. A conditional model checker takes as input the program and specification to be verified as well as a condition that describes the states that have already been checked, and it produces another such condition to encode the results of the verification. The focus of CMC is on encoding the typical limitations of model checkers, such as space-out and time-out, but it can also encode compromises such as assuming that no arithmetic overflow occurs. Beyer et al. performed a detailed experimental evaluation that demonstrates the benefits of making assumptions and partial verification results explicit, which is in line with our findings. Despite these similarities, there are significant technical differences between CMC and our approach. First, as is common in model checking, CMC is presented as a whole-program analysis, and the resulting condition may contain assumptions about the whole program. For instance, the verification of a method may depend on assumptions made in its callers. By contrast, we have demonstrated how to integrate modular static analyzers, such as Clousot, and deductive verifiers, such as Dafny and Spec#. Second, although Beyer et al. mention test case generation as a possible application of CMC, they do not explain how to generate test cases from the conditions. Since these conditions may include nonlocal assumptions, they might be used to generate *system* tests, whereas the generation of *unit* tests seems challenging. However, test case generation tools based on constraint solving (such as symbolic execution and concolic testing) do not scale well to the large execution paths that occur in system tests. By contrast, we have demonstrated how to use concolic testing to generate unit tests from our local assumptions and verification results.

A common form of tool integration is to support static checkers with inference tools, such as Houdini [15] for ESC/Java or Daikon [11] for the Java PathFinder [19] tool. Such combinations either assume that the inference is sound and thus, do not handle the compromises addressed in our work, or they verify every property that has been inferred, which is overly conservative and increases the verification effort. Our technique enables a more effective tool integration by making all design compromises explicit.

Integration of Verification and Testing. Various approaches combine verification and testing mainly to determine whether a static verification error is spurious. Check 'n' Crash [9] is an automated defect detection tool that integrates the ESC/Java static checker with the JCrasher [8] testing tool in order to decide whether errors emitted by the static checker truly exist. Check 'n' Crash was later integrated with Daikon in the DSD-Crasher tool [10]. DyTa [17] integrates the Code Contracts static checker with Pex to reduce the number of spurious errors compared to static verification alone and perform more efficiently compared to dynamic test generation alone. Confirming whether a failing verification attempt refers to a real error is also possible in our technique: The instrumentation phase of the architecture introduces assertions for each property that has not been statically verified (which includes the case of a failing verification attempt). The testing phase then uses these assertions to direct test case generation towards the unproved properties. Eventually, the testing tools might generate either a series of successful test cases that will boost the user's confidence about the correctness of their programs or concrete counterexamples that reproduce an error.

A perhaps more precise approach towards the same direction as the aforementioned tools is counterexample-guided abstraction refinement (CEGAR) [2,5].

CEGAR exploits the abstract counterexample trace of a failing proof attempt to suggest a concrete trace that might reveal a real error. If, however, the abstract trace refers to a spurious error, the abstraction is refined in such a way that subsequent verification attempts will not reproduce the infeasible abstract trace. More recently, YOGI [22], a tool for checking properties of C programs, was developed to refine CEGAR with concolic execution. Such techniques, if regarded as tool chains, address the issue of program correctness from the opposite direction than we do: they use concrete traces to refine static over-approximations, whereas, in our work, combinations of potential under-approximations made by different static checkers are checked by the testing tools. If, on the other hand, these techniques are regarded as single tools, they could also be integrated in our architecture.

6   Conclusion

We have presented a technique for collaborative verification and testing that makes compromises of static checkers explicit with a simple language extension. In our approach, the verification results give definite answers about program correctness allowing for the integration of multiple, complementary static checkers and the generation of more effective unit test suites. Our experiments suggest that our technique finds more errors and proves more properties than verification alone, testing alone, and combined verification and testing without the explicit assumptions. As future work, we plan to implement our technique for Spec# and the Code Contracts static checker and to use them for experiments on large code bases. We expect such experiments to shed light on the impact of some design compromises and suggest guidelines for the effective use of static checkers in industrial projects.

Acknowledgments. We would like to thank Alexander Summers and the anonymous reviewers for their helpful comments.

References

1. Ball, T., Hackett, B., Lahiri, S.K., Qadeer, S., Vanegue, J.: Towards Scalable Modular Checking of User-Defined Properties. In: Leavens, G.T., O'Hearn, P., Rajamani, S.K. (eds.) VSTTE 2010. LNCS, vol. 6217, pp. 1–24. Springer, Heidelberg (2010)
2. Ball, T., Rajamani, S.K.: The SLAM project: Debugging system software via static analysis. In: POPL, pp. 1–3. ACM (2002)
3. Barnett, M., Fähndrich, M., Leino, K.R.M., Müller, P., Schulte, W., Venter, H.: Specification and verification: The Spec# experience. CACM 54, 81–91 (2011)
4. Beckert, B., Hähnle, R., Schmitt, P.H. (eds.): Verification of Object-Oriented Software. The KeY Approach. LNCS (LNAI), vol. 4334. Springer, Heidelberg (2007)
5. Beyer, D., Henzinger, T.A., Jhala, R., Majumdar, R.: The software model checker BLAST: Applications to software engineering. STTT 9, 505–525 (2007)
6. Beyer, D., Henzinger, T.A., Keremoglu, M.E., Wendler, P.: Conditional model checking. CoRR, abs/1109.6926 (2011)

7. Correnson, L., Cuoq, P., Kirchner, F., Prevosto, V., Puccetti, A., Signoles, J., Yakobowski, B.: Frama-C User Manual (2011), http://frama-c.com//support.html
8. Csallner, C., Smaragdakis, Y.: JCrasher: An automatic robustness tester for Java. SPE 34, 1025–1050 (2004)
9. Csallner, C., Smaragdakis, Y.: Check 'n' Crash: Combining static checking and testing. In: ICSE, pp. 422–431. ACM (2005)
10. Csallner, C., Smaragdakis, Y., Xie, T.: DSD-Crasher: A hybrid analysis tool for bug finding. TOSEM 17, 1–37 (2008)
11. Ernst, M.D., Perkins, J.H., Guo, P.J., McCamant, S., Pacheco, C., Tschantz, M.S., Xiao, C.: The Daikon system for dynamic detection of likely invariants. Sci. Comput. Program. 69, 35–45 (2007)
12. Fähndrich, M., Barnett, M., Logozzo, F.: Embedded contract languages. In: SAC, pp. 2103–2110. ACM (2010)
13. Fähndrich, M., Logozzo, F.: Static Contract Checking with Abstract Interpretation. In: Beckert, B., Marché, C. (eds.) FoVeOOS 2010. LNCS, vol. 6528, pp. 10–30. Springer, Heidelberg (2011)
14. Filliâtre, J.-C., Marché, C.: The Why/Krakatoa/Caduceus Platform for Deductive Program Verification. In: Damm, W., Hermanns, H. (eds.) CAV 2007. LNCS, vol. 4590, pp. 173–177. Springer, Heidelberg (2007)
15. Flanagan, C., Leino, K.R.M.: Houdini, an Annotation Assistant for ESC/Java. In: Oliveira, J.N., Zave, P. (eds.) FME 2001. LNCS, vol. 2021, pp. 500–517. Springer, Heidelberg (2001)
16. Flanagan, C., Leino, K.R.M., Lillibridge, M., Nelson, G., Saxe, J.B., Stata, R.: Extended static checking for Java. In: PLDI, pp. 234–245. ACM (2002)
17. Ge, X., Taneja, K., Xie, T., Tillmann, N.: DyTa: Dynamic symbolic execution guided with static verification results. In: ICSE, pp. 992–994. ACM (2011)
18. Godefroid, P., Klarlund, N., Sen, K.: DART: Directed automated random testing. In: PLDI, pp. 213–223. ACM (2005)
19. Havelund, K., Pressburger, T.: Model checking JAVA programs using JAVA PathFinder. STTT 2, 366–381 (2000)
20. Leavens, G.T., Poll, E., Clifton, C., Cheon, Y., Ruby, C., Cok, D., Müller, P., Kiniry, J., Chalin, P., Zimmerman, D.M., Dietl, W.: JML Reference Manual (2011), http://www.jmlspecs.org/
21. Leino, K.R.M.: Dafny: An Automatic Program Verifier for Functional Correctness. In: Clarke, E.M., Voronkov, A. (eds.) LPAR-16 2010. LNCS, vol. 6355, pp. 348–370. Springer, Heidelberg (2010)
22. Nori, A.V., Rajamani, S.K., Tetali, S., Thakur, A.V.: The YOGI Project: Software Property Checking via Static Analysis and Testing. In: Kowalewski, S., Philippou, A. (eds.) TACAS 2009. LNCS, vol. 5505, pp. 178–181. Springer, Heidelberg (2009)
23. Sen, K., Marinov, D., Agha, G.: CUTE: A concolic unit testing engine for C. In: ESEC, pp. 263–272. ACM (2005)
24. Tillmann, N., de Halleux, J.: Pex–White Box Test Generation for .NET. In: Beckert, B., Hähnle, R. (eds.) TAP 2008. LNCS, vol. 4966, pp. 134–153. Springer, Heidelberg (2008)

TLA+ Proofs

Denis Cousineau[1], Damien Doligez[2], Leslie Lamport[3], Stephan Merz[4],
Daniel Ricketts[5], and Hernán Vanzetto[4]

[1] Inria - Université Paris Sud, Orsay, France**
[2] Inria, Paris, France
[3] Microsoft Research, Mountain View, CA, U.S.A.
[4] Inria Nancy & LORIA, Villers-lès-Nancy, France
[5] Department of Computer Science, University of California, San Diego, U.S.A.

Abstract. TLA+ is a specification language based on standard set theory and temporal logic that has constructs for hierarchical proofs. We describe how to write TLA+ proofs and check them with TLAPS, the TLA+ Proof System. We use Peterson's mutual exclusion algorithm as a simple example and show how TLAPS and the Toolbox (an IDE for TLA+) help users to manage large, complex proofs.

1 Introduction

TLA+ [5] is a specification language originally designed for specifying concurrent and distributed systems and their properties. It is based on Zermelo-Fraenkel set theory for modeling data structures and on the linear-time temporal logic TLA for specifying system executions and their properties. More recently, constructs for writing proofs have been added to TLA+, following a proposal for presenting rigorous hand proofs in a hierarchical style [8].

In this paper, we present the main ideas that guided the design of the proof language and its implementation in TLAPS, the TLA+ proof system [3,13]. The proof language and TLAPS have been designed to be independent of any particular theorem prover. All interaction takes place at the level of TLA+. Users need know only what sort of reasoning TLAPS's backend provers tend to be good at—for example, that SMT solvers excel at arithmetic. This knowledge is gained mostly by experience.

TLAPS has a *Proof Manager* (PM) that transforms a proof into individual proof obligations that it sends to backend provers. Currently, the main backend provers are Isabelle/TLA+, an encoding of TLA+ as an object logic in Isabelle [14], Zenon [2], a tableau prover for classical first-order logic with equality, and a backend for SMT solvers. Isabelle serves as the most trusted backend prover, and when possible, we expect backend provers to produce a detailed proof that is checked by Isabelle. This is currently implemented for the Zenon backend.

TLAPS has been integrated into the TLA+ Toolbox, an IDE (Integrated Development Environment) based on Eclipse for writing TLA+ specifications and

** This work was partially funded by Inria-Microsoft Research Joint Centre, France.

running the TLA⁺ tools on them, including the TLC model checker. The Toolbox provides commands to hide and unhide parts of a proof, allowing a user to focus on a given proof step and its context. It is also invaluable to be able to run the model checker on the same formulas that one reasons about.

We explain how to write and check TLA⁺ proofs, using a tiny well-known example: a proof that Peterson's algorithm [12] implements mutual exclusion. We start by writing the algorithm in PlusCal [6], an algorithm language that is based on the expression language of TLA⁺. The PlusCal code is translated to a TLA⁺ specification, which is what we reason about. Section 3 introduces the salient features of the proof language and of TLAPS with the proof of mutual exclusion. Liveness of Peterson's algorithm (processes eventually enter their critical section) can also be asserted and proved with TLA⁺. However, liveness reasoning makes full use of temporal logic, and TLAPS cannot yet check temporal logic proofs.

Section 4 indicates the features that make TLA⁺, TLAPS, and the Toolbox scale to realistic examples. A concluding section summarizes what we have done and our plans for future work.

2   Modeling Peterson's Algorithm in TLA⁺

Peterson's algorithm is a classic, very simple two-process mutual exclusion algorithm. We specify the algorithm in TLA⁺ and prove that it satisfies mutual exclusion: no two processes are in their critical sections at the same time.[1]

A representation of Peterson's algorithm in the PlusCal algorithm language is shown on the left-hand side of Figure 1. The two processes are named 0 and 1; the PlusCal code is embedded in a TLA⁺ module that defines an operator Not so that $Not(0) = 1$ and $Not(1) = 0$.

The **variables** statement declares the variables and their initial values. For example, the initial value of $flag$ is an array such that $flag[0] = flag[1] =$ FALSE. (Mathematically, an array is a function; the TLA⁺ notation $[x \in S \mapsto e]$ for writing functions is similar to a lambda expression.) To specify a multiprocess algorithm, it is necessary to specify what its atomic actions are. In PlusCal, an atomic action consists of the execution from one label to the next. With this brief explanation, the reader should be able to figure out what the code means.

A translator, normally called from the Toolbox, generates a TLA⁺ specification from the PlusCal code. We illustrate the structure of the TLA⁺ translation in the right-hand part of Figure 1. The heart of the TLA⁺ specification consists of the predicates $Init$ describing the initial state and $Next$, which represents the next-state relation.

The PlusCal translator adds a variable pc to record the control state of each process. The meaning of formula $Init$ in the figure is straightforward. The formula $Next$ is the disjunction of the two formulas $proc(0)$ and $proc(1)$, which are in turn defined as disjunctions of formulas corresponding to the atomic steps of the **process**. In these formulas, unprimed variables refer to the old state and

---

[1] The TLA⁺ module containing the specification and proof as well as an extended version of this paper are accessible at the TLAPS Web page [13].

--**algorithm** Peterson {
  variables
    flag = [*i* ∈ {0,1} ↦ FALSE],
    turn = 0;
  process (*proc* ∈ {0,1}) {
   a0: **while** (TRUE) {
   a1:   *flag*[*self*] := TRUE;
   a2:   *turn* := *Not*(*self*);
   a3a: **if** (*flag*[*Not*(*self*)])
          {goto *a3b*}
        else **{goto** *cs*} ;
   a3b: **if** (*turn* = *Not*(*self*))
          {goto *a3a*}
        else **{goto** *cs*} ;
   cs: **skip**; * critical section
   a4: *flag*[*self*] := FALSE;
      } * end while
  } * end process
} * end algorithm

VARIABLES *flag, turn, pc*

$$vars \triangleq \langle flag, turn, pc\rangle$$

$$Init \triangleq \wedge flag = [i \in \{0,1\} \mapsto \text{FALSE}]$$
$$\wedge turn = 0$$
$$\wedge pc = [self \in \{0,1\} \mapsto \text{"a0"}]$$

$$a3a(self) \triangleq$$
$$\wedge pc[self] = \text{"a3a"}$$
$$\wedge \text{IF } flag[Not(self)]$$
$$\text{THEN } pc' = [pc \text{ EXCEPT } ![self] = \text{"a3b"}]$$
$$\text{ELSE } pc' = [pc \text{ EXCEPT } ![self] = \text{"cs"}]$$
$$\wedge \text{UNCHANGED } \langle flag, turn\rangle$$

* remaining actions omitted

$$proc(self) \triangleq a0(self) \vee \ldots \vee a4(self)$$
$$Next \triangleq \exists\, self \in \{0,1\} : proc(self)$$
$$Spec \triangleq Init \wedge \square[Next]_{vars}$$

Fig. 1. Peterson's algorithm in PlusCal (left) and in TLA$^+$ (excerpt, right)

primed variables to the new state. The temporal formula *Spec* is the complete specification. It characterizes behaviors (ω-sequences of states) that start in a state satisfying *Init* and where every pair of successive states either satisfies *Next* or else leaves the values of the tuple *vars* unchanged.[2]

Before trying to prove that the algorithm is correct, we use TLC, the TLA$^+$ model checker, to check it for errors. The Toolbox runs TLC on a model of a TLA$^+$ specification. A model usually assigns particular values to specification constants, such as the number of processes. It can also restrict the set of states explored, which is useful if the specification allows an infinite number of reachable states. TLC easily verifies that the two processes can never both be at label *cs* by checking that the following formula is an invariant (true in all reachable states):

$$MutualExclusion \triangleq (pc[0] \neq \text{"cs"}) \vee (pc[1] \neq \text{"cs"})$$

Peterson's algorithm is so simple that TLC can check all possible executions. For more interesting algorithms that have parameters (such as the number of processes) and perhaps an infinite set of reachable states, TLC cannot exhaustively verify all executions, and correctness can only be proved deductively. Still, TLC is invaluable for catching errors, and it is much easier to run TLC than to write a formal proof.

3   Proving Mutual Exclusion for Peterson's Algorithm

The assertion that Peterson's algorithm implements mutual exclusion is formalized in TLA$^+$ as the theorem in Figure 2. The standard method of proving this

---

[2] "Stuttering steps" are allowed in order to make refinement simple [4].

THEOREM $Spec \Rightarrow \Box MutualExclusion$
$\langle 1 \rangle 1.$ $Init \Rightarrow Inv$
$\langle 1 \rangle 2.$ $Inv \wedge [Next]_{vars} \Rightarrow Inv'$
$\langle 1 \rangle 3.$ $Inv \Rightarrow MutualExclusion$
$\langle 1 \rangle 4.$ QED

Fig. 2. The high-level proof

invariance property is to find an inductive invariant Inv such that the steps $\langle 1 \rangle 1$–$\langle 1 \rangle 3$ of Figure 2 are provable.

TLA$^+$ proofs are hierarchically structured and are generally written top-down. Each proof in the hierarchy ends with a QED step that asserts the proof's goal. We usually write the QED step's proof before the proofs of the intermediate steps. The QED step follows easily from steps $\langle 1 \rangle 1$–$\langle 1 \rangle 3$ by standard proof rules of temporal logic. However, TLAPS does not yet handle temporal reasoning, so we omit that step's proof. When temporal reasoning is added to TLAPS, we expect it easily to check such a trivial proof.

Figure 3 defines the inductive invariant Inv as the conjunction of two formulas. (A definition must precede its use, so the definition of Inv appears in the module before the proof.) The first, $TypeOK$, asserts simply that the values of all variables are elements of the expected sets. (The expression $[S \rightarrow T]$ is the set of all functions whose domain is S and whose range is a subset of T.) In an untyped logic like that of TLA$^+$, almost any inductive invariant must assert type correctness. The second conjunct, I, is the interesting one that explains why Peterson's algorithm implements mutual exclusion. We again use TLC to check that Inv is indeed an invariant. In our simple example, TLC can even check that Inv is inductive, by checking that it is an (ordinary) invariant of the specification $Inv \wedge \Box [Next]_{vars}$, obtained from $Spec$ by replacing the initial condition by Inv.

We now prove steps $\langle 1 \rangle 1$–$\langle 1 \rangle 3$. We can prove them in any order; let us start with $\langle 1 \rangle 1$. This step follows easily from the definitions, and the following leaf proof is accepted by TLAPS:

BY DEF $Init$, Inv, $TypeOK$, I

$TypeOK \triangleq \wedge\ pc \in [\,\{0,1\} \rightarrow \{\,\text{"a0"}, \text{"a1"}, \text{"a2"}, \text{"a3a"}, \text{"a3b"}, \text{"cs"}, \text{"a4"}\,\}\,]$
$\qquad\qquad\quad \wedge\ turn \in \{0,1\}$
$\qquad\qquad\quad \wedge\ flag \in [\,\{0,1\} \rightarrow \text{BOOLEAN}\,]$

$I \triangleq \forall i \in \{0,1\}:$
$\qquad \wedge\ pc[i] \in \{\,\text{"a2"}, \text{"a3a"}, \text{"a3b"}, \text{"cs"}, \text{"a4"}\,\} \Rightarrow flag[i]$
$\qquad \wedge\ pc[i] \in \{\,\text{"cs"}, \text{"a4"}\,\} \Rightarrow \wedge\ pc[Not(i)] \notin \{\,\text{"cs"}, \text{"a4"}\,\}$
$\qquad\qquad\qquad\qquad\qquad\qquad\qquad\quad \wedge\ pc[Not(i)] \in \{\,\text{"a3a"}, \text{"a3b"}\,\} \Rightarrow turn = i$

$Inv \triangleq TypeOK \wedge I$

Fig. 3. The inductive invariant

⟨1⟩2. $Inv \land [Next]_{vars} \Rightarrow Inv'$
   ⟨2⟩1. SUFFICES ASSUME $Inv, Next$ PROVE Inv'
   ⟨2⟩2. $TypeOK'$
   ⟨2⟩3. I'
      ⟨3⟩1. SUFFICES ASSUME NEW $j \in \{0,1\}$ PROVE $I!(j)'$
      ⟨3⟩2. PICK $i \in \{0,1\} : proc(i)$
      ⟨3⟩3. CASE $i = j$
      ⟨3⟩4. CASE $i \neq j$
      ⟨3⟩5. QED
   ⟨2⟩4. QED

Fig. 4. Outline of a hierarchical proof of step ⟨1⟩2

TLAPS will not expand definitions unless directed to so. In complex proofs, automatically expanding definitions often leads to formulas that are too big for provers to handle. Forgetting to expand some definition is a common mistake. If a proof does not succeed, the Toolbox displays the exact proof obligation that it passed to the prover. It is then usually easy to see which definitions need to be invoked.

Step ⟨1⟩3 is proved the same way, by simply expanding the definitions of *MutualExclusion*, *Inv*, *I*, and *Not*. We next try the same technique on ⟨1⟩2. A little thought shows that we have to tell TLAPS to expand all the definitions in the module up to and including the definition of *Next*, except for the definition of *Init*. Unfortunately, when we direct TLAPS to prove the step, it fails to do so, reporting a 65-line proof obligation.

TLAPS uses Zenon and Isabelle as its default backend provers. However, TLAPS also includes an SMT solver backend [10] that is capable of handling larger "shallow" proof obligations—in particular, ones that do not contain significant quantifier reasoning. We instruct TLAPS to use the SMT backend when proving the current step by writing

   BY SMT DEF ...

The backend translates the proof obligation to the input language of SMT solvers. In this way, step ⟨1⟩2 is proved in a few seconds. For sufficiently complicated algorithms, an SMT solver will not be able to prove inductive invariance as a single obligation. Instead, the proof will have to be hierarchically decomposed. We illustrate how this is done by writing a proof of ⟨1⟩2 that can be checked using only the Zenon and Isabelle backend provers.

The outline of a hierarchical proof of step ⟨1⟩2 appears in Figure 4. The proof introduces more elements of the TLA+ proof language that we now explain.

A SUFFICES step allows a user to introduce an auxiliary assertion, from which the current goal can be proved. For example, step ⟨2⟩1 reduces the proof of the implication asserted in step ⟨1⟩2 to assuming predicates *Inv* and *Next*, and proving *Inv'*. In particular, this step establishes that the invariant is preserved by stuttering steps that leave the tuple *vars* unchanged. Steps ⟨2⟩2 and ⟨2⟩3 establish the two conjuncts in the definition of *Inv*. Whereas $\langle 2 \rangle 2$ can be proved directly by Isabelle, $\langle 2 \rangle 3$ needs some more interaction.

Following the definition of predicate I as a universally quantified formula, we introduce in step $\langle 3 \rangle 1$ a new variable j, assume that $j \in \{0, 1\}$, and prove $I!(j)'$, which denotes the body of the universally quantified formula, with j substituted for the bound variable, and with primed copies of all state variables. Similarly, step $\langle 3 \rangle 2$ introduces variable i to denote the process that makes a transition, following the definition of *Next* (which is assumed in step $\langle 2 \rangle 1$). Even after this elimination of two quantifiers, Isabelle and Zenon cannot prove the goal in a single step. The usual way of decomposing the proof is to reason separately about each atomic action $a0(i)$, ..., $a4(i)$. However, Peterson's algorithm is simple enough that we can just split the proof into the two cases $i = j$ and $i \neq j$ with steps $\langle 3 \rangle 3$ and $\langle 3 \rangle 4$. Isabelle and Zenon can now prove all the steps.

4   Writing Real Proofs

Peterson's algorithm is a tiny example. Some larger case studies have been carried out using the system [7,9,11]. Several features of TLAPS and its Toolbox interface help in coping with the complexity of large proofs.

4.1   Hierarchical Proofs and the Proof Manager

Hierarchical structure is the key to managing complexity. TLA⁺'s hierarchical and declarative proof language enables a user to keep decomposing a complex proof into smaller steps until the steps become provable by one of the backend provers. In logical terms, proof steps correspond to natural-deduction sequents that must be proved in the current context. The Proof Manager tracks the context, which is modified by non-leaf proof steps. For leaf proof steps, it sends the corresponding sequent to the backend provers, and records the result of the step's proof that they report.

Proof obligations are independent of one another, so users can develop proofs in any order and work on different proof steps independently. The Toolbox makes it easy to instruct TLAPS to check the proof of everything in a file, of a single theorem, or of any step in the proof hierarchy. Its editor helps reading and writing large proofs, providing commands that show or hide subproofs. Although some other interactive proof systems offer hierarchical proofs, we do not know of other systems that provide the Toolbox's abilities to use that structure to aid in reading and writing proofs and to prove steps in any order.

Hierarchical proofs are much better than conventional lemmas for handling complexity. In a TLA⁺ proof, each step with a non-leaf proof is effectively a lemma. One typical 1100-line invariance proof [7] contains 100 such steps. A conventional linear proof with 100 lemmas would be impossible to read.

Unlike most interactive proof assistants [15], TLAPS is independent of any specific backend prover. There is no way for a user to indicate how available facts should be used by backends. TLA⁺ proofs are therefore less sensitive to changes in any prover's implementation.

4.2 Fingerprinting: Tracking the Status of Proof Obligations

During proof development, a user repeatedly modifies the proof structure or changes details of the specification. By default, TLAPS does not re-prove an obligation that it has already proved—even if the proof has been reorganized. It can also show the user the impact of a change by indicating which parts of the existing proof must be re-proved.

The Proof Manager computes a *fingerprint* of every obligation, which it stores, along with the obligation's status, in a separate file. The fingerprint is a compact canonical representation of the obligation and the relevant part of its context. The Toolbox displays the proof status of each step, indicating by color whether the step has been proved or some obligation in its proof has failed or been omitted. The only other proof assistant that we know to offer a mechanism comparable to our fingerprinting facility is the KIV system [1].

5 Conclusion

The proof of Peterson's algorithm illustrates the main constructs of the hierarchical and declarative TLA⁺ proof language. The algorithm is so simple that we had to eschew the use of the SMT solver backend so we could write a nontrivial proof. Section 4 explains why TLAPS, used with the TLA⁺ Toolbox, can handle more complex algorithms and specifications.

A key feature of TLAPS is its use of multiple backend provers. Different proof techniques, such as resolution, tableau methods, rewriting, and SMT solving offer complementary strengths. Future versions of TLAPS will probably support additional backend provers. Because multiple backends raise concerns about soundness, TLAPS provides the option of having Isabelle certify proof traces produced by backend provers; and this has been implemented for Zenon. Still, it is much more likely that a proof is meaningless because of an error in the specification than that it is wrong because of an error in a backend. Soundness also depends on parts of the proof manager.

We cannot overstate the importance of having TLAPS integrated with the other TLA⁺ tools—especially the TLC model checker. Finding errors by running TLC on finite instances of a specification is much faster and easier than discovering them when writing a proof. Also, verifying an algorithm or system may require standard mathematical results. For example, the correctness of a distributed algorithm might depend on known facts about graphs. Engineers want to assume such results, not prove them. However, it is easy to make a mistake when formalizing mathematics. TLC can check the exact TLA⁺ formulas assumed in a proof (on finite instances), greatly reducing the chance of introducing an unsound assumption.

We are actively developing TLAPS. Our main short-term objective is to add support for temporal reasoning. We have designed a smooth extension of the existing proof language to sequents containing temporal formulas. We also plan to improve support for standard TLA⁺ data structures such as sequences.

References

1. Balser, M., Reif, W., Schellhorn, G., Stenzel, K., Thums, A.: Formal System Development with KIV. In: Maibaum, T. (ed.) FASE 2000. LNCS, vol. 1783, pp. 363–366. Springer, Heidelberg (2000)
2. Bonichon, R., Delahaye, D., Doligez, D.: Zenon: An Extensible Automated Theorem Prover Producing Checkable Proofs. In: Dershowitz, N., Voronkov, A. (eds.) LPAR 2007. LNCS (LNAI), vol. 4790, pp. 151–165. Springer, Heidelberg (2007)
3. Chaudhuri, K., Doligez, D., Lamport, L., Merz, S.: Verifying Safety Properties with the TLA$^+$ Proof System. In: Giesl, J., Hähnle, R. (eds.) IJCAR 2010. LNCS, vol. 6173, pp. 142–148. Springer, Heidelberg (2010)
4. Lamport, L.: What good is temporal logic? In: Mason, R.E.A. (ed.) Information Processing 1983. IFIP, pp. 657–668, North-Holland, Paris (September 1983)
5. Lamport, L.: Specifying Systems: The TLA$^+$ Language and Tools for Hardware and Software Engineers. Addison-Wesley (2003)
6. Lamport, L.: The PlusCal Algorithm Language. In: Leucker, M., Morgan, C. (eds.) ICTAC 2009. LNCS, vol. 5684, pp. 36–60. Springer, Heidelberg (2009)
7. Lamport, L.: Byzantizing Paxos by refinement (2011), http://research.microsoft.com/en-us/um/people/lamport/pubs/web-byzpaxos.pdf
8. Lamport, L.: How to write a 21st century proof. Journal of Fixed Point Theory and Applications (March 2012), doi:10.1007/s11784-012-0071-6
9. Lu, T., Merz, S., Weidenbach, C.: Towards Verification of the Pastry Protocol Using TLA$^+$. In: Bruni, R., Dingel, J. (eds.) FORTE 2011 and FMOODS 2011. LNCS, vol. 6722, pp. 244–258. Springer, Heidelberg (2011)
10. Merz, S., Vanzetto, H.: Automatic Verification of TLA$^+$ Proof Obligations with SMT Solvers. In: Bjørner, N., Voronkov, A. (eds.) LPAR-18 2012. LNCS, vol. 7180, pp. 289–303. Springer, Heidelberg (2012)
11. Parno, B., Lorch, J.R., Douceur, J.R., Mickens, J., McCune, J.M.: Memoir: Practical state continuity for protected modules. In: Security and Privacy, pp. 379–394. IEEE (2011)
12. Peterson, G.L.: Myths about the mutual exclusion problem. Inf. Process. Lett. 12(3), 115–116 (1981)
13. The TLAPS Project. Web page, http://msr-inria.inria.fr/~doligez/tlaps/
14. Wenzel, M., Paulson, L.C., Nipkow, T.: The Isabelle Framework. In: Mohamed, O.A., Muñoz, C., Tahar, S. (eds.) TPHOLs 2008. LNCS, vol. 5170, pp. 33–38. Springer, Heidelberg (2008)
15. Wiedijk, F. (ed.): The Seventeen Provers of the World. LNCS (LNAI), vol. 3600. Springer, Heidelberg (2006)

The Modal Transition System Control Problem*

Nicolás D'Ippolito[1], Victor Braberman[2],
Nir Piterman[3], and Sebastián Uchitel[1,2]

[1] Computing Department, Imperial College London, London, UK
[2] Departamento de Computatión, FCEyN, Universidad de Buenos Aires, Argentina
[3] Department of Computer Science, University of Leicester, Leicester, UK

Abstract. Controller synthesis is a well studied problem that attempts
to automatically generate an operational behaviour model of the system-
to-be such that when deployed in a given domain model that behaves
according to specified assumptions satisfies a given goal. A limitation
of known controller synthesis techniques is that they require complete
descriptions of the problem domain. This is limiting in the context of
modern incremental development processes when a fully described problem domain is unavailable, undesirable or uneconomical. In this paper we
study the controller synthesis problem when there is partial behaviour
information about the problem domain. More specifically, we define and
study the controller realisability problem for domains described as Modal
Transition Systems (MTS). An MTS is a partial behaviour model that
compactly represents a set of complete behaviour models in the form of
Labelled Transition Systems (LTS). Given an MTS we ask if all, none
or some of the LTS it describes admit an LTS controller that guarantees a given property. We show a technique that solves effectively the
MTS realisability problem and is in the same complexity class as the
corresponding LTS problem.

1 Introduction

Michael Jackson's Machine-World model [15] establishes a framework on which
to approach the challenges of requirements engineering. In this model, requirements R are prescriptive statements of the world expressed in terms of phenomena on the interface between the machine we are to build and the world in
which the real problems to be solved live. Such problems are to be captured with
prescriptive statements expressed in terms of phenomena in the world (but not
necessarily part of the world-machine interface) called goals G and descriptive
statements of what we assume to be true in the world (domain model D).

Within this setting, a key task in requirements engineering is to understand
and document the goals and the characteristics of the domain in which these are
to be achieved, in order to formulate a set of requirements for the machine to
be built such that assuming that the domain description and goals are valid, the
requirements in such domain entail the goals, more formally $R, D \models G$.

---

* This work was partially supported by grants ERC PBM-FIMBSE, MEALS 295261,
CONICET PIP955, UBACYT X021, and PICT PAE 2272.

D. Giannakopoulou and D. Méry (Eds.): FM 2012, LNCS 7436, pp. 155–170, 2012.

Thus, a key problem of requirements engineering can be formulated as a synthesis problem. Given a set of descriptive assumptions on the environment behaviour and a set of system goals, construct an operational model of the machine such that when composed with the environment, the goals are achieved. Such problem is known as the controller synthesis [24] problem and has been studied extensively resulting in techniques which have been used in various software engineering domains.

Controller synthesis [24] is a well studied problem that attempts to automatically generate an operational behaviour model of the system-to-be such that when deployed in a given environment that behaves according to specified assumptions satisfies a given goal. Controller synthesis techniques have been used in several domains such as safe synthesis of web services composition [14] or synthesis of adaptation strategies in self-adaptive systems [26].

In practice, requirements engineering is not a waterfall process. Engineers do not build a complete description for G and D before they construct or synthesise R. Typically D, G and R are elaborated incrementally. Furthermore, multiple variations of partial models of D, G and R are explored to asses risk, cost and feasibility [18]. In particular a key question that drives requirements engineering forward and consequently drives elaboration of a partial description of D, G and R is if it is feasible to extend them to D', G' and R' such that $R', D' \models G'$.

In this context, existing controller synthesis techniques are not such a good fit because they require complete domain descriptions. Typically, the domain is described in a formal language with its semantics defined as some variation of a two-valued state machine such as Labelled Transition Systems (LTS) [17] or Kripke structures. Thus, the domain model is assumed to be complete up to some level of abstraction (i.e, with respect to an alphabet of actions or propositions).

An appropriate formalism to support modelling when behaviour information is lacking is one in which currently unknown aspects of behaviour can be explicitly modelled [27]. A number of such formalisms exist such as Modal Transition Systems (MTS) [19] and Disjunctive MTS [20]. Partial behaviour models can distinguish between required, possible, and proscribed behaviour.

In this paper, we define controller synthesis in the context of partially specified domain models. More specifically, we study the problem of checking the existence of an LTS controller (i.e. controller realisability) capable of guaranteeing a given goal when deployed in a completely defined LTS domain model that conforms to the partially defined domain model given as an MTS.

The semantics of MTS is given in terms of a set of LTS implementations in which each LTS provides the required behaviour described in the MTS and does not provide any of the MTS proscribed behaviour. We define the *MTS control problem* as follows: given an MTS we ask if *all*, *none* or *some* of the LTS implementations it describes admit an LTS controller that guarantees a given goal given as a Fluent Linear Temporal Logic [11] formula. The realisability question we address in the context of MTS has a three valued answer.

From a model elaboration perspective, a *none* response indicates that there is no hope of building a system that satisfies the goals independently of the aspects of the domain that have been modelled as uncertain. This entails that either goals must be weakened or stronger assumptions about the domain must be made. An *all* response indicates that the partial domain knowledge modelled is sufficient to guarantee that the goals can be achieved, consequently further elaboration may not be necessary. Finally, a *some* response indicates that further elaboration is required. Feedback as to why in some domains which conform to the partial model the goal may not be realisable may be good indicators as to in which direction should elaboration proceed. Note that the latter, feedback on *some* realisability, is beyond the scope of this paper.

The technique we present yields an answer to the MTS control problem showing that, despite dealing with a potentially infinite number of LTS, the MTS control problem is actually in the same complexity class as the underlying LTS synthesis problem. The results for MTS realisability can be used with controller synthesis techniques that deal efficiently with restricted yet expressive goals such as [1,22]. Note that our results are limited to deterministic domain models.

The rest of this paper is organised as follows. In Section 2 we introduce the required concepts and notations. Then, in Section 3 we define the MTS control problem and show how to solve it. We then optimise our algorithmic solution to achieve optimal complexity bounds in Section 4. Finally, we discuss related work in Section 5 and conclude in Section 6.

Due to lack of space all proofs are omitted and given in [7].

2   Preliminaries

2.1   Transition Systems

We fix notation for labelled transition systems (LTSs) [17], which are widely used for modelling and analysing the behaviour of concurrent and distributed systems. LTS is a state transition system where transitions are labelled with actions. The set of actions of an LTS is called its communicating alphabet and constitutes the interactions that the modelled system can have with its environment.

Definition 1. (Labelled Transition Systems [17]) *Let States be the universal set of states, Act be the universal set of action labels. A* Labelled Transition System *(LTS) is a tuple* $E = (S, A, \Delta, s_0)$*, where* $S \subseteq$ *States is a finite set of states,* $A \subseteq Act$ *is a finite alphabet,* $\Delta \subseteq (S \times A \times S)$ *is a transition relation, and* $s_0 \in S$ *is the initial state.*

If for some $s' \in S$ we have $(s, \ell, s') \in \Delta$ we say that ℓ is enabled from s.

Definition 2. (Parallel Composition) *Let* $M = (S_M, A_M, \Delta_M, s_0^M)$ *and* $N = (S_N, A_N, \Delta_N, s_0^N)$ *be LTSs. Parallel composition* $\|$ *is a symmetric operator (up to isomorphism) such that* $M\|N$ *is the LTS* $P = (S_M \times S_N, A_M \cup A_N, \Delta, (s_0^M, s_0^N))$*, where* Δ *is the smallest relation that satisfies the rules below, where* $\ell \in A_M \cup A_N$*:*

$$\frac{(s,\ell,s')\in\Delta_M}{((s,t),\ell,(s',t))\in\Delta}\ell\in A_M\setminus A_N \qquad \frac{(t,\ell,t')\in\Delta_N}{((s,t),\ell,(s,t'))\in\Delta}\ell\in A_N\setminus A_M$$

$$\frac{(s,\ell,s')\in\Delta_M,\ (t,\ell,t')\in\Delta_N}{((s,t),\ell,(s',t'))\in\Delta}\ell\in A_M\cap A_N$$

Definition 3. (Traces) *Consider an LTS $L = (S, A, \Delta, s_0)$. A sequence $\pi = \ell_0, \ell_1, \ldots$ is a trace in L if there exists a sequence $s_0, \ell_0, s_1, \ell_1, \ldots$, where for every $i \geq 0$ we have $(s_i, \ell_i, s_{i+1}) \in \Delta$.*

Modal Transition System (MTS) [19] are abstract notions of LTSs. They extend LTSs by distinguishing between two sets of transitions. Intuitively an MTS describes a set of possible LTSs by describing an upper bound and a lower bound on the set of transitions from every state. Thus, an MTS defines required transitions, which must exist, and possible transitions, which may exist. By elimination, other transitions cannot exist. Formally, we have the following.

Definition 4. (Modal Transition Systems [19]) *A Modal Transition System (MTS) is $M = (S, A, \Delta^r, \Delta^p, s_0)$, where $S \subseteq States$, $A \subseteq Act$, and $s_0 \in S$ are as in LTSs and $\Delta^r \subseteq \Delta^p \subseteq (S \times A \times S)$ are the required and possible transition relations, respectively.*

We denote by $\Delta^p(s)$ the set of possible actions enabled in s, namely $\Delta^p(s) = \{\ell \mid \exists s' \cdot (s, \ell, s') \in \Delta^p\}$. Similarly, $\Delta^r(s)$ denotes the set of required actions enabled in s.

Definition 5. (Refinement) *Let $M = (S, A, \Delta^r_M, \Delta^p_M, s_0^M)$ and $N = (T, A, \Delta^r_N, \Delta^p_N, s_0^N)$ be two MTSs. Relation $H \subseteq S \times T$ is a refinement between M and N if the following holds for every $\ell \in A$ and every $(s, t) \in H$.*

- *If $(s, \ell, s') \in \Delta^r_M$ then there is t' such that $(t, \ell, t') \in \Delta^r_N$ and $(s', t') \in H$.*
- *If $(t, \ell, t') \in \Delta^p_N$ then there is s' such that $(s, \ell, s') \in \Delta^p_M$ and $(s', t') \in H$.*

We say that N refines M if there is a refinement relation H between M and N such that $(s_0^M, s_0^N) \in H$, denoted $M \preceq N$.

Intuitively, N refines M if every required transition of M exists in N and every possible transition in N is possible also in M. An LTS can be viewed as an MTS where $\Delta^p = \Delta^r$. Thus, the definition generalises to when an LTS refines an MTS. LTSs that refine an MTS M are complete descriptions of the system behaviour and thus are called *implementations* of M.

Definition 6. (Implementation and Implementation Relation) *An LTS N is an implementation of an MTS M if and only if N is a refinement of M ($M \preceq N$). We shall refer to the refinement relation between an MTS and an LTS as an implementation relation. We denote the set of implementations of M as $\mathcal{I}(M)$.*

An implementation is *deadlock free* if all states have outgoing transitions. We say that an MTS is *deterministic* if there is no state that has two outgoing possible transitions on the same label, more formally, an LTS E is *deterministic* if $(s, \ell, s') \in \Delta_E$ and $(s, \ell, s'') \in \Delta_E$ implies $s' = s''$. For a state s we denote $\Delta(s) = \{\ell \mid \exists s' \cdot (s, \ell, s') \in \Delta\}$. We refer to the set of all deterministic implementations of an MTS M as $\mathrm{I}^{det}[M]$.

2.2   Fluent Linear Temporal Logic

We describe properties using Fluent Linear Temporal Logic (FLTL) [11]. Linear temporal logics (LTL) [23] are widely used to describe behaviour requirements [11,21]. The motivation for choosing an LTL of fluents is that it provides

$$\pi,i \models Fl \quad\triangleq\quad \pi,i \models Fl$$
$$\pi,i \models \neg\varphi \quad\triangleq\quad \neg(\pi,i \models \varphi)$$
$$\pi,i \models \varphi \vee \psi \quad\triangleq\quad (\pi,i \models \varphi) \vee (\pi,i \models \psi)$$
$$\pi,i \models \mathbf{X}\varphi \quad\triangleq\quad \pi,1 \models \varphi$$
$$\pi,i \models \varphi\mathbf{U}\psi \quad\triangleq\quad \exists j \geq i \cdot \pi,j \models \psi \wedge \forall\, i \leq k < j \cdot \pi,k \models \varphi$$

Fig. 1. Semantics for the satisfaction operator

a uniform framework for specifying and model-checking state-based temporal properties in event-based models [11]. An LTL formula checked against an LTS model requires interpreting propositions as the occurrence of events in the LTS model. Some properties can be rather cumbersome to express as sequences of events, while describing them in terms of states is simpler. Fluents provide a way of defining abstract states. FLTL is a linear-time temporal logic for reasoning about fluents. A *fluent* Fl is defined by a pair of sets and a Boolean value: $Fl = \langle I_{Fl}, T_{Fl}, Init_{Fl}\rangle$, where $I_{Fl} \subseteq Act$ is the set of initiating actions, $T_{Fl} \subseteq Act$ is the set of terminating actions and $I_{Fl} \cap T_{Fl} = \emptyset$. A fluent may be initially trueor falseas indicated by $Init_{Fl}$. Every action $\ell \in Act$ induces a fluent, namely $\dot\ell = \langle \ell, Act \setminus \{\ell\}, \mathsf{false}\rangle$.

Let $\mathcal{F}$ be the set of all possible fluents over Act. An FLTL formula is defined inductively using the standard Boolean connectives and temporal operators $\mathbf{X}$ (next), $\mathbf{U}$ (strong until) as follows: $\varphi ::= Fl \mid \neg\varphi \mid \varphi \vee \psi \mid \mathbf{X}\varphi \mid \varphi\mathbf{U}\psi$, where $Fl \in \mathcal{F}$. As usual we introduce $\wedge$, $\Diamond$ (eventually), and $\Box$ (always) as syntactic sugar. Let Π be the set of infinite traces over Act. The trace $\pi = \ell_0, \ell_1, \ldots$ satisfies a fluent Fl at position i, denoted $\pi, i \models Fl$, if and only if one of the following conditions holds:

- $Init_{Fl} \wedge (\forall j \in \mathbb{N} \cdot 0 \leq j \leq i \rightarrow \ell_j \notin T_{Fl})$
- $\exists j \in \mathbb{N} \cdot (j \leq i \wedge \ell_j \in I_{Fl}) \wedge (\forall k \in \mathbb{N} \cdot j < k \leq i \rightarrow \ell_k \notin T_{Fl})$

In other words, a fluent holds at position i if and only if it holds initially or some initiating action has occurred, but no terminating action has yet occurred. The interval over which a fluent holds is *closed* on the left and *open* on the right, since actions have an immediate effect on the value of fluents.

Given an infinite trace π, the satisfaction of a formula φ at position i, denoted $\pi, i \models \varphi$, is defined as shown in Figure 1. We say that φ holds in π, denoted $\pi \models \varphi$, if $\pi, 0 \models \varphi$.

A formula $\varphi \in$ FLTL holds in an LTS E (denoted $E \models \varphi$) if it holds on every infinite trace produced by E.

Consider P, shown in Figure 2.3, and the FLTL formula $\phi = \neg idle\mathbf{U}Cooking$, where $Cooking = \langle\{cook\}, \{doneCooking\}, \mathsf{false}\rangle$, and the trace $\pi = idle, cook, doneCooking, moveToBelt, cook, doneCooking, \ldots$ of the LTS shown in Figure 2.3. Since at position 1 $idle$ holds (i.e, $\pi, 1 \models idle$) but $Cooking$ does not (i.e., $\pi, 1 \not\models Cooking$) it follows that $\pi, 0 \not\models \phi$. On the other hand, at time 2 $idle$ does not holds (i.e, $\pi, 2 \not\models idle$) but $Cooking$ does hold (i.e, $\pi, 2 \models Cooking$), hence, $\pi, 2 \models \phi$. Note that ϕ holds in P, i.e, $P \models \phi$.

In this paper we modify LTSs and MTSs by adding new actions and adding states and transitions that use the new actions. It is convenient to change FLTL formulas to ignore these changes. Consider an FLTL formula φ and a set of actions Γ such that for all fluents $Fl = \langle I_{Fl}, T_{Fl}, Init_{Fl} \rangle$ in φ we have $\Gamma \cap (I_{Fl} \cup T_{Fl}) = \emptyset$. We define the *alphabetised next* version of φ, denoted $\mathcal{X}_\Gamma(\varphi)$, as follows.

- For a fluent $Fl \in \mathcal{F}$ we define $\mathcal{X}_\Gamma(Fl) = Fl$.
- For $\varphi \vee \psi$ we define $\mathcal{X}_\Gamma(\varphi \vee \psi) = \mathcal{X}_\Gamma(\varphi) \vee \mathcal{X}_\Gamma(\psi)$.
- For $\neg\varphi$ we define $\mathcal{X}_\Gamma(\neg\varphi) = \neg\mathcal{X}_\Gamma(\varphi)$.
- For $\varphi \mathbf{U} \psi$ we define $\mathcal{X}_\Gamma(\varphi \mathbf{U} \psi) = \mathcal{X}_\Gamma(\varphi) \mathbf{U} \mathcal{X}_\Gamma(\psi)$.
- For $\mathbf{X}\varphi$ we define $\mathcal{X}_\Gamma(\mathbf{X}\varphi) = \mathbf{X}((\bigvee_{f \in \Gamma} f) \mathbf{U} \mathcal{X}_\Gamma(\varphi))$

Thus, this transformation replaces every next operator occurring in the formula by an until operator that skips uninteresting actions that are in Γ. The transformations in Section 3 force an action not in Γ to appear after every action from Γ. Thus, the difference between $\mathbf{U}$ under even and odd number of negations is not important. Given a trace $\pi = \ell_0, \ell_1, \ldots$, we say that $\pi' = \ell'_0, \ell'_1, \ldots$ is a Γ-variant of π if there is an infinite sequence $i_0 < i_1 < \ldots$ such that $\ell_j = \ell_{i_j}$ for every j. That is, π' is obtained from π by adding a finite sequences of actions from Γ between actions in π.

Theorem 1. *Given a trace $\pi = \ell_0, \ell_1, \ldots$ in $E = (S, A, \Delta, s_0)$, an FLTL formula φ and a set of actions $\Gamma \in Act$. If $\Gamma \cap A = \emptyset$ then the following holds. For every trace π' that is a Γ-variant of π we have $\pi \models \varphi$ iff $\pi' \models \mathcal{X}_\Gamma(\varphi)$.*

We note that our results hold for properties that describe sets of traces that can be modified easily to accept Γ-variants as above. We choose to focus on FLTL as it makes all complexity results concrete and is a well accepted standard.

2.3 LTS Controller Synthesis

Given a domain model, which is a description of what is known about the world, the problem of controller synthesis is to construct a machine / controller that will interact with the world and ensure that certain goals are fulfilled. In our context, the domain model is given as and LTS and the goal of the machine is defined as an FLTL formula. The interface between the machine and the domain model is given by partitioning the events that can occur to those that are controllable by the machine and those that are uncontrollable by it. Then, the controller restricts the occurrence of events it controls to ensure that its goals are fulfilled.

Definition 7. (LTS Control [8]) *Given a domain model in the form of a deterministic LTS $E = (S, A, \Delta, s_0)$, a set of controllable actions $A_c \subseteq A$, and an FLTL formula φ, a solution for the LTS control problem $\mathcal{E} = \langle E, \varphi, A_c \rangle$ is an LTS $M = (S_M, A_M, \Delta_M, s_{0_M})$ such that $A_M = A$, from every state in S_M all actions in $A_M \backslash A_c$ are enabled, $E \| M$ is deadlock free, and every trace π in $E \| M$ is such that $\pi \models \varphi$.*

That is, looking for a solution of an LTS control problem with domain model E, is to verify the existence of an LTS M such that when composed in parallel with E (i.e. $E \| M$), it does not block uncontrollable actions in E and every trace of $E \| M$ satisfies a given FLTL goal φ (i.e. $E \| M \models \varphi$).

We may refer to the solution of an LTS control problem as controller or LTS controller. Whenever such a controller exists we say that the control problem is realisable and unrealisable otherwise. In case that a domain model E is given and A_c and φ are implicit we denote by $\mathcal{E}$ the control problem $\mathcal{E} = \langle E, \varphi, A_c \rangle$.

Theorem 2. (LTS Control [24]) *Given an LTS control problem* $\mathcal{E} = \langle E, \varphi, A_c \rangle$ *it is decidable in 2EXPTIME whether* $\mathcal{E}$ *is realisable. The algorithm checking realisability can also extract a controller* M.

Note that determinism of the domain model is required. As LTS controllers guarantee the satisfaction of their goals through parallel composition, having nondeterministic domain models means that the controller would not be able to know the exact state of the domain model. This leads to imperfect information, as the controller would only be able to deduce which *set* of states the domain model is in. Translation of the existing results on synthesis with imperfect information to the context of nondeterministic LTSs is out of the scope of this paper.

For example, consider E, the simple domain model in Figure 2.3, where a ceramics cooking process is described. The aim of the controller is to produce cooked ceramics by taking raw pieces from the in-tray, placing them in the oven and moving them once cooked to a conveyor belt. In addition, raw pieces have to be cooked twice before being moved to the conveyor belt. A natural solution for such a problem is to build a controller guaranteing that raw pieces are cooked twice and moved to the conveyor belt infinitely often. The solution for this simple example is shown in Figure 2.3. Note that the controller has the memory needed to remember how many times a piece has been cooked.

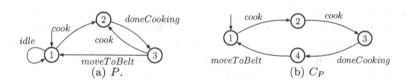

(a) P.   (b) C_P

Fig. 2. Ceramic Cooking Example

3   MTS Control Problem

The problem of control synthesis for MTS is to check whether all, none or some of the LTS implementations of a given MTS can be controlled by an LTS controller [9]. More specifically, given an MTS, an FLTL goal and a set of controllable actions, the answer to the MTS control problem is *all* if all implementations of the MTS can be controlled, *none* if no implementation can be controlled and *some* otherwise. This is defined formally below.

Definition 8. (Semantics of MTS Control) *Given a deterministic MTS* $E = (S, A, \Delta^r, \Delta^p, s_0)$, *an FLTL formula* φ *and a set* $A_c \subseteq A$ *of controllable actions, to solve the MTS control problem* $\mathcal{E} = \langle E, \varphi, A_c \rangle$ *is to answer:*

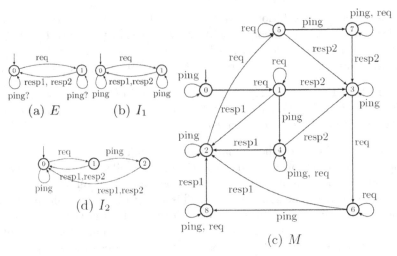

Fig. 3. Server Example.

- **All**, if for all LTS $I \in \Gamma^{det}[E]$, the control problem $\langle I, \varphi, A_c \rangle$ is realisable,
- **None**, if for all LTS $I \in \Gamma^{det}[E]$, the control problem $\langle I, \varphi, A_c \rangle$ is unrealisable,
- **Some**, otherwise.

Note that, as in the case of LTS control problem, we restrict attention to deterministic domain models. This follows from the fact that our solution for MTS realisability is by a reduction to LTS realisability.

Consider E, shown in Figure 3(a), that describes the interactions between a server and clients. Note that although it is certain that client requests can be responded by the server, definitions regarding when clients may ping the server have not been made yet. Suppose that we want to build a controller for this server such that the server guarantees that after receiving a request it will eventually yield a response and if there are enough requests, responses of both kinds will be issued. We formally describe this requirement as the FLTL formula: $\varphi = \Box\Diamond\neg ResponseOwed \wedge (\Box\Diamond r\dot{e}q \Rightarrow (\Box\Diamond r\dot{e}sp_1 \wedge \Box\Diamond r\dot{e}sp_2))$, where $ResponseOwed = \langle\{req\}, \{resp_1, resp_2\}, false\rangle$. As expected, the server can only control the response. Hence, we have the MTS control problem $\mathcal{E} = \langle E, \varphi, \{resp_1, resp_2\}\rangle$. Consider the implementation I_1, shown in Figure 3(b). The uncontrollable self loop over ping in state 1 allows the environment to flood the controller impeding it from eventually producing a response (i.e. no controller can avoid the trace $req, ping, ping, \ldots$). The implementation I_2, shown in Figure 3(d), allows only a bounded number of pings after a request, hence, the server cannot be flooded and a controller for the property exists . Since I_1 and I_2 are implementations of E such that I_2 can be controlled and I_2 cannot, it follows that the answer for the MTS control problem $\mathcal{E}$ is *some*.

A naive approach to the MTS control problem may require to evaluate an infinite number of LTS control problems. Naturally, such approach is not possible, hence, it is mandatory to find alternative ways to handle MTS control problems.

We reduce the MTS control problem to two LTS control problems. The first LTS control problem encodes the problem of whether there is a controller for each implementation described by the MTS. It does so by modelling an environment that can pick the "hardest" implementation to control. In fact, in the LTS control problem, the environment will pick at each point the subset of possible transitions of the MTS that are available. If there is a controller for this environment, there is a controller for all implementations.

The second LTS control problem encodes the problem of whether there is no controller for every implementation of the MTS. Similarly, this is done by modelling an LTS control problem in which the controller can pick the "easiest" implementation to control (in fact, it is now the controller that picks the subset of possible transitions of the MTS that are available at each point). If there is no controller in this setting, then for every implementation there is no controller.

The two LTS problems are defined in terms of the same LTS. The only difference is who controls the selection of the subset of possible actions, i.e. implementation choice. We now define the LTS E^I in which additional transition labels are added to model explicitly when either the controller or the environment choose which subset of possible transitions of the MTS are available.

Definition 9. *Given an MTS $E = (S, A, \Delta^r, \Delta^P, s_0)$. We define $E^I = (S_{E^I}, A_{E^I}, \Delta_{E^I}, s_0)$ as follows:*

- *$S_{E^I} = S \cup \{(s, i) \mid s \in S \text{ and } i \subseteq A \text{ and } \Delta^r(s) \subseteq i\}$*
- *$A_{E^I} = A \cup \overline{A}$, where $\overline{A} = \{\ell_i \mid i \subseteq A\}$*
- *$\Delta_{E^I} = \{(s, \ell_i, (s, i)) \mid s \in S \text{ and } i \subseteq \Delta^P(s) \text{ and } \Delta^r(s) \subseteq i\} \cup \{((s, i), \ell, s') \mid (s, \ell, s') \in \Delta^P \text{ and } \ell \in i\}$*

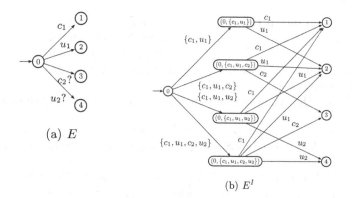

(a) E

(b) E^I

Fig. 4.

States in E^I are of two kinds. Those that are of the form s with $s \in S$ encode states in which a choice of which subset of possible transitions are implemented has to be made. Choosing a subset $i \subseteq A$, leads to a state (s, i). States of latter form (s, i) have outgoing transitions labelled with actions in i. A transition from (s, i) on an action $\ell \in i$ leads to the same state s' in E^I as taking ℓ from s in E. For example, the model in Figure 3 is obtained by applying Definition 9 to model in Figure 3.

The LTS E^I provides the basis for tractably answering the MTS control question. The following algorithm shows how to compute the solution for the MTS control problem.

Algorithm 1. (MTS Control) *Given an MTS control problem $\mathcal{E} = \langle E, \varphi, A_c \rangle$. If E^I is the LTS model obtained by applying Definition 9 to E, then the answer for $\mathcal{E}$ is computed as follows.*
  - *All, if there exists a solution for $\mathcal{E}_A^I = \langle E^I, \mathcal{X}_{\overline{A}}(\varphi), A_c \rangle$*
  - *None, if there is no solution for $\mathcal{E}_N^I = \langle E^I, \mathcal{X}_{\overline{A}}(\varphi), A_c \cup \overline{A} \rangle$*
  - *Some, otherwise.*

Algorithm 1 shows how to compute the answer for a given MTS control problem.

Consider the case in which the answer for the MTS control problem is *all*. As stated by Algorithm 1, the answer to $\mathcal{E}$ is *all*, if there is solution to the LTS control problem $\mathcal{E}_A^I$. Intuitively, if we give control over the new actions ℓ_i to the environment, it can choose the hardest implementation to control. Thus, this solves the question of whether all implementations are controllable.

Lemma 1 proves that the case *all* in Algorithm 1 is sound and complete.

Lemma 1. (All) *Given an MTS control problem $\mathcal{E} = \langle E, \varphi, A_c \rangle$ where $E = (S, A, \Delta^r, \Delta^p, s_{0_E})$. If E^I is the LTS obtained by applying Definition 9 to E, then the following holds. The answer for $\mathcal{E}$ is all iff the LTS control problem $\mathcal{E}_A^I = \langle E^I, \mathcal{X}_{\overline{A}}(\varphi), A_c \rangle$ is realisable.*

Consider the case in which the answer for the MTS control problem is *none*. The answer to $\mathcal{E}$ is *none*, if there is no solution to the LTS control problem $\mathcal{E}_N^I$. Intuitively, if we give control over the new actions ℓ_i to the controller, it can choose the easiest implementation to control. Thus, this solves the question of whether no implementation is controllable.

Lemma 2 proves that the case *none* in Algorithm 1 is sound and complete.

Lemma 2. *(None) Given an MTS control problem $\mathcal{E} = \langle E, \varphi, A_c \rangle$ where $E = (S, A, \Delta^r, \Delta^p, s_0)$. If E^I is the LTS obtained by applying Definition 9 to E, then the following holds.*

The LTS control problem $\mathcal{E}_N^I = \langle E^I, \mathcal{X}_{\overline{A}}(\varphi), A_c \cup \overline{A} \rangle$ is realisable iff there exists $I \in \mathcal{I}^{det}[E]$ such that the LTS control problem $\mathcal{I} = \langle I, \varphi, A_c \rangle$ is realisable.

The answer to $\mathcal{E}$ is *some* whenever there exists an implementation of E that can be controlled and an implementation of E that cannot be controlled.

Lemma 3. *(Some) Given an MTS control problem $\mathcal{E} = \langle E, \varphi, A_c \rangle$. The answer for $\mathcal{E}$ is some iff $\mathcal{E}_A^I$ is unrealisable and $\mathcal{E}_N^I$ is realisable.*

4   Linear Reduction into LTS Control Problems

Algorithm 1 shows that the MTS control problem can be reduced to two LTS control problems. Hence, our solution to the MTS control problem is, in general, doubly exponential in the size of E^I (cf. [24,8]). Unfortunately, the state space of E^I is exponential in the branching degree of E, which in turn is bounded by the size of the alphabet of the MTS. More precisely, for a state $s \in E^I$ the number of successors of s is bounded by the number of possible combinations of labels of maybe transitions from s in E. In this section we show that to compute the answer for $\mathcal{E}^I_A$ and $\mathcal{E}^I_N$ it is enough to consider only a small part of the states of E^I. Effectively, it is enough to consider at most linearly (in the number of outgoing transitions) many successors for every state. This leads to the MTS control problem being 2EXPTIME-complete.[1]

First, we analyse E^I in the context of $\mathcal{E}^I_A$. We define a fragment $\mathcal{E}^{I^+}_A$ of $\mathcal{E}^I_A$. Let $E^{I^+} = (S_{E^I}, A_{E^I}, \Delta^+, s_{0_{E^I}})$, where only the following transitions from Δ_{E^I} are included in Δ^+.

1. Consider a state $s \in E$ that has at least one required uncontrollable successor. In Δ^+ we add to s only the transition $(s, \ell_i, (s, i))$, where $i = \Delta^r_E(s) \cup (\Delta^p_E(s) \cap A_\mu)$. That is, in addition to required transitions from s we include all uncontrollable possible successors of s.
2. Consider a state $s \in E$ that has no required uncontrollable successors but has a required controllable successor. In Δ^+ we add to s only the transitions $(s, \ell_i, (s, i))$, where i is either $\Delta^r_E(s)$ or i is $\Delta^r_E(s) \cup (\Delta^p_E(s) \cap A_\mu)$. That is, include a transition to all required transitions from s as well as augmenting all required transitions by all uncontrollable possible transitions.
3. Consider a state $s \in E$ that has no required successors. In Δ^+ we add to s a transition to $(s, \ell_i, (s, i))$, where $i = \Delta^p_E(s) \cap A_\mu$, and for every $\ell \in \Delta^p_E(s) \cap A_c$ we add to s the transition $(s, \ell_{\{\ell\}}, (s, \{\ell\}))$. That is, we include a transition to all possible uncontrollable transitions from s and for every possible controllable transition a separate transition.
4. For a state (s, i) we add to Δ^+ all the transitions in Δ_{E^I}.

Lemma 4. *The problem $\mathcal{E}^I_A$ is realisable iff $\mathcal{E}^{I^+}_A = \langle E^{I^+}, \mathcal{X}_{\overline{A}}(\varphi), A_c \rangle$ is realisable.*

We now analyse E^I in the context of the $\mathcal{E}^I_N$. We define a fragment $\mathcal{E}^{I^-}_N$ of $\mathcal{E}^I_N$. Let $E^{I^-} = (S_{E^I}, A_{E^I}, \Delta^-, s_{0,E^I})$, where only the following transitions from Δ_{E^I} are included in Δ^-.

1. Consider a state $s \in E$ that has at least one required uncontrollable successor. In Δ^- we add to s only the transition $(s, \ell_i, (s, i))$, where $i = \Delta^r_E(s)$. That is, include only the required transitions from s.
2. Consider a state $s \in E$ that has no required uncontrollable successors. In Δ^- we add to s a transition to $(s, \ell_i, (s, i))$, where $i = \Delta^r_E(s) \cup (\Delta^p_E(s) \cap A_c)$,

---

[1]   We can avoid adding states altogether by having a per state definition of what are controllable and uncontrollable actions. For simplicity of presentation we choose to add states. The modification is not complicated. In an enumerative implementation of game analysis this would be our suggested treatment.

and for every $\ell \in \Delta_E^p(s) \cap A_\mu$ we add to s the transition to $(s, \ell_{\Delta_E^r(s) \cup \{\ell\}},$ $(s, \Delta_E^r(s) \cup \{\ell\}))$. That is, we include a transition to all controllable transitions from s and for every possible uncontrollable transition a separate transition.

3. For a state (s, i) we add to Δ^- all the transitions in Δ_{E^I}.

Lemma 5. *The problem* $\mathcal{E}_N^I$ *is realisable iff* $\mathcal{E}_N^{I^-} = \langle E^{I^-}, \mathcal{X}_{\overline{A}}(\varphi), A_c \cup \overline{A} \rangle$ *is realisable.*

Using $\mathcal{E}_A^{I^+}$ and $\mathcal{E}_N^{I^-}$ can establish the complexity of the MTS control problem.

Theorem 3. (MTS Control Complexity) *Given an MTS control problem* $\mathcal{E} = \langle E, \varphi, A_c \rangle$ *it is 2EXPTIME-complete to decide whether the answer to* $\mathcal{E}$ *is all, none, or some.*

5   Discussion and Related Work

Automated construction of event-based operational models of intended system behaviour has been extensively studied in the software engineering community.

Synthesis from scenario-based specifications (e.g. [27,6]) allows integrating a fragmented, example-based specification into a model which can be analysed via model checking, simulation, animation and inspection, the latter aided by automated slicing and abstraction techniques. Synthesis from formal declarative specification (e.g. temporal logics) has also been studied with the aim of providing an operational model on which to further support requirements elicitation and analysis [16]. The work presented herein shares the view that model elaboration can be supported through synthesis and analysis. Furthermore, analysis of a partial domain model for realisability of system goals by means of a controller allows prompting further elaboration of both domain model and goals.

Synthesis is also used to automatically construct plans that are then straightforwardly enacted by some software component. For instance, synthesis of glue code and component adaptors has been studied in order to achieve safe composition at the architecture level [14], and in particular in service oriented architectures [2]. Such approaches cannot be applied when a fully specified domain model is not available, hence their application is limited in earlier phases of development. Our approach allows the construction of glue code and adaptors earlier without necessarily requiring the effort of developing a full domain model.

In the domain of self-adaptive systems there has also been an increasing interest in synthesis as such systems must be capable of designing at run-time adaptation strategies. Hence, they rely heavily on automated synthesis of behaviour models that will guarantee the satisfaction of requirements under the constraints enforced by the environment and the capabilities offered by the self-adaptive system [26,5]. We speculate that controller synthesis techniques that support partial domain knowledge, such as the one presented here, may allow deploying self-adaptive systems that work in environments for which there is more uncertainty.

Partial behaviour models have been extensively studied. A number of such modelling formalisms exist, e.g., Modal Transition Systems (MTSs) [19] and variants such as Disjunctive MTS [20]. The results presented in this work would have to be revisited in the context of other partial behaviour formalisms. However, since many complexity results for MTS hold for extensions such as DMTS, we believe that our results could also extend naturally to these extensions.

The formal treatment of MTSs started with model checking, which received a lot of attention (cf. [3,4,12]). Initially, a version of three-valued model checking was defined [3] and shown to have the same complexity as that of model checking. Generalised model checking [4] improves the accuracy of model checking of partial specifications. Indeed, three-valued model checking may yield that the answer is unknown even when no implementations of an MTS satisfy the formula. However, complexity of generalised model checking is much higher [12].

In order to reason about generalised model checking one has to go from the model of transition systems (for 3-valued model checking) to that of a game. Our definition of MTS control is more similar to generalised model checking than to 3-valued model checking. We find it interesting that both MTS and LTS control problems are solved in the same model (that of a game) and that MTS control does not require a more general model.

Another related subject is abstraction of games. For example, in [13] abstraction refinement is generalised to the context of control in order to reason about larger games. Their main interest is in applying abstraction on existing games. Thus, they are able to make assumptions about which states are reasoned about together. We, on the other hand, are interested in the case that an MTS is used as an abstract model. In this case, the abstract MTS is given and we would like to reason about it.

Of the huge body of work on controller synthesis and realizability of temporal logic we highlight two topics. First, we heavily rely on LTS control. For example, we use the 2EXPTIME-completeness of LTL controller synthesis [24]. Second, we would like to mention explorations of restricted subsets of LTL in the context of synthesis (cf. [1,22]). These results show that in some cases synthesis can be applied in practice. Similar restrictions, if applied to MTS control combined with our reductions, would produce the same reduction in complexity.

Our previous work on usage of controller synthesis in the context of LTSs has been incorporated in the MTSA toolset [10]. We have implemented a solver to GR(1) [22] formulas in the context of the LTS control problem [8].

More specifically, from a descriptive specification of the domain model in the form of an LTS and a set of controllable actions, the solver constructs an LTS controller that when composed with the domain model satisfies a given FLTL [11] formula of the form $\Box I \wedge (\bigwedge_{i=1}^{n} \Box \Diamond A_i \rightarrow \bigwedge_{j=1}^{m} \Box \Diamond G_j)$ where $\Box I$ is a safety system goal, $\Box \Diamond A_i$ represents a liveness assumption on the behaviour of the environment, $\Box \Diamond G_j$ models a liveness goal for the system and A_i and G_j are non-temporal fluent expressions, while I is a system safety goal expressed as a Fluent Linear Temporal Logic formula. We have implemented the reductions proposed in this paper and extended MTSA to support MTS control. The tool implements the conversion of the MTS E to the LTSs E^{I^+} and E^{I^-} (cf. Section 4) and calls our implementation for the LTS control solution on both problems. The structure of specification does not change when introducing the additional actions. Thus, starting from GR(1) formulas, we can call our GR(1) LTS solver.

6   Conclusions and Future Work

We present a technique that solves the MTS control problem showing that, despite dealing with a potentially infinite number of LTS implementations, the MTS problem is actually in the same complexity class that the underlying LTS synthesis problem.

Specifically, we have defined the MTS control problem that answers if all, none or some implementations of a given MTS, modelling a partially defined domain model, admit an LTS controller that guarantees a given goal. Although an MTS has a potentially infinite number of implementations, we provide an effective algorithm to compute the answer for the MTS control problem without requiring going through all the implementations described by the MTS.

The algorithm reduces the MTS control problem to two LTS control problems in which the controller or the environment get to choose which implementation described by the MTS must be LTS controlled. In principle, both LTS control problems are exponentially larger than the original MTS model. Nevertheless, we show that the number of states of each LTS problem that must be considered is in fact linear in the alphabet of the input MTS. Hence, the MTS control problem remains in the same complexity as the LTS control problems. In fact, as mentioned before we have implemented a solver for GR(1) [22] style formulas applied to LTS control [8]. Hence, our tool checks realisability of an expressive class of MTS control problems in polynomial time.

As mentioned in previous sections, having nondeterminism in the domain model leads to synthesis with imperfect information. Such a setting is much more computationally complex than synthesis with full information. Only in recent years a few approaches towards imperfect information have started to emerge [25]. However, most of them are far from actual applications. In a setting of a nondeterministic domain model but giving the controller full information of actions and states, our technique works with no changes. Similarly, our technique can handle the setting of nondeterministic MTSs and considering only deterministic implementations. Solving the synthesis problem for nondeterministic MTS, which corresponds to imperfect information games, is not straightforward. Nevertheless, we believe that it would reduce to synthesis for nondeterministic LTS in much the same way as with the deterministic variant.

The semantics of MTS is given in terms of a set of LTS implementations. In the context of controller synthesis an MTS is interpreted as the characterisation of a set of possible problem domain models. Hence, the MTS control problem could be used as a mechanism to explicitly identify which are the behaviour assumptions in problem domain that guarantee realisability of a certain goal: We are interested in studying the problem of characterising the set of realisable implementations whenever the answer for a given MTS control problem is *some*.

Having solved the realisability of the MTS control problem, the next logical step is to an algorithm that will produce controllers if the MTS control problem is realisable. We expect that synthesising controllers for the two LTS control problems derived from the MTS control problem should serve as templates to construct controllers for specific LTSs that are implementations of the MTS.

References

1. Asarin, E., Maler, O., Pnueli, A., Sifakis, J.: Controller synthesis for timed automata. In: SSC (1998)
2. Bertolino, A., Inverardi, P., Pelliccione, P., Tivoli, M.: Automatic synthesis of behavior protocols for composable web-services. In: FSE. ACM (2009)
3. Bruns, G., Godefroid, P.: Model Checking Partial State Spaces with 3-Valued Temporal Logics. In: Halbwachs, N., Peled, D.A. (eds.) CAV 1999. LNCS, vol. 1633, pp. 274–287. Springer, Heidelberg (1999)
4. Bruns, G., Godefroid, P.: Generalized Model Checking: Reasoning about Partial State Spaces. In: Palamidessi, C. (ed.) CONCUR 2000. LNCS, vol. 1877, pp. 168–182. Springer, Heidelberg (2000)
5. Dalpiaz, F., Giorgini, P., Mylopoulos, J.: An Architecture for Requirements-Driven Self-reconfiguration. In: van Eck, P., Gordijn, J., Wieringa, R. (eds.) CAiSE 2009. LNCS, vol. 5565, pp. 246–260. Springer, Heidelberg (2009)
6. Damas, C., Lambeau, B., van Lamsweerde, A.: Scenarios, goals, and state machines: a win-win partnership for model synthesis. In: FSE. ACM (2006)
7. D'Ippolito, N.: Technical Report, http://www.doc.ic.ac.uk/~srdipi/techfm2012
8. D'Ippolito, N., Braberman, V., Piterman, N., Uchitel, S.: Synthesising non-anomalous event-based controllers for liveness goals. ACM TOSEM 22(1) (to appear, 2013)
9. D'Ippolito, N., Braberman, V.A., Piterman, N., Uchitel, S.: Synthesis of live behaviour models for fallible domains. In: ICSE. ACM (2011)
10. D'Ippolito, N., Fischbein, D., Chechik, M., Uchitel, S.: Mtsa: The modal transition system analyser. In: ASE. IEEE (2008)
11. Giannakopoulou, D., Magee, J.: Fluent model checking for event-based systems. In: FSE. ACM (2003)
12. Godefroid, P., Piterman, N.: LTL Generalized Model Checking Revisited. In: Jones, N.D., Müller-Olm, M. (eds.) VMCAI 2009. LNCS, vol. 5403, pp. 89–104. Springer, Heidelberg (2009)
13. Henzinger, T.A., Jhala, R., Majumdar, R.: Counterexample-Guided Control. In: Baeten, J.C.M., Lenstra, J.K., Parrow, J., Woeginger, G.J., et al. (eds.) ICALP 2003. LNCS, vol. 2719, pp. 886–902. Springer, Heidelberg (2003)
14. Inverardi, P., Tivoli, M.: A reuse-based approach to the correct and automatic composition of web-services. In: ESSPE. ACM (2007)
15. Jackson, M.: The world and the machine. In: ICSE. ACM (1995)
16. Kazhamiakin, R., Pistore, M., Roveri, M.: Formal verification of requirements using spin: A case study on web services. In: SEFM. IEEE (2004)
17. Keller, R.M.: Formal verification of parallel programs. CACM 19 (1976)
18. van Lamsweerde, A.: Requirements Engineering - From System Goals to UML Models to Software Specifications. Wiley (2009)
19. Larsen, K., Thomsen, B.: A Modal Process Logic. In: LICS. IEEE (1988)
20. Larsen, K.G., Xinxin, L.: Equation solving using modal transition systems. In: LICS. IEEE (1990)

21. Letier, E., van Lamsweerde, A.: Agent-based tactics for goal-oriented requirements elaboration. In: ICSE. ACM (2002)
22. Piterman, N., Pnueli, A., Sa'ar, Y.: Synthesis of Reactive(1) Designs. In: Emerson, E.A., Namjoshi, K.S. (eds.) VMCAI 2006. LNCS, vol. 3855, pp. 364–380. Springer, Heidelberg (2005)
23. Pnueli, A.: The temporal logic of programs. In: FOCS. IEEE (1977)
24. Pnueli, A., Rosner, R.: On the synthesis of a reactive module. In: POPL. ACM (1989)
25. Raskin, J.F., Chatterjee, K., Doyen, L., Henzinger, T.A.: Algorithms for omega-regular games with imperfect information. LMCS 3(3) (2007)
26. Sykes, D., Heaven, W., Magee, J., Kramer, J.: Plan-directed architectural change for autonomous systems. In: SAVCBS (2007)
27. Uchitel, S., Brunet, G., Chechik, M.: Synthesis of partial behavior models from properties and scenarios. TOSEM 35 (2009)

When Structural Refinement of Components Keeps Temporal Properties over Reconfigurations

Julien Dormoy[1], Olga Kouchnarenko[1,3], and Arnaud Lanoix[2]

[1] FEMTO-ST CNRS and University of Franche-Comté, Besançon, France
{Julien.Dormoy,Olga.Kouchnarenko}@univ-fcomte.fr
[2] LINA CNRS and Nantes University, Nantes, France
arnaud.lanoix@univ-nantes.fr
[3] INRIA/CASSIS France

Abstract. Dynamic reconfigurations increase the availability and the reliability of component-based systems by allowing their architecture to evolve at runtime. Recently, a linear temporal pattern logic, called FTPL, has been defined to express desired—architectural, event and temporal—properties over dynamic reconfigurations of component systems. This paper is dedicated to the preservation of the FTPL properties when refining components and introducing new reconfigurations. To this end, we use architectural reconfiguration models giving the semantics of component-based systems with reconfigurations, on which we define a new refinement relation. This relation combines: (i) a *structural* refinement which respects the component encapsulation within the architectures at two levels of refinement, and (ii) a *behavioural* refinement which links dynamic reconfigurations of a refined component-based system with their abstract counterparts that were possible before the refinement. The main advantage of the new refinement is that this relation *preserves* the FTPL properties. The main contributions are illustrated on the example of an HTTP server architecture.

1 Introduction

The refinement-based design and development simplifies complex system specification and implementation [1,2]. For component-based systems, it is important in practice to associate a design by refinement with a design by a composition of their components [3,4]. Dynamic reconfiguration of software architectures is an active research topic [5,6,7] motivated by practical distributed applications like, e.g., those in Fractal [8] or OSGi[1].

In this paper we propose a refinement of component-based systems with reconfigurations which preserves event and temporal properties. Our main goal is to respect component encapsulation, i.e. the refinement of a component must not cause any changes outside of this component. Moreover, we want the refinement to respect the availability of reconfigurations from an abstract level to a refined one: new reconfigurations handling new components introduced by the

---

[1] http://www.osgi.org

D. Giannakopoulou and D. Méry (Eds.): FM 2012, LNCS 7436, pp. 171–186, 2012.
© Springer-Verlag Berlin Heidelberg 2012

refinement must not take control forever, and no new deadlock is allowed. The present paper's contributions as displayed in Fig. 1, are based on our previous works [9,10,11] where the semantics of component-based architectures with dynamic reconfigurations has been given in terms of labelled transition systems (**1** in Fig. 1). The first contribution of this paper is a definition of a *structural refinement* (**2** in Fig. 1) which links two architectures at two development levels: in a refined architecture every refined component must have the same interfaces of the same types as before. This way other components do not see the difference between the refined components and their abstract versions, and thus there is no need to adapt them. The second contribution is the definition of a *reconfiguration refinement relation* (**3** in Fig. 1) linking dynamic reconfigurations of a refined component-based system with their abstract counterparts that were possible before the refinement.

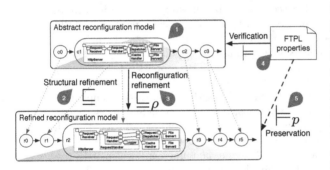

Fig. 1. Verification and preservation through refinement

Moreover, we want the refinement to preserve temporal properties. To express temporal properties over architectural reconfigurations of Fractal [8] component-based systems, a temporal pattern logic, called FTPL, has been defined [9] (**4** in Fig. 1). FTPL allows expressing architectural invariants, both event and temporal properties involving different kinds of temporal patterns which have been shown useful in practice. The third contribution of this paper consists in proving that the refinement relation—a special kind of simulation—*preserves* (**5** in Fig. 1) the FTPL properties: any property verified at a given refinement level is ensured, "for free", at the following refinement levels, provided that the refinement relation holds.

The remainder of the paper is organised as follows. We briefly recall in Sect. 2 the architectural (re-)configuration model and the FTPL syntax and semantics. We then define in Sect. 3 the structural refinement between two architectural configurations, before integrating it into the reconfiguration model refinement. Section 4 shows that the refinement relation preserves FTPL properties. Finally, Section 5 concludes and gives some perspectives.

2   Architectural Reconfiguration Model

This section briefly recalls, because of a lack of room, the architectural reconfiguration model formally given in [9,10], and the temporal pattern logic for dynamic reconfigurations, called FTPL in [9].

2.1   Component-Based Architectures

In general, the system configuration is the specific definition of the elements that define or prescribe what a system is composed of. The architectural elements we consider (components, interfaces and parameters) are the core entities of a component-based system, and relations over them express various links between these basic architectural elements. In this section we sum up formal definitions given in [9,10]. To this end, we consider a graph-based representation in Fig. 2, inspired by the model for Fractal in [6].

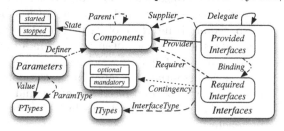

Fig. 2. Architectural elements and relations

In our model, a configuration c is a tuple $\langle Elem, Rel \rangle$ where $Elem$ is a set of architectural elements, and $Rel \subseteq Elem \times Elem$ is a relation over architectural elements. The architectural elements of $Elem$ are the core entities of a component-based system:

- *Components* is a non-empty set of the core entities, i.e. components;
- *RequiredInterfaces* and *ProvidedInterfaces* are defined to be subsets of *Interfaces*;
- *Parameters* is a set of component parameters;
- *ITypes* is the set of the types associated with interfaces;
- *PType* is a set of data types associated with parameters. Each data type is a set of data values. For the sake of readability, we identify data type names with the corresponding data domains.

The architectural relation *Rel* then expresses various links between the previously mentioned architectural elements.

- *InterfaceType* is a total function that associates a type with each interface;
- *Supplier* is a total function to determine the component of a provided or of a required interface; *Provider* is a total surjective function which gives the component having at least a provided interface of interest, whereas *Requirer* is only a total function;
- *Contingency* is a total function which indicates for each required interface whether it is *mandatory* or *optional*;
- *Definer* is a total function which gives the component of a considered parameter;
- *Parent* is a relation linking sub-components to the corresponding composite component. Composite components have no parameter, and a sub-component must not be a composite including its parent component;
- *Binding* is a partial function to connect a provided interface with a required one: a provided interface can be linked to only one required interface, whereas

a required interface can be the target of one or more provided interfaces. Moreover, two linked interfaces do not belong to the same component, but their corresponding components are sub-components of the same composite component. The considered interfaces must have the same interface type. Also, they have not been involved in a delegation yet;

- *Delegate* describes delegation links. It is a partial bijection which associates a provided (resp. required) interface of a sub-component with a provided (resp. required) interface of its parent. Both interfaces must have the same type, and they have not been involved in a binding yet;
- *State* is a total function which associates a value from {*started, stopped*} with each instantiated component: a component can be *started* only if all its mandatory required interfaces are bound or delegated;
- Last, *Value* is a total function which gives the current value of a considered parameter.

Example 1. To illustrate our model, let us consider an example of an HTTP server from [12,6]. The architecture of this server is depicted in Fig. 3. The **RequestReceiver** component reads HTTP requests from the network and transmits them to the **RequestHandler** component. In order to keep the response time as short as possible, **RequestHandler** can either use a cache (with the component **CacheHandler**) or directly transmit the request to the **RequestDispatcher** component. The number of requests (load) and the percentage of similar requests (deviation) are two parameters defined for the **RequestHandler** component:

1. The **CacheHandler** component is used only if the number of similar HTTP requests is high.
2. The memorySize for the **CacheHandler** component must depend on the overall load of the server.
3. The validityDuration of data in the cache must also depend on the overall load of the server.
4. The number of used file servers (like the **FileServer1** and **FileServer2** components) used by **RequestDispatcher** depends on the overall load of the server.

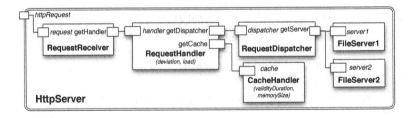

Fig. 3. HTTP Server architecture

We now introduce a set CP of configuration propositions which are constraints on the architectural elements and the relations between them. These constraints are specified using first order (FO) logic formulas over constants $\{\top, \bot\}$, variables in $\mathcal{V}$ to reason on elements of $Elem$, functions and relations from Rel, predicates $S_{\mathcal{P}} = \{\in, =, \ldots\}$, connectors $\wedge$, $\vee$, $\neg$, $\Rightarrow$, and quantifiers $\exists$, $\forall$ [13]. Then the interpretation of functions, relations, and predicates over $Elem$ is done according to basic definitions in [13] and the model definition in [9].

The configuration properties are expressed at different specification levels. At the component model level, the constraints are common to all the component architectures. Furthermore, some constraints must be expressed to restrict a family of component architectures (a profile level), or to restrict a specific component architecture (an application level).

Example 2. Let $CacheConnected$ be a configuration property defined by

$$\exists \, cache, getCache \in Interfaces. \left(\begin{array}{l} Provider(\text{cache}) = \textbf{CacheHandler} \\ \wedge \; Requirer(\text{getCache}) = \textbf{RequestHandler} \\ \wedge \; Binding(\text{cache}) = \text{getCache} \end{array} \right)$$

This property expresses that the **CacheHandler** component is connected to the **RequestHandler** component through their respective interfaces.

2.2   Reconfigurations: From a Component Architecture to Another

To make the component-based architecture evolve dynamically, we introduce reconfigurations which are combinations of primitive operations such as instantiation/destruction of components; addition/removal of components; binding/unbinding of component interfaces; starting/stopping components; setting parameter values of components. The normal running of different components also changes the architecture by modifying parameter values or stopping components. Let $\mathcal{R}_{run} = \mathcal{R} \cup \{run\}$ be a set of evolution operations, where $\mathcal{R}$ is a finite set of reconfiguration operations, and run is an action to represent running operations. Given a component architecture and $\mathcal{R}_{run}$, the possible evolutions of the component architecture are defined as a transition system over $\mathcal{R}_{run}$.

Definition 1. *The operational semantics of component systems with reconfigurations is defined by the labelled transition system* $S = \langle \mathcal{C}, \mathcal{C}^0, \mathcal{R}_{run}, \rightarrow, l \rangle$ *where* $\mathcal{C} = \{c, c_1, c_2, \ldots\}$ *is a set of configurations,* $\mathcal{C}^0 \in \mathcal{C}$ *is a set of initial configurations,* $\mathcal{R}_{run}$ *is a finite set of evolution operations,* $\rightarrow \subseteq \mathcal{C} \times \mathcal{R}_{run} \times \mathcal{C}$ *is the reconfiguration relation[2], and* $l : \mathcal{C} \rightarrow CP$ *is a total function to label each* $c \in \mathcal{C}$ *with the largest conjunction of* $cp \in CP$ *evaluated to true on* c.

Let us note $c \xrightarrow{ope} c'$ when a target configuration $c' = \langle Elem', Rel' \rangle$ is reached from a configuration $c = \langle Elem, Rel \rangle$ by an evolution operation $ope \in \mathcal{R}_{run}$. Given the model $S = \langle \mathcal{C}, \mathcal{C}^0, \mathcal{R}_{run}, \rightarrow, l \rangle$, an evolution path (or a path for short) σ of S is a (possibly infinite) sequence of configurations $c_0, c_1, c_2, \ldots$ such that $\forall i \geq 0.(\exists \, ope_i \in \mathcal{R}_{run}.(c_i \xrightarrow{ope_i} c_{i+1} \in \rightarrow))$. We write $\sigma(i)$ to denote the i-th configuration of a path σ. The notation σ_i denotes the suffix path $\sigma(i)$,

---

[2] Actually, $\rightarrow$ is a reconfiguration function because of the architectural model.

$\sigma(i+1), \ldots$, and σ_i^j denotes the segment path $\sigma(i), \sigma(i+1), \sigma(i+2), \ldots, \sigma(j-1), \sigma(j)$. The segment path is infinite in length when the last state of the segment is repeated infinitely. Let Σ denotes the set of paths, and Σ^f $(\subseteq \Sigma)$ the set of finite paths.

Example 3. For the HTTP server, the reconfiguration operations are: Add-CacheHandler and RemoveCacheHandler which are respectively used to add and remove the **CacheHandler** component; AddFileServer and removeFileServer which are respectively used to add and remove the **FileServer2** component; Memory-SizeUp and MemorySizeDown which are respectively used to increase and to decrease the MemorySize value; DurationValidityUp and DurationValidityDown to respectively increase and decrease the ValidityDuration value. A possible evolution path of the HTTP server architecture is given in Fig. 4.

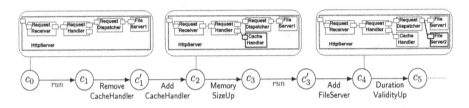

Fig. 4. Part of an evolution path of the HTTP server architecture

2.3 FTPL: A Temporal Logic for Dynamic Reconfigurations

Let us first give the FTPL syntax in Fig. 5. Basically, constraints on the architectural elements and the relations between them are specified as configuration propositions in Sect. 2.1. In addition, the language contains events from reconfiguration operations, trace properties and, finally, temporal properties. Let $Prop_{FTPL}$ denote the set of FTPL formulae.

$<temp> ::=$	**after** $<event> <temp>$
	before $<event> <trace>$
	$<trace>$ **until** $<event>$
$<trace> ::=$	**always** cp
	eventually cp
	$<trace> \land <trace>$
	$<trace> \lor <trace>$
$<event> ::=$	ope **normal**
	ope **exceptional**
	ope **terminates**

Fig. 5. FTPL syntax

Let $cp \in CP$ be a configuration property, and c a configuration. We say that c satisfies cp, written $c \models cp$, when $l(c) \Rightarrow cp$. We also say that cp is valid on c. Otherwise, we write $c \not\models cp$ when c does not satisfy cp. For example, for the *CacheConnected* configuration property from Example 2 and the path from Fig. 4, we have $c_2 \models CacheConnected$ whereas $c_1 \not\models CacheConnected$.

Definition 2 (FTPL semantics). *Let $\sigma \in \Sigma$. The FTPL semantics $\Sigma \times Prop_{FTPL} \to \mathbb{B}$ is defined by induction on the form of the formulae as follows:*

For the events:		
$\sigma(i) \models ope$ **normal**	if	$i > 0 \wedge \sigma(i-1) \neq \sigma(i) \wedge \sigma(i-1) \overset{ope}{\rightarrow} \sigma(i) \in \rightarrow$
$\sigma(i) \models ope$ **exceptional**	if	$i > 0 \wedge \sigma(i-1) = \sigma(i) \wedge \sigma(i-1) \overset{ope}{\rightarrow} \sigma(i) \in \rightarrow$
$\sigma(i) \models ope$ **terminates**	if	$\sigma(i) \models ope$ **normal** $\vee \, \sigma(i) \models ope$ **exceptional**
For the trace properties:		
$\sigma \models$ **always** cp	if	$\forall i.(i \geqslant 0 \; \Rightarrow \sigma(i) \models cp)$
$\sigma \models$ **eventually** cp	if	$\exists i.(i \geqslant 0 \wedge \sigma(i) \models cp)$
$\sigma \models trace_1 \wedge trace_2$	if	$\sigma \models trace_1 \wedge \sigma \models trace_2$
$\sigma \models trace_1 \vee trace_2$	if	$\sigma \models trace_1 \vee \sigma \models trace_2$
For the temporal properties:		
$\sigma \models$ **after** $event$ $temp$	if	$\forall i.(i \geqslant 0 \wedge \sigma(i) \models event \Rightarrow \sigma_i \models temp)$
$\sigma \models$ **before** $event$ $trace$	if	$\forall i.(i > 0 \wedge \sigma(i) \models event \Rightarrow \sigma_0^{i-1} \models trace)$
$\sigma \models trace$ **until** $event$	if	$\exists i.(i > 0 \wedge \sigma(i) \models event \wedge \sigma_0^{i-1} \models trace)$

An architectural reconfiguration model $S = \langle \mathcal{C}, \mathcal{C}^0, \mathcal{R}_{run}, \rightarrow, l \rangle$ satisfies a property $\phi \in Prop_{FTPL}$, denoted $S \models \phi$, if $\forall \sigma.(\sigma \in \Sigma(S) \wedge \sigma(0) \in \mathcal{C}^0 \Rightarrow \sigma \models \phi)$.

Example 4. The FTPL framework allows handling architectural invariants from [12,6]. The following property expresses an architectural constraint saying that at least there is always one file server component connected to **Request-Dispatcher**.

$$\textbf{always} \left(\exists \textsf{getServer} \in Interfaces. \left(\begin{array}{l} Requirer(\textsf{getServer}) = \textsf{RequestDispatcher} \\ \wedge \exists i \in Interfaces.(Binding(i) = \textsf{getServer}) \end{array} \right) \right)$$

Example 5. The following temporal property specifies that after calling up the AddCacheHandler reconfiguration operation, the **CacheHandler** component is always connected to **RequestHandler**. In other words, the *CacheConnected* configuration property from Example 2 holds on all the path after calling up AddCacheHandler:

after AddCacheHandler **normal always** *CacheConnected*

3 Refinement of Architectural Reconfiguration Models

This section defines a new notion of a structural configuration refinement between two architectural configurations, and then gives the reconfiguration model refinement as defined in the style of Milner-Park's simulation.

3.1 Structural Configuration Refinement

In this section we introduce a *structural* refinement of a component-based architecture. This refinement aims to respect component encapsulation, i.e. the refinement of a component does not cause any changes outside of this component. In fact, the refined component must have the same interfaces of the same types as before. This way other components do not see the difference between the component and its refined version, and thus there is no need to adapt them.

Example 6. Let us illustrate our goal on the example of the HTTP server. We consider the configuration c_A given Fig. 6, and we refine the **RequestHandler** by two new components: **RequestAnalyzer** and **Logger**, to obtain a new *refined* configuration c_R. **RequestAnalyzer** handles requests to determine the values of

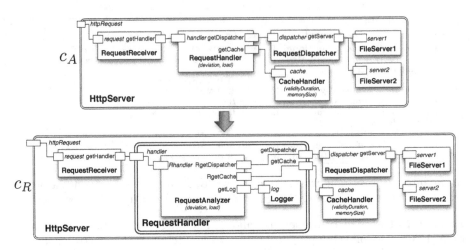

Fig. 6. A refinement of the **HttpServer** component

the deviation and load parameters. **Logger** allows **RequestAnalyzer** to memorise requests to choose either **RequestDispatcher** or **CacheHandler**, if it is available, to answer requests. The "old" **RequestHandler** component becomes a composite component which encapsulates the new components. Its interfaces remain the same as the interfaces of the old component.

Let $c_A = \langle Elem_A, Rel_A \rangle$ and $c_R = \langle Elem_R, Rel_R \rangle$ be two architectural configurations at two—an abstract and a refined—levels of refinement. To distinguish architectural elements at the abstract level and at the refined level, the elements are renamed to have $Elem_A \cap Elem_R = \varnothing$. To define the structural refinement, we have to link together an abstract and a refined configuration, i.e. express how all the architectural elements and relations are associated with their refined versions: a *gluing* predicate $gp : Elem_A \rightarrow Elem_R$ must be defined as a mapping to link the abstract and the refined elements which respects the $Elem$ signature.

In addition to this gluing predicate gp, component-based structural constraints are necessary to ensure that the proposed refinement respects the component semantics, i.e. which changes are allowed or prescribed during the refinement process. These *architectural constraints*, named AC, are defined as the conjunction of the propositions given in Table 1, with the following meanings:

- *In the system parts not concerned by the refinement, all the core entities and all the relations between them remain unchanged through refinement* (constraints (G), (H), (I) and (J));
- *The new elements introduced during the refinement process must satisfy the following constraints:*
  - In the refined architecture the new components must be subcomponents of components existing before refinement (constraint (K));
  - The new interfaces are associated with the new components (constraint (C));

Table 1. Structural refinement constraints AC

$$\forall i_A \in Interfaces_A, \atop \exists i_R \in Interfaces_R \cdot \left(\begin{array}{l} (gp(i_A) = i_R \wedge Contingency_A(i_A) = Contingency_R(i_R)) \wedge \\ \forall t_A \in ITypes_A.(InterfaceType_A(i_A) = t_A \Rightarrow \\ \exists t_R \in ITypes_R.(InterfaceType_R(i_R) = t_R \wedge gp(t_A) = t_R)) \end{array} \right) \quad (A)$$

$$\forall i_A \in Interfaces_A, \atop \forall c_A \in Components_A \cdot \left(\begin{array}{l} Supplier_A(i_A) = c_A \Rightarrow \\ \exists i_R \in Interface_R, \exists c_R \in Components_R. \\ (Supplier_R(i_R) = c_R \wedge gp(i_A) = i_R \wedge gp(c_A) = c_R)) \end{array} \right) \quad (B)$$

$$\forall i_R \in Interface_R, \atop \forall i_A \in Interface_A \cdot \left(\begin{array}{l} gp(i_A) \neq i_R \Rightarrow \\ \exists c_R \in Components_R.(Supplier_R(i_R) = c_R \wedge \\ \forall c_A \in Components_A. \, gp(c_A \neq c_R)) \end{array} \right) \quad (C)$$

$$\forall p_A \in Parameters_A, \atop \forall t_A \in PTypes_A \cdot \left(\begin{array}{l} ParameterType_A(p_A) = t_A \Rightarrow \\ \exists p_R \in Parameters_R, \exists t_R \in PTypes_R. \\ \left(\begin{array}{l} ParameterType_R(p_R) = t_R \\ \wedge Value_A(p_A) = Value_R(p_R) \\ \wedge gp(p_A) = p_R \wedge gp(t_A) = t_R) \end{array} \right) \end{array} \right) \quad (D)$$

$$\forall p_R \in Parameters_R, \atop \forall p_A \in Parameters_A \cdot \left(\begin{array}{l} gp(p_A) \neq p_R \Rightarrow \\ \exists c_R \in Components_R. \, \forall c_A \in Components_A. \\ (Definer_R(p_R) = c_R \wedge gp(c_A) \neq c_R) \end{array} \right) \quad (E)$$

$$\forall p_A \in Parameters_A, \atop \forall c_A \in Components_A \cdot \left(\begin{array}{l} Definer_A(p_A) = c_A \Rightarrow \\ \exists p_R \in Parameters_R, \exists c_R \in Components_R. \\ \left(\begin{array}{l} gp(p_A) = p_R \wedge gp(c_A) = c_R \wedge \\ (Definer(p_R) = c_R \vee ((Definer_R(p_R), c_R) \in Parent_R^+)) \end{array} \right) \end{array} \right) \quad (F)$$

$$\forall ri_A \in IRequired_A, \atop \forall pi_A \in IProvided_A \cdot \left(\begin{array}{l} Binding_A(ri_A) = pi_A \Rightarrow \\ \exists ri_R \in IRequired_R, \exists pi_R \in IProvided_R. \\ (Binding_R(ri_R) = pi_R \wedge gp(ri_A) = ri_R \wedge gp(pi_A) = pi_R) \end{array} \right) \quad (G)$$

$$\forall i_A, i_A' \in Interface_A. \left(\begin{array}{l} Delegate_A(i_A) = i_A' \Rightarrow \\ \exists i_R, i_R' \in Interface_R. \\ (Delegate_R(i_R) = i_R' \wedge gp(i_A) = i_R \wedge gp(i_A') = i_R') \end{array} \right) \quad (H)$$

$$\forall c_A, c_A' \in Components_A, \atop \exists c_R, c_R' \in Components_R \cdot \left(\begin{array}{l} (gp(c_A) = c_R \wedge gp(c_A') = c_R' \wedge (c_A', c_A) \in Parent_A) \\ \Rightarrow (c_R', c_R) \in Parent_R \end{array} \right) \quad (I)$$

$$\forall c_A \in Components_A. \left(\begin{array}{l} \exists c_R \in Components_R. \\ (gp(c_A) = c_R \wedge State_A(p_A) = State_R(p_R)) \end{array} \right) \quad (J)$$

$$\forall c_A, c_A' \in Components_A, \atop \forall c_R \in Components_R \cdot \left(\begin{array}{l} (c_A, c_A') \notin Parent_A \wedge (gp(c_A') \neq c_R) \Rightarrow \\ \exists c_R' \in Components_R. \\ (gp(c_A') = c_R' \wedge (c_R, c_R') \in Parent_R) \end{array} \right) \quad (K)$$

$$\forall c_A, c_A' \in Components_A, \atop \forall i_A' \in Interface_A \cdot \atop \forall c_R' \in Components_R \left(\begin{array}{l} (c_A, c_A') \notin Parent_A \wedge gp(c_A') = c_R' \wedge Supplier_A(i_A') = c_A' \Rightarrow \\ \exists c_R \in Components_R.((c_R, c_R') \in Parent_R) \wedge \\ \exists i_R, i_R' \in Interface_R. \\ (\, gp(i_A') = i_R \wedge Supplier_R(i_R') = c_R' \wedge i_R' = Delegate(i_R) \,) \end{array} \right) \quad (L)$$

- The new parameters are associated with the new components (constraint (E));

- *Finally, for the architectural elements existing before and impacted by the refinement, the constraints are as follows:*

  - All the interfaces of the components existing before and detailed during the refinement must be delegated interfaces, these components being composites after refinement (constraints (A), (B) and (L));
  - All the parameters of the components existing before and detailed during the refinement must be associated with the new subcomponents (constraints (D) and (F)).

Definition 3 (Structural Configuration Refinement). *Let* $c_A = \langle Elem_A, Rel_A \rangle$ *and* $c_R = \langle Elem_R, Rel_R \rangle$ *be two configurations, and AC the architectural constraints. The configuration* c_R *refines* c_A *wrt. AC, written* $c_R \sqsubseteq c_A$, *if* $l_R(c_R) \wedge AC \Rightarrow l_A(c_A)$.

3.2 Reconfiguration Models Refinement

As an architecture may dynamically evolve through reconfigurations, it concerns refined architectures, where new non primitive reconfigurations may be introduced to handle the new components. For example, in the refined system presented Fig. 6, a possible new reconfiguration RemoveLogger consists in removing the **Logger** component which does not exist at the abstract level.

We consider the new reconfigurations introduced during the refinement process as being *non observable*: they are called τ-reconfiguration. In addition, we define a one-to-one function fc to link the refined reconfiguration actions with the abstract ones as follows: $fc : \mathcal{R}_{run_R} \setminus \{\tau\} \rightarrow \mathcal{R}_{run_A}$ such that $\forall r_R.(r_R \in \mathcal{R}_{run_R} \setminus \{\tau\} \Rightarrow \exists r_A.(r_A \in \mathcal{R}_{run_A} \wedge fc(r_R) = r_A)$.

Following [14], the refinement relation ρ is defined in the style of Milner-Park [15] as a τ-simulation having the following properties[3]:

1. The new reconfiguration actions renamed by τ should not take control forever: the τ- livelocks are forbidden.
2. Moreover, the new reconfiguration actions should not introduce deadlocks.

Definition 4 (Refinement relation). *Let* $S_A = \langle \mathcal{C}_A, \mathcal{C}_A^0, \mathcal{R}_{run_A}, \rightarrow_A, l_A \rangle$ *and* $S_R = \langle \mathcal{C}_R, \mathcal{C}_R^0, \mathcal{R}_{run_R}, \rightarrow_R, l_R \rangle$ *be two reconfiguration models,* $r \in \mathcal{R}_{run_R}$ *and* σ_R *a path of* S_R. *We define the relation* $\rho \subseteq \mathcal{C}_R \times \mathcal{C}_A$ *as the greatest binary relation satisfying the following conditions: structural refinement* $(c_R \sqsubseteq c_A)$, *strict transition refinement (4.1), stuttering transition refinement (4.2), non* τ-*divergence (4.3), non introduction of deadlocks (4.4).*

---

[3] These features are common to other formalisms, like action systems refinement [16] or LTL refinement [1].

$$\forall c_A \in \mathcal{C}_A, \forall c_R, c'_R \in \mathcal{C}_R.(c_R \ \rho \ c_A \wedge c_R \xrightarrow{\tau} c'_R \ \Rightarrow \ \exists c'_A.(c_A \xrightarrow{fc(r)} c'_A \wedge c'_R \ \rho \ c'_A)) \tag{4.1}$$

$$\forall c_A \in \mathcal{C}_A, \forall c_R, c'_R \in \mathcal{C}_R.(c_R \ \rho \ c_A \wedge c_R \xrightarrow{\tau} c'_R \ \Rightarrow \ c'_R \ \rho \ c_A) \tag{4.2}$$

$$\forall k.(k \geq 0 \ \Rightarrow \ \exists k'.(k' > k \wedge \sigma_R(k' - 1) \xrightarrow{\tau} \sigma_R(k') \in \rightarrow_R)) \tag{4.3}$$

$$\forall c_A \in \mathcal{C}_A, \forall c_R \in \mathcal{C}_R.(c_R \ \rho \ c_A \wedge c_R \not\rightarrow \ \Rightarrow \ c_A \not\rightarrow) \tag{4.4}$$

We say that S_R refines S_A, written $S_R \sqsubseteq_\rho S_A$, if $\forall c_R.(c_R \in \mathcal{C}_R^0 \Rightarrow \exists c_A.(c_A \in \mathcal{C}_A^0 \wedge c_R \ \rho \ c_A))$.

As a consequence of Definition 4, we give an important property of this relation allowing to ensure the existence of an abstract path for any refined path.

Proposition 1. *Let S_A and S_R be two reconfiguration models such that $S_R \sqsubseteq_\rho S_A$. Then, $\forall c_R.(c_R \in \mathcal{C}_R \Rightarrow \exists c_A.(c_A \in \mathcal{C}_A \wedge c_R \ \rho \ c_A))$.*

Proof (Sketch). Suppose that c_R can be reached by a path σ_R such that $\sigma_R(0) \in \mathcal{C}_R^0$ and $\sigma_R(i) = c_R$. By Clause (4.3) of Def. 4 σ_R contains a finite number of τ-reconfiguration actions, and σ_R is of the form $\sigma_R(0) \xrightarrow{\tau} \ldots \xrightarrow{\tau} \sigma_R(n_1) \xrightarrow{r_1} \sigma_R(n_1 + 1) \xrightarrow{\tau} \ldots \xrightarrow{r_n} \sigma_R(i - n_m) \xrightarrow{\tau} \ldots \sigma_R(i)$. Moreover, there is a configuration $c_A \in \mathcal{C}_A^0$ such that $\sigma_R(0) \ \rho \ c_A$. We can then build a path from $c_A = \sigma_A(0)$ such that the configurations of σ_A are linked by transitions labelled by reconfigurations $fc(r_1) \ldots fc(r_n) : \sigma_A = c_A^0 \xrightarrow{fc(r_1)} c_A^1 \xrightarrow{fc(r_2)} \ldots \xrightarrow{fc(r_n)} c_A^n (= \sigma_A(j))$. This way the configuration $\sigma_A(j)$ is reached, and by Clauses (4.1) and (4.2) of Def. 4 we have $\sigma_R(i) \ \rho \ \sigma_A(j)$. $\qquad\qquad\square$

Example 7. The reconfiguration path of the HTTP server from Fig. 4 can be refined as depicted in Fig. 7, where the abstract configuration c_4 is refined by the configurations r_5 and r_6: the new reconfigurations renamed by τ concern the new component **Logger** introduced during the refinement: it is possible to add or to remove the **Logger** component.

4   Preservation of FTPL Properties through Refinement

In many formalisms supporting a design by refinement, systems properties are preserved from abstract models to their refined models [17,1,18]. In this section we show that FTPL properties are also preserved through our architectural reconfiguration models refinement. This idea is depicted by Fig. 1.

Let S_A and S_R be two reconfiguration models such that S_R refines S_A. These systems being defined over different sets of architectural elements and reconfigurations, we have to give a new validity definition to be able to deal with an abstract system at a refined level. Actually, we make use of the fc function to link reconfiguration actions, and of the ρ refinement relation to define the validity of a FTPL property by preservation, as follows.

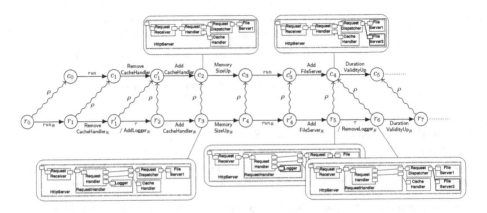

Fig. 7. A refinement of a reconfiguration path of the HTTP server

Definition 5 (FTPL semantics by preservation). *Let* $S_R = \langle \mathcal{C}_R, \mathcal{C}_R^0, \mathcal{R}_{run_R}, \rightarrow_R, l_R \rangle$ *and* $S_A = \langle \mathcal{C}_A, \mathcal{C}_A^0, \mathcal{R}_{run_A}, \rightarrow_A, l_A \rangle$ *be two reconfiguration models such that* $S_R \sqsubseteq_\rho S_A$. *Let* σ_R *be a path of* S_R, ϕ_A *a FTPL property over* S_A. *We define the validity of* ϕ_A *on* σ_R *by preservation, written* $\sigma_R \models_p \phi_A$, *by induction on the form of* ϕ_A:

$\sigma_R(i) \models_p cp_A$	if $\sigma_A(j) \models cp_A \wedge \sigma_R(i) \rho \sigma_A(j)$
$\sigma_R(i) \models_p ope_A$ **normal**	if $i > 0 \wedge \sigma_R(i-1) \neq \sigma_R(i) \wedge \sigma_R(i-1) \xrightarrow{fc^{-1}(ope_A)}_R \sigma_R(i)$
$\sigma_R(i) \models_p ope_A$ **exceptional**	if $i > 0 \wedge \sigma_R(i-1) = \sigma_R(i) \wedge \sigma_R(i-1) \xrightarrow{fc^{-1}(ope_A)}_R \sigma_R(i)$
$\sigma_R \models_p$ **always** cp_A	if $\forall i.(i \geq 0 \Rightarrow \sigma_R(i) \models_p cp_A)$
$\sigma_R \models_p$ **eventually** cp_A	if $\exists i.(i \geq 0 \wedge \sigma_R(i) \models_p cp_A)$
$\sigma_R \models_p$ **after** e_A tpp_A	if $\forall i.(i \geq 0 \wedge \sigma_R(i) \models_p e_A \Rightarrow \sigma_{i_R} \models_p tpp_A)$
$\sigma_R \models_p$ **before** e_A trp_A	if $\forall i.(i > 0 \wedge \sigma_R(i) \models_p e_A \Rightarrow \sigma_0^{i-1}{}_R \models_p trp_A)$
$\sigma_R \models_p trp_A$ **until** e_A	if $\exists i.(i > 0 \wedge \sigma_R(i) \models_p e_A \wedge \sigma_0^{i-1}{}_R \models_p trp_A)$

We note $S_R \models_p \phi_A$ when $\forall \sigma_R.(\sigma_R \in \Sigma(S_R) \wedge \sigma_R(0) \in \mathcal{C}^0 \Rightarrow \sigma_R(0) \models_p \phi_A)$.

Now, we prove that FTPL properties are preserved by the reconfiguration refinement defined in Sect. 3.

Theorem 1 (Preservation of a FTPL property on a path). *Let* S_A *and* S_R *be two reconfiguration models such that* $S_R \sqsubseteq_\rho S_A$. *Let* ϕ *be a FTPL property. Let* $\sigma_A \in \Sigma(S_A)$ *and* $\sigma_R \in \Sigma(S_R)$ *be two paths. Then we have* $\forall i, j.(0 \leq i \leq j \wedge (\sigma_R(j) \rho \sigma_A(i)) \wedge \sigma_A \models \phi \Rightarrow \sigma_R \models_p \phi)$.

Proof (Part of Theorem 1). Let $\sigma_R \in \Sigma(S_R)$ be a path refining a path $\sigma_A \in \Sigma(S_A)$ (the proof of Proposition 1 ensures that this path exists). Besides, $ope_R, ope'_R, \ldots \in \mathcal{R}_{run_R}$ label the transitions of S_R, and τ labels each transition introduced during refinement. The proof is done by structural induction on the form of ϕ; only two cases are given here because of lack of room[4].

---

[4] The whole proof can be found in [19].

1. Let us prove that ope_A **normal** is preserved by refinement. By hypothesis, $\sigma_A(i) \models ope_A$ **normal**, and so, by Def. 2 we have (i). As by hypothesis $\sigma_R(j) \; \rho \; \sigma_A(i)$, by construction there is a path σ_A such that $\sigma_R(0)$ refines $\sigma_A(0)$ and where $ope_A = fc(ope_R)$. Consequently, by Proposition 1 we have (ii). Moreover, it implies that there are two configurations $\sigma_R(j)$ and $\sigma_R(l)$ such that $\sigma_R(l) \; \rho \; \sigma_A(i-1)$ and $\sigma_R(j) \; \rho \; \sigma_A(i)$. There are two cases:

   (a) If $\sigma_R(l) \overset{ope_R}{\to}_R \sigma_R(j)$ then $l = j-1$, and immediately we can deduce (iii). Then by Def. 5, $\sigma_R \models_p ope_A$ **normal**, and we are done.

   (b) If $\sigma_R(l) \overset{\tau}{\to}_R \sigma_R(l+1)$, then by Clause (4.2) of Def. 4 we have $\sigma_R(l+1) \; \rho \; \sigma_A(i-1)$, and we can continue with the following configuration of σ_R. According to Clauses (4.3) and (4.4) of Def. 4, the reconfigurations labelled by τ cannot take control forever, and the refinement does not introduce deadlocks. So, there is a configuration $\sigma(l+n)$ such that $\sigma_R(l+n) \; \rho \; \sigma_A(i-1)$ and $\sigma_R(l+n) \overset{ope_R}{\to} \sigma_R(j)$. We set $l+n = j-1$ and consequently we have (iii). Then, by Def. 5, $\sigma_R \models_p ope_A$ **normal**.

$$i > 0 \wedge \sigma_A(i-1) \neq \sigma_A(i) \wedge (\sigma_A(i-1) \overset{fc(ope_R)}{\to}_A \sigma_A(i)) \in \to_A \qquad \text{(i)}$$

$$\forall j.(j \geq 0 \Rightarrow \exists k.(k \geq 0 \wedge \sigma_R(j) \; \rho \; \sigma_A(k))) \qquad \text{(ii)}$$

$$j > 0 \wedge \sigma_R(j-1) \neq \sigma_R(j) \wedge (\sigma_R(j-1) \overset{ope_R}{\to}_R \sigma_R(j)) \in \to_R \qquad \text{(iii)}$$

2. Let us prove that trp_A **until** e_A is preserved by refinement, with the recurrence hypotheses that trp_A and e_A are preserved by refinement. By hypothesis, we have $\sigma_A \models trp_A$ **until** e_A. So, by Def. 2 we have (iv). As by hypothesis $\sigma_R(j) \; \rho \; \sigma_A(i)$, by construction there is a path σ_A such that $\sigma_R(0)$ refines $\sigma_A(0)$ and where $ope_A = fc(ope_R)$. Consequently, by Proposition 1 we have (v). Moreover, by construction, there is a finite part $\sigma_0^{j-1}{}_R$ of σ_R whose configurations refine the configurations of a corresponding finite part $\sigma_0^{i-1}{}_A$ of σ_A, ensuring (vi). By recurrence hypotheses, trp and e are preserved by refinement. So, we have (vii). Then, by Def. 5, $\sigma_R \models_p trp_A$ **until** e_A.

$$\exists i.(i > 0 \wedge \sigma_A(i) \models e_A \Rightarrow \sigma_0^{i-1}{}_A \models trp_A) \qquad \text{(iv)}$$

$$\forall j.(j \geq 0 \Rightarrow \exists k.(k \geq 0 \wedge \sigma_R(j) \; \rho \; \sigma_A(k))) \qquad \text{(v)}$$

$$\forall k.(0 \leq k < j \Rightarrow \exists k'.(0 \leq k' < i \wedge \sigma_0^{j-1}{}_R(k) \; \rho \; \sigma_0^{i-1}{}_A(k'))) \qquad \text{(vi)}$$

$$\exists j.(j > 0 \wedge \sigma_R(j) \models_p e_A \Rightarrow \sigma_0^{j-1}{}_R \models_p trp_A) \qquad \text{(vii)}$$

$\square$

We are ready to generalise Theorem 1 from paths to reconfiguration models.

Theorem 2 (Preservation of a FTPL property by refinement). *Let $S_A = \langle \mathcal{C}_A, \mathcal{C}_A^0, \mathcal{R}_{run_A}, \to_A, l_A \rangle$ and $S_R = \langle \mathcal{C}_R, \mathcal{C}_R^0, \mathcal{R}_{run_R}, \to_R, l_R \rangle$ be two reconfiguration models such that $S_R \sqsubseteq_\rho S_A$. Let ϕ be a FTPL property. If $S_A \models \phi$ then $S_R \models_p \phi$.*

Proof. Immediate. If $S_R \sqsubseteq_\rho S_A$ then $\forall \sigma_R.(\sigma_R \in \Sigma(S_R) \wedge \sigma_R(0) \in \mathcal{C}_R^0 \Rightarrow \exists \sigma_A.(\sigma_A \in \Sigma(S_A) \wedge \sigma_A(0) \in \mathcal{C}_A^0 \wedge \sigma_R(0) \rho \sigma_A(0)))$. Moreover, if $S_A \models \phi$ then by definition $\forall \sigma_A.(\sigma_A \in \Sigma(S_A) \Rightarrow \sigma_A \models \phi)$. The reconfiguration relations of both S_R and S_A being functional, there is no abstract path different from σ_A which could be refined by σ_R. We then can apply Theorem 1.   □

Example 8. For our running example of the HTTP server, let us consider again the path refinement in Fig. 7. In this refinement, the **RequestHandler** component is refined as depicted in Fig. 6. Let us consider again the temporal property from Example 5:

$$\sigma \models \textbf{after} \; \mathsf{AddCacheHandler} \; \textbf{normal always} \; CacheConnected$$

It is easy to see that this property is valid on the abstract path depicted in Fig. 7. Moreover, as presented in this figure, the ρ refinement relation holds between the configurations of the illustrated part of the refined path and the corresponding part of the abstract path. Consequently, this property is also valid by preservation on the refined path depicted in Fig. 7.

5   Conclusion

In this paper, we have enriched a theoretical framework for dynamic reconfigurations of component architectures with a new notion of a structural refinement of architectures, which respects the component encapsulation. Then we have integrated this structural refinement into a behavioural refinement relation for dynamic reconfigurations defined in the style of Milner-Park's simulation [15] between reconfiguration models. Afterwards, we have shown that this refinement relation preserves the FTPL properties—architectural invariants, event properties and temporal properties involving different kinds of temporal patterns shown useful in practice. The preservation means that any FTPL property expressed and established for an abstract system is also established for the refined counterparts, provided that the refinement relation holds. This way we ensure the system's consistency at different refinement levels, and we free the specifier from expressing and verifying properties at these levels with new details, components, reconfigurations.

To check the structural refinement, we plan to pursue further and to extend our previous work on the verification of the architectural consistency through reconfigurations [10]. The structural refinement constraints in Table 1 could be formalised and validated in a similar manner. Another solution would be to exploit the architectural description language (ADL) describing component architectures in XML. It becomes possible then to use XML tools for checking the structural refinement between two component architectures.

To conclude, this work on property preservation is used as a hypothesis for our running work on the runtime FTPL verification [11]. We have reviewed FTPL from a runtime point of view [11] by introducing a new four-valued logic, called RV-FTPL, characterising the "potential" (un)satisfiability of the architectural and temporal constraints: potential true and potential false values are chosen whenever an observed behaviour has not yet lead to a violation or satisfiability of the property under consideration. We intend to accompany this work with a runtime checking of a "potential" reconfiguration model refinement.

References

1. Kesten, Y., Manna, Z., Pnueli, A.: Temporal Verification of Simulation and Refinement. In: de Bakker, J.W., de Roever, W.-P., Rozenberg, G. (eds.) REX 1993. LNCS, vol. 803, pp. 273–346. Springer, Heidelberg (1994)
2. Abrial, J.R., Butler, M.J., Hallerstede, S., Hoang, T.S., Mehta, F., Voisin, L.: Rodin: an open toolset for modelling and reasoning in Event-B. STTT 12(6), 447–466 (2010)
3. de Alfaro, L., Henzinger, T.: Interface-based design. In: Broy, M., et al (eds.): Engineering Theories of Software-intensive Systems. NATO Science Series: Mathematics, Physics, and Chemistry, vol. 195, pp. 83–104. Springer, Netherlands (2005)
4. Mikhajlov, L., Sekerinski, E., Laibinis, L.: Developing Components in the Presence of Re-entrance. In: Wing, J.M., Woodcock, J., Davies, J. (eds.) FM 1999. LNCS, vol. 1709, pp. 1301–1320. Springer, Heidelberg (1999)
5. Allen, R.B., Douence, R., Garlan, D.: Specifying and Analyzing Dynamic Software Architectures. In: Astesiano, E. (ed.) ETAPS 1998 and FASE 1998. LNCS, vol. 1382, pp. 21–37. Springer, Heidelberg (1998)
6. Léger, M., Ledoux, T., Coupaye, T.: Reliable Dynamic Reconfigurations in a Reflective Component Model. In: Grunske, L., Reussner, R., Plasil, F. (eds.) CBSE 2010. LNCS, vol. 6092, pp. 74–92. Springer, Heidelberg (2010)
7. Bozga, M., Jaber, M., Maris, N., Sifakis, J.: Modeling Dynamic Architectures Using Dy-BIP. In: Gschwind, T., De Paoli, F., Gruhn, V., Book, M. (eds.) SC 2012. LNCS, vol. 7306, pp. 1–16. Springer, Heidelberg (2012)
8. Bruneton, E., Coupaye, T., Leclercq, M., Quéma, V., Stefani, J.B.: The Fractal component model and its support in java. Softw., Pract. Exper. 36(11-12), 1257–1284 (2006)
9. Dormoy, J., Kouchnarenko, O., Lanoix, A.: Using Temporal Logic for Dynamic Reconfigurations of Components. In: Barbosa, L.S. (ed.) FACS 2010. LNCS, vol. 6921, pp. 200–217. Springer, Heidelberg (2010)
10. Lanoix, A., Dormoy, J., Kouchnarenko, O.: Combining proof and model-checking to validate reconfigurable architectures. In: FESCA 2011. ENTCS (2011)
11. Dormoy, J., Kouchnarenko, O., Lanoix, A.: Runtime Verification of Temporal Patterns for Dynamic Reconfigurations of Components. In: Arbab, F. (ed.) FACS 2011. LNCS, vol. 7253, pp. 115–132. Springer, Heidelberg (2012)
12. David, P.C., Ledoux, T., Léger, M., Coupaye, T.: FPath and FScript: Language support for navigation and reliable reconfiguration of Fractal architectures. Annales des Télécommunications 64(1-2), 45–63 (2009)
13. Hamilton, A.G.: Logic for mathematicians. Cambridge University Press, Cambridge (1978)
14. Bellegarde, F., Julliand, J., Kouchnarenko, O.: Ready-Simulation Is Not Ready to Express a Modular Refinement Relation. In: Maibaum, T. (ed.) FASE 2000. LNCS, vol. 1783, pp. 266–283. Springer, Heidelberg (2000)
15. Milner, R.: Communication and Concurrency. Prentice-Hall, Inc. (1989)

16. Butler, M.J.: Stepwise refinement of communicating systems. Sci. Comput. Program. 27(2), 139–173 (1996)
17. Pnueli, A.: System specification and refinement in temporal logic. In: Proceedings of the 12th Conference on Foundations of Software Technology and Theoretical Computer Science, pp. 1–38. Springer, London (1992)
18. Lamport, L.: The temporal logic of actions. ACM Trans. Program. Lang. Syst. 16(3), 872–923 (1994)
19. Dormoy, J.: Contributions à la spécification et à la vérification des reconfigurations dynamiques dans les systémes à composants. PhD thesis, Université de Franche-Comté, France (December 2011)

Error Invariants

Evren Ermis[1], Martin Schäf[2,*], and Thomas Wies[3]

[1] University of Freiburg
[2] United Nations University, IIST, Macau
[3] New York University

Abstract. Localizing the cause of an error in an error trace is one of the most time-consuming aspects of debugging. We develop a novel technique to automate this task. For this purpose, we introduce the concept of *error invariants*. An error invariant for a position in an error trace is a formula over program variables that over-approximates the reachable states at the given position while only capturing states that will still produce the error, if execution of the trace is continued from that position. Error invariants can be used for slicing error traces and for obtaining concise error explanations. We present an algorithm that computes error invariants from Craig interpolants, which we construct from proofs of unsatisfiability of formulas that explain why an error trace violates a particular correctness assertion. We demonstrate the effectiveness of our algorithm by using it to localize faults in real-world programs.

1 Introduction

A central element of a programmer's work routine is spending time on debugging. Particularly time-consuming (and often the most frustrating part of debugging) is the task of *fault localization* [1, 3, 9, 10, 13, 14, 18, 20, 21], i.e., isolating the cause of an error by inspecting a failed execution of the program. This task encompasses, for instance, the identification of the program statements that are relevant for the error, and determining the variables whose values should be tracked in order to understand the cause of the error.

In this paper, we present a novel technique that enables automated fault localization and the automatic generation of concise error explanations. The input to our technique is a an *error trace* of the program, which consists of the sequence of program statements whose execution produced an error, and formulas describing the initial states of the trace and the expected output states (i.e., the assertion that was violated). Such error traces can be obtained either from failing test cases or from counterexamples produced by static analysis tools. Our technique is based on the new concept of *error invariants*. An invariant for a given position in a trace is a formula satisfied by all states reaching that position in an execution of the trace. An error invariant is an invariant for a position in an error trace that only captures states that will still produce the error, if execution of the trace is continued from that position. Hence, an error invariant provides an explanation for the failure of the trace at the given position. We observe that *inductive* error

---

* Supported in part by the projects ARV and COLAB, funded by Macau Science and Technology Development Fund.

D. Giannakopoulou and D. Méry (Eds.): FM 2012, LNCS 7436, pp. 187–201, 2012.

invariants, which are those error invariants that hold for consecutive positions in an error trace, characterize statements in the trace that are irrelevant for the error. That is, if an error invariant holds for an interval of consecutive positions, no relevant changes have occurred to error relevant variables in that interval. A statement that is enclosed by an inductive error invariant can thus be replaced by any other statement that preserves the invariant, without changing the nature of the error. Hence, inductive error invariants can be used to compute slices of error traces that contain only relevant statements and information about reachable states that helps to explain the cause of an error. Moreover, error invariants characterize the relevant variables whose values should be tracked along the execution of the error trace.

To compute inductive error invariants, we build on the idea of *extended trace formulas* [14] to obtain an unsatisfiable formula from an error trace. We then compute Craig interpolants for each position in the trace from the proof of unsatisfiability of this formula. These Craig interpolants serve as candidate error invariants which we subsequently propagate through the trace to check their inductiveness. Thus, we build on existing techniques for synthesizing inductive invariants in program verification [12] to compute inductive error invariants. We implemented our technique in a prototype tool and evaluated it on error traces taken from the literature as well as real-world examples. For the error traces that we have considered, the error invariants computed by our technique capture the precise cause of the error.

Related Work. Minimizing error traces to aid debugging is an active area of research. Recently, static techniques for identifying relevant fragments of error traces have been developed. Closest to our approach is Bug-Assist [13, 14], which uses a MAX-SAT based algorithm to identify a maximal subset of statements from an error trace that cannot be responsible for the failing of the execution. The remaining statements then form an error trace such that removing any statements from this trace will result in a trace that has normally terminating executions. One benefit of this approach is that a compact error trace can be computed with a single MAX-SAT query while our approach requires several calls to a theorem prover. On the other hand, our approach can further simplify the error traces obtained by Bug-Assist because it may replace some of the remaining statements with error invariants. For instance, if a relevant variable is incremented several times in a row (e.g., in a loop), our approach may replace all these statement by one invariant stating that the incremented variable is within a certain bound. Also, error invariants identify variables that should be tracked during debugging and that highlight the relevant changes to the program state. This is particularly useful for *dense errors*, where the length of the error trace cannot be reduced significantly. A common limitation of our approach and Bug-Assist is that control-relevant variables might not be considered relevant. This, however, depends on the way error traces are encoded as formulas.

Another way to minimize error traces is to compare failing with successful executions (e.g., [1, 9, 10, 17, 18, 20]). Ball et al. [1] present an algorithm for isolating parts of an error trace that do not occur on feasible traces. Groce et al. [9–11] use distance metrics for program executions to find minimal abstractions of error traces. For a given counterexample, they find a passing execution that is as similar to the counterexample as possible. The deviations between the passing and failing executions are then presented

```
int y=0;                        int foo(int a, int b, int x) {
                                   x = x + a;
void testFoo() {                   x = x + b;
    int res = foo(0,-2,1);         y = y + a;
    CU_ASSERT(res>=0);             return x;
}                               }
```

Fig. 1. Example of a failing unit test

as an explanation for the error. The major difference of these approaches to ours is that they require passing executions that are similar to the failing execution as an additional input. Hence, these approaches are limited to cases where it is possible to find adequate passing runs that cover large portions of the original error trace.

Dynamic approaches can be used to reduce the cognitive load for the programmer. Delta Debugging (e.g., [3]) compares failing executions with passing executions to identify relevant inputs that can be blamed for the failing of the execution. Dynamic slicing (see, e.g., [21] for an overview) removes irrelevant fragments from error traces based on dynamic control and data dependencies. Both approaches return a compact representation of the original error trace. Hence, our approach of using error invariants is orthogonal to delta debugging and dynamic slicing. Similar to Bug-Assist, dynamic techniques can be used to compute a compressed error trace that serves as input to our static analysis algorithm, which then computes further information about the error.

2 Overview and Illustrative Example

We demonstrate how error invariants can help to produce a more compact representation of an error trace using the illustrative example in Figure 1. We call this compact representation an *abstract error trace*. The figure shows a procedure foo and a unit test testFoo, which checks if foo returns a certain value when it is called on a particular input. The tested procedure foo adds the variables a and b to x before returning the new value of x. Further, foo increments the global variable y. The unit test testFoo calls foo on an initial state where a=0, b=-2, and x=1, and then checks if foo returns a value greater or equal to 0. However, this is not the case and the unit test fails. From the failing test case we can derive the following error trace (ψ, π, ϕ), where the path π is the sequence of statements executed on the trace:

$$\psi \equiv (a = 0 \wedge b = -2 \wedge x = 1 \wedge y = 0) \qquad \phi \equiv x \geq 0$$
$$\pi = \ell_0 : x = x + a; \quad \ell_1 : x = x + b; \quad \ell_2 : y = y + a; \quad \ell_3 :$$

To understand why the post-condition $x \geq 0$ of our unit test is violated, we first compute a *trace formula* for the error trace, which is a conjunction of the pre-condition ψ, the post-condition ϕ, and a formula representation $\mathbf{TF}(\pi)$ of the path π, such that the satisfying assignments of the trace formula exactly correspond to the possible executions of the path π that satisfy the pre and post-condition. The resulting formula

$$(a=0)\wedge(b=-2)\wedge(x=1)\wedge(y=0)\wedge(x'=x+a)\wedge(x''=x'+b)\wedge(y'=y+a)\wedge(x'' \geq 0)$$

is unsatisfiable, as the execution of the test case violates the assertion at the end of the error trace. From the proof of unsatisfiability, we compute a sequence of formulas $I_0, \ldots, I_3$, where each I_i is an error invariant for position ℓ_i of the error trace. This means that for each i, the formula $\psi \wedge \mathbf{TF}(\pi[0, i]) \Rightarrow I_i$ is valid and the formula $I_i \wedge \mathbf{TF}(\pi[i, 3]) \wedge \phi$ is unsatisfiable, where $\pi[0, i]$ is the prefix of the trace up to position i and $\pi[i, 3]$ the corresponding suffix. For our example, a possible sequence of error invariants is as follows:

$$I_0 \equiv (x = 1) \wedge (a = 0) \wedge (b = -2) \qquad I_2 \equiv (x = -1)$$
$$I_1 \equiv (x = 1) \wedge (b = -2) \qquad\qquad I_3 \equiv (x = -1)$$

An error invariant I_i can be seen as an abstraction of the set of post states of the prefix trace $\pi[0, i]$ such that any execution of the suffix trace $\pi[i, 3]$ that starts in a state satisfying I_i will still fail. Thus, for each point of the error trace, the error invariant can provide a concise explanation why the trace fails when the execution is continued from that point. In particular, error invariants provide information about which variables are responsible for an execution to fail and which values they have at each point. In our example, I_0 is a summary of the initial state and indicates that the variable a, b, and x are responsible for the error. After executing $x = x + b$, we can see from I_2 that a and b are no longer relevant and only x has to be considered. Further, we can see that the value of variable y does not matter at all. Error invariants also help to identify irrelevant statements in an error trace. Note that the formula I_1 is a valid error invariant for both positions ℓ_2 and ℓ_3. That is, I_2 is *inductive* with respect to the statement y = y + a and any execution of the suffix trace $\pi[2, 3]$ that starts in a state satisfying I_2 will still fail. The fact that I_2 is an error invariant for both ℓ_2 and ℓ_3 implies that the formula $\psi \wedge \mathbf{TF}(\pi) \wedge \phi$ will remain unsatisfiable even if y = y + a is removed from the trace π. Thus, this statement is irrelevant for the error.

In the following sections, we formalize the concept of error invariants and present an algorithm that synthesizes error invariants to compute concise abstractions of error traces.

3   Preliminaries

We present programs and error traces using formulas in first-order logic. We assume standard syntax and semantics of such formulas and use $\top$ and $\bot$ to denote the Boolean constants for *true* and *false*, respectively. Let X be a set of program variables. A *state* is a valuation of the variables from X. A *state formula* F is a first-order constraint over free variables from X. A state formula F represents the set of all states s that satisfy F and we write $s \models F$ to denote that a state s satisfies F.

For a variable $x \in X$ and $i \in \mathbb{N}$, we denote by $x^{\langle i \rangle}$ the variable obtained from x by adding i primes to it. The variable $x^{\langle i \rangle}$ models the value of x in a state that is shifted i time steps into the future. We extend this shift function from variables to sets of variables, as expected, and we denote by X' the set of variables $X^{\langle 1 \rangle}$. For a formula F with free variables from Y, we write $F^{\langle i \rangle}$ for the formula obtained by replacing each occurrence of a variable $y \in Y$ in F with the variable $y^{\langle i \rangle}$. We denote by $x^{\langle -i \rangle}$ the inverse operation of $x^{\langle i \rangle}$, which we also extend to formulas. A *transition formula* T is a first-order constraint over free variables from $X \cup X'$, where the variables X' denote the values of the variables from X in the next state. A transition formula T represents a binary relation on states and we write $s, s' \models T$ to denote that the pair of states (s, s') is in the relation represented by T.

A *program* $\mathcal{P}$ over variables X is simply a finite set of transition formulas over $X \cup X'$. Each transition formula $T \in \mathcal{P}$ models the semantics of a single program statement. Note that control can be model implicitly via a dedicated program variable $\mathrm{pc} \in X$ for the program counter. The correctness assertion of a program can be stated as a relation between the pre and the post states of the program's executions. A witness of the incorrectness of the program is given by an error trace. An error trace consists of a state formula, describing the initial states from which a failed execution can start, a path of the program describing the statements of the failed execution, and a state formula, which describes the violated correctness assertion.

Formally, a *path* π of a program $\mathcal{P}$ is a finite sequence of transition formulas in $\mathcal{P}$. Let $\pi = T_0, \ldots, T_{n-1}$ be a path. For $0 \leq i \leq j \leq n$, we denote by $\pi[i, j]$ the subpath $T_i, \ldots, T_{j-1}$ of π that goes from position i to position j. We use $\pi[i]$ to represent the i-th transition formula T_i of path π. A *trace* τ of a program $\mathcal{P}$ is a tuple (ψ, π, ϕ) where π is a path of $\mathcal{P}$ and ψ and ϕ are state formulas. We say that τ has length n if π has length n. An *execution* of a trace (ψ, π, ϕ) is a sequence of states $\sigma = s_0 \ldots s_n$ such that (1) $s_0 \models \psi$, (2) $s_n \models \phi$, and (3) for all $0 \leq i < n$, $s_i, s_{i+1} \models \pi[i]$. The *trace formula* $\mathbf{TF}(\tau)$ of a trace $\tau = (\psi, \pi, \phi)$ of length n is the formula $\psi \wedge (\pi[0])^{\langle 0 \rangle} \wedge \ldots \wedge (\pi[n-1])^{\langle n-1 \rangle} \wedge \phi^{\langle n \rangle}$. Thus, there is a one-to-one correspondence between the executions of τ and the models of $\mathbf{TF}(\tau)$. For a path π we write $\mathbf{TF}(\pi)$ as a shorthand for the trace formula $\mathbf{TF}((\top, \pi, \top))$. A trace τ is called *feasible*, if its trace formula $\mathbf{TF}(\tau)$ is satisfiable. A trace is called *error trace* if it is infeasible.

4 Error Invariants

An error trace provides sufficient information to repeat the program's behavior that violates the correctness assertion. There are many ways to obtain error traces, e.g., from a failing test case, from a counterexample returned by a static analysis tool [15], or when debugging, by manually marking a particular state as violation of the correctness assertion. By limiting the scope to only one control-flow path, error traces can help the programmer to detect the cause of the unexpected behavior. However, the error trace itself does not give any insight into which transitions on the path of the trace are actually responsible for the incorrect behavior. Further, the trace does not say which variables on this path should be tracked to identify the cause of the error. This is particularly challenging for error traces of large programs, where the number of transitions and variables might become intractable for the programmer.

In this paper, we propose the concept of *error invariants* as a means to rule out irrelevant transitions from an error trace, to identify the program variables that should be tracked along the path in order to understand the error, and to obtain a compact representation of the actual cause of an error.

Definition 1 (Error Invariant). *Let* $\tau = (\psi, \pi, \phi)$ *be an error trace of length* n *and let* $i \leq n$ *be a position in* π. *A state formula* I *is an* error invariant *for position* i *of* τ, *if the following two formulas are valid:*

1. $\psi \wedge \mathbf{TF}(\pi[0, i]) \Rightarrow I^{\langle i \rangle}$
2. $I \wedge \mathbf{TF}(\pi[i, n]) \wedge \phi^{\langle n-i \rangle} \Rightarrow \bot$

An error invariant for a position in an error trace can be understood as an abstract representation of the *reason* why the execution will fail if it is continued from that position. We next explain how error invariants can be used to identify transitions and program variables that are relevant for the fault in the error trace.

Using Error Invariants for Fault Localization. In the following, let τ be an error trace. We say that a state formula I is an *inductive* error invariant for positions $i \leq j$, if I is an error invariant for both i and j. Given such an inductive error invariant, we can argue that the execution of the path of the error trace will still fail for the same reason, even if the transitions between positions i and j are not executed. Thus, we can use inductive error invariants to identify irrelevant transitions in error traces. Inductive error invariants further help to identify the relevant program variables that should be tracked while debugging an error trace. Namely, if I is an inductive invariant for positions $i < j$, then only the program variables appearing in I should be tracked for the trace segment between the positions i and j. We can make these observations formal.

Abstract Error Traces. We say that a trace $\tau^{\#}$ *abstracts* a trace τ if for every n-step execution σ of τ there exists an m-step execution $\sigma^{\#}$ of $\tau^{\#}$ such that $\sigma^{\#}[0] = \sigma[0]$, $\sigma^{\#}[m] = \sigma[n]$, and $\sigma^{\#} \preceq \sigma$. Here, $\preceq$ denotes the *subsequence ordering*, i.e., $a_0 \ldots a_m \preceq b_0 \ldots b_n$ iff $a_0 = b_{i_0}, \ldots, a_m = b_{i_m}$ for some indices $0 \leq i_0 < \ldots < i_m \leq n$. The problem we are attempting to solve in this paper, is to find for a given error trace $\tau = (\psi, \pi, \phi)$ an error trace $\tau^{\#} = (\psi, \pi^{\#}, \phi)$ such that $\tau^{\#}$ abstracts τ and $\pi^{\#}$ concisely explains why π is failing for (ψ, ϕ). We use inductive error invariants to define such abstract error traces.

Let $\pi^{\#} = I'_0, T_1, I'_1, \ldots, T_k, I'_k$ be an alternating sequence of primed state formulas I'_j and transition formulas T_j. Note that a primed state formula I' can be interpreted as a transition formula that models transitions in which all program variables are first non-deterministically updated and then assumed to satisfy the formula I. Thus, $\pi^{\#}$ is also a path. We call $(\psi, \pi^{\#}, \phi)$ an *abstract error trace* for (ψ, π, ϕ) if there exist positions $i_0 < \ldots < i_{k+1}$ such that $i_0 = 0$, $i_{k+1} = n + 1$, for all j with $1 \leq j \leq k$, $T_j = \pi[i_j]$, and for all j with $0 \leq j \leq k$, I_j is an inductive error invariant for i_j and $i_{j+1} - 1$.

Theorem 2. *If* $\tau^{\#}$ *is an abstract error trace for an error trace* τ, *then* $\tau^{\#}$ *abstracts* τ.

In the next section, we show how abstract error traces can be computed using Craig interpolants, which we obtain automatically from the unsatisfiability proof of the extended path formula.

5   Error Invariants from Craig Interpolants

There are different ways to obtain error invariants for error traces. For instance, given an error trace $\tau = (\psi, \pi, \phi)$ of length n, the weakest error invariant for position i in

π is given by the weakest (liberal) precondition of the negated post-condition and the suffix of the path starting from i: $\mathsf{wlp}(\pi[i,n], \neg\phi)$. However, weakest error invariants are typically not inductive, nor do they provide compact explanations for the cause of an error. What we are really interested in are *inductive* error invariants.

Error invariants are closely related to the concept of *Craig interpolants* [5]. Let A and B be formulas whose conjunction is unsatisfiable. A formula I is a *Craig interpolant* for A and B, if the following three conditions hold: (a) $A \Rightarrow I$ is valid, (b) $I \wedge B$ is unsatisfiable, and (c) all free variables occurring in I occur free in both A and B. Thus, given a position i in an error trace, we can split the unsatisfiable path formula $\psi \wedge \mathbf{TF}(\pi) \wedge \phi^{\langle n \rangle}$ into two conjuncts $A = \psi \wedge \mathbf{TF}(\pi[0,i])$ and $B = \mathbf{TF}(\pi[i,n])^{\langle i \rangle} \wedge \phi^{\langle n \rangle}$, for which we can then obtain interpolants[1].

Proposition 3. *Let (ψ, π, ϕ) be an error trace of length n, let i be a position in π, and let $A = \psi \wedge \mathbf{TF}(\pi[0,i])$ and $B = \mathbf{TF}(\pi[i,n])^{\langle i \rangle} \wedge \phi^{\langle n \rangle}$. Then for every interpolant I of A, B, the formula $I^{\langle -i \rangle}$ is an error invariant for i.*

Interpolants are always guaranteed to exist for first-order logical formulas A and B whose conjunction is unsatisfiable [5]. In fact, for many first-order theories there always exist quantifier-free interpolants that can be directly constructed from the proof of unsatisfiability of the conjunction $A \wedge B$ [2, 16]. Interpolants constructed in this way often give concise explanations for the infeasibility of a trace. For this reason, they have shown to be useful for finding inductive invariants in program verification [12]. We argue that the same is true for error traces and show how to find interpolants that are, both, inductive error invariants and useful for fault localization.

Computing Abstract Error Traces. In the following, let (ψ, π, ϕ) be an error trace with $\pi = (T_i)_{0 \leq i < n}$. The problem we want to solve is to compute an abstract error trace for (ψ, π, ϕ), i.e., an alternating sequence of inductive error invariants and transitions $I_0, T_{i_1}, I_1, \ldots, T_{i_k}, I_k$ where the T_{i_j} are the relevant transition formulas in π and each I_j abstracts the intermediate sequences of irrelevant transition formulas between the T_{i_j}. Given the unsatisfiable trace formula $\psi \wedge T_0 \wedge \ldots \wedge T_{n-1}^{\langle n-1 \rangle} \wedge \phi^{\langle n \rangle}$, we can use a single call to an interpolating theorem prover to obtain a sequence of interpolants $I_0, \ldots, I_n$ such that each I_i is an error invariant for position i in the error trace. The basic idea underlying our algorithm is to use these interpolants as candidates for the inductive error invariants that occur in the computed abstract error trace. A naive algorithm to obtain the abstract error trace from the computed interpolants is to compute an $(n+1) \times (n+1)$ matrix $\mathcal{I}$ where an entry $\mathcal{I}_{ij}$ indicates whether interpolant I_i is an error invariant for position j of the error trace. The matrix $\mathcal{I}$ can then be used to obtain an abstract error trace by replacing maximal sequences of transition formulas $T_{i_1}, \ldots, T_{i_2}$ in the error trace by interpolant I_j, if I_j was found to be inductive for $i_1 < i_2$.

We have applied this naive algorithm to a number of example error traces and have found that it produces abstract error traces that concisely explain the cause of the error. The only problem with this naive algorithm is that it can be expensive: the number of theorem prover calls that is needed to compute the matrix $\mathcal{I}$ is quadratic in the length of the error trace. We have therefore developed an algorithm that obtains a better running

---

[1] Note that whenever we say *interpolant* we always mean *Craig interpolant*.

time. This improved algorithm is based on an observation that we made during the evaluation of the naive algorithm: if an interpolant I is an inductive error invariant for positions $i < j$ of an error trace, then it is also often an error invariant for all intermediate positions between i and j. Thus, instead of checking for each position i and interpolant I_j, whether I_j is an error invariant for i, we instead compute for each I_j the end positions of the interval of π on which I_j holds. Using a binary search, this can be done with fewer theorem prover calls than required by the naive algorithm.

Algorithm 1. Algorithm for computing abstract error traces

Input: error trace $\tau = (\psi, \pi, \phi)$ of length n
Output: abstract error trace for τ

def $search(low : \mathsf{Int}, high : \mathsf{Int}, incLow : \mathsf{Int} \to \mathsf{Boolean}) : \mathsf{Int} = \{$
    if $(high < low)$ **return** low
    val $mid = (low + high)/2$
    if $(incLow(mid))$ $search(mid + 1, high, incLow)$
    else $search(low, mid - 1, incLow)$ $\}$
def $isErrInv(I : \mathsf{Formula}, i : \mathsf{Int}) : \mathsf{Boolean} =$
    $valid(\psi \wedge \mathbf{TF}(\pi[0, i]) \Rightarrow I^{\langle i \rangle}) \wedge valid(I \wedge \mathbf{TF}(\pi[i, n]) \wedge \phi^{\langle n-i \rangle} \Rightarrow \bot)$
var $interpolants = \mathrm{interpolate}(\mathbf{TF}(\tau))$
var $intervals = interpolants$ map $(\lambda I_j . \{ start = search(0, j, (\lambda i. \neg isErrInv(I_j, i)))$
                                     $end = search(j, n, (\lambda i. isErrInv(I_j, i))) - 1$
                                     $inv = I_j \})$
var $sortedIntervals = intervals$ sortWith $(\lambda(a, b). a.start \leq b.start)$
var $maxInterval = sortedIntervals[0]$
var $prevEnd = 0$
for $(currInterval \leftarrow sortedIntervals)$ $\{$
  if $(currInterval.start > prevEnd)$ $\{$
    yield $maxInterval.inv$
    if $(maxInterval.end < n)$ **yield** $\pi[maxInterval.end]$
    $prevEnd = maxInterval.end$
    $maxInterval = currInterval$
  $\}$ **else if** $(currInterval.end > maxInterval.end)$ $maxInterval = currInterval$
$\}$

Algorithm 1 shows the pseudo code for our improved algorithm in a syntax akin to the Scala programming language. The algorithm takes an error trace τ as input and returns an abstract error trace for τ. It first computes a sequence of candidate error invariants *interpolants* by calling the interpolating theorem prover. It then computes for each interpolant I_j in *interpolants* a maximal interval on which I_j is inductive. Each interval is represented as a record with fields *start* and *end* storing the start and end position of the interval, and field *inv* storing the actual interpolant I_j. The interval boundaries are computed using a binary search that is implemented by the function *search*. The binary search is parameterized by a function *incLow*, which guides the search depending on which of the two interval bounds is to be computed. In either case, the function *incLow* is implemented using the function *isErrInv*, which checks whether the given formula I is an error invariant for the given position i. The algorithm then computes a minimal subset of the intervals that cover all positions of the error trace. This is done by first sorting the computed intervals according to their start time and then selecting maximal intervals to cover all positions. The latter step is implemented in the final for-comprehension, which directly yields the error invariants and relevant transition formulas of the resulting abstract error trace.

Note that each binary search requires at most $\mathcal{O}(\log n)$ theorem prover calls, which gives $\mathcal{O}(n \log n)$ theorem prover calls in total (as opposed to $\mathcal{O}(n^2)$ for the naive algorithm). Also the sorting of the intervals can be done in time $\mathcal{O}(n \log n)$, which gives total running time $\mathcal{O}(n \log n)$, if we factor out the actual running time of the theorem prover calls.

6   Evaluation

We have implemented a prototype of Algorithm 1 on top of the interpolating theorem prover SMTInterpol [2] and applied it to compute abstractions of several error traces that we obtained from real-world programs. In the following, we present two of these examples in detail.

6.1   Faulty Sorting

Our first example is a faulty implementation of a sorting algorithm that sorts a sequence of integer numbers. This program is taken from [3] and shown in Figure 2. The program takes an array of numbers as input and is supposed to return a sorted sequence of these numbers. An error is observed when the program is called on the sequence $11, 14$. Instead of the expected output $11, 14$, the program returns $0, 11$. The corresponding error trace consists of the precondition $\psi \equiv (a[0] = 11 \wedge a[1] = 14)$, the post-condition $\phi \equiv (a'[0] = 11 \wedge a'[1] = 14)$ and the path π containing the sequence of 27 statements shown in Figure 3.

We translated each statement in path π into a corresponding transition formula. While there exist interpolation procedures for reasoning about arrays, SMTInterpol does not yet provide an implementation of such a procedure. We therefore encoded arrays using uninterpreted function symbols and added appropriate axioms for the array updates. Before calling the theorem prover, we instantiated all axioms with the ground terms occurring in the path formula. This resulted in an unsatisfiable quantifier-free formula which we used as input for our algorithm.

The theorem prover computed 28 interpolants, one for each position in the error trace. Table 1 shows the error invariant matrix for these interpolants. The matrix indicates for each computed interpolant I_i at which positions I_i is a valid error invariant. Note that the matrix is not actually computed by our algorithm. Instead, Algorithm 1 only computes for each I_i the boundaries of the interval of positions for which I_i is a valid error invariant. The marked interpolants I_1, I_{10}, I_{12}, I_{19}, I_{22}, and I_{26} are the ones that our algorithm selects for the computation of the abstract error trace. Thus, the only relevant statements for the error are the statements at positions 6, 11, 13, 20, 23, as well as the post-condition.

```
static void shell_sort(int a[], int size) {    int main(int argc, char *argv[]) {
  int i, j;                                       int i = 0;
  int h = 1;                                      int *a = NULL;
  do {
    h = h * 3 + 1;                                a = (int*)malloc((argc-1) *
  } while (h <= size);                                            sizeof(int));
  do {                                            for (i = 0; i < argc - 1; i++)
    h /= 3;                                         a[i] = atoi(argv[i + 1]);
    for (i = h; i < size; i++) {                  shell_sort(a, argc);
      int v = a[i];
      for (j = i; j >= h &&                       for (i = 0; i < argc - 1; i++)
        a[j - h] > v; j -= h)                       printf("%d", a[i]);
        a[j] = a[j-h];                            printf("\n");
      if (i != j) a[j] = v;
    }                                             free(a);
  } while (h != 1);                               return 0;
}                                               }
```

Fig. 2. Faulty implementation of a sort algorithm taken from [3]. The faulty behavior can be observed, e.g., for the input value sequence 11, 14.

```
0   int i,j, a[];              14   j=i;
1   int size=3;                15   assume (j>=h && a[j-h]>v);
2   int h=1;                   16   a[j]=a[j-h];
3   h = h*3+1;                 17   j-=h;
4   assume !(h<=size);         18   assume (j>=h && a[j-h]>v);
5   h/=3;                      19   a[j]=a[j-h];
6   i=h;                       20   j-=h;
7   assume (i<size);           21   assume !(j>=h && a[j-h]>v);
8   v=a[i];                    22   assume (i!=j);
9   j=i;                       23   a[j]=v;
10  assume !(j>=h && a[j-h]>v); 24   i++;
11  i++;                       25   assume !(i<size);
12  assume (i<size);           26   assume (h==1);
13  v=a[i];
```

Fig. 3. Error path π of the program in Figure 2 for the input sequence 11, 14

Table 1. Error invariant matrix for the error trace of the program in Figure 2

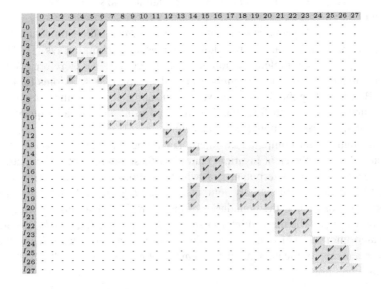

$\boxed{\texttt{a[2]=0}}$
```
6:i=h;
```
$\boxed{\texttt{a[2]=0} \land \texttt{h=1} \land \texttt{i=h}}$
```
11:i = i + 1;
```
$\boxed{\texttt{a[2]=0} \land \texttt{h=1} \land \texttt{i=2}}$
```
13:v = a[i];
```
$\boxed{\texttt{h=1} \land \texttt{i=2} \land \texttt{v=0} \land \texttt{h}\leq\texttt{j} \land \texttt{j}\leq\texttt{1}}$
```
20:j = j - h;
```
$\boxed{\texttt{h=1} \land \texttt{i=2} \land \texttt{v=0} \land \texttt{j=0}}$
```
23:a[j] = v;
```
$\boxed{\texttt{a[0]=0}}$
```
27:assert (a[0]=11 ∧ a[1]=14);
```

Fig. 4. Abstract error trace for the error path in Figure 3

The resulting abstract error trace is shown in Figure 4. We use boxed code such as $\boxed{\texttt{a[2]=0}}$ to highlight the error invariants. From the first error invariant a[2]=0 we can see that the only information we need to track until position 6 of our error trace is the value at index 2 of the array a. This error invariant is also the summary of the relevant part of the failing initial state ψ. Hence, we do not need to mention ψ explicitly in our abstract error trace. At position 6, the variable i is initialized. The error invariant no longer holds after this statement. The new error invariant now also states that h=1 and i=h hold up to position 11. The next statement, which cannot be rendered irrelevant, is i = i + 1 and sets i to 2. This statement already indicates the problem, as i should always be strictly smaller than the array bounds of a. The next error invariant now states that i=2. This error invariant holds up to position 13, where the value a[2] is stored in the local variable v. The new error invariant I_{20} keeps track of v=0, while the current content of the array a is completely irrelevant for the following parts of the error trace. The error invariant I_{20} also states that j=1. This property is temporarily violated from positions 14 to 17 but reestablished at position 18. The context of the variable j is abstracted away as all necessary information about j is provided by the error invariants. One could also think of a different algorithm that does not allow error invariants to be temporarily violated. Such an algorithm would further add the statements ℓ_{14} :j=i and ℓ_{17} :j=j-h to the error trace because we cannot find an invariant that holds at the enclosing positions of these statements. However, the relevant information about the variable j is provided by the error invariant. Hence, these statements can be omitted. The new error invariant holds up to position 20, when j is set to 0. This is recorded in the new error invariant, which holds up to position 23, when a[0] is finally set to 0. This is the only information we need to keep track of for the remainder of the error trace, as it contradicts the post-condition. Hence, Algorithm 1 is able to reduce the error trace from its original 27 statements to only six statements. The computed error invariants further highlight the information about the state that is crucial for the error at each point of the error trace.

For comparison with the state of the art, we have also applied the tool Bug-Assist [13, 14] to the error trace in Figure 3. Bug-Assist returns a set of *potential bugs*, each of

```
0    int OLEV = 600;
1    int MAXALTDIFF = 600;
2    int MINSEP = 300;
3    int NOZCROSS = 300;
4    int NO_INTENT = 0;
5    int DO_NOT_CLIMB = 1;
6    int DO_NOT_DESCEND = 2;
7    int TCAS_TA = 1;
8    int OTHER = 2;
9    int UNRESOLVED = 0;
10   int UPWARD_RA = 1;
11   int DOWNWARD_RA = 2;
12   int Positive_RA_Alt_Thresh = 740;
13   bool enabled = High_Confidence && (Own_Tracked_Alt_Rate <= OLEV) &&
         (Cur_Vertical_Sep > MAXALTDIFF);
14   bool tcas_equipped = (Other_Capability == TCAS_TA);
15   bool intent_not_known = (Two_of_Three_Reports_Valid&&(Other_RAC==NO_INTENT));
16   int alt_sep = UNRESOLVED;
17   assume(enabled && ((tcas_equipped && intent_not_known) || !tcas_equipped));
18   assume(Climb_Inhibit);
19   inhibitBiasedClimb = Up_Separation + NOZCROSS;
20   ownBelowThreat = (Own_Tracked_Alt < Other_Tracked_Alt);
21   ownAboveThreat = (Other_Tracked_Alt < Own_Tracked_Alt);
22   upward_preferred = (inhibitBiasedClimb > Down_Separation);
23   assume(upward_preferred);
24   nonCrossingBiasedClimb = !(ownBelowThreat) || ((ownBelowThreat) &&
                                  (!(Down_Separation > Positive_RA_Alt_Thresh)));
25   need_upward_RA = nonCrossingBiasedClimb && ownBelowThreat;
26   upward_preferred = inhibitBiasedClimb > Down_Separation;
27   assume(upward_preferred);
28   nonCrossingBiasedDescend = ownBelowThreat && (Cur_Vertical_Sep >= MINSEP) &&
         (Down_Separation >= Positive_RA_Alt_Thresh);
29   need_downward_RA = nonCrossingBiasedDescend && ownAboveThreat;
30   assume !(need_upward_RA && need_downward_RA);
```

Fig. 5. Error path π for faulty TCAS produced by the model checker ULTIMATE

which is a statement in the input error trace. If ordered by their location, these statements form a reduced error trace. For our example, this reduced error trace still contains 18 statements.

6.2 Faulty TCAS

Our second example is a faulty implementation of the Traffic Alert and Collision Avoidance System (TCAS). TCAS is an aircraft collision detection system used by all US commercial aircraft. The TCAS example can be found in [8] and has been used in many papers to test algorithms that explain error traces (e.g., [10, 11, 13, 17, 19]). The error in this TCAS implementation is inflicted by a wrong inequality in the function Non_Crossing_Biased_Climb(). On some inputs, the error causes the Boolean variable need_upward_RA to become true. The effect is that the controlled aircraft will eventually rise even though its altitude is lower than the other aircraft's altitude. This may potentially lead to a collision.

To obtain an appropriate error trace for this error we applied the software model checker ULTIMATE [7] to the faulty TCAS implementation. The correctness condition that exposes the error in the implementation has been taken from [4] and is as follows:

need_upward_RA ⇒(¬(Up_Separation < Positive_RA_Alt_Thresh)∧

(Down_Separation ≥ Positive_RA_Alt_Thresh))

This property is also the post-condition ϕ of our error trace (ψ, π, ϕ). When we checked this property with ULTIMATE, the model checker produced the error path π shown in Figure 5.

Note that the statement at position 24 is the problematic statement from function Non_Crossing_Biased_Climb() that causes the error. The strict inequality > should be replaced by >= for the implementation to be correct.

In order to obtain a suitable precondition ψ for our error trace, we used the SMT solver Z3 [6] to produce a model for the formula $\mathbf{TF}(\pi) \wedge \neg\phi$. We then encoded this model in a corresponding formula ψ. Applying our algorithm to the resulting error trace produces the abstract error trace shown in Figure 6. The error invariant matrix in Table 2 highlights the five interpolants that are selected for the abstract error trace.

Table 2. Error invariant matrix for the error trace of the TCAS example

The abstract error trace shows how the infliction at position 24 affects the value assigned to need_upward_RA at position 25 and eventually leads to the error. The last error invariant forces the execution to take the then branch of the conditional, which is encoded as an implication in the post condition ϕ. The algorithm reduces the error trace from 31 to 4 statements. These statements are sufficient to understand the causality between the erroneous line and the error. The abstract error trace depends only on 7 instead of 37 variables. The number of input variables is reduced from 12 to 5. The abstract error trace thus significantly simplifies the search for the erroneous statement at position 24. For the purpose of comparison, we also ran Bug-Assist on the TCAS example. The reduced error trace thus obtained still contained 14 statements. We therefore believe that error invariants provide a valuable instrument that improves upon the state of the art.

7 Conclusion

We have introduced the concept of error invariants for reasoning about the relevancy of portions of an error trace. Error invariants provide a semantic argument why certain

> Up_Separation = 441 ∧ Down_Separation = 740 ∧ Own_Tracked_Alt = -1 ∧
> Other_Tracked_Alt = 0

12:Positive_RA_Alt_Thresh = 740;

> Positive_RA_Alt_Thresh = 740∧ Up_Separation = 441 ∧Down_Separation = 740 ∧
> Own_Tracked_Alt = -1 ∧ Other_Tracked_Alt = 0

20:ownBelowThreat = Own_Tracked_Alt < Other_Tracked_Alt;

> ownBelowThreat ∧Positive_RA_Alt_Thresh = 740 ∧Up_Separation = 441 ∧
> Down_Separation = 740 ∧ Own_Tracked_Alt = -1 ∧ Other_Tracked_Alt = 0

24:nonCrossingBiasedClimb = !ownBelowThreat ||
        (ownBelowThreat && (!(Down_Separation > Positive_RA_Alt_Thresh))));

> nonCrossingBiasedClimb ∧ownBelowThreat ∧ Positive_RA_Alt_Thresh =740 ∧
> Up_Separation = 441 ∧ Down_Separation = 740

25:need_upward_RA = nonCrossingBiasedClimb && ownBelowThreat;

> need_upward_RA ∧ Positive_RA_Alt_Thresh = 740 ∧ Up_Separation = 441 ∧
> Down_Separation = 740

31:assert (need_upward_RA ==> !(Up_Separation < Positive_RA_Alt_Thresh) &&
            (Down_Separation >= Positive_RA_Alt_Thresh));

Fig. 6. Abstract error trace of the TCAS example

portions of an error trace are irrelevant to the search for the cause of an error. Removing those irrelevant portions from the error trace will not alter the observable error. This is in contrast to related static approaches for slicing error traces that are based on computing unsatisfiable cores of extended path formulas. We have presented an algorithm that synthesizes error invariants from Craig interpolants and uses them to obtain compact abstractions of error traces. Our evaluation has shown that our algorithm can indeed help programmers understand the cause of an error more easily. We therefore believe that our algorithm will be a useful component in future debugging tools.

We see many opportunities to further improve the performance of the presented algorithm, which will be subject to our future work. For instance, our approach can be used on already reduced error traces, to further compress them. Also, many theorem prover calls during the binary search can be avoided by first syntactically checking whether a candidate invariant speaks about variables that do not occur in both the prefix and suffix of the trace. In this case, it is not necessary to invoke the theorem prover because the candidate invariant cannot be a Craig interpolant. Further optimizations are possible if the theorem prover is not treated as a black box. In particular, we will explore different approaches to compute Craig interpolants from unsatisfiable path formulas. If we have more control over the structure of the computed interpolants, this will allow us to build more efficient algorithms for computing inductive error invariants.

References

1. Ball, T., Naik, M., Rajamani, S.K.: From symptom to cause: localizing errors in counterexample traces. SIGPLAN Not., 97–105 (2003)
2. Christ, J., Hoenicke, J.: Instantiation-based interpolation for quantified formulae. In: SMT Workshop Proceedings (2010)
3. Cleve, H., Zeller, A.: Locating causes of program failures. In: ICSE 2005, pp. 342–351 (2005)

4. Coen-Porisini, A., Denaro, G., Ghezzi, C., Pezze, M.: Using symbolic execution for verifying safety-critical systems (2001)
5. Craig, W.: Three uses of the Herbrand-Gentzen theorem in relating model theory and proof theory. The Journal of Symbolic Logic, 269–285 (1957)
6. de Moura, L., Bjørner, N.S.: Z3: An Efficient SMT Solver. In: Ramakrishnan, C.R., Rehof, J. (eds.) TACAS 2008. LNCS, vol. 4963, pp. 337–340. Springer, Heidelberg (2008)
7. Ermis, E., Hoenicke, J., Podelski, A.: Splitting via Interpolants. In: Kuncak, V., Rybalchenko, A. (eds.) VMCAI 2012. LNCS, vol. 7148, pp. 186–201. Springer, Heidelberg (2012)
8. Graves, T.L., Harrold, M.J., Kim, J.-M., Porter, A., Rothermel, G.: An empirical study of regression test selection techniques. ACM Trans. Softw. Eng. Methodol, 184–208 (2001)
9. Groce, A.: Error Explanation with Distance Metrics. In: Jensen, K., Podelski, A. (eds.) TACAS 2004. LNCS, vol. 2988, pp. 108–122. Springer, Heidelberg (2004)
10. Groce, A., Kroening, D.: Making the Most of BMC Counterexamples. ENTCS, pp. 67–81 (2005)
11. Groce, A., Kroning, D., Lerda, F.: Understanding Counterexamples with `explain`. In: Alur, R., Peled, D.A. (eds.) CAV 2004. LNCS, vol. 3114, pp. 453–456. Springer, Heidelberg (2004)
12. Jhala, R., Mcmillan, K.L.: Interpolant-Based Transition Relation Approximation. In: Etessami, K., Rajamani, S.K. (eds.) CAV 2005. LNCS, vol. 3576, pp. 39–51. Springer, Heidelberg (2005)
13. Jose, M., Majumdar, R.: Bug-Assist: Assisting Fault Localization in ANSI-C Programs. In: Gopalakrishnan, G., Qadeer, S. (eds.) CAV 2011. LNCS, vol. 6806, pp. 504–509. Springer, Heidelberg (2011)
14. Jose, M., Majumdar, R.: Cause clue clauses: error localization using maximum satisfiability. In: PLDI 2011, pp. 437–446. ACM (2011)
15. Leino, K.R.M., Millstein, T., Saxe, J.B.: Generating error traces from verification-condition counterexamples. Sci. Comput. Program., 209–226 (2005)
16. McMillan, K.L.: An interpolating theorem prover. Theor. Comput. Sci, 101–121 (2005)
17. Qi, D., Roychoudhury, A., Liang, Z., Vaswani, K.: Darwin: an approach for debugging evolving programs. In: ESEC/SIGSOFT FSE, pp. 33–42 (2009)
18. Renieris, M., Reiss, S.P.: Fault localization with nearest neighbor queries. In: ASE, pp. 30–39 (2003)
19. Wang, C., Yang, Z.-J., Ivančić, F., Gupta, A.: Whodunit? Causal Analysis for Counterexamples. In: Graf, S., Zhang, W. (eds.) ATVA 2006. LNCS, vol. 4218, pp. 82–95. Springer, Heidelberg (2006)
20. Zeller, A.: Isolating cause-effect chains from computer programs. In: SIGSOFT FSE, pp. 1–10 (2002)
21. Zhang, X., He, H., Gupta, N., Gupta, R.: Experimental evaluation of using dynamic slices for fault location. In: AADEBUG 2005, pp. 33–42. ACM (2005)

Correctness of Pointer Manipulating Algorithms Illustrated by a Verified BDD Construction

Mathieu Giorgino and Martin Strecker

IRIT, Université de Toulouse[*]

Abstract. This paper is an extended case study using a high-level approach to the verification of graph transformation algorithms: To represent sharing, graphs are considered as trees with additional pointers, and algorithms manipulating them are essentially primitive recursive traversals written in a monadic style. With this, we achieve almost trivial termination arguments and can use inductive reasoning principles for showing the correctness of the algorithms. We illustrate the approach with the verification of a BDD package which is modular in that it can be instantiated with different implementations of association tables for node lookup. We have also implemented a garbage collector for freeing association tables from unused entries. Even without low-level optimizations, the resulting implementation is reasonably efficient.

Keywords: Verification of imperative algorithms, Pointer algorithms, Modular Program Development, Binary Decision Diagram.

1 Introduction

There is now a large range of verification tools for imperative and object-oriented (OO) languages. Most of them have in common that they operate on source code of a particular programming language like C or Java, annotated with pre- and post-conditions and invariants. This combination of code and properties is then fed to a verification condition generator which extracts proof obligations that can be discharged by provers offering various degrees of automation (see below for a more detailed discussion).

This approach has an undeniable success when it comes to showing that a program is well-behaved (no null-pointer accesses, index ranges within bounds, deadlock-freedom of concurrent programs etc.). Program verification and in particular static analysis often amounts to showing the absence of undesirable situations with the aid of a property language that is considerably more expressive than a traditional type system, but nevertheless has a restricted set of syntactic forms for program verification that cannot be user-extended unless the imperative programming language is embedded into a general purpose proof-assistant.

These limitations turn out to be a hindrance when one has to build up a larger "background theory" capable of expressing deeper semantic properties of

---

[*] Part of this research has been supported by the *Climt* project (ANR-11-BS02-016-02).

D. Giannakopoulou and D. Méry (Eds.): FM 2012, LNCS 7436, pp. 202–216, 2012.

the data structures manipulated by the program (such as the notions of interpretation and validity of a formula used in this paper). Even worse, high-level mathematical notions (such as "sets" and "trees") are often not directly available in the specification language. Even if they are, recovering an algebraic data type from a pointer structure in the heap is not straightforward: one has to ensure, for example, that a structure encoding a list is indeed an instance of a data type and not cyclic.

In this paper, we explore the opposite direction: we start from high-level data structures based on inductive data types, which allows for an easy definition of algorithms with the aid of primitive recursion and for reasoning principles based on structural induction and rewriting. References are added explicitly to these data structures, which makes it possible to express sharing of subtrees with a simple notion of reference equality as well as associating mutable content to nodes. The notion of state is manipulated with a state-exception monad (see Section 2), thus allowing for a restricted form of object manipulation (in particular object creation and modification).

We illustrate our approach with the development of a Binary Decision Diagram (BDD) package. After recalling the basic notions and the semantics of BDDs in Section 3, we describe a first, non-optimized version of the essential algorithms in Section 4 and the implementation of association tables in Section 6. Section 5 introduces a garbage collector and memoization, which lead to a substantial speed-up.

As formal framework, we use the Isabelle proof assistant [16] and its extension Imperative_HOL [8], together with its Isabelle-to-Scala code extractor. Our algorithms are therefore executable in Scala and, as witnessed by the performance evaluation of Section 7, within the realm of state-of-the-art BDD packages.

A further gain in efficiency might be achieved by mapping our still rather coarse-grained memory model to a fine-grained memory model, which would allow us to introduce bit-level optimizations. Even though this is compatible with our approach, we have refrained from it here because it would lead to a considerable increase in complexity and is not central to the approach of this paper. The formal development is available on the authors' home pages[1] and more detailed discussions of some topics will appear in the first author's forthcoming PhD thesis [11].

Related Work – Program Verification: There are roughly two broad classes of program verifiers - those aiming at a mostly automatic verification, as Spec# [2], VCC [9], Frama-C[2] or Why3 [4], or at mostly interactive proofs, such as the ones based on Dynamic Logic like KeY[3], KIV[3] or codings of programming languages and their associated Hoare logics in proof assistants [10,19]. The borderline is not clear-cut, since some of the "automatic" tools can also be interfaced with interactive proof assistants such as Coq and Isabelle, as in [5].

---

[1] http://www.irit.fr/~Mathieu.Giorgino/Publications/GiSt2012BDD.html

[2] http://frama-c.com/

[3] http://www.informatik.uni-augsburg.de/lehrstuehle/swt/se/kiv/

The work that comes closest to ours is the extension of Isabelle with OO features [6]. It is at the same time more complete and considerably more complex, since it has the ambition to simulate genuine OO capabilities such as late binding, which requires, among others, the management of dynamic type tags of objects. Our approach remains confined to what can be done within a conventional polymorphic functional type system. Our aim is not to be able to verify arbitrary programs in languages such as Java or Scala, but to export programs written and verified in a functional style with stateful features to a language such as Scala. We thus hope to reduce the proof burden, while still obtaining relatively efficient target code in an idiomatic style (using subtyping and inheritance) and compatible with a widely used language.

Related Work – Verification of BDDs: Binary Decision Diagrams (BDDs) [7] are a compact format for representing Boolean formulas, making extensive use of sharing of subtrees and thus achieving a canonical representation of formulas, and a verified BDD package might become useful for the formal verification of decision procedures

Even without such an application in mind, BDDs have become a favorite case study for the verification of pointer programs. As mentioned above, all the approaches we are aware of use a low-level representation of BDDs as linked pointer structures. The idea of representing the state space in monadic style is introduced in [13], but ensuring the termination of the functions poses a problem because termination and well-formedness of the state space are closely intertwined.

There is a previous verification [18] in the Isabelle proof assistant, starting from an algorithm written in a C-like language. As in our case, it is possible to take semantic properties of BDDs into account, but the proof of correctness has a considerable complexity. By a tricky encoding, the PVS formalization in [21] can avoid the use of the notion of "state" altogether, but the encoding creates huge integers even for a small number of BDD nodes, so that the approach might not scale to larger examples.

The most comprehensive verification [20] (apart from ours) describes a verification in the Coq proof assistant, including some optimizations and a garbage collector. The state space is explicitly represented and manipulated by a functional program, and also the OCaml code extracted from Coq is functional. This seems to account for the lower performance (slower execution and faster exhaustion of memory) as compared to genuine imperative code.

2   Memory and Object Models

We first present a shallow embedding of an OO management of references in Isabelle. As a basis we use the Imperative_HOL theory [8] belonging to the Isabelle library. This theory provides imperative features to Isabelle/HOL by defining a state-exception monad with syntax facilities like do-notation. We then add object-oriented features that should eventually improve code generation to Scala. In the following, we put the Isabelle keywords corresponding to the discussed concepts in parentheses.

Language. Imperative programs returning values of type $'a$ have type $'a\ Heap$. They can manipulate references of type $'b\ ref$ using the usual ML syntax to allocate ($ref\ a$), read ($!r$) and write ($r := a$) references. On the logical level, the term $effect\ m\ h\ h'\ v$ states that if m terminates, it transforms the heap h (of type $heap$) into h' and returns the value v.

To get closer to an OO development, a reference to a record should be seen as a handle to an object, without giving the ability in the language to retrieve the record itself. To do this, we define accessors (of type $'a \rhd 'b$ where $'a$ and $'b$ are respectively the types of the record and the field) as a means to describe an abstract attribute in an object. These allow us to introduce primitives *lookup* (denoted $r \cdot ac$) and *update* ($r \cdot ac := v$) to read and write fields of the record referenced by r, which can be seen as attributes of an object. A '$\$$' character will start accessor names to avoid name clashes with other identifiers.

For example, with the definition of accessors $\$fst$ and $\$snd$ for the first and second components of pairs, the definition $m\ p \equiv do\{\ a \leftarrow p \cdot \$fst;\ p \cdot \$snd := a;\ p \cdot \$fst\ \}$ defines a monadic operation m replacing the second component of the pair referenced by p by its first component and returns it.

We also note that in Isabelle/HOL, implication is written at object or meta level as $\longrightarrow$ or $\Longrightarrow$ but can be read indifferently as implication.

Objects and Classes as Types. Hierarchical definition of data (with sub-typing) is provided by extensible records (**record**) as described in [15]. A record *runit* is used as a top element of a record hierarchy, in the same way as Object in Java or Any in Scala are the top classes of their class hierarchies. In contrast to the implicit object sub-typing, record types are explicitly parameterized by their extension types as for example $'a$ in $'a\ runit\text{-}scheme$.

Methods and Classes as Modules. Locales (**locale**) [1] allows the creation of a context parameterized by constants (**fixes**) and assumptions (**assumes**). We use them to define functions in the context of a reference called *this* in the same way as for OO languages. Then the functions defined in this locale and used from the outside take an additional argument being a reference to the record.

locale *object* = **fixes** *this* :: $'a\ ref$

They can also be used as an equivalent of interfaces or abstract classes. They can be built upon each other with multiple inheritance ($+$) for which assumptions (including types of constants) can be strengthened (**for**). Finally they can be instantiated by several implementations.

In This Development. Objects and classes are used at two levels:

- for the state of the BDD factory containing the two *True* and *False* leaves and the association tables for maximal sharing and memoization. This state and its reference is unique in the context of the algorithms and provided by the locale *object* as a *this* constant parameter.

– for the nodes, each one containing a reference to a mutable extension of itself. This extension is initially empty and called *runit* to be extended later to *refCount* to store the reference counter for the garbage collection.

Figures 1a and 1b present the hierarchies of records and locales used in this development. We also take advantage of locales to specify the logical functions used only in proofs (locale *bddstate*) and the abstract methods (locales *bddstate-mk* and *bddstate-mk-gc*).

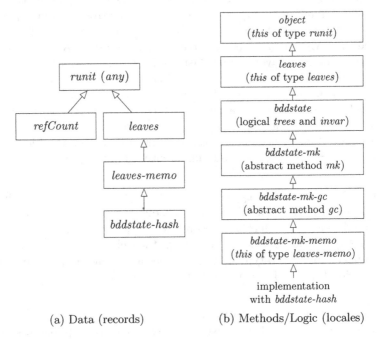

(a) Data (records)   (b) Methods/Logic (locales)

Fig. 1. Hierarchies of data and methods

3   Binary Decision Diagrams

3.1   Tree Structure and Interpretation

BDDs are used to represent and manipulate efficiently Boolean expressions. We will use them as starting point of our algorithms, by defining a function constructing BDDs from their representation of type $('v, bool)$ *expr* in which $'v$ is the type of variable names. The definition of expressions is rather standard:

datatype $('v,'a)$ *expr* =
  Var $'v$ | *Const* $'a$ | *BExpr* $('a \Rightarrow 'a \Rightarrow 'a)$ $(('v,'a)$ *expr*$)$ $(('v,'a)$ *expr*$)$

and their interpretation is done by *interp-expr* taking as extra argument the variable instantiations represented as a function from variables to values:

fun *interp-expr* :: $('v, 'a)$ *expr* $\Rightarrow$ $('v \Rightarrow 'a)$ $\Rightarrow$ $'a$ **where**
  interp-expr (*Var v*) *vs* = *vs v*
| *interp-expr* (*Const a*) *vs* = *a*
| *interp-expr* (*BExpr bop* e_1 e_2) *vs* = *bop* (*interp-expr* e_1 *vs*) (*interp-expr* e_2 *vs*)

We now define BDDs as binary trees where the two subtrees represent the BDDs resulting from the instantiation of the root variable to *False* or *True* :

datatype $('a, 'b)$ *tree* = *Leaf* $'a$ | *Node* $'b$ $(('a, 'b)$ *tree*) $(('a, 'b)$ *tree*)
type-synonym $('a,'b,'c)$ *rtree* = $('a \times 'c$ *ref*, $'b::linorder \times 'c$ *ref*) *tree*

$('a, 'b, 'c)$ *rtree* is the type of referenced trees with leaf content of type $'a$, node content of type $'b$ and mutable extension of type $'c$. These trees contain a reference to this mutable extension that will be used as an identifier. Each node contains a variable index whose type is equipped with a linear order (as indicated by Isabelle's sort annotation ::*linorder*) and each leaf contains a value of any type instantiated later in the development (for interpretations) to Booleans.

BDDs can be interpreted (*i. e.* evaluated) by giving values to variables which is what the *interp* function does (*l* and *h* abbreviate *low* and *high*):

fun *interp* :: $('a, 'v, 'r)$ *rtree* $\Rightarrow$ $('v \Rightarrow bool)$ $\Rightarrow$ $'a$ **where**
  interp (*Leaf* (*b,r*)) *vs* = *b*
| *interp* (*Node* (*v,r*) *l h*) *vs* = (*if vs v then interp h vs else interp l vs*)

3.2 Sharing

We first illustrate the concept of subtree-sharing by an example. A non-shared BDD (thus, in fact, just a decision tree) representing the formula $(x \wedge y) \vee z$ is given by the tree on the left of Figure 2.

There is a common subtree (shaded) which we would like to share. We therefore adorn the tree nodes with references, using the same reference for structurally equal trees. The result of sharing is illustrated on the right of Figure 2.

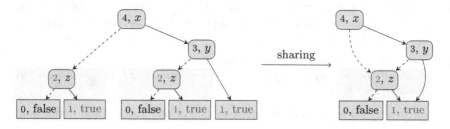

Fig. 2. Sharing nodes in a tree

In this way, as long as subtrees having identic references are the same, we can represent sharing. To ensure this property giving meaning to references, we use the predicate *ref-unique ts*:

definition *ref-unique* :: $('a, 'v, 'r)$ *rtree set* $\Rightarrow$ *bool* **where** *ref-unique ts* $\equiv$
$\forall t_1\ t_2.\ t_1 \in ts \longrightarrow t_2 \in ts \longrightarrow$ (*ref-equal* $t_1\ t_2 \longleftrightarrow$ *struct-equal* $t_1\ t_2$)

in which *ref-equal* means that two trees have the same reference attribute, and *struct-equal* is structural equality neglecting references, thus corresponding to the typical notion of equality of data in functional languages.

While the left-to-right implication of this equivalence is the required property (two nodes having the same reference are the same), the other implication ensures maximal sharing (same subtrees are shared, *i. e.* have the same reference).

3.3   Ordering and Reducedness

With this definition, and without any other property, BDDs would be rather hard to manipulate. For one, same variable indices could appear several times on paths from root to leaves. Also, variables would not be in the same order, making comparison of BDDs harder. Moreover, a lot of space would be wasted. To circumvent this problem, one often imposes a strict order on variables, the resulting BDDs being called ordered (OBDDs). We define this property using the *tree-vars* constant to collect all variables of a tree:

fun *ordered* :: $('a, 'v{::}linorder, 'r)$ *rtree* $\Rightarrow$ *bool* **where**
    ordered (*Leaf b*) = *True*
| *ordered* (*Node* $(i, r)\ l\ h$) =
    $((\forall\ j \in (tree\text{-}vars\ l \cup tree\text{-}vars\ h).\ i < j) \wedge ordered\ l \wedge ordered\ h)$

An additional important property is to avoid redundant tests, which occur when the two children of a node have the same interpretation. All the nodes satisfying this property can be removed. In this case, the OBDD is said to be reduced (ROBDD).

fun *reduced* :: $('a, 'v, 'r)$ *rtree* $\Rightarrow$ *bool* **where**
    reduced (*Node vr l h*) = $((interp\ l \neq interp\ h) \wedge reduced\ l \wedge reduced\ h)$
| *reduced* (*Leaf b*) = *True*

This property uses a high-level definition (*interp*), but it can be deduced (*cf.* Lemma 1) from the three low-level properties *ref-unique*, *ordered* (already seen) and *non-redundant*:

fun *non-redundant* :: $('a, 'v, 'r)$ *rtree* $\Rightarrow$ *bool* **where**
    non-redundant(*Node vr l h*)=$((\neg ref\text{-}equal\ l\ h) \wedge non\text{-}redundant\ l \wedge non\text{-}redundant\ h)$
| *non-redundant*(*Leaf b*) = *True*

We then merge these properties into two definitions *robdd* (high-level) and *robdd-refs* (low-level):

definition *robdd t* $\equiv$ (*ordered t* $\wedge$ *reduced t*)
definition *robdd-refs t* $\equiv$ (*ordered t* $\wedge$ *non-redundant t* $\wedge$ *ref-unique* (*treeset t*))

From these definitions, we finally show that ROBDDs are a canonical representation of Boolean expressions, *i. e.* that two equivalent ROBDDs are structurally equal at high (*robdd*) and low (same with *robdd-refs*) level:

Theorem 1 (canonic_robdd)

$robdd\ t_1 \wedge robdd\ t_2 \wedge interp\ t_1 = interp\ t_2 \implies struct\text{-}equal\ t_1\ t_2$

Proof. By induction on the pair of trees: the leaves case is trivial, heterogeneous cases (leaf and node or nodes of different levels) lead to contradictions, and the remaining case (two nodes of same level) is proved by applying the induction hypothesis on subtrees.

Also high- and low-level properties are related in Theorem 2 as a consequence of Lemma 1:

Lemma 1 (non_redundant_imp_reduced)

$ordered\ t \wedge non\text{-}redundant\ t \wedge ref\text{-}unique\ (treeset\ t) \implies reduced\ t$

Proof. By induction on t: the leaf case is trivial and the node case is proved by applying the induction hypothesis on the subtrees and proving that trees with different references are structurally different (from definitions of *non-redundant* and *ref-unique*) and then have different interpretations (with contrapositive of Theorem 1).

Theorem 2 (robdd_refs_robdd)

$ref\text{-}unique\ (treeset\ t) \implies robdd\text{-}refs\ t = robdd\ t$

4   Constructing BDDs

The simplest BDDs are the leaves corresponding to the *True* and *False* values. These ones have to be unique in order to permit sharing of nodes. We put them in the BDD factory whose data is this record:

record $('v, 'c)$ *leaves* $= runit\ +$
    leafTrue :: $(bool, 'v, 'c)$ *rtree*
    leafFalse :: $(bool, 'v, 'c)$ *rtree*

We define the context of this state by constraining the type of the referenced record *this*. This context together with the *leaves* record would be equivalent to a class definition **class Leaves extends Object** in Java where type of **this** is constrained from **Object** to **Leaves**.

locale *leaves* $=$ *object this* **for** *this* :: $('v, 'c, 'a)$ *leaves-scheme ref*

Then we extend it to add logical abstractions *trees* and *invar* that will be instantiated during the implementation to provide the correctness arguments we will rely on in the proofs. The *trees* parameter abstracts the set of trees already constructed in the state. The *invar* parameter is the invariant of the data-structures that will be added to the heap by the implementation and that will have to be preserved by BDD operations.

locale *bddstate = leaves +*
  fixes *trees :: heap* ⇒ *(bool, 'v, 'c) rtree set*
  fixes *invar :: heap* ⇒ *bool*

To be well-formed (*wf-heap*), the heap needs to follow the abstract implementation invariant *invar* and its trees need to contain the leaves and to be maximally shared and closed for the subtree relation.

definition *wf-heap :: heap* ⇒ *bool* **where**
wf-heap s ≡ (*invar s* ∧ *ref-unique (trees s)* ∧ *subtree-closed (trees s)* ∧ *leaves-in s*)

Finally we add an abstract function *mk* and its specification (*mk-spec*) especially ensuring that *mk i l h* constructs a ROBDD whose interpretation is correct under the precondition that the heap is well-formed, level *i* is consistent with levels of *l* and *h* and trees in the heap are already ROBDDs. It uses the function *levelOf* returning the level of a BDD.

locale *bddstate-mk = bddstate +*
  fixes *mk :: 'v* ⇒ *(bool, 'v, 'r) rtree* ⇒ *(bool, 'v, 'r) rtree* ⇒ *(bool, 'v, 'r) rtree Heap*
  assumes *mk-spec: effect (mk i l h) s s' t* ∧ *wf-heap s* ∧ {*l,h*} ⊆ *trees s* ⟹ (
  (*LevNode i* < *Min (levelOf '* {*l,h*}) ∧ (∀ *t'* ∈ *trees s. robdd-refs t'*) ⟶ *robdd-refs t*)
  ∧ (∀ *vs. interp t vs* = (*if vs i then interp h vs else interp l vs*))
  ∧ (*wf-heap s'*) ∧ (*trees s'* = *insert t (trees s)*)))

In this context we define the *app* function which applies a binary Boolean operator to two BDDs. If these BDDs are both leaves, it returns a leaf corresponding to the application of the binary Boolean operator to their contents. Else it returns a new BDD constructed with *mk* from its recursive calls to the left and right subtrees of BDDs with the same level. For this purpose it uses the *select* function which returns two pairs of BDDs corresponding to the subtrees (*split-lh*) of the BDD(s) with the smallest level and the duplication (*dup*) of the other (if any). It also uses the function *varOfLev* retrieving the variable corresponding to the level of a node.

function *app :: (bool* ⇒ *bool* ⇒ *bool)*
  ⇒ ((*bool, 'v, 'r) rtree * (bool, 'v, 'r) rtree)* ⇒ *(bool, 'v, 'r) rtree Heap* **where**
  app bop (n₁, n₂) = *do* {
    if tpair is-leaf (n₁, n₂) then (constLeaf (bop (leaf-contents n₁) (leaf-contents n₂)))
      else (do {
        let ((l₁, h₁), (l₂, h₂)) = *select split-lh dup (n₁, n₂)*;
        l ← app bop (l₁, l₂); *h ← app bop (h₁, h₂)*;
        mk (varOfLev (min-level (n₁, n₂))) l h })}

This is the only function whose termination proof is not automatic, but still very simple: it suffices to show that *select split-lh dup* decreases the sum of the sizes of the trees in the pair. Indeed by representing BDDs as an inductive structure instead of pointers in the heap, the termination condition does not appear anymore in the implicit nested recursion on the heap like in [13] and we do not need to add a phantom parameter as a bound like in [20].

Finally, we define the *build* function which is a simple traversal recursively constructing BDDs for sub-expressions and then joining them with *app*.

primrec *build* :: $('v, bool)$ *expr* $\Rightarrow$ $(bool, 'v, 'r)$ *rtree Heap* **where**
  build $(Var\ i)$ = $(do\{\ cf \leftarrow constLeaf\ False;\ ct \leftarrow constLeaf\ True;\ mk\ i\ cf\ ct\})$
| *build* $(Const\ b)$ = $(constLeaf\ b)$
| *build* $(BExpr\ bop\ e_1\ e_2)$ = $(do\{\ n_1 \leftarrow build\ e_1;\ n_2 \leftarrow build\ e_2;\ app\ bop\ (n_1, n_2)\})$

The verification of these functions involves the preservation of the well-formedness of the heap (Theorems 3 and 4) – implying that the returned BDD (as well as the others in the heap) is a ROBDD and that it is interpreted like the expression – and the construction of canonical BDDs (Theorem 5) – implying for example that a tautology constructs *Leaf True*.

Theorem 3 (wf_heap_app)

wf-heap $s \wedge \{t_1, t_2\} \subseteq$ *trees* $s \wedge$ *effect* $(app\ f\ (t_1, t_2))\ s\ s'\ t \Longrightarrow$
interp $t\ vs = f$ $(interp\ t_1\ vs)$ $(interp\ t_2\ vs) \wedge$ *insert* t $(trees\ s) \subseteq$ *trees* $s' \wedge$ *wf-heap* s'

Proof. We use the induction schema generated from the termination proof of *app* working on a pair of trees – following the order relation infered from *select split-lh dup*. If both trees are leaves, the BDD is a leaf already in the unchanged state. Else the induction hypotheses hold for the subtrees provided by *select*. The specification of *mk* and the transitivity of $\subseteq$ finish the proof.

Theorem 4 (wf_heap_build)

effect $(build\ e)\ s\ s'\ t \wedge$ *wf-heap* $s \Longrightarrow$
interp $t =$ *interp-expr* $e \wedge$ *insert* t $(trees\ s) \subseteq$ *trees* $s' \wedge$ *wf-heap* s'

Proof. By induction on the expression: In the cases of *Const* or *Var*, the result is immediate from the specification of *mk* and the definition of *constLeaf*. In the case of *BExpr*, the induction hypotheses hold for the sub-expressions and the result is obtained from Theorem 3.

Theorem 5 (build_correct)

$(\forall\ t \in trees\ s_1.\ robdd\text{-}refs\ t) \wedge$ *wf-heap* $s_1 \Longrightarrow$
$(\forall\ t \in trees\ s_2.\ robdd\text{-}refs\ t) \wedge$ *wf-heap* $s_2 \Longrightarrow$
effect $(build\ e_1)\ s_1\ s_1'\ t_1 \wedge$ *effect* $(build\ e_2)\ s_2\ s_2'\ t_2 \Longrightarrow$
struct-equal $t_1\ t_2 = (interp\text{-}expr\ e_1 = interp\text{-}expr\ e_2)$

Proof. In the same way as for Theorem 4, by proving a similar property for *app*.

5   Optimizations: Memoization and Garbage Collection

The *app* and *build* functions have been presented in their simplest form and without optimizations. We present in this section the two optimizations we have made to them.

Memoization During the BDD construction, several identical computations can appear. This happens mostly within the recursive calls of the *app* function during which the binary operation stays the same and identical pairs of BDDs can arise by simplifications and sharing. In order to avoid these redundant computations, the immediate solution is to use a memoization table – recording the arguments and the result for each of its calls and returning directly the result in case the arguments already have an entry in the table. This optimization is essential as it cuts down the complexity of the construction of highly shared BDD.

We add this memoization table to the state by extending the record containing the leaves. Then the only changes to the *app* function are the memoization table lookup before the eventual calculation and the table update after.

By adding an invariant on all the trees in the memoization table ensuring the properties desired for the resulting tree (mostly the conclusion of Theorem 3), the changes in the proof follow the changes of the function. With a case distinction on the result of the table lookup for the arguments, if there is an entry for them, the result follows the invariant, else the original proof remains and the result following the invariant is stored in the table.

Garbage Collection. Using an association table avoids duplication of nodes and allows us to share them. However, recording all created nodes since the start of the algorithm can lead to a very huge memory usage. Indeed keeping a reference to a node in an association table prevents the JVM garbage collector to collect nodes that could have been discarded during BDD simplifications.

We chose to remove these unused nodes from the association table by a reference counting variant. The principle of reference counting is simply to store for each node the number of references to it. Instead of counting references for all nodes, we only count them for the BDD roots. This allows us to keep the *mk* function independent of the reference count. Then, we parametrized the development with a garbage collection function *gc* whose specification ensures the preservation of used nodes (*i. e.* nodes reachable from a node with a non-null reference count). We call it in the *build* function when the association table becomes too large.

For this improvement, the proof additions were substantial. Indeed, several mutations to the reference counters appear in the functions, causing inner modifications in proofs. Moreover the invariant *insert t (trees s)* $\subseteq$ *trees s'* for *build* had to be weakened to *insert t (reachable s)* $\subseteq$ *reachable s'* . These difficulties attributable to mutability highlight the simplifications provided by the encoding of BDDs as inductive datatypes instead of nodes and pointers.

6   Implementation of Abstract Functions

It is now time to implement the abstract function *mk* as well as the logical functions *invar* and *trees*. We wrote two implementations and present the most efficient one using a hash-map provided by the Collection Framework [14].

Following its specification, *mk* needs to ensure the maximal sharing of nodes. To do this, we add in the state a table associating the components of a node (its children and variable name) to itself. Then by looking in this table, we know whether a BDD that could be returned has already been created.

record $('v, 'c)$ *bddstate-hash* =
$('v,('c$ *ref* $\times$ $'c$ *ref*, $(bool,'v,'c)$ *rtree*) *hashmap*, $'c$) *leaves-memo* +
hash :: $('v \times 'c$ *ref* $\times$ $'c$ *ref*, $(bool, 'v, 'c)$ *rtree*) *hashmap*

We also define two auxiliary monadic functions *add* and *lookup* adding and looking for nodes of the table in the state. For example, the lookup function is:

definition *lookup* **where**
lookup $i\ l\ h = do\{ hm \leftarrow this\cdot\$hash; return\ (ahm\text{-}lookup\ (i, ref\text{-}of\ l, ref\text{-}of\ h)\ hm)\ \}$

They are used in the definition of *mk*:

definition *mk* **where**
$mk\ i\ l\ h = (if\ ref\text{-}equal\ l\ h\ then\ return\ l\ else$
$do\{ to \leftarrow lookup\ i\ l\ h;\ (case\ to\ of\ None \Rightarrow add\ i\ l\ h\ |\ Some\ t \Rightarrow return\ t)\ \})$

The garbage collector *gc* is then also implemented using two auxiliary monadic functions *referencedSet* – computing the set of nodes reachable from a node with a non-null reference count – and *hash-restrict* – restricting the domain of the hash table to the set given as argument:

definition *gc* :: *unit Heap* **where** $gc = do\ \{ hs \leftarrow referencedSet;\ hash\text{-}restrict\ hs\ \}$

To avoid too frequent calls to the garbage collector, it is triggered only when the table size exceeds 10000 which is an acceptable condition for preliminary tests but that could be improved by adding a counter in the state.

We finally use these functions satisfying the specifications of the locales to obtain instantiated *app* and *build* functions for which we can generate code.

7 Performance Evaluation

Finally we evaluate the performance of our BDD construction development.

As a comparison point we developed a BDD package directly in Scala whose code would be naively expected from the code generation from the Isabelle theories. This allows us to evaluate the efficiency of the default code generation of Isabelle into Scala wrt our encoding of objects. We also compare these two implementations with a third one being a highly optimized BDD library called JavaBDD[4] providing a Java interface to several BDD libraries written in C or Java. The results are given in Figure 3.

For this evaluation we construct BDDs for two kinds of valid formulas both of which are standard benchmarks. The first one is the Urquhart's formulae U_n defined by $x_1 \Leftrightarrow (x_2 \Leftrightarrow \ldots (x_n \Leftrightarrow (x_1 \Leftrightarrow \ldots (x_{n-1} \Leftrightarrow x_n))))$. The second one is a formulae P_n stating the pigeonhole principle for $n + 1$ pigeons in n holes *i. e.* given that $n+1$ pigeons are in n holes, at least one hole contains two pigeons.

---

[4] http://javabdd.sourceforge.net/

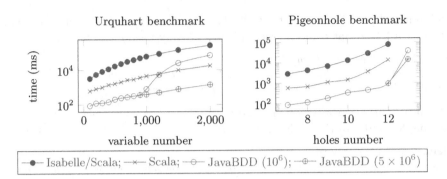

Fig. 3. Evaluation of the generated code efficiency by comparison with a direct implementation and the JavaBDD library

In the Scala version, we use the standard hash map of the Scala library (`scala.collection.mutable.HashMap`) which has an adaptable size. Its garbage collection is triggered when the table size exceeds a threshold value initially set to 1000 and increased by one half when unavoidable.

On the other side, JavaBDD lets the user choose the right table size which is increased, if necessary, after garbage collections by an initially fixed value. In the benchmarks, we set it to 10^6 and 5×10^6. We can see that increasing the initial table size for the JavaBDD version leads to better performances for large expressions but then more space is needed even for smaller ones.

As it can be seen on the pigeonhole benchmark, the memory consumption is still a limiting factor of the Scala versions compared to the JavaBDD one which manages to construct the BDD for 13 pigeon-holes. Also while the generated code is 100 times slower than the JavaBDD one (using low-level optimizations), it is only 10 times slower than the hand-written code that was the lower bound for its efficiency – the algorithms being identical. We suspect several causes of inefficiency and space usage introduced by the code extraction:

- Monad operations are converted into method calls. The presence of monadic operators at each line could explain some performance penalties.
- A "Ref" class is introduced to allow reference manipulations in Scala. This is unnecessary for objects as long as we don't use references on primitive types and referenced values are accessed only through accessors.
- Record extensions are translated to class encapsulations leading to waste of space and several indirections at the time of attribute accesses.

Improving on these points is current work and we think that these optimizations in the code generation could improve the general performances, to the point that the generated code would be comparable to the hand-written code. However, the confidence in the code generator is an essential component of the whole process that makes it hard to modify. More details on possible solutions will be discussed in [11].

8 Conclusions

This paper has presented a verified development of a BDD package in the Isabelle proof assistant, with fully operational code generated for the programming language Scala. It represents BDDs by trees containing references allowing for easy definitions and proofs – done by natural induction schemas and rewriting. The development time for the formalization itself (around 6 person months) is difficult to estimate exactly, because it went hand in hand with the development of the methodology. In the light of the performance of the code obtained, the result is encouraging, and we expect to explore the approach further for the development of verified decision procedures.

As mentioned in the outset, bit-level optimizations could be introduced, at the price of adding one or several refinement layers, with corresponding simulation proofs. Even though feasible, this is not our current focus, since we aim at a method for producing reasonably efficient verified code with a very moderate effort. Indeed this development stretches over about 7500 lines – 5000 before optimizations – among them about 1500 are generic and concern object management. This compares very favorably with the verification in Coq of the same algorithm including optimizations [20] (about 15000 lines), and with the verification of normalization of BDDs in Isabelle/HOL [18] (about 10000 lines).

Consequently, our method is not a panacea. As far as the class and object model is concerned: The type system has intentionally been kept simple in the sense that classes are essentially based on record structures and inductive data types as found in ML-style polymorphism. Such a choice is incompatible with some OO features such late method binding, which appears to be acceptable in the context of high-integrity software. As mentioned in Section 7, we are aware of some inefficiencies that arise during code extraction to Scala, and which have as deeper cause a mismatch between pointer-manipulating languages (as incorporated in the Imperative_HOL framework) and "all is object" languages, such as Java and Scala. We will address this issue in our future work.

Finally, even though the representation "trees with sharing" appears to be a severe limitation at first glance, its combination with cute functional data structures [17] allows to represent quite general pointer meshes (see for example the verification of the Schorr-Waite algorithm [12] using a "zipper" data structure).

References

1. Ballarin, C.: Locales and Locale Expressions in Isabelle/Isar. In: Berardi, S., Coppo, M., Damiani, F. (eds.) TYPES 2003. LNCS, vol. 3085, pp. 34–50. Springer, Heidelberg (2004)
2. Barnett, M., Fähndrich, M., Leino, K.R.M., Müller, P., Schulte, W., Venter, H.: Specification and verification: the Spec# experience. Commun. ACM 54(6), 81–91 (2011)
3. Beckert, B., Hähnle, R., Schmitt, P.H. (eds.): Verification of Object-Oriented Software. LNCS (LNAI), vol. 4334. Springer, Heidelberg (2007)

4. Bobot, F., Filliâtre, J.-C., Marché, C., Paskevich, A.: Why3: Shepherd Your Herd of Provers. In: Boogie 2011: First International Workshop on Intermediate Verification Languages, Wrocław, Poland (August 2011)
5. Böhme, S., Moskal, M., Schulte, W., Wolff, B.: HOL-Boogie — An Interactive Prover-Backend for the Verifying C Compiler. Journal of Automated Reasoning 44(1-2), 111–144 (2010)
6. Brucker, A.D., Wolff, B.: Semantics, Calculi, and Analysis for Object-Oriented Specifications. Acta Informatica 46(4), 255–284 (2009)
7. Bryant, R.E.: Graph-based algorithms for Boolean function manipulation. IEEE Transactions on Computers C-35, 677–691 (1986)
8. Bulwahn, L., Krauss, A., Haftmann, F., Erkök, L., Matthews, J.: Imperative Functional Programming with Isabelle/HOL. In: Mohamed, O.A., Muñoz, C., Tahar, S. (eds.) TPHOLs 2008. LNCS, vol. 5170, pp. 134–149. Springer, Heidelberg (2008)
9. Cohen, E., Dahlweid, M., Hillebrand, M., Leinenbach, D., Moskal, M., Santen, T., Schulte, W., Tobies, S.: VCC: A Practical System for Verifying Concurrent C. In: Berghofer, S., Nipkow, T., Urban, C., Wenzel, M. (eds.) TPHOLs 2009. LNCS, vol. 5674, pp. 23–42. Springer, Heidelberg (2009)
10. Filliâtre, J.-C., Marché, C.: The Why/Krakatoa/Caduceus Platform for Deductive Program Verification. In: Damm, W., Hermanns, H. (eds.) CAV 2007. LNCS, vol. 4590, pp. 173–177. Springer, Heidelberg (2007)
11. Giorgino, M.: Proofs of pointer algorithms by an inductive representation of graphs. PhD thesis, Université de Toulouse (forthcoming, 2012)
12. Giorgino, M., Strecker, M., Matthes, R., Pantel, M.: Verification of the Schorr-Waite Algorithm – From Trees to Graphs. In: Alpuente, M. (ed.) LOPSTR 2010. LNCS, vol. 6564, pp. 67–83. Springer, Heidelberg (2011)
13. Krstić, S., Matthews, J.: Verifying BDD Algorithms through Monadic Interpretation. In: Cortesi, A. (ed.) VMCAI 2002. LNCS, vol. 2294, pp. 182–195. Springer, Heidelberg (2002)
14. Lammich, P., Lochbihler, A.: The Isabelle Collections Framework. In: Kaufmann, M., Paulson, L.C. (eds.) ITP 2010. LNCS, vol. 6172, pp. 339–354. Springer, Heidelberg (2010)
15. Naraschewski, W., Wenzel, M.T.: Object-Oriented Verification Based on Record Subtyping in Higher-Order Logic. In: Grundy, J., Newey, M. (eds.) TPHOLs 1998. LNCS, vol. 1479, pp. 349–366. Springer, Heidelberg (1998)
16. Nipkow, T., Paulson, L.C., Wenzel, M.T.: Isabelle/HOL. A Proof Assistant for Higher-Order Logic. LNCS, vol. 2283. Springer, Heidelberg (2002)
17. Okasaki, C.: Purely functional data structures. Cambridge University Press (1998)
18. Ortner, V., Schirmer, N.W.: Verification of BDD Normalization. In: Hurd, J., Melham, T. (eds.) TPHOLs 2005. LNCS, vol. 3603, pp. 261–277. Springer, Heidelberg (2005)
19. Schirmer, N.: Verification of Sequential Imperative Programs in Isabelle/HOL, PhD thesis, Technische Universität München (2006)
20. Verma, K.N., Goubault-Larrecq, J., Prasad, S., Arun-Kumar, S.: Reflecting BDDs in Coq. In: Kleinberg, R.D., Sato, M. (eds.) ASIAN 2000. LNCS, vol. 1961, pp. 162–181. Springer, Heidelberg (2000)
21. von Henke, F.W., Pfab, S., Pfeifer, H., Rueß, H.: Case Studies in Meta-Level Theorem Proving. In: Grundy, J., Newey, M. (eds.) TPHOLs 1998. LNCS, vol. 1479, pp. 461–478. Springer, Heidelberg (1998)

A Formal Framework for Modelling Coercion Resistance and Receipt Freeness

James Heather and Steve Schneider

University of Surrey, Guildford, Surrey, GU2 7XH, UK

Abstract. Coercion resistance and receipt freeness are critical properties for any voting system. However, many different definitions of these properties have been proposed, some formal and some informal; and there has been little attempt to tie these definitions together or identify relations between them.

We give here a general framework for specifying different coercion resistance and receipt freeness properties using the process algebra CSP. The framework is general enough to accommodate a wide range of definitions, and strong enough to cover both randomization attacks and forced abstention attacks. We provide models of some simple voting systems, and show how the framework can be used to analyze these models under different definitions of coercion resistance and receipt freeness. Our formalisation highlights the variation between the definitions, and the importance of understanding the relations between them.

Keywords: secure voting, CSP, coercion-resistance, receipt-freeness.

1 Introduction

Much work has been published over the last couple of decades concerning secure voting protocols. Many proposals come with claims that they meet appropriate security guarantees; but the properties in question are often poorly defined, and for the most part any proofs offered have been informal at best.

More recently, there have been attempts to formalize some of the desirable properties of voting systems [MN06, DKR09, DLL11]. These results have been useful, because they have been able to give precise answers to previously vague questions about the security of various systems. The approach has been to construct a model, and to verify it against a formalization of the relevant property.

However, since the informal definitions vary considerably, these formal definitions inevitably capture what is meant by some authors' use of the terms, and not others'; consequently, one can debate whether the formalisms really have captured the 'right' understanding of the various properties.

Our approach here is a little different. We take two commonly discussed properties—coercion resistance and receipt freeness—and construct a framework that is rich enough to cope with a large variety of definitions. This has the advantage of allowing us to formalize many definitions and analyze a voting system to see which definitions it satisfies and which it does not. A simplified CSP model of Prêt à Voter is then considered against a range of coercion resistance properties expressed in our framework. Two further examples of voting systems are presented to highlight differences between definitions in the literature.

D. Giannakopoulou and D. Méry (Eds.): FM 2012, LNCS 7436, pp. 217–231, 2012.
© Springer-Verlag Berlin Heidelberg 2012

1.1   Characterisations

Characterisations of coercion resistance and receipt freeness are plentiful in the literature, but rarely do two definitions coincide. The following characterisations are examples from the literature. They are a mixture of coercion resistance and receipt freeness definitions; once we have seen the flavour of some of these definitions, then we will consider the differences. They apply to systems which voters interact with in order to cast votes, and which potential coercers may also observe and interact with.

Characterisation 1 (Okamoto [RF]). *For any two candidates c and c', a voter can vote for c in a way that is consistent (from the coercer's point of view) with having voted for c' [Oka97].*

Characterisation 2 (Benaloh/Tuinstra [RF]). *A voter should be unable to prove that a vote was cast in a particular way [BT94].*

Characterisation 3 (Delaune/Kremer/Ryan [CR]). *Coercion resistance holds if a coerced voter behaving as instructed is indistinguishable from one voting a different way, to a coercer interacting with the voter [DKR09]. (A weaker notion of receipt freeness is also provided.)*

The issue here is what can qualify as instruction. The difference between coercion resistance and receipt freeness is usually phrased in terms of the coercer's ability to interact with the voter during the voting process: coercion resistance includes protection against a coercer who can interact in this way, whereas receipt freeness does not. This is a slippery distinction, for two reasons. First, interacting with the voter *before* the voting process, and interacting *during* the voting process, are hard to distinguish cleanly. For instance, there is nothing in principle to stop the coercer from interacting before voting takes place, and providing the voter with a flowchart showing how the voter is to act in any given situation. Secondly, it is not clear what constitutes interaction. If it is known to me that someone is offering money for receipts that show a vote for a particular candidate, does the fact that the knowledge has reached me (by whatever means) constitute interaction with the coercer?

Since coercion resistance is generally considered to be a stronger property than receipt freeness, the approach we will take in this paper is to see receipt freeness properties as a subclass of coercion resistance properties. We will assume that receipt freeness deals with a coercer who is concerned only with deducing information about how someone voted from receipts and any public information, but who does not give detailed instructions on how to cast the vote. Coercion resistance, on the other hand, includes dealing with a coercer who gives details not just on which candidate to vote for but also on how to cast the vote.

This understanding of receipt freeness has the advantage that it can be modelled in the same way as coercion resistance. Receipt freeness, on this definition, is equivalent to coercion resistance against a coercer who can specify which candidate the voter should choose, but cannot specify how the voter should make the choice. If the voting process is deterministic (as it is, for example, in Prêt à Voter), then these two notions will coincide, but if it is non-deterministic (as, for example, in ThreeBallot [Riv06]) then they might not.

Because receipt freeness properties are, on this understanding, a subclass of coercion resistance properties, we will focus on the larger problem of coercion resistance. Receipt freeness is discussed in more detail in an expanded and more technical version of this paper [HS12].

2 Modelling Voting Systems in CSP

CSP (Communicating Sequential Processes) provides a language for describing concurrent systems, and a theory for reasoning about them, in terms of events that they can perform. Events can be atomic, e.g., *start*, or they can be structured with several fields, e.g., *vote.i.p.v*. The language of processes includes:

- $a \to P$, which can perform a and then behave as P;
- $c?v \to P(v)$ which inputs value v over channel c and then behaves as $P(v)$;
- $c!v \to P$ which outputs v on channel c;
- $P \setminus A$ which hides the set of events in A, which are performed internally;
- *Stop* is the process that does nothing.
- *Chaos*(H) is the process that can nondeterministically perform or refuse to perform any event from H at any time.
- $P \sqcap Q$ makes an internal (nondeterministic) choice between P and Q;
- $P \square Q$ offers an external choice between P and Q;
- $P \parallel Q$ runs P and Q in parallel, synchronising on their common events.

The last three operators also have indexed forms. The language also includes recursive definitions $N = P$.

The theory provides a hierarchy of semantic models, including the Stable Failures model, which models a process as the set of traces (sequences of events) and subsequent sets of events that can be refused and the Failures/Divergences model which also includes information about divergent (infinite internal) behaviour. A process P is refined by another process Q, written $P \sqsubseteq_F Q$ (or $Q \sqsupseteq_F P$), and $P \sqsubseteq_{FD} Q$ for the respective models, if all observations of Q in that model are also observations of P. See [Ros98, Sch99] for further details.

Throughout this section, we shall assume that voting systems are modelled as follows. The system as a whole is modelled by a CSP process *SYSTEM*; this will be responsible for receiving votes, publishing receipts, tallying, publishing audit data, and whatever else the system in question may need to do.

Voters will interact with the system by being placed in parallel with it. We will model voter behaviour by a process *VOTER*(i, c), which represents the most general behaviour of a voter with ID i who chooses to vote for candidate c.

Preferential voting systems allow voters to rank the candidates, rather than asking them to choose one candidate. The framework presented here is expressive enough to allow for this: c would be the vote in whatever form it might take, rather than necessarily being a specific candidate, and each possible ranking would effectively be treated as a separate 'candidate'. However, for clarity of exposition, we will continue to talk in terms of votes for particular candidates.

We will consider coercion resistance and receipt freeness from the perspective of an arbitrarily chosen voter, to whom we will give the name of Zara and the ID of 0. Thus, roughly speaking, we will want to know whether a coercer can distinguish $SYSTEM \parallel VOTER(0, c)$ from $SYSTEM \parallel VOTER(0, c')$. In the first case, the target voter casts a vote for c; in the second case, for c'.

However, we start by observing that no voting system can be coercion resistant from voter 0's perspective if every other voter is under the complete control of the coercer. The coercer will know what the tally should be without voter 0's vote, and so he will be able to establish how voter 0 voted by seeing how the tally has changed. We will need to assume that there is at least one other voter who lies outside the control of the coercer. Since we will need to reason about this voter, we will identify him by the name of Juan and the ID of 1. This approach is also taken in the formalisations given in [DKR09].

The idea will be that Juan will cover Zara's tracks. Consider the case where the coercer instructs Zara to vote for Alice. Coercion resistance will mean that the coercer is unable to distinguish between Zara's compliance by voting for Alice and Juan's voting for Bob, and Zara's disobedience by voting for Bob and Juan's voting for Alice. The underlying assumption is that there is at least one voter (whom we will call Juan) who, as far as the coercer is concerned, might or might not vote for Alice, but who in fact does so. As long as at least one voter casts a vote for Alice but is not known by the coercer to have done so, then Zara's non-compliance will be masked. The precise masking behaviour will vary according to the voting system and the model of coercion resistance.

We are now ready to state the formal definition. We start with some assumptions on the model of the system and the model of a general voter. We denote the set of all candidates by $CANDIDATES$. This set includes the special value abs; a voter who 'chooses' the candidate abs chooses to abstain from voting.

Assumption 4 (System Model). *The system is modelled by a process $SYSTEM$, and the most general behaviour of a voter with ID i who chooses to vote for candidate c is modelled by $VOTER(i, c)$. Voter behaviour is also defined for a set of candidates: the most general behaviour of a voter who chooses non-deterministically from the set $CANDS \neq \emptyset$ of candidates is*

$$VOTER(i, CANDS) = \bigsqcap_{c \in CANDS} VOTER(i, c)$$

These processes must meet the following conditions:

$$SYSTEM \setminus (\Sigma \setminus \{open, close\}) =_{FD} open \rightarrow close \rightarrow Stop$$

$$VOTER(i, CANDIDATES) \setminus (\Sigma \setminus \{open, close\}) =_{FD} open \rightarrow close \rightarrow Stop$$

$$SYSTEM \parallel (\parallel_{i \in IDS} VOTER(i, CANDIDATES)) \setminus (\Sigma \setminus \{open, close\})$$
$$=_{FD} open \rightarrow close \rightarrow Stop$$

One consequence of these assumptions is that voter behaviour and overall system behaviour are both finitary. This rules out, for instance, unbounded auditing of ballot papers in a system like Prêt à Voter [CRS05], or unbounded re-voting in a system like Helios [Adi08]. This is not unreasonable, since in practice polling closes at a fixed time, meaning that systems and voters must eventually terminate their interaction.

What is more important from a technical point of view is that it eliminates the possibility of divergence in any of the processes involved in the model. When we consider the coercer's view of the system, we will abstract away all of the events that the coercer cannot see; if unbounded sequences of such events were allowed, then the abstraction would introduce divergence. By ensuring that every process is divergence free, we will be able to analyze the model in stable failures without concerning ourselves with divergence. Hence for the remainder of this paper we will use the stable failures semantic model.

Definition 5 (Coercer's control). *We use 'H' for the set of events invisible to the coercer. The only restriction is that* $\{open, close\} \cap H = \emptyset$; *in other words, the coercer must be able to see the opening and closing of the election.*

Definition 6 (Candidates and abstentions). *The set of all candidates under consideration is denoted by 'C'. This will denote all the candidates for whom Zara may wish to vote, and all of the candidates for whom the coercer may wish her to vote. Typically we will have either* $C = CANDIDATES \setminus \{abs\}$, *if we do not want to consider abstentions, or* $C = CANDIDATES$ *if we do.*

We now define the set of all instructions the coercer might give Zara. Instructions will come in the form of a process whose behaviour Zara must mimic; for compliance to be possible, the process must be a refinement of $VOTER(0, C)$, Zara's most general behaviour.

Definition 7. *We use 'I' to denote the set of instructions that the coercer might give Zara. It must be a subset of the set of all possible instructions that the coercer could give Zara, with the set C of candidates under consideration:*

$$I \subseteq \{P \mid P \sqsupseteq_F VOTER(0, C)\}$$

Definition 8 (Coercion resistance [CR]). *Suppose that we are given some system model SYSTEM (with associated voter model* $VOTER(i, c)$*). We say that SYSTEM meets* $CR(I, C, H, mask)$*, with*

$$I \subseteq \{P \mid P \sqsupseteq_F VOTER(0, C)\}$$
$$C \subseteq CANDIDATES$$
$$H \subseteq \Sigma \setminus \{open, close\}$$
$$mask \subseteq (H \times H) \cup (\bar{H} \times \bar{H})$$

if, for all $c \in C$ *and* $Z_x \in I$*, there exist some* $Z_c \sqsupseteq_F VOTER(0, c)$ *and* $J_x \sqsupseteq_F VOTER(1, C)$ *such that*

$$\mathcal{L}_H(mask(SYSTEM \parallel Z_x \parallel VOTER(1, C)))$$
$$\sqsubseteq_F \quad \mathcal{L}_H(mask(SYSTEM \parallel Z_c \parallel J_x)) \tag{1}$$

In this definition, J is a shorthand for $VOTER(1, C)$, Juan's most general behaviour. The set I represents the set of processes that the coercer is able to choose from when giving instructions to Zara; we must have $I \subseteq \{P \mid P \sqsupseteq_F VOTER(0, C)\}$ if Zara is to be able to comply. The second parameter, C, determines the set of candidates under consideration; in particular, the flavour of coercion resistance will change if this contains the special abs candidate. If abs $\in C$, then Zara must be able to abstain if she so wishes, and the coercer may try to force her to abstain.

The coercer's view is controlled by the third parameter, H. The $\mathcal{L}_H$ function is *lazy abstraction*, and is defined in [Ros98]; it provides a mechanism for masking all of the events (in traces and in refusals) from the hidden set H. It is defined as $\mathcal{L}_H(P) = (P \parallel Chaos(H)) \setminus H$. Essentially, by applying lazy abstraction over the set H, we ensure that events from the set H are invisible, so that the coercer can neither see such events nor see the refusal to engage in such events. This is a stronger form of abstraction than simply hiding events, for which hidden events cannot be refused.

The purpose of the fourth parameter, *mask*, is to allow us to model semantic security of an encryption function. There will be times when we want to say that encryptions are essentially opaque to an observer: he cannot learn anything from seeing an encryption, including determining whether two encryptions represent the same value. The *mask* function is applied to events, and then lifted to whole processes; usually it will involve mapping all encryptions to a single value. The conditions on it state that it should act reasonably with respect to the events that are being entirely abstracted away: it will not move a whole event from hidden (in H) to visible (in $\Sigma \setminus H$) or from visible to hidden. For most of the models in this paper, we will use the identity function id as the mask, because there is no encryption to deal with; but for the Prêt à Voter model in Section 4, we will need to mask encryptions from the observer's view.

What Definition 8 states, then, is that whatever candidate c Zara wishes to vote for, and whatever instructions Z_x the coercer might give her from the set I, there is some possible behaviour Z_c of hers that casts a vote for c, and some possible behaviour J_x of Juan, such that, when we abstract away the set of all hidden events H, any behaviour of the system when Zara acts as Z_c and Juan acts as J_x is also a possible behaviour of the system when Zara acts as instructed by the coercer.

An alternative definition replaces the refinement relation with equality:

Definition 9 (Coercion resistance [CR^*]). *The coercion resistance property $CR^*(I, C, H, mask)$ has the same definition as CR of Definition 8 except that it uses equality instead of refinement, replacing Line (1) with the following:*

$$\exists J_c \sqsupseteq_F VOTER(1, c) . \mathcal{L}_H(mask(SYSTEM \parallel Z_x \parallel J_c))$$
$$=_F \mathcal{L}_H(mask(SYSTEM \parallel Z_c \parallel J_x))$$

In Definition 8, the question is whether some strategy of Zara's is sufficient to allow her to vote according to her own wishes whilst claiming plausibly to have obeyed the coercer; in Definition 9, the question is whether *every* observation that the coercer might make of a compliant voter is also possible for a voter voting for c. Definition 9 is stronger than Definition 8 since equality implies refinement. For most voting systems there will be no difference; but we will see in Section 4.1 that this is not always the case. Hence we illustrate the difference between approaches based on CR and those based on CR^*.

The line we will adopt here is to use Definition 8 for the bulk of our work, to illustrate how the definition can be applied. Similar results hold for Definition 9.

3 Definitions of Coercion Resistance

In this section, we will give formal definitions within our framework of several different informal definitions of coercion resistance and receipt freeness, including some of those found in Section 1.1. In each case, we will give the definition of the set I of instructions that the coercer can give. This set will be defined in terms of C, the set of candidates under consideration. We will then give a useful result that allows us to compare definitions; this will enable us to set up a hierarchy of definitions of coercion resistance and receipt freeness.

Since the definitions are in terms of the set I of instructions, they can apply equally to CR and to CR^*.

3.1 Formal Definitions

For convenience, we will attach a superscript of 'abs' when the definition includes the special abstention candidate. The definitions below are given in their undecorated form; but later we will use the decorated forms of some of these definitions when we want to consider abstentions.

One notion of coercion resistance that is not given a formal definition below is that of resistance to *randomization attacks*, in which the coercer attempts to force Zara to vote randomly. This type of attack can occur in a system like Prêt à Voter, where the coercer can insist that Zara bring back a receipt with a cross in the top box, without the coercer knowing which candidate the top box will represent. The formal definition of such attacks varies according to the system in question, so we cannot give a general definition, but we will discuss randomization attacks further in Section 4.

We start with the definition of a general kind of receipt freeness property, in the context of a voter who wishes to deceive the coercer where possible.

Definition 10 (Receipt Absence). *Our informal definition of receipt absence allows the coercer to specify the content of the vote, but not how to cast the vote. In its most general form, the coercer may specify any non-empty subset X of candidates, and require the voter to cast the vote for a candidate from X. The set of instructions that the coercer may give, then, is*

$$I_{RFGEN} = \{ VOTER(0, X) \mid X \subseteq C \wedge X \neq \emptyset \}$$

We shall shortly give some results that enable us to say when one definition is stronger than another.

Definition 11 (Okamoto). *Characterisation 1 is encapsulated formally by using the following set within the definition of CR or CR∗:*

$$I_{OK} = \{ VOTER(0, c) \mid c \in C \}$$

The coercer may specify a candidate to vote for, but may not specify how the voter is to cast it. This turns out to be equivalent to I_{RFGEN}.

Definition 12 (Benaloh/Tuinstra). *We here give the formal definition of coercion resistance for Characterisation 2. This holds when a voter aiming to deceive the coercer can avoid leaking information about how the vote was cast. The Benaloh/Tuinstra definition is encapsulated by using the following set within the definition of CR or CR^*:*

$$I_{BT} = \{ P \mid P \sqsupseteq VOTER(0, c) \wedge c \in C \}$$

This is stronger than the Okamoto definition. Here, the coercer can require specific evidence that Zara has complied with specific instructions not just on voting for c but on voting for c in a particular way.

Definition 13 (Delaune/Kremer/Ryan). *Characterisation 3 says that a system is coercion resistant if the coercer cannot tell whether a coerced voter has behaved as instructed or voted differently. This leaves open the question of what possible instructions the coercer may give, but it appears that in their model a coercer's instructions must always be instructions to vote for a particular candidate, possibly in a specific way. The formal definition of the set I within our framework is then the same as that for the Benaloh/Tuinstra definition: the coercer can choose any candidate, then specify any refinement of the process that always casts a vote for that candidate. Note that Delaune, Kremer and Ryan use observational equivalence, so CR^* will always be the appropriate definition corresponding to theirs.*

Definition 14 (Forced abstention attacks). *A forced abstention attack is an attack in which the coercer attempts to force Zara to abstain. Since it makes sense only when abstentions are under consideration, we give the formal definition in its decorated form: $I^{abs} = \{ VOTER(0, abs) \}$.*

Definition 15 (Maximum strength). *Our framework finds its strongest possible notion of coercion resistance in the set of all refinements of Zara's most general behaviour, $VOTER(0, C)$. This includes everything covered by Benaloh/Tuinstra, but it also includes randomization attacks, and any other sort of instruction that Zara is able to follow: for instance, an instruction to use the last digit of the ballot serial number to determine which candidate to vote for. When $abs \in C$, it also includes instructions to abstain, or instructions to participate.*

$$I_{MAX} = \{ P \mid P \sqsupseteq_F VOTER(0, C) \} \quad \text{where } abs \notin C$$
$$I_{MAX}^{abs} = \{ P \mid P \sqsupseteq_F VOTER(0, C) \} \quad \text{where } abs \in C$$

The possibility of randomisation attacks is dependent on the particular system under consideration, and there is not a generic characterisation. We see an example of a randomisation set I_{RND} in the next section, under Proposition 20.

3.2   Relationships between Definitions

Some of the associated CR and $CR*$ definitions are stronger than others. We now state some results that allow us to formalize relations between notions of coercion resistance. Proofs of the results given in this paper can be found in [HS12].

Definition 16 (Dominance). *Suppose that I_1 and I_2 are sets of processes. We say that I_1 dominates I_2 if $\forall P_2 \in I_2. \exists P_1 \in I_1. P_2 \sqsubseteq_F P_1$.*

Theorem 17 (CR and dominance). *Suppose that I_1 dominates I_2, and $SYSTEM$ meets $CR(I_1, C, H, mask)$. Then it also meets $CR(I_2, C, H, mask)$.*

Corollary 18 (CR and subset). *Suppose that $I_2 \subseteq I_1$, and $SYSTEM$ meets $CR(I_1, C, H, mask)$. Then it also meets $CR(I_2, C, H, mask)$.*

These results allow us to give a hierarchy of definitions, whose relationships are shown in Figure 1.

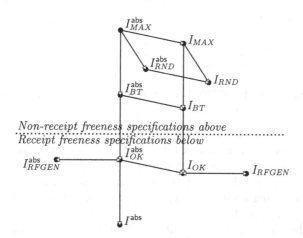

Fig. 1. Hierarchy of definitions of coercion resistance

4   Example: Simplified Prêt à Voter

Figure 2 shows the CSP for a simplified model of Prêt à Voter running a referendum. Voters receive a value $b \in \{0, 1\}$ on channel *ballot*, which indicates the ordering of the boxes on the ballot form: 0 or 1 means that the top box represents 'yes' or 'no' respectively. They also receive a pair of encryptions, the first (second) of which will decrypt to the value represented by the top (bottom)

$$BOOTH = open \rightarrow WAITING(\emptyset, \emptyset)$$

$$WAITING(VTD, BOX) = arrive?id : IDS \setminus VTD \rightarrow VOTING(VTD, BOX, id)$$
$$\square \; close \rightarrow mix.1!BOX \rightarrow Stop$$

$$VOTING(VTD, BOX, id) = newBallot \rightarrow genBallot?b?encs \rightarrow ballot.id!b!encs$$
$$\rightarrow \underset{v \in \{0,1\}}{\square} (vote.id.v.encs[v] \rightarrow write!encs[v] \rightarrow$$
$$WAITING(VTD \cup \{id\}, BOX \cup \{encs[v]\}))$$

$$MIX(n) = close \rightarrow mix.n?BOX \rightarrow REMIX(n, BOX, \emptyset)$$

$$REMIX(n, \emptyset, NEW) = mix.(n+1)!NEW \rightarrow Stop$$

$$REMIX(n, OLD, NEW) = \underset{v \in OLD}{\bigcap} reenc.n!v \rightarrow genReenc.n?v' \rightarrow$$
$$REMIX(n, OLD \setminus \{v\}, NEW \cup \{v'\})$$

$$DEC = mix.(K+1)?BOX \rightarrow announce!cnt(BOX, 0).cnt(BOX, 1) \rightarrow Stop$$

$$SYSTEM = \left(BOOTH \parallel \left(\underset{1 \leqslant i \leqslant K}{\parallel} MIX(i)\right) \parallel ENCSVR(RAND) \parallel DEC\right)$$
$$\setminus \{|newBallot, genBallot, reenc, genReenc|\}$$

$$ENCSVR(R) = newBallot \rightarrow \underset{b \in \{0,1\}}{\bigcap} genBallot!b!\langle Enc.b.R[0], Enc.(1-b).R[1]\rangle \rightarrow ENCSVR(R[2..])$$
$$\square \; reenc?n?Enc.b.r \rightarrow genReenc!n!Enc.b.R[0] \rightarrow ENCSVR(R[1..])$$

$$VOTER(i, c) = open \rightarrow if \; (c \neq \mathsf{abs}) \; then$$
$$arrive!i \rightarrow ballot.i?b?xs \rightarrow vote.i.c \oplus b.xs[c \oplus b] \rightarrow close \rightarrow Stop$$
$$else \; close \rightarrow Stop$$

$$cnt(BOX, b) = \#\{r \mid Enc.b.r \in BOX\}$$

Fig. 2. A simplified model of Prêt à Voter: defining the system and voter behaviour

box. They then submit an ID from the finite set *IDS* of all voter IDs, and the encryption associated with the box they want to choose; the system returns this encryption to them, and then stores the encrypted value.

When voting closes, the set of votes is passed through each of the K mix servers in turn, which each re-encrypt them all. The votes are then decrypted and the totals announced.

Here and throughout, '$\bar{v}$' represents $1 \oplus v$, where '$\oplus$' is bitwise exclusive-or. (The special candidate abs is treated as invariant under this operation.) The ballots and re-encryptions are produced by *ENCSVR*, which models the assumption that no two encryptions ever have the same randomness. It is initialized with an infinite sequence *RANDS* of distinct random numbers, and it uses these to generate new ballots and re-encryptions of existing ballots.

The voter process is finitary (Assumption 4) because it is non-recursive. The system is finite because on each step the number of people who have voted strictly increases, and cannot exceed $\#IDS$.

Our Prêt à Voter model is rich enough to allow for analysis under various definitions of coercion resistance. We consider several here. Initially, we will not take abstentions into account.

For what follows, we define the function *mask* to model the semantic security of the encryption: it abstracts the system so that all encryptions appear as the value '$\perp$'. This prevents agents from 'reading' inside the encryptions:

$$mask(ballot.i.b.E) = ballot.i.b.\langle \perp \mid e \in E \rangle \quad mask(mix.n.B) = mix.n.\{\perp \mid b \in B\}$$
$$mask(vote.i.p.v) = vote.i.p.\perp \qquad\qquad mask(write.v) = write.\perp$$

Proposition 19 (Okamoto and PaV, no abs).

The set of candidates under consideration, when abstentions are not taken into account, is $C_2 = \{0, 1\}$.

The Okamoto definition in this setting is encapsulated by $I_{OK} = \{VOTER(0, c) \mid c \in C_2\}$.

Suppose that we set $H_{PUB} = \{|ballot|\}$. In other words, the coercer cannot see the ordering of the names on the ballot paper (the ballot channel), but can see who arrives to vote (the arrive channel) and who ticks which box (the masked vote channel). We use the name 'H_{PUB}' because this models a scenario in which it is made public which voter is associated with each encrypted receipt.

The simplified Prêt à Voter model meets $CR(I_{OK}, C_2, H_{PUB}, mask)$.

Proposition 20 (Randomization attacks and PaV, no abs). *To mount a randomization attack, the coercer specifies a particular box to be ticked (for instance, the top box). The coercer cannot know whether this box represents a 'yes' or a 'no' vote. Such an attack is represented in our model by setting*

$$I_{RND} = \{ open \rightarrow arrive!0 \rightarrow ballot.0?b?xs \rightarrow$$
$$vote.i.xs[v] \rightarrow close \rightarrow Stop \mid v \in \{0, 1\}\}$$

We consider candidates in $C_2 = \{0, 1\}$, and $H_{PUB} = \{|ballot|\}$. The coercer can see which box Zara ticks, but not which candidate it represents.

Our simplified model of Prêt à Voter does not meet $CR(I_{RND}, C_2, H_{PUB}, mask)$.

Corollary 21 (I_{MAX} and PaV, no abs). *It is an immediate corollary of Proposition 20 and Corollary 18 that our simplified Prêt à Voter does not meet $CR(I_{MAX}, C_2, H_{PUB}, mask)$.*

Any set of coercer instructions must be a subset of I_{MAX}, so Corollary 18 tells us that if Prêt à Voter met $CR(I_{MAX}, C_2, H_{PUB}, mask)$ then it would meet $CR(I, C_2, H_{PUB}, mask)$ for any I. But Proposition 20 shows that it does not meet $CR(I_{RND}, C_2, H_{PUB}, mask)$; therefore, it cannot meet $CR(I_{MAX}, C_2, H_{PUB}, mask)$.

We now return to the question of abstentions. In what follows, we will use $C_2^{abs} = C_2 \cup \{abs\}$, and establish what effect this has on coercion resistance. Including abs has two consequences. First, Zara may now want to abstain; coercion resistance will imply that she is able to abstain if she wishes, without the coercer knowing that she has not complied. If the coercer can force Zara not to abstain, then we have a *forced participation* attack. Secondly, the coercer may insist on Zara's abstention; coercion resistance will imply that she is able to vote if she wants to, without the coercer knowing that she has not abstained. If the coercer can force Zara to abstain, then we have a *forced abstention* attack. The model is rich enough to handle these cases independently. However, they are naturally treated together, and we will treat them together here.

Proposition 22 (Okamoto and PaV, C_2^{abs}).
The Okamoto definition, with abs included, is modelled by

$$I_{OK}^{abs} = \{\, VOTER(0, c) \mid c \in C_2^{abs} \,\}$$

By including abs in the set of candidates, we also allow for the possibility that Zara wishes to abstain. We continue to set $H_{PUB} = \{|ballot|\}$, so that the coercer can see all voter actions but cannot see the candidate ordering on the ballot paper.

Our simplified Prêt à Voter model does not meet $CR(I_{OK}^{abs}, C_2^{abs}, H_{PUB}, mask)$. If the coercer can see anything that includes the voter's ID, then there is no hope of resistance to forced abstention attacks.

Corollary 23 (I_{MAX}^{abs} and PaV, C_2^{abs}). *The strongest definition, with abs included, is modelled by $I_{MAX}^{abs} = \{P \mid P \sqsupseteq_{FD} VOTER(0, c) \mid c \in C_2^{abs}\}$*
Our model does not meet $CR(I_{MAX}^{abs}, C_2^{abs}, H_{PUB}, mask)$.

Finally we ask what happens if we change the level of abstraction, so that the coercer can see fewer events. We will allow the coercer to see votes being posted up (on the *write* channel), but not arrivals or vote casting. We will set $H_{SEC} = \{|arrive, ballot, vote|\}$.

Proposition 24 (I_{MAX} and PaV, C_2^{abs}, H_{SEC}). *Our simplified Prêt à Voter model meets $CR(I_{MAX}, C_2^{abs}, H_{SEC}, mask)$. In other words, when all events containing voter IDs are abstracted away, our model satisfies the strongest possible definition of coercion resistance in our framework.*

It is evident from this one example that the framework we have constructed is able to handle a wide variety of notions of coercion resistance, by varying the values of I, C and H. A summary of results is shown in Table 1.

Table 1. Summary of results for simplified Prêt à Voter model

Definition	Abs?	Invisible	Formalism	Met by PaV?
Okamoto	No	$\{|ballot|\}$	$CR(I_{OK}, C_2, H_{PUB}, mask)$	Yes
Randomization	No	$\{|ballot|\}$	$CR(I_{RND}, C_2, H_{PUB}, mask)$	No
Strongest	No	$\{|ballot|\}$	$CR(I_{MAX}, C_2, H_{PUB}, mask)$	No
Okamoto / forced abs	Yes	$\{|ballot|\}$	$CR(I_{OK}^{abs}, C_2^{abs}, H_{PUB}, mask)$	No
Strongest	Yes	$\{|ballot|\}$	$CR(I_{MAX}^{abs}, C_2^{abs}, H_{PUB}, mask)$	No
Strongest	Yes	$\{|arrive, ballot, vote|\}$	$CR(I_{MAX}^{abs}, C_2^{abs}, H_{SEC}, mask)$	Yes

4.1   Further Examples

Two further toy examples illustrate the differences between types of coercion resistance. 'Two-receipt' shows the difference between the definitions of Okamoto (where it holds) and Benaloh/Tuinstra (where it does not hold). 'Opt-receipt' shows the difference between the two characterisations of coercion resistance, CR and CR^*. In each case, we give here the informal definitions and state the properties the systems meet; the CSP models can be found in [HS12].

Two-Receipt. This system gives voters a receipt containing two names (in arbitrary order): the name of the candidate who received the vote, and one other candidate of the voter's choice. The intention is that the inclusion of an alternative name on the receipt allows the voter to mask who received her vote.

Two-receipt meets the property $CR(I_{OK}, \{c_1, c_2, c_3\}, \{|vote, dummy|\}, id)$. A voter instructed to vote for c' can vote for c in a way consistent with a vote for c'. Conversely, Two-receipt does not meet the Benaloh and Tuinstra characterisation as captured by the property $CR(I_{BT}, \{c_1, c_2, c_3\}, \{|vote, dummy|\}, id)$. This is consistent with our expectations. A voter is able to vote for her preferred candidate c in a way consistent with a vote for c', as required by Okamoto's definition. On the other hand, if the coercer can require a vote to be cast in a particular way, then the voter might not be able to vote in her preferred way consistent with this. Our formal characterisation captures this distinction.

Opt-Receipt. The following example is attributed to Ron Rivest. On accepting a vote, the system chooses whether or not to offer a receipt. If offered, the voter chooses whether or not to accept the receipt. Hence the voter might obtain a receipt of exactly how they voted. However, they can also vote for their preferred candidate consistently with any instructions a coercer might give them, by declining any receipt, and claiming that the system did not offer one.

The voter has a strategy for voting without production of a receipt, and so Opt-receipt meets $CR(I_{MAX}, C, H_{OPT}, id)$, where $H_{OPT} = \{|vote, noreceipt, offerreceipt, accept, reject|\}$. However, it does not meet $CR^*(I_{MAX}, C, H_{OPT}, id)$. This example thus highlights the difference between CR, which requires the existence of a coercion resistance strategy for a voter, and CR^*, which requires that information about the vote should not leak whatever the voter does.

5   Discussion

As commented in Section 1, there are a variety of definitions in the literature to receipt-freeness and coercion-resistance, and a range of approaches to analysing proposed voting protocols and systems. They all hinge on the required inability of a coercer to tell whether the coerced voter has followed instructions or not.

The game-based approach typically applied to cryptographic schemes has been applied with respect to coercion-resistance in [JCJ05, GGR09, KTV10]. In this approach, coercion-resistance is captured in terms of a game with a specific goal, e.g. [GGR09] considers Indistinguishability of Encoded Votes. The nature of the goal and the coercer's possible instructions characterises whether abstention and randomisation attacks are included, and so the hierarchy of Figure 1 also applies to the range of possibilities expressible using the game-based approach.

Coercion resistance has also been characterised in the Universal Composability (UC) framework, for example in [MN06], [UMQ10], [dMPQ07]. This approach uses an idealised system in which voters choose whether or not to obey the coercer, and then defines a coercion-resistant system to be one in which an adversary cannot enable a distinguisher to tell the difference between the real system and the idealised system. Though in a different setting, this gives the same sense of coercion-resistance as Definition 3. The hierarchy of definitions of Figure 1 for the UC setting corresponds to what the coercer can require of the voter in the idealised system. Abstention attacks fall naturally within this setting, but randomisation attacks will perhaps be more difficult to characterise.

Others take a more symbolic approach. Okamoto's original formulation [Oka97] was epistemic. More recently the epistemic approach of [KT09] requires that for any instructions provided by the coercer, there is a counter-strategy for the voter to achieve their own goal, where the coercer cannot tell whether or not his instructions were followed. The hierarchy of definitions arises naturally with this approach, as the possible instructions and observations of the coercer vary. A quantitative approach based on knowledge reasoning is given in [JMP09], which gives a measure of voter privacy.

The process algebraic approaches of [DKR09, BHM08] and this paper are also symbolic. In these approaches an observational equivalence is used for indistinguishability, and coercion-resistance is captured as the equivalence of two processes, one where the voter complies and one where he does not. The models in [DKR09] provide a general framework to include the weaker properties of receipt-freeness and privacy, but unlike our approach they do not handle abstention or randomisation attacks since they are characterised in terms of a coercer selecting a particular candidate. The extended framework of [BHM08] does explicitly handle forced abstention attacks, but not randomisation attacks.

Our approach is most closely related to the epistemic characterisation in [KT09], but ours is cast in a process algebraic setting. This allows a higher level description of a voting system design in CSP. Further, our emphasis is on the hierarchy of definitions rather than the proposal of any specific one.

Acknowledgements. We are grateful to the reviewers for their careful reviewing and their valuable comments and suggestions. Thanks are also due to Chris Culnane, Murat Moran, Sriram Srinivasan and Zhe (Joson) Xia. This work was conducted while the first author was a Royal Society/Leverhulme Trust Senior Research Fellow. The research was funded by EPSRC under grant EP/G025797/1.

References

[Adi08]   Adida, B.: Helios: Web-based open-audit voting. In: van Oorschot, P.C. (ed.) USENIX Security Symposium, pp. 335–348 (2008)

[BHM08]   Backes, M., Hritcu, C., Maffei, M.: Automated verification of remote electronic voting protocols in the applied pi-calculus. In: CSF, pp. 195–209. IEEE Computer Society (2008)

[BT94]   Benaloh, J.C., Tuinstra, D.: Receipt-free secret-ballot elections (extended abstract). In: STOC, pp. 544–553 (1994)

[CRS05]   Chaum, D., Ryan, P.Y.A., Schneider, S.: A practical voter-verifiable election scheme. In: di Vimercati, S.d.C., Syverson, P.F., Gollmann, D. (eds.) ESORICS 2005. LNCS, vol. 3679, pp. 118–139. Springer, Heidelberg (2005)

[DKR09]   Delaune, S., Kremer, S., Ryan, M.: Verifying privacy-type properties of electronic voting protocols. Journal of Computer Security 17(4), 435–487 (2009)

[DLL11]   Dreier, J., Lafourcade, P., Lakhnech, Y.: A formal taxonomy of privacy in voting protocols. Technical Report TR-2011-10, Verimag (2011)

[dMPQ07]   de Marneffe, O., Pereira, O., Quisquater, J.-J.: Simulation-Based Analysis of E2E Voting Systems. In: Alkassar, A., Volkamer, M. (eds.) VOTE-ID 2007. LNCS, vol. 4896, pp. 137–149. Springer, Heidelberg (2007)

[GGR09]   Gardner, R.W., Garera, S., Rubin, A.D.: Coercion Resistant End-to-end Voting. In: Dingledine, R., Golle, P. (eds.) FC 2009. LNCS, vol. 5628, pp. 344–361. Springer, Heidelberg (2009)

[HS12]   Heather, J., Schneider, S.A.: A formal framework for modelling coercion resistance and receipt freeness. Technical report, University of Surrey (2012)

[JCJ05]   Juels, A., Catalano, D., Jakobsson, M.: Coercion-resistant electronic elections. In: WPES, pp. 61–70 (2005)

[JMP09]   Jonker, H.L., Mauw, S., Pang, J.: A formal framework for quantifying voter-controlled privacy. J. Algorithms 64(2-3), 89–105 (2009)

[KT09]   Küsters, R., Truderung, T.: An epistemic approach to coercion-resistance for electronic voting protocols. In: IEEE Symposium on Security and Privacy, pp. 251–266. IEEE Computer Society (2009)

[KTV10]   Küsters, R., Truderung, T., Vogt, A.: A game-based definition of coercion-resistance and its applications. In: CSF, pp. 122–136. IEEE Computer Society (2010)

[MN06]   Moran, T., Naor, M.: Receipt-Free Universally-Verifiable Voting with Everlasting Privacy. In: Dwork, C. (ed.) CRYPTO 2006. LNCS, vol. 4117, pp. 373–392. Springer, Heidelberg (2006)

[Oka97]   Okamoto, T.: Receipt-Free Electronic Voting Schemes for Large Scale Elections. In: Christianson, B., Lomas, M. (eds.) Security Protocols 1997. LNCS, vol. 1361, pp. 25–35. Springer, Heidelberg (1998)

[Riv06]   Rivest, R.L.: The ThreeBallot Voting System (2006),
           http://theory.lcs.mit.edu/~rivest/
           Rivest-TheThreeBallotVotingSystem.pdf

[Ros98]   Roscoe, A.W.: Theory and Practice of Concurrency. Prentice-Hall (1998)

[Sch99]   Schneider, S.: Concurrent and Real-time Systems. Wiley (1999)

[UMQ10]   Unruh, D., Müller-Quade, J.: Universally Composable Incoercibility. In: Rabin, T. (ed.) CRYPTO 2010. LNCS, vol. 6223, pp. 411–428. Springer, Heidelberg (2010)

Using Time to Add Order
to Distributed Testing*

Robert M. Hierons[1], Mercedes G. Merayo[2], and Manuel Núñez[2]

[1] Department of Information Systems and Computing, Brunel University
Uxbridge, Middlesex, UB8 3PH United Kingdom
`rob.hierons@brunel.ac.uk`
[2] Departamento de Sistemas Informáticos y Computación
Universidad Complutense de Madrid, Madrid, Spain
`mgmerayo@fdi.ucm.es,mn@sip.ucm.es`

Abstract. Many systems interact with their environment at physically distributed interfaces called ports. In testing such a system we might use a distributed approach in which there is a separate tester at each port. If the testers do not synchronise during testing then we cannot always determine the relative order of events observed at different ports and corresponding implementation relations have been developed for distributed testing. One possible method for strengthening the implementation relation is for testers to synchronise through exchanging coordination messages but this requires sufficiently fast communications channels and can increase the cost of testing. This paper explores an alternative in which each tester has a local clock and timestamps its observations. If we know nothing about how the local clocks relate then this does not help while if the local clocks agree exactly then we can reconstruct the sequence of observations made. In practice, however, we are likely to be between these extremes: the local clocks will not agree exactly but we have assumptions regarding how they can differ. This paper explores several such assumptions and derives corresponding implementation relations.

1 Introduction

Testing is the most widely used method to increase the confidence regarding the correctness of software systems. Testing has traditionally been a manual activity. This characteristic strongly increases the cost of complex software systems, where testing might take up to 50% of the project budget. As a result, there has been increasing interest in the development of techniques to automate, as much as possible, the different testing activities. One important such approach is to use formal testing methods [1,2]. In the context of the integration of formal methods

---

* Research partially supported by the Spanish MICINN project TESIS (TIN2009-14312-C02-01) and the UK EPSRC project Testing of Probabilistic and Stochastic Systems (EP/G032572/1). This research was carried out while the second author was visiting Brunel University supported by a grant *Fundación Caja Madrid para movilidad de profesores de universidades públicas de Madrid.*

D. Giannakopoulou and D. Méry (Eds.): FM 2012, LNCS 7436, pp. 232–246, 2012.
© Springer-Verlag Berlin Heidelberg 2012

and testing it is important to define suitable *implementation relations*, that is, formal ways to express what it means for a system to be correct with respect to a specification. Currently, the *standard* implementation relation is **ioco** [3], a well-established framework where a system under test (SUT) is correct with respect to a specification if for every sequence of actions σ that both the SUT and the specification can produce, we have that the outputs that the SUT can show after performing σ are a subset of those that the specification can show.

Many systems interact with their environment at physically distributed ports. Examples of such systems include communications protocols, web-services, cloud systems and wireless sensor networks. Users perceive these systems as black-boxes and user requirements are thus expressed at this level: users are not interested in the internal structure of a system, only in whether it delivers the services they require. In testing such systems we place a tester at each port and we are then using a distributed test architecture [4]. The use of the distributed test architecture can have a significant impact on testing and this topic has received much attention. Much of this work has concerned controllability problems, where the observations of the tester at a port p are not sufficient for it to know when to supply an input. There has also been interest in observability problems, where it is impossible to reconstruct the real order in which events were produced at different ports. A different line of work involves providing implementation relations that appropriately capture the special characteristics of the distributed test architecture. The underlying assumption in **dioco** [5], an extension of **ioco** to the distributed setting, is that we cannot compare global traces, obtained at different ports, by using equality. The idea is that if a trace is a reordering of another one where the order of events at each port has been preserved, then these two traces are indistinguishable in a distributed framework and therefore must be considered equivalent. The **dioco** framework reflects the situation in which separate agents interact with the SUT, these agents record their observations but we cannot know the causalities between events observed by different agents. However, sometimes we wish to use a framework where it is possible to establish information regarding causalities between events observed at different ports through the testers at these ports exchanging messages [6,7]. In particular, if the testers can exchange synchronisation messages with an external agent then it is possible to use such messages to establish the exact order in which events occurred [8]. However, the assumption that the testers can synchronise (effectively, message exchange takes no time) does not seem appropriate if the testers are physically distributed.

This paper considers an alternative perspective to providing additional information regarding the causality between actions performed at different ports. We use time information: if we label actions with the time when they were observed then we can obtain additional information regarding the order in which they occurred. We can consider two possibilities to include time information in the distributed test architecture. The first one assumes the existence of a global clock. However, usually we cannot assume that there exists a global clock. We therefore consider a weaker assumption under which there is a local clock at each port. But, how do these clocks work? If we assume that the clocks are *perfect*, then **dioco** and **ioco** almost coincide. Nevertheless, this is again a very unrealistic assumption. If we make no assumptions regarding how the times given by these local clocks relate, then they add nothing and so we have **dioco**. This paper investigates different assumptions regarding how the local clocks relate and the corresponding implementation relations.

The use of timestamps to decorate actions is not new [9,10] and the problems concerning the synchronisation of different clocks has also been studied [11]. Moreover, it has been shown that the use of timestamps has limitations since not all the causality relations can be captured [12]. Adding timestamps to actions is a common mechanism in formalisms such as process algebras to represent concurrent timed systems [13]. In this paper we investigate the use of timing information when testing from an input output transition system (IOTS).

The rest of the paper is structured as follows. Section 2 provides preliminary material. Sections 3 and 4 define implementation relations that correspond to different assumptions regarding how the clocks relate. Finally, in Section 5 we present our conclusions and some lines for future work.

2   Preliminaries

In this section we present the main concepts used in the paper. First, we define input output transition systems and notation to deal with sequences of actions that can be performed by a system. Then, we review the main differences between *classical* testing and testing in the distributed architecture.

2.1   Notation on Sequences

Given a set A, we let A^* denote the set of finite sequences of elements of A; $\epsilon \in A^*$ denotes the empty sequence. Given a sequence $\sigma \in A^*$ and $1 \le r \le |\sigma|$, $\sigma_r \in A$ denotes the r-th element of σ. Finally, let $\sigma \in A^*$ and $a \in A$. We have that σa denotes the sequence σ followed by a and $a\sigma$ denotes the sequence σ preceded by a.

2.2   Input Output Transition Systems

An input output transition system is a labelled transition system in which we distinguish between input and output. We use this formalism to define processes.

Definition 1. *Let $\mathcal{P} = \{1, \ldots, m\}$ be a set of ports. An* input output transition system *(IOTS) is defined by a tuple $s = (Q, I, O, T, q_{in})$ in which Q is a countable set of states, $q_{in} \in Q$ is the initial state, I is a countable set of inputs, O is a countable set of outputs, and $T \subseteq Q \times (I \cup O \cup \{\tau\}) \times Q$, where τ represents an internal (unobservable) action, is the transition relation. A transition (q, a, q'), also denoted by $q \xrightarrow{a} q'$, means that from state q it is possible to move to state q' with action $a \in I \cup O \cup \{\tau\}$.*

We say that a state $q \in Q$ is quiescent *if from q it is not possible to take a transition whose action is an output or τ without first receiving input. We extend T, the transition relation, by adding the transition (q, δ, q) for each quiescent state q. We say that s is* input-enabled *if for all $q \in Q$ and $?i \in I$ there is some $q' \in Q$ such that $(q, ?i, q') \in T$. We say that a system s is* output *divergent if it can reach a state from which there is an infinite path that contains only outputs and internal actions.*

The sets I and O are partitioned into sets $I_1, \ldots, I_m$ and $O_1, \ldots, O_m$ such that for all $p \in \mathcal{P}$, I_p and O_p are the sets of inputs and outputs at port p, respectively. We assume that $I_1, \ldots I_m, O_1, \ldots, O_m$ are pairwise disjoint.

We let $\mathcal{A}ct$ denote the set of observable actions, that is, $\mathcal{A}ct = I \cup O \cup \{\delta\}$. Given port $p \in \mathcal{P}$, $\mathcal{A}ct_p$ denotes the set of observations that can be made at p, that is, $\mathcal{A}ct_p = I_p \cup O_p \cup \{\delta\}$.

We let $\texttt{IOTS}(I, O, \mathcal{P})$ denote the set of IOTSs with input set I, output set O and port set $\mathcal{P}$. Processes can be identified with its initial state and we can define a process corresponding to a state q of s by making q the initial state. Thus, we use states and process and their notation interchangeably. An $\texttt{IOTS}$ can be represented by a diagram in which nodes represent states of the $\texttt{IOTS}$ and transitions are represented by arcs between the nodes. In order to distinguish between input and output we usually precede the name of an input by ? and precede the name of an output by !.

In this paper, whenever we compare two elements of $\texttt{IOTS}(I, O, \mathcal{P})$ we will assume that they have the same $\mathcal{A}ct_p$ for all $p \in \mathcal{P}$. Moreover, when we relate two $\texttt{IOTSs}$ we will assume that they have the same port set. As usual, we assume that implementations are input-enabled.[1] We also consider that specifications are input-enabled since this assumption simplifies the analysis. However, it is possible to remove this restriction in our framework [5]. Next we introduce a system that will be used as a running example along the paper.

Example 1. The specification depicted in Figure 1 represents a simplified version of an online travel agency that sells products and services to customers on behalf of suppliers such as airlines, car rentals, hotels, etc. We focus on the functionality associated with the process that begins at the moment a client request that some services are booked and receives the confirmation. A client must ask for a flight ticket and a booking of a hotel room. Additionally, the customer can request either an airport transfer or to rent a car and, optionally, a day trip. The system presents five different ports that correspond to the different suppliers. All of them are connected to the central server where the information of the products related to each client is collected. We denote by $\texttt{TA}$ the specification of the Travel Agency and the alphabets of the different ports are

- Airlines: $I_a = \{?data\_flight\}$, $O_a = \{!req\_flight\}$
- Hotels: $I_h = \{?data\_hotel\}$, $O_h = \{!req\_hotel\}$

---

[1] If an input cannot be applied in some state of the SUT, then we can assume that there is a response to the input that reports that this input is blocked.

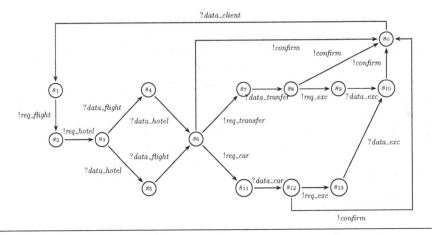

Fig. 1. Running example: travel agency

- *Transport:* $I_t = \{?data\_transfer, ?data\_car\}$, $O_t = \{!req\_transfer, !req\_car\}$
- *Excursions:* $I_e = \{?data\_exc\}$, $O_e = \{!req\_exc\}$
- *Client:* $I_c = \{?data\_client\}$, $O_c = \{!confirm\}$

In distributed testing each tester observes only the events at its port and this corresponds to a projection of the global trace that occurred.

Definition 2. *Let* $s = (Q, I, O, T, q_{in})$ *be an IOTS with port set* $\mathcal{P} = \{1, \ldots, m\}$. *Let* $p \in \mathcal{P}$ *and* $\sigma \in Act^*$ *be a sequence of visible actions. We let* $\pi_p(\sigma)$ *denote the projection of* σ *onto port* p *and* $\pi_p(\sigma)$ *is called a* local trace. *Formally,*

$$\pi_p(\sigma) = \begin{cases} \epsilon & \text{if } \sigma = \epsilon \\ a\pi_p(\sigma') & \text{if } \sigma = a\sigma' \wedge a \in Act_p \\ \pi_p(\sigma') & \text{if } \sigma = a\sigma' \wedge a \in Act \setminus Act_p \end{cases}$$

Given $\sigma, \sigma' \in Act^*$ *we write* $\sigma \sim \sigma'$ *if* σ *and* σ' *cannot be distinguished when making local observations, that is, for all* $p \in \mathcal{P}(s)$ *we have that* $\pi_p(\sigma) = \pi_p(\sigma')$.

The equivalence relation $\sim$ among sequences is fundamental to defining our original implementation relation **dioco** [5] that we give in the next section.

In distributed testing quiescent states can be used to combine the traces observed at each port and reach a verdict. This is because we assume that quiescence can be observed and, in addition, the testers can choose to stop testing in a quiescent state. The use of distributed testers also leads to the requirement for us to compare the set of local observations made with the global traces from the specification; if we make observations in non-quiescent states then we cannot know that the observed local traces are all projections of the same global trace of the SUT and we will distinguish processes that are observationally equivalent. For example, consider the processes r and s such that r can do $!o_1!o_2$ and then can only receive input ($!o_1$ and $!o_2$ are at different ports) and s can do $!o_2!o_1$ and then can only receive input. We have that r can do $!o_1$ while

s cannot. Therefore, if we consider that non quiescent traces can be used to compare processes then these two processes are not equivalent. However, in a distributed environment we cannot distinguish between these two processes if we do not have additional information (e.g. a timestamp indicating which action was performed before). Note that if a process is output-divergent then it can go through an infinite sequence of non-quiescent states, so that local traces cannot be combined. In addition, output-divergence is similar to a livelock and will generally be undesirable. We therefore restrict attention to processes that are not output divergent[2].

A *trace* is a sequence of observable actions that can be performed, possibly interspersed with τ actions, from the initial state of a process. Let s be an IOTS. Given a finite sequence of observable actions $\sigma \in \mathcal{A}ct^*$, we write $s \overset{\sigma}{\Longrightarrow} q$ if σ is a trace of s that ends in the state q. We let $\mathcal{T}r(s)$ denote the set of *traces* of s (in particular, $\epsilon \in \mathcal{T}r(s)$). Given a trace $\sigma \in \mathcal{A}ct^*$, s **after** σ denotes the set of states that can be reached from the initial state of s and after performing σ; given a state q, $\mathbf{out}(q)$ denotes the set of outputs (including quiescence) that can be performed from q possibly preceded by the performance of τ actions. The function $\mathbf{out}$ can be extended to deal with sets in the expected way, that is, $\mathbf{out}(Q') = \cup_{q \in Q'}\mathbf{out}(q)$. The interested reader is referred either to our previous work [5] or to the original **ioco** framework [3] for complete formal definitions. Next we present the standard implementation relation for testing from an IOTS [3] where information about different ports is not taken into account.

Definition 3. *Let r, s be IOTSs. We write r **ioco** s if for every $\sigma \in \mathcal{T}r(s)$ we have that $\mathbf{out}(r$ **after** $\sigma) \subseteq \mathbf{out}(s$ **after** $\sigma)$.*

2.3   Adding Timestamps

We assume that there is a local clock at each port and that an event at port p is timestamped with the current time of the local clock at port p. Therefore, timed traces collected from the SUT are sequences of inputs and outputs annotated with the local time at which events were observed. We assume that actions need a minimum amount of time to be performed (this is a real assumption since we can always consider a clock cycle as this bound) and therefore it is not possible to have Zeno processes. As a consequence of this assumption, if two events are produced at the same port, then one has to be produced first and, therefore, we cannot have two events in the same port timestamped with the same value.

It is clear how a tester can timestamp inputs and outputs. In contrast, quiescence is typically observed through timeouts: the system is deemed to be quiescent if it fails to produce output for a given period of time. As a result, quiescence is not observed at a particular time and so we do not include quiescence in timed traces. Naturally, corresponding untimed traces with quiescence can be produced

---

[2] It is possible to consider infinite traces rather than quiescent traces [5] but this complicates the exposition.

from the timed traces. Our not including quiescence in timed traces might seem to reduce the power of testing. However, all our implementation relations will have two parts: one part considers untimed traces, which might contain quiescence, and the other part considers a set of timed traces. As a result of the first part, occurrences of δ can be safely removed from our timed traces.

Definition 4. *We consider that the time domain includes all non-negative real numbers, that is,* Time $= I\!\!R_+$. *Given* $(a, t) \in Act \times$ Time *we have that* $\text{act}(a, t) = a$ *and* $\text{time}(a, t) = t$. *Let I and O be sets of inputs and outputs, respectively. Let $\sigma \in ((I \cup O) \times$ Time$)^*$ be a sequence of (observable action, time) pairs. We let* $\text{untime}(\sigma)$ *denote the trace produced from σ by removing the time stamps associated with actions.*

Let $s \in IOTS(I, O, \mathcal{P})$. A timed trace of s is a sequence $\sigma \in ((I \cup O) \times$ Time$)^*$ such that there exists $\sigma' \in \mathcal{T}r(s)$ such that $\sigma' \sim \text{untime}(\sigma)$, and if there exists $p \in \mathcal{P}$ such that $\text{act}(\sigma_{j_1}), \text{act}(\sigma_{j_2}) \in I_p \cup O_p$ and $j_1 < j_2$ then $\text{time}(\sigma_{j_1}) < \text{time}(\sigma_{j_2})$.

Let σ be a timed trace of s. We let $\pi_p(\sigma)$ denote the projection of σ onto port p and $\pi_p(\sigma)$ is called a timed local trace *(the formal definition of π_p is similar to the one given in Definition 2 for untimed traces and we therefore omit it).*

We use σ both to denote timed and untimed traces: we will state what type of sequence it represents unless this is clear from the context. We only require that timed traces can be produced by the system, that is, its untimed version is observationally equivalent to a trace of the system, and that actions at a port are sorted according to the available time information. Note that the timestamps define the exact order in which actions were produced at a given port.

2.4 Traces and Event Sets

A (timed or untimed) global trace defines a set of *events*, each event being either input or output (possibly with a timestamp) or the observation of quiescence. We will use information regarding timestamps to impose a partial order on the set of observed events and we therefore reason about *partially ordered sets (posets)*. In this section we only consider sequences of events that do not include quiescence since quiescence is not timestamped.

We first consider untimed traces, before generalising the definitions to timed traces. Since we wish to use a set of events we need notation to distinguish between two events with the same action and we achieve this through defining a function e from untimed traces to sets of events. We will compare traces that are equivalent under $\sim$ and so we want a representation under which 'corresponding' events for traces $\sigma \sim \sigma'$ have the same names; this will mean that we do not have to rename events when comparing traces. We achieve this by adding a label to each event, with the label for event a, preceded by σ', being k if this is the kth instance of a in $\sigma'a$.

Definition 5. *Let* $\sigma = a_1 \ldots a_n \in Act^*$ *be an untimed trace. We define* e_σ : $\mathbb{N} \longrightarrow Act \times \mathbb{N}$ *as* $e_\sigma(i) = (a_i, k)$ $(1 \leq i \leq n)$ *if there are exactly* $k - 1$ *occurrences of* a_i *in* $a_1 \ldots a_{i-1}$. *This says that the ith element of* σ *is the kth instance of* a_i *in* σ. *Then we let* $e(\sigma) = \{e_\sigma(1), \ldots, e_\sigma(n)\}$.

Example 2. Consider the untimed trace

$$\sigma = ?data\_client!req\_flight!req\_hotel?data\_hotel?data\_flight!confirm?data\_client$$

$$!req\_flight!req\_hotel?data\_flight?data\_hotel!req\_transfer?data\_transfer!confirm$$

For example, the second occurrence of $?data\_client$ in σ is represented by the event $e_\sigma(7) = (?data\_client, 2)$ and the event set associated with σ is

$$e(\sigma) = \left\{ \begin{array}{l} (?data\_client, 1), (!req\_flight, 1), (!req\_hotel, 1), (?data\_hotel, 1), \\ (?data\_flight, 1), (!confirm, 1), (?data\_client, 2), (!req\_flight, 2), \\ (!req\_hotel, 2), (?data\_hotel, 2), (?data\_flight, 2), (!req\_transfer, 1), \\ (?data\_transfer, 1), (!confirm, 2) \end{array} \right\}$$

The tester at port p observes a projection of a global trace σ and so can place a total order on the events at p. We can combine these orders to obtain a partial order $<_\sigma$.

Definition 6. *Let* $\sigma = a_1 \ldots a_n \in Act^*$ *be an untimed trace. We define the partial order* $<_\sigma$ *by: given* $1 \leq i, j \leq n$ *we have that* $e_\sigma(i) <_\sigma e_\sigma(j)$ *if and only if* $i < j$ *and there exists a port* p *such that* $a_i, a_j \in Act_p$.

Given a partially ordered set $(E, <)$ *with* $E = \{e_1, \ldots, e_n\}$ *we let* $L(E, <)$ *denote the set of linearisations of* $(E, <)$, *that is, the set of sequences* $e_{\rho(1)} \cdots e_{\rho(n)}$ *that are permutations of* $e_1 \ldots e_n$ *and that are consistent with* $<$: *if* $e_i < e_j$ *then this ordering is preserved by the permutation* $(\rho^{-1}(i) < \rho^{-1}(j))$.

In a slight abuse of notation, given $\sigma, \sigma' \in Act^*$, *with* $\sigma' = a_1 \ldots a_n$, *we say that* $\sigma' \in L(e(\sigma), <_\sigma)$ *if there exists* $\sigma'' \in L(e(\sigma), <_\sigma)$ *and* $k_1, \ldots, k_n \in \mathbb{N}$ *such that* $\sigma'' = (a_1, k_1), \ldots, (a_n, k_n)$.

Given a timed trace $\sigma = (a_1, t_1), \ldots, (a_n, t_n)$, *we let* $e(\sigma)$ *denote* $e(\text{untime}(\sigma))$ *and* $<_\sigma$ *denote* $<_{\text{untime}(\sigma)}$. *Given* $1 \leq i \leq n$ *and event* $e = e_\sigma(i)$, *we let* $\eta_\sigma(e) = t_i$, *that is, the timestamp associated with* e.

Note that $(e(\sigma), <_\sigma)$ is a partially ordered set; $<_\sigma$ is irreflexive, transitive and antisymmetric. We have an interesting property, whose proof can be found in the extended version of the paper [14], that will allow us to simplify several definitions and results, since we can quantify over all traces equivalent to σ by considering the set $L(e(\sigma), <_\sigma)$.

Proposition 1. *Let* $\sigma, \sigma' \in (I \cup O)^*$. *We have that* $\sigma \sim \sigma'$ *if and only if* $L(e(\sigma), <_\sigma) = L(e(\sigma'), <_{\sigma'})$.

3   Implementation Relations for Clocks with Imprecision Bounded by a Constant

In this section we study approaches to adapt our previous implementation relation **dioco** in order to take into account time information obtained from observing the behaviour of the SUT. We assume that each tester has a local clock but there is no global clock. Under **dioco** we cannot order the events at different ports but in this section we will show that more can be done if we have additional information regarding how the local clocks relate.

First, let us note that the addition of time does not modify our implementation relation **pdioco** [5]. This implementation relation assumes a framework where the agents at the ports of the SUT are entirely independent: no external agent or system can receive information regarding observations made at more than one port of the SUT. Thus, an agent at a port can observe only the local trace at that port but has no information about the observations made at the other ports. In determining whether the behaviour of the SUT is acceptable, all an agent can do is compare the observed local trace with the local traces that can be produced by the specification. Therefore, in this framework, time information cannot be used to establish causality relations between actions performed at different ports and, therefore, the addition of time does not change the implementation relation.

The implementation relation **dioco** [5] allows the set of local traces observed to be compared with the global traces of the specification. If information regarding observations made at different ports can be combined, then it is appropriate to use a stronger implementation relation.

Definition 7. *Let* r, s *be* IOTSs. *We write* r **dioco** s *if and only if for every quiescent trace* $\sigma\delta \in \mathcal{T}r(r)$, *there exists a trace* $\sigma' \in \mathcal{T}r(s)$ *such that* $\sigma' \sim \sigma\delta$.

As we pointed out in the previous section, the implementation relation **dioco** only considers traces that end with quiescence; we will call these *quiescent traces*. It is straightforward to prove that for the processes that we consider in this paper, input-enabled and non output divergent, r **ioco** s implies r **dioco** s but the reverse implication does not hold.

Recall that given an untimed trace σ we have the partial order $<_\sigma$ on $e(\sigma)$ and that $L(e(\sigma), <_\sigma)$ is the corresponding set of linearisations. Based on this we have the following alternative characterisation of **dioco**.

Proposition 2. *Given* $r, s \in$ IOTS$(I, O, \mathcal{P})$, *we have that* r **dioco** s *if and only if for every quiescent trace* $\sigma\delta \in \mathcal{T}r(r)$, *there exists a quiescent trace* $\sigma' \in \mathcal{T}r(s)$ *such that* $\sigma' \in L(e(\sigma), <_\sigma)$.

Next we present how timed traces, instead of just traces, can be used to provide a more refined implementation relation. The idea is simple: if we have timestamps then we can try to determine the order in which events were produced at different ports. Consider a specification that states that a correct system must produce output $!o_U$ at port U followed by $!o_L$ at port L. If the SUT produces $!o_L$ followed by $!o_U$ then, since these two outputs were produced at different ports, we have a correct system with respect to **dioco** because we have no means of determining that the actions were produced in the wrong order. Assume now that in addition to the actions produced at each port we are provided with timestamps. For example, let us suppose that we receive $(!o_U, 100)$ and $(!o_L, 98)$. If we have a global clock or local clocks that work perfectly, then we can claim that the SUT is not correct since $!o_L$ was performed before $!o_U$. However, if we consider a more realistic scenario where local clocks need not be synchronised, then we might consider that the difference is so small that it might be the case indeed that $!o_L$ was produced after $!o_U$ but that the clock at port U is running faster than the one placed at port L. Therefore, we need a variety of implementation relations to cope with the different alternatives.

We first assume the existence of a global clock or, equivalently, that local clocks work perfectly.

Definition 8. *Let I and O be sets of inputs and outputs, respectively. Given timed trace $\sigma = (a_1, t_1) \ldots (a_n, t_n) \in ((I \cup O) \times \text{Time})^*$, $\ll_\sigma$ is the partial order on $e(\sigma)$ such that for all $1 \leq i, j, \leq n$ with $i \neq j$ we have that $e_\sigma(i) \ll_\sigma e_\sigma(j)$ if and only if $t_j > t_i$.*

*Let $r, s \in \text{IOTS}(I, O, \mathcal{P})$ and $\mathcal{T} \in \mathcal{P}(((I \cup O) \times \text{Time})^*)$ be a set of quiescent timed traces of r. We write r **tdioco**$(\mathcal{T})$ s if r **dioco** s and for every $\sigma \in \mathcal{T}$ there exists a quiescent trace $\sigma' \in \mathcal{T}r(s)$ such that $\sigma' \in L(e(\sigma), \ll_\sigma)$.*

Here a timed trace σ is a quiescent timed trace if $\text{untime}(\sigma)$ is a quiescent trace. This new implementation relation requires **dioco** to hold since the intention is to strengthen **dioco** by including a set $\mathcal{T}$ of timed traces that have been observed in testing. As we already explained, timed traces do not contain quiescence since quiescence is not timestamped; including **dioco** ensures that the observation of quiescence is not ignored.

Example 3. Consider our running example and an SUT producing the sequence $?data\_client!req\_hotel!req\_flight$. Since $!req\_hotel$ and $!req\_flight$ were produced at different ports, the system is correct with respect to **dioco**. However, if the actions produced at each port are provided with timestamps, for example $(!req\_hotel, 40)$ and $(!req\_flight, 42)$, we can claim that the system is not correct since $!req\_hotel$ was performed before $!req\_flight$.

We now assume that there is a known value α such that the local clocks differ by at most α. We will show how this information can be used to deduce the relative ordering of events at different ports. We will express this through a partial order on the set of events observed.

Definition 9. *Let I and O be sets of inputs and outputs, respectively. Given timed trace $\sigma = (a_1, t_1) \ldots (a_n, t_n) \in ((I \cup O) \times \text{Time})^*$ and $\alpha \in \mathbb{R}_+$, $\ll_\sigma^\alpha$ is the partial order on $e(\sigma)$ such that for all $1 \leq i, j, \leq n$ with $i \neq j$ we have that $e_\sigma(i) \ll_\sigma^\alpha e_\sigma(j)$ if and only if one of the following holds.*

- *There exists $p \in \mathcal{P}$ such that $a_i, a_j \in I_p \cup O_p$ and $i < j$.*
- *We have that $t_j - t_i > \alpha$.*

This says that we know that event $e_\sigma(i)$ was before event $e_\sigma(j)$ if either they were observed at the same port and $e_\sigma(i)$ was observed first or they were observed at different ports but the timestamp for $e_\sigma(i)$ was earlier than that for $e_\sigma(j)$ by more than α. In the second case, our assumption that the local clocks differ by at most α allows us to know that $e_\sigma(i)$ was observed before $e_\sigma(j)$.

This additional information, regarding the order in which events occurred, can be used to define a more refined implementation relation. This operates in the situation in which a set of timed traces has been observed, with timestamps having been produced using local clocks that can differ by at most α. As with **dioco**, we only consider quiescent traces since for these we know that the testers have observed projections of the same trace of the SUT.

Definition 10. *Let $r, s \in IOTS(I, O, \mathcal{P})$, $\mathcal{T} \in \mathcal{P}(((I \cup O) \times \text{Time})^*)$ be a set of quiescent timed traces of r, and $\alpha \in \mathbb{R}_+$ be a positive real number. We write r **tdioco**$_\alpha(\mathcal{T})$ s if r **dioco** s and for every $\sigma \in \mathcal{T}$ there exists a quiescent sequence $\sigma' \in \mathcal{T}r(s)$ such that $\sigma' \in L(e(\sigma), \ll_\sigma^\alpha)$.*

Example 4. Let r be an SUT such that r **dioco** TA. Let $\mathcal{T}$ be a set of timed traces obtained from the testing process of the system and containing, in particular, the quiescent timed trace

$$\sigma = (?data\_client, 0.5), (!req\_hotel, 1.3), (!req\_flight, 1.7), (?data\_flight, 3),$$
$$(?data\_hotel, 4), (!req\_excursion, 5.8), (!req\_transfer, 6.2)$$

We have that r **tdioco**$(\mathcal{T})$ TA does not hold but if local clocks differ by at most $\alpha = 0.5$ units of time, then r **tdioco**$_\alpha(\mathcal{T})$ TA.

We can compare implementation relations using the following relation $\sqsubseteq$.

Definition 11. *Given two implementation relations imp_1 and imp_2, we write $imp_1 \sqsubseteq imp_2$ if and only if for all IOTSs r, s we have that r imp_2 s implies r imp_1 s.*

Proposition 3. *Let $\mathcal{T}$ be a set of quiescent timed traces and $\alpha \in \mathbb{R}_+$ be a positive real number. We have that **dioco** $\sqsubseteq$ **tdioco**$_\alpha(\mathcal{T})$ but it may be that we do not have **tdioco**$_\alpha(\mathcal{T}) \sqsubseteq$ **dioco**.*

Proof. The first part is immediate from the definitions. For the second part it is sufficient to consider a process s that has trace $!o_1!o_2\delta$, a process r that has trace $!o_2!o_1\delta$ and a timed trace of r with timestamps that allow us to deduce that $!o_2$ was produced before $!o_1$.

If we abuse the notation slightly, to allow α to take on the value of 0, then we obtain the following result.

Proposition 4. *Given a set $\mathcal{T}$ of quiescent timed traces, we have that r **ioco** s only if r **tdioco**$_0(\mathcal{T})$ s. Similarly, given $\alpha \in \mathbb{R}_+$ we have that r **dioco** s if and only if r **tdioco**$_\alpha(\emptyset)$ s.*

The following gives a more general condition under which we can compare two implementation relations defined using different values for α and $\mathcal{T}$. The proof can be found in the extended version of the paper [14].

Proposition 5. *Given $\alpha_1, \alpha_2 \in \mathbb{R}_+$ and sets $\mathcal{T}_1$ and $\mathcal{T}_2$ of quiescent timed traces, we have that $\mathbf{tdioco}_{\alpha_1}(\mathcal{T}_1) \sqsubseteq \mathbf{tdioco}_{\alpha_2}(\mathcal{T}_2)$ if for all $\sigma_1 \in \mathcal{T}_1$ there exists $\sigma_2 \in \mathcal{T}_2$ such that $e(\sigma_2) = e(\sigma_1)$ and $\ll_{\sigma_1}^{\alpha_1} \subseteq \ll_{\sigma_2}^{\alpha_2}$.*

We now say what it means for a set of timed traces to be valid for a process r given α; these are the set of timed traces that can be produced if the clocks are within α of one another.

Definition 12. *Given $\alpha \in \mathbb{R}_+$ and timed trace σ, we say that σ is valid for process r given α if there exists a trace $\sigma' = a'_1 \ldots a'_n \in \mathcal{T}r(r)$ with $e(\text{untime}(\sigma)) = e(\sigma')$ such that for all $1 \leq i < j \leq n$ we have that $\eta_\sigma(e_{\sigma'}(i)) - \eta_\sigma(e_{\sigma'}(j)) \leq \alpha$.*

This condition requires that if $e_\sigma(i)$ is before $e_\sigma(j)$ in σ' then the timestamp for $e_\sigma(i)$ is less than the timestamp for $e_\sigma(j)$ in σ or the time difference is sufficiently small for it to be possible that $e_\sigma(i)$ occurred before $e_\sigma(j)$. We now have the following result.

Proposition 6. *Given $r, s \in IOTS(I, O, \mathcal{P})$, $\alpha \in \mathbb{R}_+$ and a set $\mathcal{T}$ of quiescent timed traces that are valid for r given α, then $\mathbf{tdioco}_\alpha(\mathcal{T}) \sqsubseteq \mathbf{ioco}$.*

We have seen that our new implementation relation lies between **ioco** and **dioco**: it can be more powerful than **dioco** and can be less powerful than **ioco**. In the extended version of the paper [14] we give results that explore this issue further, showing how in the limit it can approach **ioco** and also how it can be reduced to **dioco** even if we have many timed traces. Specifically, we show that if the set of timed traces parameterising our implementation relations contains appropriate instances of all the traces of the system then the stronger **ioco** implementation relation can be fully captured. We also show that *irrelevant* time values do not add distinguishing power to the collected set of traces, so that we still obtain the **dioco** relation.

4   Clocks with Variable Imprecision

In the previous section we defined an implementation relation based on the assumption that there is a known $\alpha \in \mathbb{R}_+$ that is an upper bound on the differences between the local clocks. However, in practice we expect there to be drift: some clocks will progress faster than others. As a result, the potential difference will grow with time. Therefore, in this section we devise implementation relations for this more general scenario.

For our next relation we assume that there is a bound α on the potential difference between the clocks at the beginning of testing and for the difference to be able to grow with time based on another value β. Even for small bounds, we think that this is a very realistic assumption. As we will see later, even though we are not able to fully capture the original ordering in which events are performed at different ports, we can still fix the occurrence of actions that were performed far apart. First we define the corresponding partial order on events.

Definition 13. *Let I and O be sets of inputs and outputs, respectively. Given timed trace $\sigma = (a_1, t_1) \ldots (a_n, t_n) \in ((I \cup O) \times \text{Time})^*$ and $\alpha, \beta \in \mathbb{R}_+$, $\ll_\sigma^{\alpha,\beta}$ is the partial order on $e(\sigma)$ such that for all $1 \le i, j, \le n$ with $i \ne j$ we have that $e_\sigma(i) \ll_\sigma^{\alpha,\beta} e_\sigma(j)$ if and only if one of the following holds.*

- *There exists $p \in \mathcal{P}$ such that $a_i, a_j \in I_p \cup O_p$ and $i < j$.*
- *We have that $t_j - t_i > \alpha + \beta \cdot \max(t_i, t_j)$.*

*Let $r, s \in \text{IOTS}(I, O, \mathcal{P})$, $\mathcal{T} \in \mathcal{P}(((I \cup O) \times \text{Time})^*)$ be a set of quiescent timed traces of r, and $\alpha, \beta \in \mathbb{R}_+$ be positive real numbers. We write r **tdioco**$_{\alpha,\beta}(\mathcal{T})$ s if r **dioco** s and for every $\sigma \in \mathcal{T}$ there exists a quiescent trace $\sigma' \in \mathcal{T}r(s)$ such that $\sigma' \in L(e(\sigma), \ll_\sigma^{\alpha,\beta})$.*

The next relation is a generalisation of **tdioco**$_{\alpha,\beta}(\mathcal{T})$ where potential difference in clocks can accumulate in a non-linear way. We capture this by using an increasing function to place a bound on the relative imprecision of clocks.

Definition 14. *Let I and O be sets of inputs and outputs, respectively. Given timed trace $\sigma = (a_1, t_1) \ldots (a_n, t_n) \in ((I \cup O) \times \text{Time})^*$ and a monotonically increasing function $h : \mathbb{R}_+ \longrightarrow \mathbb{R}_+$, $\ll_\sigma^h$ is the partial order on $e(\sigma)$ such that for all $1 \le i, j, \le n$ with $i \ne j$ we have that $e_\sigma(i) \ll_\sigma^h e_\sigma(j)$ if and only if one of the following holds.*

- *There exists $p \in \mathcal{P}$ such that $a_i, a_j \in I_p \cup O_p$ and $i < j$.*
- *We have that $t_j - t_i > h(\max(t_i, t_j))$.*

*Let $r, s \in \text{IOTS}(I, O, \mathcal{P})$, $\mathcal{T} \in \mathcal{P}(((I \cup O) \times \text{Time})^*)$ be a set of quiescent timed traces of r and $h : \mathbb{R}_+ \longrightarrow \mathbb{R}_+$ be a monotonically increasing function. We write r **tdioco**$_h(\mathcal{T})$ s if r **dioco** s and for every $\sigma \in \mathcal{T}$ there exists a quiescent trace $\sigma' \in \mathcal{T}r(s)$ such that $\sigma' \in L(e(\sigma), \ll_\sigma^h)$.*

Example 5. Consider the specification of the travel agency depicted in Figure 1. Let r be a SUT such that its conformance to the TA specification with respect to **dioco** has been established. Assume that while testing r we obtained the following set $\mathcal{T}$ of timed sequences

$tr_1 = (?data\_client, 0.5)(!req\_flight, 1)(!req\_hotel, 2)(?data\_flight, 3)(?data\_hotel, 4)$
$\qquad (!req\_car, 5)(?data\_car, 6)$
$tr_2 = (?data\_client, 1.5)(!req\_hotel, 3.4)(!req\_flight, 4.4)$
$tr_3 = (?data\_client, 1)(!req\_hotel, 1.3)(!req\_flight, 2)(?data\_flight, 3)(?data\_hotel, 4.6)$
$\qquad (!req\_transfer, 5.1)(!req\_excursion, 5.3)$

The sequences tr_2 and tr_3 show that r **tdioco**$(\mathcal{T})$ TA does not hold since $!req\_hotel$ was produced before $!req\_flight$. Besides, r **tdioco**$_\alpha(\mathcal{T})$ TA holds if $\alpha \ge 1$, while if $\alpha < 1$ the conformance does not hold. If we assume that the difference between clocks grows with time, then for any value assigned to β when $\alpha \ge 1$ we have that r **tdioco**$_{\alpha,\beta}(\mathcal{T})$ TA holds; however if, for example, $\alpha = 0.2$ and $\beta = 0.2$ then the sequence tr_3 shows that r is not correct.

Proposition 7. *Let $r, s \in IOTS(I, O, \mathcal{P})$, $\mathcal{T}$ be a set of timed traces and $\alpha, \beta \in \mathbb{R}_+$ be positive real numbers. If r $\textbf{tdioco}_\alpha(\mathcal{T})$ s then r $\textbf{tdioco}_{\alpha,\beta}(\mathcal{T})$ s. However, we might have that r $\textbf{tdioco}_{\alpha,\beta}(\mathcal{T})$ s but not r $\textbf{tdioco}_\alpha(\mathcal{T})$ s.*

In order to conclude the paper, we would like to point out that if we consider single-port systems then all the timed implementation relations introduced in this paper coincide with **ioco**. The proof is easy and relies on the fact that **ioco** and **dioco** are equal for single-port, input-enabled and non output-divergent systems.

5 Conclusions and Future Work

Many systems interact with their environment at physically distributed interfaces, which we call ports. In distributed testing we place a separate tester at each port and the tester at port p only observes events that occur at p. As a result, it may not be possible to determine the relative order of events observed at different ports and this has led to the development of implementation relations such as **dioco** that reflect this.

This paper has explored the situation in which each tester has a local clock and adds timestamps to the observations it makes. If we have no information regarding how the local clocks relate then this does not help us. However, in practice we are likely to have some information, in the form of assumptions, regarding how much the local clocks can differ. We considered several such assumptions. In one extreme case the local clocks are known to agree and so we can reconstruct the sequence of events. However, this assumption appears to be unrealistic. We also considered the case where there is a known upper bound α on how much the clocks can differ. An alternative scenario is when there is an initial bound α and the bound on the differences between the clocks can grow linearly. We also considered the generalisation when there is a monotonically increasing function h such that at time t the differences between the clocks is at most $h(t)$. For each scenario we defined a corresponding implementation relation and we explored how these relate.

There are several possible lines of future work. First, we can integrate our approach with methods for establishing local clocks through message exchange. We might consider the case where the specification contains timing requirements. Distributed testing in the situation in which there are timing requirements is likely to be challenging, especially if there are requirements regarding the relative timing of events at different ports. In the same line, there is a need to consider the implications of time for test generation. Another direction worth investigating is to study the limits of timed implementation relations. By taking into account time we are able to distinguish processes that were undistinguishable under **dioco** but it would be interesting to explore implementation relations closer to **ioco** in the current framework. One issue that we did not consider in this paper is the computational complexity of deciding the different implementation relations, in particular, it would be important to consider the trade-off between distinguishing power and the complexity of checking whether a given relation holds.

Acknowledgements. We would like to thank the reviewers of the paper for the careful reading and for pointing out interesting lines to continue the research in this topic.

References

1. Hierons, R.M., Bogdanov, K., Bowen, J., Cleaveland, R., Derrick, J., Dick, J., Gheorghe, M., Harman, M., Kapoor, K., Krause, P., Luettgen, G., Simons, A., Vilkomir, S., Woodward, M., Zedan, H.: Using formal methods to support testing. ACM Computing Surveys 41(2) (2009)
2. Grieskamp, W., Kicillof, N., Stobie, K., Braberman, V.: Model-based quality assurance of protocol documentation: tools and methodology. Software Testing, Verification and Reliability 21(1), 55–71 (2011)
3. Tretmans, J.: Model Based Testing with Labelled Transition Systems. In: Hierons, R.M., Bowen, J.P., Harman, M. (eds.) FORTEST. LNCS, vol. 4949, pp. 1–38. Springer, Heidelberg (2008)
4. ISO/IEC JTC 1, J.T.C.: International Standard ISO/IEC 9646-1. Information Technology - Open Systems Interconnection - Conformance testing methodology and framework - Part 1: General concepts. ISO/IEC (1994)
5. Hierons, R.M., Merayo, M.G., Núñez, M.: Implementation relations and test generation for systems with distributed interfaces. Distributed Computing 25(1), 35–62 (2012)
6. Cacciari, L., Rafiq, O.: Controllability and observability in distributed testing. Information and Software Technology 41(11-12), 767–780 (1999)
7. Rafiq, O., Cacciari, L.: Coordination algorithm for distributed testing. The Journal of Supercomputing 24(2), 203–211 (2003)
8. Jard, C., Jéron, T., Kahlouche, H., Viho, C.: Towards automatic distribution of testers for distributed conformance testing. In: TC6 WG6.1 Joint Int. Conf. on Formal Description Techniques and Protocol Specification, Testing and Verification, FORTE 1998, pp. 353–368. Kluwer Academic Publishers (1998)
9. Lamport, L.: Time, clocks, and the ordering of events in a distributed system. Communications of the ACM 21(7), 558–565 (1978)
10. Jard, C., Jéron, T., Tanguy, L., Viho, C.: Remote testing can be as powerful as local testing. In: 19th Joint Int. Conf. on Protocol Specification, Testing, and Verification and Formal Description Techniques, FORTE/PSTV 1999, pp. 25–40. Kluwer Academic Publishers (1999)
11. Lamport, L., Melliar-Smith, P.: Synchronizing clocks in the presence of faults. Journal of the ACM 32(1), 52–78 (1985)
12. Fidge, C.: A limitation of vector timestamps for reconstructing distributed computations. Information Processing Letters 68(2), 87–91 (1998)
13. Baeten, J., Middelburg, C.: Process algebra with timing. EATCS Monograph. Springer (2002)
14. Hierons, R.M., Merayo, M.G., Núñez, M.: Using time to add order to distributed testing (2012),
    http://antares.sip.ucm.es/manolo/papers/fm2012_extended.pdf

A Verification Toolkit for Numerical Transition Systems
Tool Paper*

Hossein Hojjat[1], Filip Konečný[2,4], Florent Garnier[2],
Radu Iosif[2], Viktor Kuncak[1], and Philipp Rümmer[3]

[1] Swiss Federal Institute of Technology Lausanne (EPFL)
[2] Verimag, Grenoble, France
[3] Uppsala University, Sweden
[4] Brno University of Technology, Czech Republic

Abstract. This paper presents a publicly available toolkit and a benchmark suite for rigorous verification of *Integer Numerical Transition Systems* (INTS), which can be viewed as control-flow graphs whose edges are annotated by Presburger arithmetic formulas. We present FLATA and ELDARICA, two verification tools for INTS. The FLATA system is based on precise acceleration of the transition relation, while the ELDARICA system is based on predicate abstraction with interpolation-based counterexample-driven refinement. The ELDARICA verifier uses the PRINCESS theorem prover as a sound and complete interpolating prover for Presburger arithmetic. Both systems can solve several examples for which previous approaches failed, and present a useful baseline for verifying integer programs. The infrastructure is a starting point for rigorous benchmarking, competitions, and standardized communication between tools.

1 Introduction

Common representation formats, benchmarks, and tool competitions have helped research in a number of areas, including constraint solving, theorem proving, and compilers. To bring such benefits to the area of software verification, we are proposing a standardized logical format for programs, in terms of hierarchical infinite-state transition systems. The advantage of using a formally defined common format is avoiding ambiguities of programming language semantics and helping to separate semantic modeling from designing verification algorithms. This paper focuses on systems whose transition relation is expressed in Presburger arithmetic. Integer Numerical Transition Systems, (denoted INTS in this paper), also known as counter automata, counter systems, or counter machines, are an infinite-state extension of the model of finite-state *boolean transition systems*, a model extensively used in the area of software verification [8]. The interest for INTS comes from the fact that they can encode various classes of systems with unbounded (or very large) data domains, such as hardware circuits, cache

---

* Supported by the Rich Model Toolkit initiative, http://richmodels.org, the Czech Science Foundation (projects P103/10/0306 and 102/09/H042), the Czech Ministry of Education (COST OC10009 and MSM 0021630528), the EU/CzechIT4Innovations Centre of Excellence project CZ.1.05/1.1.00/02.0070, the BUT project FIT-12-1 and the Microsoft Innovation Cluster for Embedded Software.

D. Giannakopoulou and D. Méry (Eds.): FM 2012, LNCS 7436, pp. 247–251, 2012.

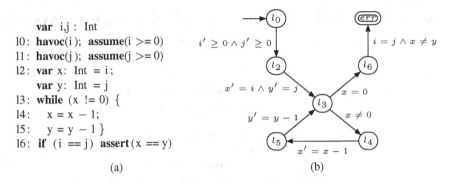

```
        var i,j : Int
10:  havoc(i); assume(i >= 0)
11:  havoc(j); assume(j >= 0)
12:  var x: Int = i;
        var y: Int = j
13:  while (x != 0) {
14:       x = x − 1;
15:       y = y − 1 }
16:  if (i == j) assert(x == y)
```

(a)   (b)

Fig. 1. Example Program and its Numerical Transition System (NTS) Representation. By convention, if a variable v does not appear in the transition relation formula, we implicitly assume that the frame condition $v = v'$ is conjoined. The states l_1 and l_2 have been merged in the NTS.

memories, or software systems with variables of non-primitive types, such as integer arrays, pointers and/or recursive data structures. Any Turing-complete class of systems can, in principle be simulated by an INTS. A number of recent works have revealed cost-effective approximate reductions of verification problems for several classes of complex systems to decision problems phrased in terms on INTS. Examples of systems that can be effectively verified by means of integer programs include: specifications of hardware components [10], programs with singly-linked lists [1], trees [6], and integer arrays [2].

Consider the program in Figure 1(a). Most programmers would have little difficulty observing that the assertion will always succeed, but many tools, including non-relational abstract interpretation, as well as predicate abstraction with arbitrary interpolation can fail to prove the assertion to hold [9]. The integer numerical transition system for this program is in Figure 1(b). We have developed a toolkit for producing and manipulating such representations, as well as two very different analyzers that can analyze such transition systems. Both analyzers, ELDARICA and FLATA, in fact succeed for this example, as well as for several other interesting examples. Our experiments show that the two tools are complementary in general, so users benefit from different techniques that use the same input format.

2   The INTS Infrastructure

We have developed a toolkit for rigorous automated verification of programs in INTS format. The unifying component is the INTS library[1], which defines the syntax of the INTS representation by providing a parser and a library of abstract syntax tree classes. For the purposes of this paper, the INTS syntax is considered to be a textual description of a control flow graph labeled by Presburger arithmetic formulae, as in Figure 1 (b).

At this point, there are several tools supporting the INTS format, as input and/or output language. The INTS library is designed for easy bridging with new tools, which can be either front-ends (translators from mainstream programming languages into INTS),

---

[1] http://richmodels.epfl.ch/ntscomp/ntslib

back-ends (verification tools), or both. Currently, there exist tools to generate INTS from sequential and concurrent C, Scala, and Verilog. We present two tools that can verify INTS programs: Flata and Eldarica.

Flata Verifier. FLATA[2] is a verification tool for hierarchical non-recursive INTS models. The tool computes the summary relation for each INTS independently of its calling context, thus avoiding the overhead of procedure inlining. The verification is based on computing transitive closure of loops. Classes of integer relations for which transitive closures can be computed precisely include: (1) *difference bounds relations*, (2) *octagons*, and (3) *finite monoid affine transformations*. For these three classes, the transitive closures can be effectively defined in Presburger arithmetic. FLATA integrates the transitive closure computation method for difference bounds and octagonal relations from [3] in a semi-algorithm computing the summary relation incrementally, by eliminating control states and composing incoming with outgoing relations.

Eldarica Verifier.   ELDARICA[3] implements predicate abstraction with Counter-Example Guided Abstraction Refinement (CEGAR). It generates an abstract reachability tree (ART) of the system on demand, using lazy abstraction with Cartesian abstraction, and uses interpolation to refine the set of predicates [7]. For checking the feasibility of paths, and constructing abstractions, ELDARICA employs the provers Z3[4] and Princess.[5] In addition, ELDARICA uses caching of previously explored states and formulae to prevent unnecessary reconstruction of trees. Large block encoding can be performed to reduce the number of calls to the interpolating theorem prover.

Eldarica refines abstractions with the help of *Craig Interpolants*, extracted from infeasibility proofs for spurious counterexamples. The complete interpolation procedure for Presburger arithmetic was proposed in [4], and is implemented as part of Princess.

3   Experimental Comparison of the FLATA and ELDARICA Tools

We next give an experimentally compare FLATA and ELDARICA on six sets of examples extracted automatically from different sources: (a) C programs with arrays provided as examples of divergence in predicate abstraction [9], (b) INTS extracted from programs with singly-linked lists by the L2CA tool [1], (c) INTS extracted from VHDL models of circuits following the method of [10], (d) verification conditions for programs with arrays, expressed in the SIL logic of [2] and translated to INTS, (e) C programs provided as benchmarks in the NECLA static analysis suite, and (f) C programs with asynchronous procedure calls translated into INTS using the approach of [5] (the examples with extension .optim are obtained via an optimized translation method). Experiments were ran on an Intel®Core™2 Duo @ 2.66GHz with 3GB RAM. The two tools behaved in a complementary way. In some cases (examples (a)) the predicate abstraction method fails due to an unbounded number of loop unrollings required by refinement. In these cases, acceleration was capable to find the needed invariant rather quickly. On

---

the other hand (examples (f)), the acceleration approach was unsuccessful in reducing loops with linear but non-octagonal relations. In these cases, the predicate abstraction found the needed Presburger invariants for proving correctness, and error traces, for the erroneous examples.

Model	Time [s]		Model	Time [s]		Model	Time [s]	
	Flata	Eld.		Flata	Eld.		Flata	Eld.
(a) Examples from [9]			**(c) VHDL models from [10]**			**(f) Examples from [5]**		
anubhav (C)	0.8	2.0	counter (C)	0.1	1.7	h1 (E)	-	5.7
copy1 (E)	1.8	13.9	register (C)	0.2	1.2	h1.optim (E)	0.6	1.3
cousot (C)	12.0	-	synlifo (C)	16.4	20.3	h1h2 (E)	-	19.0
loop1 (E)	1.3	12.0	**(d) Verification conditions**			h1h2.optim (E)	0.9	4.3
loop (E)	1.9	10.6	**for array programs [2]**			simple (E)	-	6.1
scan (E)	2.5	-	rotation_vc.1 (C)	0.8	2.0	simple.optim (E)	0.6	1.3
string_concat1 (E)	4.7	-	rotation_vc.2 (C)	1.1	2.2	test0 (C)	-	30.6
string_concat (E)	4.7	-	rotation_vc.3 (C)	1.2	0.3	test0.optim (C)	0.3	5.3
string_copy (C)	0.4	-	rotation_vc.1 (E)	1.1	1.4	test0 (E)	-	5.0
substring1 (E)	0.6	5.5	split_vc.1 (C)	3.8	3.0	test0.optim (E)	0.6	1.3
substring (E)	1.6	0.7	split_vc.2 (C)	2.8	2.2	test1.optim (C)	0.6	8.5
(b) Examples from L2CA [1]			split_vc.3 (C)	2.6	0.6	test1.optim (E)	1.4	6.8
bubblesort (E)	14.1	2.5	split_vc.1 (E)	30.2	2.2	test2_1.optim (E)	1.2	4.6
insdel (E)	0.1	0.3	**(e) NECLA benchmarks**			test2_2.optim (E)	2.8	4.6
insertsort (E)	1.9	0.8	inf1 (E)	0.2	0.4	test2.optim (C)	6.3	72.9
listcounter (C)	0.3	-	inf4 (E)	0.9	0.6	wrpc.manual (C)	0.6	1.2
listcounter (E)	0.3	0.3	inf6 (C)	0.1	0.4	wrpc (E)	-	9.5
listreversal (C)	4.8	0.6	inf8 (C)	0.3	0.6	wrpc.optim (E)	-	3.0

Fig. 2. Benchmarks for **Fla**ta and **Eld**arica. The letter after the model name distinguishes **C**orrect from models with a reachable **E**rror state. Items with "-" led to a timeout for the respective tool.

References

1. Bouajjani, A., Bozga, M., Habermehl, P., Iosif, R., Moro, P., Vojnar, T.: Programs with Lists Are Counter Automata. In: Ball, T., Jones, R.B. (eds.) CAV 2006. LNCS, vol. 4144, pp. 517–531. Springer, Heidelberg (2006)
2. Bozga, M., Habermehl, P., Iosif, R., Konečný, F., Vojnar, T.: Automatic Verification of Integer Array Programs. In: Bouajjani, A., Maler, O. (eds.) CAV 2009. LNCS, vol. 5643, pp. 157–172. Springer, Heidelberg (2009)
3. Bozga, M., Iosif, R., Konečný, F.: Fast Acceleration of Ultimately Periodic Relations. In: Touili, T., Cook, B., Jackson, P. (eds.) CAV 2010. LNCS, vol. 6174, pp. 227–242. Springer, Heidelberg (2010)
4. Brillout, A., Kroening, D., Rümmer, P., Wahl, T.: An Interpolating Sequent Calculus for Quantifier-Free Presburger Arithmetic. In: Giesl, J., Hähnle, R. (eds.) IJCAR 2010. LNCS, vol. 6173, pp. 384–399. Springer, Heidelberg (2010)
5. Ganty, P., Majumdar, R.: Algorithmic verification of asynchronous programs. CoRR, abs/1011.0551 (2010)
6. Habermehl, P., Iosif, R., Rogalewicz, A., Vojnar, T.: Proving Termination of Tree Manipulating Programs. In: Namjoshi, K.S., Yoneda, T., Higashino, T., Okamura, Y. (eds.) ATVA 2007. LNCS, vol. 4762, pp. 145–161. Springer, Heidelberg (2007)

7. Henzinger, T.A., Jhala, R., Majumdar, R., McMillan, K.L.: Abstractions from proofs. In: POPL, pp. 232–244. ACM (2004)

8. Henzinger, T.A., Jhala, R., Majumdar, R., Sutre, G.: Lazy abstraction. In: POPL (2002)

9. Jhala, R., McMillan, K.L.: A Practical and Complete Approach to Predicate Refinement. In: Hermanns, H. (ed.) TACAS 2006. LNCS, vol. 3920, pp. 459–473. Springer, Heidelberg (2006)

10. Smrčka, A., Vojnar, T.: Verifying Parametrised Hardware Designs Via Counter Automata. In: Yorav, K. (ed.) HVC 2007. LNCS, vol. 4899, pp. 51–68. Springer, Heidelberg (2008)

Satellite Rendezvous and Conjunction Avoidance: Case Studies in Verification of Nonlinear Hybrid Systems*

Taylor T. Johnson[1], Jeremy Green[1], Sayan Mitra[1], Rachel Dudley[2], and Richard Scott Erwin[3]

[1] University of Illinois at Urbana-Champaign
Urbana, IL 61801, USA
{johnso99,jdgreen4,mitras}@illinois.edu
[2] Iowa State University, Ames, IA 50011, USA
rfdudley@iastate.edu
[3] Air Force Research Laboratory
Albuquerque, NM 87116, USA

Abstract. Satellite systems are beginning to incorporate complex autonomous operations, which calls for rigorous reliability assurances. Human operators usually plan satellite maneuvers in detail, but autonomous operation will require software to make decisions using noisy sensor data and problem solutions with numerical inaccuracies. For such systems, formal verification guarantees are particularly attractive. This paper presents automatic verification techniques for providing assurances in satellite maneuvers. The specific reliability criteria studied are rendezvous and conjunction avoidance for two satellites performing orbital transfers. Three factors pose challenges for verifying satellite systems: (a) incommensurate orbits, (b) uncertainty of orbital parameters after thrusting, and (c) nonlinear dynamics. Three abstractions are proposed for contending with these challenges: (a) quotienting of the state-space based on periodicity of the orbital dynamics, (b) aggregation of similar transfer orbits, and (c) overapproximation of nonlinear dynamics using hybridization. The method's feasibility is established via experiments with a prototype tool that computes the abstractions and uses existing hybrid systems model checkers.

1 Introduction

As greater numbers of satellites are deployed and maintained in space, there is a growing need for autonomy in their operation. Software-based control systems enable autonomy by performing routine tasks automatically and minimize the need for human supervision. Given the high cost of space systems, a high level of reliability assurance is crucial. To provide such assurances, formal methods can complement traditional testing and simulation-based methods, and can also help find defects early in the design process.

* Most of this research was conducted under the Air Force's 2011 Summer Faculty Fellowship Program and Space Scholars Program at the Air Force Research Laboratory at Kirtland Air Force Base. The Illinois researchers were also supported by NSF CAREER Grant 1054247.

D. Giannakopoulou and D. Méry (Eds.): FM 2012, LNCS 7436, pp. 252–266, 2012.

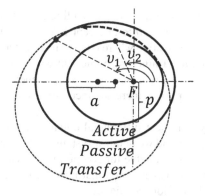

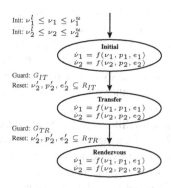

Fig. 1. Orbital transfer for two satellites: ν_1 and ν_2 are the angular positions of the passive and active satellite, respectively, a is the *semi-major axis* (max distance from the ellipse center to the ellipse edge), and p is the *semi-latus rectum* (distance from foci F to ellipse in direction perpendicular to the semi-major axis).

Fig. 2. Hybrid automaton for a two-stage rendezvous maneuver. The angular positions of the passive (ν_1) and active (ν_2) satellites evolve according to the nonlinear dynamics $\dot{\nu}_i = f(\nu_i, p_i, e_i) = \sqrt{\mu/p_i^3}(1 + e_i \cos \nu_i)^2$. Initial conditions are nondeterministically selected from the indicated ranges.

In this paper, we propose and validate a methodology for verifying autonomous operations between a pair of satellites. To the best of our knowledge, this is the first application of automatic verification to autonomously maneuvering satellite systems. The sound overapproximation approach presented in this paper allows us to nondeterministically model inaccuracies due to sensor measurements and numerical errors, which can cause serious errors in simulations. A *passive satellite* moves in a specific orbit, and an *active satellite* performs a software-controlled orbital transfer (see Fig. 1). Orbital transfers are performed when, for example, one satellite services (refuels or repairs) another satellite [9]. We aim to verify two properties: (A) **conjunction avoidance**: two passive (non-thrusting) satellites do not come closer than a certain distance, and (B) **rendezvous**: given a passive and an active satellite, the two satellites come closer than a certain distance of each other during a specified interval of time.

Our approach for verification is first to compute the reach set of an abstraction of the system and then to check that this set satisfies the above properties. Consider two satellites on different orbits with periods T_1 and T_2. The state of the satellites on their orbits is completely specified by the angular positions ν_1 and ν_2. In verifying rendezvous or conjunction avoidance, we are interested in computing the set of angular position pairs (ν_1, ν_2) that are reachable from a given set of initial angular positions. However, we have to overcome the following technical challenges in computing the reach set.

First, we observe that for *incommensurate orbits* (orbits with an irrational ratio of periods T_1/T_2) the unbounded-time reach set is dense in the set of all possible relative angular positions, $[0, 2\pi]^2$. This means that for incommensurate orbits, all (ν_1, ν_2) pairs are eventually visited arbitrarily closely. Therefore, we will focus on bounded-time versions of rendezvous or conjunction avoidance. In conjunction avoidance, for example, it suffices to verify safety up to a certain time horizon because new ground-based measurements are available that can be used as updated initial conditions.

Second, for the active satellite 2 to rendezvous with the passive satellite 1, 2 must burn its thrusters to enter a new orbit called a *transfer orbit* to intercept 1 (see Fig. 1). The transfer orbit 2 follows depends crucially on the position where it burns its thrusters. The magnitude and direction of the thrusting are determined by numerically solving a standard orbital dynamics problem called *Lambert's problem*. Due to such numerical methods and other sources of inaccuracy like sensor noise, there are uncertainties in the transfer orbit parameters.

Third, satellite trajectories are described by nonlinear differential equations. With orbital transfers, these differential equations change, and we obtain a system description as a nonlinear hybrid automaton. The software tools available for computing the reach set of such automata are limited, and thus, we resort to overapproximating the reach set. To address these challenges, we present three abstraction techniques.

Sequence of abstractions: Satellite orbits exhibit periodic motion, so the angular position of the satellite can be bounded between 0 and 2π. The transfer orbit parameters are determined by numerical methods and orbit determination measurements use noisy sensors. Thus, an exact transfer orbit may not be known, so we develop an abstraction for parameter uncertainty. The concrete model nondeterministically specifies the movement of the satellite along all (infinitely many) transfer orbits. That is, there may be infinitely many modes of the concrete hybrid automaton. Since the active satellite stays in the transfer orbit for a short period of time—an upper time bound is an input to Lambert's problem—we aggregate the motion along all such transfer orbits into a single mode of the hybrid system where the continuous evolution is defined by differential and algebraic equations. To accomplish this, we exploit monotonicity of the transfer orbit dynamics. For computing overapproximations of the reach set, nonlinear dynamics can be overapproximated by linear or rectangular hybrid automata. We employ the (now standard) *hybridization* technique [6,10]. The state space of each mode of the original automaton is partitioned into a set of zones $\mathcal{Z}$, and within each zone $Z \in \mathcal{Z}$, the nonlinear differential equation $\dot{x} = f(x)$ is abstracted by simpler dynamics.

Contributions: The abstraction methods we develop—particularly transfer orbit aggregation—allow us to perform verification that compensates for numerical errors in the methods used to solve problems without analytic solutions that frequently arise in astrodynamics. We developed an automated abstraction tool to work on the class of periodic hybrid automata used to model systems like the satellite case studies in this paper. The abstraction tool is fully automatic, generating inputs to existing reachability tools for hybrid automata (HyTech [15], PHAVer [12], and SpaceEx [13]), and allows us to automatically verify time-bounded safety properties. Specifically for the case studies, we verified conjunction avoidance and rendezvous for several realistic examples, such as non-coaxial orbits, non-coplanar orbits, low-earth orbits, medium earth orbits, geosynchronous orbits, and geostationary orbits. The experimental results demonstrate the utility of different approximation methods and their associated complexities. The abstractions we defined are useful by themselves and can be applied independently or together for other systems that require hybridization, are periodic, or are dependent on numerical solutions. Finally, we believe that the family of nonlinear hybrid models presented here can serve as realistic benchmarks for future verification research.

Related Work: Most prior work on formal verification of satellite systems requires manual reasoning, but we mention a couple of semi-automatic methods. The algebraic framework based on Gröbner, described in [14] and extended in [1], can be used to determine the global minimum and maximum separation between two satellites. In contrast, our technique provides guarantees about all reachable states up to a bounded time horizon. Other recent work uses verified integration methods and interval analysis for proving collision avoidance of satellite systems [21]. None of these works handle orbital transfers.

There are a variety of hybrid systems reachability algorithms. We use the hybridization method from [6], which was extended to handle larger classes of nonlinear dynamics in [10]. Another hybridization method is developed in [2], which was applied to a truck rollover example with nonlinear dynamics in [3]. There is some theoretical work on periodic hybrid systems [11], and some case studies from circuits use reachability analysis for periodic hybrid systems [4]. Our work does not use an on-the-fly hybridization approach like some of the works just referenced, but we believe this was reasonable due to the periodicity of the examples studied.

2   Astrodynamics and Hybrid Systems Background

In this paper, a *satellite* is an object moving around the Earth under the influence of the latter's gravitational force. By Kepler's first law, the orbit of a satellite is an ellipse with the Earth at one of the foci, called the *main focus*, and thus the satellite remains in the same plane in 3-dimensional space.[1] Different orbits may or may not be coplanar or coaxial. Given the masses of the Earth and the satellite, and the relative position and velocity of the satellite (with respect to Earth), the orbit is uniquely defined.

Fixing an orbit, a satellite's motion in polar coordinates is given by the following equation, which captures Kepler's law of equal areas:

$$\dot{\nu} = f(\nu, p, e) = \sqrt{\frac{\mu}{p^3}}(1 + e \cos \nu)^2, \tag{1}$$

where ν is the angle of the satellite with respect to the major axis as measured from the main focus (known as the *true anomaly*), e is the *eccentricity*, $p = a(1 - e^2)$ is called the *semi-latus rectum*, a is the *semi-major axis*, and μ is the geocentric gravitational parameter. See Fig. 1 for a graphical depiction of these quantities. We refer the interested reader to [22,8,7] for derivations of this equation. Given an angle ν, Cartesian coordinates of the satellite are specified by

$$r = \frac{p}{1 + e \cos \nu}, \quad x = r \cos \nu, \text{ and } y = r \sin \nu. \tag{2}$$

We consider verification of pairs of satellites performing the rendezvous operation (refer to Fig. 1). One passive and one active satellite each begin in respective initial orbits. In order to rendezvous with the passive satellite, when the active satellite arrives at a certain pre-calculated angular position, it switches (by firing its thrusters) to a transfer

---

[1] Generally, an orbit is some conic section, but we assume orbits are circular or elliptical (the eccentricity e of the orbit satisfies $0 \leq e < 1$).

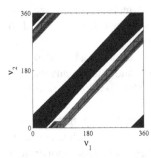
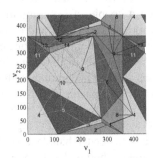
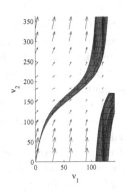

Fig. 3. Verification of conjunction avoidance over a single period for $d = 5000$km. The set $P_d(o_1, o_2)$ of (ν_1, ν_2) points where the distance between the two orbits is at most d is shown in black, and the time-bounded reach set is in red. The orbits are described by the parameters $e_1 = 0.05$, $p_1 = 7074$km, $e_2 = 0.10$, and $p_2 = 7748$km.

Fig. 4. Visualization of abstract system $\mathcal{B}$. The polygons due to the hybridization abstraction $\mathcal{A}_3$ partition the state space, and green lines are transitions between partitions. Black lines between centers of partitions are quotient transitions due to $\mathcal{A}_1$. Partitions on the post-state of a quotient transition are duplicated (e.g., see blue triangle labeled 11).

Fig. 5. Reach$_{\mathcal{B}}^\delta$ for a pair of elliptical orbits with parameters $e_1 = 0.33$, $a_1 = 2$, $e_2 = 0.5$, and $a_2 = 1$. Black arrows are a vector field of the nonlinear dynamics. Error due to overapproximation of dynamics grows with time. Partition size was 15×15 degrees.

orbit. We will verify properties related to the proximity of the two satellites measured by their Euclidean distance in 3-dimensional space. Given two orbits o_1, o_2, and a distance threshold d, we define the set $P_d(o_1, o_2) \subseteq \mathbb{R}^2$ to be all (ν_1, ν_2) values at which the distance between the orbits is at most d. For coplanar orbits,

$$P_d(o_1, o_2) \triangleq \{(\nu_1, \nu_2) : \|(x_1, y_1) - (x_2, y_2)\| \leq d\} \tag{3}$$

where $\|\cdot\|$ is the 2-norm, and the Cartesian coordinates of each point on the orbit are determined by (2). See Fig. 3 for an example of this set. For non-coaxial and non-coplanar orbit pairs, the expression for $P_d(o_1, o_2)$ is analogous, albeit more complex.[2]

While thrusters typically actuate by burning over an interval of time, it is standard practice to model the actuation as an instantaneous change in dynamics due to the short duration of this burn time compared with the timescales involved in orbital motion. However, we note that approaches have been formulated to consider these finite-duration effects [20]. To rendezvous with the passive satellite, usually the active satellite performs two burns. The first burn puts the active satellite on an intermediate *transfer orbit* that intersects the passive satellite's orbit. This burn is modeled as an instantaneous switch from the initial orbit parameters (e_I, p_I) to the transfer orbit parameters (e_T, p_T), and causes an instantaneous switch in the dynamics of $\dot{\nu}_2$ in (1). The second burn makes the active and passive satellites' orbits coincide and is modeled by another

---

[2] Descriptions of non-coaxial and non-coplanar orbits require the introduction of more orbital parameters, which for brevity we chose not to do, but we note that all the methods presented in this paper apply for non-coaxial and non-coplanar orbits.

switch. One way to determine the transfer orbit parameters is by solving a problem called *Lambert's problem*, which is discussed in more detail in Section 4. Next, we discuss how such orbital transfers can naturally be modeled in the hybrid automata framework.

A *hybrid automaton (HA)* is a (possibly nondeterministic) state machine with state that can evolve both instantaneously (through *discrete transitions*) and over intervals of time (according to *trajectories*). In the satellite system model, the continuous variables of the HA model the angular positions of the satellites, and the discrete variables model the orbital parameters. The HA of Fig. 2 shows a two-burn rendezvous maneuver described earlier. Informally, when the HA is in a certain location (shown by the ellipses), the satellites move along specific orbits. That is, their angular positions evolve according to the differential equations corresponding to that location. The discrete transitions (shown by arrows) model the instantaneous burns.

The HA models the angular positions ν_1, ν_2 of two satellites. The passive satellite (ν_1) always moves along the same orbit specified by constant semi-latus rectum p_1 and eccentricity e_1. The active satellite (ν_2) begins in an initial orbit specified by parameters p_I and e_I. If the *guard* predicate G_{IT} is satisfied, then the active satellite must execute a burn that puts it on a transfer orbit. The transfer orbit is specified by the *reset map* R_{IT} that changes the valuations of p_2, e_2, and ν_2. Resetting the variable ν_2 is needed to model transfer orbits that are not coaxial with the initial orbit. That is, the same point in Cartesian coordinates may no longer correspond to the same polar coordinates because the transfer orbit may not be coaxial with the initial orbit. The second burn is modeled in an identical fashion, and sequences of burns can be modeled similarly.

Now we define the HA formally based on previous HA modeling frameworks [5,18,16]. Variables are associated with types and are used as names for state components, such as the angular positions and the orbital parameters. For a set of variables V, a valuation $\mathbf{v}$ is a function that maps each variable $v \in V$ to a point in its type. The set of all possible valuations is $val(V)$. For a valuation $\mathbf{x}$, we use $\mathbf{x}.x$ to denote the value of the variable $x \in V$.

The *concrete HA* is a tuple $\mathcal{A} \triangleq \langle V, Q, \Theta, Edg, Grd, Rst, Flow, Inv \rangle$, where: (a) $V \triangleq \{X, loc, p_1, e_1, p_2, e_2\}$. V is a set of variables, where $X \triangleq \{\nu_1, \nu_2\}$ are real-valued continuous variables, p_1, e_1, p_2, and e_2 are real-valued discrete variables modeling the orbit parameters, and $loc \in L$ is a discrete variable of type $L \triangleq \{I, T, R\}$, where elements represent respectively the initial, transfer, and rendezvous orbits. (b) $Q \triangleq val(V)$ is the set of states. For a state $\mathbf{x} \in Q$, the valuation of $\mathbf{x}.loc$ is called the *location*; along with the valuations of the discrete variables p_1, e_1, p_2, e_2, it describes the discrete state. The valuation of the continuous variables X, that is $\{\mathbf{x}.x : x \in X\}$, is called the *continuous state* and is referred to as $\mathbf{x}.X$. (c) $\Theta \subseteq Q$ is a set of *initial states*. (d) $Edg = \{(I, T), (T, R)\}$ is the set of *edges*. (e) $Grd : Edg \to Q$ is a function that associates a *guard* (a valuation of V that must be satisfied) with each edge. The guards are shown in Fig. 2. $Grd((I, T)) \triangleq G_{IT}(\nu_1, \nu_2)$ and $Grd((T, R)) \triangleq G_{TR}(\nu_1, \nu_2)$; that is, they are left as parameters. (f) $Rst : Edg \to (Q \to 2^Q)$ is a function, called the *reset map*, associated with each edge. A reset map associates a set of states with each edge: $Rst((I, T)) \triangleq \nu_2' = R_{IT}(\nu_1, \nu_2)$ and $Rst((T, R)) \triangleq \nu_2' = R_{TR}(\nu_1, \nu_2)$. (g) $Flow : L \to (Q \to 2^Q)$ associates a *flow map* with each location. Here, for

$l \in L$ and where f is from (1), we have $Flow(l) = [f(\nu_1, p_1, e_1); f(\nu_2, p_2, e_2)]$.
(h) $Inv : L \to 2^Q$ associates an *invariant* with each location. Here we assume urgency, so $Inv(I) = \mathbb{R}^2 \setminus Grd((I, T))^\circ$ and $Inv(T) = \mathbb{R}^2 \setminus Grd((T, R))^\circ$, where, for a real-valued set R, R° is the interior of R.

The semantics of HA $\mathcal{A}$ are defined in terms of sets of *transitions* and *trajectories*. The set of transitions $\mathcal{D} \subseteq Q \times Q$ is defined as follows. We have $(\mathbf{v}, \mathbf{v}') \in \mathcal{D}$ if and only if for $e = (\mathbf{v}.loc, \mathbf{v}'.loc)$, (a) $e \in Edg$, (b) $\mathbf{v} \in Grd(e)$, and (c) $\mathbf{v}' \in Rst(e)(\mathbf{v}.X)$. A *trajectory* for $\mathcal{A}$ is a function $\tau : [0, t] \to Q$ that maps an interval of time to states such that the following hold. (a) For all $t' \in [0, t]$, $\tau(t').loc = \tau(0).loc$, that is, the discrete state remains constant. (b) $(\tau \downarrow X)$, that is, the restriction of τ to X is a solution of the differential equation specified by the flow function $\dot{X} = Flow(\tau(0).loc)(\tau(0))$. (c) For all $t' \in [0, t]$, $\tau(t') \in Inv(\tau(0).loc)$. The set of all the trajectories of $\mathcal{A}$ is written $\mathcal{T}$.

An *execution* of $\mathcal{A}$ is a sequence $\alpha = \tau_0 \tau_1 \ldots$, such that (a) each $\tau_i \in \mathcal{T}$, (b) for each i, $(\tau_i(t), \tau_{i+1}(0)) \in \mathcal{D}$, where t is the right endpoint of the domain of τ_i, and (c) $\tau_0 \in \Theta_0$. The set of all executions of $\mathcal{A}$ is denoted by $\mathsf{Execs}_\mathcal{A}$. A state $\mathbf{v} \in Q$ is said to be *reachable* if there exists a closed execution α that ends at $\mathbf{v}$. The set of all reachable states of $\mathcal{A}$ is denoted by $\mathsf{Reach}_\mathcal{A}$. The set of states reachable of $\mathcal{A}$ within δ time is denoted by $\mathsf{Reach}_\mathcal{A}^\delta$ and is called the set of bounded-time reachable states (see Fig. 5 as an example). We define $\mathsf{Reach}_\mathcal{A}(t)$ as the set of states that are reachable by executions of $\mathcal{A}$ at exactly t time, and for $t \leq \delta$, $\mathsf{Reach}_\mathcal{A}^\delta(t)$ is defined analogously.

We write $\mathcal{D}_\mathcal{A}, \mathcal{T}_\mathcal{A}, Rst_\mathcal{A}, V_\mathcal{A}$, etc., for the components of $\mathcal{A}$ if the automaton is not clear from context. Similarly, when necessary to disambiguate components of HA $\mathcal{A}$ from those of HA $\mathcal{B}$, we use subscripts such as $Q_\mathcal{A}, Inv_\mathcal{A}, Rst_\mathcal{B}$, etc. Given a pair of HA $\mathcal{A}$ and $\mathcal{B}$, $\mathcal{B}$ is said to be an *abstraction* for $\mathcal{A}$ if $\mathsf{Execs}_\mathcal{A} \subseteq \mathsf{Execs}_\mathcal{B}$. It follows that if $\mathcal{B}$ is an abstraction of $\mathcal{A}$, then $\mathsf{Reach}_\mathcal{A} \subseteq \mathsf{Reach}_\mathcal{B}$. Also, if $\mathcal{B}$ is safe with respect to some property (set), then so is $\mathcal{A}$.

3   Abstractions and Analysis

To verify conjunction avoidance and rendezvous properties, we compute bounded reach sets, which is difficult for nonlinear HA. In this section, we describe three independent abstractions of periodic, nonlinear HA (quotienting, transfer orbit aggregation, and hybridization), and then apply their composition.

Quotienting: The quantities ν_1 and ν_2 model the angular position of the satellites on their orbits, which are periodic with period 2π. We define a quotient HA $\mathcal{A}_1$ based on an equivalence relation $\sim$:

$$\mathbf{x} \sim \mathbf{x}' \iff \exists k_1, k_2, \forall i \in \{1, 2\}, \mathbf{x}.\nu_i = \mathbf{x}'.\nu_i + k_i 2\pi.$$

Using $\sim$, we reduce the unbounded state space to a bounded one by adding transitions to each mode of the concrete HA $\mathcal{A}$. If some ν_i reaches the 2π boundary, it is reset to 0. These are the only edges and resets we add, since $\dot{\nu}_1 > 0$ and $\dot{\nu}_2 > 0$ (the angular positions are monotonically increasing), but in general, it may be necessary to add transitions when $\nu_i = 0$ if $\dot{\nu}_i < 0$. $\mathcal{A}_1$ is bisimilar to $\mathcal{A}$.

Transfer orbit aggregation: Solving the Lambert problem yields a unique transfer orbit, where the trajectory of the active satellite would begin from a ν_2 angle called the *burn point*. There is also a constraint on the passive satellite's angle so that the two satellites can rendezvous, so the burn point is a pair of (ν_1, ν_2) values. However, the burn point is not known precisely, so a burn actually takes place within a range of (ν_1, ν_2) values. Each (ν_1, ν_2) pair will place the active satellite on a slightly different transfer orbit. Thus, the transfer mode must take into account a set of different possible transfer orbits. The following abstraction aggregates this set of transfer orbit parameters into a single location of the HA.

First, we define the set of possible transfer orbits that could be reached by burning at different points.

Definition 1. *For any set $\mathcal{O}$ of transfer orbit parameter pairs $o \triangleq (p, e) \in \mathcal{O}$, consider $R_i \subseteq \mathbb{R}$ for $i \in \{1, 2, \ldots, k\}$ such that $\cup_i R_i = \mathbb{R}$, where $\forall i \in \{1, 2, \ldots, k\}$,*

(i) $\exists (p_{min}, e_{min})$ such that $\forall o = (p, e) \in \mathcal{O}, \forall \nu_2 \in R_i$, we have $f_{min}(\nu_2) \triangleq f(\nu_2, p_{min}, e_{min}) \le f(\nu_2, p, e)$, and

(ii) $\exists (p_{max}, e_{max})$ such that $\forall o = (p, e) \in \mathcal{O}, \forall \nu_2 \in R_i$, we have $f_{max}(\nu_2) \triangleq f(\nu_2, p_{max}, e_{max}) \ge f(\nu_2, p, e)$.

That is, $f_{min}(\nu_2)$ and $f_{max}(\nu_2)$ are lower and upper bounds of the $\dot{\nu}_2$ dynamics for a particular region R_i.

Given a collection $\{R_i\}$ that satisfies the requirements in Definition 1, the *HA with transfer orbit aggregation* is a tuple $\mathcal{A}_2 \triangleq \langle V, Q, \Theta, Edg, Grd, Rst, Flow, Inv \rangle$, where: (a) $V = V_\mathcal{A}$, (b) $Q = Q_\mathcal{A}$, (c) $\Theta = \Theta_\mathcal{A}$, (d) $Edg = Edg_\mathcal{A}$, (e) $Grd : Grd_\mathcal{A}$, and (f) $Rst : Rst_\mathcal{A}$, but now the guard and reset maps between modes correspond to sets of ν_1, ν_2 values. (g) $Flow_{\mathcal{A}_2}$: Using the set of all (p, e) pairs of $\mathcal{O}$, the $\dot{\nu}_2$ dynamics for the active satellite in the transfer mode are defined piecewise over all R_i such that for each R_i, we have $\dot{\nu}_2 \in [f_{min}(\nu_2), f_{max}(\nu_2)]$.

The dynamics of $\mathcal{A}_2$ and $\mathcal{A}$ are identical except when the active satellite is in the transfer mode. For that mode, the dynamics corresponding to any execution of $\mathcal{A}$ are contained within the dynamics of $\mathcal{A}_2$ by construction, since $\mathcal{A}_2$ creates piecewise upper and lower bounds on $\dot{\nu}_2$. Thus we have that $\mathcal{A}_2$ is an abstraction of $\mathcal{A}$.

Hybridization: Our approach for both verification problems relies on computing the reachable states $Reach_\mathcal{A}$ of the HA $\mathcal{A}$. Since the software tools for computing the reach set of nonlinear HA are not as well-developed as those for linear and rectangular HA, we abstract the given nonlinear HA by a HA with simpler dynamics. We employ the *hybridization* approach [6,10], where the state-space of $\mathcal{A}$ is partitioned into a finite number of zones (see the polygons in Fig. 4). The nonlinear dynamics are conservatively approximated within each zone with simpler dynamics—in our case either (a) rectangular or (b) linear (affine) dynamics.

Given HA $\mathcal{A}$ and a partition function P that returns, for each location $l \in L$, a partition $\{I_1, \ldots, I_k\}$ such that $\cup_{j=1}^{k} I_j = Inv(l)$, we define the *hybridization abstraction* as the tuple $\mathcal{A}_3 \triangleq \langle V, Q, \Theta, Edg, Grd, Rst, Flow, Inv \rangle$, where: (a) $V = V_\mathcal{A} \cup zone$, where $zone$ is a discrete variable of type $Z_l = \{1, \ldots, k\}$ and identifies the partitions of each mode. (b) $Q = val(V_{\mathcal{A}_3})$ is the set of states. Now, for $\mathbf{x} \in Q$, the valuations of $\mathbf{x}.loc$, $\mathbf{x}.zone$, and the orbit parameter variables describe the discrete state. (c) $\Theta \subset Q$. (d) $Edg \subseteq (L \times Z) \times (L \times Z)$ is defined as follows: $((l, z), (l', z')) \in Edg$

if and only if either (i) $l' = l$ and $I_{z'}$ is adjacent to I_z, or (ii) $l' \neq l$ and I_z is contained in $I_{z'}$. (e) $Grd : Edg \to Q$ is defined as $Grd(((l, z), (l', z'))) = Inv_{\mathcal{A}}(l) \cap I_z$. (f) $Rst : Edg \to (Q \to 2^Q)$ is defined as (i) if $l = l'$, then the reset is the identity, and (ii) $Rst_{\mathcal{A}}(l, l')$, otherwise. (g) $Flow : (L \times Z) \to (Q \to 2^Q)$ is the flow map defined as follows. For each satellite $i \in \{1, 2\}$, location l, and zone z, we associate either (i) rectangular differential inclusions: $\dot{\nu}_i \in [a_i, b_i]$ for

$$a_i = \min_{\mathbf{x}.\nu_i \in I_z} Flow_{\mathcal{A}}(l)(\mathbf{x}) \text{ and } b_i = \max_{\mathbf{x}.\nu_i \in I_z} Flow_{\mathcal{A}}(l)(\mathbf{x}),$$

or (ii) affine (linear) differential inclusions: $\dot{\nu} = A\nu + b \pm \epsilon$, for

$$A = \nabla Flow_{\mathcal{A}}(l)(\mathbf{x})|_c \cdot (\nu - c), \ b = f(c), \ \epsilon = \max_{\mathbf{x}.\nu \in I_z} ||Flow_{\mathcal{A}}(l)(\mathbf{x}) - A\nu - b||,$$

where $c \in \mathbb{R}^2$ is the centroid of z, and $\nabla Flow_{\mathcal{A}}(l)(\mathbf{x})|_c$ is the Jacobian evaluated at c of $Flow_{\mathcal{A}}(l)(\mathbf{x})$. (h) $Inv : (L \times Z) \to 2^{val(X)}$ is $Inv_{\mathcal{A}_3}(l, z) \triangleq Inv(l) \cap I_z$.

By construction, the dynamics of $\mathcal{A}$ are contained in the conservative overapproximation, and a proof that $\mathcal{A}_3$ is an abstraction of $\mathcal{A}$ appears in [6]. Each of the individual abstractions are sound and can be implemented independently of one another. Thus, applying the abstractions $\mathcal{A}_1$, $\mathcal{A}_2$, and $\mathcal{A}_3$ sequentially to $\mathcal{A}$ yields another HA called $\mathcal{B}$ (visualized in Fig. 4), which is an abstraction of $\mathcal{A}$, since the composition of abstractions is sound.

Impossibility of unbounded model checking: Consider two arbitrary orbits o_1 and o_2 with periods T_1 and T_2. These two orbits are said to be *relatively periodic* if $\frac{T_1}{T_2}$ is rational; otherwise, they are said to be *incommensurate*. For circular orbits, the right-hand side of (1) reduces to a constant, and consequently, the reach set can be computed exactly. However, if the ratio of the orbits' periods is irrational, this is impossible. The proof of this follows from the mathematical result that the reach set of a point with irrational slope on the unit torus (or the unit square with billiards reflections at edges) is dense [19].

4   Computation of Abstractions

In this section, we describe how the transfer orbit aggregation abstraction is computed in our abstraction tool. We use boldface to indicate vectors.

First, we summarize how an ideal thrust vector ΔV is computed by numerically solving Lambert's problem. Then, we show how ΔV is applied to points nearby the original burn point. This yields uncountably infinitely many transfer orbits, each denoted by o_i, where $i \in \mathcal{O}$ for an uncountably infinite index set $\mathcal{O}$. We collapse this set of transfer orbits to a single mode by overapproximating the dynamics to include all possible transfer orbits.

Computation of ideal thrust vector ΔV: To calculate the orbit of the active satellite following a burn, we use an equivalent representation of the orbit dynamics—the position and velocity of the satellite in 3-dimensional Cartesian space. Recall that a satellite's orbit is completely described by (1) with parameters p, e, and angular position ν. In Cartesian coordinates, the satellite is described by a position vector r and

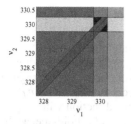 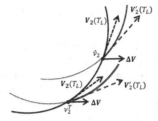 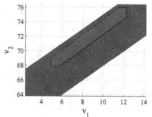

Fig. 6. Reach set of the initial orbit is plotted in blue. Black region is the expanded Grd_{IT} determined by transfer orbit aggregation around the original burn guard $(330, 330)$.

Fig. 7. Transfer orbit calculation: Lambert burn vector $\boldsymbol{\Delta V}$ applied to the original burn angle ν_2^T and neighboring point $\hat{\nu}_2$. Resulting velocity vectors and transfer orbits shown.

Fig. 8. Example verification of rendezvous for $d = 500$km. Blue set is the distance set Γ_d. Red set is the time intersection reach set, $\mathsf{Reach}_B^A(t)$ for $t = T_R$, the rendezvous time.

velocity vector $\boldsymbol{V}$. We will use both of these representations in the following procedure to calculate the transfer orbit.

Let T_L be the time when the (instantaneous) burn occurs, and let the angular positions of the two satellites at T_L be $(\nu_1(T_L), \nu_2(T_L))$. Let the time-to-rendezvous be T_R. The next sequence of steps describes how to compute the magnitude and direction of force that the burn applies to the active satellite. (a) $\boldsymbol{r}_i(T_L)$ and $\boldsymbol{V}_i(T_L)$ are computed at the passive and active satellites' initial positions $\nu_i(T_L)$. (b) Given the time of transfer T_R, $\nu_1(T_L + T_R)$ is computed by numerical integration of (1), and then the rendezvous location, $\boldsymbol{r}_1(T_L + T_R)$, is computed using $\nu_1(T_L + T_R)$. (c) The active satellite's states $\boldsymbol{r}_2(T_L)$ and $\boldsymbol{V}_2(T_L)$, and desired position for rendezvous $\boldsymbol{r}_2(T_L + T_R) = \boldsymbol{r}_1(T_L + T_R)$, are used to solve Lambert's problem to determine the velocity $\boldsymbol{V}'_2(T_L)$ that defines the transfer orbit. We then convert this velocity $\boldsymbol{V}'_2(T_L)$ to the transfer orbit parameters e_T and p_T needed to achieve rendezvous.

From the transfer orbit parameters, the required change in velocity at T_L is $\boldsymbol{\Delta V} = \boldsymbol{V}'_2(T_L) - \boldsymbol{V}_2(T_L)$. In reality, the time of and angular positions at burning are not known exactly, and as a result, the calculated $\boldsymbol{\Delta V}$ puts the active satellite on one of a collection of transfer orbits.

Expanding the Lambert burn angle to a range of angles: To construct $\mathcal{A}_2$ for rendezvous, we have to instantiate Grd_{IT}. Consider a point representing the minimum energy burn in the ν_1, ν_2 state space. Uncertainties in initial conditions, measurements, and numerical errors in position estimation cause the concrete system to have a larger guard. Thus, this is also incorporated into the abstract system. As a result, a given execution of the automaton may perform the burn within a set of different angular positions (and velocities). Also, the partitioning scheme around this minimum burn point must be adjusted to accommodate the larger guard, as shown in Fig. 6. Next, we outline the details of calculating transfer orbits of $\mathcal{O}$ for points within a small neighborhood of an ideal Lambert burn point. Let $(\nu_1^T, \nu_2^T) = G_{IT}$ be the ideal Lambert burn point. In general, we will add $\boldsymbol{\Delta V}$ to neighboring points to obtain a new $\boldsymbol{V}$ and then convert to the equivalent angular representation as shown in Fig. 7. The following calculations pertain only to the active satellite for some $\hat{\nu}_2$ location. Hence, we denote all initial orbit quantities with subscript I and transfer orbit quantities with subscript T, so $V_2(T_L) = V_I$ and $V_2'(T_L) = V_T$.

(a) Determine nearby points within guard set of the active satellite: $\hat{\nu}_2 \in \Lambda \triangleq [\nu_2^T - \epsilon, \nu_2^T + \epsilon]$. (b) For $\hat{\nu}_2$, calculate the position and velocity vectors in Cartesian coordinates using the orbital parameters of the initial orbit. For converting between the angular representation and Cartesian representation, we introduce an eccentricity vector e_I and angular momentum vector h_I [22]. The vectors e_I and h_I give direction with respect to the axes of the elliptical orbit. We write e_I, h_I, etc., without vector boldface, as the magnitude of the corresponding vector. The conversion is done by computing: $p_I = a_I(1 - e_I^2)$, $e_I = [e_I; \ 0; \ 0]$, $h_I = [0; \ 0; \ \sqrt{\mu p_I}]$, and

$$V_I = \frac{\mu}{h_I^2} h_I \times (e_I + [\cos(\hat{\nu}_2); \ \sin(\hat{\nu}_2); \ 0]),$$

$$r_I = \frac{p_I}{1 + e_I \cos(\hat{\nu}_2)}, \quad \text{and } r_I = r_I[\cos(\hat{\nu}_2); \ \sin(\hat{\nu}_2); \ 0].$$

(c) Now, add the Lambert burn vector ΔV corresponding to the angle ν_2^T to the velocity vector V_I at $\hat{\nu}_2$, $V_T = V_I + \Delta V$. (d) From the position (note that $r_I = r_T$) and resultant velocity vectors at $\hat{\nu}_2$, calculate the corresponding transfer orbit parameters:

$$h_T = V_T \times r_T, \qquad e_T = \frac{1}{\mu}(V_T \times h_T) - \frac{r_T}{r_T}, \qquad a_T = \frac{h_T^2}{\mu}(1 - e_T^2),$$

$$p_T = a_T(1 - e_T^2), \quad \text{and} \quad \nu_2' = \arctan\left(\frac{e_T[2]}{e_T[1]}\right),$$

where for a vector x, the notation $x[j]$ accesses the jth component of that vector. Here, ν_2' is the reset value for ν_2, which corresponds to the angular shift in the coordinate frame of a single transfer orbit. Since there is a transfer orbit for each $\hat{\nu}_2 \in \Lambda$, the reset for ν_2 will be in a range defining the reset R_{IT}.

Now that we can calculate transfer orbits for points from Λ, there are two issues to address. First, the dynamics of the transfer mode in the abstraction $\mathcal{A}_2$ must include all possible transfer orbit dynamics. To address this, we revisit (1). The parameters e_T and p_T for the transfer orbit are now defined in terms of $\hat{\nu}_2$ for $\hat{\nu}_2 \in \Lambda$. That is, $p(\hat{\nu}_2)$ and $e(\hat{\nu}_2)$ are functions representing all possible transfer orbit parameters. Thus, the non-linear differential inclusion describing all transfer orbits of the active satellite is $\dot{\nu}_2 = \sqrt{\mu/p(\hat{\nu}_2)^3}(1 + e(\hat{\nu}_2)\cos(\nu_2))^2$. In general, the definition of $\mathcal{A}_2$ requires the dynamics to be described by a function with upper and lower bounds. Thus, rectangular dynamics satisfy this definition, although we could use any appropriate upper and lower bounded function, e.g., the linear overapproximation used in hybridization. We construct rectangular dynamics for $\mathcal{A}_2$ by solving the following optimization problem:

$$\dot{\nu}_{2min} = \min_{\nu_2 \in R_i \,\wedge\, \hat{\nu}_2 \in \Lambda} f(\nu_2, p(\hat{\nu}_2), e(\hat{\nu}_2)), \quad \dot{\nu}_{2max} = \max_{\nu_2 \in R_i \,\wedge\, \hat{\nu}_2 \in \Lambda} f(\nu_2, p(\hat{\nu}_2), e(\hat{\nu}_2)).$$

For a particular partition in the transfer mode, we first minimize or maximize $\cos(\hat{\nu}_2)$. Now, replacing $\cos(\nu_2)$ with this optimized value in $\dot{\nu}_2$ will allow optimization over the single variable $\hat{\nu}_2$.

The second issue is that since there are a continuum of possible transfer orbits, we must generalize the distance threshold set P_d from (3) that was previously defined for a single pair of orbits. If the active satellite is on one of many possible transfer orbits, then to ensure the rendezvous property is satisfied, the satellites must be within d for each of these possible orbits. We ensure this by calculating a distance set Γ_d that holds for every transfer orbit. The active satellite's position is defined in terms of the functions $p(\hat{\nu}_2), e(\hat{\nu}_2)$ such that:

$$\Gamma_d \triangleq \{(\nu_1, \nu_2) \; : \; \|(x_1, y_1) - (x_2(p(\hat{\nu}_2), e(\hat{\nu}_2)), y_2(p(\hat{\nu}_2), e(\hat{\nu}_2)))\| \leq d\}. \tag{4}$$

In practice, we form this as an optimization problem by maximizing the norm from (4) over $\hat{\nu}_2$ for any particular point (ν_1, ν_2) in the state space. If this maximum distance is within the threshold d, then for any transfer orbit, the active satellite at that point is within d of the passive satellite. For both of these issues, when there is not an analytic solution to the optimization, we can introduce an error bound ϵ to the function being optimized to preserve soundness. For instance, if ϵ is the maximum error in the optimization of the distance equation, we would compute $\Gamma_{d-\epsilon}$ to ensure that any potential verified rendezvous satisfies the actual distance threshold d.

We now summarize the procedure for verifying rendezvous maneuvers. With a set of initial conditions for ν_1, ν_2, initial orbits o_1, o_2, and a Lambert burn point, the abstract HA $\mathcal{B}$ is computed as just described. Next, using $\mathcal{B}$ as input to HyTech, PHAVer, or SpaceEx, calculate $\text{Reach}_{\mathcal{B}}^{\delta}$ for a bounded time δ. Then, take a time intersection $\text{Reach}_{\mathcal{B}}^{\delta}(t)$ for a possible rendezvous time $t < \delta$. If $\text{Reach}_{\mathcal{B}}^{\delta}(t) \subseteq \Gamma_d$, then the reachable set of states at time t is within the distance threshold d. An example $\text{Reach}_{\mathcal{B}}^{\delta}(t)$ and Γ_d are shown in Fig. 8.

5   Experimental Results

We present experimental results for verifying conjunction avoidance and rendezvous using the three abstractions applied to the original system.

Once the abstract system $\mathcal{B}$ is constructed using our tool, the conjunction avoidance and rendezvous properties can be verified by computing $\text{Reach}_{\mathcal{B}}^{\delta}$ for some bounded time δ. Our prototype tool is written in Matlab and experiments were carried out on a modern laptop running Windows 7 with 4GB RAM and a 2.0GHz dual-core Intel i5 processor. We used PHAVer [12] and SpaceEx [13] for verification of $\mathcal{B}$.[3] SpaceEx runs in a virtual machine, and we also ran HyTech and PHAVer in an Ubuntu virtual machine. Overall, our results using HyTech, PHAVer, and SpaceEx suggest that tools allowing for relatively complex discrete dynamics and large numbers of locations need to be complemented with more scalable continuous reachability methods. We previously showed conjunction avoidance verification for one set of parameters in Fig. 3. Our test cases included Low Earth Orbits (LEO, altitude below 2000km), Medium Earth Orbits (MEO, 2000km to 35,786km), Geo Stationary (GEO), and Geo Synchronous (GSO) orbits with varying eccentricities. We were able to verify rendezvous for LEOs with eccentricities between 0 and 0.1.

Table 1 shows some successful rendezvous test cases, which used a rendezvous distance $d = 500$km, rectangular overapproximation of dynamics, and PHAVer. The first column is the initial state of the continuous variables. The second column is the ideal guard G_{IT} around which the abstracted guard Λ is built. The initial orbit parameters

---

[3] We found HyTech [15] to be unusable for elliptical orbits due to numerical overflows.

Table 1. Rendezvous experiments for $d = 500$km, $\epsilon = 0.25$ for guard Λ, and partition size 20×20 degrees. AT is abstraction run time (sec). PT is PHAVer run time (sec). RT is the time interval of rendezvous (sec), with the burn occurring in time at the lower bound of this interval. The underline and overlined parameters e_T or p_T are respectively the min and max of the nondeterministic parameter values.

Initial (ν_1, ν_2)	Guard (ν_1^T, ν_2^T)	Initial Orbit $(e_1, p_1[km], e_I, p_I[km])$	Transfer Orbit $(\underline{e}_T, \overline{e}_T, \underline{p}_T[km], \overline{p}_T[km])$	AT (s)	PT (s)	RT (s)
$(270, 267.5)$	$(330, 330)$	$(0, 6718, 0.05, 7340)$	$(0.05849, 0.05853, 6766, 6769)$	811	3.01	$(950, 1200)$
$(250, 246.5)$	$(330, 330)$	$(0, 6718, 0.05, 7340)$	$(0.05849, 0.05853, 6766, 6769)$	811	3.23	$(1050, 1300)$
$(300, 299)$	$(333, 333)$	$(0.05, 7074, 0.10, 7748)$	$(0.06468, 0.06486, 7114, 7116)$	801	3.4	$(500, 1250)$
$(300, 299)$	$(327, 327)$	$(0, 6718, 0.10, 7748)$	$(0.06186, 0.06202, 6982, 6984)$	834	3.37	$(440, 990)$

Table 2. Reachability experiments for different overapproximation techniques. Initial condition is $(\nu_1, \nu_2) = (0, 0)$. RA and AA columns are the abstraction times in seconds for rectangular and affine dynamics, respectively. PR, SR, and SA columns are, respectively, the run time in seconds of PHAVer with rectangular dynamics, SpaceEx with rectangular dynamics, and SpaceEx with affine (linear) dynamics. The number subscript for the SpaceEx runs determine the sampling time used in the reachability algorithm. These experiments ran until the time bound T equal to the satellite period.

Parameters $(e_1, p_1[km], e_2, p_2[km])$	Partition Size	RA	AA	PR	SR_{20}	SR_{100}	SA_{20}	SA_{100}
$[0.05, 7056, 0.10, 7670]$	60 x 60	4.42	5.89	0.26	979	249	193	140
$[0.10, 7467, 0.10, 7670]$	60 x 60	9.8	9.92	0.35	1076	263	384	191

are shown as well as the parameter ranges that define the continuum of transfer orbits in the second mode. The RT column shows the time intersection of the reach set where the rendezvous was satisfied. To verify smaller rendezvous distances, smaller partitioning sizes can be used. This will minimize the error accumulated in the approximation, but will result in increased abstraction and reach set computation time. The bounded reach set, $\text{Reach}_{\mathcal{B}}^{\delta}$, is not completely contained in Γ_d, and only its intersection for a range of times ($\text{Reach}_{\mathcal{B}}^{\delta}(t)$ for $t \in [T_R - \rho, T_R + \rho]$) is completely contained. For instance, one input to Lambert's problem is the time T_R for rendezvous to occur, and we can verify rendezvous for a range of times ρ around T_R.

Table 2 compares different hybridization schemes—rectangular versus linear overapproximations of dynamics—for conjunction avoidance. We fix the partitioning of the hybridization and are comparing only rectangular versus linear dynamics for the same partition shape and size. Usually, the reach sets from linear overapproximation are smaller than rectangular. However, the support function algorithm implemented in SpaceEx allows the user to configure the amount of error in the overapproximation. Lower error comes at the cost of higher runtime, and we summarize runtime comparisons in Table 2. We can decrease this runtime cost by configuring SpaceEx, but this may come at the expense of the rectangular overapproximation being as good, if not better, than the linear overapproximation.

6   Conclusion and Future Work

In this paper, we developed abstraction techniques used to enable automatic verification of bounded-time safety properties for nonlinear satellite systems. The abstractions account for uncertainties in observation times, sensor measurements, and thrusting. We also showed that the unbounded model-checking of incommensurate orbits is impossible. However, the reach set for circular commensurate orbits can be computed exactly. While we do not have space to present it here, we (a) can verify unbounded properties of eccentric commensurate orbits by using forward and backward reachability techniques, and (b) have verified time-bounded safety properties for nearby satellites using the Clohessy-Wiltshire-Hill (CWH) dynamics in the ellipsoidal toolbox [17].

One of the primary roadblocks for analyzing more eccentric elliptical orbits or multiple-transfer satellite maneuvers is the granularity with which we are able to partition the state space. If we are able to approximate the dynamics over smaller intervals, we will be better equipped to analyze these more complex systems. An important feature yet to be taken advantage of is that the dynamics between the satellites is loosely coupled. A new approach we are exploring is to decompose the multi-satellite system into individual satellite automata, which would allow for much finer partitioning. With each automata containing a synchronized clock variable, we are developing algorithmic techniques that act on the individual reach sets to enable compositional verification of the global safety properties.

References

1. Allgeier, S.E., Fitz-Coy, N.G., Erwin, R.S., Lovell, T.A.: Metrics for mission planning of formation flight. In: Proc. AAS/AIAA Astrodynamics Specialist Conference, Girdwood, AK (July 2011)
2. Althoff, M., Stursberg, O., Buss, M.: Reachability analysis of nonlinear systems with uncertain parameters using conservative linearization. In: 47th IEEE Conference on Decision and Control (CDC), pp. 4042–4048 (December 2008)
3. Althoff, M., Le Guernic, C., Krogh, B.H.: Reachable set computation for uncertain time-varying linear systems. In: Hybrid Systems: Computation and Control (HSCC), pp. 93–102. ACM, New York (2011)
4. Althoff, M., Rajhans, A., Krogh, B., Yaldiz, S., Li, X., Pileggi, L.: Formal verification of phase-locked loops using reachability analysis and continuization. In: IEEE/ACM International Conference on Computer-Aided Design, ICCAD (2011)
5. Alur, R., Courcoubetis, C., Halbwachs, N., Henzinger, T.A., Ho, P.-H., Nicollin, X., Olivero, A., Sifakis, J., Yovine, S.: The algorithmic analysis of hybrid systems. Theoretical Computer Science 138(1), 3–34 (1995)
6. Asarin, E., Dang, T., Girard, A.: Hybridization methods for the analysis of nonlinear systems. Acta Informatica 43, 451–476 (2007)
7. Bate, R.R., Mueller, D.D., White, J.E.: Fundamentals of Astrodynamics. Dover (1971)
8. Battin, R.H.: An introduction to the mathematics and methods of astrodynamics. AIAA education series. American Institute of Aeronautics and Astronautics (1999)
9. Bosse, A.B., Barnds, W.J., Brown, M.A., Creamer, N.G., Feerst, A., Henshaw, C.G., Hope, A.S., Kelm, B.E., Klein, P.A., Pipitone, F., Plourde, B.E., Whalen, B.P.: Sumo: Spacecraft for the Universal Modification of Orbits. In: Proc. of SPIE, vol. 5419, pp. 36–46 (2004)

10. Dang, T., Maler, O., Testylier, R.: Accurate hybridization of nonlinear systems. In: Hybrid Systems: Computation and Control (HSCC), pp. 11–20. ACM, New York (2010)

11. Flieller, D., Riedinger, P., Louis, J.P.: Computation and stability of limit cycles in hybrid systems. Nonlinear Analysis: Theory, Methods, & Applications 64(2), 352–367 (2006)

12. Frehse, G.: PHAVer: Algorithmic Verification of Hybrid Systems Past HyTech. In: Morari, M., Thiele, L. (eds.) HSCC 2005. LNCS, vol. 3414, pp. 258–273. Springer, Heidelberg (2005)

13. Frehse, G., Le Guernic, C., Donzé, A., Cotton, S., Ray, R., Lebeltel, O., Ripado, R., Girard, A., Dang, T., Maler, O.: SpaceEx: Scalable Verification of Hybrid Systems. In: Gopalakrishnan, G., Qadeer, S. (eds.) CAV 2011. LNCS, vol. 6806, pp. 379–395. Springer, Heidelberg (2011)

14. Gurfil, P., Kholshevnikov, K.V.: Manifolds and metrics in the relative spacecraft motion problem. Journal of Guidance Control and Dynamics 29(4), 1004–1010 (2006)

15. Henzinger, T.A., Ho, P.-H., Wong-Toi, H.: Hytech: a model checker for hybrid systems. Journal on Software Tools for Technology Transfer 1, 110–122 (1997)

16. Kaynar, D.K., Lynch, N., Segala, R., Vaandrager, F.: The Theory of Timed I/O Automata. Synthesis Lectures in Computer Science. Morgan & Claypool (2006)

17. Kurzhanskiy, A.A., Varaiya, P.: Ellipsoidal toolbox. In: 45th IEEE Conference on Decision and Control (CDC), pp. 1498–1503 (December 2006)

18. Lynch, N., Segala, R., Vaandrager, F.: Hybrid i/o automata. Inf. Comput. 185(1), 105–157 (2003)

19. Masur, H., Tabachnikov, S.: Rational billiards and flat structures. In: Hasselblatt, B., Katok, A. (eds.) Handbook of Dynamical Systems, Handbook of Dynamical Systems, vol. 1 Part A, ch. 13, pp. 1015–1089. Elsevier Science (2002)

20. Ocampo, C.: Finite burn maneuver modeling for a generalized spacecraft trajectory design and optimization system. Annals of the New York Academy of Sciences 1017(1), 210–233 (2004)

21. Römgens, B.A., Mooij, E., Naeije, M.C.: Verified interval orbit propagation in satellite collision avoidance. In: Proc. AIAA Guidance, Navigation, and Control, Portland, OR (2011)

22. Vallado, D.A., McClain, W.D.: Fundamentals of astrodynamics and applications. Space technology library. Microcosm Press (2001)

Executing Formal Semantics with the $\mathbb{K}$ Tool[*]

David Lazar[1], Andrei Arusoaie[2], Traian Florin Şerbănuţă[1,2], Chucky Ellison[1],
Radu Mereuta[2], Dorel Lucanu[2], and Grigore Roşu[1,2]

[1] University of Illinois at Urbana-Champaign
{lazar6,tserban2,celliso2,grosu}@illinois.edu
[2] University Alexandru Ioan Cuza of Iaşi
{andrei.arusoaie,traian.serbanuta,radu.mereuta,dlucanu}@info.uaic.ro

Abstract. This paper describes the $\mathbb{K}$ tool, a system for formally defining programming languages. Formal definitions created using the $\mathbb{K}$ tool automatically yield an interpreter for the language, as well as program analysis tools such as a state-space explorer. The modularity of $\mathbb{K}$ and the design of the tool allow one semantics to be used for several applications.

1 Introduction

Programming languages are the key link between computers and the software that runs on them. While syntax is typically formally defined for almost any programming language, semantics is most often given in natural language, and only rarely using mathematical language. However, without a formal semantics, it is impossible to rigorously reason about programs in that language. Moreover, a formal definition of a language is a specification offering its users and implementers a solid basis for agreeing on the meaning of programs. Unfortunately, tools for creating and working with formal definitions are poor and unfriendly, causing language designers to prefer writing reference manuals or reference implementations over formal definitions.

This paper presents a tool that makes it easy to write formal definitions for large languages and use them for analysis and verification. This tool, known as the $\mathbb{K}$ tool, is an executable implementation of the $\mathbb{K}$ framework [2], a formal specification language that is simultaneously expressive, modular, and analyzable. We extend an earlier implementation [4] with a mechanism for guided state-space search and an easy-to-use frontend that supports input and output. These key features allow users to experiment with language design and specification by means of testing and exhaustive non-deterministic behavior exploration.

Besides didactic and prototypical languages (such as System F and Agent), the $\mathbb{K}$ tool has been used to completely formalize C and Scheme. Several other languages are currently being defined using the $\mathbb{K}$ tool, including Haskell, Javascript, LLVM IR, and Python. The $\mathbb{K}$ tool has also been used in the development of several analysis tools, including a new program verification tool using program assertions based on matching logic, a model checking tool based on the CEGAR

---

[*] This work is supported by Contract 161/15.06.2010, SMISCSNR 602-12516 (DAK).

D. Giannakopoulou and D. Méry (Eds.): FM 2012, LNCS 7436, pp. 267–271, 2012.

cycle, and several runtime verification tools. References and links to these tools and definitions can be found on the $\mathbb{K}$ tool website, http://k-framework.org.

2   The $\mathbb{K}$ Tool: Basics

$\mathbb{K}$ definitions of programming languages can be written in machine-readable ASCII. The $\mathbb{K}$ tool provides facilities to manipulate such definitions, including typesetting them into their LaTeX mathematical representation, and generating execution and analysis tools. For example, Figure 1 gives the definition of a simple calculator language with variables, input, and output. We assume this definition is saved in a file called exp.k for the following examples.

```
module EXP
  configuration
    ⟨k⟩ $PGM:K ⟨/k⟩
    ⟨state⟩ $STATE:Map ⟨/state⟩
    ⟨streams⟩
      ⟨in stream="stdin"⟩ .List ⟨/in⟩
      ⟨out stream="stdout"⟩ .List ⟨/out⟩
    ⟨/streams⟩

  syntax KResult ::= Int

  syntax K ::= K + K [strict]
            |  K / K [strict]

  rule I1:Int + I2:Int  =>  I1 +Int I2
  rule I1:Int / I2:Int  =>  I1 /Int I2
    when I2 =/=Int 0

  syntax K ::= Id

  rule ⟨k⟩ X:Id => I ···⟨/k⟩
       ⟨state⟩··· X |-> I:Int ···⟨/state⟩

  syntax K ::= read
            |  print K [strict]

  rule ⟨k⟩ read => I ···⟨/k⟩
       ⟨in⟩ ListItem(I:Int)  =>  .List ···⟨/in⟩

  rule ⟨k⟩ print I:Int => I ···⟨/k⟩
       ⟨out⟩··· .List  =>  ListItem(I) ⟨/out⟩
end module
```

MODULE EXP

CONFIGURATION

$\langle\ \$PGM\ \rangle_k\ \langle\ \$STATE\ \rangle_{state}$

$\langle\ \langle\ \cdot\ \rangle_{in}\ \langle\ \cdot\ \rangle_{out}\ \rangle_{streams}$

SYNTAX $KResult ::= Int$

SYNTAX $K ::= K + K$ [strict]
          $|\ K\ /\ K$ [strict]

RULE $I_1 + I_2 \Rightarrow I_1 +_{Int} I_2$

RULE $I_1\ /\ I_2 \Rightarrow I_1 \div_{Int} I_2$ when $I_2 \neq_{Int} 0$

SYNTAX $K ::= Id$

RULE $\langle\ \underset{I}{X}\ \cdots\rangle_k\ \langle\cdots X \mapsto I\ \cdots\rangle_{state}$

SYNTAX $K ::=$ read
          $|$ print K [strict]

RULE $\langle$ read $\cdots\rangle_k\ \langle\cdots \underset{I}{I}\ \cdots\rangle_{in}$
          $\qquad\quad \overline{\cdot}$

RULE $\langle$ print $I\ \cdots\rangle_k\ \langle\cdots \underset{I}{\cdot}\ \rangle_{out}$
          $\qquad\quad \overline{I}$

END MODULE

Fig. 1. $\mathbb{K}$ definition of a calculator language with variables and I/O (left: ASCII source; right: LaTeX generated by the tool)

For execution and analysis purposes, the definitions are translated into Maude rewrite theories. To obtain the rewrite theory associated to exp.k, we use the kompile tool:

```
$ kompile exp.k
Compiled version written in exp-compiled.maude.
```

Once the definition is compiled, it can be used for interpretation and analysis. Consider the program p1.exp:

```
print((read + read + read) / 3)
```

which reads three numbers and outputs their (truncated) mean. We can test this program using the krun tool:

```
$ echo "3 14 15" | krun p1.exp
10
```

Notice the use of the operating system's standard input/output streams.

Consider now the program p2.exp:

```
print(x + y)
```

which prints the sum of two externally defined variables x and y. If we forget to pass in a value for x at the start of the program's execution:

```
$ krun p2.exp --STATE="y |-> 2"
<k> x ~> □ + 2 ~> print □ </k>
<state> y |-> 2 </state>
```

the tool prints a configuration indicating that the execution got stuck. The contents of the k cell tells us that the next computation to perform is the lookup of x. Since x is not present in the state, the rule for variable lookup can not apply so the execution is unable to proceed. If we instead type --STATE="y |-> 2 x |-> 3", the tool prints the expected result of 5.

These examples demonstrate a new and important feature of the K tool: the ability to associate cells in the configuration with data from the outside world. In the definition above, the in and out cells are linked to standard input/output (via the **stream** attribute) to achieve interactive I/O. This feature allows K definitions to easily be tested for correctness using existing test suites and test frameworks. Similarly, the state cell is initialized to the $STATE variable. This allows the contents of the cell to be manipulated from the command-line, as in the previous example. Incidentally, the k cell is also initialized to a variable, $PGM, which is always mapped to the input program.

3   The K Tool: Analysis

The K tool is more than an interpreter front-end. Consider the program p3.exp:

```
print(print(read) + print(read))
```

The definition of EXP in Figure 1 says the value returned by print is the printed number. Therefore, the program should read two numbers, print them, and then print their sum. If we just execute the program as before, we see what we expect:

```
$ echo "3 14" | krun p3.exp
31417
```

However, the definition also says that the evaluation order of + (specified by the `strict` annotation on its syntax) is nondeterministic. If we search for all possible behaviors of `p3.exp`, we obtain two final configurations with differing out cells: one where "3" is printed first and one where it is printed second:

```
$ echo "3 14" | krun p3.exp --search
Search results:
```

```
Solution 1, state 4:          Solution 2, state 9:
<k> 17 </k>                   <k> 17 </k>
<state> . </state>            <state> . </state>
<streams>                     <streams>
  <in> "" </in>                 <in> "" </in>
  <out> "31417" </out>          <out> "14317" </out>
</streams>                    </streams>
```

The state-space exploration functionality provided by `krun --search` can be used to explore all possible thread interleavings of multi-threaded programs. It is also used to find undefined behaviors in programs (particularly C programs).

In addition to the functionality shown in the examples above, the $\mathbb{K}$ tool gives $\mathbb{K}$ definitions access to the exploration, analysis, and proving tools available for all Maude rewrite theories [1], allowing programs written in the defined programming languages to also be debugged, traced, and model checked, all without modifying the definition.

4 Conclusion

The modularity and executability features provided by the $\mathbb{K}$ tool have made it possible to completely define large languages like C. These features also make it easy to experiment with language design in order to create new languages and make modifications to existing languages. Regardless of the language being defined, the same $\mathbb{K}$ definition that is tested by executing programs is used to do program analysis and is used to do proofs about the language. One semantics is used for all applications.

In this paper, we have shown only a subset of the features offered by the $\mathbb{K}$ tool. To learn more about it, or to start developing a programming language, download the $\mathbb{K}$ tool from our open source project page, `http://k-framework.googlecode.com`, and start by reading the $\mathbb{K}$ Primer [3].

References

1. Clavel, M., Durán, F., Eker, S., Lincoln, P., Martí-Oliet, N., Meseguer, J., Talcott, C.: All About Maude - A High-Performance Logical Framework. LNCS, vol. 4350. Springer, Heidelberg (2007)
2. Roşu, G., Şerbănuţă, T.F.: An overview of the K semantic framework. J. Logic and Algebraic Programming 79, 397–434 (2010)

3. Şerbănuţă, T.F., Arusoaie, A., Lazar, D., Ellison, C., Lucanu, D., Roşu, G.: The K primer (version 2.5). In: Proceedings of the 2nd Intl. K Wkshp. (K 2011). Electronic Notes in Theoretical Computer Science (to appear, 2012)
4. Şerbănuţă, T.F., Roşu, G.: K-Maude: A Rewriting Based Tool for Semantics of Programming Languages. In: Ölveczky, P.C. (ed.) WRLA 2010. LNCS, vol. 6381, pp. 104–122. Springer, Heidelberg (2010)

Automatic Compositional Verification of Timed Systems

Shang-Wei Lin[1], Yang Liu[1], Jun Sun[2], Jin Song Dong[3], and Étienne André[4]

[1] Temasek Laboratories, National University of Singapore*
{tsllsw,tsllliuya}@nus.edu.sg
[2] Singapore University of Technology and Design
sunjun@sutd.edu.sg
[3] National University of Singapore
dongjs@comp.nus.edu.sg
[4] LIPN, CNRS UMR 7030, Université Paris 13, France
Etienne.Andre@lipn.univ-paris13.fr

Abstract. Specification and verification of real-time systems are important research topics with crucial applications; however, the so-called state space explosion problem often prevents model checking to be used in practice for large systems. In this work, we present a self-contained toolkit to analyze real-time systems specified using *event-recording automata* (ERAs), which supports system modeling, animated simulation, and fully automatic compositional verification based on learning techniques. Experimental results show that our tool outperforms the state-of-the-art timed model checker.

1 Introduction

Ensuring the correctness of safety-critical systems with timing requirements is crucial and challenging. Model checking is emerging as an effective verification method and has been widely used for timed system. However, model checking suffers from the infamous state space explosion problem, and the problem is even graver in timed model checking because of the timed transitions.

To alleviate this problem, we proposed an automatic learning-based compositional verification framework for timed systems (cf. technical repoert [7]). We focus on timed systems that are modeled by *event-recording automata* (ERAs) [1], which is a determinizable class of timed automata. ERAs are as powerful as timed transition systems and are sufficiently expressive to model many interesting timed systems. The proposed framework consists of a compositional verification based on the non-circular assume-guarantee (AG-NC) proof rule [9] and uses a learning algorithm, TL* [8], to automatically generate timed assumptions for *assume-guarantee reasoning* (AGR).

Our engineering efforts realize the proposed techniques into a self-contained toolkit for analyzing real-time systems, which is built as the ERA module (can be downloaded

* This work is mainly supported by TRF Project "Research and Development in the Formal Verification of System Design and Implementation" from Temasek Lab@National University of Singapore; partially supported by project IDG31100105/IDD11100102 from Singapore University of Technology and Design, project MOE2009-T2-1-072 from School of Computing@National University of Singapore, and Merlion Project R-252-000-482-133.

D. Giannakopoulou and D. Méry (Eds.): FM 2012, LNCS 7436, pp. 272–276, 2012.

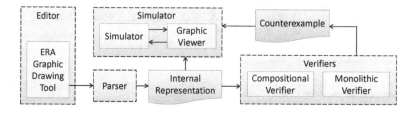

Fig. 1. Architecture of the ERA Module in PAT

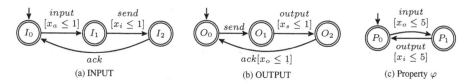

Fig. 2. Models and property of the I/O system

at [6]) in the PAT model checker [10]. Fig. 1 shows the architecture of our tool, which consists of four components, namely the *editor*, the *parser*, the *simulator* and *verifiers*. The editor is featured with a powerful graphic drawing component that allows users to design system models and specify properties by drawing ERAs. The editor also supports syntax highlighting, intellisense, and undo/redo functionality such that designers can efficiently model the systems. The parser compiles both the system models and the properties (in the form of ERAs) into internal representations for simulation and verification. The simulator allows users to perform various simulation tasks on the input model such as user interactive simulation, trace replay and so on. Most importantly, compositional verification is fully automated for *safety* properties specified using ERAs. To the best of our knowledge, our tool is the first one supporting fully automatic compositional verification for timed systems. Our tool also supports the traditional monolithic approach that generates the global state space based on zone abstraction. Users can choose to use either the monolithic or our compositional approach inside the verification interface. If the verification result is false, counterexamples will be produced and can be visualized using the simulator. Experimental results (Section 3) show that our tool of compositional verification for real-time systems outperforms traditional timed monolithic approaches in many cases.

2 Compositional Verification of ERAs

An *event-recording automaton* (ERA) is a special case of timed automaton where each event a on a transition is associated with a corresponding event-recording clock x_a recording the time elapsed since the last occurrence of event a. Each event-recording clock x_a is implicitly and automatically reset when a transition with event a is taken.

Fig. 2 gives an I/O system with two components, INPUT and OUTPUT, modeled by ERAs. The pairs of event-recording clocks and the corresponding events are x_i : *input*, x_s : *send*, x_o : *output*, and x_a : *ack*. The model of the INPUT component is

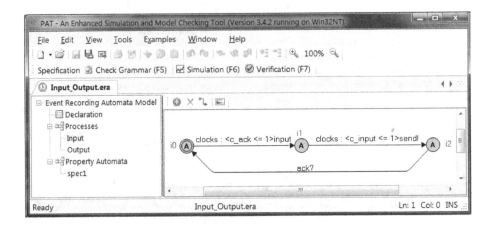

Fig. 3. GUI of the PAT Model Checker

shown in Fig. 2 (a). It performs an *input* event within one time unit once it receives an *ack* event from OUTPUT. Subsequently, it performs a *send* event to notify OUTPUT and waits for another *ack* event from OUTPUT. The model of OUTPUT is shown in Fig. 2 (b), which is similar to INPUT. The system property φ, as shown in Fig. 2 (c), is that *input* and *output* events should alternate and the time difference between every two consecutive events should not exceed five time units. Fig. 3 shows the INPUT component modeled in PAT, where a double circle represents the initial state and a state labeled with "**A**" represents an accepting state.

The flow of the proposed timed compositional verification is a two-phase process using the TL* algorithm [8] to automatically learn the timed assumption needed by AGR. The first, *untimed verification*, phase constructs the untimed assumption, and then the second, *timed verification*, phase refines the untimed assumption into timed one and concludes the verification result. The flow is complete, i.e., users are guaranteed to get the verification result. Interested readers are referred to the technical report [7]. After verification, PAT shows that the I/O system satisfies the property φ.

3   Experimental Results and Discussion

To show the feasibility and scalability of our tool, we present verification results of four different applications, namely the CSS, GSS, FMS, and AIP systems, in Table 1. The details of the four systems, their models, and the verified properties can be found in [6]. The experimental results were obtained by running PAT on a Windows 7 machine with a 2.27 GHz Intel(R) Core(TM) i3 processor and 4 GB RAM. We also compared our approach with the UPPAAL model checker [11]; however, we do not list the verification time of UPPAAL for verifying the AIP system because UPPAAL does not support events on transitions such that the AIP system cannot be modeled in UPPAAL. When the system size is small, compositional approach does not outperform monolithic verification or UPPAAL because of the overhead of learning iterations; when the number of components increases, the learning iterations compensate for the large global state

Table 1. Verification Results

System	n	$|C_\Sigma|$	$\dfrac{|P_{\not\models}|}{|P|}$	Monolithic				Compositional				UPPAAL
				$|L|_{max}$	$|\delta|_{max}$	Time (secs)	Mem (MB)	$|L|_{max}$	$|\delta|_{max}$	Time (secs)	Mem (MB)	Time (secs)
CSS	3	6	0/6	11	20	0.03	0.16	19	50	0.06	0.77	0.05
GSS	3	3	2/3	29	46	0.03	0.13	56	107	0.03	0.69	0.06
FMS-1	5	3	1/3	193	514	0.03	1.18	60	138	0.03	0.89	0.08
FMS-2	10	6	3/6	76, 305	396, 789	40.71	114.08	1, 492	4, 952	0.66	6.60	2.05
FMS-3	11	6	5/7	201, 601	1, 300, 566	70.02	295.89	3, 150	16, 135	1.14	12.07	9.87
FMS-4	14	8	3/9	−	−	−	ROM	26, 320	127, 656	51.02	41.41	ROM
AIP	10	4	5/10	104, 651	704, 110	78.05	149.68	2, 992	12, 971	1.90	7.39	N/A

n: # of components; $|C_\Sigma|$: # of event-recording clocks; $|P|$: # of properties; $|P_{\not\models}|$: # of violated properties; $|L|_{max}$: # of visited locations during verification; $|\delta|_{max}$: # of visited transitions during verification; ROM: run out of memory

space and compositional approach can reduce the verification time and the memory usage significantly. For the FMS-4 system, the monolithic approach and UPPAAL cannot even finish the verification using 4 GB memory.

Discussion. AGR has been applied to model checking to alleviate the state space explosion problem [3]. However, the construction of the assumptions for AGR usually requires nontrivial creativity and experience, which limits the impact of AGR. Cobleigh et al. [4] proposed a framework that generates the assumptions of components automatically using the L* algorithm [2]. This work was a breakthrough of automating compositional verification for untimed systems. Grinchtein et al. [5] proposed three algorithms for learning ERAs; however, the time complexity of the algorithms depend exponentially on the largest constant appearing in the time constraints. In [8], we proposed a more efficient polynomial time algorithm, TL*, for learning ERAs. Starting from 2010, ERA module in PAT has come to a stable stage with solid testing. We successfully applied it to verify real-time systems ranging from classical concurrent algorithms to real world problems. In the future, we plan to use different techniques to generate the assumptions and to extend the framework using other proof rules of AGR.

References

1. Alur, R., Fix, L., Henzinger, T.A.: Event-clock automata: A determinizable class of timed automata. Theoretical Computer Science 211(1-2), 253–273 (1999)
2. Angluin, D.: Learning regular sets from queries and counterexamples. Information and Computation 75(2), 87–106 (1987)
3. Clarke, E.M., Long, D.E., MacMillan, K.L.: Compositional model checking. In: LICS, pp. 353–362 (1989)
4. Cobleigh, J.M., Giannakopoulou, D., Păsăreanu, C.S.: Learning Assumptions for Compositional Verification. In: Garavel, H., Hatcliff, J. (eds.) TACAS 2003. LNCS, vol. 2619, pp. 331–346. Springer, Heidelberg (2003)
5. Grinchtein, O., Jonsson, B., Leucker, M.: Learning of event-recording automata. Theoretical Computer Science 411(47), 4029–4054 (2010)
6. Lin, S.W.: https://sites.google.com/site/shangweilin/era-pat
7. Lin, S.W.:
https://sites.google.com/site/
shangweilin/technical-reports

8. Lin, S.-W., André, É., Dong, J.S., Sun, J., Liu, Y.: An Efficient Algorithm for Learning Event-Recording Automata. In: Bultan, T., Hsiung, P.-A. (eds.) ATVA 2011. LNCS, vol. 6996, pp. 463–472. Springer, Heidelberg (2011)
9. Namjoshi, K.S., Trefler, R.J.: On the Completeness of Compositional Reasoning. In: Emerson, E.A., Sistla, A.P. (eds.) CAV 2000. LNCS, vol. 1855, pp. 139–153. Springer, Heidelberg (2000)
10. Sun, J., Liu, Y., Dong, J.S., Pang, J.: PAT: Towards Flexible Verification under Fairness. In: Bouajjani, A., Maler, O. (eds.) CAV 2009. LNCS, vol. 5643, pp. 709–714. Springer, Heidelberg (2009)
11. UPPAAL, http://www.uppaal.org/

Applying Software Model Checking Techniques for Behavioral UML Models

Orna Grumberg[1], Yael Meller[1], and Karen Yorav[2]

[1] Computer Science Department, Technion, Haifa, Israel
{orna,ymeller}@cs.technion.ac.il
[2] IBM Haifa Research Laboratory, Haifa, Israel
yorav@il.ibm.com

Abstract. This work presents a novel approach for the verification of Behavioral UML models, by means of software model checking.

We propose adopting *software model checking* techniques for verification of UML models. We translate UML to *verifiable* C code which preserves the high level structure of the models, and abstracts details that are not needed for verification. We combine of static analysis and bounded model checking for verifying LTL safety properties and absence of livelocks.

We implemented our approach on top of the bounded software model checker CBMC. We compared it to an IBM research tool that verifies UML models via a translation to IBM's hardware model checker RuleBasePE. Our experiments show that our approach is more scalable and more robust for finding long counterexamples. We also demonstrate the usefulness of several optimizations that we introduced into our tool.

1 Introduction

This work presents a novel approach for the verification of Behavioral UML models, by means of software model checking.

The *Unified Modeling Language* (UML) [4] is a widely accepted modeling language that is used to visualize, specify, and construct systems. It provides means to represent a system as a collection of objects and to describe the system's internal structure and behavior. UML has been accepted as a standard object-oriented modeling language by the Object Management Group (OMG) [12]. It is becoming the dominant modeling language for embedded systems. As such, the correct behavior of systems represented as UML models is crucial and verification techniques for such models are required.

Model checking [6] is a successful automated verification technique for checking whether a given system satisfies a desired property. Model checking traverses *all* system behaviors, and either confirms that the system is correct w.r.t. the checked property, or provides a *counterexample* demonstrating an erroneous behavior.

Model checking tools expect the checked system to be presented in an appropriate description language. Previous works on UML model checking translate UML models to SMV [5,7] or VIS[1] [25], both particularly suitable for hardware; to PROMELA (the input language of SPIN) [17,16,20,10,1,14,11]), which is mainly suitable for communication protocols; or to IF[3] [18], which is oriented to real-time systems.

---

[1] These works were developed as part of the European research project OMEGA [19].

D. Giannakopoulou and D. Méry (Eds.): FM 2012, LNCS 7436, pp. 277–292, 2012.

We believe that behavioral UML models mostly resemble high-level software systems. We therefore choose to translate UML models to C and adopt *software model checking* techniques for their verification. Our translation indeed preserves the high-level structure of the UML system: event-driven objects communicate with each other via an *event queue*. An execution consists of a sequence of *Run To Completion* (RTC) steps. Each RTC step is initiated by the event queue by sending an event to its target object, which in turn executes a maximal series of enabled transitions.

Model checking assumes a finite-state representation of the system in order to guarantee termination with a definite result. One approach for obtaining finiteness is to *bound* the length of the traversed executions by an iteratively increased bound. This is called *Bounded Model Checking* (BMC) [3]. BMC is highly scalable, and widely used, and is particularly suitable for bug hunting. We find this approach most suitable for UML models, which are inherently infinite due to the unbound size of the event queue[2].

We emphasize that our goal is to translate the UML model into *verifiable* C code that suits model checking, rather than produce executable code. Also, we only wish to verify user-created artifacts. When translating to C, we therefore simplify implementation details that are irrelevant for verification. For instance, the event queue is described at a high level of abstraction, and code is sometimes duplicated to avoid pointers and simplify the verification. The resulting code is significantly easier for model checking than automatically generated code produced by UML tools such as Rhapsody [23].

Recall that the verifiable C code will be checked by BMC with some bound k. We choose k to count the number of RTC steps. This implies that along an execution of size k only the first k events in the queue are consumed, even if more were produced. It is therefore sufficient to hold an event queue of size k. We thus obtain a finite-state model without losing any precision. Counterexamples are also returned as a sequence of RTC steps, but zooming in to intermediate states is available upon request.

We verify two types of properties: LTL safety properties and livelocks. Safety properties require that the system never arrives at bad states, such as deadlock states, states violating mutual exclusion, or states from which the execution can continue nondeterministically. *LTL safety properties* can further require that no undesired finite execution occurs. Checking (LTL) safety properties can be reduced to traversing the reachable states of the system while searching for bad states. We apply *Bounded reachability* with increasing bounds for finding bad states. Our method can also be extended to proving the absence of bad states, using k-induction [26].

Another interesting type of properties is the absence of livelocks. *Livelocks* are a generalization of deadlocks. While in *deadlock* states the *full system* cannot progress, in livelock states part of the system is "stuck" forever while other parts continue to run. Livelocks can be hazardous in safety critical systems and often indicate a faulty design.

Scalable bounded model checking tools mostly handle *safety* or linear-time properties. However, absence of livelocks is neither safety nor linear-time property and is therefore not amenable to bounded model checking. We identify an important subclass of livelocks, which we refer to as *cycle-livelocks*, and show that they can be found by combining static analysis and bounded reachability.

---

[2] Variables are treated as finite width bit vectors and therefore do not hurt the model finiteness.

The property of deadlock has been the subject of many works. In the context of UML, [15] presents model checking for deadlocks via process algebra. The SPIN model checker itself supports checking for deadlocks. To the best of our knowledge, absence of livelocks has never been verified in the context of behavioral UML models.

We implemented our approach to verifying UML models with respect to LTL safety properties and cycle-livelocks in a tool called soft-UMC (**soft**ware-based **U**ML **M**odel **C**hecking). Our tool is built on top of the software model checker CBMC [8] which applies BMC to C programs and safety properties. We ran it on several UML examples and interesting properties, and found erroneous behaviors and livelocks. For safety properties, we also compared soft-UMC with an IBM research tool that verifies UML models via a translation to IBM's hardware model checker RuleBasePE [24]. Our experiments show that soft-UMC is more scalable and more robust for finding long counterexamples. Our experimental results also demonstrate the usefulness of the optimizations applied in the creation of the verifiable C code.

The rest of the paper is organized as follows. In Sec. 2 we present some background. Our translation to verifiable C code is presented in Sec. 3, and our method for verification of (LTL) safety properties and cycle-livelocks is presented in Sec 4. We show our experimental results in Sec 5, and conclude in Sec. 6.

2 Preliminaries

2.1 Behavioral UML Models

We use a running example describing a flight ticket ordering system to explain UML. The *class diagram* in Fig. 1(a)[3] shows the classes *DB* and *Agent* and the connection between them. The *object diagram* in Fig. 1(b) defines four objects, two of each class. These diagrams also show the attributes (variables) of each class and their *event receptions*. E.g., objects of class *DB* have two attributes ($isMyFlt$ and $space$) and are able to receive events of type $evReqOwnership$, $evReqFlt$, and $evGrantOwnership$.

UML objects process events. Event processing is defined by *statecharts* [13], which extend conventional state machines with hierarchy, concurrency and communication. The statecharts of DB and Agent classes are presented in Fig. 2.

Objects communicate by sending events (asynchronous messages). An event is a pair $(ev, trgt)$, where ev is the type of the sent event and $trgt$ is the target object of the event. Events are kept in an *event queue* (EQ), managed by an *event queue manager* (EQ-mgr). When object A sends an event to object B, the event is inserted into the EQ. The EQ-mgr executes a never-ending event-loop, taking an event from the EQ, and dispatching it to the target object. If the target object cannot process the event, the event is *discarded*. Otherwise, the event is *consumed* and the target object makes a *run-to-completion (RTC) step*, where it processes the event, and continues execution until it cannot continue anymore. Only when the target object finishes its RTC step, the EQ-mgr dispatches the next event available in the EQ[4].

---

[3] We used Rhapsody [23] to generate the drawings in this paper, and will accordingly use some of Rhapsody's terms and conventions.

[4] The order in which events are executed is under-specified in UML. We choose to follow the Rhapsody semantics, and implement event processing as a FIFO.

Every object is associated with a single EQ. In a multi-threaded model, there are several EQ-mgrs, and objects from different threads can communicate with each other. In this paper we focus on the case of a single thread, and will henceforth ignore the multi-threaded case.

Objects send events via the operation $GEN()$. For example, in the statechart of DB (Fig. 2(a)), when $db1$ executes the operation $itsA \rightarrow GEN(evFltAprv())$, an event of type $evFltAprv$ is sent to the target object on the relevant link. From the object diagram (Fig. 1(b)), we see that the target object is $a1$.

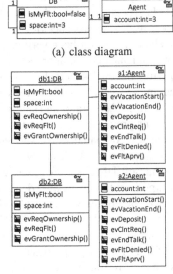

(a) class diagram

(b) object diagram

Fig. 1. Ticket Ordering System

Statecharts: The behavior of each object in the system is described by the *hierarchical statechart* associated with the class of the object. Hierarchical statecharts for classes DB and Agent are given in Fig. 2. For simplicity, in the rest of this section, notions related to statecharts and semantics are first defined for non-hierarchical statecharts. Needed definitions and notations are then extended for hierarchical statecharts as well.

We first define the following notions: A *guard* is a boolean expression over a set of attributes. The trivial guard is *true*. A *trigger* is the name of some event type. An *action* is a possibly empty sequence of statements in some programming language. A statechart of class Cls is a tuple $sc = (Q, T, init)$, where Q is a finite set of states, $init \in Q$ is the initial state, and T is a finite set of transitions. For every $t \in T$, $t = (q, b, e, a, q')$ where $q \in Q$ is the source state, b is a guard, e is either a trigger or nil, a is an action, and $q' \in Q$ is the destination state.

Transitions whose trigger is nil and whose guard is *true* are referred to as *null-transitions*. In a graphical representation of a statechart, states are marked as squares. Every transition t is marked with $trig[grd]/act$, representing the trigger, guard and action of t. If trigger is nil, guard is *true* or action is empty then they are omitted from the representation. The initial state is marked with a transition with no source (●▶).

We place a few restrictions on the statecharts language. We assume that every loop in a statechart includes at least one transition with a trigger. We also place restrictions on the action language and disallow dynamic allocation of objects and memory, dynamic pointers, unbounded loops, and recursion. This defines a restricted case of behavioral UML models, which is nevertheless relevant for embedded software. These restrictions enable us to focus on software based verification for UML models, while avoiding orthogonal issues such as termination and pointer analysis.

The Semantics of Behavioral UML Models: Let o be an object with statechart $sc(o)$, and attribute evaluation $\nu(o)$, where $\nu(o)$ is a function mapping all attributes of o to a value in the relevant domain. We say that a transition $t = (q, b, e, a, q')$ in $sc(o)$ is

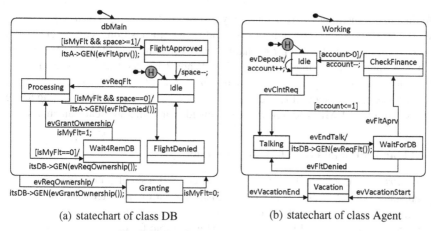

Fig. 2. Ticket Ordering System - Statecharts

enabled w.r.t. $\nu(o)$ and an event $ev = (e', o)$ if the following holds: b evaluates to *true* under $\nu(o)$, and e is either *nil* or $e = e'$. Let (e, o) be an event that was taken from the queue. Then q, the current state of $sc(o)$, and $\nu(o)$ determine how this event is processed. A transition t can be executed if its source is q and t is enabled w.r.t. $\nu(o)$ and (e, o). If there exists one or more transitions that can be executed from q, then one is executed non-deterministically. When transition t is executed from q, the *action* of t is executed, and the statechart reaches state q', which is the destination state of t.

Let (e, o) be an event dispatched to o, whose current state is q. An RTC step is a sequence of enabled transitions starting from q. The first transition in the sequence can be marked with a trigger or not[5]. The rest of the transitions are not marked with triggers. An RTC step terminates at a state q' that has no enabled outgoing transitions.

The following terminology will be needed later. Objects that can send some event (ev, o) are called *producers* of (ev, o). In our example, the (only) producer of event $(evReqOwnership, db1)$ is $db2$. Objects that can modify some attribute x of object o are called *modifiers* of (x, o). Let b be a guard in $sc(o)$, where b includes attributes $\{x_1, ..., x_m\}$. The set of modifiers of all attributes in b are called the modifiers of (b, o).

Hierarchical Statecharts: In hierarchical statecharts states can be either *simple* or *composite*. A composite state consists of a set of states, called its *substates*. A simple state has no substates. Every composite state includes an initial state. A composite state can also be defined with *history data*[6], marked by ⊕ in the statechart. This represents the most recent active substate of q.

Every hierarchical statechart includes a unique *top* state, which is not a substate of any other state. Hierarchical statecharts are denoted by $sc = (Q, T, top)$. A *h-state* $\bar{q} = (q_1, ..., q_n)$ of sc describes a full hierarchical path in sc, where $q_1 = top$, q_n is a simple state and for every $i > 0$, q_i is a substate of q_{i-1}. The initial h-state of sc is $\bar{q} = (q_1, ..., q_n)$ s.t. for every composite state q_i, q_{i+1} is the initial state of q_i.

---

[5] This point is under-specified in UML. We chose to follow the Rhapsody semantics.
[6] In this work we only consider shallow history.

We disallow transitions to cross hierarchy levels, i.e. for $t = (q, b, e, a, q')$, q and q' are substates of the same state. Given $\nu(o)$ and (e, o), a transition t can execute from h-state $\bar{q} = (q_1, ..., q_n)$ of $sc(o)$ if t is enabled w.r.t. $\nu(o)$ and (e, o) from q_i, $1 \leq i \leq n$, and no t' is enabled from any q_j, $i < j \leq n$. When t is executed, $sc(o)$ reaches the destination h-state $\bar{q}' = (q'_1, ..., q'_m)$ for some $m \geq i$ s.t.: (1) $\forall j.1 \leq j < i$, $q'_j = q_j$, (2) q'_i is the destination state of t, and (3) $\forall j.i < j \leq m$, q'_j is defined according to the history semantics of UML. From now on we consider only hierarchical statecharts.

2.2   LTL and Automata Based Model Checking

A *Kripke structure* is a tuple $M = (S, I_0, R)$, where S is a set of states, $I_0 \subseteq S$ is a set of initial states, and $R \subseteq S \times S$ is a total transition relation. An *execution* of M is an infinite set of states $s_0, s_1, ...$ s.t. for every $i \geq 0$, $(s_i, s_{i+1}) \in R$. .

The Linear-time Temporal Logic (LTL) [21] is suitable for expressing properties of a system along an execution path. We assume the reader is familiar with LTL. In this work we restrict ourselves to a fragment of LTL, in which only *safety properties* are expressible. These are properties whose violation occurs along a finite execution. [27] gives a syntactic characterization of safety properties.

A Kripke structure M satisfies an LTL formula ψ, denoted $M \models \psi$, if every execution of M starting at an initial state satisfies ψ. A general method for on-the-fly verification of LTL safety properties is based on a construction of a regular automaton $A_{\neg\psi}$, which accepts exactly all the executions that violate ψ. Given M and ψ, we construct $M \times A_{\neg\psi}$ to be the product of M and $A_{\neg\psi}$. A path in $M \times A_{\neg\psi}$ from an initial state (s, q) to a state (s', q') where q' is an accepting state in $A_{\neg\psi}$ represents an execution of M, and a word accepted by $A_{\neg\psi}$. It therefore represents an execution showing why M does not satisfy ψ. Such executions are called *counterexamples* for ψ.

2.3   Bounded Model Checking

Bounded Model Checking (BMC) [3] is an iterative process for checking models against LTL formulas. The transition relations for a Kripke structure M and its specification are jointly unwound for k steps and are represented by a boolean formula that is satisfiable iff there exists an execution of M of length k that violates the specification. The formula is then checked by a SAT solver. If the formula is satisfiable, a counterexample is extracted from the output of the SAT procedure. Otherwise, k is increased.

BMC is widely used for finding bugs in large systems, including software systems ([8,2,9]). BMC for software is performed by unwinding the loops in the program for k times, and verifying the required property. The property is often described by an assertion added to the program text. The model checker then searches for a program execution that violates the assertion. Our method for verifying UML models relies on invoking a software BMC tool. We require that the tool supports assumptions on the program, given as $assume(b)$ commands, where b is some boolean condition. Having $assume(b)$ at location ℓ of the program means that only executions π that satisfy b when passing at ℓ are considered. If b is violated then π is ignored.

2.4 Notations and Abbreviations

Throughout the rest of the paper we will use the following notations and abbreviations. A model includes N objects $\mathcal{M} = \{o_1, ..., o_N\}$. Every object o_i is associated with a statechart $sc(o_i) = (Q_i, T_i, top_i)$. For $t_i = (q, b, e, a, q')$ a transition in T_i: $grd(t_i) = b$, $ev(t_i) = e$ and $act(t_i) = a$. Given a state $q \in Q_i$:

- $trn(q) \subseteq T_i$ is the set of transitions whose source is q.
- $evnts(q) = \bigcup_{t \in trn(q)} \{(ev(t), i)\} \setminus \{(nil, i)\}$ is the set of triggers on $trn(q)$.
- $grds(q) = \bigcup_{t \in trn(q)} \{(grd(t), i)\}$ is the set of guards on $trn(q)$.
- $prod(q) \subseteq \{1, ..., n\}$ denotes indexes of producers of all events in $evnts(q)$. For example, if $evnts(q') = \{(ev, j)\}$, and the producers of (ev, o_j) are $\{o_{i_1}, ..., o_{i_k}\}$, then $prod(q') = \{i_1, ..., i_k\}$.
- $modif(q) \subseteq \{1, ..., n\}$ denotes indexes of modifiers of all guards in $grds(q)$.

These abbreviations are generalized to denote the transitions, events, guards, producers, and modifiers of an h-state and of a *subset* of states.

3   Translation to Verifiable Bounded C

We translate behavioral UML models to C. Our goal is to create code that is most suitable for verification, rather then an efficient implementation of the system. Moreover, we verify our code using a BMC verifier, therefore our code describes a bounded run of the model. In order to create code suitable for verification we avoid as much as possible the use of pointers or of methods called with different parameters. This results in code which is longer in lines-of-code. However, the model created by the verification tool is

```
1: method RunRTCStep_i(ev)
2: while (j < maxRTClen) do
3:   if (!enabled(currSt, ν_i, ev)) return
4:   choose Transition t
5:   assume(t ∈ trn(currSt))
6:   assume(val(t, currSt, ν_i, ev))
7:   execute act(t)
8:   ev := nil
9:   incr j
```

Fig. 3. $RunRTCStep_i$ method of o_i

smaller, and the model checker can then perform optimizations more efficiently.

The atomic unit in our translation is a *single RTC step*, rather than a single transition. Every object is translated into a method, representing the behavior of its associated statechart. When an event ev is dispatched to object o_i, the method associated with o_i executes a single RTC step of o_i.

Fig. 3 presents $RunRTCStep_i$, the pseudo-code for a single RTC step of o_i. $currSt$ is the current h-state of o_i in $sc(o_i)$. $enabled(currSt, \nu_i, ev)$ is *true* iff there exists an enabled transition $t \in trn(currSt)$ w.r.t. ν_i and event ev. The method terminates when there are no enabled transitions to execute. The while loop iterates up to $maxRTClen$ iterations. $maxRTClen$ represents the maximum number of transitions of any RTC step of o_i. If this value cannot be extracted by static analysis, then the condition is replaced by *true*, and the length of the RTC step is bounded by the BMC bound, k.

$val(t, currSt, \nu_i, ev)$ is *true* iff t can be executed from $currSt$ w.r.t. ν_i and event ev. Lines 4-6 amount to a non-deterministic choice of a transition t, which can be executed from $currSt$. When choosing a transition (line 4), no constraints are assumed on it. Line 5 restricts the program executions to those where t is a transition from $currSt$. Line 6 restricts the remaining program executions to those where t can execute. In line 7 the action of the transition is executed. Executing the action updates the $currSt$ according to the destination state of t. Note line 8, where we set the event to nil. This is done since the event is consumed once, and only in the first transition of the RTC step. The rest of the transitions of the RTC step can be executed only if their trigger is nil.

The EQ is represented as a bounded array. The main method of the program executes the never-ending loop of taking an event from the EQ, and dispatching it to the relevant target object. Fig. 4 presents the pseudo-code for the main method. In line 3 an event ev whose target is o_i is taken from the EQ. In line 4 an RTC step of o_i is initiated.

When applying BMC on the main method in Fig. 4, the while loop is unrolled k times, which means that the model is verified for k RTC steps. Generally, placing a bound on the EQ can make the model inaccurate due to overflows. However, k is the exact bound for a k-bounded verification over k RTC steps, since only the first k events that are sent will be dispatched during k RTC steps.

```
1: method main
2: while (true) do
3:    (ev, o_i) := popEv()
4:    RunRTCStep_i(ev)
```

Fig. 4. main method

Another verification oriented optimization we introduce is in the implementation of the environment. The array is initialized with k environment events, but with $head = tail = 1$. When a system event evS is sent, the tail is incremented non-deterministically, after which evS is added to the EQ, overriding the environment event there. This models inserting to the EQ a non-deterministic number of environment events that arrive prior to the addition of evS to the EQ.

C code can be automatically generated by UML tools such as Rhapsody, but this code would not be suitable for verification. Automatically generated code includes generic code, and means for communicating with different libraries and with the operating system. We, on the other hand, are interested in verifying only the user-created behavior of the system, and therefore we can abstract the event queue and the operating system. We exploit features of the model-checker, such as the assume construct, to make the verification more efficient. Assuming a static model allows us to implement links by direct calls rather than using pointers.

4   Model Verification

We now describe our method for verification of a given behavioral UML model. The model includes N objects $\mathcal{M} = \{o_1, ..., o_N\}$. Verification is done using assertions on the code describing the model. We support verification in a granularity of transition level or RTC level. First, we define the notion of *configuration* (CONF) of a UML model.

Definition 1. *A configuration (CONF) of $\mathcal{M}$ is $C = (q, \nu, EQ)$, where:*

- $q = (\bar{q}_1, ..., \bar{q}_N)$ *is a* system state *where $\bar{q}_i$ is a h-state of $sc(o_i)$.*

- $\nu = (\nu(o_1), ..., \nu(o_N))$ *is an* evaluation vector; $\nu(o_i)$ *is attribute evaluation of* o_i.
- $EQ = ((e_1, i_1), ..., (e_m, i_m))$ *is an event queue with m elements, where* (ev_j, i_j) *represents event ev_j whose target is o_{i_j}. (e_1, i_1) is the top, denoted top(EQ).*

A behavioral UML model $\mathcal{M}$ can be viewed as a Kripke structure $M = (S, I_0, R)$, where S is the set of all possible CONFs in $\mathcal{M}$. R can be defined either at the *RTC level* (denoted R_{RTC}) or at the *transition level* (denoted R_t). $(C, C') \in R_{RTC}$ iff C' is reachable from C in a single RTC step. $(C, C') \in R_t$ iff C' is reachable from C in an execution of a single transition. Executions are defined at *RTC* or *transition* level.

Definition 2. $\pi_r = C_0, C_1, ...$ *is an* execution at the RTC level (RTC-execution) *iff for every $n > 0$, $(C_{n-1}, C_n) \in R_{RTC}$.*

Definition 3. $\pi_t = C_0, C_1, ...$ *is an* execution at the transition level (t-execution) *iff for every $n > 0$, $(C_{n-1}, C_n) \in R_t$, and π_t represents an execution of RTC steps. That is, for every $i \geq 0$, there exist $j \leq i$ and $m \geq i$ s.t. $C_j, ..., C_m$ represents a single RTC step.*

For the rest of the paper, when an execution is either a t-execution or an RTC-execution, we refer to it as an *execution*. In the following we first present how model checking of an LTL safety property over a given behavioral UML model is done. We then continue to present our algorithm for verifying cycle-livelocks.

4.1 Verifying LTL Safety Properties

We now show how to verify safety LTL properties over behavioral UML models using an automata based approach. We assume the atomic propositions of the property are predicates over the CONFs of the model. We extend the C program created from $\mathcal{M}$ with a method representing the automaton $A_{\neg\psi}$. The method runs in lock step with the system, and identifies property violations.

A safety property can be verified either at the RTC level or at the transition level, by placing the call to the automaton method either at the end of each RTC step (within the method $main$) or at the end of each transition (within the method $RunRTCStep_i$). The choice of the level for verification depends on the property to be verified. For example, in our running example we might want to guarantee that, at the end of RTC steps $isMyFlt$ cannot be $true$ for both $db1$ and $db2$ at the same time. This property must not necessarily hold during an RTC step. We would therefore verify $AG^7(db1.isMyFlt = 0 \lor db2.isMyFlt = 0)$ at the RTC level. If we want to check for dead states (unreachable states) we need to work at the transition level in order to recognize as reachable also those states that are passed through during the RTC step.

Note that our method for BMC can be extended to proof by k-induction [26] in a straightforward manner. The base case is a BMC of k steps, which is done in the way we described above. The step is a BMC run of $k + 1$ steps with the initial state completely non-deterministic, looking for a run in which a property violation occurs at the $k + 1$ step after k steps with no violation. In the initial state of the step case we assume there may already be any number of events in the queue, of any type. We can

---

^{7} G is the temporal operator with the meaning of "globally".

still bound the event queue to $k + 1$ entries because no more than $k + 1$ events will be dispatched in $k + 1$ steps, making it sound to ignore the content of the queue beyond $k + 1$ entries.

4.2   Verify Cycle-Livelocks

A Livelock describes the case where *part of the system* cannot progress, even though the other parts of the system do. In this section we focus on finding livelocks in behavioral UML models. As mentioned before, absence of livelocks in neither safety nor LTL property and therefore cannot be handled by scalable bounded model checking tools. For that reason, we identify a subclass of livelocks, and present a method for finding such livelocks within our framework. This is done by a reduction to a safety property, which requires a preceding syntactic analysis of the UML model.

We first define the notion of a *livelock CONF* in behavioral UML models.

Definition 4. *Given a CONF $C = (q, \nu, EQ)$, where $q = (\bar{q}_1, ..., \bar{q}_N)$. We say that o_i is disabled under C if no transition $t \in trn(\bar{q}_i)$ is enabled.*

Definition 5. *Given a CONF C, object o_i is stuck at C if for every RTC-execution $\pi = C_0, C_1, ...$ s.t. $C_0 = C$ the following holds: for every $C_j = (q, \nu, EQ)$ s.t. $j \geq 0$, if $top(EQ) = (ev, i)$ then o_i is disabled under C_j.*

Thus, an object o_i is stuck if whenever the event at the top of the queue is targeted at o_i, meaning it is o_i's turn to execute, o_i is disabled and cannot make any progress.

Definition 6. *A CONF C is a* livelock CONF *if at least one object is stuck at C.*

Following, we present a characterization for a subclass of livelock CONFs, which we call *cycle-livelocks*. Intuitively, a CONF C is a cycle-livelock if there is a subset of objects that are stuck at C, and for every object o in the subset all of the producers of events that o is stuck on, and all of the modifiers of the guards that o is stuck on, are in the subset as well.

Definition 7. *Let $C = (q, \nu, EQ)$ where $q = (\bar{q}_1, ..., \bar{q}_N)$. A $q' = (\bar{q}'_1, ..., \bar{q}'_N)$ is a* partial state *of C if for every $1 \leq i \leq N$, $\bar{q}'_i = nil$ or $\bar{q}'_i = \bar{q}_i$.*

Definition 8. *Let C be a livelock CONF, and let $q' = (\bar{q}'_1, ..., \bar{q}'_N)$ be partial state of C. q' is a* livelock state *of C if $\forall i.1 \leq i \leq N$, if $\bar{q}'_i \neq nil$ then o_i is stuck at C.*

Definition 9. *CONF C is a* cycle-livelock *if there exists a livelock state of C, $q' = (\bar{q}'_1, ..., \bar{q}'_N)$ s.t. for all $j \in prod(q') \cup modif(q')$, $q'_j \neq nil$.*

Intuitively, the partial state describes a set of objects that are stuck and will stay stuck forever. This is because all objects that may "release" a stuck object by producing an event or changing a guard are in the same set. That is, they are stuck as well.

Our goal is to find *reachable* cycle-livelock CONFs. To achieve scalability, we use SAT-based BMC and only find livelock CONFs that are reachable within k RTC steps. Our method for finding reachable cycle-livelocks consists of two stages. We first identify system states that are *cycle-states*. This is a *syntactic* identification and can thus be checked independently of a CONF. This stage is performed during the analysis of the UML model. We then search for a reachable cycle-livelock CONF. This is done by adding an assertion describing the fact that the current CONF is a cycle-livelock. We then apply BMC to search for a violation of the assertion. Next we define the syntactic notion of cycle-state.

Finding Cycle-States: An object o_i cannot be stuck at $C = (q, \nu, EQ)$ if $\bar{q}_i \in q$ has a null-transition, or if q_i has a transition that can be enabled by an environment event.

Definition 10. *An h-state $\bar{q}$ is potentially stuck if for every $t \in trn(\bar{q})$, t is not a null-transition, and if $ev(t)$ is an environment event, then $grd(t) \neq true$.*

Intuitively, a *cycle-state* represents a subset of objects that are all potentially stuck and dependant on each other, i.e. all the necessary producers are inside this subset.

Definition 11. *A cycle-state is a vector $q = (\bar{q}_1, ..., \bar{q}_N)$ s.t. $\forall 1 \leq i \leq N$, $\bar{q}_i = nil$ or $\bar{q}_i$ is a h-state of $sc(o_i)$, and the following holds for every $\bar{q}_i \neq nil$: (1) $\bar{q}_i$ is a potentially stuck h-state, and (2) There is no $j \in prod(\bar{q}_i) \cup modif(\bar{q}_i)$ s.t. $\bar{q}_j = nil$, and (3) q is minimal. That is, let $q' = (\bar{q}'_1, ..., \bar{q}'_N)$ be a system state vector where $\forall 1 \leq i \leq N$, $\bar{q}'_i \neq nil \Rightarrow \bar{q}'_i = \bar{q}_i$. If $q' \neq q$ then req. 2 does not hold for q'.*

The requirement of minimality (requirement (3)) is introduced for the sake of efficiency. It reduces the number of states to be considered and also simplifies the encoding in BMC. Further, it reduces the number of similar counterexamples returned to the user.

Note that this definition is *syntactic*. That is, it depends only on the system state vector. It does not depend on the evaluation vector or the event queue, which can be determined along an execution. As a result, the set of all cycle-states can be identified independently of any configuration. We generate this set from the syntactic structure of the model, as part of the analysis of the UML model.

Lemma 1. *The set of cycle-states is* complete. *Meaning for every cycle-livelock configuration C there exists a partial state of C, q, that is a cycle-state.*

The set of CONFs is infinite, because the size of the EQ is not limited, and the domain of the evaluation vector can be infinite. However, the set of cycle-states is finite.

Bounded Search for Cycle-Livelocks: We observe that if a given CONF includes a cycle-state s.t. for every transition in the cycle-state either the guard is false or the trigger is a system event which is not in the EQ, then this CONF is a cycle-livelock.

We adapt the translation of UML models to C (Sec. 3) to allow checking whether a cycle-livelock CONF is reachable by adding assertions at the RTC level. When the model checker finds an execution violating the assertion, the last CONF in the execution is a cycle-livelock CONF. Fig. 5 presents the pseudo-code of the modified method. Line 5 and 6 show the added code.

$currC = (q, \nu, EQ)$ represents the current CONF of the system. At every iteration of the `while` loop $currC$ changes (due to the RTC step). The method $partSt(q, C)$ receives a cycle-state q and a CONF C, and returns $true$ iff q is a partial state of C. The method $grdFalse(grd, \nu)$ returns $true$ iff grd is $false$ w.r.t. ν_i. The method $notInQ(ev, EQ)$ returns $true$ iff ev is a system event which is not in the EQ. The assertion is violated on C if C is a cycle-livelock.

There is one subtle point that still needs to be solved: We need a finite representation of the queue. Recall that for verifying safety properties, for k-bounded executions we bound the queue to k. However, when searching for cycle-livelocks this is incorrect because a configuration is a cycle-livelock if there are *no future* executions that can release the stuck states. Thus, we must keep track of *all* events inserted into the queue (within k RTC steps). However, only the first k events are dispatched, and therefore their

---

```
1: method FindCycleLivelock()
2: while (true) do
3:    (ev, i) := popEv()
4:    RunRTCStep_i(ev)
5:    for each cycle-state q' do
6:       assert(!(partSt(q', currC)∧
             for all t ∈ trn(q') :
               notInQ(ev(t), EQ)∨
               grdFalse(grd(t), ν)))
```

Fig. 5. $FindCycleLivelock$ method

relative order is important. For the rest of the events, we only need to know whether they were sent or not. indicating whether or not an instance of that event exists in the "actual" queue. The method $notInQ(ev, EQ)$ returns $true$ iff the flag of event ev is $false$, indicating that no such event is in the "actual" queue.

We exemplify our method on our running example. The events $evVacationStart$ and $evVacationEnd$, which are consumed by class Agent, are both environment events. Note that none of the h-states associated with the statechart of Agent are potentially stuck h-states. Thus, $a1$ and $a2$ can never be stuck. The system state vector $(Wait4RemDB, Wait4RemDB, nil, nil)$ is a cycle-state because the producer of state $Wait4RemDB$ of $db1$ is $db2$, and vice-versa. Note that for finding $prod(Wait4RemDB)$, we include the producers of both $Wait4RemDB$ and $dbMain$, since $Wait4RemDB$ is a substate of $dbMain$. For this cycle-state, we add the following assertion:

$$assert(!(!InEQ(evGrantOwnership, 1) \wedge !InEQ(evGrantOwnership, 2) \wedge$$
$$!InEQ(evReqOwnership, 1) \wedge !InEQ(evReqOwnership, 2) \wedge$$
$$partSt((Wait4RemDB, Wait4RemDB, nil, nil), currC)))$$

Note that it is possible to skip the first stage of our algorithm, that finds the set of cycle-states, and incorporate it within the second stage. However, this would be inefficient due to the number of checks that would need to be done during the model checking stage. Further, since the first stage is applied to the UML model, it is quite "light weight". Model checking, on the other hand, is applied to a low-level description and is a heavy task. Thus, the first stage is essential for the scalability of our method.

5   Experimental Results

We have implemented the algorithm described above in a tool called Soft-UMC (**soft**ware-based **U**ML **M**odel **C**hecking). The implementation reads a UML (version 2.0) model, and translates it to verifiable C code. Static analysis is applied at this stage, according to the type of property to be checked: (LTL) safety or livelock. We then apply CBMC[8] (version 4.1) as our C verifier.

First, we compared our implementation to one translating the model to the input language of RuleBasePE[24], IBM's hardware model checker (we call this solution HWMC). HWMC represents the EQ as a bounded FIFO, where the size of the FIFO is relative to the maximum number of events generated in a single RTC step. It also preserves the hierarchical structure of the model.

To compare the performance of Soft-UMC and HWMC we used the following four examples. (1) A variant of the railroad crossing system from [22], including a gate object and three track objects that communicate with the gate, (2) The ticket ordering model (Figs. 1,2), (3) A dishwasher machine (inspired by the example provided with Rhapsody), (4) A locking model, including a manager and three lock clients. We have checked several safety properties on the models. In Fig. 6 we present a comparison of the runtime for finding a counterexample in Soft-UMC and HWMC. It can be seen that HWMC is better on short counterexamples. However, on long ones Soft-UMC achieves results in shorter times. This can be explained by the initialization time of CBMC which is significant for short counterexamples but becomes negligible on long ones.

	Soft-UMC		HWMC	
prop.	time	#RTCs	time	# trans
RC1	155	10	44	34
RC2	198	11	145	39
RC3	868	17	2315	57
TO1	17	6	14	8
TO2	23	7	14	13
TO3	51	10	28	31
TO4	514	22	1425	67
DW1	263	12	58	37
DW2	304	18	40	95
DW3	986	30	1345	155
LM1	18	7	12	19
LM3	101	16	79	86
LM2	158	14	1320	37
LM4	555	34	645	176

Fig. 6. Soft-UMC vs. HWMC. time in secs. $\sharp$RTC and $\sharp$trans is number of RTC steps and transitions in counterexamples.

To check the scalability of our tool compared to HMWC, we considered three parameterized examples: The ticket ordering model, and variations of the dishwasher machine and the locking model. E.g., for the ticket ordering model, the attribute *account* of *Agent* is used as the parameter, and the checked property is non-determinism. For increasing initial values of *account*, the counterexample leading to a non-deterministic state is of increasing length. This allows us to experiment on the same model with different lengths of counterexamples. In all examples, a counterexample for a model with parameter i is of length $\sim 2*i$ RTC steps. Each RTC step is composed of 3-5 transitions. We used a timeout of 1 hour. Results are presented in Fig 7. From the comparison it is clear that HWMC is better for shallow examples, however our tool is more scalable.

We also evaluated the performance impact of two of our optimizations, the EQ (Sec. 3) and the hierarchical model. We compared a naive implementation of the EQ against our optimized implementation. To analyze the impact of maintaining the hierarchy of the model we created a flat model of the ticket ordering model. The flat model has 24 states and 54 transitions, whereas the hierarchical model has 26 states and 36 transitions. The flat model is missing the

param	Soft-UMC TO	HWMC TO	Soft-UMC DW	HWMC DW	Soft-UMC LM	HWMC LM
5	49	21	82	23	34	30
8	113	92	242	34	101	71
11	202	380	475	66	192	180
14	364	1830	825	254	328	187
17	693	3470	1326	810	555	613
20	1740	T.O	1964	T.O	766	789
23	T.O	T.O	2900	T.O	1153	889
26	T.O	T.O	T.O	T.O	1657	1876
29	T.O	T.O	T.O	T.O	1859	2142
32	T.O	T.O	T.O	T.O	3049	T.O

Fig. 7. Compare scalability. time in secs.

hierarchical states. However, it has an additional attribute for maintaining the history. Fig 8 shows the results of the comparison. We compared the runtime of 4 different implementations: Hierarchical model with optimized EQ (H-OP-EQ), flat model with

optimized EQ (F-OP-EQ), hierarchical model with naive EQ (H-NV-EQ) and flat model
with naive EQ (F-NV-EQ).

We verified three different properties, and modified the model s.t. counterexample is reached at different bounds. 1,3 are safety properties. 2 is a livelock check, checked on a slightly modified model: the guard of transition from *Processing* to *FlightApproved* of *DB* (Fig. 2(a)) is modified to [*isMyFlt* && (*space* > 1)]. This introduces a reachable livelock state, when *db*1 and *db*2 are in state *Processing*, *space* = 1 and *isMyFlt* = *true* for both objects. Each row in Fig 8 represents a different setting defined by the property and the initial values of the attributes, which determine the

#RTC	H-OP-EQ	F-OP-EQ	H-NV-EQ	F-NV-EQ
#1 6	21	31	369	396
10	63	94	3362	T.O
18	224	420	T.O	T.O
26	524	1235	T.O	T.O
#2 10	88	133	T.O	T.O
20	818	3157	T.O	T.O
#3 6	21	32	371	420
10	72	103	T.O	T.O
14	275	550	T.O	T.O

Fig. 8. Optimizations on ticket ordering. Bound in RTC steps; time in secs.

length of the counterexample (in RTC steps). Time limit is set to 1 hour. It is clear that the optimized implementation of the EQ scales much better w.r.t. the naive EQ implementation. This is because the naive implementation includes a loop representing the addition of a non-deterministic number of environment events to the EQ. In the optimized implementation this amounts to a non-deterministic increment of the tail. The comparison also shows that the hierarchical implementation scales better than the flat one. Our conjecture is that flattening increases the number of transitions in the model, and therefore increases the search space. [11] presents similar results when comparing verification of hierarchical UML models to flat models. The above shows the significance of optimizations. We expect to be able to further improve performance of our solution with other optimizations.

6   Conclusions

This work is a first step in exploiting software model checking techniques for the verification of behavioral UML models. By translating UML models to C we could preserve the high-level structure of the model. We intend to further exploit this structure in techniques such as abstraction and modularity in order to enhance UML verification.

Our translation to *verifiable* C code rather than executable one significantly eased the workload of the model checker. This is demonstrated, for instance, by the comparison of our optimized representation of the event queue with a naive one. In our translation we also took advantage of the fact that *bounded* model checking is applied, and obtained a finite representation in spite of the unbounded size of the queue. Nevertheless, our method can be extended to *unbounded* model checking by means of k-induction.

The comparison with IBM's hardware oriented tool for UML verification demonstrates that our approach is superior for long counterexamples.

Our approach to finding cycle-livelocks in UML models is novel. Static analysis identifies *syntactically* potential cycle-livelock states. A suitable finite representation of the event queue then enables to apply BMC for finding reachable such states. We expect similar approaches to be useful for proving additional non-safety properties.

References

1. Majzik, I., Darvas, A., Beny, B.: Verification of UML Statechart Models of Embedded Systems. In: DDECS (2002)
2. Armando, A., Mantovani, J., Platania, L.: Bounded Model Checking of Software Using SMT Solvers Instead of SAT Solvers. STTT 11(1) (2009)
3. Biere, A., Cimatti, A., Clarke, E., Zhu, Y.: Symbolic Model Checking without BDDs. In: Cleaveland, W.R. (ed.) TACAS 1999. LNCS, vol. 1579, pp. 193–207. Springer, Heidelberg (1999)
4. Booch, G., Rumbaugh, J.E., Jacobson, I.: The Unified Modeling Language User Guide. J. Database Manag. 10(4) (1999)
5. Chan, W., Anderson, R.J., Beame, P., Burns, S., Modugno, F., Notkin, D., Reese, J.D.: Model Checking Large Software Specifications. IEEE Trans. Software Eng. 24(7) (1998)
6. Clarke, E.M., Grumberg, O., Peled, D.A.: Model Checking. MIT Press (1999)
7. Clarke, E.M., Heinle, W.: Modular Translation of Statecharts to SMV. Technical Report, CMU (2000)
8. Clarke, E., Kroning, D., Lerda, F.: A Tool for Checking ANSI-C Programs. In: Jensen, K., Podelski, A. (eds.) TACAS 2004. LNCS, vol. 2988, pp. 168–176. Springer, Heidelberg (2004)
9. Cordeiro, L., Fischer, B., Marques-Silva, J.: SMT-Based Bounded Model Checking for Embedded ANSI-C Software. In: ASE (2009)
10. Csertán, G., Huszerl, G., Majzik, I., Pap, Z., Pataricza, A., Varró, D.: VIATRA - Visual Automated Transformations for Formal Verification and Validation of UML Models. In: ASE (2002)
11. Dubrovin, J., Junttila, T.A.: Symbolic Model Checking of Hierarchical UML State Machines. In: ACSD (2008)
12. Object Management Group. OMG Unified Modeling Language (UML) Infrastructure, version 2.4. ptc/2010-11-16 (2010)
13. Harel, D.: Statecharts: A Visual Formalism for Complex Systems. Sci. Comp. Prog. 8(3) (1987)
14. Jussila, T., Dubrovin, J., Junttila, T., Latvala, T., Porres, I.: Model Checking Dynamic and Hierarchical UML State Machines. In: MoDeVa (2006)
15. Kaveh, N.: Using Model Checking to Detect Deadlocks in Distributed Object Systems. In: Emmerich, W., Tai, S. (eds.) EDO 2000. LNCS, vol. 1999, pp. 116–128. Springer, Heidelberg (2001)
16. Latella, D., Majzik, I., Massink, M.: Automatic Verification of a Behavioural Subset of UML Statechart Diagrams Using the SPIN Model-checker. Formal Asp. Comput. 11(6) (1999)
17. Mikk, E., Lakhnech, Y., Siegel, M., Holzmann, G.J.: Implementing Statecharts in PROMELA/SPIN. In: WIFT (1998)
18. Ober, I., Graf, S., Ober, I.: Validating Timed UML Models by Simulation and Verification. STTT 8(2) (2006)
19. IST-2001-33522 OMEGA (2001), http://www-omega.imag.fr
20. Lilius, J., Paltor, I.P.: Formalising UML State Machines for Model Checking. In: France, R.B. (ed.) UML 1999. LNCS, vol. 1723, pp. 430–444. Springer, Heidelberg (1999)
21. Pnueli, A.: The Temporal Logic of Programs. In: FOCS (1977)
22. Prashanth, C.M., Shet, K.C., Elamkulam, J.: An Efficient Event Based Approach for Verification of UML Statechart Model for Reactive Systems. In: ADCOM (2008)
23. Rhapsody, http://www-01.ibm.com/software/awdtools/rhapsody

24. RuleBasePE,
http://www.haifa.ibm.com/projects/
verification/RB_Homepage/
25. Schinz, I., Toben, T., Mrugalla, C., Westphal, B.: The Rhapsody UML Verification Environment. In: SEFM (2004)
26. Sheeran, M., Singh, S., Stålmarck, G.: Checking Safety Properties Using Induction and a SAT-Solver. In: Johnson, S.D., Hunt Jr., W.A. (eds.) FMCAD 2000. LNCS, vol. 1954, pp. 108–125. Springer, Heidelberg (2000)
27. Sistla, A.P.: Safety, Liveness and Fairness in Temporal Logic. Formal Asp. Comput. 6(5) (1994)

Reachability Analysis of the HTML5 Parser Specification and Its Application to Compatibility Testing

Yasuhiko Minamide and Shunsuke Mori

University of Tsukuba, Japan

Abstract. A draft standard for HTML, HTML5, includes the detailed specification of the parsing algorithm for HTML5 documents, including error handling. In this paper, we develop a reachability analyzer for the parsing specification of HTML5 and automatically generate HTML documents to test compatibilities of Web browsers. The set of HTML documents are extracted using our reachability analysis of the statements in the specification. This analysis is based on a translation of the specification to a conditional pushdown system and on a new algorithm for the reachability analysis of conditional pushdown systems.

In our preliminary experiments, we generated 353 HTML documents automatically from a subset of the specification and found several compatibility problems by supplying them to Web browsers.

1 Introduction

A draft standard for HTML, HTML5 [Con12], includes the detailed specification of the parsing algorithm for HTML5 documents, including error handling. Although it is intended that this will solve compatibility issues in HTML parsing, several current implementations of Web browsers and parsing libraries have compatibility issues caused by the complexity of the specification.

In this paper, we develop an analyzer for the specification that checks the reachability of statements in the specification. We then apply the analyzer to generate a set of HTML documents automatically, which are used to test compatibilities of Web browsers with respect to the specification. The set of generated HTML documents enables path testing. That is, the tests cover both true and false cases for all conditional statements in the specification. The reachability analysis is based on a translation of the specification to a *conditional pushdown system* [LO10] and on a new algorithm for the reachability analysis of conditional pushdown systems.

In the first step of the development, we introduce a specification language to describe the parsing algorithm of HTML5 formally. We concentrate on the stage of parsing that follows tokenization, called tree construction in the specification. The algorithm for the tree-construction stage is specified in terms of a stack machine, with the behaviour for each input token being described informally in English. We formalize the specification by introducing an imperative programming language with commands for manipulating the stack. The distinctive

D. Giannakopoulou and D. Méry (Eds.): FM 2012, LNCS 7436, pp. 293–307, 2012.

feature of the specification is that the specification inspects not only the top of the stack, but also the contents of the whole stack. Furthermore, the parsing algorithm destructively modifies the stack for elements called formatting elements. However, we exclude formatting elements from our formalized specification because of difficulties with the destructive manipulation of the stack. This is the main limitation of our work.

Our reachability analysis of the specification is based on that for conditional pushdown systems. Esparza *et al.* introduced pushdown systems with checkpoints that has the ability to inspect the contents of the whole stack and showed that they can be translated to ordinary pushdown systems [EKS03]. Li and Ogawa reformulated their definition and called them conditional pushdown systems [LO10]. The translation to ordinary pushdown systems causes the size of the stack alphabet to increase exponentially, which makes direct translation infeasible for the implementation of the reachability analysis. To overcome this problem, we design a new algorithm for reachability analysis that is a direct extension of that for ordinary pushdown systems [BEM97, EHRS00]. Our algorithm is obtained by extending $\mathcal{P}$-automata that describe a set of configurations to automata with regular lookahead. Although it still has an exponential complexity, it avoids the exponential blowup caused by the translation before applying the reachability analysis.

We have developed a reachability analyzer for the HTML5 parser specification based on the translation to a conditional pushdown system and on the reachability analysis on it. A nontrivial subset of the tree-construction stage consisting of 24 elements and 9 modes is formalized in our specification language. In our preliminary experiments, we have generated 353 HTML documents automatically from the subset of the specification and found several compatibility problems by supplying them to Web browsers.

This paper is organized as follows. Section 2 reviews the HTML5 parser specification and introduces our language for formalizing the specification. The reachability analysis of the specification and its application to test-case generation are also discussed in this section. We introduce conditional pushdown systems and present a new algorithm for their reachability analysis in Section 3. The translation from the specification language to conditional pushdown systems is described in Section 4. In Section 5, we describe our implementation and present our experimental results. Finally, we discuss related work and conclude.

2   HTML5 Parser Specification and Reachability Analysis

2.1   HTML5 Parser Specification

The algorithm for the HTML5 parsing is specified as a stack machine whose behaviour depends on a variable called the *insertion mode*. The insertion mode keeps track of the part of an HTML document that the parser is processing, such as "initial", "in body", or "in table". The *stack of open elements* stores elements that have not yet been closed during parsing, and is used to match corresponding end tags and to handle errors. When the parser inserts a new HTML element, it appends the new element to the top element of the stack and pushes it onto the stack as follows.

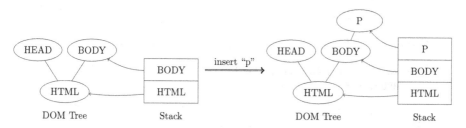

The specification is written in English and is quite complex. The following is part of the HTML5 specification for the "in body" insertion mode.

> ↪ *A start tag whose tag name is one of: ..., "p", ...*
> *If the stack of open elements has a p element in button scope, then act as if an end tag with the tag name "p" had been seen. Insert an HTML element for the token.*

The specification is sometimes rather difficult to interpret precisely, and it is not possible to analyze the specification mechanically.

The first step in the analysis of the specification is to introduce a specification language. Figure 1 is an example of a formalized specification using our specification language. The specification comprises a set of mode definitions, with each mode definition containing specifications of the behaviour for start and end tags in the mode. The behaviour for each tag is described as an imperative program that manipulates the stack of open elements with commands including PUSH and POP. We also allow the following commands:

- MODE[mode] changes the insert mode to mode. The change of mode affects the behaviour of the PSEUDO command below.
- PSEUDO[t] is basically a procedure call and the parser acts as if a tag t had been seen.
- ERROR records that an error is encoutered during parsing and does nothing in our model.

In the specification for each tag, the variable me refers to the element name for the tag. The command insertElement is currently defined as follows.

```
sub insertElement [target] = PUSH [target]
```

This definition is used because we are currently interested only in the reachability analysis of the specification and are ignoring the construction of the DOM tree.

The most notable feature of the specification language is the inspection of the current stack content. In the example, the current contents of the stack are inspected by a regular expression match[{H1 | H2} .*], where regular expression {H1 | H2} .* represents stacks whose top element is either H1 or H2.

```
mode inbody{
  <p> : {
    if isInScope[ buttonScopeElements, {P} ] then
      PSEUDO[</p>];
    insertElement[me]
  }
  <h1>, <h2> : {
    ...
    if match[ {H1 | H2} .* ] then{
      ERROR; POP
    };
    insertElement[me]
  }
  <table> : {
    insertElement[{Table}];
    MODE["intable"]
  }
  ...
}
```

Fig. 1. Example of a formalized specification

The stack of open elements is said to have an element in a specific scope consisting of a list of element types list when the following algorithm terminates in a match state:

1. Initialize node to be the current node (the bottommost node of the stack).
2. If node is the target node, terminate in a match state.
3. Otherwise, if node is one of the element types in list, terminate in a failure state.
4. Otherwise, set node to the previous entry in the stack of open elements and return to step 2. (This will never fail, since the loop will always terminate in the previous step if the top of the stack — an html element — is reached.)

Fig. 2. The algorithm of "have a element in a specific scope"

The real capability stack inspection is utilized in the definition for `<p>` as `isInScope[ buttonScopeElements, {P} ]`. It is the formalization of "have an element in a specific scope" and its specification is shown in Figure 2. Although the algorithm is rather complicated, the property can be checked by the following inspection of the stack using a regular expression:

```
fun isInScope [list,target] = match[ (element \ list)* target .* ]
```

where `element` is a variable representing the set of all elements, and therefore the set `element \ list` contains elements that exclude those in `list`.

In the formalization of the HTML5 specification, we also make explicit some of the implicit assumptions that appear in the specification. In the following example, it is assumed that, at this point, the stack of open elements will have either a "td" or "tr" element in the table scope.

```
mode inbody {
 <select> : { PUSH[ me ]; MODE["inselect"] }
}
mode inselect {
 <option>, <optgroup> : { PUSH[ me ] }

 </optgroup> : {
    if match[ {Option} {Optgroup} .* ] then
      POP    // (A)
    else
      NOP;   // (B)
    if match[ me .* ] then
      POP    // (C)
    else
      ERROR  // (D)
  }
}
```

Fig. 3. Example for reachability analysis

*If the stack of open elements has a td element in table scope, then act as
if an end tag token with the tag name "td" had been seen.
Otherwise, the stack of open elements **will have a th element in table
scope**; act as if an end tag token with the tag name "th" had been seen.*

We formalize this specification by using the command FATAL and show that
FATAL is not reachable by applying our reachability analyzer. Please note that
it is normal to reach an ERROR command because it just records the parser
encounter an ill-formed HTML document.

```
if isInTableScope [ { Td } ] then ...
else if isInTableScope [ { Th } ] then ...
else FATAL
```

2.2 Reachability Analysis and Test Generation

We analyze the reachability of specification points via translation to a conditional pushdown system. The main application is to test the compatibility of
HTML5 parsing with Web browsers and parsing libraries. Our reachability analyzer generates test cases that cover both true and false cases for all conditional
statements in the specification.

Let us consider the example shown in Figure 3. To cover both true and false
cases for all conditional statements, our reachability analyzer must check the
reachability of the points (A)–(D). By translating the specification to a conditional pushdown system and applying the reachability analysis described in
Section 3.2, the analyzer finds that the point (A) is reachable from the initial
state of inbody with the empty stack by the following input.

```
<select><optgroup><option></optgroup>
```

A test document is generated from this input by appending appropriate end tags as follows. By executing the interpreter of the specification language, we compute the stack after the execution for the above input. Before the execution of (A), we have stack Option, Optgroup, Select. The pop statements at (A) and (C) are then executed. The execution for the input then results in stack Select. We therefore generate the following HTML document as a test case by appending the end tag of Select.

```
<select><optgroup><option></optgroup></select>
```

By applying the same method, we obtain the following test cases for (B)–(D).

```
<select></optgroup></select>                // (B)
<select><optgroup></optgroup></select> // (C)
<select></optgroup></select>                // (D)
```

We can then test the compatibility of Web browsers by supplying test cases generated in this manner as HTML documents.

3 Conditional Pushdown Systems and Reachability Analysis

We translate our specification language into conditional pushdown systems of Li and Ogawa [LO10], which are a reformulation of pushdown systems with checkpoints [EKS03]. Conditional pushdown systems extend ordinary pushdown systems with the ability to check the contents of the whole stack against a regular language.

3.1 Regular Languages and Derivatives

We briefly review the theory of regular languages with a focus on the derivatives of regular languages [Brz64]. The theory of derivatives has drawn renewed attention as an implementation technique for parsing and decision procedures on regular languages [ORT09, KN11]. Let $\mathrm{Reg}(\Gamma)$ be the set of regular languages over Γ.

For $L \subseteq \Gamma^*$ and $w \in \Gamma^*$, the *derivative*[1] of L with respect to w is written as $w^{-1}L$ and defined as follows.

$$w^{-1}L = \{w' \mid ww' \in L\}$$

Brzozowski showed that there are a finite number of types of derivatives for each regular language. More precisely, the set $\{w^{-1}L \mid w \in \Gamma^*\}$ is finite for any regular language L over Γ. This fact is the key to the termination of our algorithm for the reachability analysis of conditional pushdown systems.

---

[1] The derivative $w^{-1}L$ is also called the left quotient in many litterateurs.

In this paper, regular languages are often described in terms of regular expressions. The syntax of regular expressions over Γ is defined as follows[2]:

$$R ::= \emptyset \mid \epsilon \mid \gamma \mid R \cdot R \mid R + R \mid R^*$$

where $\gamma \in \Gamma$. We write $L(R)$ for the language of regular expression R. We say that a regular expression R is nullable if $\epsilon \in L(R)$. We characterize nullable expressions in terms of following function $\nu(R)$.

$$\nu(\emptyset) = \emptyset \qquad\qquad \nu(\epsilon) = \epsilon$$
$$\nu(\gamma) = \emptyset \qquad\qquad \nu(R^*) = \epsilon$$
$$\nu(R_1 + R_2) = \nu(R_1) + \nu(R_2) \qquad \nu(R_1 \cdot R_2) = \nu(R_1) \cdot \nu(R_2)$$

Brzozowski showed that the derivative $\gamma^{-1}R$ of a regular expression can be computed symbolically using $\nu(R)$, as follows:

$$\gamma^{-1}\emptyset = \emptyset \qquad\qquad \gamma^{-1}\epsilon = \emptyset$$
$$\gamma^{-1}\gamma = \epsilon \qquad\qquad \gamma^{-1}\gamma' = \emptyset$$
$$\gamma^{-1}R^* = (\gamma^{-1}R)R^* \qquad \gamma^{-1}(R_1 + R_2) = \gamma^{-1}R_1 + \gamma^{-1}R_2$$

$$\gamma^{-1}R_1 \cdot R_2 = (\gamma^{-1}R_1)R_2 + \nu(R_1)(\gamma^{-1}R_2)$$

The derivative of a regular expression can be extended for words with $\epsilon^{-1}R = R$ and $(\gamma w)^{-1}R = w^{-1}(\gamma^{-1}R)$. We then have $w^{-1}L(R) = L(w^{-1}R)$.

Our implementation utilizes regular expressions extended with intersection and complement. The derivatives of extended regular expressions are computed similarly, as described in [ORT09]. The automaton corresponding to a regular expression is constructed only when we decide the language inclusion between two regular expressions.

3.2   Conditional Pushdown Systems

We now review conditional pushdown systems that have the ability to check the current stack contents against a regular language, and then present a new algorithm for the reachability analysis.

Definition 1. *A conditional pushdown system $\mathcal{P}$ is a structure $\langle P, \Gamma, \Delta \rangle$, where P is a finite set of states, Γ is a stack alphabet, and $\Delta \subseteq P \times \Gamma \times P \times \Gamma^* \times \mathrm{Reg}(\Gamma)$ is a set of transitions.*

A configuration of conditional pushdown system $\mathcal{P}$ is a pair $\langle p, w \rangle$ where $p \in P$ and $w \in \Gamma^*$. The set of all configurations is denoted by $\mathcal{C}$. We write $\langle p, \gamma \rangle \overset{R}{\hookrightarrow} \langle p', w \rangle$ if $\langle p, \gamma, p', w, R \rangle \in \Delta$. The reachability relation is defined as an extension of that for ordinary pushdown systems. A configuration $\langle p, \gamma w' \rangle$ is an immediate predecessor of $\langle p', ww' \rangle$ if $\langle p, \gamma \rangle \overset{R}{\hookrightarrow} \langle p', w \rangle$ and $w' \in R$: the regular language R

---

[2] For regular expressions in our specification language, we write alternation as $R_1 | R_2$ instead of $R_1 + R_2$.

inspects the current stack contents excluding its top. The reachability relation $\Longrightarrow$ is the reflexive and transitive closure of the immediate successor relation. Then, the predecessor function $\mathrm{pre}^* : 2^C \to 2^C$ is defined by $\mathrm{pre}^*(C) = \{c \mid \exists c' \in C.c \Longrightarrow c'\}$.

Let us consider the following conditional pushdown system $\mathcal{P}_1$ shown below. A transition labeled with $\gamma/w|R$ from p to p' denotes transition rule $\langle p, \gamma \rangle \overset{R}{\hookrightarrow} \langle p', w \rangle$, and a transition labeled with γ/w is an abbreviation of $\gamma/w|\Gamma^*$.

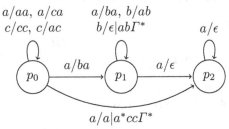

In the transition from p_0 to p_2, the condition $a^*cc\Gamma^*$ is used to check that two c's were pushed at p_0 consecutively. In the transition from p_1 to p_1, the condition $ab\Gamma^*$ is used to prevent the popping of the last b on the stack.

As discussed by Esparz *et al.* [EKS03], a conditional pushdown system can be translated into an ordinary pushdown system by expanding its stack alphabet. However, the translation causes the size of the stack alphabet and the transition relation to grow exponentially, and it is therefore not feasible to apply the translation for the reachability analysis directly.

3.3   New Algorithm for Reachability Analysis

We describe our new algorithm for the reachability analysis of conditional pushdown systems. The reachability analysis of ordinary pushdown systems represents a regular set of configurations with $\mathcal{P}$-automata [BEM97, EHRS00]. We directly extend the algorithm by representing a regular set of configurations with $\mathcal{P}$-automata using regular lookahead.

Given a conditional pushdown system $\mathcal{P} = \langle P, \Gamma, \Delta \rangle$, a $\mathcal{P}$-automaton uses P as a set of initial states and Γ as the input alphabet.

Definition 2. *A $\mathcal{P}$-automaton with regular lookahead is a structure $\mathcal{A} = \langle \Gamma, Q, \delta, P, F \rangle$, where Q is a finite set of states satisfying $P \subseteq Q$, $\delta \subseteq Q \times \Gamma \times Q \times \mathrm{Reg}(\Gamma)$ is a set of transition rules, and F is a set of final states.*

We introduce the transition relation of the form $q \overset{w|w'}{\longrightarrow} q$ for $\mathcal{P}$-automata with regular lookahead: it means that, at the state q, the automaton may consume w and change its state to q' if the rest of the input is w'. This is defined as follows:

- $q \overset{\epsilon|w}{\longrightarrow} q$ for any $q \in Q$ and any $w \in \Gamma^*$,
- $q \overset{\gamma|w}{\longrightarrow} q'$ if $\langle q, \gamma, q', R \rangle \in \delta$ and $w \in R$,
- $q \overset{w\gamma|w'}{\longrightarrow} q'$ if $q \overset{w|\gamma w'}{\longrightarrow} q''$ and $q'' \overset{\gamma|w'}{\longrightarrow} q'$.

Then, the set of configurations represented by $\mathcal{A}$ is defined as $\mathrm{Conf}(\mathcal{A}) = \{\langle p, w \rangle \mid p \in P \text{ and } p \xrightarrow{w|\epsilon} q \text{ for some } q \in F\}$.

To formulate our new algorithm for reachability analysis, we also extend the transition rules to those involving many steps, namely $q \xrightarrow{w|R} q'$, as follows:

- $q \xrightarrow{\epsilon|\Gamma^*} q$,
- $q \xrightarrow{\gamma|R} q'$ if $\langle q, \gamma, q', R \rangle \in \delta$,
- $q \xrightarrow{w\gamma|\gamma^{-1}R_1 \cap R_2} q'$ if $q \xrightarrow{w|R_1} q''$ and $q'' \xrightarrow{\gamma|R_2} q'$.

In the third case of the above definition, the two transition rules are combined by composing two lookahead sets via quotient and intersection: $\gamma^{-1}R_1 \cap R_2$. At the state q', $\gamma^{-1}R_1$ must be satisfied because the symbol γ is consumed by the transition from q'' to q'. The following lemma relates the extended transition rules to transitions.

Lemma 1.

- If $q \xrightarrow{w|R} q'$ and $w' \in R$, then $q \xrightarrow{w|w'} q'$.
- If $q \xrightarrow{w|w'} q'$, then $q \xrightarrow{w|R} q'$ and $w' \in R$ for some R.

The $\mathcal{P}$-automaton $\mathcal{A}_{\mathrm{pre}^*}$ representing $\mathrm{pre}^*(\mathrm{Conf}(\mathcal{A}))$ can be computed by extending the *saturation rule* of [BEM97]. That is, $\mathcal{A}_{\mathrm{pre}^*}$ is obtained by adding new transitions according to the following extended saturation rule:

- If $\langle p, \gamma \rangle \xhookrightarrow{R_1} \langle p', w \rangle$ and $p' \xrightarrow{w|R_2} q$ in the current automaton, add a transition rule $p \xrightarrow{\gamma|R_1 \cap R_2} q$.

Based on this saturation rule, we have also extended the efficient algorithm for the reachability analysis [EHRS00] in a straightforward manner.

The following lemma and the finiteness of derivatives of a regular language guarantee the termination of the application of the saturation rule.

Lemma 2. Let $\mathcal{R} = \{R \mid \langle q, \gamma, q', R \rangle \in \delta \text{ for some } q, \gamma, q'\}$.

If $q \xrightarrow{w|R} q''$, then $R = \bigcap \mathcal{R}'$ for some $\mathcal{R}' \subseteq \{w^{-1}R \mid R \in \mathcal{R} \wedge w \in \Gamma^*\}$.

Let us consider the previous conditional pushdown system $\mathcal{P}_1$. We apply the saturation algorithm to $\mathcal{P}_1$ to check the reachability to the set of configurations $C_1 = \{\langle p_2, w \rangle \mid w \in L(c(a + c)^* b\Gamma^*)\}$. The $\mathcal{P}_1$-automaton in Figure 4 excluding the dashed transitions represents C_1 by using lookahead. The dashed transitions are added by applying the saturation rule. The three transitions from p_0 to q_f are added from the top. This shows that the configuration C_1 is reachable from p_0 with a stack satisfying $(a + c)^+ b\Gamma^*$.

4 Translation to Conditional Pushdown Systems

In this section, we present the translation of the specification language to conditional pushdown systems.

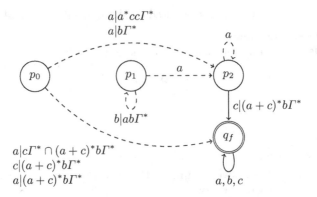

Fig. 4. $\mathcal{P}_1$-automaton obtained by the saturation algorithm

4.1 Expanding Pseudo Statements

The first step of the translation is to expand pseudo statements PSEUDO[t] at non-tail positions. This is necessary because PSEUDO[t] is basically a procedure call and its simulation requires another stack that is not synchronized with the stack of open elements. Pseudo inputs at tail positions can be translated directly into transitions of a pushdown automaton. To avoid infinite chains of inline expansion, we do not expand PSEUDO[t] inside the code for the tag t. In the following example, PSEUDO[</p>] in <p> and PSEUDO[<p>] in </p> should be expanded because they are not at tail positions.

```
<p> : {
  if isInButtonScope[ {P} ] then
    PSEUDO[</p>];
  insertElement[me]
}
</p> : {
  if !isInButtonScope [ {P} ] then {
    PSEUDO[<p>];   PSEUDO[</p>]
  } else {
    popuntil[{P}]
  }
}
```

We obtain the following code by expanding them. Because we cannot expand PSEUDO[<p>] in the code for <p>, it is translated into FATAL. If the FATAL introduced in this translation is reachable, then the translation will not be faithful. However, this is not the case in this example because PSEUDO[<p>] is constrained by isInButtonScope[{P}] and !isInButtonScope[{P}].

```
<p> : {
  if isInButtonScope[ {P} ] then {
    if !isInButtonScope [ {P} ] then {
      PSEUDO[<p>];   => FATAL
      PSEUDO[</p>]
```

```
  } else {
     popuntil[{P}]
  }
 }
 insertElement[me]
}
...
```

In order to check that **FATAL** statements introduced by this expansion are not reachable, we check their reachability after the translation to a conditional pushdown system. For the subset of the HTML5 specification we have formalized, our reachability analyzer showed that they are not reachable.

4.2 Translation to Conditional Pushdown Systems

After expansion of pseudo statements, a specification is translated to a conditional pushdown automaton. Then, a conditional pushdown system is obtained by forgetting the input of the pushdown automaton. Let us consider the following specification as an example.

```
</p> : {
  if match[ {Li}*{P}.* ] then {
    while !match[{P} .*] do POP; POP
  }
}
<p> : { PUSH[{P}] }
```

This can be converted into the following state transition diagram, where each transition is labeled with a tag indicating input, push, pop, or the condition under which the transition occurs.

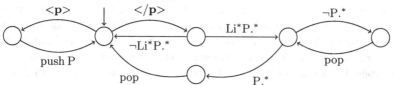

The transitions labeled with a tag, push, or pop can be translated directly to those of pushdown automata. The transition label with a regular expression representing the condition under which it occurs is translated as follows. Let us consider a transition labeled with a regular expression R from q to q'.

- For each γ in the stack alphabet, a transition $\langle q, \gamma \rangle \overset{\gamma^{-1}R}{\hookrightarrow} \langle q', \gamma \rangle$ is added to the pushdown automaton.

In this example, the previous state transition diagram is translated to the following conditional pushdown automaton under the stack alphabet $\{P, Li\}$:

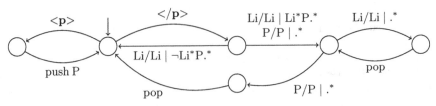

where push and pop are not translated for simplicity. The following derivatives are used in the translation.

$$Li^{-1}(Li^*P.^*) = (Li^{-1}(Li^*))P.^* + \nu(Li^*)Li^{-1}(P.^*) = Li^*P.^*$$
$$P^{-1}(Li^*P.^*) = (P^{-1}(Li^*))P.^* + \nu(Li^*)P^{-1}(P.^*)\ \ = .^*$$

5   Experimental Results

We have implemented the reachability analyzer of our specification language. It performs the translation from the specification language to conditional pushdown systems and reachability analyses for these systems. It is implemented in OCaml and based on the library for automata used in the PHP string analyzer [Min05].

The main application of the analyzer is to generate automatically a set of HTML test documents from a specification. It is also used to check the consistency of the specification and the translation. The current implementation checks for consistency in the following two respects.

- The execution of the specification cannot cause stack underflow.
- FATAL statements in the specification or introduced by the translation are unreachable.

The analyzer showed that these properties hold for the subset of the HTML5 parser specification described below.

We have formalized a nontrivial subset of the tree-construction stage of the HTML5 specification. It is 438 lines in length, excluding comments and empty lines, and contains the specification of 24 elements and 9 modes. This specification can be obtained from http://www.score.cs.tsukuba.ac.jp/~minamide/html5spec/model.html5. As we mentioned in the Introduction, this subset excludes the specification of formatting elements, which is one of the main limitations of our work to date.

We applied our reachability analyzer to the specification using a Linux PC with an Intel Xeon processor (3.0 GHz) and 16 GB memory. The specification is translated to a conditional pushdown automaton with 487 states, and there are 1186 specification points[3] whose reachability had to be checked. For these points, our reachability analyzer showed that 828 points were reachable from the initial state and generated 353 HTML documents excluding duplicates. In the following table, the first row shows the length of an input sequence of tags and

---

[3] In the implementation, a specification point is represented by a pair comprising a state and a regular expression. We may therefore have more specification points than states.

the second row shows the number of points. For example, there are 380 points for which the analyzer found an input sequence of length 3.

Length	1	2	3	4	5	6
# Points	46	167	380	198	35	2

The reachability of the specification points was checked by applying the algorithm described in Section 3.2 by adding the final states corresponding to them in the $\mathcal{P}$-automaton. It took 82 minutes to check the reachability of all the points and required more than 3 Gbyte of memory during the computation.

We conducted compatibility tests on the following Web browsers and HTML5 parser libraries: html5lib [htm] is implemented in Python and closely follows the specification, and htmlparser, the Validator.nu HTML parser [Val], is implemented in Java and has been used for HTML5 in the W3C markup validation service. The experiment was conducted on Mac OS X, version 10.7.3. The following table shows the number of incompatibilities found when using the generated set of 353 HTML documents. The numbers in parentheses are obtained after merging similar incompatibilities.[4]

	Safari	Firefox	Opera	IE [5]	html5lib	htmlparser
Version	5.1.3	10.0.1	11.61	–	0.95	1.3.1
# Incompatibilities	1	6	0	0	3	6
	(1)	(2)	–	–	(1)	(2)

The three main incompatibilities found in this experiment are listed below. The lines labeled 'Test' and 'Spec' are the HTML documents generated by our analyzer and the serialized representation of the results of parsing with the HTML5 specification, respectively. The incompatible results are shown following the Spec lines.

```
Test : <body><dd><optgroup><dd></dd></body>
Spec : <body><dd><optgroup></optgroup></dd><dd></dd></body>
       Safari, Opera, html5lib, IE
     : <body><dd><optgroup><dd></dd></optgroup></dd></body>
       Firefox, htmlparser
Test : <body><ruby><button><rp></rp></button></ruby></body>
Spec : <body><ruby><button><rp></rp></button></ruby></body>
       Opera, html5lib, IE
     : <body><ruby><button></button><rp></rp></ruby></body>
       Safari, Firefox, htmlparser
Test : <body><table><li><li></li></table></body>
Spec : <body><li></li><li></li><table></table></body>
       Safari, Firefox, Opera, htmlparser, IE
       <body><li></li><table><li></li></table></body>
       html5lib
```

---

[4] Some of the incompatibilities are caused by differences between versions of the HTML5 specification, which is discussed below.

[5] Consumer Preview, version 10.0.8250.0.

We have investigated the second case for Firefox. The specification for the start rp tag can be written as follows.

```
if isInScope[{Ruby}] then {
  generateImpliedEndTag[];
  if !match[ {Ruby} .* ] then ERROR
};
insertElement[me]
```

The code of Firefox does not correspond to this, but to the specification below. We found that this is compatible with the latest *published version* of the specification, W3C Working Draft 25 May 2011, although we were working with the Editor's Draft 22 February 2012.

```
if isInScope[{Ruby}] then {
  generateImpliedEndTag[];
  if !match[ {Ruby} .* ] then ERROR
  while !match[ {Ruby} .*] do POP;    <== Extra code in Firefox
};
insertElement[me]
```

6   Related Work

The reachability analysis of pushdown systems with checkpoints was studied by Esparza *et al.* as an application of LTL model checking of pushdown systems with regular valuations [EKS03]. They presented a translation to ordinary pushdown systems. Although reachability can be decided via the translation, it is not practical to apply the translation because of exponential blowup of the size of pushdown systems. They also showed that the reachability problem of pushdown systems with checkpoints is EXPTIME-complete.

Reachability can also be decided by translation to extensions of pushdown systems such as alternating pushdown systems and stack automata [GGH67]. An analysis for alternating pushdown systems is given in [BEM97] and that for stack automata is given in [HO08] as reachability analysis for higher-order pushdown systems. Although the translations to those systems do not incur exponential blowup, their algorithms are more complicated than our reachability analysis for conditional pushdown systems. An efficient algorithm for alternating pushdown systems was developed in [SSE06, Suw09]. However, only an algorithm for a restricted class with polynomial time complexity was implemented.

7   Conclusions

We have developed a reachability analyzer for the HTML5 parser specification based on the analysis of conditional pushdown systems. The analysis is applied to the automated generation of HTML documents for path testing of the specification. Several compatibility issues in Web browsers and HTML5 parsing libraries are found by supplying the documents to them.

One of the limitations of our work is that we cannot handle the specification for formatting elements. This is because their specification requires destructive manipulation of the stack. We are planning to address this limitation by checking the reachability to the first point where a destructive operation on the stack is required.

References

[BEM97] Bouajjani, A., Esparza, J., Maler, O.: Reachability Analysis of Pushdown Automata: Application to Model-Checking. In: Mazurkiewicz, A., Winkowski, J. (eds.) CONCUR 1997. LNCS, vol. 1243, pp. 135–150. Springer, Heidelberg (1997)

[Brz64] Brzozowski, J.: Derivatives of regular expressions. J. ACM 11, 481–494 (1964)

[Con12] World Wide Web Consortium. HTML5: Editor's draft 22 (February 2012), http://dev.w3.org/html5/spec/Overview.html

[EHRS00] Esparza, J., Hansel, D., Rossmanith, P., Schwoon, S.: Efficient Algorithms for Model Checking Pushdown Systems. In: Emerson, E.A., Sistla, A.P. (eds.) CAV 2000. LNCS, vol. 1855, pp. 232–247. Springer, Heidelberg (2000)

[EKS03] Esparza, J., Kucera, A., Schwoon, S.: Model checking LTL with regular valuations for pushdown systems. Information and Computation 186(2), 355–376 (2003)

[GGH67] Ginsburg, S., Greibach, S.A., Harrison, M.A.: Stack automata and compiling. J. ACM 14(1), 172–201 (1967)

[HO08] Hague, M., Ong, C.-H.L.: Symbolic backwards-reachability analysis for higher-order pushdown systems. Logical Methods in Computer Science 4, 1–45 (2008)

[htm] html5lib, http://code.google.com/p/html5lib/

[KN11] Krauss, A., Nipkow, T.: Proof pearl: Regular expression equivalence and relation algebra. J. Automated Reasoning (March 2011) (published online)

[LO10] Li, X., Ogawa, M.: Conditional weighted pushdown systems and applications. In: Proceedings of the 2010 ACM SIGPLAN Workshop on Partial Evaluation and Program Manipulation, pp. 141–150 (2010)

[Min05] Minamide, Y.: Static approximation of dynamically generated Web pages. In: Proceedings of the 14th International World Wide Web Conference, pp. 432–441. ACM Press (2005)

[ORT09] Owens, S., Reppy, J., Turon, A.: Regular-expression derivatives reexamined. J. of Functional Programming 19, 173–190 (2009)

[SSE06] Suwimonteerabuth, D., Schwoon, S., Esparza, J.: Efficient Algorithms for Alternating Pushdown Systems with an Application to the Computation of Certificate Chains. In: Graf, S., Zhang, W. (eds.) ATVA 2006. LNCS, vol. 4218, pp. 141–153. Springer, Heidelberg (2006)

[Suw09] Suwimonteerabuth, D.: Reachability in Pushdown Systems: Algorithms and Applications. PhD thesis, Technischen Universität München (2009)

[Val] Validator.nu. The validator.nu html parser, http://about.validator.nu/htmlparser/

Theory and Techniques for Synthesizing Efficient Breadth-First Search Algorithms

Srinivas Nedunuri[1], Douglas R. Smith[2], and William R. Cook[1]

[1] University of Texas at Austin
[2] Kestrel Institute

Abstract. Although Breadth-First Search (BFS) has several advantages over Depth-First Search (DFS) its prohibitive space requirements have meant that algorithm designers often pass it over in favor of DFS. To address this shortcoming, we introduce a theory of efficient BFS (EBFS), along with a simple recursive program schema for carrying out the search. The theory is based on dominance relations, a long standing technique from the field of search algorithms. We also show that greedy and greedy-like algorithms form a very useful and important sub-category of EBFS. Finally, we show how the EBFS class can be used for semi-automated program synthesis by introducing some techniques for demonstrating that a given problem is solvable by EBFS. We illustrate our approach on several examples.

1 Introduction

Program synthesis is experiencing something of a resurgence [SGF10, SLTB+06, GJTV11] [PBS11, VY08, VYY10] following negative perceptions of its scalability in the early 90s. Many of the current approaches aim for near-automated synthesis. In contrast, the approach we follow, we call *guided program synthesis*, also incorporates a high degree of automation but is more user-guided. The basic idea is to identify interesting classes of algorithms and capture as much *generic* algorithm design knowledge as possible in one place. The user instantiates that knowledge with problem-specific *domain* information. This step is often carried out with machine assistance. The approach has been applied to successfully derive scores of efficient algorithms for a wide range of practical problems including scheduling [SPW95], concurrent garbage collection [PPS10], and SAT solvers [SW08].

One significant class of algorithms that has been investigated is search algorithms. Many interesting problems can be solved by application of search. In such an approach, an initial search space is partitioned into subspaces, a process called *splitting*, which continues recursively until a *feasible* solution is found. A feasible solution is one that satisfies the given problem specification. Viewed as a search tree, spaces form nodes, and the subspaces after a split form the children of that node. The process has been formalized by Smith [Smi88, Smi10]. Problems which can be solved by global search are said to be in the Global Search (GS) class. The enhancements in GS over standard branch-and-bound include

D. Giannakopoulou and D. Méry (Eds.): FM 2012, LNCS 7436, pp. 308–325, 2012.
© Springer-Verlag Berlin Heidelberg 2012

a number of techniques designed to improve the quality of the search by eliminating unpromising avenues. One such technique is referred to as *dominance relations*. Although they do not appear to have been widely used, the idea of dominance relations goes back to at least the 70s [Iba77]. Essentially, a dominance relation is a relation between two nodes in the search tree such that if one dominates the other, then the dominated node is guaranteed to lead to a worse solution than the dominating one, and can therefore be discarded. Establishing a dominance relation for a given problem is carried out by a user. However this process is not always obvious. There are also a variety of ways in which to carry out the search, for example Depth-First (DFS), Breadth-First (BFS), Best-First, etc. Although DFS is the most common, BFS actually has several advantages over DFS were it not for its exponential space requirement. The key to carrying out BFS space-efficiently is to limit the size of the frontier at any level. However, this has not been investigated in any systematic manner up to now.

This paper has two main contributions:

- We show how to limit the size of the frontier in search using dominance relations, thereby enabling space-efficient BFS. Additionally, we show that limiting the size of the undominated frontier to a constant results in a useful class of *greedy* algorithms.
- Even though our method is not automatic, we believe that the process should be straightforward to apply, without requiring Eureka steps. For this reason, we have devised techniques that address roadblocks in derivations, which are illustrated on some simple but illuminating examples. Further examples are in [NSC12]

2   Background To Guided Program Synthesis

2.1   Process

The basic steps in guided program synthesis are:

1. Start with a logical specification of the problem to be solved. A specification is a quadruple $\langle D, R, o, c \rangle$ where D is an input type, R an output or result type, $o : D \times R$ is a predicate relating correct or feasible outputs to inputs, and $c : D \times R \to Int$ is a cost function on solutions. An example specification is in Eg. 1 (This specification is explained in more detail below)
2. Pick an algorithm class from a library of algorithm classes (GLOBAL SEARCH, LOCAL SEARCH, DIVIDE AND CONQUER, FIXPOINT ITERATION, etc). An algorithm class comprises a *program schema* containing operators to be instantiated and an *axiomatic theory* of those operators (see [Ned12] for details). A schema is analogous to a template function in Java/C++ with the difference that both the template and template arguments are formally constrained.

3. Instantiate the operators of the program schema using information about the problem domain and in accordance with the axioms of the class theory. To ensure correctness, this step can be carried out with mechanical assistance. The result is an efficient algorithm for solving the given problem.
4. Apply low-level program transforms such as finite differencing, context-dependent simplification, and partial evaluation, followed by code generation. Many of these are automatically applied by Specware [S], a formal program development environment.

The result of Step 4 is an efficient program for solving the problem which is guaranteed correct by construction. The power of the approach stems from the fact that the common structure of many algorithms is contained in *one* reusable program schema and associated theory. Of course the program schema needs to be carefully designed, but that is done once by the library designer. The focus of this paper is the GLOBAL SEARCH class, and specifically on how to methodically carry out Step 3 for a wide variety of problems. Details of the other algorithm classes and steps are available elsewhere [Kre98, Smi88, PPS10].

Example 1. Specification of the Shortest Path problem is shown in Fig. 2.1 (The $\mapsto$ reads as "instantiates to") The input D is a structure with 3 fields, namely a start node, end node and a set of edges. The result R is a sequence of edges ($[]$ notation). A correct result is one that satisfies the predicate *path?* which checks that a path z must be a contiguous path from the start node to the end node (simple recursive definition not shown). Finally the cost of a solution is the sum of the costs of the edges in that solution. Note that fields of a structure are accessed using the '.' notation.

2.2   Global Search

Before delving into a program schema for Global Search, it helps to understand the structures over which the program schema operates. In [Smi88], a *search space* is represented by a descriptor of some type $\widehat{R}$, which is an abstraction of the result type R. The initial or starting space is denoted $\bot$. There are also two predicates *split*: $D \times \widehat{R} \times \widehat{R}$, writ-

$$D \mapsto \langle start : Node, end : Node, edges : \{Edge\}\rangle$$
$$Edge = \langle f : Node, t : Node, cost : Nat\rangle$$
$$R \mapsto [Edge]$$
$$o \mapsto \lambda(x, z) \cdot path?(z, x.start, x.end)$$
$$path?(p, s, f) = ...$$
$$c \mapsto \lambda(x, z) \cdot \sum\nolimits_{edge \in z} edge.cost$$

Fig. 2.1. Specification of Shortest Path problem

ten $\pitchfork$, and *extract*: $\widehat{R} \times R$, written χ. Split defines when a space is a subspace of another space, and extract captures when a solution is extractable from a space. We say a solution z is *contained* in a space y (written $z \in y$) if it can be extracted after a finite number of splits. A feasible space is one that contains feasible solutions. We often write $\pitchfork (x, y, y')$ as $y \pitchfork_x y'$ for readability, and even drop the subscript when there is no confusion. *Global*

Search theory (GS-theory) [Smi88] axiomatically characterizes the relation between the predicates $\perp$, ń and χ, as well as ensuring that the associated program schema computes a result that satisfies the specification. In the sequel, the symbols $\widehat{R}, \perp, \text{ń}, \chi, \oplus$ are all assumed to be drawn from GS-theory.

Example 2. Instantiating GS-theory for the Shortest Path problem requires instantiating the free terms in the theory. The type of solution spaces $\widehat{R}$ is the same as the result type R. However, there is a covariant relationship between an element of $\widehat{R}$ and of R. For example, the initial space, corresponding to all possible paths, is the empty list. A space is split by adding an edge to the current path - that is the subspaces are the different paths that result from adding an edge to the parent path. Finally a solution can be trivially extracted from any space by setting the result z to the space p. This is summarized in Fig. 2.2 ($[]$ denotes the empty list, and $+\!\!+$ denotes list concatenation).

2.3   Dominance Relations

$$\widehat{R} \mapsto R$$
$$\perp \mapsto \lambda x \cdot []$$
$$\text{ń} \mapsto \lambda(x, p, pe) \cdot \exists e \in x.edges \cdot pe = p +\!\!+ [e]$$
$$\chi \mapsto \lambda(z, p) \cdot p = z$$

Fig. 2.2. GS instantiation for Shortest Path

As mentioned in the introduction, a dominance relation provides a way of comparing two subspaces in order to show that one will always contain at least as good a solution as the other. (Goodness in this case is measured by some cost function on solutions). The first space is said to *dominate* ($\rhd$) the second, which can then be eliminated from the search. Letting c^* denote the cost of an optimal solution in a space, this can be formalized as (all free variables are assumed to be universally quantified):

$$y \rhd y' \Rightarrow c^*(x, y) \le c^*(x, y') \tag{2.1}$$

Another way of expressing the consequent of (2.1) is

$$\forall z' \in y' \cdot o(x, z') \Rightarrow \exists z \in y \cdot o(x, z) \wedge c(x, z) \le c(x, z') \tag{2.2}$$

To derive dominance relations, it is often useful to first derive a semi-congruence relation [Smi88]. A semi-congruence between two partial solutions y and y', written $y \rightsquigarrow y'$, ensures that any way of extending y' into a feasible solution can also be used to extend y into a feasible solution. Like ń, $\rightsquigarrow$ is a ternary relation over $D \times \widehat{R} \times \widehat{R}$ but as we have done with ń and many other such relations in this work, we drop the input argument when there is no confusion and write it as a binary relation for readability. Before defining semi-congruence, we introduce two concepts. One is the idea of *useability* of a space. A space y is is useable, written $o^*(x, y)$, if $\exists z. \chi(y, z) \wedge o(x, z)$, meaning a feasible solution can be extracted from the space. The second is the notion of incorporating sufficient information into a space to make it useable. This is defined by an operator $\oplus : \widehat{R} \times t \to \widehat{R}$ that takes a space and some additional information of type t and returns a more defined space. The type t depends on $\widehat{R}$. For example if $\widehat{R}$ is the type of lists, then t might also be the same type. Now the formal definition of semi-congruence is:

$$y \rightsquigarrow y' \Rightarrow o^*(x, y' \oplus e) \Rightarrow o^*(x, y \oplus e)$$

That is, $y \rightsquigarrow y'$ is a sufficient condition for ensuring that if y' can be extended into a feasible solution than so can y *with the same extension*. Now if c is compositional (that is, $c(s \oplus t) = c(s) + c(t)$) then it can be shown [Ned12] that if $y \rightsquigarrow y'$ and y is cheaper than y', then y *dominates* y' (written $y \triangleright y'$). Formally:

$$y \rightsquigarrow y' \wedge c(x, y) \leq c(x, y') \Rightarrow y \triangleright y' \tag{2.3}$$

Dominance relations are a part of GS-theory [Smi88].

Example 3. Shortest Path between two given nodes in a graph. If there are two paths p and p' leading from the start node, if p and p' both terminate in the same node then $p \rightsquigarrow p'$. The reason is that any path extension e (of type $t = [Edge]$) of p' that leads to the target node is also a valid path extension for p. Additionally if p is shorter than p' then p dominates p', which can be discarded. Note that this does not imply that p leads to the target node, simply that no optimal solutions are lost in discarding p'. This dominance relation is formally derived in Eg. 5

Example 4. 0-1 Knapsack
   The 0-1 Knapsack problem is, given a set of items each of which has a weight and utility and a knapsack that has some maximum weight capacity, to pack the knapsack with a subset of items that maximizes utility and does not exceed the knapsack capacity. Given combinations k, k', if k and k' have both examined the same set of items and k weighs less than k' then any additional items e that can be feasibly added to k' can also be added to k, and therefore $k \rightsquigarrow k'$. Additionally if k has at least as much utility as k' then $k \triangleright k'$.

The remaining sections cover the original contributions of this paper .

3   A Theory of Space-Efficient Breadth-First Search (EBFS)

While search can in principle solve any computable function, it still leaves open the question of how to carry it out effectively. Various search strategies have been investigated over the years; two of the most common being Breadth-First Search (BFS) and Depth-First Search (DFS). It is well known that BFS offers several advantages over DFS. Unlike DFS which can get trapped in infinite paths[1], BFS will always find a solution if one exists. Secondly, BFS does not require backtracking. Third, for deeper trees, BFS will generally find a solution at the

---

[1] Resolvable in DFS with additional programming effort.

earliest possible opportunity. However, the major drawback of BFS is its space requirement which grows exponentially. For this reason, DFS is usually preferred over BFS.

Our first contribution in this paper is to refine GS-theory to identify the conditions under which a BFS algorithm can operate space-efficiently. The key is to show how the size of the undominated frontier of the search tree can be polynomially bounded. Dominance relations are the basis for this.

In [Smi88], the relation $⋔^l$ for $l \geq 0$ is recursively defined as follows:

$$y \mathrel{⋔^0} y' = (y = y')$$
$$y \mathrel{⋔^{l+1}} y' = \exists y'' \cdot y \mathrel{⋔} y'' \wedge y'' \mathrel{⋔^l} y'$$

From this the next step is to define those spaces at a given frontier level that are not dominated. However, this requires some care because dominance is a pre-order, that is it satisfies the reflexivity and transitivity axioms as a partial order does, but not the anti-symmetry axiom. That is, it is quite possible for y to dominate y' and y' to dominate y but y and y' need not be equal. An example in Shortest Path is two paths of the same length from the start node that end at the same node. Each path dominates the other. To eliminate such cyclic dominances, define the relation $y \approx y'$ as $y \rhd y' \wedge y' \rhd y$. It is not difficult to show that $\approx$ is an equivalence relation. Now let the *quotient frontier* at level l be the quotient set $frontier_l / \approx$. For type consistency, let the *representative* frontier $rfrontier_l$ be the quotient frontier in which each equivalence class is replaced by some arbitrary member of that class. The representative frontier is the frontier in which cyclic dominances have been removed. Finally then the *undominated* frontier $undom_l$ is $rfrontier_l - \{y \mid \exists y' \in rfrontier_l \cdot y' \rhd y\}$.

Now given a problem in the GS class, if it can be shown that $\|undom_l\|$ for any l is polynomially bounded in the size of the input, a number of benefits accrue: (1) BFS can be used to tractably carry out the search, as implemented in the raw program schema of Alg. 1, (2) The raw schema of Alg. 1 can be transformed into an efficient tail recursive form, in which the entire frontier is passed down and (3) If additionally the tree depth can be polynomially bounded (which typically occurs for example in *constraint satisfaction problems* or CSPs [Dec03]) then, under some reasonable assumptions about the work being done at each node, the result is a polynomial-time algorithm for the problem.

3.1   Program Theory

A program theory for EBFS defines a recursive function which given a space y, computes a non-trivial subset $F_x(y)$ of the optimal solutions contained in y, where

$$F_x(y) = opt_c\{z \mid z \in y \wedge o(x, z)\}$$

opt_c is a subset of its argument that is the optimal set of solutions (w.r.t. the cost function c), defined as follows:

$$opt_c S = \{z \mid z \in S \wedge (\forall z' \in S \cdot c(z) \leq c(z'))\}$$

Algorithm 1. pseudo-Haskell Program Schema for EBFS (schema parameters underlined)

```
solve :: D -> {R}
solve(x) = bfs x {initial(x)}

bfs :: D -> {RHat}-> {R}
bfs x frontier =
  let localsof y = let z = extract x y
                   in if z!={} && o(x,z) then z else {}
      locals = (flatten.map) localsof frontier
      allsubs = (flatten.map) (subspaces x) frontier
      undom = {yy : yy∈allsubs &&
                     (yy'∈subs && yy' 'dominates' yy ⇒ yy==yy')}
      subsolns = bfs x undom
  in opt(locals ∪ subsolns)

subspaces :: D -> RHat -> {RHat}
subspaces x y = {yy: split(x,y,yy))

opt :: {R} -> {R}
opt zs = min {c x z | z ∈zs}
```

Also let $undom(y)$ be $undom_{l(y)+1} \cap \{yy \mid y \pitchfork yy\}$ where $l(y)$ is the level of y in the tree. The following theorem defines a recurrence that serves as the basis for computing $F_x(y)$:

Theorem 3.1. *Let $\pitchfork$ be a well-founded relation of GS-theory and $G_x(y) = opt_c(\{z \mid \chi(y,z) \wedge o(x,z)\} \cup \bigcup_{yy \in undom(y)} G_x(yy)\})$ be a recurrence. Then $G_x(y) \subseteq F_x(y)$.*

The theorem states that if the feasible solutions immediately extractable from a space y are combined with the solutions obtained from G_x of each undominated subspace yy, and the optimal ones of those retained, the result is a subset of $F_x(y)$. The next theorem demonstrate non-triviality[2] of the recurrence by showing that if a feasible solution exists in a space, then one will be found.

Theorem 3.2. *Let $\pitchfork$ be a well-founded relation of GS-Theory and G_x be defined as above. Then*

$$F_x(y) \neq \emptyset \Rightarrow (\{z \mid \chi(y,z) \wedge o(x,z)\} \cup \bigcup_{yy \in undom(y)} G_x(yy)\}) \neq \emptyset$$

Proofs of both theorems are in [NSC12]. From the characteristic recurrence we can straightforwardly derive a simple recursive function `bfs` to compute a non-trivial subset of F_x for a given y, shown in Alg. 1

The final program schema that is included in the Specware library is the result of incorporating a number of other features of GS such as necessary filters, bounds tests, and propagation, which are not shown here. Details of these and other techniques are in [Smi88].

---

[2] Non-triviality is similar but not identical to completeness. Completeness requires that every optimal solution is found by the recurrence, which we do not guarantee.

3.2   A Class of Strictly Greedy Algorithms (SG)

A greedy algorithm [CLRS01] is one which repeatedly makes a locally optimal choice. For some classes of problems this leads to a globally optimum choice. We can get a characterization of optimally greedy algorithms within EBFS by restricting the size of $undom_l$ for any l to 1. If $undom_l \neq \emptyset$ then the singleton member y^* of $undom_l$ is called the *greedy* choice.

A perhaps surprising result is that our characterization of greedy algorithms is broader than a well-known characterization of greedy solutions, namely the Greedy Algorithm over algebraic structures called *greedoids* [BZ92], which are themselves more general than *matroids*. We demonstrated this in earlier work [NSC10] although at the time we were not able to characterize the greedy class as a special case of EBFS.

Another interesting result is that even if $\|undom_l\|$, for any l, cannot be limited to one but can be shown to be some constant value, the resulting algorithm, we call *Hardly Strictly Greedy*[3] *(HSG)*, still has the same complexity as a strictly greedy one. A number of interesting problems have the HSG property, and these are discussed later. Note that for problems in the SG class, there is no longer any "search" in the conventional sense.

4   Methodology

We strongly believe that every formal approach should be accompanied by a methodology by which it can be used by a competent developer, without needing great insights. Guided program synthesis already goes a long way towards meeting this requirement by capturing design knowledge in a reusable form. The remainder of the work to be done by a developer consists of instantiating the various parameters of the program schema. The second main contribution of this paper is to describe some techniques, illustrated with examples, that greatly simplify the instantiation process. We wish to reiterate that once the dominance relation and other operators in the schema have been instantiated, *the result is a complete solution to the given problem.* We focus on dominance relations because they are arguably the most challenging of the operators to design. The remaining parameters can usually be written down by visual inspection.

The simplest form of derivation is to reason backwards from the conclusion of $y \rightsquigarrow y' \Rightarrow o^*(x, y' \oplus e) \Rightarrow o^*(x, y \oplus e)$, while assuming $o^*(x, y' \oplus e)$. The additional assumptions that are made along the way form the required semi-congruence condition. The following example illustrates the approach.

Example 5. Derivation of the semi-congruence relation for Shortest Path in Eg. 1 is fairly straightforward calculation as shown in Fig 4.1. It relies on the specification of Shortest Path given in Eg. 1 and the GS-theory in Eg. 2.

The calculation shows that a path y is semi-congruent to y' if y and y' both end at the same node and additionally y is itself a valid path from the start node

---

[3] This name inspired by that of the *Hardly Strictly Bluegrass* festival held annually in San Francisco.

$o^*(x, y \oplus e)$
$= \{\text{defn of } o^*\}$
$\exists z \cdot \chi(y \oplus e, z) \wedge o(x, z)$
$= \{\text{defn of } \chi\}$
$o(x, y \oplus e)$
$= \{\text{defn of } o\}$
$path?(y \oplus e, x.start, x.end)$
$= \{\text{distributive law for } path?\}$
$\exists n \cdot path?(y, x.start, n) \wedge path?(e, n, x.end)$
$\Leftarrow \{o^*(x, y' \oplus e), \text{ie.} \exists m \cdot path?(y', x.start, m) \wedge path?(e, m, x.end).$
Let m be a witness for $n\}$
$path?(y, x.start, m) \wedge path?(e, m, x.end)$
$= \{m = last(y).t, \text{ (where } last \text{ returns the last element of a sequence)}\}$
$last(y).t = last(y').t \wedge path?(y, x.start, n)$

Fig. 4.1. Derivation of semi-congruence relation for Shortest Path

to its last node. Since the cost function is compositional, this immediately produces a dominance relation $y \rhd y' = last(y) = last(y') \wedge path?(y, x.start, n) \wedge \sum_{edge \in y} edge.cost \leq \sum_{edge' \in y'} edge'.cost$. Note the use of the distributive law for $path?$ in step 4. Such laws are usually formulated as part of a domain theory during a domain discovery process, or even as part of the process of trying to carry out a derivation such as the one just shown. Given an appropriate constructive prover (such as the one in KIDS [Smi90]) such a derivation could in fact be automated. Other examples that have been derived using this approach are Activity Selection [NSC10], Integer Linear Programming [Smi88], and variations on the Maximum Segment Sum problem [NC09]. The next two sections deal with situations in which the derivation is not so straightforward.

4.1   Technique 1: An Exchange Tactic

In the example just considered, and many such others, the derivation process was free of *rabbits* (Dijkstra's term for magic steps that appear seemingly out of nowhere). However, some cases are a little more challenging. As an example consider the following problem:

Example 6. One-Machine Scheduling. This is the problem of scheduling a number of jobs on a machine so as to minimize the sum of the completion times of the jobs (because dividing the sum of the completion times by the number of jobs gives the average amount of time that a job waits before being processed). A schedule is a permutation of the set of input jobs $\{J_1, J_2, \ldots J_n\}$. The input to the problem is a set of tasks, where a task consists of a pair of an *id* and duration, p. The result is a sequence of tasks. The output condition o requires that every task (and only those tasks) in the input be scheduled, ie placed at a unique position in the output sequence. Finally the cost of a solution, as stated above, is the sum of the completion times of the tasks. The problem specification is therefore:

$$D \mapsto \{Task\}$$
$$R \mapsto [Task]$$
$$Task = \langle id : Id, p : Time \rangle$$
$$o \mapsto \lambda(x, z) \cdot asBag(z) = x$$
$$c \mapsto \lambda(x, z) \cdot \sum_{i=1}^{n} ct(z, i)$$
$$ct(z, i) = \sum_{j=1}^{i} z_j.p$$

The instantiation of terms in GS-theory is similar to that of Shortest Path:

$$\widehat{R} \mapsto R$$
$$\bot \mapsto \lambda x \cdot []$$
$$\pitchfork \mapsto \lambda(x, s, ss) \cdot \exists t \in x. \, ss = s \mathbin{+\!\!+} [t]$$
$$\chi \mapsto \lambda(z, p) \cdot p = z$$
$$\rhd \mapsto ?$$

However, attempting to derive a semi-congruence relation in the same manner as we did for the Shortest Path problem by comparing two schedules αa and αb will not work. This is because every task must be scheduled, so any extension ω that extends say αa must contain b but as each task can be scheduled only once, such an extension will not be feasible for αb. Such situations are very common in scheduling and planning problems[4]. For such problems, note that when $\widehat{R}$ is a sequence type, every possible way a (called a *choice*) of extending some sequence α ie. $\alpha \mathbin{+\!\!+} [a]$, written αa for conciseness, forms a subspace of α. A simple example is the problem of generating all bit strings. If the current space is some bit string say [1,0,0,1] then the two subspaces are [1,0,0,1]$\mathbin{+\!\!+}$[0] and [1,0,0,1]$\mathbin{+\!\!+}$[1] , written 10010 and 10011 resp. Another example occurs in CSP. If α is the sequence of assignments to the first i variables, then αv for every v in $\mathcal{D}_{i+1}$ is a subspace of α. The tactic to try in such situations is to compare two partial solutions that are permutations of each other. This idea is backed up by the following theorem.

Theorem 4.1. *Suppose it can be shown that any feasible extension of αa must eventually be followed by some choice b. That is, any feasible solution contained in αa must be contained in $\alpha a \beta b$ for some β. Let $\alpha b \beta a$ be the partial solution obtained by exchanging a and b. If $R(\alpha, a, b)$ is an expression for the semi-congruence relation $\alpha b \beta a \rightsquigarrow \alpha a \beta b$ and $C(\alpha, a, b)$ is an expression for $c(\alpha b \beta a \gamma) \leq c(\alpha a \beta b \gamma)$, for any α, β, then $R(\alpha, a, b) \wedge C(\alpha, a, b)$ is a dominance relation $\alpha b \rhd \alpha a$.*

Proof. See [Ned12]

□

Example 6 Revisited. We now show how to derive a dominance relation for this problem. The tactic above suggests the following: Suppose some partial schedule is extended by picking task a to assign in the next position and this is

---

[4] In planning, actions that must occur after another action to achieve a feasible plan are called *action landmarks*.

followed subsequently by some task b. When is this better than picking b for the next position and a subsequently? Let $y = \alpha a \beta b$ and $y' = \alpha b \beta a$. It is not difficult to show that y and y' are unconditionally semi-congruent. To apply Theorem 4.1 it is necessary to derive an expression for $c(\alpha b \beta a \gamma) \leq c(\alpha a \beta b \gamma)$. Let $z = y\gamma$ and $z' = y'\gamma$ and let i be the position of a (b) in y (resp. y') and j be the position of b (a) in y (resp. y'). As shown in Fig. 4.2, the calculation is simple enough to be automated. The derivation shows that for any feasible solution $\alpha b \beta a \omega$

$c(z) \leq c(z')$
= {unfold defn of c}
   $c(\alpha) + ct(z,i) + c(\beta) + ct(z,j) + c(\gamma) \leq c(\alpha) + ct(z,j) + c(\beta) + ct(z,i) + c(\gamma)$
= {unfold defn of ct. Realize that $c(\alpha) = \sum_{i=1}^{\|\alpha\|} \sum_{j=1}^{i} \alpha_j.p$ and let $pt(\alpha) = \sum_{j=1}^{\|\alpha\|} \alpha_j.p$}
   $c(\alpha) + pt(\alpha) + a.p + c(\beta) + pt(\alpha) + a.p + pt(\beta) + b.p$
   $\leq$
   $ct(\alpha) + pt(\alpha) + b.p + c(\beta) + pt(\alpha) + b.p + pt(\beta) + a.p$
= {algebra}
   $2(a.p) + b.p \leq 2(b.p) + a.p$
= {algebra}
   $a.p \leq b.p$

Fig. 4.2. Calculation of cost comparison relation for 1 mach. scheduling.

extending αb there is a cheaper feasible solution $\alpha a \beta b \omega$ that extends αa provided $a.p \leq b.p$. By Theorem 4.1, this constitutes the dominance relation $\alpha a \rhd \alpha b$. Finally, as $\leq$ is total order, there must be a choice that dominates all other choices, namely the task with the least processing time. Therefore the problem is in the SG class. Following this greedy choice at every step therefore leads to the optimum solution. Instantiating the library schema derived from Alg. 1 with such a dominance relation (along with the other parameters) immediately results in a greedy algorithm for this problem. The result corresponds to the Shortest Processing Time (SPT) rule, discovered by W.E. Smith in 1956. We have shown how it can be systematically derived.

We have applied the tactic above to derive other scheduling algorithms, for example an algorithm for the scheduling problem $1//L_m$ in which the goal is to minimize the maximum lateness of any job (amount by which it misses its due date), as well as variant of it to derive dominance relations for planning problems [Ned12].

4.2   Technique 2: General Dominance

There are situations in which the above tactic will fail. Consider the following problem from [CLRS01] and [Cur03]:

Example 7. Professor Midas's Driving Problem

Professor Midas wishes to plan a car journey along a fixed route. There are a given number of gas stations along the route, and the professor's gas tank when full can cover a given number of miles. Derive an algorithm that minimizes the number of refueling stops the professor must make.

The input data is assumed to be a sequence of cumulative distances of gas stations from the starting point (cds) along with the car's tank capacity $(cap,$ measured in terms of distance). The variables will represent the gas stations along the route, that is variable i will be the ith gas station. A stop at a gas station is indicated in the result by assigning the corresponding variable $true$, and $false$ otherwise. The start and finish are considered mandatory stops (that is z_1 and z_n are required to be $true$). Finally, the cost of a solution is a simple count of the number of variables assigned $true$. An obvious requirement on the input is that the distance between any two stations not exceed the tank capacity of the car. These ideas are captured in the following specification (in the cost function $false$ is interpreted as 0 and $true$ as 1). Note that a type $\langle \ldots \mid P \rangle$ denotes a predicate subtype in which the type members must satisfy the predicate P.

$$D \mapsto \langle cds : [Nat], cap : Nat \mid \forall x \in D \cdot \forall i < \|x.cds\| \cdot x.cds[i+1] - x.cds[i] \leq x.cap \rangle$$
$$R \mapsto [Boolean]$$
$$o \mapsto \|z\| = \|x.cds\| \wedge fsok(x,z)$$
$$\qquad fsok(x,z) = \forall i,j \cdot i \leq j \cdot didntStop(z,i,j) \Rightarrow span(x,i,j) \leq x.cap$$
$$\qquad didntStop(z,a,b) = \forall i \cdot a \leq i \leq b \cdot \neg z_i$$
$$\qquad span(x,i,j) = x.cds[j+1] - x.cds[i-1]$$
$$c \mapsto \lambda x, z \cdot \sum_{i=1}^{\|z\|} z_i$$

The instantiation of GS-theory, with the exception of $\rhd$, is as it was for the machine scheduline example (Eg. 6). Attempting to apply the Exchange tactic described above and derive a semi-congruence relation between $\alpha T \beta F$ and $\alpha F \beta T$ (T is $true$ and F is $false$) that does not depend on β will fail. The counterexample of Fig 4.3 shows why (boxes represent variables, shading means the variable was set true): it is possible that there is some extension e to αT which delays a stop but which is too long a span for αF. In such situations, we have found it useful to try to establish *general dominance* (Def. 2.2).

As before, it is useful to identify any distributive laws. In this case, the combination of partial solutions r and s satisfies $fsok$ provided each partial solution independently satisfies $fsok$ and where they abut satisfies $fsok$. Expressing the law formally requires broadening the definition of $fsok$ somewhat to take into account the offset t of a particular sequence from the start, that is:
$fsok(x,z,t) = \forall i,j \cdot i \leq j \wedge didntStop(z,i,j) \Rightarrow span(x,i+t,j+t) \leq x.cap.$
Then:

$$fsok(x, y \oplus e, 0) = fsok(x,y,0) \wedge fsok(x,e,\|y\|) \wedge fs2ok(x,y,e)$$

where $fs2ok$ deals with the boundary between y and e and can be shown to be

$$fs2ok(x,y,e) = fsok(x, lfs(y) + ffs(e), \|y - lfs(y)\|)$$

where *ffs* (resp. *lfs*) denotes the initial (resp. last) false span of a segment, if any.

Now consider the two possible solutions after a split again, namely αT and αF. To demonstrate $o(x, \alpha F e)$ for some e, the usual backwards inference procedure can be applied, assuming $\alpha T e'$ for some e' (for brevity, the input x to *fsok* has been dropped)

$o(x, \alpha F e)$
$= \{\text{defn }\}$
$fsok(\alpha F e, 0)$
$= \{\text{defn }\}$
$fsok(\alpha, 0) \wedge fsok(F, \|\alpha\|) \wedge fs2ok(\alpha, F) \wedge fsok(e, \|\alpha\| + 1) \wedge fs2ok(\alpha F, e)$
$= \{fsok(\alpha, 0) \text{ because } o(x, \alpha T e'), fsok(F, -) \text{ because of restriction on } D\}$
$fs2ok(\alpha, F) \wedge fsok(e, \|\alpha\| + 1)) \wedge fs2ok(\alpha F, e)$
$= \{\text{see below}\}$
$fs2ok(\alpha, F)$

To demonstrate both $fsok(e, \|\alpha\| + 1)$ and $fs2ok(\alpha F, e)$, let $e = e'[1 = T]$ (e' with the first variable assigned $true$). Clearly $fsok(e, \|\alpha\| + 1)$ if $fsok(e', \|\alpha\| + 1)$ and $fs2ok(\alpha F, e)$ if $fs2ok(\alpha, F)$ because $ffs(e)$ is empty. As αF has one stop less than αT and e has at most one extra, it follows that $c(x, \alpha F e) \leq c(x, \alpha T e')$. Therefore αF dominates αT

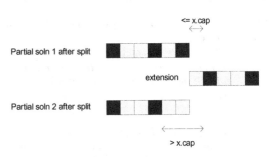

Fig. 4.3. Counter-example: extension works for the 1st partial soln but not for the 2nd

provided there is sufficient fuel to make it to the next stop. As there are only two branches following a split, the greedy choice is clear. Informally this rule is to travel as far as possible without stopping.

Other algorithms we have derived by applying general dominance have been a SG algorithm for Shortest Path similar to Dijkstra's algorithm, and SG algorithms similar to Prim and Kruskal for Minimum Spanning Trees [NSC12].

4.3 Technique 3: Feasibility Problems

Finally, we show that the notion of greediness applies not only to optimality problems, but also feasibility problems. By letting the "cost" of a solution be its correctness and using the standard ordering on Booleans, namely that $false < true$, we can derive a feasibility dominance criterion for $y \rhd_F y'$, namely $o(x, y') \Rightarrow o(x, y)$ [Ned12]. One way to use this constraint is derive conditions under which $o(x, y')$ is false, ensuring y' is dominated. An example of this follows.

Example 8. Searching for a key in an ordered sequence. A combined problem specification and GS-theory instantiation is:

$$D \mapsto \langle seq : [Int], key : Int \mid unique(key, seq) \wedge ordered(seq) \rangle$$
$$R \mapsto Nat$$
$$o \mapsto \lambda(x, z) \cdot x.seq[z] = x.key$$
$$\widehat{R} \mapsto (Nat, Nat)$$
$$⋔ \mapsto \lambda(x, (i, j), (k, l)) \cdot (k = i \wedge l = (i + j) \ div \ 2)) \vee$$
$$(k = (i + j) \ div \ 2) + 1 \wedge l = j)$$
$$\chi \mapsto \lambda(y, z) \cdot z = y$$

The input D provides the sequence and the key, requiring that the sequence be ordered and the key occur uniquely in the sequence. The result is the index of the desired key. The two subspaces after a split are the sequence from the start i of the parent sequence to the midway point and from some point immediately after the midway to the end j of the parent sequence. (This split relation is derived in [Smi10]). In general, there could be an n-way split, or a split at any chosen point in the range but for simplicity, only the binary midpoint case is illustrated. There are only two subspaces after a split denoted L and R. Fig 4.4 derives the condition under which $o(x, \alpha L)$ holds. Negating this condition, ie. $x.key > x.seq[(i+j) \ div \ 2]$ determines when $o(x, \alpha L)$ is false and αL is dominated, leaving at most one undominated child, αR. Completing the instantiation of GS-theory with this dominance condition provides the bindings for the parameters of the program schema of Alg. 1. Since the depth of the search is $O(\log n)$, the result is an $O(\log n)$ greedy algorithm that implements Binary Search.

4.4 HSG Problems

$$o(x, \alpha L)$$
$$= \{\text{defn. of } o\}$$
$$\exists z \in \alpha L \cdot o(x, z)$$
$$= \{\text{defn. of } o\}$$
$$\bigvee_{p=i}^{(i+j)/2} x.seq[p] = x.key$$
$$\Rightarrow \{\text{ordered elements}\}$$
$$x.key \leq x.seq[(i + j) \ div \ 2]$$

Fig. 4.4. Derivation of greedy dominance relation for binary search

The problems illustrated so far have all been Strictly Greedy (SG). This was intentional. For one thing, many problems have a greedy solution (or a greedy approximation). Additionally, as one moves down an algorithm hierarchy, the narrower class generally has a more efficient algorithm. The price to be paid is that it is usually more difficult to establish the conditions necessary for membership in a tighter class. The techniques we have demonstrated for establishing membership in SG apply equally well to the broader category of HSG and indeed the catch-all one of EBFS. Although problems in the broader categories are seemingly sparser, we have demonstrated several problems are in HSG ; for example, 2-SAT (Boolean satisfiability in which there are at most 2 variables per clause) [Ned12] as well as a family of Segment Sum problems [NC09]. Noteworthy is that the run-time performance of the solutions we derived for the Segment

Sum problems consistently exceeded those obtained by program transformation [SHT00, SHT01, SOH05]. Genetic algorithms in which the descendant population is maintained at a constant level are another example of HSG algorithms.

5 Related Work

Gulwani et al. [SGF10, GJTV11] describe a powerful program synthesis approach called *template-based synthesis*. A user supplies a template or outline of the intended program structure, and the tool fills in the details. A number of interesting programs have been synthesized using this approach, including Bresenham's line drawing algorithm and various bit vector manipulation routines. A related method is inductive synthesis [IGIS10] in which the tool synthesizes a program from examples. The latter has been used for inferring spreadsheet formulae from examples. All the tools rely on powerful SMT solvers. The Sketching approach of Solar-Lezama et al [PBS11] also relies on inductive synthesis. A *sketch*, similar in intent to a template, is supplied by the user and the tool fills in such aspects as loop bounds and array indexing. Sketching relies on efficient SAT solvers. To quote Gulwani et al. the benefit of the template approach is that "the programmer only need write the structure of the code and the tool fills out the details" [SGF10].Rather than the programmer supplying an arbitrary template, though, we suggest the use of a program schema from the appropriate algorithm class (refer to Step 2 of the process in Sec. 2.1). We believe that the advantage of such an approach is that, based on a sound theory, much can already be inferred at the abstract level and this is captured in the theory associated with the algorithm class. Furthermore, knowledge of properties at the abstract level allows specialization of the program schema with information that would otherwise have to either be guessed at by the programmer devising a template or inferred automatically by the tool (e.g. tail recursive implementation or efficient implementation of dominance testing with hashing). We believe this will allow semi-automated synthesis to scale up to larger problems such as constraint solvers (SAT, CSP, LP, MIP, etc.), planning and scheduling, and O/S level programs such as garbage collectors [PPS10].

Program verification is another field that shares common goals with program synthesis - namely a correct efficient program. The difference lies in approach - we prefer to construct the program in a way that is guaranteed to be correct, as opposed to verifying its correctness after the fact. Certainly some recent tools such as Dafny [Lei10] provide very useful feedback in an IDE during program construction. But even such tools requires significant program annotations in the form of invariants to be able to automatically verify non-trivial examples such as the Schorr-Waite algorithm [Lei10]. Nevertheless, we do not see verification and synthesis as being necessarily opposed. For example, ensuring the correctness of the instantiation of several of the operators in the program schema which is usually done by inspection is a verification task, as is ensuring correctness of the schema that goes in the class library. We also feel that recent advances in verification via SMT solvers will also help guided synthesis by increasing the degree of automation.

Refinement is generally viewed as an alternative to synthesis. A specification is gradually refined into an efficient executable program. Refinement methods such as Z and B have proved to be very popular. In contrast to refinement, guided program synthesis already has the program structure in place, and the main body of work consists of instantiating the schema parameters followed by various program transformations many of which can be mechanically applied. Both refinement and synthesis rely extensively on tool support, particularly in the form of provers. We expect that advances in both synthesis and refinement will benefit the other field.

Curtis [Cur03] presents a classification scheme for greedy algorithms. Each class has some conditions that must be met for a given algorithm to belong to that class. The greedy algorithm is then automatically correct and optimal. Unlike Curtis, our results extend beyond strictly greedy algorithms. We also rely extensively on calculational proofs for problem instances.

Another approach has been taken by Bird and de Moor [BM93] who show that under certain conditions a dynamic programming algorithm simplifies into a greedy algorithm. Our characterization in can be considered an analogous specialization of (a form of) branch-and-bound. The difference is that we do not require calculation of the entire program, but specific operators, which is a less onerous task.

6   Summary and Future Work

We have shown how Breadth-First Search can be carried out efficiently by relying on dominance relations. This is an important result as Breadth-First Search has several advantages over Depth-First Search. Secondly, we demonstrated some techniques by which dominance relations can be derived and illustrated them on several problems. We hope to identify and collect more techniques over time and catalogue then in the style of design patterns [GHJV95].

Nearly all the derivations shown in this paper have been carried out by hand. However, they are simple enough to be automated. We plan on building a prover that incorporates the ideas mentioned in here. We are encouraged by the success of a similar prover that was part of KIDS, a predecessor to Specware.

We are currently applying some of these ideas to the problem of synthesizing fast planners that produce good quality plans. We hope to report on this work in the near future.

References

[BM93]   Bird, R.S., De Moor, O.: From Dynamic Programming to Greedy Algorithms. In: Möller, B., Schuman, S., Partsch, H. (eds.) Formal Program Development. LNCS, vol. 755, pp. 43–61. Springer, Heidelberg (1993)

[BZ92]   Björner, A., Ziegler, G.M.: Introduction to greedoids. In: White, N. (ed.) Matroid Applications. Cambridge University Press (1992)

[CLRS01] Cormen, T., Leiserson, C., Rivest, R., Stein, C.: Introduction to Algorithms, 2nd edn. MIT Press (2001)

[Cur03]   Curtis, S.A.: The classification of greedy algorithms. Sci. Comput. Program. 49(1-3), 125–157 (2003)

[Dec03]   Dechter, R.: Constraint Processing. Morgan Kauffman (2003)

[GHJV95]   Gamma, E., Helm, R., Johnson, R., Vlissides, J.: Design patterns: elements of reusable object-oriented software. Addison-Wesley Professional (1995)

[GJTV11]   Gulwani, S., Jha, S., Tiwari, A., Venkatesan, R.: Synthesis of loop-free programs. In: PLDI, pp. 62–73 (2011)

[Iba77]   Ibaraki, T.: The power of dominance relations in branch-and-bound algorithms. J. ACM 24(2), 264–279 (1977)

[IGIS10]   Itzhaky, S., Gulwani, S., Immerman, N., Sagiv, M.: A simple inductive synthesis methodology and its applications. In: OOPSLA, pp. 36–46 (2010)

[Kre98]   Kreitz, C.: Program synthesis. In: Bibel, W., Schmitt, P. (eds.) Automated Deduction – A Basis for Applications, vol. III, ch. III.2.5, pp. 105–134. Kluwer (1998)

[Lei10]   Leino, K.R.M.: Dafny: An Automatic Program Verifier for Functional Correctness. In: Clarke, E.M., Voronkov, A. (eds.) LPAR-16 2010. LNCS, vol. 6355, pp. 348–370. Springer, Heidelberg (2010)

[NC09]   Nedunuri, S., Cook, W.R.: Synthesis of fast programs for maximum segment sum problems. In: Intl. Conf. on Generative Prog. and Component Engineering (GPCE) (October 2009)

[Ned12]   Nedunuri, S.: Theory and Techniques for Synthesizing Efficient Breadth-First Search Algorithms. PhD thesis, Univ. of Texas at Austin (2012)

[NSC10]   Nedunuri, S., Smith, D.R., Cook, W.R.: A Class of Greedy Algorithms and Its Relation to Greedoids. In: Cavalcanti, A., Deharbe, D., Gaudel, M.-C., Woodcock, J. (eds.) ICTAC 2010. LNCS, vol. 6255, pp. 352–366. Springer, Heidelberg (2010)

[NSC12]   Nedunuri, S., Smith, D.R., Cook, W.R.: Theory and techniques for synthesizing graph algorithms using breadth-first search. In: 1st Workshop on Synthesis (SYNT) in Computer Aided Verification, CAV (to appear, 2012)

[PBS11]   Pu, Y., Bodík, R., Srivastava, S.: Synthesis of first-order dynamic programming algorithms. In: OOPSLA, pp. 83–98 (2011)

[PPS10]   Pavlovic, D., Pepper, P., Smith, D.R.: Formal Derivation of Concurrent Garbage Collectors. In: Bolduc, C., Desharnais, J., Ktari, B. (eds.) MPC 2010. LNCS, vol. 6120, pp. 353–376. Springer, Heidelberg (2010)

[S]   Specware, http://www.specware.org

[SGF10]   Srivastava, S., Gulwani, S., Foster, J.S.: From program verification to program synthesis. In: POPL, pp. 313–326 (2010)

[SHT00]   Sasano, I., Hu, Z., Takeichi, M.: Make it practical: A generic linear-time algorithm for solving maximum-weightsum problems. In: Intl. Conf. Functional Prog. (ICFP) (2000)

[SHT01]   Sasano, I., Hu, Z.: Generation of Efficient Programs for Solving Maximum Multi-marking Problems. In: Taha, W. (ed.) SAIG 2001. LNCS, vol. 2196, pp. 72–91. Springer, Heidelberg (2001)

[SLTB+06] Solar-Lezama, A., Tancau, L., Bodik, R., Seshia, S., Saraswat, V.: Combinatorial sketching for finite programs. In: Proc. of the 12th Intl. Conf. on Architectural Support for Prog. Lang. and Operating Systems (ASPLOS), pp. 404–415 (2006)

[Smi88]   Smith, D.R.: Structure and design of global search algorithms. Tech. Rep. Kes. U.87.12, Kestrel Institute (1988)

[Smi90]   Smith, D.R.: Kids: A semi-automatic program development system. IEEE Trans. on Soft. Eng., Spec. Issue on Formal Methods 16(9), 1024–1043 (1990)

[Smi10]   Smith, D.R.: Global search theory revisited. Unpublished (December 2010)

[SOH05]   Sasano, I., Ogawa, M., Hu, Z.: Maximum Marking Problems with Accumulative Weight Functions. In: Van Hung, D., Wirsing, M. (eds.) ICTAC 2005. LNCS, vol. 3722, pp. 562–578. Springer, Heidelberg (2005)

[SPW95]   Smith, D.R., Parra, E.A., Westfold, S.J.: Synthesis of high-performance transportation schedulers. Technical report, Kestrel Institute (1995)

[SW08]   Smith, D.R., Westfold, S.: Synthesis of propositional satisfiability solvers. Final proj. report, Kestrel Institute (2008)

[VY08]   Vechev, M., Yahav, E.: Deriving linearizable fine-grained concurrent objects. In: PLDI 2008, pp. 125–135 (2008)

[VYY10]   Vechev, M., Yahav, E., Yorsh, G.: Abstraction-guided synthesis of synchronization. In: POPL 2010, pp. 327–338 (2010)

Improved BDD-Based Discrete Analysis
of Timed Systems

Truong Khanh Nguyen[2], Jun Sun[1], Yang Liu[2], Jin Song Dong[2], and Yan Liu[2]

[1] Information System Technology and Design,
Singapore University of Technology and Design
sunjun@sutd.edu.sg
[2] School of Computing
National University of Singapore
{truongkhanh,liuyang,dongjs,yanliu}@comp.nus.edu.sg

Abstract. Model checking timed systems through digitization is relatively easy, compared to zone-based approaches. The applicability of digitization, however, is limited mainly for two reasons, i.e., it is only sound for *closed* timed systems; and clock ticks cause state space explosion. The former is mild as many practical systems are subject to digitization. It has been shown that BDD-based techniques can be used to tackle the latter to some extent. In this work, we significantly improve the existing approaches by *keeping the ticks simple* in the BDD encoding. Taking advantage of the 'simple' nature of clock ticks, we fine-tune the encoding of ticks and are able to verify systems with many ticks. Furthermore, we develop a BDD library which supports not only encoding/verifying of timed state machines (through digitization) but also composing timed components using a rich set of composition functions. The usefulness and scalability of the library are demonstrated by supporting two languages, i.e., closed timed automata and Stateful Timed CSP.

1 Introduction

Model checking of real-time systems has been studied extensively. One popular approach is zone abstraction [1,2]. The scalability and effectiveness of the zone-based approach have been proved with successful industrial applications, e.g., [3]. Meanwhile, it is known that for a large class of timed verification problems, correctness can be established using an integral model of time (digital clocks) as oppose to a dense model of time [4]. For instance, Lamport argued that model checking of real-time systems can be really simple if digitization is adopted [5]. Digitization translates a real-time verification problem to a discrete one by using clock ticks to represent elapsed time. The advantage is that the techniques which are developed for classic automata verification can be applied without the added complexity of zone operations. One particularly interesting example is model checking with the assumption of non-Zenoness. A timed execution is Zeno if infinitely many discrete steps are taken within finite time. For obvious reasons, Zeno executions are impractical and must be ruled out during the system verification. It is, however, nontrivial to check whether an execution is Zeno or not based on zone graphs [6,7]. The problem is much simpler with digitization. An execution of a digitized

D. Giannakopoulou and D. Méry (Eds.): FM 2012, LNCS 7436, pp. 326–340, 2012.

system is non-Zeno if and only if it contains infinitely many clock ticks. Thus a finite-state system is non-Zeno if on any of its control cycles, time advances with at least one time unit. In other words, this cycle contains at least one clock tick transition, which can be determined efficiently with cycle-detection algorithms. Further, the experiment in [8] showed that BDD-based model checking of digitized systems is more robust with the increment in the number of processes, compared with zone-based approaches.

The disadvantage of digitization is that the number of reachable states of the digitized system is an increasing function of the number of clock ticks, which is determined by the upper-bound of the timing constraints. The experiments in [5] showed that UP-PAAL has a clear advantage (over TLC or Spin in verifying the digitized systems) when the time upper-bound is bigger than 10. The same experiments showed that the symbolic model checker SMV is more robust with the increment in time upper-bounds. The question is then: Can BDD-based symbolic model checker scale better with large time upper-bounds? In [9], it has been shown that the size of BDD is very sensitive to time upper-bounds through a theoretical analysis. As a result, the time upper-bounds were thus kept very small in their experiments, i.e., no more than 16.

In this work, we re-visit the problem in order to develop efficient model checking techniques for timed systems. Our investigation shows that if we keep clock ticks simple, *by avoiding clock variables altogether*, we are able to obtain a small BDD encoding of all ticks in a system which scales significantly better than existing approaches. We are able to verify systems with time upper-bounds in the order of thousands. Furthermore, to make this technique available for different timed modeling languages, we build a BDD library for encoding and composing digitized timed systems. The motivation is that complex timed systems are often composed of many components at multiple levels of hierarchies. We propose to use *timed finite-state machines* (TFSMs) to model timed system components, which are designed to capture useful system features like different ways of communication among system components. Next, we define a rich set of system composition functions accordingly based on TFSMs. The library further complements the previous approaches (e.g., UPPAAL, Rabbit [8]) by supporting linear temporal logic (LTL), LTL with weak/strong fairness, non-Zenoness, etc. The usefulness of the library is evidenced by showing that it can be readily used to build model checkers for two different timed modeling languages, e.g., closed timed automata and Stateful Timed CSP [10].

We evaluate the efficiency of the library using benchmark systems with different settings. In the first experiment, systems are modeled and verified with an increment in time upper-bounds. The objective is to show that, by taking advantage of characteristics of clock ticks, our library is reasonably robust with larger number of clock ticks than Rabbit. In the second experiment, the systems are verified with the increment in the number of processes so as to show that our model checker scales up better than model checkers like UPPAAL. Lastly, we show that our model checker verifies LTL properties, with/without non-Zenoness, efficiently.

The rest of the paper is organized as follows. Section 2 presents the design of the library. Section 3 presents the work on supporting two languages. Section 4 evaluates the performance of the library. Section 5 concludes the work.

2 System Models and BDD Encoding

A timed system may be built from the bottom up by gradually composing system components. We propose to model system components using timed finite-state machines (TFSMs), which are designed to capture a variety of system features. In the following, we introduce TFSM and system compositions based on TFSMs. Furthermore, we show abstractly how to generate a BDD encoding of TFSMs in a compositional way.

2.1 Timed Finite-State Machines

Definition 1. *A TFSM is a tuple* $\mathcal{M} = (GV, LV, S, init, Act, Ch, T)$ *such that* GV *is a set of finite-domain shared variables;* LV *is a set of finite-domain local variables such that* $GV \cap LV = \varnothing$; S *is a finite set of control states;* $init \in S$ *is the initial state;* Act *is the alphabet;* Ch *is a set of synchronous channels[1]; and* T *is a labeled transition relation. A transition label is of the form* $[guard]\,evt\{prog\}$ *where* $guard$ *is an optional guard condition constituted by variables in* GV *and* LV; evt *is either an event name, a channel input/output or the special tick event (which denotes 1-unit elapsed time); and* $prog$ *is an optional transaction, i.e., a sequential program which updates global/local variables.*

A transaction (which may contain program constructs like *if-then-else* or *while-do*) associated with a transition is to be executed atomically. A non-atomic operation is thus to be broken into multiple transitions. TFSMs support many system features. For instance, TFSMs may communicate with each other through shared variables GV, multiparty event synchronization (common events in parallel composition are synchronized) or pair-wise channel communication.

The semantics of $\mathcal{M}$ is a labeled transition system $(C, init_c, \rightarrow)$ such that C contains finitely many configurations of the form (σ_g, σ_l, s) such that σ_g is the valuation of GV and σ_l is the valuation of LV and $s \in S$ is a control state; $init_c = (init_g, init_l, init)$ where $init_g$ is the initial valuation of GV and $init_l$ is the initial valuation of LV; and $\rightarrow$ is defined as follows: for any (σ_g, σ_l, s), if $(s, [guard]e\{prog\}, s') \in T$, then $(\sigma_g, \sigma_l, s) \stackrel{e}{\rightarrow} (\sigma_g', \sigma_l', s')$ if the following holds: $guard$ is true given σ_g and σ_l; e is not a synchronous channel input/output; and $prog$ updates σ_g and σ_l to σ_g' and σ_l' respectively. Notice that synchronous input/output cannot occur on its own. Rather, it must be jointly performed by different TFSMs which execute concurrently. Furthermore, $\rightarrow$ contains transitions labeled with events to be synchronized, which later will be synchronized with corresponding transitions from other TFSMs. We remark that timing constraints are captured explicitly by allowing/disallowing transitions labeled with *tick*. For instance, an urgent state is a state which disallows ticks.

Example 1. Fig. 1 shows a TFSM which models a process in Fischer's mutual exclusion protocol. The double-lined circle denotes the initial state. GV contains two variables. Variable id denotes the identifier of the latest process attempting to access the critical session. It is initially 0, which means that no process is attempting. Variable

---

[1] Asynchronous channels can be mimicked using shared variables.

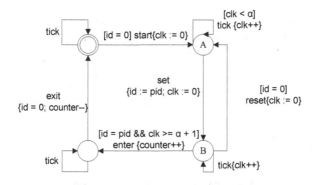

Fig. 1. A TFSM model with clock variables

counter counts the number of processes currently accessing the critical session. By design, *counter* should be always less than 2. The local variable *pid* is a unique process identifier which is a constant. In addition, variable $clk \in LV$ is a clock variable which tracks the passage of time. Initially, the TFSM awaits until $id = 0$ and then performs event *start*. At state A, it can set id to its pid (indicating that it is trying to get into the critical session). Event *set* must occur within α time units as the *tick* transition is guarded by $clk < \alpha$. At state B, the TFSM waits for at least $\alpha + 1$ time units and then checks whether id is still same as its pid. If so, it enters the critical session; otherwise, it restarts from the beginning via the *reset* event.   □

TFSM can be encoded in BDD following the standard approach. That is, a BDD can be used to encode symbolically the system configuration including valuation of global and local variables as well as the control states. Using two sequences of Boolean variables $\overrightarrow{x}$ and $\overrightarrow{x}'$ (which represent system configurations before and after a transition respectively), transitions of TFSMs can be encoded as BDDs constituted by $\overrightarrow{x}$ and $\overrightarrow{x}'$. An encoded transition is of the form: $g \wedge e \wedge t$ such that g (over $\overrightarrow{x}$) is the encoded guard condition; e is the encoded event and t (over $\overrightarrow{x}$ and $\overrightarrow{x}'$) is the encoded transaction. Interested readers are referred to [11] for details on encoding TFSM.

The encoding of a TFSM is a tuple $\mathcal{B} = (\overrightarrow{V}, \overrightarrow{v}, Init, Trans, Out, In, Tick)$. $\overrightarrow{V}$ is a set of unprimed Boolean variables encoding global variables, event names including the clock tick, channel names, and channel buffers, which are calculated for the whole system before encoding. $\overrightarrow{v}$ is a set of variables encoding local variables and local control states; *Init* is a formula over $\overrightarrow{V}$ and $\overrightarrow{v}$, which encodes the initial valuation of the variables. *Trans* is a set of encoded transitions *excluding tick transitions*. *Out* (*In*) is a set of encoded transitions labeled with synchronous channel output (input). Note that transitions in *Out* and *In* cannot occur by itself, but must be paired with corresponding input/output communication of other components. *Out* and *In* are separated from the rest of the transitions so that they can be matched with corresponding input/output transitions later. Lastly, *Tick* is a BDD which encodes all the tick transitions. Note that tick transitions must be synchronized among all concurrent TFSMs. Keeping tick transitions separated allows us to realize dedicated optimizations (see below).

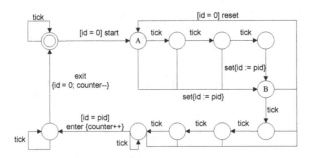

Fig. 2. A TFSM model without clock variables

2.2 Keeping Ticks Simple

In order to handle systems with large time upper-bounds, it is important that we keep the encoding of tick transitions small. There are different ways of capturing timing constraints. For instance, in Fig. 1, the timing constraints at state A and B are captured by using 'clock' clk, i.e., by increasing clk with the tick transitions and guarding system transitions with conditions on clk. Another way of modeling timing constraints is to use only tick transitions without clock variables. For instance, assuming α is 3 in Example 1, Fig. 2 models the same TFSM without clock variables. At state A, at most three tick transitions are allowed to occur before event set occurs, which captures that set must occur within three time units.

We argue that clock variables should be avoided altogether if possible for the following reason. Without clock variables, both the tick transitions and other transitions become simpler since there is no need to introduce a new variable clk; or have transactions to increment clk or to have transition guards on clk. Moreover by generating explicitly the model with tick transitions, we can reduce the state space of the problem. For instance, given the encoding in Figure 1, the total number of potential states (i.e., the product of the control state and the clock value) is 20, whereas with the encoding in Figure 2, it is only 11. This latter encoding thus allows us to save one boolean variable in encoding of one TFSM. This reduction is due to the fact that the latter encodes more 'domain knowledge'. For instance, some of the 20 states are in fact not reachable (e.g., state $(A, clk = 4)$ assuming α is 3) or bi-similar to each other (e.g., state $(init, clk = 0)$ and $(init, clk = 1)$ where $init$ is the initial state).

However if tick transitions are used instead of the clock variables, the number of tick transitions in one TFSM is bigger, linear to the product of all clock ceilings in that TFSM. If we store $Tick$ as a disjunctive partitioned transition function [12], the number of BDDs to encode tick transitions in a system can grow exponentially. Given a system with n TFSMs, each of which has m tick transitions, $Tick$ of the resulted composition has m^n BDDs which are implicitly disjuncted. As a result, the number of BDD-based pre-image and post-image operations grows exponentially too. Thus we store $Tick$ as a single BDD to encode all the tick transitions in a TFSM. It reduces the time spending on BDD-based computation by taking one complex operation instead of m^n simpler operations. Lastly, we compare the two different approaches of encoding timing con-

Table 1. Compare two different approaches of encoding timing constraints

#proc		4	5	6	7	8
time (s)	without clock variables	0	0	0.1	0.2	0.4
	with clock variables	0.6	15	513	×	×
memory (Mb)	without clock variables	21	22	23	24	26
	with clock variables	32	70	425	×	×

straint (i.e., with or without clock variables) and show that avoiding clock variables leads to a smaller BDD (as suggested by the memory consumption) and subsequently significantly more efficient verification (as suggested by the verification time). Table 1 summarizes the experiment results on Fischer's protocol using the model in Figure 1 and 2. Thus, in the following, we always avoid clock variables whenever possible.

2.3 System Composition

A complicated system may consist of many components at multiple levels of hierarchies; and components at the same level may be composed in many ways. In the following, we define a few common system composition functions and show how to generate encodings of these functions without constructing the composed TFSM. We fix two TFSMs $\mathcal{M}_i = (GV, LV_i, S_i, init_i, Act_i, Ch_i, T_i)$ where $i \in \{0, 1\}$, and $\mathcal{B}_i = (\overrightarrow{V}, \overrightarrow{v}_i, Init_i, Trans_i, Out_i, In_i, Tick_i)$ which encodes $\mathcal{M}_i$ respectively. Notice that $\overrightarrow{v}_0$ and $\overrightarrow{v}_1$ are disjoint and $\overrightarrow{V}$ is always shared.

Parallel Composition The parallel composition of $\mathcal{M}_0$ and $\mathcal{M}_1$ is a TFSM $\mathcal{M} = (GV, LV, S, init, Act, Ch, T)$ such that $LV = LV_0 \cup LV_1$; $S = S_0 \times S_1$; $init = (init_0, init_1)$; $Act = Act_0 \cup Act_1$; $Ch = Ch_0 \cup Ch_1$; T is the minimum transition relation such that for any $(s_0, [g_0]e_0\{prog_0\}, s_0') \in T_0$; $(s_1, [g_1]e_1\{prog_1\}, s_1') \in T_1$,

- if $e_0 \notin (Act_0 \cap Act_1) \cup \{tick\}$, $((s_0, s_1), [g_0]e_0\{prog_0\}, (s_0', s_1)) \in T$;
- if $e_1 \notin (Act_0 \cap Act_1) \cup \{tick\}$, $((s_0, s_1), [g_1]e_1\{prog_1\}, (s_0, s_1')) \in T$;
- $((s_0, s_1), [g_0 \wedge g_1]e_0\{prog_0;\ prog_1\}, (s_0', s_1')) \in T$ if $e_0 = e_1$ and $e_0 \in (Act_0 \cap Act_1) \cup \{tick\}$. In order to prevent data race, we assume that $prog_0$ and $prog_1$ do not conflict, i.e., update the same variables to different values.
- if $e_0 = ch!v$ is an output on channel ch with value v; and $e_1 = ch?x$ is a matching channel input, $((s_0, s_1), [g_0 \wedge g_1]ch.v\{prog_0;\ prog_1\}, (s_0', s_1')) \in T$;
- if $e_1 = ch!v$ is a channel output; and $e_0 = ch?x$ is a matching channel input, $((s_0, s_1), [g_0 \wedge g_1]ch.v\{prog_1;\ prog_0\}, (s_0', s_1')) \in T$;

Notice that a channel input/output from $\mathcal{M}_i$ may be matched with an output/input from $\mathcal{M}_{1-i}$ to form a transition in T. It is promoted to Ch at the same time because a channel input/output from $\mathcal{M}_i$ may synchronize with another TFSM in the rest of the system. In the contrast, an event in $(Act_0 \cap Act_1) \cup \{tick\}$ must be synchronized by both machines. If $Act_0 \cap Act_1 = \varnothing$, then $\mathcal{M}_0$ and $\mathcal{M}_1$ communicate only through shared variables or channels, which is often referred to as interleaving. For instance, Fischer's protocol is the interleaving of multiple TFSMs defined in Fig. 1.

Let $(\overrightarrow{V}, \overrightarrow{v}, Init, Trans, Out, In, Tick)$ be the BDD encoding the parallel composition of $\mathcal{B}_0$ and $\mathcal{B}_1$. We have $\overrightarrow{v} = \overrightarrow{v}_0 \cup \overrightarrow{v}_1$; $Init = Init_0 \wedge Init_1$. $Trans$ contains three kinds of transitions.

- local transition: if $g_i \wedge e_i \wedge t_i$ is a transition in $Trans_i$ and e_i is an event which is not to be synchronized (i.e., $e_i \notin (Act_0 \cap Act_1) \cup \{tick\}$), $Trans$ contains a transition $g_i \wedge e_i \wedge t_i \wedge (\overrightarrow{v}_{1-i} = \overrightarrow{v}'_{1-i})$, where $(\overrightarrow{v}_{1-i} = \overrightarrow{v}'_{1-i})$ denotes that the local variables of $\mathcal{B}_{1-i}$ are unchanged.
- channel communication: if $g_i \wedge e_i \wedge t_i$ is a transition in Out_i; and $g_{1-i} \wedge e_{1-i} \wedge t_{1-i}$ is a transition in In_{1-i}; and e_i and e_{1-i} are matching channel input/output, $Trans$ contains a transition $g_i \wedge g_{1-i} \wedge e_i \wedge t_i \wedge t_{1-i}{}^2$.
- barrier synchronization: if $g_i \wedge e_i \wedge t_i$ is a transition in $Trans_i$ and $g_{1-i} \wedge e_i \wedge t_{1-i}$ is a transition in $Trans_{1-i}$ and $e_i \in (Act_0 \cap Act_1)$ is a synchronization barrier and t_i and t_{1-i} do not conflict, $Trans$ contains transition $g_i \wedge g_{1-i} \wedge e_i \wedge t_i \wedge t_{1-i}$.

Out/In contains a transition $g_i \wedge e_i \wedge t_i \wedge (\overrightarrow{v}_{1-i} = \overrightarrow{v}'_{1-i})$ if $g_i \wedge e_i \wedge t_i$ is a transition in Out_i/In_i respectively. These transitions could be paired with matching input/output from other TFSMs running in parallel later. Lastly, $Tick$ contains the transition $g_i \wedge g_{1-i} \wedge tick \wedge t_i \wedge t_{1-i}$ if $g_i \wedge tick \wedge t_i$ is a transition in $Tick_i$ and $g_{1-i} \wedge tick \wedge t_{1-i}$ is in $Tick_{1-i}$.

Unconditional Choice An unconditional choice between $\mathcal{M}_0$ and $\mathcal{M}_1$ is a TFSM $\mathcal{M} = (GV, LV, S, init, Act, Ch, T)$ such that $LV = LV_0 \cup LV_1$; $S = ((S_0 \cup \{done\}) \times (S_1 \cup \{done\}))$; $init = (init_0, init_1)$; $Act = Act_0 \cup Act_1$; $Ch = Ch_0 \cup Ch_1$; and T is the minimum transition relation defined as follows. Notice that we introduce a special state *done* which denotes the state of one component after the other component is chosen. For any $(s_0, [g_0]e_0\{prog_0\}, s'_0) \in T_0$; any $(s_1, [g_1]e_1\{prog_1\}, s'_1) \in T_1$,

- if $e_0 = e_1 = tick$, $((s_0, s_1), [g_0 \wedge g_1]tick\{prog_0; prog_1\}, (s'_0, s'_1)) \in T$;
- if $e_0 \neq tick$, $((s_0, s), [g_0]e_0\{prog_0\}, (s'_0, done)) \in T$ for all $s \in S_1 \cup \{done\}$;
- if $e_1 \neq tick$, $((s, s_1), [g_1]e_1\{prog_1\}, (done, s'_1)) \in T$ for all $s \in S_0 \cup \{done\}$;
- if $e_0 = tick$, $((s_0, done), [g_0]tick\{prog_0\}, (s'_0, done)) \in T$;
- if $e_1 = tick$, $((done, s_1), [g_1]tick\{prog_1\}, (done, s'_1)) \in T$;

Initially when the choice is not resolved, if both components take a tick transition, then so does the choice. Only after one of the components takes an action, the choice is resolved and the other component goes to the *done* state.

Let $(\overrightarrow{V}, \overrightarrow{v}, Init, Trans, Out, In, Tick)$ be the BDD encoding of the choice between $\mathcal{B}_0$ and $\mathcal{B}_1$ such that $\overrightarrow{v} = \overrightarrow{v}_0 \cup \overrightarrow{v}_1 \cup \{choice\}$ where $choice \in \{-1, 0, 1\}$ is a fresh integer variable of value -1 (i.e., the choice is not resolved), 0 (i.e., $\mathcal{M}_0$ has been chosen), or 1 (i.e., $\mathcal{M}_1$ has been chosen); $Init = Init_0 \wedge Init_1 \wedge (choice = -1)$; $Trans, Out, In$ contain the transition $(choice = -1 \vee choice = i) \wedge g_i \wedge e_i \wedge t_i \wedge (choice' = i)$ if $g_i \wedge e_i \wedge t_i$ is a transition in $Trans_i$, Out_i or In_i respectively. Lastly, a transition $(choice = -1) \wedge g_i \wedge g_{1-i} \wedge tick \wedge t_i \wedge t_{1-i} \wedge (choice' = -1)$ is in $Tick$ if $g_i \wedge tick \wedge t_i$ is a transition in $Tick_i$ and $g_{1-i} \wedge tick \wedge t_{1-i}$ is a transition in $Tick_{1-i}$. Moreover $Tick$ also contains tick transitions from $\mathcal{M}_i$ when the choice is already resolved, $(choice = i) \wedge g_i \wedge tick \wedge t_i \wedge (choice' = i)$.

---

[2] In our encoding, matching synchronous input/output are labeled with the same event.

Timeout A common timed composition function is timeout, i.e., if a system component is not responding within certain time units, then another component takes over control. Given $\mathcal{M}_0$ and $\mathcal{M}_1$ and a constant d, the timeout is a TFSM $\mathcal{M} = (GV, LV, S, init, Act, Ch, T)$ such that $LV = LV_0 \cup LV_1$; $S = S_0 \cup S_1 \cup \{state_i \mid 1 \leq i \leq t\}$; $init = init_0$; $Act = Act_0 \cup Act_1$; $Ch = Ch_0 \cup Ch_1$; and T is the minimum transition relation defined as follows. Notice that we introduce t states to remember the time passage while the $\mathcal{M}_0$ delays its first action. For any $(s_0, [g_0]e_0\{prog_0\}, s_0') \in T_0$; any $(s_1, [g_1]e_1\{prog_1\}, s_1') \in T_1$, T is defined as follow

- $(init_0, tick, state_1) \in T$
- $(state_i, tick, state_{i+1}) \in T$ where $1 \leq i \leq t-1$
- $(state_t, \tau, init_1)$. The timeout occurs and the control is passed to $\mathcal{M}_1$.
- $(s, [g_0]e_0\{prog_0\}, s_0') \in T$ for all $s \in init_0 \cup \{state_1, ..., state_t\}$ where $s_0 = init_0$, e_0 is not a tick. Actions from initial state can happen during the d-unit-long period.
- $(s_0, [g_0]e_0\{prog_0\}, s_0')$ where $s_0 \neq init_0$
- $(s_1, [g_1]e_1\{prog_1\}, s_1') \in T$

The corresponding encoding of $\mathcal{M}$ is built in the standard way. Notice that *timeout* can be equivalently defined by adopting an integer clock variable *clk* which is updated by every tick transition and guarding every transition of $\mathcal{M}_0$ with a constraint on *clk*. The above definition, however, keeps tick transitions simple by avoiding clock variables.

Deadline A timed system requirement may put a bound on the execution time of a component, i.e., a component must terminate before certain time units. A TFSM $\mathcal{M}_0$ with a deadline d is a TFSM $\mathcal{M} = (GV, LV, S, init, Act, Ch, T)$ such that $LV = LV_0$; $S = S_0 \times \{0, 1, \cdots, d\}$ where the numbers represent the number of elapsed time units; $init = (init_0, 0)$; $Act = Act_0$; $Ch = Ch_0$; and T is the minimum transition relation such that:

- for any $(s, [g]e\{prog\}, s') \in T_0$ and $e \neq tick$, $((s, d_0), [g]e\{prog\}, (s', d_0)) \in T$ for all $d_0 \in \{0, 1, \cdots, d\}$.
- for any $(s, [g]tick\{prog\}, s') \in T_0$, $((s, d_0), [g]tick\{prog\}, (s', d_0 + 1)) \in T$ for all $d_0 \in \{0, 1, \cdots, d-1\}$.

Similarly, the corresponding BDD encoding of $\mathcal{M}$ is built in the standard way.
Through literature survey and case studies, we collected and defined more than twenty composition functions. Other functions like time/event interrupt, sequential composition, conditional choice, repetition, etc., are similarly defined. Interested readers can refer to [11] for the complete list. We remark that the compositions remain as TFSM and therefore not only system components can be composed repeatedly but also the library of system composition functions is extensible.

3   Case Studies

In this section, we show how to support model checking of two fairly different languages, i.e., closed timed automata and Stateful Timed CSP, using our library.

3.1 Closed Timed Automata

Given a set of clocks C, the set $\Phi(C)$ of closed clock constraints δ is defined inductively by: $\delta := x \sim n \mid \neg\delta \mid \delta \wedge \delta$ where $\sim \in \{=, \leq, \geq\}$; x is a clock in C and $n \in \mathbb{R}^+$ is a constant. Without loss of generality (Lemma 4.1 of [13]), we assume that n is an integer constant. The set of downward closed constraints obtained with $\sim = \leq$ is denoted as $\Phi_\leq(C)$. A clock valuation v for a set of clocks C is a function which assigns a real value to each clock. A clock valuation v satisfies a clock constraint δ, written as $v \models \delta$, if and only if δ evaluates to true using the clock values given by v. For $d \in \mathbb{R}_+$, let $v + d$ denote the clock valuation v' such that $v'(c) = v(c) + d$ for all $c \in C$. For $X \subseteq C$, let clock resetting notion $[X \mapsto 0]v$ denote the valuation v' such that $v'(c) = v(c)$ for all $c \in C \setminus X$ and $v'(x) = 0$ for all $x \in X$.

Definition 2. *A closed timed automaton $\mathcal{A}$ is a tuple $(S, init, \Sigma, C, L, \rightarrow)$ where S is a finite set of states; $init \in S$ is an initial state; Σ is an alphabet; C is a finite set of clocks; $L : S \rightarrow \Phi_\leq(C)$ is a function which associates an invariant with each state; $\rightarrow: S \times \Sigma \times \Phi(C) \times 2^C \times S$ is a labeled transition relation.*

A transition $(s, e, \delta, X, s') \in \rightarrow$ is fired only if δ and $L(s)$ are satisfied by the current clock valuation v and $[X \mapsto 0]v$ satisfies $L(s')$. After event e occurs, clocks in X are set to zero. Given any clock c in C, the upper-bound of time constraints associated with a clock c, denoted as $\lceil c \rceil$, is called its ceiling. A closed timed automaton can be digitized [4] and interpreted as a TFSM $\mathcal{M} = (\varnothing, \varnothing, St, x_{init}, Act, \varnothing, T)$ which is defined as follows. A state in St is a pair (s, v) where $s \in S$ and v is the valuation of all the clocks in C such that for every clock $c \in C$, $v(c)$ is a number in $\{0, \cdots, \lceil c \rceil\}$; $x_{init} = (init, v_0)$ where v_0 is a clock valuation which assigns every clock value 0; and T contains two kinds of transitions.

- event-transitions: for any $(s, e, \delta, X, s') \in \rightarrow$, $((s, v), e, (s', v')) \in T$ if v satisfies δ and $L(s)$ and $v' = [X \mapsto 0]v$ and v' satisfies $L(s')$.
- time-transitions: for any $(s, v) \in S$, $((s, v), tick, (s, v')) \in T$ such that for any $c \in C$, $v'(c) = v(c) + 1$ if $v(c) < \lceil c \rceil$ or $v'(c) = v(c)$ otherwise; and v' satisfies $L(s)$.

Notice that timing constraints are captured using tick transitions and therefore in the event-transitions above, the transitions are *not* guarded. It is obvious that our library can be used to support verification of closed timed automata as well as many additional features introduced in UPPAAL. For instance, interleaving of multiple closed timed automata can be encoded using the parallel composition function; pair-wise synchronous channel communications can be captured using channels supported in the library; etc. Furthermore, it is straightforward to support hierarchical timed automata [14,15] using our library (by applying the corresponding composition functions) as long as all clock constraints are closed.

It is worth mentioning that a clock which is shared by multiple timed automata is modeled as a shared variable (ranging from 0 to $\lceil c \rceil$) in GV rather than resolved using tick transitions, due to arbitrary clock resetting. A tick transition in the composition is associated with a program which increases every shared clock except those which have reached their ceilings. This encoding complicates the encoding of tick transitions. Nonetheless, we observe that many real-world timed systems use local clocks only.

3.2   Stateful Timed CSP

Stateful Timed CSP (STCSP) [10] extends Timed CSP to capture hierarchical timed systems with non-trivial data structures and operations. Different from timed automata, STCSP relies on implicit clocks to capture timed aspects of system behaviors. It has been shown that STCSP, like Timed CSP, is equivalent to closed timed automata with τ-transitions [10], and thus can be potentially supported by our library.

A STCSP model is a tuple $\mathcal{S} = (Var, init_G, P)$ where Var is a finite set of *finite-domain* global variables, $init_G$ is the initial valuation of the variables and P is a timed process. Process P can be defined using a rich set of process constructs. The following shows a core subset of them.

$$P = Stop \mid Skip \mid e \to P \mid a\{program\} \to P \mid if\ (b)\ \{P\}\ else\ \{Q\} \mid P;\ Q$$
$$\mid P \setminus X \mid (P \mid Q) \mid P \parallel[\ X\ ]\mid Q \mid Wait[d] \mid P\ timeout[d]\ Q$$
$$\mid P\ interrupt[d]\ Q \mid P\ within[d] \mid P\ deadline[d] \mid Q$$

The un-timed process operators are either borrowed from CSP [16] or self-explanatory. We thus focus on the timed operators. Assume that d is a positive integer constant. Process $Wait[d]$ idles for exactly d time units (and becomes $Skip$ afterwards). Process $P\ timeout[d]\ Q$ behaves exactly as P if the first observable event of P occurs before d time units (since process $P\ timeout[d]\ Q$ is activated). Otherwise, Q takes over control after exactly d time units. In process $P\ interrupt[d]\ Q$, if P terminates before d time units, $P\ interrupt[d]\ Q$ behaves exactly as P. Otherwise, $P\ interrupt[d]\ Q$ behaves as P until d time units and then Q takes over. In contrast to $P\ timeout[d]\ Q$, P may engage in multiple observable events before it is *interrupted*. Process $P\ within[d]$ must react within d time units, i.e., an observable event must be engaged by process P within d time units. In process $P\ deadline[d]$, P must terminate within d time units, possibly after engaging in multiple observable events.

Example 2. Fischer's mutual exclusion algorithm can be modeled as a STCSP model $(V, v_i, Protocol)$ where V contains two variables id and $counter$, which play the same roles as in Example 1.

$$Proc(pid) \quad \widehat{=} \mathbf{if}\ (id = 0)\ \{$$
$$Started(pid)$$
$$\}$$
$$Started(pid) \widehat{=} (set\{id := pid\} \to Wait[\alpha + 1])\ within[\alpha];$$
$$\mathbf{if}\ (id = pid)\ \{$$
$$enter\{counter := counter + 1\} \to$$
$$exit\{counter := counter - 1;\ id := 0\} \to Proc(pid)$$
$$\}\ \mathbf{else}\ \{$$
$$reset \to Started(pid)$$
$$\}$$

Process *Protocol* is the parallel composition of the process, i.e., $Proc(1) \parallel \cdots \parallel Proc(n)$ where n is a constant representing the number of processes. Process $Proc(pid)$ models a process with a unique integer identifier pid. If id is 0 (i.e., no other process is attempting), id is set to be pid by action set. Note that set must occur within α time units (captured by $within[\alpha]$). Next, the process idles for $\alpha + 1$ time units (captured by $Wait[\alpha + 1]$). It then checks whether id is still pid. If so, it enters the critical section and leaves later. Otherwise, it restarts from the beginning via $reset$ action.

Given a STCSP model $\mathcal{S} = (Var, init_G, P)$, its discrete operational semantics are defined through a set of firing rules. Elapsed time is defined explicitly through transitions labeled with tick. Interested readers are referred to [10]. Supporting STCSP with our library is not trivial due to two reasons. Firstly, STCSP is capable of specifying irregular or even non-context-free languages (due to unbounded recursion, refer to [16] for concrete examples), which are beyond the expressiveness of our library. We thus focus on a subset of STCSP models which are *finite-state*, as defined in [10]. Secondly, it is not clear what are primitive system components given a STCSP model. Notice that auxiliary variables are sometimes introduced in the BDD composition, which may result in a *non-optimal* encoding. Given a simple system with 1000 simple choices, ideally, 10 Boolean variables are sufficient to capture all outcomes. If the choice pattern is applied each time instead, then 999 Boolean variables are added. This example may suggest that the composition functions should be avoided, whereas we argue that the composition functions may be inevitable as knowing the exact number of states in the composition is as hard as reachability analysis. In order to minimize the overall time, one thus has to find a balance between quick encoding (which may imply more verification time) and fast verification (which may be implied by an optimal encoding).

In this work, given a STCSP model, static system analysis is firstly performed so as to identify maximum sub-systems which do not contain a parallel composition. For instance, in Example 2, the identified maximum sub-system is $Proc(pid)$ where $pid \in \{1, \cdots, n\}$. Next, one TFSM is generated systematically from the maximum sub-systems, according to the firing rules, and then encoded using BDD. Finally, the BDD encodings are composed using the respective composition functions so as to generate the BDD encoding of the model. Notice that extending our library with functions to support process constructs in STCSP is straightforward based on its formal operational semantics.

4 Evaluation

The BDD library [11] has been implemented as part of the PAT framework [17,18]. It is based on the CUDD package, with about thirty classes and thousands of lines of C# code. A range of properties are supported, e.g., reachability analysis or LTL with or without non-Zenoness assumptions or fairness assumptions, etc. Verification of LTL with non-Zenoness assumption is based on a symbolic implementation of the automata-based approach [19], with an additional checking for non-Zenoness (i.e., a strongly connected component is accepting if it is not only Büchi fair but also contains at least one tick transition).

In the following, we evaluate the model checker for closed timed automata developed based on the library, by comparing its performance with existing timed automata model checkers. An automatic translator is developed to translate timed automata into TFSM using the approach documented in Section 3.1. Notice that there is limited tool

Table 2. Fischer's protocol with 4 processes

bound		32	64	128	256	512	1024	2048	3096
time	PAT	0.5	1.4	5	17	68	293	1297	3018
	Rabbit	5.5	44	570	×	×	×	×	×
memory	PAT	16	21	41	49	104	298	494	519

Table 3. Railway control system with 4 stations

bound		20	40	80	160	320	640	1280	2560
time	PAT	0.5	1.3	4	9	29	105	428	1853
	Rabbit	2.6	5.3	13.4	54.4	256	1510	×	×
memory	PAT	17	24	31	35	62	122	303	446

support (other than our own) for STCSP. Three benchmark systems are used: Fischer's protocol, a railway control system and the CSMA/CD protocol. All models are available online [11]. The test bed is a PC with Intel Core 2 Duo E6550 CPU at 2.33GHz and 2GB RAM. Because the maximal memory for Rabbit is 800MB, in the first two experiments, PAT and Rabbit are both allocated 800MB memory. For other cases, tools are set to run until the memory exhausts.

The first question is how well the library scales with the number of clock ticks. In the first experiment, we exponentially increase the upper bound of the timing constraints while keeping the number of processes constant. Table 2, 3 and 4 summarize the verification time, which includes both system encoding time and searching time (in seconds), and peak memory usage (in Megabytes). × means either out of memory or running more than 2 hours.

All of the properties verified are safety condition which are unreachable from the initial state. The row *bound* shows the maximum time upper-bound. The *bound* in CSMA/CD protocol is in the form m/n where m is the time for signal propagation and n is the time for data transmission. The memory consumption of Rabbit is not available from the tool.

The data confirm that time and memory consumptions do increase with the number of tick transitions. Nonetheless, PAT is more robust than Rabbit, e.g., Rabbit exhausts the memory earlier, whereas PAT is able to handle relatively large time upper bounds (e.g., more than one thousand for all three cases). This outperformance can come from of our strategy of Keeping Ticks Simple (section 2.2). Zone-based approaches like the one implemented in UPPAAL are more robust to the increment of the *bound*. UPPAAL's time/memory consumption remains constant (i.e., about one second and 30Mb) as expected. However, notice that UPPAAL's performance could be sensitive to the ratio of time bounds in a model (even if the bounds are small), which is not the case for digitization-based approaches. We refer the readers to [5] for details.

In the second experiment, we increase the number of processes (while keeping the time upper bounds constant) and compare the performance of PAT, UPPAAL and Rabbit. The verification results are summarized in Table 5, 6 and 7. It can be seen that both PAT and Rabbit offer significantly better performance than UPPAAL on Fischer's protocol and the CSMA/CD protocol. For railway control system, PAT and Rabbit take more

Table 4. CSMA/CD with 4 processes

bound		8/248	12/372	16/497	20/621	26/808	40/1243
time	PAT	5	10	21	35	67	205
	Rabbit	10	32.7	67	90	342	1160
memory	PAT	31	72	126	245	468	518

Table 5. Fischer's protocol with time upper-bound 4

	#proc	8	12	16	24	32	40	50
time	PAT	0.4	1.1	4	20	61	195	531
	UPPAAL	1	200	×	×	×	×	×
	Rabbit	1.6	4.4	12	60	180	473	1142
memory	PAT	17	26	47	136	278	386	757
	UPPAAL	29	629	×	×	×	×	×

time than UPPAAL for less than 10 processes. It is likely due to the queue data structure in the model, which is costly to support using BDD. Compared with Rabbit, in this experiment, PAT is better than Rabbit in Fischer's protocol and railway control system whereas Rabbit is faster than PAT in CSMA/CD protocol

In addition to reachability analysis, our library offers verification of the full set of LTL formulae, LTL with non-Zenoness assumption, etc. In the following, we compare the performance of verifying liveness properties, with non-Zenoness (row -Zeno) or without non-Zenoness (row +Zeno). Two approaches are compared, i.e., zone-based approach implemented in UPPAAL and the BDD-based approach proposed in this work (i.e., row PAT). The liveness properties are all progress properties which are supported by UPPAAL. Notice that verification with non-Zenoness is not supported in UPPAAL. Furthermore, Rabbit does not support liveness.

As shown in Table 8, BDD-based approach can handle more processes than UP-PAAL for Fischer's protocol and CSMA/CD. It is, however, slower than UPPAAL for railway control system. Encoding the queue data structure symbolically, e.g., pushing and popping an element, makes the BDD of the transition function complex. Thus the BDD-based operations over the transition functions are slow. In addition, the experiments suggest that checking non-Zenoness does incur computational overheads. The reason of these overheads is that the additional computation to discard the strongly connected components which do not contain any tick transition.

5 Discussion

The technical contribution is twofold. Firstly, we develop a BDD library which supports verification of timed systems based on digitization. The library is shown to be reasonably robust with a large number of tick transitions and efficient in verifying benchmark systems. Secondly, based on the library, two model checkers are developed to support two different timed modeling languages.

Table 6. Railway control system with time upper-bound 5

	#proc	6	7	8	9	10
time	PAT	1.8	6	16	58	169
	UPPAAL	0.2	1.1	7.9	83.1	×
	Rabbit	53	805	×	×	×
memory	PAT	33	64	170	460	715
	UPPAAL	26	36	111	835	×

Table 7. CSMA/CD with time upper-bound 1/4

	#proc	8	10	12	14	16	32	64	128
time	PAT	0.3	0.3	0.4	0.6	0.8	5	45	593
	UPPAAL	0.4	3.0	22.9	163	×	×	×	×
	Rabbit	1	1	1.3	1.4	1.5	3	16.1	80
memory	PAT	16	17	18	25	28	73	312	661
	UPPAAL	29	51	292	1894	×	×	×	×

Table 8. LTL model checking with/without non-Zenoness

Model		Fischer						Railway Control				CSMA/CD			
#proc		6	8	10	12	14	16	6	7	8	9	4	6	8	9
+Zeno	PAT	5	39	177	599	1653	4345	14	48	157	887	0.2	3	24	106
	UPPAAL	2.3	6711	×	×	×	×	0.4	2.6	24.1	242	0	0.6	662	×
-Zeno	PAT	9	59	269	980	3014	×	21	66	207	1006	0.4	5	55	368

This work follows the line of research on using digital clocks for modeling and verifying timed systems. In [4], the usefulness and limitations of digital clocks have been formally established, which forms the theoretical background of this work. In contrast to the approach in [5] where integer clock variables are used, we use tick transitions only and avoid clock variables so as to obtain a smaller BDD encoding of tick transitions. As a result, we are able to verify systems with many more ticks or processes. In the name of improving modularity, Lamport's method is slightly improved by work in [20]. This work continues the line of work by Beyer [9,8] to cope with large time upper-bounds and supports liveness properties and liveness with fairness/non-Zenoness. This work is remotely related to work on symbolic model checking of timed systems [21]. As for future work, we are constantly optimizing the library so as to encode further state reduction techniques, e.g., symmetry reduction and, more importantly, compositional verification techniques.

Acknowledgement. We would like to thank anonymous reviewers for their extremely valuable comments. This research is partially supported by project IDG31100105/IDD11100102 from Singapore University of Technology and Design, and TRF project 'Research and Development in the Formal Verification of System Design and Implementation'.

References

1. Berthomieu, B., Menasche, M.: An Enumerative Approach for Analyzing Time Petri Nets. In: IFIP Congress, pp. 41–46 (1983)
2. Dill, D.L.: Timing Assumptions and Verification of Finite-State Concurrent Systems. In: Sifakis, J. (ed.) CAV 1989. LNCS, vol. 407, pp. 197–212. Springer, Heidelberg (1990)
3. Havelund, K., Skou, A., Larsen, K.G., Lund, K.: Formal Modeling and Analysis of an Audio/video Protocol: an Industrial Case Study using UPPAAL. In: RTSS, pp. 2–13 (1997)
4. Henzinger, T.A., Manna, Z., Pnueli, A.: What Good Are Digital Clocks? In: Kuich, W. (ed.) ICALP 1992. LNCS, vol. 623, pp. 545–558. Springer, Heidelberg (1992)
5. Lamport, L.: Real-Time Model Checking Is Really Simple. In: Borrione, D., Paul, W. (eds.) CHARME 2005. LNCS, vol. 3725, pp. 162–175. Springer, Heidelberg (2005)
6. Tripakis, S.: Verifying Progress in Timed Systems. In: Katoen, J.-P. (ed.) AMAST-ARTS 1999, ARTS 1999, and AMAST-WS 1999. LNCS, vol. 1601, pp. 299–314. Springer, Heidelberg (1999)
7. Herbreteau, F., Srivathsan, B., Walukiewicz, I.: Efficient Emptiness Check for Timed Büchi Automata. In: Touili, T., Cook, B., Jackson, P. (eds.) CAV 2010. LNCS, vol. 6174, pp. 148–161. Springer, Heidelberg (2010)
8. Beyer, D., Lewerentz, C., Noack, A.: Rabbit: A Tool for BDD-Based Verification of Real-Time Systems. In: Hunt Jr., W.A., Somenzi, F. (eds.) CAV 2003. LNCS, vol. 2725, pp. 122–125. Springer, Heidelberg (2003)
9. Beyer, D., Noack, A.: Can Decision Diagrams Overcome State Space Explosion in Real-Time Verification? In: König, H., Heiner, M., Wolisz, A. (eds.) FORTE 2003. LNCS, vol. 2767, pp. 193–208. Springer, Heidelberg (2003)
10. Sun, J., Liu, Y., Dong, J.S., Liu, Y., Shi, L., André, E.: Modeling and Verifying Hierarchical Real-time Systems using Stateful Timed CSP. ACM Transactions on Software Engineering and Methodology (2011) (to appear)
11. Nguyen, T.K., Sun, J., Liu, Y., Dong, J.S., Liu, Y.: BDD-based Discrete Analysis of Timed Systems, http://www.comp.nus.edu.sg/%Epat/bddlib/
12. Burch, J.R., Clarke, E.M., Long, D.E.: Symbolic Model Checking with Partitioned Transistion Relations. In: VLSI, pp. 49–58 (1991)
13. Alur, R., Dill, D.L.: A Theory of Timed Automata. Theoretical Computer Science 126, 183–235 (1994)
14. Jin, X.L., Ma, H.D., Gu, Z.H.: Real-Time Component Composition Using Hierarchical Timed Automata. In: QSIC, pp. 90–99. IEEE (2007)
15. David, A., David, R., Möller, M.O.: From HUPPAAL to UPPAAL - A Translation from Hierarchical Timed Automata to Flat Timed Automata. Technical report, Department of Computer Science, University of Aarhus (2001)
16. Hoare, C.A.R.: Communicating Sequential Processes. International Series in Computer Science. Prentice-Hall (1985)
17. Sun, J., Liu, Y., Dong, J.S., Pang, J.: PAT: Towards Flexible Verification under Fairness. In: Bouajjani, A., Maler, O. (eds.) CAV 2009. LNCS, vol. 5643, pp. 709–714. Springer, Heidelberg (2009)
18. Liu, Y., Sun, J., Dong, J.S.: Developing Model Checkers Using PAT. In: Bouajjani, A., Chin, W.-N. (eds.) ATVA 2010. LNCS, vol. 6252, pp. 371–377. Springer, Heidelberg (2010)
19. Vardi, M.Y., Wolper, P.: An Automata-Theoretic Approach to Automatic Program Verification. In: LICS, pp. 332–344. IEEE Computer Society (1986)
20. Wang, H., MacCaull, W.: Verifying Real-Time Systems using Explicit-time Description Methods. In: QFM. EPTCS, vol. 13, pp. 67–78 (2009)
21. Morbé, G., Pigorsch, F., Scholl, C.: Fully Symbolic Model Checking for Timed Automata. In: Gopalakrishnan, G., Qadeer, S. (eds.) CAV 2011. LNCS, vol. 6806, pp. 616–632. Springer, Heidelberg (2011)

Experience Report on Designing and Developing Control Components Using Formal Methods

Ammar Osaiweran[1], Tom Fransen[2], Jan Friso Groote[1],
and Bart van Rijnsoever[2]

[1] Eindhoven University of Technology, Eindhoven, The Netherlands
{a.a.h.osaiweran,j.f.groote}@tue.nl
[2] Philips Healthcare, BU Interventional X-ray, Best, The Netherlands
{tom.fransen,bart.van.rijnsoever}@philips.com

Abstract. This paper reports on experiences from an industrial project related to developing control components of an interventional X-ray system, using formal techniques supplied by the Analytical Software Design approach, of the company Verum. We illustrate how these formal techniques were tightly integrated with the standard development processes and the steps accomplished to obtain verifiable components using model checking. Finally, we show that applying these formal techniques could result in quality software and we provide supporting statistical data for this regard.

Keywords: Formal methods in industry; Analytical Software Design.

1 Introduction

This paper demonstrates experiences of developing control components of an interventional X-ray imaging system, using a formal development approach, called the Analytical Software Design (ASD). The work was carried out in one of industrial projects of the business unit Interventional X-ray (iXR), at Philips Healthcare.

Figure 1 presents an example of such type of systems, depicting a number of movable parts such as the patient table, the stand that holds the X-ray collimator and the image detector. It also depicts graphical user interfaces that facilitate managing details of patients and their clinical examinations and visualizing live images.

The X-ray equipment is used to support minimally invasive, image-guided surgeries to, for instance, improve throughput of patient blood vessels by inserting a stent via a catheter where the physician is guided by X-ray images. This way open heart surgeries are avoided resulting in increasing productivity, more effective treatments and reduce healthcare costs by shorter hospital stays and higher throughput.

Since the healthcare domain is quickly evolving, many challenges are imposed to such type of X-ray systems. This includes, for example, rapidly supporting the increasing amount of medical innovations, new clinical procedures and smooth

D. Giannakopoulou and D. Méry (Eds.): FM 2012, LNCS 7436, pp. 341–355, 2012.
© Springer-Verlag Berlin Heidelberg 2012

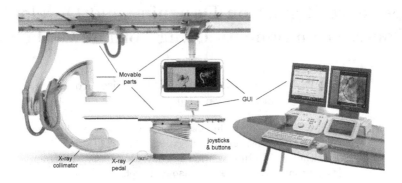

Fig. 1. Interventional X-ray system

integration with products of third part suppliers. Indeed, this requires a flexible software architecture that can be easily extended and maintained without the need of constructing the software from scratch.

To achieve this goal, Philips Healthcare is gradually shifting to a component-based architecture with formally specified and verified interfaces. The development of such type of components is supported by a commercial formal verification tool called the ASD:Suite, supplied by the company Verum [17]. The aim is to build high quality components that are mathematically verified at the design phase by eliminating defects as early as possible in the development life cycle, and thus reducing the effort and shortening the time devoted to testing and integration.

A report has shown that applying the ASD formal techniques resulted in better quality code compared to software developed in more conventional approaches [6]. Therefore, these formal techniques are becoming more and more credible for developing software at Philips Healthcare [5,1,12,7].

The X-ray machines comprise embedded software which includes a number of software modules. One of the key modules is the Backend Orchestration, which is mainly responsible of controlling workflow steps required to achieve the clinical examinations using X-ray.

The purpose of this paper is to report on our experience of how we tightly integrated the ASD approach and its formal techniques with the standard development processes for developing control components of the Orchestration module. It also focuses on the steps followed to design components of the Orchestration module that preceded the steps of modeling and developing the components using the ASD technology. Furthermore, we highlight the limitations encountered during the design process.

The paper demonstrates how these design steps effectively helped us designing verifiable components. We illustrate peculiarities of these components that facilitate verifying them compositionally following the ASD recipe, avoiding the state space explosion problem of the behavioral verification using model checking supported by the ASD:Suite. Finally, the paper investigates the effectiveness of using ASD to the end quality of the module and we show that the module is stable and reliable even during the evolution of requirements.

This paper is structured as follows. Section 2 introduces the ASD approach to the limit needed in this paper. In Section 3 the context of the Orchestration module within the X-ray system is demonstrated. Section 4 introduces the steps of incorporating the ASD approach to the standard development processes for developing the components of the Orchestration module. Section 5 details the steps accomplished for designing components of the module, and the peculiarities that facilitate verifying them easily using model checking. Section 6 details the end quality results of the module.

2   Principles of Analytical Software Design

ASD is a component-based, model-driven technology that incorporates formal mathematical methods such as Sequence-Based Specification (SBS) [13], Communicating Sequential Processes (CSP) [14] and its model checker Failure Divergence Refinement (FDR2) [2] to software development.

A common design practice in ASD is to identify a software design as interacting components, communicating with one another or their environment via communication channels (interfaces). Using ASD, the functionality of a system is distributed among responsible components in levels (e.g., hierarchical structure), to facilitate systematic construction and verification of components in isolation.

At the left of Figure 2 an example structure of components is depicted. It includes a controller (Ctr) that controls a motor and a sensor assumed to be attached to the patient table. Here, we assume that the motor component is responsible of moving the table to the left and to the right. The sensor sends signals to the top controller in case there is an object in the course of a movement to prevent collisions with patients or other parts of the system. We use this example system along with the description of the ASD approach in this section.

Any ASD component is developed using two types of models complementing each other: the interface and the design models. The specification of both models is supported by the ASD:Suite tool. The interface model of a component does not only include signatures of methods to be invoked on the component but also the externally visible behavior and the protocol of interaction exposed to client components at an upper level. It excludes any behavior with lower-level components. The interface model can also be used to describe the external behavior of components not developed using ASD, representing legacy code, hardware and manually coded modules.

The actual detailed behavior of the component is described by a design model, which extends the interface specification with interactions with used components at a lower level.

The ASD interface and design models are state machines, described in similar tabular notations. Each model consists of a number of tables, each of which represents a state in the state machine. An example specification of the interface model of the motor component is presented in Figure 3. It describes the external

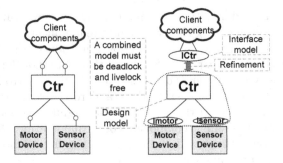

Fig. 2. Example of structured components

behavior of the motor towards the top controller providing the behavior of the very basic movements.

The specification includes two tables that represent two states: *UnInitialized* and *Ready*. Every table comprises a number of rows called rule cases, each of which includes a number of items, such as the interface name (channel), stimulus event, a list of responses and a transition to a new state.

	Channel	Stimulus event	Predicate	Response	State update	Next state	Comment	Tag
1	UnInitialized< >		state					
2	IMotorCtr	initialize		IMotorCtr.NullRet		Ready		
3	IMotorCtr	uninitialize		Illegal		-		
4	IMotorCtr	moveLeft		Illegal		-		
5	IMotorCtr	moveRight		Illegal		-		
6	IMotorCtr	stopMovement		Illegal		-		
7	Ready<IMotorCtr initialize>		state					
8	IMotorCtr	initialize		Illegal		-		
9	IMotorCtr	uninitialize		IMotorCtr.NullRet		UnInitialized		
10	IMotorCtr	moveLeft		IMotorCtr.NullRet		Ready		
11	IMotorCtr	moveRight		IMotorCtr.NullRet		Ready		
12	IMotorCtr	stopMovement		IMotorCtr.NullRet		Ready		

Fig. 3. The tabular specification of the Motor interface in the ASD:Suite

As can be seen from the specification, all possible input stimuli are listed in each table, so that ASD users are forced to fill-in all corresponding items for the sake of specification completeness. The main aim is to find newly unaddressed scenarios and thus initiating discussions with different stakeholders in early phases of the development life cycle.

The ASD:Suite ensures consistency and correctness by automatically generating the tabular specification to corresponding mathematical CSP models [8] and source code implementation in different languages such as C++ or C#, following the state machine pattern of [4]. Usually, any changes to the generated

CSP models or the source code are not recommended. Details of such systematic translations are irrelevant for this paper.

ASD components are built and formally verified in isolation to allow, for instance, parallel, multi-site development. The isolated, compositional verification is especially essential to circumvent the state space explosion problem when FDR2 is used for formal verification. Below we summarize the steps and the recipe required to develop an ASD component, considering developing the *Ctr* component in the structure of models depicted in Figure 2 at the right as an example.

1. External behavior specification. Initially, the interface model of the component is created. Interactions with used components at a lower level are excluded from this specification. For instance *ICtr* is the interface model of the *Ctr* component, where interactions with the sensor and the motor interfaces are not included. *ICtr* specifies how the clients are supposed to use *Ctr*.

2. External specification of boundary components. Likewise, interface models of used components at the lower level are specified. These models describe the external behavior exposed to the component being developed. For instance, *Isensor* and the *Imotor* interface models specifies the hardware external behavior visible to the *Ctr* component. Any internal interactions not visible to *Ctr* are not included.

3. Concrete, functional specification. Upon the completion of specifying the external behavior, a design model of the component is constructed. It includes detailed behavior and interactions with used components. For instance, design model of *Ctr* comprises method invocations from and to the *Motor* and the *Sensor* components.

4. Formal behavioral verification. In this step the ASD:Suite translates all ASD models to corresponding CSP processes for verification using the FDR2 model checker. Verification includes an exhaustive check on the absence of deadlocks (crashes or failure to proceed with any action), livelocks (hanging due to entering an endless loop of internal events and not responding to external commands), and illegal (unexpected) interactions for a combined CSP model that includes the design and the used interface models. When an error is detected by FDR2, ASD:Suite visualizes a sequence diagram and allows users to trace the source of error back in the models. To clarify this step using the *Ctr* component example, the ASD:Suite systematically constructs a combined model that composes *Ctr*, *Imotor* and *Isensor*. Then, the behavioral verification checks whether *Ctr* uses the motor and the sensor interfaces correctly, by checking deadlocks, livelocks, illegal calls and race conditions.

5. Formal refinement check of external specifications. After that, ASD:Suite checks whether the combined model created in step 4 correctly refines the interface model of step 1 using failures and failures-divergences refinement. Errors are also visualized and traced to the models to allow easy debugging. Once the formal refinement check is succeeded, the interface model represents all lower level components. For instance, when the *Ctr* combined model of step 4 refines the *ICtr* interface of step 1, *ICtr* formally represents all lower level components including *Ctr*, the Motor and the Sensor.

6. Code generation. After all formal verification checks succeeded, source code of the component can be generated and integrated with the rest of the code.

7. Iterative development of components. Each interface model can be used as a building block for refinement of new design models. Hence, this allows developing ASD components top-down, middle-out or bottom-up, in parallel with developing the manually coded modules.

3   The Context of the Orchestration Module

The embedded software of the X-ray equipment is divided into concurrent subsystems; among these are the Backend, the Frontend and the Image Processing (IP), see the deployment in Figure 4. The subsystems communicate with one another via standardized, formally verified ASD interfaces. These interfaces are made formal in order to ensure equal understanding of the intended behavior among separate teams developing the subsystems and to reduce communication overhead.

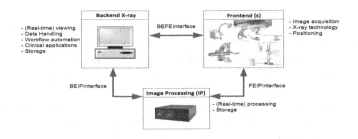

Fig. 4. Subsystems with distinct responsibilities and formal interfaces

Each subsystem comprises a number of software units, each of which includes various modules that encapsulate a number of software components, with well-defined interfaces and responsibilities. Below we briefly address the functionality of the subsystems from a high-level perspective to the extent required for introducing components of the Orchestration module.

The Backend subsystem houses graphical user interfaces (GUI), patients databases and a number of predefined X-ray settings used to achieve required clinical examinations. Through the GUI, clinical users can manage patients' data and exam details and can review related X-ray images. The Backend is also responsible of supporting different types of Frontends.

The Frontend subsystem controls motorized movements of the table where patients can lay and the stands that hold X-ray collimators and image detectors. It is also in charge of calibrating these components upon requests sent remotely by the Backend, based on the predefined X-ray settings, selected from the GUI.

When all components are calibrated and prepared, the Frontend demands the Backend to prepare its internal units before it asks for permission to start image acquisition. Upon obtaining permission, the Frontend starts acquiring X-ray images and sends related data to the IP subsystem for further processing. After that, the IP subsystem sends the processed images to the Backend for viewing on various screens and for local storage to facilitate future references.

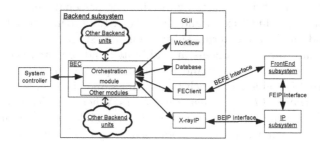

Fig. 5. Relation of the Orchestration as a black-box with other units

The Backend includes a total of 12 software units. One of these units is the Backend controller (BEC), which includes the Orchestration module as one of its control modules. Figure 5 depicts the deployment of the Orchestration module in the Backend surrounded by a number of concurrent (i.e., multiple processes include multiple threads) units on the boundary (e.g., the FEClient unit).

The impetus of introducing the Orchestration module was the result of migrating from decentralized architecture, where units were working on their own, observing changes in the system through a shared blackboard and then react upon them, to a more centralized one. The main challenge imposed on the decentralize architecture was the need to know the overall state of the entire system and whether all units are synchronized with one another in predefined states. Further, maintainability was complex to achieve and utterly challenging.

Therefore, the Orchestration module is used as a central module that is responsible of coordinating a number of phases required to achieve the clinical examinations and harmonizing the flow of events between the concurrent interacted subsystems, preventing potential deadlocks, livelocks, race conditions, and illegal interactions. These phases are summarized below.

The Initialization phase. At the start up of the system, the system controller instructs the Orchestration module to start the initialization phase of the system. Consequently, the Orchestration module initializes and activates a number of internal units of the Backend and the external subsystems through boundary units. This includes ensuring that all required services and configurations are loaded, proper messages and indicators are displayed on user terminals and further that the Backend is connected to compatible, supported subsystems.

The Selection phase. After the Orchestration module ensures that all components of the system are fully activated, the Orchestration accepts selection requests related to the patients and to the clinical examinations and subsequently enters the Selection mode. In this mode patient's data can be selected and sent by the GUI to the Orchestration module through the workflow controller. At the moment of receiving a selection request, the Orchestration checks whether it is allowed (e.g., there is no active image acquisition) to start the selection procedures and then distributes the data to internal units of the Backend and to the external subsystems.

The data includes information about a patient and is applied throughout the system in steps. This briefly starts by distributing personal data of the patient followed by the predefined exam and then the X-ray settings to internal units of the Backend and to the external subsystems. Based on these settings various software and hardware components are calibrated and prepared such as the X-ray collimators, image detectors and performing proper automatic positioning of the motorized movable parts such as the tables and the stands.

The Preparation and Image Acquisition phases. When the selection procedures are successfully accomplished, the Orchestration module can enter the preparation phase. This starts when the Frontend sends corresponding settings back to the Backend in order to properly prepare and program the IP subsystem. After that, the Frontend asks permission to start the generation of X-ray for image acquisition (practically the user presses the X-ray pedal).

When the Orchestration module ensures that all internal units of the Backend and the IP subsystem are prepared for receiving incoming images, the Orchestration module gives permission to the Frontend subsystem to start image acquisition. Based on that, the Frontend acquires the image data and sends them to the IP subsystem for further processing. The processed images are sent to the Backend for viewing on different terminals synchronized by the Backend.

4 Developing the Orchestration Module

We detail the activities performed to develop components of the Orchestration module, through a total of six consecutive increments. The development process involved 2 full-time and 2 part-time team members. Each increment included two members who were involved not only in developing the Orchestration module but also in building other modules of the BEC unit. The team attended ASD training courses, to learn the fundamentals of the approach and its accompanying tool. Team members had sufficient programming skills, but limited background in formal mathematical methods. During the first three increments one ASD consultant was present who devoted half of his time helping the team to quickly understand the ASD approach.

Steps of developing components of the Orchestration module. The development process within the context of iXR is an evolutionary iterative process. That is, the entire software is developed through consecutive increments, each of which requires regular review and acceptance meetings by several stakeholders. Figure 6 depicts the flow of events performed in a single increment for developing components of the Orchestration module. It demonstrates how the formal ASD approach was combined with the standard development approach in industry.

At the start of each increment, lead architects identify a list of features to be implemented together with related requirements. After the features and the requirements are approved by various stakeholders, the development team provides project and team leaders with work breakdown estimations that include, for instance, required functionalities to be implemented, necessary time, potential risks and effort, and dependencies with other units that may block the development progress of these features.

Based on the work breakdown estimations, team and project leaders prepare an incremental plan, which includes the features to be implemented in a chronological order, scheduled with strict deadlines to achieve each of them. Team leaders use the plan as a reference to monitor the development tasks during regular weekly progress meetings.

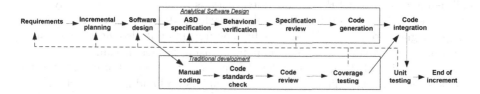

Fig. 6. Integrating ASD processes in a development increment

The actual building of software components begins with an approved design that includes components with well-defined interfaces and responsibilities. Such a design often results from iterative design sessions and a number of drafts.

When the intention is to use ASD, the design differentiates between control (state machines) components and non-control components (e.g., data manipulation, computation and algorithms, (de-)serializing xml strings ..etc). Non-control components are developed using conventional development methods, while control components are usually constructed using ASD.

Non-control components are coded manually, so that checking coding standards is mandatory. Such a check is performed automatically using the TIOBE technology [16]. After that, the code is thoroughly reviewed by team members before it becomes a target of coverage testing.

For coverage testing, development teams are required to provide at least 80% statement coverage and 100% function coverage for the manually written code, using the NCover technology [15]. Upon the completion of coverage testing, the code is integrated with the rest of product code, including the automatically generated code from ASD models. For ASD components, formal verification takes the place of coverage testing, which is typically not necessary for the ASD generated code.

Then, the entire unit becomes a target of unit test, usually accomplished as a black-box. The entire code is then delivered to the main code archive, managed by the IBM clearcase technology [9], where the code is integrated with the code delivered by other team members responsible of developing other units. At the end of each increment developers solve problems and fix defects reported during the construction of the components.

Below we concentrate more on the design phase detailing steps of designing and constructing the components of the Orchestration module using ASD.

5   Design of the Orchestration Module

The Orchestration module was one of the first modules which were built using ASD. At the time of the first increment the ASD tooling used to construct the models was still very immature and difficult to use since it required manual interventions to the CSP models and the generated code. Apart from that the team members were new to ASD and were confronted with the steep learning curve although all formal details were hidden from end users. After the third increment all required manual CSP and code interventions were done automatically.

There was a lack of design cookbooks, guidelines, design patterns or steps that help designers to not only design quality components but also more importantly to construct formally verifiable components using model checking. As a result the first version of the module suffered from some problems. For example, some models were over-specified, too complex to understand and model checking took a substantial amount of time for verification. During a subsequent development increment we decided to refactor the module based on the knowledge gained.

The next section discusses the steps followed to get to a better (ASD) design and the peculiarities of the components that facilitate verifying them compositionally following the previously addressed ASD recipe (see Section 2).

5.1   Design Steps

Designing software is a creative process and typically requires several iterations to come to a final design. So although there is no fixed recipe there are steps that can guide this process. During the design of the Orchestration module we applied the following steps. Consider that although the steps are described in a linear fashion the process is iterative. Even the requirements phase might be revisited because of questions that arise during design.

Setting the stage: the context diagram. As a first step we defined the context diagram of the Orchestration module as a black-box. The context diagram depicts the module and its external environment i.e., all other components it interacts with. Using the requirement documents we constructed the list of messages/stimuli that the module exchanges with the external environment, in other words its input and outputs. The context diagram was used to draw the main sequence diagrams (between the module and its external environment) including the sequence diagrams for the non-happy flow.

Divide and concur: decomposition. As a second step we decomposed the black box of step 1 into smaller components. The decomposition was done by identifying different aspects of the problem domain. As Orchestration is about controlling and coordinating changes in the overall system state (e.g., selecting a new patient or starting image acquisition) we decided to use one overall controller controlling the system state and separate controllers which control details of the state transition when moving from one state to another.

Defining responsibilities. We then re-iterated the list of requirements allocated to the Orchestration module and assigned each requirement to one (if possible) or more of its components. While doing so new components were identified, e.g., the one guarding the connection to the front-end subsystem.

Repeat the process. For each of the individual components the process was repeated. We defined the context diagram, input and output messages/stimuli and the main sequence diagrams for each individual component.

Define Interfaces. Based on the previous step we identified the provided and used interfaces of each component. After that we prepared initial drafts of state machines for each component.

Identify handwritten components and their interfaces. As we are using ASD which does not deal very well with data it is important to factor out code that is responsible for data related operations or code that interfaces to legacy code. In the case of Orchestration the module distributes information which is needed for the state transition (e.g., a reference to the patient to be selected for acquisition). This requires retrieving data from a repository which has to be written by hand.

Constructing ASD models. After all these steps the ASD models (interface and design) were constructed based on draft state machine for each component. In parallel, the code of handwritten components was written.

During the creation of the ASD models, requirements were referenced in ASD tables using tags. Since ASD forces specification completeness, a number of new (missing) requirements were found, e.g., network outages after a failed case selection (so we asked should we reselect default or failed case after reconnection?). This revealed omissions and gaps in requirements early, before verification or even implementation.

5.2   The Resulting ASD Components

The final structure of the Orchestration components is depicted in Figure 7. Below we detail their peculiarities that effectively had helped verifying them compositionally in a reasonable time using the ASD:Suite.

The *BEFacade* component includes a high abstract state machine that captures the overall system states, seen at that level. This state machine knows only whether the system is initialized, activated or deactivated. It includes events that only affect these global states. The detailed behavior that refines these states is pushed down to the Orchestration controller component.

The *Orchestration* controller state machine includes states that capture the overall modes of the system. That is, whether the system is busy activating, performing selection procedures, or performing image acquisition. The Orchestration controller, for instance, does not know which particular type of selection is performed but it knows that the selection procedure is active or has finally succeeded or failed. Detailed procedures of these phases are the responsibility of lower-level components. The same concept applies to all other modes, e.g., activation and acquisition. The Orchestration controller component mainly coordinates the behavior of the used components positioned at the lower-level, give permissions to start certain phase and ensures that certain procedures are

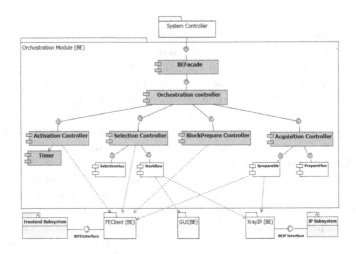

Fig. 7. Decomposition of the Orchestration components

mutually exclusive and run to completion. It also ensures that units are syn-chronized back to a predefined state when a connection with other subsystems is re-established (e.g., reselecting previously selected patient).

The *Selection* controller is in charge of performing detailed selection pro-cedures with other subsystems after getting permission from the Orchestration controller. The Selection controller knows which part of the system has succeeded with the selection. It includes internal components (e.g., the *SelectionMux*) used to distribute selection related signals to other units, gather their responses and reports back the end result to the selection controller. The selection controller informs the Orchestration controller about the end result of the selection, i.e., whether succeeded or failed.

The *Activation* controller handles detailed initialization behavior, by peri-odically checking connections with other subsystems. The Activation controller retries to establish the connection in the presence of network outage and informs the Orchestration with the connection state. When the activation is succeeded, the Backend knows that compatible, supported subsystems are connected, and thus accepts requests to proceed to the following phase.

Other ASD components follow the same concept and related details to their behavior can be found in [11].

5.3   Constructing the ASD Components Following the ASD Recipe

The ASD components of the Orchestration module were realized in a mixture of top-down and bottom-up fashions. Each ASD design model is verified in isolation with the direct interface models of lower-level components, providing that these interface models are refined by corresponding design and other interface models. The compositional construction and verification is visualized in Figure 8 and is self-explainable. Both the Orchestration and the FEClient units were constructed concurrently. The FEClient team provided the *IFEClient* ASD interface model to the Orchestration team as a formal external specification describing the protocol of interaction between the two units, and the allowable and forbidden sequences of events crossing the boundary.

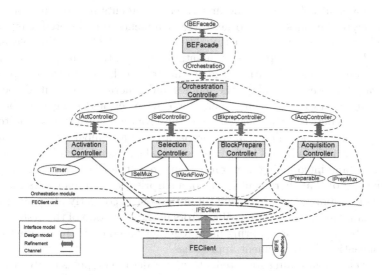

Fig. 8. Compositional construction and verification of components

Table 1 includes statistical data related to the number of ASD models, specified rule cases, generated states and transitions plus time required for verification by FDR2 and the number of (executable) lines of generated code for each ASD component. As can be seen from the table, the models are easy to verify using model checking and the time needed for verification ranges between 1 second to 20 minutes, using the ASD:Suite version 6.2.0.

Table 1. The ASD models of the Orchestration

Component	ASD models	Rule cases	States	Transitions	Time (sec)	Total LOC	Exec. LOC
AcquisitionController	9	458	576296	2173572	30	4151	3891
ActivationController	5	622	351776	1512204	28	2188	2062
BECFacadeICC	2	85	28	33	1	590	502
BlockPrepareController	2	33	16484	55298	1	838	784
OrchestrationController	8	448	9948256	42841904	1111	2940	2580
SelectionController	8	807	2257180	9657242	110	3450	3190
SelectionState	2	42	665	2393	1	622	566
ASD runtime	-	-	-	-	-	852	746
Total	36	2495	-	-	-	15631	14321

The sum of hours spent for developing the module was nearly 1624 hours, with average productivity of 8.8 lines of code per hour.

6   Quality Results of the Orchestration Module

The development activities of the first three increments resulted in a release of the product to the market. The other three increments were devoted to extending the module with additional functionalities and new features. Notable is that developed components were easy to maintain and to extend due to the high-level description of ASD specification, and the abstract behavior of the components. In general, it was easy to adapt the models and generate new verified code.

For example, in the fifth increment there were serious changes in the standard interface between the Backend and the Frontend subsystems, due to evolution of requirements. The changes propagated to a number of units including the Orchestration module. These changes caused substantially adapting existing components and introducing new components (e.g., the *BlockPrepare* controller).

At the end of that increment it was of a surprise to team members especially to those developing other units that all units worked correctly after integration, from the first run, without any visible errors in the execution of the system. They spend a substantial effort to bring units together based on their experience with more conventional development approaches.

The development team submitted a total of 8 detailed reports related to errors encountered along the construction of the module. We refer to [11] for the details of such errors. In general, these errors were easy to locate and fix, not deep design errors.

The development activities of the module yield 19,601 LOC, with an average rate of 0.4 defect per KLOC. This favorably compares to the standard of 1-25 defects per KLOC for software developed in industrial settings [10].

The quality of the ASD code depends on many factors, including thorough specification reviews and behavioral verification. The model checking technology covered all potential execution scenarios, so that defects were found early and quickly with the click of a button. It further took the place of manual testing which is typically time consuming and uncertain.

The quality of the manually coded components depends on many other factors such as code reviews, automatic code standard checks and coverage testing. Unit testing had provided key benefits of preparing coverage reports, detecting potential memory leaks and optimizing memory usage. The total number of test code written for the Orchestration module is 3966 lines of code.

Although there were delays on the deliverable of the module due to spending more time in learning ASD and obtaining verifiable design, there was less time spent in testing and resolving problems compared to the other manually coded modules of the same and other units [3].

Finally, feedbacks from team and project leaders were very positive, and the module appeared to be stable and reliable. The module was robust against the increasing evolution and the frequent changes of requirements. Team members appreciated the end quality of the software, relating that to the firm specification and formal verification technologies provided by the ASD approach.

References

1. Broadfoot, G.H.: ASD Case Notes: Costs and Benefits of Applying Formal Methods to Industrial Control Software. In: Fitzgerald, J.S., Hayes, I.J., Tarlecki, A. (eds.) FM 2005. LNCS, vol. 3582, pp. 548–551. Springer, Heidelberg (2005)
2. FDR homepage (2012), http://www.fsel.com
3. Folmer, B.: Personal communication (backend project leader) (2010)
4. Gamma, E., Helm, R., Johnson, R., Vlissides, J.: Design patterns: elements of reusable object-oriented software. Addison-Wesley Professional (1995)
5. Groote, J.F., Osaiweran, A., Wesselius, J.H.: Experience report on developing the front-end client unit under the control of formal methods. In: Proceedings of ACM SAC-SE 2012, Riva del Garda, Italy, March 25-29 (in press, 2012)
6. Groote, J.F., Osaiweran, A., Wesselius, J.H.: Analyzing the effects of formal methods on the development of industrial control software. In: Proceedings of the 27th IEEE Int. Conf. on Soft. Maint (ICSM 2011), pp. 467–472 (2011)
7. Hooman, J., Huis in 't Veld, R., Schuts, M.: Experiences with a compositional model checker in the healthcare domain. In: (FHIES 2011), pages 92–109, 2011.
8. Hopcroft, P.J., Broadfoot, G.H.: Combining the box structure development method and CSP for software development. ENTCS, vol. 128(6), pp. 127–144 (2005)
9. IBM ClearCase (2012), http://www-01.ibm.com/software/awdtools/clearcase/
10. McConnell, S.: Code Complete, 2nd edn. Micr. Press, Redmond (2004)
11. Osaiweran, A., Fransen, T., Groote, J.F., Rijnsoever, B.: Experience report on designing and developing control components using formal methods. CS-Report 12-04. Eindhoven University of Technology (2012)
12. Osaiweran, A., Schuts, M., Hooman, J., Wesselius, J.: Incorporating formal techniques into industrial practice: an experience report. In: Proceedings FESCA 2012, Tallinn, Estonia, March 31 (in press, 2012)
13. Prowell, S.J., Poore, J.H.: Foundations of sequence-based software specification. IEEE Transactions on Software Engineering 29(5), 417–429 (2003)
14. Roscoe, A.W.: The theory and practice of concurrency. Prentice Hall (1998)
15. The NCover home page (2012), http://www.ncover.com/
16. TIOBE homepage (2012), http://www.tiobe.com
17. Verum homepage (2012), http://www.verum.com

Automatic Dimensional Analysis of Cyber-Physical Systems[*]

Sam Owre[1], Indranil Saha[2], and Natarajan Shankar[1]

[1] Computer Science Laboratory, SRI International, Menlo Park, CA 94025, USA
owre@csl.sri.com, shankar@csl.sri.com
[2] Computer Science Department, UCLA, CA 90095, USA
indranil@cs.ucla.edu

Abstract. The first step in building a cyber-physical system is the construction of a faithful model that captures the relevant behaviors. Dimensional consistency provides the first check on the correctness of such models and the physical quantities represented in it. Though manual analysis of dimensions is used in physical sciences to find errors in formulas, this approach does not scale to complex cyber-physical systems with many interacting components. We present DimSim, a tool to automatically check the dimensional consistency of a cyber-physical system modeled in Simulink. DimSim generates a set of constraints from the Simulink model for each subsystem in a modular way, and solves them using the Gauss-Jordan elimination method. The tool depends on user-provided dimension annotations, and it can detect both inconsistency and underspecification in the given dimensional constraints. In case of a dimensional inconsistency, DimSim can provide a minimal set of constraints that captures the cause of the inconsistency. We have applied DimSim to numerous examples from different embedded system domains. Experimental results show that the dimensional analysis in DimSim is scalable and is capable of uncovering critical errors in models of cyber-physical systems.

Keywords: Cyber-Physical Systems, Simulink, Dimensional Analysis, Gauss-Jordan Elimination, Unsatisfiable Core.

1 Introduction

Cyber-physical systems are complex computing systems that interact with physical processes. As the physical processes are closely coupled with the system, it cannot be developed without keeping the physical process in the loop. Thus the first step in building a cyber-physical system is the construction of a faithful

---

[*] This work was supported by NSF Grant CSR-EHCS(CPS)-0834810 and NASA Cooperative Agreement NNX08AY53A. We received useful feedback from our colleagues Bruno Dutertre and Ashish Tiwari and from Professor Martin Hofmann of LMU Munich. We are especially grateful to the anonymous reviewers for their constructive and insightful feedback.

D. Giannakopoulou and D. Méry (Eds.): FM 2012, LNCS 7436, pp. 356–371, 2012.
© Springer-Verlag Berlin Heidelberg 2012

model that captures the relevant behaviors. Physical quantities have associated dimensions that can be represented in terms of some set of base dimensions, for example, force can be given a dimension $mass \times length/(time \times time)$, where *length*, *mass* and *time* are base dimensions. Dimensions can be further classified into units so that length can be measured in inches or metres and mass in pounds or kilograms. Dimensions are used in the physical sciences to check the feasibility of computative formulas for physical laws for dimensional consistency [13]. Such laws also satisfy *dimensional invariance* so that they hold even under changes of units through scaling. Dimensions also provide a heuristic for suggesting such laws. Finally, dimensional analysis can be used to refactor a law involving n variables with dimensions built from d base dimensions in terms of $n - d$ dimensionless product terms.

As cyber-physical systems deal with physical processes, the variables associated with the model of a system often represent the numerical values of physical quantities. While constructing the model of a cyber-physical system, many common errors are indicated by mismatches in dimensions. Dimensional consistency provides the first check on the correctness of such models and the physical quantities represented in it. Manual analysis of dimensions is used in physical science to find errors, but this approach does not scale to complex cyber-physical systems with many interacting components. We present DimSim, a tool to automatically check dimensional consistency of a cyber-physical system modeled in Simulink. DimSim relies on user-provided dimension annotations for a small subset of the variables in the model. As type discipline plays a fundamental role in writing software programs, dimension discipline can play the same role for the design of cyber-physical systems where each variable has a physical meaning attached to it. We argue that dimension discipline eliminates a common source of errors in designing cyber-physical systems. The techniques used in DimSim are general and can be used for languages other than Simulink.

DimSim generates a set of constraints on the dimensions of the inputs and the outputs of the system as given by the interconnection of the system components. Depending on the provided dimension annotations, the dimensions of all the variables may or may not be uniquely determined. If the dimensions of all the variables can be uniquely determined, the dimensional safety question is reduced to the unique satisfiability question. Though the unique satisfiability problem is in general NP-hard [19], dimensional analysis does not have disjunctive constraints, and the resulting constraints can be solved in polynomial time. DimSim uses the Gauss-Jordan Elimination method [16] to solve the constraints and infer (possibly polymorphic) dimensions for all the variables. If the dimensions cannot be determined uniquely (modulo the dimensions of the external, i.e., input and output, variables of the block under analysis), the unification algorithm finds the most general dimension assignment for the variables. If the set of dimensional constraints is found to be inconsistent, DimSim provides a minimal subset of constraints that helps pinpoint the source of the error.

One of our goals is to provide a tool that is scalable to large models. As the Gauss-Jordan Elimination method takes cubic time to solve the constraints, we cannot solve the constraints generated from large models using this technique in reasonable time. To make DimSim scalable to large systems, we adopt a compositional strategy. In Simulink, one can model a cyber-physical system in a modular way by using subsystems. DimSim analyzes one subsystem at a time, and the constraints on the inputs and outputs of a subsystem are propagated to its parent subsystem. While analyzing a higher level subsystem DimSim looks only at the dimensional constraints of the inputs and outputs of each component subsystem.

We have applied DimSim to a number of examples including a house heating model, a collision detection algorithm from the aerospace domain, and a number of automotive control systems. Our results show that DimSim is scalable and is capable of uncovering critical errors in the model.

In Section 2, we introduce the basic concepts of Simulink through an example, and provide the problem statements. In Section 3, we present our dimension analysis technique: we describe our dimensional constraint solver, and how the solver detects dimensional inconsistency and underspecification of dimensional annotations. In Section 4, we present experimental results on numerous examples. In Section 5 we outline the related work, and compare and contrast our approach.

2   Example and Problem Definitions

In this section, we introduce the basic terminology that is used in the rest of the paper, and formally define our problem.

2.1   Simulink Model

Simulink is used to model cyber-physical systems. A Simulink model of a cyber-physical system is composed of a number of blocks connected by wires. A block may be an elementary block that does not contain any other block, or it may be a subsystem that is composed of a number of elementary blocks and subsystems. Each occurrence of a block in a subsystem has a unique name.

Example. Figure 1 depicts the Simulink model of a cruise control system [3]. The objective of this control system is to maintain the speed of the car at a reference point. Thus the input to the model is the *reference speed* and the output is the *actual speed* of the vehicle. The model has two main subsystems: the *Controller* subsystem generates the control signal depending on the reference speed and the actual speed of the car, and the *VehicleDynamics* subsystem models the response of the vehicle to the control inputs.

We now introduce a few terms that are used in describing the dimensional analysis.

Source Block. A Simulink block that does not have an input port is a Source block. For example, in Figure 1, *ReferenceSpeed* is a source block.

Sink Block. A Simulink block that does not have an output port is called a Sink block. For example, *VehicleSpeed* is a sink block.

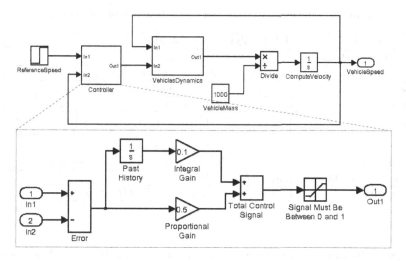

Fig. 1. Simulink model of a cruise control system

Value Parameter. If a Simulink block requires an external value as a parameter, the parameter is called a Value parameter. For example, the constant in *VehicleMass* is a value parameter.

Port Variables. As we explain later, the dimensions of the input and the output ports are represented by dimensional variables. The dimension variables corresponding to the input and output ports of a block are named with suffixes, e.g., _In1 and _Out1. For example, the variables corresponding to the ports of the *Divide* block are *Divide_In1*, *Divide_In2* and *Divide_Out1*, respectively.

Interface Variables. This set of variables covers the dimensions of the output ports of the Source blocks, the input ports of the Sink blocks, and the variables used to hold the parameter values. The user is expected to provide dimension annotations for some of these variables.

External Variables. The variables representing the dimensions of the input and output ports of a subsystem in a model are called external variables for the subsystem. For example, in Figure 1, *In1_Out1* (i.e., the output of the source block *In1*), *In2_Out1* and *Out1_In1* are external variables in the *Controller* subsystem. Note that the set of external variables of a subsystem is a subset of its interface variables.

Internal Variables. In a subsystem, all port variables that are not external variables are internal variables. For example, in Figure 1, *Error_Out1* is an example of internal variable in the *Controller* subsystem.

2.2 Dimensional Constraints

Each port in a block in a Simulink subsystem is assigned a dimension variable. A dimension variable denotes a vector of rational numbers, where each position

Table 1. Dimensional constraints for different Simulink blocks

Simulink Block	Block Type	Constraints
Abs, Unary Minus	$[D_1 \rightarrow D_2]$	$D_2 = D_1$
Add, Subtract	$[D_1, D_2 \rightarrow D_3]$	$D_2 = D_1, D_3 = D_1$
Product	$[D_1, D_2 \rightarrow D_3]$	$D_3 = add\_dim(D_1, D_2)$
Divide	$[D_1, D_2 \rightarrow D_3]$	$D_3 = add\_dim(D_1, inv\_dim(D_2))$
Trigonometric Function	$[D_1 \rightarrow D_2]$	$extract\_dim(D_1, \delta) = \begin{cases} 1 \text{ if } \delta = angle \\ 0 \text{ if } \delta \neq angle \end{cases}$ $D_2 = dimensionless$
Relational Operator	$[D_1, D_2 \rightarrow D_3]$	$D_2 = D_1, D_3 = dimensionless$
Memory, Unit Delay	$[D_1 \rightarrow D_2]$	$D_2 = D_1$
Integrator	$[D_1 \rightarrow D_2]$	$D_2 = inc\_dim(D_1, time, 1)$

corresponds to an exponent of a base dimension. For example, if the base dimensions are length, mass, and time, then the dimension for force will be a vector $\langle L = 1, M = 1, T = -2 \rangle$. Note, however, that the set of base dimensions can be defined for each specific dimensional analysis problem.

In Table 1, we present the dimensional constraints generated from some basic Simulink blocks. DimSim handles many other Simulink blocks that are used in different embedded system domains. The dimension type of a Simulink block is a relation between the dimension variables representing the input ports of the block and the dimension variables representing the output ports. The function add_dim takes two dimension vectors as inputs and computes the output dimension vector element-wise by adding the exponents of the base dimensions of the inputs. The function inv_dim takes a dimension vector as input and returns a dimension vector whose components are obtained by negating the components of the input vector. The function $extract\_dim$ takes as argument, a dimension vector D and a base dimension δ, and returns the exponent value of the base dimension δ in the dimension vector D. The function inc_dim takes as input a dimension vector D_1, a base dimension δ which appears in D_1 and an integer k and returns a dimension vector D_2 which is obtained by adding k to the exponent of δ in D_1, and leaving the other base dimensions in D_1 unchanged.

As an example, the dimensional constraints from the cruise control model are shown in Figure 2.

2.3 Problem Definition

A user may provide a dimension annotation for an interface variable of a Simulink block. For example, the dimension of the source *ReferenceSpeed* is $\langle L = 1, M = 0, T = -1 \rangle$ and the dimension of the output of the Constant block *VehicleMass* is $\langle L = 0, M = 1, T = 0 \rangle$, where L, M, and T denote the exponent of the base dimensions *length*, *mass*, and *time*, respectively. We do not use a fixed set of base dimensions in DimSim, but instead extract the set of base dimensions from those used in the model.

$(\texttt{VehicleDynamics\_\_In1} = \langle \texttt{L} = 1,\ \texttt{M} = 0,\ \texttt{T} = -1 \rangle) \wedge (\texttt{VehicleDynamics\_\_In2} =$
$\langle \texttt{L} = 0,\ \texttt{M} = 0,\ \texttt{T} = 0 \rangle) \wedge (\texttt{VehicleDynamics\_\_Out1} = \langle \texttt{L} = 1,\ \texttt{M} = 1,\ \texttt{T} = -2 \rangle) \wedge$
(constraints from VehicleDynamics Subsystem)
$(\texttt{Controller\_\_In1} = \texttt{Controller\_\_In2}) \wedge (\texttt{Controller\_\_Out1} = \langle \texttt{L} = 0,\ \texttt{M} = 0,\ \texttt{T} = 0 \rangle) \wedge$
(constraints from Controller Subsystem)
$(\texttt{ReferenceSpeed\_\_Out1} = \langle\ \texttt{L} = 1,\ \texttt{M} = 0,\ \texttt{T} = -1 \rangle) \wedge (\texttt{VehicleMass\_\_Out1} =$
$\langle\ \texttt{L} = 0,\ \texttt{M} = 1,\ \texttt{T} = 0 \rangle) \wedge (\texttt{VehicleSpeed\_\_In1} = \langle\ \texttt{L} = 1,\ \texttt{M} = 0,\ \texttt{T} = -1 \rangle) \wedge$
(constraints provided for interface variables)
$(\texttt{Controller\_\_In1} = \texttt{ReferenceSpeed\_\_Out1}) \wedge$
$(\texttt{Controller\_\_In2} = \texttt{ComputeVelocity\_\_Out1}) \wedge$
$(\texttt{VehicleDynamics\_\_In1} = \texttt{ComputeVelocity\_\_Out1}) \wedge$
$(\texttt{VehicleDynamics\_\_In2} = \texttt{Controller\_\_Out1}) \wedge$
$(\texttt{Divide\_\_In1} = \texttt{VehicleDynamics\_\_Out1}) \wedge (\texttt{Divide\_\_In2} = \texttt{VehicleMass\_\_Out1}) \wedge$
$(\texttt{Divide\_\_Out1} = add\_dim(\texttt{Divide\_\_In1},\ inv\_dim(\texttt{Divide\_\_In2}))) \wedge$
$(\texttt{ComputeVelocity\_\_Out1} = inc\_dim(\texttt{Divide\_\_Out1}, \texttt{time}, 1)) \wedge$
$(\texttt{Out1\_\_In1} = \texttt{ComputeVelocity\_\_Out1})$
(constraints for polymorphic blocks)

Fig. 2. Dimensional constraints generated from Cruise Control model

Dimensional Safety. For a Simulink subsystem, if the port variables of the blocks can be assigned dimensions without violating any dimensional constraint for the basic Simulink blocks in the model, then the Simulink model is dimensionally safe.

DimSim solves the following three problems related to dimension analysis:

Problem 1. Given a Simulink model, find out if it is dimensionally safe, i.e., is there any solution to the set of dimensional constraints. If there is a solution, is there a compact way to represent the set of all solutions. Furthermore, determine the unique solution if there is one.

Problem 2. When a subsystem in a Simulink model is not dimensionally safe, i.e., there is no solution to the dimensional constraints, then provide a succinct explanation of the inconsistency.

Problem 3. When the dimensions of all the variables cannot be uniquely determined from the user provided annotations, compute a minimal set of variables for which the user should provide dimension annotations to determine the dimension of all the variables uniquely. We omit the details of the solution in order to focus on the solutions to the first two problems.

3   Dimension Analysis through Constraint Solving

Our objective is to find out if a Simulink model is dimensionally safe, by which we mean that it is possible to assign dimensions to all the variables in the Simulink model without any conflict. Our dimension analysis algorithm is modular and is executed on a Simulink model in a bottom-up manner. Dimensional safety analysis of a subsystem is performed when all the subsystems inside it have already been analyzed.

DimSim accepts a Simulink model annotated by dimensions. The required constraints are generated by a static analysis of the model, and the generated constraints are solved using Gauss-Jordan Elimination. There may be three outcomes of solving the constraints for a Simulink subsystem - there is no solution, there is a unique solution, and there is an infinite number of solutions. In case there is no solution, the Simulink subsystem is dimensionally inconsistent, and we present to the user a minimal subset of constraints that explain the inconsistency. In case there is a unique solution the values of all dimension variables are known. And in case there are an infinite number of solutions, the Simulink subsystem is dimensionally consistent, but the dimensions of some variables are known only in terms of other dimension variables. Our objective is to determine if there is a unique dimension assignment for all the ports in a subsystem (modulo the dimensions of the external variables). We provide the user with a minimal set of dimension variables that should be annotated for obtaining such a unique dimension assignment of all the variables in the subsystem.

Constraints are solved in a modular manner so that each subsystem is analyzed exactly once using the externally visible constraints exported by each of its component subsystems. The solver also indicates if the dimensional assignment for the signals in a subsystem is unique relative to the dimensional assignment for the external variables of the subsystem.

A static analysis of each subsystem yields a set of constraints (as shown in Section 2.2) over the external and internal variables of the subsystem. For example, a subsystem b of the form $z = u + w; u = xy$ with output variable z, a set of input variables $\{x, y, w\}$, and internal variable u, yields the constraints $Z = U = W; U = X + Y$, where X is a *dimension variable*. Here, each dimension variable X represents a vector $\langle x_1, \ldots, x_d \rangle$ for base dimensions $\delta_1, \ldots, \delta_d$, where x_i is the value for x on the dimension δ_i. The dimension solver transforms these constraints on dimension variables into a reduced row-echelon form. The dimension variables are ordered so that an external dimension variable, i.e., a dimension variable X corresponding to an external variable x, is never solved in terms of an internal dimension variable, i.e., a dimension variable Y corresponding to an internal variable y. In the above example, this yields the solved form $U = W, Z = W, X = W - Y$. This solved form also shows that there is a unique solution to the dimensional constraints modulo the assignment of dimensions to the external variables since it contains no internal non-basic (i.e., free) dimension variables. We can then project out the solved form on the external dimension variables to obtain $Z = W, X = W - Y$. This projected set of constraints, suitably renamed in terms of port variables, is exported to the subsystems that use b. If, for example, the dimension of w in the parent subsystem is identified as $\langle L = 1, M = 1, T = 0 \rangle$, and the dimension of x is identified as $\langle L = 1, M = 1, T = -1 \rangle$, then we can infer that the dimension of y is $\langle L = 0, M = 0, T = 1 \rangle$ and the dimension of u and z is $\langle L = 1, M = 1, T = 0 \rangle$. We represent constant dimension vectors with labels L, M, and T for mnemonic convenience, but a vector $\langle L = 1, M = 1, T = 0 \rangle$ would just be $\langle 1, 1, 0 \rangle$, if the dimensions are length, mass, and time, in that order. Also, the vector $\langle L = 0, M = 0, T = 0 \rangle$ is written as 0.

A dimensional inconsistency can arise when an expression such as $x + \int x\, dt$ generates the unsolvable constraint $X = X + \langle L = 0, M = 0, T = 1 \rangle$. A set of constraints is underspecified if the dimension of some internal variable of a subsystem is not uniquely determined by the dimensions of its external variables. Dimensional underspecification can be ruled out for *well-formed* systems where each value parameter has a given dimension, and each delay element is initialized by such a value parameter with an associated dimension. Underspecification can arise in the absence of well-formedness. For example, suppose a subsystem with input variables x and y and output variable z defines internal variables u and v such that initially, $u_0 = v_0 = 0$, and $u' = u + ux/(x+y)$ and $v' = v + vy/(x-y)$, and $z = u/(1 + v)$, where u' and v' denote the values of the internal variables u and v in the next time step. Since 0 is a dimensionally polymorphic constant, this yields the dimensional constraints $Z = U - V; X = Y$, and there is no way to determine the values of U and V from the dimensional assignment to x, y, and z.

We describe below the details of our modular analysis where we solve the constraints for each subsystem in terms of the solutions provided by analyzing its component subsystems. The dimension solver maintains a table T that contains an entry for each subsystem b in the design that records its

1. Set of external variables Θ_b
2. Set of internal variables Υ_b (disjoint from Θ_b)
3. An array S_b of reduced row-echelon solved forms

For each subsystem b, the solver takes as input the external variables Θ_b, internal variables Υ_b, the constraints Γ_b, and the imported subsystems $b_1 \rho_1, \ldots, b_N \rho_N$, where each ρ_i is the wiring that maps the external variables of b_i to $\Theta_b \cup \Upsilon_b$. Each constraint in Γ_b is a sum of monomials, where each monomial is either of the form $k_i X_i$ for some rational coefficient k_i and $X_i \in \Theta_b \cup \Upsilon_b$ or of the form $k\langle L = 1, M = m, T = t \rangle$ for rational constants k, l, m, and t. For example $X - 2Y - \langle L = 1, M = 0, T = -2 \rangle$ is a possible constraint. The interpretation is that this represents the condition $X - 2Y - \langle L = 1, M = 0, T = -2 \rangle = \langle L = 0, M = 0, T = 0 \rangle$, where the summation operation $X + Y$ represents vector addition, and kX represents scaling. The constraints imported from each block b_i are renamed using ρ_i so as to map the external variables of b_i to the variables of b. For example, an adder block of the form $z = x + y$ might be used in a larger block with the x and y inputs renamed as u and the output z renamed as v. In this case ρ will be $\{x \mapsto u, y \mapsto u, z \mapsto v\}$.

The modular solver builds S_b by computing $solve(\Theta_b, \Upsilon_b, \Gamma_b \cup \bigcup_{i=1}^N \rho_i(\hat{S}_{b_i}))$. Here, Γ_b represents the constraints from subsystem b on the variables in $\Theta_b \cup \Upsilon_b$, $\hat{S}_{b_i}$ is the set of equations exported from S_{b_i}, and $\rho_i(\hat{S}_{b_i})$ is the result of renaming the equations $\hat{S}_{b_i}$ using the map ρ_i. If $\rho_i(x) = z$, then correspondingly, $\rho_i(X) = Z$ on the dimensional variables. In placing these constraints into a reduced row-echelon solved form, the variables are ordered so that internal variables are basic variables in preference to external variables. This is done by numbering the variables so that external variables are assigned smaller numbers than internal ones, and solving each equation in terms of its largest variable. The solving process can fail signalling an inconsistency when, for example, an equation of the form $v = 0$ is introduced, where v is a non-zero vector, i.e., of the form $\langle L = 1, M = \mathbf{m}, T = \mathbf{t}\rangle$ where $\mathbf{l}$, $\mathbf{m}$, or $\mathbf{t}$ is non-zero. In this case, the solver returns $\bot$. If we have a non-$\bot$ solved form S_b the exported constraints $\hat{S}_b$ are those constraints of S_b in the external variables Θ_b.

We use a simple incremental Gauss–Jordan solver for building S_b. For a set of constraints over $\Theta_b \cup \Upsilon_b$, we order the variables so that those in Θ_b are below those in Υ_b. For example, if $\Theta_b = \{x, w\}$ and $\Upsilon_b = \{y, z, u\}$, then we can order the variables as $X < W < Y < Z < U$. We assume that all linear polynomials are always represented as ordered sum of monomials, where each monomial is either of the form kX for a nonzero rational coefficient k or is a constant monomial kv with a nonzero k and a vector constant v, so that $k_1 X_1$ precedes $k_2 X_2$ iff $X_1 > X_2$, and the constant monomial always occurs last. For example, if a polynomial is of the form $(2Z - \langle L = 1, M = 0, T = -2\rangle + 3X - 4W) - (5Y - 2U + 4Z)$, its ordered sum of monomials has the form $3X + (-4)W + (-5)Y + (-2)Z + 2U + \langle L = 1, M = 0, T = -2\rangle$.

The input set of polynomial constraints have the form $\{p_0 = 0, \ldots, p_n = 0\}$. The solved form is a polynomial constraint of the form $\{g_0 = 0, \ldots, g_m = 0\}$, where the leading monomial in each polynomial g_i has a distinct variable X_i, i.e., the basic variable in g_i, so that $X_i \not\equiv X_j$ for $i \neq j$, and no X_i occurs in g_j for $i \neq j$. If Ψ is a solved form, then $\Psi(p)$ represents the result of replacing each occurrence X_i in p by g_i'/k_i, where X_i is a basic variable in a polynomial $g_i = 0$ in Ψ of the form $k_i X_i + g_i'$. This substitution operation can be extended to sets of polynomials so that $\Psi(\Pi)$ is just the image of Π with respect to Ψ. The $solve$ procedure can be defined as follows.

$$solve(\Theta, \Upsilon, \Pi) = incsolve(\Pi, \emptyset)$$

$$incsolve(\{p\} \cup \Pi', \Psi) = \begin{cases} \bot, \text{if } p' \equiv k, \text{ for } k \neq 0 \\ incsolve(\Pi', \Psi), \text{if } p' \equiv k, \text{ for } k = 0 \\ incsolve(\Pi', \{p'\}(\Psi) \cup \{p'\}) \end{cases}$$

$$\text{where } p' \equiv \Psi(p)$$

In this procedure, the initial solved form is empty, and hence there are no basic variables. If we have processed i input constraints, then we have a state Ψ_i to which we add the input constraint $p_{i+1} = 0$. We first place p_{i+1} in an ordered sum of monomials form with monomials ordered in decreasing order of their variables with the constant monomial placed last. We then obtain p_{i+1}' as $\Psi_i(p_{i+1})$, the result of substituting each basic variable X of Ψ_i in p_{i+1} by $\Psi_i(X)$ and placing the result in an ordered sum of products form. Note that all the variables in p'_{i+1} are non-basic in Ψ_i. If the resulting p'_{i+1} is just a constant vector v, then either $v = 0$, the equation is redundant, or $v \neq 0$ and we have an inconsistency and $\Psi_{i+1} = \bot$. Otherwise, p'_{i+1} has the form $kX + p''$ with X as the maximal variable, then we obtain Ψ_{i+1} by adding $p'_{i+1} = 0$ to Ψ_i and replacing each occurrence of X in Ψ_i by $-p''/k$ so that X is now a basic variable in Ψ_{i+1}.

For example, with Θ_b, Υ_b as before, if we start with an empty solution set Ψ_0, we can add $X + 2Y - U = 0$ by normalizing it as $U - X - 2Y = 0$ and adding it to Ψ_0 to obtain Ψ_1. Next, we can add $3W - 2U + X = 0$ by normalizing and substituting the solution for U to get $3W - 2(X + 2Y) + X = 0$. This is normalized as $4Y - 3W + X = 0$ which is added to Ψ_1 after replacing each occurrence of Y in g_1 by $\frac{3}{4}W - \frac{1}{4}X$ to obtain $U - \frac{3}{2}W - \frac{1}{2}X$ so that Ψ_2 is $\{U - \frac{3}{2}W - \frac{1}{2}X, Y - \frac{3}{4}W + \frac{1}{4}X\}$. If there are n constraints in Γ_b, then either $S_b = \bot$ if $\Psi_i = \bot$ for some i, or $S_b = \Psi_n$.

We can now sketch the argument for the correctness of the solver. The dimensional constraints of b are given by $\Gamma_b \wedge \bigwedge_{i=1}^{N} \exists \Upsilon_{b_i}.\rho_i(\Gamma_{b_i})$, where $b_1\rho_1, \ldots, b_N\rho_N$ are the subsystems appearing in b, and $\rho_i(\Gamma_{b_i})$ renames each external variable X of Γ_{b_i} to $\rho_i(X)$.

Proposition 1. $incsolve(\Pi, \emptyset) = \bot$, *iff the set of constraints Π is unsatisfiable.*

It can be easily checked that in each step of the *incsolve* procedure going from Π, Ψ to Π', Ψ', every solution of Π, Ψ, i.e., an assignment of dimensional vector values to variables in Π, Ψ, is a solution for Π', Ψ', and vice versa. In particular, note that every variable in Π, Ψ also occurs in Π', Ψ', and vice versa.

Proposition 2. *For a subsystem b_i, any assignment satisfying $\hat{S}_{b_i}$ can be extended to an assignment satisfying S_{b_i}.*

This is because the non-basic internal dimension variables in S_{b_i} can be freely assigned any value, e.g., the vector 0, and the assignments for the basic internal dimension variables are computed from those of the external variables and the non-basic ones. Strictly speaking, we disallow such internal non-basic variables in S_{b_i} since it implies underspecification (see below).

Proposition 3. $S_b = solve(\Theta_b, \Upsilon_b, \Gamma_b \cup \bigcup_{i=1}^{N} \rho_i(\hat{S}_{b_i})) = \bot$ *iff the set of constraints $\Gamma_b \wedge \bigwedge_{i=1}^{N} \exists \Upsilon_{b_i}.\rho_i(\Gamma_{b_i})$ is unsatisfiable.*

If we replace Π in Proposition 1 by $\Gamma_b \cup \bigcup_{i=1}^{N} \rho_i(\hat{S}_{b_i})$, we know that the latter set of constraints is satisfiable iff $solve(\Theta_b, \Upsilon_b, \Gamma_b \cup \bigcup_{i=1}^{N} \rho_i(\hat{S}_{b_i})) \neq \bot$. If $\Gamma_b \wedge \bigwedge_{i=1}^{N} \exists \Upsilon_{b_i}.\rho_i(\Gamma_{b_i})$ is satisfiable, then so is $\Gamma_b \cup \bigcup_{i=1}^{N} \rho_i(\hat{S}_{b_i})$ since the latter is a subset of the former. For the converse, any solution of $\Gamma_b \cup \bigcup_{i=1}^{N} \rho_i(\hat{S}_{b_i})$ yields a solution of $\hat{S}_{b_i}$ by assigning each external variable X in Θ_{b_i} the value of $\rho_i(X)$. By Proposition 2, the latter solution can be recursively extended to a solution for $\Gamma_b \wedge \bigwedge_{i=1}^{N} \exists \Upsilon_{b_i}.\rho_i(\Gamma_{b_i})$.

We say that a subsystem b is underspecified if either one of its component subsystems b_i, for $1 \leq i \leq N$ is underspecified or the assignment of the internal variables of b cannot be uniquely determined from those of Θ_b.

Proposition 4. *If $S_b = solve(\Theta_b, \Upsilon_b, \Gamma_b \cup \bigcup_{i=1}^{N} \rho_i(\hat{S}_{b_i})) \neq \bot$, then $\Gamma_b \cup \bigcup_{i=1}^{N} \rho_i(\hat{S}_{b_i})$ is underspecified iff S_b contains a non-basic internal variable or for some i, $1 \leq i \leq N$, the component constraint set S_{b_i} is underspecified.*

If S_b contains a non-basic internal variable, then by the same argument as the one given for Proposition 2, this variable can be freely assigned any constant dimensional vector value. This assignment is independent of the assignments to the external variables since for each polynomial g_i in S_b where an external variable is basic, i.e., maximal, g_i must only contain external variables. Conversely, if S_b contains no non-basic internal variables, then each basic internal variable Y only occurs in a polynomial of the form $kY + g'$ in S_b, where all the variables in g' are external. Hence, any assignment of values to the external variables is easily extended to an assignment for the basic internal variables.

Finding an Unsatisfiable Core.

We can also augment the solver to identify the unsatisfiable core in the case of an inconsistency. This is done by the conventional technique of associating each input constraint with a *zero-slack* variable ω_i. For example, if the first input constraint is $X + 2Y = 0$ and the second one is $2X + 4Y + \langle L = 0, M = 1, T = 0 \rangle = 0$, then these are added with zero slacks ω_1 and ω_2 so that the first equation is rewritten as $X + 2Y + \omega_1 = 0$ and solved as $Y = -(1/2)X - (1/2)\omega_1$. When this solution is substituted into the second equation $2X + 4Y + \langle L = 0, M = 1, T = 0 \rangle + \omega_2 = 0$, it yields the normalized form $-2\omega_1 + \omega_2 + \langle L = 0, M = 1, T = 0 \rangle = 0$. Since zero-slack variables are never basic variables, this indicates that the input equations 1 and 2 projected on the d dimensions form an unsatisfiable core. In fact, if the inconsistent equation is of the form $k_1\omega_{i_1} + \ldots + k_n\omega_{i_n} + v = 0$, where each k_i and vector v are nonzero, then if we take the corresponding input equations $p_{i_1} = 0, \ldots, p_{i_n} = 0$, we get that $k_{i_1}p_{i_1} + \ldots + k_{i_n}p_{i_n} + v = 0$, yielding the contradiction $v = 0$. The unsatisfiable core given by the set of zero slacks is minimal: if one of the input equations, say $p_{i_j} = 0$, could be dropped from the unsatisfiable core, this means that the M entry of ω_{i_j} can be given any nonzero value. In particular, if ω_{i_j} is assigned $-v/k_j$, that is, $\langle -v_1/k_j, \ldots - v_d/k_j \rangle$ where $v = \langle v_1, \ldots, v_d \rangle$ for d base dimensions, then the equation $k_1\omega_{i_1} + \ldots + k_n\omega_{i_n} + v = 0$ is consistent. Furthermore, this assignment can then be extended to solution set by assigning 0 to all the non-basic variables other than ω_{i_j}. Hence, the constraint $p_{i_j} = 0$ is necessary.

Proposition 5. *If $S_b = solve(\Theta_b, \Upsilon_b, \Gamma_b \cup \bigcup_{i=1}^{N} \rho_i(\hat{S}_{b_i})) = \bot$, and the inconsistency arises when an input constraint $p_i = 0$ is normalized as $k_{i_1}\omega_{i_1} + \ldots + k_{i_j}\omega_{i_j} + v = 0$, where v is a non-zero dimension vector and $k_{i_1}, \ldots, k_{i_j}$ are nonzero rational coefficients, then normalizing $k_{i_1}p_{i_1} + \ldots + k_{i_j}p_{i_j}$ yields $-v$. Thus, $\{p_{i_1} = 0, \ldots, p_{i_j} = 0\}$ forms an unsatisfiable core of input constraints that is minimal.*

4   Experiments

DimSim performs two major operations: constraints generation and constraints solving. To generate constraints from a Simulink model, DimSim parses the model using Simulink's model construction APIs provided by Mathworks, for example, *find_system* and *get_param*. Using these APIs, DimSim generates constraints sets which are solved using a solver written in Common LISP. The source code for DimSim and the examples are available at http://www.csl.sri.com/~shankar/dimsim.tgz.

Categories of Errors. Through dimension analysis, DimSim can discover errors of the following categories:

Erroneous Annotation. The user provides the annotations for the interface variables, and erroneous annotations can lead to dimensional inconsistency.

Erroneous Design. A wrong design can be detected through dimensional analysis. For example, in the implementation of an *if-then-else* block, the value returned from the *then* block and *else* block should have the same dimension, otherwise the system has some design error. Design errors include missing blocks (e.g., a missing integrator) or an extraneous block.

Incorrect Blocks Usage. A Simulink model may contain a wrong block in place of a correct block. This may happen due to adding a wrong block from the library, for example, a Product block is used where a Sum block is required. It may also be due to an incorrect selection of parameters, for example, the Product block may be used for both multiplication and division operations, but to use it for division, the proper sign should be provided for the denominator parameters.

We illustrate the usefulness of DimSim on the following examples: Thermal Model of a House (TMH) [17], Collision Detection System (CD2D) [6], Cruise Control System (CC) [3], Rotating Clutch System (RC) [17], Engine Timing Control System (ETC) [17] and Transmission Control System (TC) [4]. Table 2 summarizes the size of the models,the amount of time taken by different components of Dim-Sim to solve different subproblems related to dimension analysis, and number of dimensional mismatches found in the model. For each model, we report the number of subsystems, number of blocks, number of port variables and number of constraints generated to indicate the size of the model. To compute the time costs, we carried out the experiments in a notebook running Mac OS X version 10.6.7, with 2.26 GHz Intel Core 2 Duo processor and 2GB 1067MHz DDR3 memory. The results show that DimSim is capable of handling large Simulink models in reasonable time.

We found dimensional mismatches in two of our example models. In Table 3, we present the mismatches found, their type, number of constraints in the generated unsatisfiable core and the effectiveness of the unsatisfiable core. The effectiveness of the unsatisfiable core w.r.t. the subsystem for which the set of constraints are inconsistent is defined as the ratio of the number of constraints

Table 2. Model size, time cost and mismatches found

Model	Model Size				Time Cost		Mismatches found
	No. of Subsystems	No. of Blocks	No. of Variables	No. of Constraints	Constraint Generation	Constraint Solving	
TMH	3	48	79	126	0.663s	0.045s	0
CD2D	9	93	164	212	1.285s	0.142s	1
CC	6	74	139	197	1.028s	0.321s	0
RC	10	102	201	346	1.463s	0.376s	0
ETC	12	113	220	362	1.848s	0.369s	0
TC	34	930	1935	4234	13.984s	11.716s	1

Table 3. Error Data

Error	Model	Type of Error	No. of UC Constraints	Effectiveness w.r.t.	
				subsystem Constraints	total constraints
Error1	CD2D	Erroneous Design	5	19.23%	2.36%
Error2	TC	Erroneous Design	11	5.76%	0.26%

in the unsatisfiable core and the number of constraints generated from the subsystem. The effectiveness of the unsatisfiable core w.r.t. the model is defined in the similar way. The mismatch in the CD2D model is because the two subsystems corresponding to an *if-then-else* block return variables with different dimensions.[1] In TC, the problem arises for the two input ports of an *Add* block with differing dimensions. The reason is a possible omission of a block that could neutralize the difference.

5   Related Work

Computer Science has a very rich literature on dimension analysis, particularly in the context of general-purpose programming languages, for example, Pascal [5], Ada [8], C++ [18], Fortran [12], Java [20,7], Fortress [1] and C [9]. For functional languages, Wand and O'Keefe [21] add dimensions and dimension variables to the simply-typed lambda calculus and Kennedy designed dimension types [10] for ML-style languages. Dimensional analysis was also undertaken for simulation language gPROMS [15] and spreadsheets [2]. Mainly two approaches have been used for dimension analysis: (1) Modification of the program source code either based on language extension [5,20,1], or using existing language features [8,18,12], and (2) Enhancement of the type system using dimensional types and application of unification algorithms using Gaussian elimination to infer dimension types [21,10,15,2,9,7].

---

[1] CD2D is a parametric algorithm where these two branches of the *if-then-else* expression correspond to two distinct modes of the system, each of which is dimensionally consistent. We are grateful to Cesar Muñoz for this clarification.

SimCheck [14], a contract type system for Simulink, supports dimensional analysis of Simulink models through the translation of the model to a set of constraints and uses off-the-shelf decision procedure to solve the constraints. The major differences between SimCheck and DimSim are that SimCheck does not support compositional analysis, cannot detect underspecification and always provides solution in concrete values if feasible, cannot produce an unsatisfiable core in case of an inconsistency, and the analysis in SimCheck is based on a fixed set of dimensions.

DimSim uses a bottom-up compositional strategy to deal with large systems. Among the previous works, only Unifi by Hangal and Lam [7] uses an inter-procedural analysis. However, the goal of DimSim is different from that of Unifi. DimSim verifies dimensional consistency in one version of a Simulink model based on user-provided annotations, whereas Unify monitors dimensional relationships between program variables as the program evolves.

Kennedy has developed a dimensional analysis for F# inspired by type inference in ML [11]. In his approach, dimensional constraints are expressed in the theory of Abelian Groups where there is an associative and commutative operator $*$ with an inverse operation $\{\}^{-1}$. For example, the dimensional constraint $m * \alpha^2 = s^2 * \beta$ would express a constraint where m is a constant representing metres, s is a constant representing seconds, and α and β are dimensional variables. Units as used in F# correspond to dimensions in our system in the sense that *metre* is just a name for the length dimension. Finding the most general solution to a dimensional constraint is equivalent to finding the most general unifier for a constraint $u = v$ in the theory of Abelian Groups using a form of Gaussian elimination. For example, unifying $\alpha * metre^2$ with *second* yields $\alpha = metre^{-2} \times second$. In our approach, we solve directly using Gauss–Jordan elimination to obtain $\alpha = \langle L = -2, M = 0, T = 1 \rangle$. This leads to a simpler solver and more informative error reporting. Unlike all previous works based on constraints solving using linear algebra, DimSim provides a concrete explanation of an inconsistency in dimensions and helps the user pinpoint the root cause of such inconsistency.

DimSim also takes a slightly different approach to polymorphic dimensional inference. For example, Kennedy provides an analog of let-polymorphism, where in a function of the form $\lambda y.let\ smult = (\lambda x.x * x * y)\ in\ (smult\ l)/(smult\ t)$, with l representing a length, t a time, and β the dimension of the variable y, the function is given the polymorphic type $\forall \alpha.[\alpha {\rightarrow} \alpha^2 * \beta]$. Our analysis can also be adapted to admit this kind of let-polymorphism. For example, the expression $x * x * y$ can be seen as having input variables x and y, and a dummy output variable z. This yields the dimensional constraint $Z = 2X + Y$ so that *smult* has the type $\forall X.[X {\rightarrow} [Z : Z = 2X + Y]]$. The dimension of $(smult\ l)$ is $[Z : Z = 2\langle L = 1, M = 0, T = 0 \rangle + Y]$, and that of $(smult\ t)$ is $[Z : Z = 2\langle L = 0, M = 0, T = 1 \rangle + Y]$. The quotient $(smult\ l)/(smult\ t)$ can be given the dimension $[W : W = 2\langle L = 1, M = 0, T = -1 \rangle]$, and the entire lambda-expression has the dimension $[Y {\rightarrow} [W : W = 2\langle L = 1, M = 0, T = -1 \rangle]]$.

6   Conclusions

We have presented DimSim , an automatic dimension analyzer for cyber-physical systems modeled in Simulink. DimSim employs compositional analysis technique to deal with large size Simulink model, and in case of an inconsistency, provides a proof of the inconsistency locally on the offending subsystems. Our case studies on numerous examples show that DimSim does find modeling errors and has the potential to be used in the industrial context.

Our approach to dimensions is pragmatic. We have focused on finding dimension errors in Simulink models of cyber-physical systems. Our dimension system is parametric in the choice of the base dimensions. As an example, in physical terms, angles are treated as dimensionless, but in our system, it is possible to introduce angles as a base dimension. Using angles as a dimension allows certain classes of bugs to be found, but it could be incompatible with calculations of values of trigonometric functions based on their Taylor expansion.

We have not yet extended DimSim to handle units of dimensions such as feet and metres. There are several approaches to incorporating units. One approach (e.g., Kennedy [11]) is to treat each such basic unit as an independent basic dimension so that it is possible to mix different units within a single dimension expression and use arbitrary conversions between units. Another approach is to report an error when different units for the same dimension are mixed. We could also restrict conversions between units to those that are derived using specific scaling and offset operations. We plan to experiment with several different approaches to units in DimSim in order to identify the criteria that works best with cyber-physical models.

References

1. Allen, E., Chase, D., Luchangco, V., Maessen, J., Steele Jr., G.L.: Object-oriented units of measurement. In: Proceedings of OOPSLA, pp. 384–403 (2004)
2. Antoniu, T., Steckler, P.A., Krishnamurthi, S., Neuwirth, E., Felleisen, M.: Validating the unit correctness of spreadsheet programs. In: Proceedings of ICSE, pp. 439–448 (2004)
3. Astrom, K.J., Murray, R.M.: Feedback Systems: An Introduction for Scientists and Engineers. Princeton University Press (2009)
4. Chutinan, A., Butts, K.R.: Smart vehicle baseline report - dynamic analysis of hybrid system models for design validation. Technical report (2002)
5. Dreiheller, A., Mohr, B., Moerschbacher, M.: PHYSCAL: Programming Pascal with physical units. SIGPLAN Not. 21, 114–123 (1986)
6. Galdino, A.L., Muñoz, C., Ayala-Rincón, M.: Formal Verification of an Optimal Air Traffic Conflict Resolution and Recovery Algorithm. In: Leivant, D., de Queiroz, R. (eds.) WoLLIC 2007. LNCS, vol. 4576, pp. 177–188. Springer, Heidelberg (2007)
7. Hangal, S., Lam, M.S.: Automatic dimension inference and checking for object-oriented programs. In: Proceedings of ICSE, pp. 155–165 (2009)
8. Hilfinger, P.N.: An ADA package for dimensional analysis. ACM Trans. Program. Lang. Syst. 10, 189–203 (1988)

9. Jiang, L., Su, Z.: Osprey: A practical type system for validating dimensional unit correctness of C programs. In: Proceedings of ICSE, pp. 262–271 (2006)
10. Kennedy, A.: Dimension Types. In: Sannella, D. (ed.) ESOP 1994. LNCS, vol. 788, pp. 348–362. Springer, Heidelberg (1994)
11. Kennedy, A.: Types for Units-of-Measure: Theory and Practice. In: Horváth, Z., Plasmeijer, R., Zsók, V. (eds.) CEFP 2009. LNCS, vol. 6299, pp. 268–305. Springer, Heidelberg (2010)
12. Petty, G.W.: Automated computation and consistency checking of physical dimensions and units in scientific programs. Softw. Pract. Exper. 31, 1067–1076 (2001)
13. Roche, J.J.: The Mathematics of Measurement: A Critical History. Springer (1998)
14. Roy, P., Shankar, N.: SimCheck: A contract type system for Simulink. ISSE 7(2), 73–83 (2011)
15. Sandberg, M., Persson, D., Lisper, B.: Automatic dimensional consistency checking for simulation specifications. In: Proceedings of SIMS (2003)
16. Strang, G.: Introduction to Linear Algebra, 3rd edn. Wellesley-Cambridge Press (2003)
17. The MathWorks. Simulink - Demos,
    http://www.mathworks.com/products/simulink/demos.html
18. Umrigar, Z.D.: Fully static dimensional analysis with C++. SIGPLAN Not. 29, 135–139 (1994)
19. Valiant, L., Vazirani, V.: NP is as easy as detecting unique solutions. Theoretical Computer Science, 85–93 (1986)
20. Van Delft, A.: A Java extension with support for dimensions. Softw. Pract. Exper. 29, 605–616 (1999)
21. Wand, M., O'Keefe, P.: Automatic dimensional inference. In: Computational Logic-Essays in Honor of Alan Robinson, pp. 479–483 (1991)

Validating B,Z and TLA+ Using ProB and Kodkod

Daniel Plagge and Michael Leuschel

Institut für Informatik, Universität Düsseldorf*
Universitätsstr. 1, D-40225 Düsseldorf
{plagge,leuschel}@cs.uni-duesseldorf.de

Abstract. We present the integration of the Kodkod high-level interface to SAT-solvers into the kernel of ProB. As such, predicates from B, Event-B, Z and TLA+ can be solved using a mixture of SAT-solving and ProB's own constraint-solving capabilities developed using constraint logic programming: the first-order parts which can be dealt with by Kodkod and the remaining parts solved by the existing ProB kernel. We also present an empirical evaluation and analyze the respective merits of SAT-solving and classical constraint solving. We also compare to using SMT solvers via recently available translators for Event-B.

Keywords: B-Method, Z, TLA, Tool Support, SAT, SMT, Constraints.

1 Introduction and Motivation

TLA+ [10], B [1] and Z are all state-based formal methods rooted in predicate logic, combined with arithmetic and set theory. The animator and model checker ProB [12] can be applied to all of these formalisms and is being used by several companies, mainly in the railway sector for safety critical control software [13,14]. At the heart of ProB is a kernel dealing with the basic data types of these formalisms, i.e., integers, sets, relations, functions and sequences. An important feature of ProB is its ability to solve constraints; indeed constraints can arise in many situations when manipulating a formal specification: the tool needs to find values of constants which satisfy the stipulated properties, the tool needs to find acceptable initial values of a model, the tool has to determine whether an event or operation can be applied (i.e., is there a solution for the parameters which make the guard true) or whether a quantified expression is true or not. Other tasks involve more explicit constraint solving, e.g., finding counterexamples to invariant preservation or deadlock freedom proof obligations [7]. While ProB is good at dealing with large data structures and also at solving certain kinds of complicated constraints [7], it can fare badly on certain other constraints,

---

* Part of this research has been sponsored by the EU funded FP7 projects ADVANCE and 214158: DEPLOY (Industrial deployment of advanced system engineering methods for high productivity and dependability).

D. Giannakopoulou and D. Méry (Eds.): FM 2012, LNCS 7436, pp. 372–386, 2012.

in particular relating to relational composition and transitive closure. (We will illustrate this later in the paper.)

Another state-based formalism is Alloy [8] with its associated tool which uses the Kodkod [21] library to translate its relational logic predicates into propositional formulas which can be fed into SAT solvers. Alloy can deal very well with complicated constraints, in particular those involving relational composition and transitive closure. Compared to B, Z and TLA$^+$, the Alloy language and the Kodkod library only allow first-order predicates, e.g., they do not allow relations over sets or sets of sets.

The goal of this work is to integrate Kodkod into PROB, providing an alternative way of solving B, Z and TLA$^+$ constraints. Note that we made sure that the animation and model checking engine as well as the user interface of PROB are agnostic as to how the underlying constraints are solved. Based on this integration we also conduct a thorough empirical evaluation of the performance of Kodkod compared to solving constraints with the existing constraint logic programming approach of PROB. As we will see later in the paper, this empirical evaluation provides some interesting insights. Our approach also ensures that the whole of B is covered, by delegating the untranslatable higher-order predicates to the existing PROB kernel.

2   B, Z, TLA$^+$ and Kodkod in Comparison

PROB can support Z and TLA$^+$ by translating those formalisms to B, because these formalisms have a common mathematical foundation. In the case of TLA$^+$ a readable B machine is actually generated, whereas a Z specification is translated to PROB's internal representation because some Z constructs did not have a direct counterpart in B's syntax. In the next sections we refer only to B, but because all three notations share the same representation in PROB, all presented techniques can be applied likewise to the two other specification languages.

If we specify a problem in B, we basically have a number of variables, each of a certain type and a predicate. The challenge for PROB is then to find values for the variables that fulfil the predicate. For simplicity, we ignore B's other concepts like machines, refinement, etc.

Kodkod provides a similar view on a problem. We have to specify a number of relations (these correspond to our variables in B) and a formula (which corresponds to a predicate in B) and Kodkod tries to find solutions for the relations.

From this point of view, the main difference between B and Kodkod is the type system: Instead of having some basic types and operations like power set and Cartesian product to combine these, Kodkod has the concept of a universe consisting of atoms. To use Kodkod, we must define a list of atoms and for each relation we must specify a *bound* that determines a range of atoms that can be in the relation.

The bound mechanism can also be used to assign an exact value to a relation. This is later useful when we have already computed some values by PROB.

3   Architecture

3.1   Overview

We use a small example to illustrate the basic mechanism how Kodkod and SAT solving is integrated into PROB's process to find a model for a problem. Details about the individual components are presented below after this overview.

Our small problem is taken from the "dragon book" [2] and formalised in B. The aim is to find loops in a control flow graph of a program (see Figure 1).

We model the basic blocks as an enumerated set *Blocks* with the elements b_1, b_2, b_3, b_4, b_5, b_6, b_{entry}, b_{exit}. The successor relation is represented by a variable *succs*, the set of the nodes that constitute the loop by L and the entry point of the loop by *lentry*. The problem is described by the B predicate:

$$succs = \{b_{entry} \mapsto b_1, b_1 \mapsto b_2, b_2 \mapsto b_3, b_3 \mapsto b_3,$$
$$b_3 \mapsto b_4, b_4 \mapsto b_2, b_4 \mapsto b_5,$$
$$b_5 \mapsto b_6, b_6 \mapsto b_6, b_6 \mapsto b_{exit}\}$$
$$\wedge\ lentry \in L$$
$$\wedge\ succs^{-1}[L \setminus \{lentry\}] \subseteq L$$
$$\wedge\ \forall l.(l \in L \Rightarrow lentry \in (L \lhd succs \rhd L)^+[\{l\}])$$

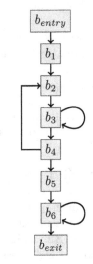

Fig. 1.   Control flow graph of a program

In total, there are seven different solutions to this problem, for instance $L = \{b_2, b_3, b_4\}$ with *lentry* = b_2.

After parsing and type checking the predicate, we start a static analysis (the box "Analysis" in Fig. 2) to determine the integer intervals of all integer expressions. In our simple case, the analysis is not necessary. In Section 3.4 we describe how this analysis works and under which circumstances it is needed.

In the next phase, we try to translate the formula from B to Kodkod ("Translation" in Fig. 2). First we have a look at the used variables and their types: *succs* is of type $\mathbb{P}(Blocks \times Blocks)$, L of type $\mathbb{P}(Blocks)$ and *lentry* of type *Blocks*. *Blocks* is here the only basic type that is used. Thus we have to reserve 8 atoms in the Kodkod universe to represent this type; each atom in the universe corresponds directly to a block b_i. The variables can be represented by binary (*succs*) and unary (L and *lentry*) relations, where we have to keep in mind that the relation for *lentry* must contain exactly one element. The B predicate can be completely translated to a Kodkod problem. In Section 3.2 we will describe the translation in more detail. It can be useful to keep a part of the formula untranslated: since the part *succs* = $\{...\}$ is very easy to compute by PROB, we leave it untranslated. The translated formula has the form:

```
one lentry &&
lentry in L &&
```

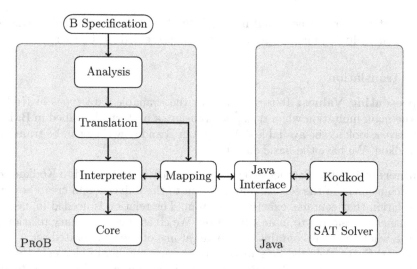

Fig. 2. Overview of the architecture

```
((L-lentry) . ~succs) in L &&
all l: one Blocks | (l in L =>
  lentry in (l.^(((L->Blocks)&succs)&(Blocks->L)))))
```

The translated description of the formula is then stored and a mapping between PROB's internal representation and Kodkod's representation of values is constructed ("Mapping" in Fig. 2). The message "new problem with following properties..." is sent to the Java process.

The Kodkod problem gets a unique identifier and the translated part of the B predicate is replaced by a reference to the problem, i.e., $succs = \{...\} \wedge$ kodkod(ID), and then given to the B interpreter of PROB.

When the PROB interpreter starts to evaluate the predicate, it prioritises which parts should be computed first. It chooses $succs = \{...\}$ because it can be computed deterministically by PROB's core and finds a value for $succs$. Then a message "We have these values for $succs$, try to find values for the other variables" is sent to the Java process.

The Java process has now a complete description of the problem. It consists of the universe (with 8 atoms) and relations for the variables and the type *Blocks* itself. The bounds define the value of $succs$ and *Blocks* and ensure that all relations contain only atoms that match their corresponding types. This information is then given together with the formula to the solver of the Kodkod library ("Kodkod" in Fig. 2) that translates the problem into a SAT problem and passes this to the SAT solver.

The SAT solver finds solutions that are transformed by Kodkod to instances of the relations that fulfil the given formula The values of the previously unknown relations that represent L and *lentry* are sent back in an answer to the PROB process. The answer is then mapped to PROB's internal representation of values.

The B interpreter can now continue with the found values. Now all predicates have been evaluated and the solutions can be presented to the user.

3.2 Translation

Representing Values. It turns out that the available data types in Kodkod are the main limitation when trying to translate a problem described in B. Let's first have a look at the available data types in B and how they can be translated to Kodkod. We have the basic data types:

Enumerated Sets. Enumerated sets can directly be translated to Kodkod. For each element of the set, we add an atom to the universe and create a unary relation that contains exactly that atom. The relation is needed in case the element is referred to in an expression. We create another unary relation for the whole set that contains exactly all atoms of the enumerated set.

Deferred Sets. Deferred Sets in B can have any number of elements that are not further specified. For animation, PROB chooses a fixed finite cardinality for the set, either by an analysis of the axioms or by using user preferences. Then we can treat deferred sets just like a special case of enumerated sets.

Booleans. The set of Booleans is a special case of an enumerated set with two elements TRUE and FALSE.

Integer. Integers in B represent mathematical numbers, they can be arbitrary large. It is possible to represent integer values in Kodkod, but the support is very limited and special care has to been taken. We describe the handling of integers in Section 3.3 in detail.

Thus, we can map a B variable of a basic data type to a Kodkod relation. Since Kodkod treats every relation as a set, we must ensure explicitly that the relations for such variables contain exactly one element.

Example. Let's assume that we use two types in our specification, an enumerated set $E = \{a, b, c\}$ and BOOL. Treating the Booleans as enumerated set $BOOL = \{TRUE, FALSE\}$, we have the following universe with five atoms:

		E		BOOL	
B value	a	b	c	TRUE	FALSE
atom	0	1	2	3	4

We can now represent a variable of type E by a unary relation r1 whose elements are bounded to be a subset of the atoms $0 .. 2$. We also have to add the Kodkod formula one r1.

In B, two or more basic types can be combined with the Cartesian product. Variables of such a type can be represented by a relation.

Example. If we have a variable of type $(E \times E) \times$ BOOL, we can represent it by a ternary relation r2 whose elements are bound to subsets of the atoms $0 .. 2 \times 0 .. 2 \times 3 .. 4$. Like in the example above, we have to add the condition one r2.

We can construct the power set $\mathbb{P}(\alpha)$ for any type α in B. A variable of type $\mathbb{P}(\alpha)$ can be mapped to a Kodkod relation if α is itself not a set. A relation for $\mathbb{P}(\alpha)$ is defined exactly as a relation for α but without the additional restriction that it must contain exactly one element.

Finally, let's have a look at what we *cannot* translate. All "higher-order" data-types, i.e. sets of sets are not translatable. E.g a function $f \in A \nrightarrow \mathbb{P}(B)$ cannot be handled.

It turned out that unary and binary relations are handled very well. With relations of a higher arity we encounter the problem that many operators in Kodkod are restricted to binary relations. Thus it is not as easy to translate many properties using these data types.

Translating Predicates and Expressions. One of the central tasks in combining PROB and Kodkod is the translation of the B predicate that specifies the problem to a Kodkod formula. Many of B's most common operators can be directly translated to Kodkod, especially when basic set theory and relational algebra is used. It is not strictly necessary to cover all operators that B provides, because we always have the possibility to fall back to PROB's own constraint solving technique. Of course, we strive to cover as many operators as possible.

Operators on Predicates. The basic operators that act on predicates like conjunction, disjunction, etc. have a direct counterpart in Kodkod. This includes also universal and existential quantification.

Arithmetic Operators. Addition, subtraction and multiplication of integers can also directly be translated, whereas division is not supported by Kodkod. Other supported integer expressions are constant numbers and the cardinality of a set. If we want a variable to represent an integer, we have to convert explicitly between a relation that describes the value and an integer expression (see Section 3.3).

Relational Operators. Many operators that act on sets and relations can be translated easily to Kodkod.

Figure 3a shows a list of operators that have a direct counterpart in Kodkod. With $\mathcal{T}(A)$ we denote the translated version of the expression A. Please note that the expressions $A \in B$ and $A \subseteq B$ are translated to the same expression in Kodkod. This is due to the fact that single values are just a special case in Kodkod where a set contains just one element. The same effect can be found at the Cartesian product $(A \times B)$ and a pair $(A \mapsto B)$ and at the relational image $(A[B])$ and the function application $(A(B))$.

Other operators need a little bit more work. They can be expressed by combining other operators. Figure 3b shows a selection of such operators. In the table, we use an operator $\mathcal{A}(E)$ to denote the arity of the relation that represents the expression E. Again we can see that different operators in B (e.g. dom and prj_1) lead to the same result.

B	Kodkod	B	Kodkod
$A \in B$	$\mathcal{T}(A)$ in $\mathcal{T}(B)$	$\text{dom}(A)$	$\texttt{prj[1:}\mathcal{A}(\alpha)\texttt{]}(\mathcal{T}(A))$
$A \subseteq B$	$\mathcal{T}(A)$ in $\mathcal{T}(B)$		with A being of type $\mathbb{P}(\alpha \times \beta)$
$A \times B$	$\mathcal{T}(A)$ -> $\mathcal{T}(B)$	$\text{ran}(A)$	$\texttt{prj[}\mathcal{A}(\alpha)\texttt{+1:}\mathcal{A}(A)\texttt{]}(\mathcal{T}(A))$
$A \mapsto B$	$\mathcal{T}(A)$ -> $\mathcal{T}(B)$		with A being of type $\mathbb{P}(\alpha \times \beta)$
$A \cap B$	$\mathcal{T}(A)$ & $\mathcal{T}(B)$	$\text{prj}_1(A)$	$\mathcal{T}(\text{dom}(A))$
$A \cup B$	$\mathcal{T}(A)$ + $\mathcal{T}(B)$	$\text{prj}_2(A)$	$\mathcal{T}(\text{ran}(A))$
$A \setminus B$	$\mathcal{T}(A)$ - $\mathcal{T}(B)$	$A \lhd B$	$(\mathcal{T}(A)$ -> $\mathcal{T}(\beta))$ & $\mathcal{T}(B)$
$A[B]$	$\mathcal{T}(B).\mathcal{T}(A)$		with B being of type $\mathbb{P}(\alpha \times \beta)$
$A(B)$	$\mathcal{T}(B).\mathcal{T}(A)$	$A \lessdot B$	$((\texttt{univ-}\mathcal{T}(A))$->$\mathcal{T}(\alpha))$ & $\mathcal{T}(B)$
$A \mathbin{\lhd\kern-0.4em-} B$	$\mathcal{T}(A)$++$\mathcal{T}(B)$		with B being of type $\mathbb{P}(\alpha \times \beta)$
A^{-1}	$\char"7E\mathcal{T}(A)$	$\text{bool}(P)$	if $\mathcal{T}(P)$ then $\mathcal{T}(\text{TRUE})$ else $\mathcal{T}(\text{FALSE})$
A^{+}	$\char"5E\mathcal{T}(A)$	$f \in A \nrightarrow B$	$\texttt{pfunc(}\mathcal{T}(f),\mathcal{T}(A),\mathcal{T}(B))$
		$f \in A \rightarrow B$	$\texttt{func(}\mathcal{T}(f),\mathcal{T}(A),\mathcal{T}(B))$
		$f \in A \rightarrowtail B$	$\texttt{func(}\mathcal{T}(f),\mathcal{T}(A),\mathcal{T}(B))$ &&
			$(\mathcal{T}(f).\char"7E\mathcal{T}(f))$ in iden

(a) direct translation	(b) more complex rules

Fig. 3. Examples for translation rules

3.3 Integer Handling in Kodkod

Kodkod provides only a very limited support for integers. The reason for this is twofold. Since SAT solvers are used as the underlying technology, integers are encoded by binary numbers. Operations like addition then have to be encoded as boolean formulas. This makes the use of integers ineffective and cumbersome. Another reason is that the designers of Alloy – where Kodkod has its origin – argue [8] that integers are often not very useful and an indication of lack of abstraction when modeling systems.

Our intention is to make our tool applicable to as many specifications as possible, and many of the B specifications we tried contained some integer expressions. Indeed, integers are used to model sequences in B or multi-sets in Z.

When using Kodkod with integers, we have to specify the number of bits used in integer expressions. Integer overflows are silently ignored, e.g. the sum of two large naturals can be negative when the maximum integer size is exceeded. Thus we need to ensure that we use only integers in the specified range to prevent faulty results.

Kodkod distinguishes between relational and integer expressions. An integer expression is for example a constant integer or the sum of two integer expressions. Comparison of integer expressions like "less than" is also supported. In case we want a relation (i.e. a variable) that represents an integer, we must first assign values to some atoms. Figure 4 shows an example with a universe consisting of 9 atoms $i_0, \ldots, i_8$ that represent integers.

atom ...	binary numbers								
	for integer sets								
	i_0	i_1	i_2	i_3	i_4	i_5	i_6	i_7	i_8 ...
associated integer value ...	-1	0	3	5	1	2	4	8	-16 ...

Fig. 4. Mapping atoms to integer values

We have basically two options when we want represent integers by a relation:

- We can represent sets of integers in the interval $a .. b$ by having an atom for each number in $a .. b$. Then the relation simply represents the integers of its atoms.

  E.g. with the universe in Figure 4, we can represent arbitrary subsets of $-1 .. 5$ by using a relation that is bounded to the atoms $i_0, \ldots, i_4$.

  The downside of this approach is that the number of atoms can become easily very large.

- Single integers can be represented more compactly by using a binary number. E.g. with the universe in Figure 4, we can represent a number of the interval $-16 .. 15$ by using a relation that is bounded to the atoms $i_4 .. i_8$. A relation that consists of the atoms i_4, i_6, i_8 would represent the sum $1 + 4 + (-16) = -9$. Kodkod provides an operator to summarise the atoms of a relation, yielding an integer expression.

  With this approach large numbers can be handled easily. The downside is that we cannot represent sets of numbers.

The atoms in the universe seen in Figure 4 are ordered in a way that we can use both approaches to represent integers in the same specification.

It can be seen that we need an exact knowledge of the possible size of integer expressions in the specification. To get the required information, a static analysis is applied to the specification before the translation. See below in Section 3.4 for details of the analysis.

Another problem that arises from having two kinds of integer representations, is that we have to ensure the consistency of formulas that use integer expressions. We briefly describe the problem in Section 3.5.

3.4 Predicate Analysis

In case that integers are used in the model, we need to know how large they can get in order to translate the expressions. To get this information we apply a static analysis on the given problem.

The first step of the analysis is that we create a graph that describes a constraint problem. For each expression in the abstract syntax tree, we create some of nodes depending on the expression's type that contain relevant information associated to the syntax node. E.g. this might be the possible interval for integers, the interval of the cardinality for sets or the interval in which all elements of a set lie.

By applying pattern matching on the syntax tree, we add rules that describe the flow of information in the graph. E.g. if we have a predicate $A \subset B$, we can propagate all information about elements of B to nodes that contain information about A. We evaluate all rules until a fixpoint or a maximum number of evaluation steps is reached.

Example. Let's take the predicate $A \subseteq 3 \mathbin{..} 6 \wedge card(A) > 1$. For each integer node $(1, 3, 6, card(A))$ we create a node containing the integer range. For each of the sets A and $3 \mathbin{..} 6$ we create two nodes: One contains the range of the set's cardinality, the other describes the integer range of the set's elements. Figure 5 shows the resulting graph. In the upper part of each node the expression is shown, in the lower part the kind of information that is stored in the node. The edges without any labels denote rules that pass information just from one node to another. Those which are labeled with $\leq, \geq, <, >$ express a relation between integer ranges of the source and target node. There is a special rule marked $i \rightarrow c$ ("interval to cardinality") which deduces a maximum cardinality from the allowed integers in a set. E.g. if all elements of a set I are in the range $x \mathbin{..} y$, we know that $card(I) \leq y - x + 1$. The graph in Figure 5 shows the information we have about each node after the analysis. In particular, we know the bounds of all integer expressions.

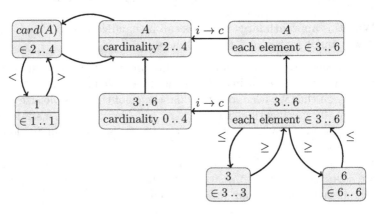

Fig. 5. Constraint system for $A \subseteq 3 \mathbin{..} 6 \wedge card(A) > 1$

Currently the analysis is limited to integer intervals and cardinality, because this was the concrete use case given by our translation to Kodkod. We plan to re-use the analysis for other aspects of PROB. E.g. if we can deduce the interval of a quantified integer variable, PROB can limit the enumeration of values to that range if it must test a predicate for all possible values of that variable.

Other types of information nodes are also of interest. For instance, we could infer the information if an expression is a function or sequence to assist PROB when evaluating predicates.

3.5 Integer Representations

We have seen above in Section 3.3 that we have two distinct forms of representing integers. Additionally we have Kodkod's integer expressions when we want to compare, add, subtract or multiply them. During the translation process we must ensure that the correct representation is chosen for each expression and that the representations are consistently used. If the take a simple equality $A = B$ with A, B being integers as an example, we must ensure that both sides use the same representation.

Internally, the result of the translation is an abstract syntax tree that describes the formula. Some expressions in this syntax tree have annotations about the needed integer representation. E.g., if the original expression in B is a set of integers, it has the annotation that the integer set representation and not the the binary number representation must be used. We now impose a kind of type checking on this syntax tree to infer if conversions between different integer representations have to be inserted in the formula.

3.6 Extent of the Translation: Partitioning

Theoretically we can take any translatable sub-predicate of a specification and replace it with a call to Kodkod. But usually, the overhead due to the communication between the processes can easily get so large that incorporating Kodkod has no advantage over using PROB alone.

A more sensible approach for a specification that is a conjunction of predicates $P_1 \wedge \ldots \wedge P_n$ is to apply the translation to every P_i. All translatable predicates are then replaced by one single call to Kodkod. But even here we made the experience that the communication overhead can become large if not all predicates are translated.

Our current approach is to create a partition of the predicates $P_1, \ldots, P_n$. Two predicates are then in the same set of the partition if they both use the same variable. We translate only complete partitions to keep the communication overhead small. There is one exception: We do not translate simple equations where one side is a variable and the other side an easy to compute constant. Such deterministic equations are computed first by the constraint solver, so the value for such a variable will be computed before the call to Kodkod is made. This keeps the translated formula small even for a large amount of data.

4 Experiments

We have chosen a number of problems to compare the performance of PROB's constraint solving technique and Kodkod's SAT solving approach. We have only used problems that can be completely translated. Completely translated models are still fully integrated into ProB, the results are converted to PROB's internal format and can be used for further animation and model checking. The results can be seen in Table 1.[1] All experiments were conducted on a dual-core Intel i7

---

[1] The source code of the examples are available in the technical report at:
http://www.stups.uni-duesseldorf.de/w/Special:Publication/
PlaggeLeuschel_Kodkod2012 .

2.8 GHz processor running under Linux. MiniSat was used as a SAT solver. The measured times do not contain time for starting up PROB and for loading, parsing and type-checking the model. We measured the time to compute all solutions to each problem. For Kodkod, we measured two different times: The "total time" includes the translation of the problem, the communication between the two processes and the time needed by the solver to produce solutions. The "solver time" is the time that the Kodkod solver itself needs to find solutions, without the overhead of translation and communication between the processes.

Table 1. Comparing PROB and Kodkod (in milliseconds)

Model	PROB	Kodkod total	solver
Who Killed Agatha?	177	123	12
Crew Allocation	timeout*	297	112
20–Queens	110	8223	8076
Graph Colouring (integer sets)	50	2323	1859
Graph Colouring (enumerated sets)	50	1037	818
Graph Isomorphism	13	553	379
Loop detection in control flow	23037	117	12
SAT instance	11830	4143	588
Send More Money	7	1773	1578
Eratosthenes' sieve (1 step)	7	5833	5712
Union of two sets (2000 elements)	33	4880	4659
Requirements WRSPM model	timeout*	333	89
BPEL deadlock check	20	337	68

*: interrupted after 60 seconds

4.1   Analysis

Relational Operators. Let's have a look at those problems where Kodkod is much faster than PROB. These are "crew allocation", "loop detection" and "WR-SPM". In all these problems we search for instances for sets or relations and the problem is described by relational operators and universal quantification. In this scenario, PROB sometimes starts to enumerate possible instances for the sets or relations which leads to a dramatic decrease of performance.

Arithmetic and Large Relations. The arithmetic problems ("Send More Money", "Eratosthenes' Sieve") are solved by ProB much faster than by Kodkod. The first two problems deal with arithmetic. PROB uses internally a very efficient finite domain solver (CLP/FD) to tackle such problems. On the other side, arithmetic is one of the weaknesses of Kodkod, as we already pointed out.

Kodkod does not seem to scale well when encountering large relations (e.g. "union of two sets"). This has only been relevant for certain applications of PROB, such as the property verification on real data [13].

The graph colouring, graph isomorphism and 20-Queens problems are clearly faster solved by PROB. The structure of the problem is somehow fixed (by having e.g. total functions) and constraint propagation is very effective.

Room for Optimization. It can be seen that the graph colouring problem needs less than half the time when it is encoded with enumerated sets instead of integers. This indicates that the translation is not yet as effective as it should be. For the "SAT" problem, the translation and communication takes six time as long as the computation of the problem itself. This shows that we should investigate if we can optimize the communication.

4.2 SMT and other Tools

Very recently, an Event-B to SMT-Lib converter has become available for the Rodin platform [4]. This makes it possible to use SMT solvers (such as veriT, CVC and Z3 [3]; we used version 3.2 of the latter within the Rodin SMT Solvers Plug-in 0.8.0r14169 in our experiments below) on Event-B proof obligations. We have experimented with the translator on the examples from Table 1.[2] This is done by adding a theorem 1=2 to the model: this generates an unprovable proof obligation which in turn produces a satisfiable SMT formula encoding the problem. For "Send More Money" from Table 1 Z3 initially reported "unknown". After rewriting the model (making the inequalities explicit), Z3 was able to determine the solution after about 0.250 seconds. It is thus faster than Kodkod, but still slower than ProB. Surprisingly, Z3 was unable to solve the SMT-Lib translations for most of the other examples, such as the "Who killed Agatha" example, the "Set Union" example or the "Graph Colouring" example. Similarly, for the "Crew Allocation" example, Z3 was unable to find a solution already for three flights.[3] Furthermore, for the constraint solving tasks related to deadlock checking, Z3 was not able to solve the translations of the simpler examples from [7]. It is too early for a conclusive result, but it seems that more work needs to be put into the B to SMT-Lib translator for this approach to be useful for model finding, animation or constraint-based checking.

Other tools for B are AnimB [17], Brama and BZTT [11]. They all have much weaker constraint-solving capabilities (see [13,14]) and are unable to solve most of the problems in Table 1. Another tool is TLC [24] for TLA+. It is very good at model checking, but constraints are solved by pure enumeration. As such, TLC is unable to solve, e.g., a 20 variable SAT problem, the NQueens problem for N>9 and takes more than 2 hours for a variation of the graph isomorphism problem from Table 1.

5   More Related Work, Discussion and Conclusion

5.1   Alternative Approaches

Before starting our translation to Kodkod, we had experimented with several other alternate approaches to solve constraints in ProB. [22] offers the user a

---

[2] Apart from "loop" which cannot be easily translated to Event-B due to the use of transitive closure.

[3] ProB solves this version in 0.06 seconds; Table 1 contains the problem for 20 flights.

Datalog-like language that aims to support program analysis. It uses BDDs to represent relations and compute queries on these relations. In particular, one has to represent a state of the model as a bit-vector and events have to be implemented as relations between two of those bit-vectors. These relations have to be constructed by creating BDDs directly with the underlying BDD library (JavaBDD) and storing them into a file. Soon after starting experimenting with BDDBDDB it became apparent that due to the lack of more abstract data types than bit vectors, the complexity of a direct translation from B to BDDBDDB was too high, even for small models, and this avenue was abandoned.

SAL [20] is a model-checking framework combining a range of tools for reasoning about systems. The SAL tool suite includes a state of the art symbolic (BDD-based) and bounded (SAT-based) model checkers. Some first results were encouraging for a small subset of the Event-B language, but the gap between B and SAL turned out to be too big in general and no realistic way was found to handle important B operators.[4] More details about these experiments can be found in [19]. For Z, there is an ongoing attempt to use SAL for model checking Z specifications [5,6]. The examples presented in [5,6] are still relatively simple and pose no serious challenge in constraint solving. As the system is not publicly available, it is unclear how it will scale to more complicated specifications and constraints.

5.2   More Related Work

The first hand-translation of B to Alloy was undertaken in [18]. The paper [16] contains first experiments in translating Event-B to Alloy; but the work was also not pursued. Later, [15] presented a prototype Z to Alloy converter. The current status of this system is available at the website `http://homepages.ecs.vuw.ac.nz/~petra/zoy/`; the applicability seems limited by the lack of type inference and limited support for schemas. In contrast to these works, we translate directly to Kodkod and have a fully developed system, covering large subsets of B, Event-B, Z and TLA^+ and delegating the rest to the PROB kernel.

A related system that translates a high-level logic language based on inductive definitions to SAT is IDP [23]. Another recent addition is Formula from Microsoft [9], which translates to the SMT solver Z3 [3].

5.3   Future Work

Currently our translation is only applicable for finding constraints satisfying the axioms as well as for constraint based deadlock checking. We are, however, working to also make it available for computing enabled events as well as for more general constraint-based testing and invariant checking.

Another avenue is to enlarge the area of applicability to some recurrent patterns of higher-order predicates. For example, many B specifications use total

---

[4] Private communication from Alexei Iliasov and Ilya Lopatkin, March 6th, 2012.

functions of the type `f : DOM --> POW(RAN)` which cannot be translated as such to Kodkod. However, such functions can often be translated to relations of the form `fr : DOM <-> RAN` by adapting the predicates accordingly (e.g., translating `f(x)` to `fr[{x}]`). More work is also needed on deciding automatically when to attempt the Kodkod translation and when predicates should be better left to the existing ProB kernel. Finally, inspired by the experiments, we also plan to improve the ProB kernel for better solving constraints over relational operators such as composition and closure.

5.4 Conclusion

After about three years of work and several attempts our translation to Kodkod is now mature enough to be put into practice and has been integrated into the latest version of the ProB toolset. The development required a considerable number of subsidiary techniques to be implemented. As our experiments have shown that the translation can be highly beneficial for certain kinds of constraints, and as such opens up new ways to analyze and validate formal specifications in B, Z and TLA⁺. However, the experiments have also shown that the constraint logic programming approach of ProB can be superior in a considerable number of scenarios; the translation to Kodkod and down to SAT is not (yet) the panacea. The same can be said of the existing translations from B to SMT. As such, we believe that much more research is required to reap the best of both worlds (SAT/SMT and constraint programming). An interesting side-effect of our work is that the ProB toolset now provides a double-chain (relying on technology developed independently and using different programming languages and paradigms) of validation for first-order predicates, which should prove relevant in high safety integrity level contexts.

Acknowledgements. We want to thank Sebastian Krings for helping us in the SMT experiments. We also thank Alexei Iliasov and Ilya Lopatkin for their earlier experiments involving translating Event-B to SAL and the insights gained in that work. We are also grateful for discussions with Daniel Jackson and Emina Torlak, in particular relating to encoding integers in Kodkod.

References

1. Abrial, J.-R.: The B-Book. Cambridge University Press (1996)
2. Aho, A.V., Lam, M.S., Sethi, R., Ullman, J.D.: Compilers. Principles, Techniques, and Tools, 2nd edn. Addison Wesley (2007)
3. de Moura, L., Bjørner, N.: Z3: An Efficient SMT Solver. In: Ramakrishnan, C.R., Rehof, J. (eds.) TACAS 2008. LNCS, vol. 4963, pp. 337–340. Springer, Heidelberg (2008)
4. Déharbe, D., Fontaine, P., Guyot, Y., Voisin, L.: SMT Solvers for Rodin. In: Derrick, J., Fitzgerald, J., Gnesi, S., Khurshid, S., Leuschel, M., Reeves, S., Riccobene, E. (eds.) ABZ 2012. LNCS, vol. 7316, pp. 194–207. Springer, Heidelberg (2012)

5. Derrick, J., North, S., Simons, A.J.H.: Z2SAL - Building a Model Checker for Z. In: Börger, E., Butler, M., Bowen, J.P., Boca, P. (eds.) ABZ 2008. LNCS, vol. 5238, pp. 280–293. Springer, Heidelberg (2008)

6. Derrick, J., North, S., Simons, A.J.H.: Z2SAL: a translation-based model checker for Z. Formal Asp. Comput. 23(1), 43–71 (2011)

7. Hallerstede, S., Leuschel, M.: Constraint-based deadlock checking of high-level specifications. TPLP 11(4–5), 767–782 (2011)

8. Jackson, D.: Alloy: A lightweight object modelling notation. ACM Transactions on Software Engineering and Methodology 11, 256–290 (2002)

9. Jackson, E.K., Tiham, Balasubramanian, D.: Reasoning about Metamodeling with Formal Specifications and Automatic Proofs. In: Whittle, J., Clark, T., Kühne, T. (eds.) MODELS 2011. LNCS, vol. 6981, pp. 653–667. Springer, Heidelberg (2011)

10. Lamport, L.: Specifying Systems, The TLA+ Language and Tools for Hardware and Software Engineers. Addison-Wesley (2002)

11. Legeard, B., Peureux, F., Utting, M.: Automated Boundary Testing from Z and B. In: Eriksson, L.-H., Lindsay, P.A. (eds.) FME 2002. LNCS, vol. 2391, pp. 21–40. Springer, Heidelberg (2002)

12. Leuschel, M., Butler, M.: ProB: A Model Checker for B. In: Araki, K., Gnesi, S., Mandrioli, D. (eds.) FME 2003. LNCS, vol. 2805, pp. 855–874. Springer, Heidelberg (2003)

13. Leuschel, M., Falampin, J., Fritz, F., Plagge, D.: Automated Property Verification for Large Scale B Models. In: Cavalcanti, A., Dams, D.R. (eds.) FM 2009. LNCS, vol. 5850, pp. 708–723. Springer, Heidelberg (2009)

14. Leuschel, M., Falampin, J., Fritz, F., Plagge, D.: Automated property verification for large scale B models with ProB. Formal Asp. Comput. 23(6), 683–709 (2011)

15. Malik, P., Groves, L., Lenihan, C.: Translating Z to Alloy. In: Frappier, M., Glässer, U., Khurshid, S., Laleau, R., Reeves, S. (eds.) ABZ 2010. LNCS, vol. 5977, pp. 377–390. Springer, Heidelberg (2010)

16. Matos, P.J., Marques-Silva, J.: Model Checking Event-B by Encoding into Alloy (Extended Abstract). In: Börger, E., Butler, M., Bowen, J.P., Boca, P. (eds.) ABZ 2008. LNCS, vol. 5238, pp. 346–346. Springer, Heidelberg (2008)

17. Métayer, C.: AnimB 0.1.1 (2010), http://wiki.event-b.org/index.php/AnimB

18. Mikhailov, L., Butler, M.: An Approach to Combining B and Alloy. In: Bert, D., Bowen, J.P., Henson, M.C., Robinson, K. (eds.) B 2002 and ZB 2002. LNCS, vol. 2272, pp. 140–161. Springer, Heidelberg (2002)

19. Plagge, D., Leuschel, M., Lopatkin, I., Romanovsky, A.: SAL, Kodkod, and BDDs for validation of B models. lessons and outlook. In: Proceedings AFM 2009, pp. 16–22 (2009)

20. Symbolic Analysis Laboratory (SAL) website, http://sal.csl.sri.com/

21. Torlak, E., Jackson, D.: Kodkod: A Relational Model Finder. In: Grumberg, O., Huth, M. (eds.) TACAS 2007. LNCS, vol. 4424, pp. 632–647. Springer, Heidelberg (2007)

22. Whaley, J., Lam, M.S.: Cloning-based context-sensitive pointer alias analysis using binary decision diagrams. In: Pugh, W., Chambers, C. (eds.) Proceedings PLDI 2004, pp. 131–144. ACM Press, New York (2004)

23. Wittocx, J., Mariën, M., Denecker, M.: Grounding FO and FO(ID) with bounds. J. Artif. Intell. Res. (JAIR) 38, 223–269 (2010)

24. Yu, Y., Manolios, P., Lamport, L.: Model Checking TLA+ Specifications. In: Pierre, L., Kropf, T. (eds.) CHARME 1999. LNCS, vol. 1703, pp. 54–66. Springer, Heidelberg (1999)

From Hoare Logic to Matching Logic Reachability[*]

Grigore Roşu[1,2] and Andrei Ştefănescu[1]

[1] University of Illinois at Urbana-Champaign, USA
[2] Alexandru Ioan Cuza University, Iaşi, Romania
{grosu,stefane1}@illinois.edu

Abstract. Matching logic reachability has been recently proposed as an alternative program verification approach. Unlike Hoare logic, where one defines a language-specific proof system that needs to be proved sound for each language separately, matching logic reachability provides a *language-independent* and *sound* proof system that directly uses the trusted operational semantics of the language as axioms. Matching logic reachability thus has a clear practical advantage: it eliminates the need for an additional semantics of the same language in order to reason about programs, and implicitly eliminates the need for tedious soundness proofs. What is not clear, however, is whether matching logic reachability is as powerful as Hoare logic. This paper introduces a technique to mechanically translate Hoare logic proof derivations into equivalent matching logic reachability proof derivations. The presented technique has two consequences: first, it suggests that matching logic reachability has no theoretical limitation over Hoare logic; and second, it provides a new approach to prove Hoare logics sound.

1 Introduction

Operational semantics are undoubtedly one of the most accessible semantic approaches. Language designers typically do not need an extensive theoretical background in order to define an operational semantics to a language, because they can think of it as if "implementing" an interpreter for the language. For example, consider the following two rules from the (operational) reduction semantics of a simple imperative language:

$$\text{while}(e)\,s \;\Rightarrow\; \text{if}(e)\,s;\,\text{while}(e)\,s\,\text{else skip}$$
$$\text{proc}() \;\Rightarrow\; \text{body} \qquad \text{where "proc()\,body" is a procedure}$$

The former says that loops are unrolled and the second says that procedure calls are inlined (for simplicity, we assumed no-argument procedures and no local variables). In addition to accessibility, operational semantics have another major advantage: they can be efficiently executable, and thus testable. For example, one can test an operational semantics as if it was an interpreter or a compiler, by executing large test suites of programs. This way, semantic or design flaws can be detected and confidence in the semantics can be incrementally build. We refer the interested reader to [1, 3, 6] for examples of large operational semantics (for C) and examples of how they are tested. Because of all the above, it is quite common that operational semantics are considered

---

[*] Full version of this paper, with proofs, available at http://hdl.handle.net/2142/31335

D. Giannakopoulou and D. Méry (Eds.): FM 2012, LNCS 7436, pp. 387–402, 2012.

trusted reference models of the programming languages they define, and thus serve as a formal basis for language understanding, design, and implementation.

With few notable exceptions, e.g. [10], operational semantics are typically considered inappropriate for program verification. That is to a large extent due to the fact that program reasoning with an operational semantics typically reduces to reasoning within the transition system associated to the operational semantics, which can be quite low level. Instead, semantics which are more appropriate for program reasoning are typically given to programming languages, such as axiomatic semantics in the form of Hoare logic proof systems for deriving Hoare triples {*precondition*} code {*postcondition*}. For example, the proof rules below correspond to the operational semantics rules above:

$$\frac{\mathcal{H} \vdash \{\psi \wedge e \neq 0\}\, s\, \{\psi\}}{\mathcal{H} \vdash \{\psi\}\, \texttt{while(e)}\, s\, \{\psi \wedge e = 0\}}$$

$$\frac{\mathcal{H} \cup \{\psi\}\, \texttt{proc()}\, \{\psi'\} \vdash \{\psi\}\, \texttt{body}\, \{\psi'\}}{\mathcal{H} \vdash \{\psi\}\, \texttt{proc()}\, \{\psi'\}} \quad \text{where "proc() body" is a procedure}$$

The second rule takes into account the fact that the procedure `proc` might be recursive (the claimed procedure specification is assumed as hypothesis when deriving its body's property). One may need to use several instances of this rule in order to derive the properties of mutually recursive procedures. Both proof rules above define the notion of an invariant, the former for while loops (we assume a C-like language, where zero means false and non-zero means true) and the latter for recursive procedures. These proof rules are so compact only because we are making (unrealistic) simplifying assumptions about the language. Hoare logic proof systems for real languages are quite involved (see, e.g., [1] for C and [9] for Java), which is why, for trusted verification, one needs to prove them sound with respect to more trusted (typically operational) semantics; the state-of-the-art approaches in mechanical verification do precisely that [1, 8–10, 12, 18].

Matching logic reachability [16] is a new program verification approach, based on operational semantics. Instead of proving properties at the low level of a transition system, matching logic reachability provides a high-level proof system for deriving program properties, like Hoare logic. State properties are specified as *(matching logic) patterns* [17], which are program configuration terms with variables, containing both program and state fragments like in operational semantics, but the variables can be constrained using logical formulae, like in Hoare logic. Program properties are specified as *reachability rules* $\varphi \Rightarrow \varphi'$ between patterns φ and φ'; intuitively, $\varphi \Rightarrow \varphi'$ states that a program configuration γ that *matches* pattern φ takes zero, one or more steps in the associated transition system to reach a configuration γ' that *matches* φ'. Unlike in Hoare logic, the matching logic reachability proof rules are all *language-independent*, taking as axioms an operational semantics given as a set of reachability rules. The key proof rule of matching logic reachability is Circularity, which language-independently captures the various circular behaviors in languages, due to loops, recursion, etc.

$$\frac{\mathcal{A} \vdash \varphi \Rightarrow^+ \varphi'' \quad \mathcal{A} \cup \{\varphi \Rightarrow \varphi'\} \vdash \varphi'' \Rightarrow \varphi'}{\mathcal{A} \vdash \varphi \Rightarrow \varphi'}$$

$\mathcal{A}$ initially contains the operational semantics rules. Circularity adds new reachability rules to $\mathcal{A}$ during the proof derivation process, which can be used in their own proof!

Its correctness is given by the fact that progress is required to be made (indicated by $\Rightarrow^+$ in $\mathcal{A} \vdash \varphi \Rightarrow^+ \varphi''$) before a circular reasoning step is allowed.

Everything else being equal, matching logic reachability has a clear pragmatic advantage over Hoare logic: it eliminates the need for an additional semantics of the same language, and implicitly eliminates the need for non-trivial and tedious correctness proofs. The soundness of matching logic reachability has already been shown in [16]. Its practicality and usability have been demonstrated by the MatchC automatic program verifier for a C fragment [14], which is a faithful implementation of the matching logic reachability proof system. What is missing is a formal treatment of its *completeness*. Since Hoare logic is relatively complete [5], any semantically valid program property expressed as a Hoare triple can also be derived using the Hoare logic proof system (provided an oracle that knows all the properties of the state model is available). Of course, since Hoare logic is language-specific, its relative completeness needs to be proved for each language individually. Nevertheless, such relative completeness proofs are quite similar and not difficult to adapt from one language to another.

This paper addresses the completeness of matching logic reachability. A technique to mechanically translate Hoare logic triples into reachability rules and Hoare logic proof derivations into equivalent matching logic reachability proof derivations is presented and proved correct. The generated matching logic reachability proof derivations are within a linear factor larger in size than the original Hoare logic proofs. Because of the language-specific nature of Hoare logic, we define and prove our translation in the context of a specific but canonical imperative language, IMP. However, the underlying idea is general. We also apply it to an extension with mutually recursive procedures.

Although we can now regard Hoare logic as a methodological fragment of matching logic reachability, where any Hoare logic proof derivation can be mimicked using the matching logic reachability proof system, experience with MatchC tells us that in general one should *not* want to verify programs following this route in practice. Specifying program properties and verifying them directly using the matching logic reachability capabilities, without going through its Hoare logic fragment, gives us shorter and more intuitive specifications and proofs. Therefore, in our view, the result of this paper should be understood through its theoretical value. First, it shows that matching logic reachability has no theoretical limitation over Hoare logic, in spite of being language-independent and working directly with the trusted operational semantics. Second, it provides a new and abstract way to prove Hoare logics sound, where one does not need to make use of low-level transition systems and induction, instead relying on the soundness of matching logic reachability (proved generically, for all languages).

The reminder of this paper is organized as follows. Section 2 recalls operational semantics and Hoare logic, by means of the IMP language. Section 3 recalls matching logic notions, including the sound proof system for matching logic reachability. Section 4 illustrates the differences between Hoare logic and matching logic reachability. Section 5 presents our translation technique and proves its correctness. Section 6 concludes.

2   IMP: Operational Semantics and Hoare Logic

Here we recall operational semantics, Hoare logic, and related notions, and introduce our notation and terminology for these. We do so by means of the simple IMP

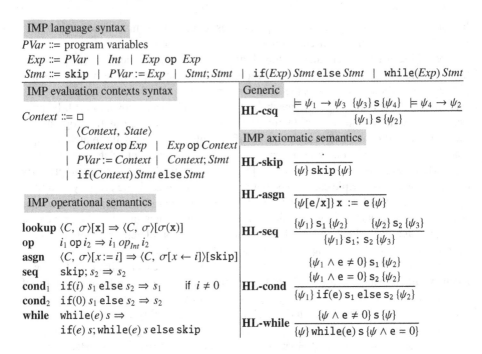

Fig. 1. IMP language syntax (top), operational semantics (left) and Hoare logic (right)

imperative language. Figure 1 shows its syntax, an operational semantics based on evaluation contexts [7], and a Hoare logic for it. IMP has only integer expressions, which can also be used as conditions of $\mathtt{if}$ and $\mathtt{while}$ (zero means false and non-zero means true, like in C). Expressions are built with integer constants, program variables, and conventional arithmetic constructs. For simplicity, we only show a generic binary operation, op. IMP statements are the variable assignment, $\mathtt{if}$, $\mathtt{while}$ and sequential composition.

The IMP program configurations are pairs $\langle code, \sigma \rangle$, where code is a program fragment and σ is a state term mapping program variables into integers. As usual, we assume appropriate definitions of the domains of integers (including arithmetic operations $i_1 \, op_{Int} \, i_2$, etc.) and of maps (including lookup $\sigma(x)$ and update $\sigma[x \leftarrow i]$ operations). IMP's operational semantics has seven reduction rule schemas between program configurations, which make use of first-order variables: σ is a variable of sort *State*; x is a variable of sort *PVar*; i, i_1, i_2 are variables of sort *Int*; e is a variable of sort *Exp*; s, s_1, s_2 are variables of sort *Stmt*. A rule mentions a context and a redex, which form a configuration, and reduces the said configuration by rewriting the redex and possibly the context. As a notation, the context is skipped if not used. E.g., the rule **op** is in fact $\langle C, \sigma \rangle[i_1 \, op \, i_2] \Rightarrow \langle C, \sigma \rangle[i_1 \, op_{Int} \, i_2]$. The code context meta-variable C allows us to instantiate a schema into reduction rules, one for each redex of each code fragment. For example, $\langle \mathtt{x := 5; y := 0}, \, x \mapsto 0 \rangle$ can be split as $\langle \Box; \mathtt{y := 0}, \, x \mapsto 0 \rangle[\mathtt{x := 5}]$, which by **asgn** reduces to $\langle \Box; \mathtt{y := 0}, \, x \mapsto 5 \rangle[\mathtt{skip}]$, or equivalently to $\langle \mathtt{skip; y := 0}, \, x \mapsto 5 \rangle$.

We can therefore regard the operational semantics of IMP above as a (recursively enumerable) set of reduction rules of the form "$l \Rightarrow r$ if b", where l and r are program configurations with variables constrained by boolean condition b. There are several operational semantics styles based on such rules. Besides the popular reduction semantics with evaluation contexts, we also have the chemical abstract machine [2] and $\mathbb{K}$ [13]. Large languages have been given semantics with only rules of the form "$l \Rightarrow r$ if b", including C [6] (defined in $\mathbb{K}$ with more than 1200 such rules). The matching logic reachability proof system works with any such rules (taking them as axioms), and is agnostic to the particular semantics or any other method used to produce them.

The major role of an operational semantics is to yield a canonical and typically trusted model of the defined language, as a transition system over program configurations. Such transition systems are important in this paper, so we formalize them here. We also recall some mathematical notions and notations, although we generally assume the reader is familiar with basic concepts of algebraic specification and first-order logic. Given an *algebraic signature* Σ, T_Σ denotes the *initial Σ-algebra* of ground terms (terms without variables), $T_\Sigma(Var)$ the *free Σ-algebra* of terms with variables in *Var*, and $T_{\Sigma,s}(Var)$ the set of Σ-terms of sort s. Valuations $\rho : Var \to \mathcal{T}$ with $\mathcal{T}$ a Σ-algebra extend uniquely to *morphisms of Σ-algebras* $\rho : T_\Sigma(Var) \to \mathcal{T}$. These notions extend to algebraic specifications. Many mathematical structures needed for language semantics have been defined as initial Σ-algebras: boolean algebras, natural/integer/rational numbers, lists, sets, bags (or multisets), maps (used as IMP's states), trees, queues, stacks, etc. We refer the reader to the CASL [11] and Maude [4] manuals for examples.

Let us fix the following: (1) an algebraic signature Σ, associated to some desired configuration syntax, with distinguished sorts *Cfg* and *Bool*; (2) a sort-wise infinite set of variables *Var*; and (3) a Σ-algebra $\mathcal{T}$, the *configuration model*, which may but need not necessarily be the initial or free Σ-algebra. As usual, $\mathcal{T}_{Cfg}$ denotes the elements of $\mathcal{T}$ of sort *Cfg*, which we call (concrete) *configurations*. Let S (for "semantics") be a set of reduction rules "$l \Rightarrow r$ if b" like above, where $l, r \in T_{\Sigma,Cfg}(Var)$ and $b \in T_{\Sigma,Bool}(Var)$.

Definition 1. *S yields a **transition system** $(\mathcal{T}, \Rightarrow_S^{\mathcal{T}})$ on the configuration model $\mathcal{T}$, where $\gamma \Rightarrow_S^{\mathcal{T}} \gamma'$ for $\gamma, \gamma' \in \mathcal{T}_{Cfg}$ if and only if there exist a reduction rule "$l \Rightarrow r$ if b" in S and a valuation $\rho : Var \to \mathcal{T}$ such that $\rho(l) = \gamma$, $\rho(r) = \gamma'$ and $\rho(b)$ holds.*

$(\mathcal{T}, \Rightarrow_S^{\mathcal{T}})$ is a conventional transition system, i.e. a set with a binary relation on it (in fact, $\Rightarrow_S^{\mathcal{T}} \subseteq \mathcal{T}_{Cfg} \times \mathcal{T}_{Cfg}$), and captures the operational behaviors of the language defined by S.

Hence, an operational semantics defines a set of reduction rules which can be used in some implicit way to yield program behaviors. On the other hand, a Hoare logic defines a proof system that explicitly tells how to derive program properties formalized as Hoare triples. Operational semantics are easy to define, test and thus build confidence in, since we can execute them against benchmarks of programs; e.g., the C semantics have been extensively tested against compiler test-suites [3, 6]. On the other hand, Hoare logics are more involved and need to be proved sound w.r.t. another, more trusted semantics.

Definition 2. *(**partial correctness**) For the IMP language in Fig. 1, a Hoare triple $\{\psi\}$ code $\{\psi'\}$ is **semantically valid**, written $\models \{\psi\}$ code $\{\psi'\}$, if and only if for all states σ and σ', it is the case that if $\sigma \models \psi$ and $\langle$code, $\sigma\rangle$ terminates in $(\mathcal{T}, \Rightarrow_S^{\mathcal{T}})$ and*

$\langle code, \sigma \rangle \Rightarrow^{*T}_{S} \langle skip, \sigma' \rangle$ *then* $\sigma' \models \psi'$. *The Hoare logic proof system in Fig. 1 is* **sound** *if and only if* $\vdash \{\psi\} code \{\psi'\}$ *implies* $\models \{\psi\} code \{\psi'\}$.

In Definition 2, we tacitly identified the ground configurations $\langle code, \sigma \rangle$ and $\langle skip, \sigma' \rangle$ with their (unique) interpretation in the configuration model $\mathcal{T}$. First-order logic (FOL) validity, both in Definition 2 and in the **HL-csq** in Fig. 1, is relative to $\mathcal{T}$. Partial correctness says the postcondition holds only when the program terminates. We do not address total correctness (i.e., the program must also terminate) in this paper.

3   Matching Logic Reachability

This section recalls matching logic and matching logic reachability notions and notations from [16, 17]. In matching logic reachability, *patterns* specify configurations and *reachability rules* specify operational transitions or program properties. A language-independent *proof system* takes a set of reachability rules (operational semantics) as axioms and derives new reachability rules (program properties). Matching logic is parametric in a model of program configurations. For example, as seen in Section 1, IMP's configurations are pairs $\langle code, \sigma \rangle$ with code a fragment of program and σ a *State*.

Like in Section 1, let us fix an algebraic signature Σ (of configurations) with a distinguished sort *Cfg*, a sort-wise infinite set of variables *Var*, and a (configuration) Σ-model $\mathcal{T}$ (which need not be the initial model T_Σ or the free model $T_\Sigma(Var)$).

Definition 3. *[17] A matching logic formula, or a **pattern**, is a first-order logic (FOL) formula which allows terms in $T_{\Sigma,Cfg}(Var)$, called **basic patterns**, as predicates. We define the satisfaction $(\gamma, \rho) \models \varphi$ over configurations $\gamma \in \mathcal{T}_{Cfg}$, valuations $\rho : Var \to \mathcal{T}$ and patterns φ as follows (among the FOL constructs, we only show $\exists$):*

$(\gamma, \rho) \models \exists X \varphi$ *iff* $(\gamma, \rho') \models \varphi$ *for some* $\rho' : Var \to \mathcal{T}$ *with* $\rho'(y) = \rho(y)$ *for all* $y \in Var \setminus X$
$(\gamma, \rho) \models \pi$ *iff* $\gamma = \rho(\pi)$ *where* $\pi \in \mathcal{T}_{\Sigma,Cfg}(Var)$
We write $\models \varphi$ *when* $(\gamma, \rho) \models \varphi$ *for all* $\gamma \in \mathcal{T}_{Cfg}$ *and all* $\rho : Var \to \mathcal{T}$.

A basic pattern π is satisfied by all the configurations γ that *match* it; the ρ in $(\gamma, \rho) \models \pi$ can be thought of as the "witness" of the matching, and can be further constrained in a pattern. If SUM is the IMP code "s:=0; while(n>0)(s:=s+n; n:=n-1)", then $\exists s (\langle SUM, (s \mapsto s, n \mapsto n) \rangle \wedge n \geq_{Int} 0)$ is a pattern matched by the configurations with code SUM and state mapping program variables s,n into integers s,n with n positive. Note that we use typewriter for program variables in *PVar* and *italic* for mathematical variables in *Var*. Pattern reasoning reduces to FOL reasoning in the model $\mathcal{T}$ [16].

Definition 4. *A (matching logic) **reachability rule** is a pair $\varphi \Rightarrow \varphi'$, where φ (the **left-hand side**, or **LHS**) and φ' (the **right-hand side**, or **RHS**), are matching logic patterns (with free variables). A **reachability system** is a set of reachability rules. A reachability system S induces a **transition system** $(\mathcal{T}, \Rightarrow^T_S)$ on the configuration model: $\gamma \Rightarrow^T_S \gamma'$ for $\gamma, \gamma' \in \mathcal{T}_{Cfg}$ iff there exist $\varphi \Rightarrow \varphi'$ in S and $\rho : Var \to \mathcal{T}$ with $(\gamma, \rho) \models \varphi$ and $(\gamma', \rho) \models \varphi'$. Configuration $\gamma \in \mathcal{T}_{Cfg}$ **terminates** in $(\mathcal{T}, \Rightarrow^T_S)$ iff there is no infinite $\Rightarrow^T_S$-sequence starting with γ. A rule $\varphi \Rightarrow \varphi'$ is **well-defined** iff for any $\gamma \in \mathcal{T}_{Cfg}$ and $\rho : Var \to \mathcal{T}$ with $(\gamma, \rho) \models \varphi$, there exists $\gamma' \in \mathcal{T}_{Cfg}$ with $(\gamma', \rho) \models \varphi'$. Reachability system S is **well-defined** iff each rule is well-defined, and is **deterministic** iff $(\mathcal{T}, \Rightarrow^T_S)$ is deterministic.*

Rules of operational nature	Rules of deductive nature

Reflexivity :

$$\frac{\cdot}{\mathcal{A} \vdash \varphi \Rightarrow \varphi}$$

Axiom :

$$\frac{\varphi \Rightarrow \varphi' \in \mathcal{A}}{\mathcal{A} \vdash \varphi \Rightarrow \varphi'}$$

Substitution :

$$\frac{\mathcal{A} \vdash \varphi \Rightarrow \varphi' \qquad \theta : Var \to \mathcal{T}_{\Sigma}(Var)}{\mathcal{A} \vdash \theta(\varphi) \Rightarrow \theta(\varphi')}$$

Transitivity :

$$\frac{\mathcal{A} \vdash \varphi_1 \Rightarrow \varphi_2 \qquad \mathcal{A} \vdash \varphi_2 \Rightarrow \varphi_3}{\mathcal{A} \vdash \varphi_1 \Rightarrow \varphi_3}$$

Case Analysis :

$$\frac{\mathcal{A} \vdash \varphi_1 \Rightarrow \varphi \qquad \mathcal{A} \vdash \varphi_2 \Rightarrow \varphi}{\mathcal{A} \vdash \varphi_1 \vee \varphi_2 \Rightarrow \varphi}$$

Logic Framing :

$$\frac{\mathcal{A} \vdash \varphi \Rightarrow \varphi' \qquad \psi \text{ is a (patternless) FOL formula}}{\mathcal{A} \vdash \varphi \wedge \psi \Rightarrow \varphi' \wedge \psi}$$

Consequence :

$$\frac{\models \varphi_1 \to \varphi_1' \qquad \mathcal{A} \vdash \varphi_1' \Rightarrow \varphi_2' \qquad \models \varphi_2' \to \varphi_2}{\mathcal{A} \vdash \varphi_1 \Rightarrow \varphi_2}$$

Abstraction :

$$\frac{\mathcal{A} \vdash \varphi \Rightarrow \varphi' \qquad X \cap FreeVars(\varphi') = \emptyset}{\mathcal{A} \vdash \exists X \, \varphi \Rightarrow \varphi'}$$

Rule for circular behavior

Circularity : $\dfrac{\mathcal{A} \vdash \varphi \Rightarrow^+ \varphi'' \qquad \mathcal{A} \cup \{\varphi \Rightarrow \varphi'\} \vdash \varphi'' \Rightarrow \varphi'}{\mathcal{A} \vdash \varphi \Rightarrow \varphi'}$

Fig. 2. Matching logic reachability proof system (nine language-independent proof rules)

Operational semantics defined with rules "$l \Rightarrow r$ if b", like those in Section 2, are particular well-defined reachability systems with rules of the form $l \wedge b \Rightarrow r$. Intuitively, the first rule states that a ground configuration γ which is an instance of the term l and satisfies the boolean condition b reduces to an instance γ' of r. Matching logic was designed to express terms with constraints: $l \wedge b$ is satisfied by exactly all the γ above. Thus, matching logic reachability naturally captures reduction semantics (see [16] for more details). Reachability rules can also specify program properties. The rule

$$\exists s (\langle \text{SUM}, (s \mapsto s, n \mapsto n) \rangle) \wedge n \geq_{Int} 0) \Rightarrow \langle \text{skip}, (s \mapsto n *_{Int} (n +_{Int} 1)/_{Int} 2, n \mapsto 0) \rangle$$

specifies the property of SUM. Unlike Hoare triples, which only specify properties about the final states of programs, reachability rules can also specify properties about intermediate states (see the end of Section 4 for an example). Hoare triples correspond to particular rules with all the basic patterns in the RHS holding the code skip, like above.

Definition 5. *Let S be a reachability system and $\varphi \Rightarrow \varphi'$ a reachability rule. We define $S \models \varphi \Rightarrow \varphi'$ iff for all $\gamma \in \mathcal{T}_{Cfg}$ such that γ terminates in $(\mathcal{T}, \Rightarrow_S^{\mathcal{T}})$ and for all $\rho : Var \to \mathcal{T}$ such that $(\gamma, \rho) \models \varphi$, there exists some $\gamma' \in \mathcal{T}_{Cfg}$ such that $\gamma \Rightarrow_S^{\star \mathcal{T}} \gamma'$ and $(\gamma', \rho) \models \varphi'$.*

Intuitively, $S \models \varphi \Rightarrow \varphi'$ specifies reachability: any terminating configuration matching φ transits, on some execution path, to a configuration matching φ'. If S is deterministic, then "some path" is equivalent to "all paths", and thus $\varphi \Rightarrow \varphi'$ captures partial correctness. If φ' has the empty code skip, then so does γ' in the definition above, and, in the case of IMP, γ' is unique and thus we recover the Hoare validity as a special case.

The above reachability rule for SUM is valid, although the proof is tedious, involving low-level IMP transition system details and induction. Figure 2 shows the *language-independent* matching logic reachability proof system which derives such rules while avoiding the transition system. Initially, $\mathcal{A}$ contains the operational semantics of the target language. Reflexivity, Axiom, Substitution, and Transitivity have an operational nature and derive concrete and (linear) symbolic executions. Case Analysis, Logic Framing, Consequence and Abstraction have a deductive nature. The Circularity proof rule has a coinductive nature and captures the various circular behaviors that appear in languages, due to loops, recursion, etc. Specifically, we can derive $\mathcal{A} \vdash \varphi \Rightarrow \varphi'$ whenever we can derive $\varphi \Rightarrow \varphi'$ by starting with one or more steps in $\mathcal{A}$ ($\Rightarrow^+$ means derivable without Reflexivity) and continuing with steps which can involve both rules from $\mathcal{A}$ and the rule to be proved itself, $\varphi \Rightarrow \varphi'$. For example, the first step can be a loop unrolling in the case of loops, or a function invocation in the case of recursive functions.

Theorem 1. *(soundness) [16] Let S be a well-defined matching logic reachability system (typically corresponding to an operational semantics), and let $S \vdash \varphi \Rightarrow \varphi'$ be a sequent derived with the proof system in Fig. 2. Then $S \models \varphi \Rightarrow \varphi'$.*

4 Hoare Logic versus Matching Logic Reachability

This section prepares the reader for our main result, by illustrating the major differences between Hoare logic and matching logic reachability using examples. We show how the same program property can be specified both as a Hoare triple and as a matching logic reachability rule, and then how it can be derived using each of the two proof systems.

Recall the SUM program "s:=0; while(n>0)(s:=s+n; n:=n-1)" in IMP. Fig. 3 gives a Hoare logic proof that SUM adds the first natural numbers (bottom left column) and a matching logic reachability proof of the same property (bottom right column). The top contains some useful macros. For the explanations of these proofs below, "triple *n*" refers to the Hoare triple numbered with *n* in the bottom left column, and "rule *m*" refers to the matching logic sequent numbered with *m* in the bottom right column in Fig. 3.

The behavior of SUM can be specified by the Hoare triple $\{\psi_{\text{pre}}\}$ SUM $\{\psi_{\text{post}}\}$, that is

$$\{n = \text{oldn} \wedge n \geq 0\} \text{ SUM} \{s = \text{oldn}*(\text{oldn+1})/2 \wedge n = 0\}$$

The oldn variable is needed in order to remember the initial value of n. Let us derive this Hoare triple using the Hoare logic proof system in Fig. 1. We can derive our original Hoare triple by first deriving triples 1 and 5, namely

$$\{n = \text{oldn} \wedge n \geq 0\} \text{ s:=0} \{\psi_{\text{inv}}\} \qquad \{\psi_{\text{inv}}\} \text{ LOOP} \{s = \text{oldn}*(\text{oldn+1})/2 \wedge n = 0\}$$

and then using the proof rule **HL-seq** in Fig. 1. Triple 1 follows by **HL-asgn** and **HL-csq**. Triple 5 follows by **HL-while** from triple 4, which in turn follows from triples 2 and 3 by **HL-seq**. Finally, triples 2 and 3 follow each by **HL-asgn** and **HL-csq**.

Before we discuss the matching logic reachability proof derivation, let us recall some important Hoare logic facts. First, Hoare logic makes no theoretical distinction between program variables, which in the case of IMP are *PVar* constants, and mathematical variables, which in the case of IMP are variables of sort *Var*. For example, in the proof above, n as a program variable, n as an integer variable appearing in the state specifications, and oldn which appears only in state specifications but never in

Code macros:

```
SUM  ≡ s:=0; while(n>0) (s:=s+n; n:=n-1)
LOOP ≡ while(n>0) (s:=s+n; n:=n-1)
BODY ≡ s:=s+n; n:=n-1
  IF ≡ if(n>0) (s:=s+n; n:=n-1; while(n>0) (s:=s+n; n:=n-1)) else skip
  S₁ ≡ s:=s+n; n:=n-1; while(n>0) (s:=s+n; n:=n-1)
  S₂ ≡ n:=n-1; while(n>0) (s:=s+n; n:=n-1)
```

Hoare logic formula macros:

$\psi_{pre} \equiv$ n = oldn $\wedge$ n $\geq$ 0
$\psi_{post} \equiv$ s = oldn*(oldn+1)/2 $\wedge$ n = 0
$\psi_{inv} \equiv$ s = (oldn-n)*(oldn+n+1)/2 $\wedge$ n $\geq$ 0
$\psi_1 \equiv \psi_{inv} \wedge$ n > 0
$\psi_2 \equiv$ s = (oldn-n+1)*(oldn+n)/2 $\wedge$ n > 0

Matching logic pattern macros:

$\varphi_{LHS} \equiv \langle SUM, (s \mapsto s, n \mapsto n) \rangle \wedge n \geq_{Int} 0$

$\varphi_{RHS} \equiv \langle skip, (s \mapsto n *_{Int} (n +_{Int} 1)/_{Int}2, n \mapsto 0) \rangle$

$\varphi_{inv} \equiv \langle LOOP, (s \mapsto (n -_{Int} n') *_{Int} (n +_{Int} n' +_{Int} 1)/_{Int}2, n \mapsto n') \rangle \wedge n' \geq_{Int} 0$

$\varphi_{if} \equiv \langle IF, (s \mapsto (n -_{Int} n') *_{Int} (n +_{Int} n' +_{Int} 1)/_{Int}2, n \mapsto n') \rangle \wedge n' \geq_{Int} 0$

$\varphi_{true} \equiv \langle IF, (s \mapsto (n -_{Int} n') *_{Int} (n +_{Int} n' +_{Int} 1)/_{Int}2, n \mapsto n') \rangle \wedge n' >_{Int} 0$

$\varphi_{false} \equiv \langle IF, (s \mapsto n *_{Int} (n +_{Int} 1)/_{Int}2, n \mapsto 0) \rangle$

$\varphi_1 \equiv \langle S_1, (s \mapsto (n -_{Int} n') *_{Int} (n +_{Int} n' +_{Int} 1)/_{Int}2, n \mapsto n') \rangle \wedge n' >_{Int} 0$

$\varphi_2 \equiv \langle S_2, (s \mapsto (n -_{Int} n' +_{Int} 1) *_{Int} (n +_{Int} n')/_{Int}2, n \mapsto n') \rangle \wedge n' >_{Int} 0$

$\varphi_{body} \equiv \langle LOOP, (s \mapsto (n -_{Int} n' +_{Int} 1) *_{Int} (n +_{Int} n')/_{Int}2, n \mapsto n' -_{Int} 1) \rangle \wedge n' >_{Int} 0$

$\mathcal{A}_{LOOP} \equiv \mathcal{S}_{IMP} \cup \{\varphi_{inv} \Rightarrow \varphi_{RHS}\}$

Hoare logic proof			Matching logic reachability proof		
Hoare triple	**Proof rule**	**Adtl. Steps**	**Reachability**	**ASLF with**	**Steps**
1.$\{\psi_{pre}\}$ s:=0 $\{\psi_{inv}\}$	**HL-asgn**	1/17	1.$\mathcal{S}_{IMP} \vdash \exists s\, \varphi_{LHS} \Rightarrow \exists n'\, \varphi_{inv}$	**asgn$_s$, seq**	1/0/1/1/0
2.$\{\psi_1\}$ s:=s+n $\{\psi_2\}$	**HL-asgn**	1/17	2.$\mathcal{S}_{IMP} \vdash \varphi_{inv} \Rightarrow^+ \varphi_{if}$	**while**	0/0/0/0/0
3.$\{\psi_2\}$ n:=n-1 $\{\psi_{inv}\}$	**HL-asgn**	1/17	3.$\mathcal{A}_{LOOP} \vdash \varphi_{true} \Rightarrow \varphi_1$	**lookup$_n$, op$_>$, cond$_1$**	2/0/0/0/0
4.$\{\psi_1\}$ BODY $\{\psi_{inv}\}$	**HL-seq(2, 3)**	0/0	4.$\mathcal{A}_{LOOP} \vdash \varphi_1 \Rightarrow \varphi_2$	**lookup$_n$, lookup$_s$, op$_+$, asgn$_n$, seq**	4/0/0/0/0
5.$\{\psi_{inv}\}$ LOOP $\{\psi_{post}\}$	**HL-while(4)**	1/0	5.$\mathcal{A}_{LOOP} \vdash \varphi_2 \Rightarrow \varphi_{body}$	**lookup$_n$, op$_-$, asgn$_n$, seq**	3/0/1/0/0
6.$\{\psi_{pre}\}$ SUM $\{\psi_{post}\}$	**HL-seq(1, 5)**	0/0	6.$\mathcal{A}_{LOOP} \vdash \varphi_{body} \Rightarrow \varphi_{RHS}$	$\varphi_{inv} \Rightarrow \varphi_{RHS}$	0/0/0/0/0
			7.$\mathcal{A}_{LOOP} \vdash \varphi_{false} \Rightarrow \varphi_{RHS}$	**lookup$_n$, op$_>$, cond$_2$**	2/0/1/0/0
			8.$\mathcal{A}_{LOOP} \vdash \varphi_{if} \Rightarrow \varphi_{RHS}$		3/1/1/0/0
			9.$\mathcal{S}_{IMP} \vdash \varphi_{inv} \Rightarrow \varphi_{RHS}$		0/0/0/0/1
			10.$\mathcal{S}_{IMP} \vdash \exists n'\, \varphi_{inv} \Rightarrow \varphi_{RHS}$		0/0/0/1/0
			11.$\mathcal{S}_{IMP} \vdash \exists s\, \varphi_{LHS} \Rightarrow \varphi_{RHS}$		1/0/0/0/0

Fig. 3. Side-by-side proofs for the property of SUM using the Hoare logic proof system (left) and, respectively, the matching logic reachability proof system (right). The Adtl. Steps for the Hoare proof mean: Consequence rules / substitution steps. The Steps for the matching logic reachability proof mean: Transitivity / Case Analysis / Consequence / Abstraction / Circularity.

the program, were formally treated the same way. Second, the same applies to language arithmetic constructs versus mathematical domain operations. For example, there is no distinction between the + construct for IMP expressions and the $+_{Int}$ operation that the integer domain provides. Third, Hoare logic takes FOL substitution for granted (see **HL-asgn**), which in reality adds a linear complexity in the size of the FOL specification to the proof. These and other simplifying assumptions make proofs like above look simple and compact, but come at a price: expressions cannot have side effects. Since in many languages expressions do have side effects, programs typically suffer (possibly error-prone) transformations that extract and isolate the side effects into special statements. Also, in practice program verifiers do make a distinction between language constructs and mathematical ones, and appropriately translate the former into the latter in specifications.

Let S_{IMP} be the operational semantics of IMP in Fig. 1. Now we show how the proof system in Fig. 2, using S_{IMP} as axioms, can derive $S_{IMP} \vdash \exists s\, \varphi_{LHS} \Rightarrow \varphi_{RHS}$, the reachability rule specifying the behavior of SUM already discussed in Section 3, namely

$$\exists s\, (\langle \text{SUM}, (s \mapsto s, n \mapsto n) \rangle) \wedge n \geq_{Int} 0) \Rightarrow \langle \text{skip}, (s \mapsto n *_{Int} (n +_{Int} 1)/_{Int}2, n \mapsto 0) \rangle$$

This rule follows by Transitivity with rules 1 and 10. By Axiom **asgn$_s$** (Fig. 1) followed by Substitution with $\theta(\sigma) = (s \mapsto s, n \mapsto n)$, $\theta(x) = s$ and $\theta(i) = 0$, followed by Logic Framing with $n \geq_{Int} 0$, we derive $\varphi_{LHS} \Rightarrow \langle \text{skip}; \text{LOOP}, (s \mapsto 0, n \mapsto n) \rangle \wedge n \geq_{Int} 0$. This "operational" sequence of Axiom, Substitution and Logic Framing is quite common; we abbreviate it ASLF. Further, by ASLF with **seq** and Transitivity, we derive $\varphi_{LHS} \Rightarrow \langle \text{LOOP}, (s \mapsto 0, n \mapsto n) \rangle \wedge n \geq_{Int} 0$. Then rule 1 follows by Consequence and Abstraction with $X = \{s\}$. Rule 10 follows by Abstraction with $\{n'\}$ from rule 9. We derive rule 9 by Circularity with rules 2 and 8. Rule 2 follows by ASLF with **while**. Rule 8 follows by Case Analysis with $\varphi_{true} \Rightarrow \varphi_{RHS}$ and $\varphi_{false} \Rightarrow \varphi_{RHS}$. The latter follows by ASLF (**lookup$_n$, op$_>$, cond$_2$**) together with some Transitivity and Consequence steps (the rule added by Circularity not needed yet). The former follows by repeated Transitivity with rules 3, 4, 5, 6. Similarly as before, rules 3, 4, 5 follow by ASLF (**lookup$_n$, op$_>$, cond$_1$, lookup$_n$, lookup$_s$, op$_+$, asgn$_s$, seq, lookup$_n$, op$_-$, asgn$_n$, seq**) together with Transitivity and Consequence steps. Rule 6, namely $S_{IMP} \cup \{\varphi_{inv} \Rightarrow \varphi_{RHS}\} \vdash \varphi_{body} \Rightarrow \varphi_{RHS}$, follows by Axiom ($\varphi_{inv} \Rightarrow \varphi_{RHS}$) and Substitution ($\theta(n') = n' -_{Int} 1$). Note that rule 6 is in fact rule 9 with $n' -_{Int} 1$ instead of n', but now the axioms include rule 9, so we are done. Welcome to the magic of Circularity!

The table in Fig. 3 shows the number of Hoare logic language-dependent proof rules (6) and the number of Hoare logic language-independent proof rules (4 **HL-csq** rules and 51 low-level steps due to traversing the FOL formulae as part of the application of substitutions in **HL-asgn**) used in proving the property of SUM, for a total of 61 steps. We count the number of low-level substitution steps for the Hoare proof because those steps, which in practice do not come for free anyway, in fact do not exist in the matching logic reachability proof, being replaced by actual reasoning steps using the proof system. Fig. 3 also shows the number of matching logic reachability proof rules (80) used in proving the same example. At a first glance, the matching logic reachability proof above may appear low-level when compared to the Hoare logic proof. However, it is quite mechanical, the only interesting part being to provide the invariant pattern

φ_{inv}, same like in the Hoare logic proof. Out of the 80 steps, 19 uses of the ASLF sequence (rule 6 only uses the Axiom and Substitution rules; each other ASLF step means 3 proof rule applications) and 16 of Transitivity account for most of them (72). Notice that the applications of ASLF and Transitivity are entirely syntax driven, and thus completely mechanical. There are 1 step of Case Analysis (for splitting on the symbolic condition of an `if` statement), and 2 steps of Abstraction (for eliminating existentially quantified variables), which are also mechanical. That leaves us with 4 steps of Consequence, and one step of Circularity (for dealing with the loop), which is similar to the number of steps used by the Hoare logic proof. In general, a matching logic reachability proof follows the following pattern: apply the operational rules whenever they match, except for circularities, which are given priority; when the redex is an `if`, do Case Analysis; if there are existentially quantified variables, skolemize. Our current MatchC implementation can prove the SUM example automatically, as well as much more complex programs [14, 16]. Although the paper Hoare logic proofs for simple languages like IMP may look more compact, as discussed above they make (sometimes unrealistic) assumptions which need to be addressed in implementations. Finally, note that the matching logic reachability rules are more expressive than the Hoare triples, since they can specify reachable configurations which are not necessarily final. E.g.,

$$\langle \text{SUM}, (\text{s} \mapsto s, \text{n} \mapsto n) \rangle \wedge n >_{Int} 0 \Rightarrow \langle \text{LOOP}, (\text{s} \mapsto n, \text{n} \mapsto n -_{Int} 1) \rangle$$

is also derivable and states that if the value n of n is strictly positive, then the loop is taken once and, when the loop is reached again, s is n and n is $n -_{Int} 1$.

5 From Hoare Logic Proofs to Matching Logic Reachability Proofs

Here we show how proof derivations using the IMP-specific Hoare logic proof system in Fig. 1 can be translated into proof derivations using the language-independent matching logic reachability proof system in Fig. 2 with IMP's operational semantics in Fig. 1 as axioms. The sizes of the two proof derivations are within a linear factor. We refer the reader to [15] for the proofs of the lemmas and theorems in this section.

5.1 Translating Hoare Triples into Reachability Rules

Without restricting the generality, we make the following simplifying assumptions about the Hoare triples $\{\psi\}$ `code` $\{\psi'\}$ that appear in the Hoare logic proof derivation that we translate into a matching logic reachability proof: (1) the variables appearing in `code` belong to an arbitrary but fixed finite set $\text{X} \subset PVar$; (2) the additional variables appearing in ψ and ψ' but not in `code` belong to an arbitrary but fixed finite set $\text{Y} \subset PVar$ such that $\text{X} \cap \text{Y} = \emptyset$. In other words, we fix the finite disjoint sets $\text{X}, \text{Y} \subset PVar$, and they have the properties above for all Hoare triples that we consider in this section. Note that we used a `typewriter` font to write these sets, which is consistent with our notation for variables in *PVar*. We need these disjointness restrictions because, as discussed in Section 4, Hoare logic makes no theoretical distinction between program and mathematical variables, while matching logic does. These restrictions do not limit the capability of Hoare logic, since we can always pick X to be the union of all the variables appearing in the program about which we want to reason and Y to be the union of all the remaining variables occurring in all the state specifications in any triple anywhere in the Hoare logic proof, making sure that the names of the variables used for stating mathematical properties of the state are always chosen different from those of the variables used in programs.

Definition 6. *Given a Hoare triple* $\{\psi\}$ *code* $\{\psi'\}$, *we define*

$$H2M(\{\psi\}\,code\,\{\psi'\}) \stackrel{def}{=} \exists X\,(\langle code,\ \sigma_X\rangle \wedge \psi_{X,Y}) \Rightarrow \exists X\,(\langle skip,\ \sigma_X\rangle \wedge \psi'_{X,Y})$$

where:

1. $X, Y \subset Var$ *(written using italic font) are finite sets of variables corresponding to the sets* $\mathsf{X}, \mathsf{Y} \subset PVar$ *fixed above, one variable* x *or* y *in Var (written using italic font) for each variable* x *or* y *in PVar (written using typewriter font);*
2. σ_X *is the state mapping each* $\mathsf{x} \in \mathsf{X}$ *to its corresponding* $x \in X$; *and*
3. $\psi_{X,Y}$ *and* $\psi'_{X,Y}$ *are* ψ *and respectively* ψ' *with* $\mathsf{x} \in \mathsf{X}$ *or* $\mathsf{y} \in \mathsf{Y}$ *replaced by its corresponding* $x \in X$ *or* $y \in Y$, *respectively, and each expression construct* op *replaced by its mathematical correspondent* op_{Int}.

The *H2M* mapping in Definition 6 is quite simple and mechanical, and can be implemented by a linear traversal of the Hoare triple. In fact, we have implemented it as part of the MatchC program verifier, to allow users to write program specifications in a Hoare style when possible (see, e.g., the simple folder of examples on the online MatchC interface at http://fsl.cs.uiuc.edu/index.php/Special:MatchCOnline).

It is important to note that, like $\mathsf{X}, \mathsf{Y} \subset PVar$, the sets of variables $X, Y \subset Var$ in Definition 6 are also fixed and thus the same for all Hoare triples considered in this section. For example, suppose that $\mathsf{X} = \{\mathsf{s}, \mathsf{n}\}$ and $\mathsf{Y} = \{\mathsf{oldn}, \mathsf{z}\}$. Then the Hoare triple

$$\{n = oldn \wedge n \geq 0\}\,\mathsf{SUM}\,\{s = oldn*(oldn+1)/2 \wedge n = 0\}$$

from Section 4 is translated into the following reachability rule:

$$\exists s, n\,(\langle \mathsf{SUM},\ (\mathsf{s} \mapsto s,\ \mathsf{n} \mapsto n)\rangle \wedge n = oldn \wedge n \geq_{Int} 0)$$
$$\Rightarrow \exists s, n\,(\langle \mathsf{skip},\ (\mathsf{s} \mapsto s,\ \mathsf{n} \mapsto n)\rangle \wedge s = oldn *_{Int} (oldn +_{Int} 1)/_{Int}2 \wedge n = 0)$$

Not surprisingly, we can use the proof system in Fig. 2 to prove this rule equivalent to the one for SUM in Section 4. Using FOL and Consequence the above is equivalent to

$$\exists s\,(\langle \mathsf{SUM},(\mathsf{s}\mapsto s, \mathsf{n}\mapsto oldn)\rangle \wedge oldn \geq_{Int}0) \Rightarrow \langle \mathsf{skip}, (\mathsf{s}\mapsto oldn*_{Int}(oldn+_{Int}1)/_{Int}2, \mathsf{n}\mapsto 0)\rangle$$

which, by Substitution ($n \leftrightarrow oldn$), is equivalent to the rule in Section 4.

We also show an (artificial) example where the original Hoare triple contains a quantifier. Consider the same $\mathsf{X} = \{\mathsf{s}, \mathsf{n}\}$ and $\mathsf{Y} = \{\mathsf{oldn}, \mathsf{z}\}$ as above. Then

$$H2M(\{true\}\,\mathsf{n}\!:=\!4*\mathsf{n}+3\,\{\exists \mathsf{z}\,(\mathsf{n} = 2*\mathsf{z}+1)\})$$

is the reachability rule

$$\exists s, n\,(\langle \mathsf{n}\!:=\!4*\mathsf{n}+3,\ (\mathsf{s} \mapsto s, \mathsf{n} \mapsto n)\rangle \wedge true)$$
$$\Rightarrow \exists s, n\,(\langle \mathsf{skip},\ (\mathsf{s} \mapsto s, \mathsf{n} \mapsto n)\rangle \wedge \exists z\,(n = 2 *_{Int} z +_{Int} 1))$$

Using FOL reasoning and Consequence, this rule is equivalent to

$$\exists s, n\,\langle \mathsf{n}\!:=\!4*\mathsf{n}+3,\ (\mathsf{s} \mapsto s, \mathsf{n} \mapsto n)\rangle \Rightarrow \exists s, z\,\langle \mathsf{skip},\ (\mathsf{s} \mapsto s, \mathsf{n} \mapsto 2 *_{Int} z +_{Int} 1)\rangle$$

5.2 Helping Lemmas

The following holds for matching logic in general:

Lemma 1. *If $S \vdash \varphi \Rightarrow \varphi'$ is derivable then $S \vdash \exists X \varphi \Rightarrow \exists X \varphi'$ is also derivable.*

The following lemma states that symbolic evaluation of IMP expressions is actually formally derivable using the matching logic reachability proof system:

Lemma 2. *If $e \in Exp$ is an expression, $C \in Context$ an appropriate context, and $\sigma \in State$ a state term binding each program variable in PVar of e to a term of sort Int (possibly containing variables in Var), then the following sequent is derivable:*

$$S_{IMP} \vdash \langle C, \sigma \rangle[e] \Rightarrow \langle C, \sigma \rangle[\sigma(e)]$$

where $\sigma(e)$ replaces each $x \in PVar$ in e by $\sigma(x)$ (i.e., a term of sort Int) and each operation symbol op by its mathematical correspondent in the Int domain, op_{Int}.

Intuitively, the following lemma states that if we append some extra statement to the code of φ, then the execution of the original code is still possible, making abstraction of the appended statement. This holds because of the specific (simplistic) nature of IMP and may not hold in more complex languages (for example in ones with support for reflection or self-generation of code). A direct consequence is that we can (symbolically) execute a compound statement $s_1; s_2$ by first executing s_1 until we reach skip and then continuing from there with s_2.

Lemma 3. *If $S_{IMP} \vdash \varphi \Rightarrow \varphi'$ is derivable and $s \in Stmt$ then $S_{IMP} \vdash$ APPEND$(\varphi, s) \Rightarrow$ APPEND(φ', s) is also derivable, where* APPEND(φ, s) *is the pattern obtained from φ by replacing each basic pattern $\langle code, \sigma \rangle$ with the basic pattern $\langle (code; s), \sigma \rangle$.*

5.3 The Main Result

Theorem 2 below states that, for the IMP language, any Hoare logic proof derivation of a Hoare triple $\{\psi\}$ code $\{\psi'\}$ yields a matching logic reachability proof derivation of the corresponding reachability rule $H2M(\{\psi\}$ code $\{\psi'\})$. This proof correspondence is constructive and the resulting proof derivation is linear in the size of the original proof derivation. For example, to generate the matching logic reachability proof corresponding to a proof step using the Hoare logic proof rule for while loop, **HL-while**, we do the following (see the proof of Theorem 2 in [15] for all the details):

1. We inductively assume a proof for the reachability rule corresponding to the Hoare triple for the while loop body;
2. We apply the Axiom step with **while** (Fig. 1), followed by Substitution, Logic Framing, and Lemma 1, and this way we "unroll" the while loop into its corresponding conditional statement (in the logical context set by the Hoare triple);
3. Since the conditional statement contains the original while loop in its true branch and since 2. above does not use Reflexivity, we issue a Circularity proof obligation and thus add the claimed reachability rule for while to the set of axioms;

4. We "evaluate" symbolically the condition, by virtue of Lemma 2;
5. We apply a Case Analysis for the conditional, splitting the proof task in two sub-tasks, the one corresponding to the false condition being trivial to discharge;
6. To discharge the care corresponding to the true condition, we use the proof given by 1. by virtue of Lemma 3, then the Axiom for **seq**, and then the reachability rule added by Circularity and we are done.

Theorem 2. *(see [15] for the proof) Let S_{IMP} be the operational semantics of IMP in Fig. 1 viewed as a matching logic reachability system, and let $\{\psi\}$ code $\{\psi'\}$ be a triple derivable with the IMP-specific Hoare logic proof system in Fig 1. Then we have that $S_{IMP} \vdash H2M(\{\psi\}$ code $\{\psi'\})$ is derivable with the language-independent matching logic proof system in Fig. 2.*

Theorem 2 thus tells us that anything that can be proved using Hoare logic can also be proved using the matching logic reachability proof system. Furthermore, it gives us a novel way to prove soundness of Hoare logic proof systems, where the low-level details of the transition system corresponding to the target programming language, including induction on path length, are totally avoided and replaced by an abstract, small and fixed proof system, which is sound for all languages.

5.4   Adding Recursion

In this section we add procedures to IMP, which can be mutually recursive, and show that proof derivations done with the corresponding Hoare logic proof rule can also be done using the generic matching logic proof system, with the straightforward operational semantics rule as an axiom. We consider the following syntax for procedures:

$$ProcedureName ::= \texttt{proc} \mid \ldots$$
$$Procedure ::= ProcedureName()\, Stmt$$
$$Stmt ::= \ldots \mid ProcedureName()$$

Our procedures therefore have the syntax "proc() body", where proc is the name of the procedure and body the body statement. Procedure invocations are statements of the form "proc()". For simplicity, and to capture the essence of the relationship between recursion and the Circularity rule of matching logic, we assume only no-argument procedures.

The operational semantics of procedure calls is trivial:

> **call**   proc() $\Rightarrow$ body   where "proc() body" is a procedure

The Hoare logic proof rule needs to take into account that procedures may be recursive:

$$\frac{\mathcal{H} \cup \{\psi\}\, \texttt{proc()}\, \{\psi'\} \vdash \{\psi\}\, \texttt{body}\, \{\psi'\}}{\mathcal{H} \vdash \{\psi\}\, \texttt{proc()}\, \{\psi'\}}$$ where "proc () body" is a procedure

This rule states that if the body of a procedure is proved to satisfy its contract while assuming that the procedure itself satisfies it, then the procedure's contract is indeed valid. If one has more mutually recursive procedures, then one needs to apply this rule several times until all procedure contracts are added to the hypothesis $\mathcal{H}$, and then each procedure body proved. The rule above needs to be added to the Hoare logic proof system in Fig. 1, but in order for that to make sense we need to first replace each Hoare triple $\{\psi\}$ code $\{\psi'\}$ in Fig. 1 by a sequent "$\mathcal{H} \vdash \{\psi\}$ code $\{\psi'\}$".

Theorem 3. *(see [15] for the proof) Let S_{IMP} be the operational semantics of IMP in Fig. 1 extended with the rule **call** for procedure calls above, and let $\mathcal{H} \vdash \{\psi\}$ code $\{\psi'\}$ be a sequent derivable with the extended Hoare logic proof system. Then we have that $S_{IMP} \cup H2M(\mathcal{H}) \vdash H2M(\{\psi\}$ code $\{\psi'\})$ is derivable with the matching logic reachability proof system in Fig. 2.*

6   Conclusion

Matching logic reachability provides a sound and language-independent program reasoning method, based solely on the operational semantics of the target programming language [16]. This paper addressed the other important aspect of matching logic reachability deduction, namely its completeness. A mechanical and linear translation of Hoare logic proof trees into equivalent matching logic reachability proof trees was presented. The method was described and proved correct for a simple imperative language with both iterative and recursive constructs, but the underlying principles of the translation are general and should apply to any language. The results presented in this paper have two theoretical consequences. First, they establish the relative completeness of matching logic reachability for a standard language, by reduction to the relative completeness of Hoare logic, and thus show that matching logic reachability is at least as powerful as Hoare logic. Second, they give an alternative approach to proving soundness of Hoare logics, by reduction to the generic soundness of matching logic reachability.

Acknowledgements. We thank Michael Whalen and Cesare Tinelli for the interesting discussions we had at Midwest Verification Day 2011, which stimulated this research. We also thank the members of the $\mathbb{K}$ team (http://k-framework.org) and the anonymous reviewers for their valuable comments on a previous version of this paper. The work in this paper was supported in part by NSA contract H98230-10-C-0294, by NSF grant CCF-0916893 and by (Romanian) SMIS-CSNR 602-12516 contract no. 161/15.06.2010.

References

1. Appel, A.W.: Verified Software Toolchain. In: Barthe, G. (ed.) ESOP 2011. LNCS, vol. 6602, pp. 1–17. Springer, Heidelberg (2011)
2. Berry, G., Boudol, G.: The chemical abstract machine. Theoretical Computer Science 96(1), 217–248 (1992)
3. Blazy, S., Leroy, X.: Mechanized semantics for the Clight subset of the C language. Journal of Automated Reasoning 43(3), 263–288 (2009)
4. Clavel, M., Durán, F., Eker, S., Lincoln, P., Martí-Oliet, N., Meseguer, J., Talcott, C.: All About Maude - A High-Performance Logical Framework. LNCS, vol. 4350. Springer, Heidelberg (2007)

5. Cook, S.A.: Soundness and completeness of an axiom system for program verification. SIAM Journal on Computing 7(1), 70–90 (1978)
6. Ellison, C.: Roşu, G.: An executable formal semantics of C with applications. In: POPL, pp. 533–544 (2012)
7. Felleisen, M., Findler, R.B., Flatt, M.: Semantics Engineering with PLT Redex. MIT (2009)
8. George, C., Haxthausen, A.E., Hughes, S., Milne, R., Prehn, S., Pedersen, J.S.: The RAISE Development Method. BCS Practitioner Series. Prentice-Hall (1995)
9. Jacobs, B.: Weakest pre-condition reasoning for Java programs with JML annotations. The Journal of Logic and Algebraic Programming 58(1-2), 61–88 (2004)
10. Liu, H., Moore, J.S.: Java Program Verification via a JVM Deep Embedding in ACL2. In: Slind, K., Bunker, A., Gopalakrishnan, G.C. (eds.) TPHOLs 2004. LNCS, vol. 3223, pp. 184–200. Springer, Heidelberg (2004)
11. Mosses, P.D. (ed.): CASL Reference Manual. LNCS, vol. 2960. Springer, Heidelberg (2004)
12. Nipkow, T.: Winskel is (almost) right: Towards a mechanized semantics textbook. Formal Aspects of Computing 10, 171–186 (1998)
13. Roşu, G., Şerbănuţă, T.F.: An overview of the K semantic framework. The Journal of Logic and Algebraic Programming 79(6), 397–434 (2010)
14. Roşu, G., Ştefănescu, A.: Matching logic: A new program verification approach (NIER track). In: ICSE, pp. 868–871 (2011)
15. Roşu, G., Ştefănescu, A.: From Hoare logic to matching logic reachability. Tech. Rep. Univ. of Illinois (June 2012), http://hdl.handle.net/2142/31335
16. Roşu, G., Ştefănescu, A.: Towards a Unified Theory of Operational and Axiomatic Semantics. In: Czumaj, A., Mehlhorn, K., Pitts, A., Wattenhofer, R. (eds.) ICALP 2012, Part II. LNCS, vol. 7392, pp. 351–363. Springer, Heidelberg (2012)
17. Roşu, G., Ellison, C., Schulte, W.: Matching Logic: An Alternative to Hoare/Floyd Logic. In: Johnson, M., Pavlovic, D. (eds.) AMAST 2010. LNCS, vol. 6486, pp. 142–162. Springer, Heidelberg (2011)
18. Sasse, R., Meseguer, J.: Java+ITP: A verification tool based on Hoare logic and algebraic semantics. Electronic Notes in Theoretical Computer Science 176(4), 29–46 (2007)

Distribution of Modal Transition Systems

German E. Sibay[1], Sebastián Uchitel[1,2], Victor Braberman[2], and Jeff Kramer[1]

[1] Imperial College London, London, U.K.
[2] Universidad de Buenos Aires, FCEyN, Buenos Aires, Argentina

Abstract. In order to capture all permissible implementations, partial models of component based systems are given as at the system level. However, iterative refinement by engineers is often more convenient at the component level. In this paper, we address the problem of decomposing partial behaviour models from a single monolithic model to a component-wise model. Specifically, given a Modal Transition System (MTS) M and component interfaces (the set of actions each component can control/monitor), can MTSs $M_1, \ldots, M_n$ matching the component interfaces be produced such that independent refinement of each M_i will lead to a component Labelled Transition Systems (LTS) I_i such that composing the I_is result in a system LTS that is a refinement of M? We show that a sound and complete distribution can be built when the MTS to be distributed is deterministic, transition modalities are consistent and the LTS determined by its possible transitions is distributable.

Keywords: Modal Transition Systems, Distribution.

1 Introduction

Partial behaviour models such as Modal Transition Systems (MTS) [LT88] extend classical behaviour models by introducing transitions of two types: required or must transitions and possible or may transitions. Such extension supports interpreting them as sets of classical behaviour models. Thus, a partial behaviour model can be understood as describing the set of implementations which provide the behaviour described by the required transitions and in which any other additional implementation behaviour is possible in the partial behaviour model.

Partial behaviour model refinement can be defined as an implementation subset relation, thus naturally capturing the model elaboration process in which, as more information becomes available (e.g. may transitions are removed, required transitions are added), the set of acceptable implementations is reduced. Such notion is consistent with modern incremental development processes where fully described problem and solution domains are unavailable, undesirable or uneconomical.

The family of MTS formalisms has been shown to be useful as a modeling and analysis framework for component-based systems. Significant amount of work has been devoted to develop theory and algorithmic support in the

D. Giannakopoulou and D. Méry (Eds.): FM 2012, LNCS 7436, pp. 403–417, 2012.
© Springer-Verlag Berlin Heidelberg 2012

context of MTS, MTS-variants, and software engineering applications. Developments include techniques for synthesising partial behaviour models from various specification languages (e.g. [FBD+11, SUB08, KBEM09]), algorithms for manipulating such partial behaviour models (e.g. [KBEM09, BKLS09b]), refinement checks [BKLS09a], composition operators including parallel composition and conjunction (e.g. [FBD+11]), model checking results(e.g. [GP11]), and tools (e.g. [Sto05, DFFU07]).

Up to now, an area that had been neglected is that of model decomposition or distribution. Distributed implementability and synthesis has been studied for LTS [Mor98, CMT99, Ste06, HS05] for different equivalences notion like isomorphism, language equivalence and bisimulation. On the other hand, work on MTSs has mostly assumed a monolithic system model which is iteratively refined until an implementation in the form of a LTS is reached.

Problems related to MTS distribution were studied by some authors [KBEM09, QG08, BKLS09b] and we compare their work to ours in Section 4. However the general problem of how to move from an MTS that plays the role of a monolithic partial behaviour model to component-wise partial behaviour model (set of MTSs) has not been studied. We study the distribution problem abstractly from the specification languages used to describe the MTS to be distributed. Those languages may allow description of behaviour that is not distributable [UKM04] and a distribution is not trivial. Furthermore we study the problem of finding all possible distributed implementations. Appropriate solutions to this problem would enable engineers to move from iterative refinement of a monolithic model to component-wise iterative refinement.

More specifically, we are interested in the following problem: given an MTS M and component interfaces (the set of actions each component can control/ monitor), can MTSs $M_1, \ldots, M_n$ matching the component interfaces be produced such that independent refinement of each M_i will lead to a component LTS I_i such that composing the I_is result in a system LTS that is a refinement of M? We show that a sound and complete distribution can be built when the MTS to be distributed is deterministic, transition modalities are consistent and the LTS determined by its possible transitions is distributable.

We present various results that answer the above questions to some extent. The main result of the paper is an algorithm that, under well-defined conditions, produces component MTSs of a monolithic partial system behaviour model without loss of information. That is, the independent refinement of the component MTSs to LTSs and their parallel composition results in exactly the set of distributable implementations of the monolithic MTS.

2   Background

We start with the familiar concept of labelled transition systems (LTSs) which are widely used for modelling and analysing the behaviour of concurrent and distributed systems [MK99]. An LTS is a state transition system where transitions are labelled with actions. The set of actions of an LTS is called its *alphabet* and constitutes the interactions that the modelled system can have with its environment. An example LTS is shown in Figure 5(a).

Definition 1. (Labelled Transition System) *Let States be a universal set of states, and Act be the universal set of action labels. An LTS is a tuple $I = \langle S, s^0, \Sigma, \Delta \rangle$, where $S \subseteq States$ is a finite set of states, $\Sigma \subseteq Act$ is the set of labels, $\Delta \subseteq (S \times \Sigma \times S)$ is a transition relation, and $s^0 \in S$ is the initial state.*

Definition 2. (Bisimilarity) [Mil89] *Let LTSs I and J such that $\alpha I = \alpha J$. I and J are bisimilar, written $I \sim J$, if (I, J) is contained in some bisimilarity relation B, for which the following holds for all $\ell \in Act$ and for all $(I', J') \in B$:*

1. $\forall \ell \cdot \forall I'' \cdot (I' \overset{\ell}{\longrightarrow} I'' \implies \exists J'' \cdot J' \overset{\ell}{\longrightarrow} J'' \wedge (I'', J'') \in B)$.
2. $\forall \ell \cdot \forall J'' \cdot (J' \overset{\ell}{\longrightarrow} J'' \implies \exists I'' \cdot I' \overset{\ell}{\longrightarrow} I'' \wedge (I'', J'') \in B)$.

Definition 3 (Modal Transition System). $M = \langle S, s^0, \Sigma, \Delta^r, \Delta^p \rangle$ *is an MTS where $\Delta^r \subseteq \Delta^p$, $\langle S, s^0, \Sigma, \Delta^r \rangle$ is an LTS representing required behaviour of the system and $\langle S, s^0, \Sigma, \Delta^p \rangle$ is an LTS representing possible (but not necessarily required) behaviour.*

Every LTS $\langle S, s^0, \Sigma, \Delta \rangle$ can be embedded into an MTS $\langle S, s^0, \Sigma, \Delta, \Delta \rangle$. Hence we sometimes refer to MTS with the same set of required and possible transitions as LTS. We refer to transitions in $\Delta^p \setminus \Delta^r$ as *maybe* transitions, depict them with a question mark following the label. An example MTS is shown in Figure 2(a). We use $\alpha M = \Sigma$ to denote the communicating alphabet of an MTS M.

Given an MTS $M = \langle S, s^0, \Sigma, \Delta^r, \Delta^p \rangle$ we say M becomes M' via a required (possible) transition labelled by ℓ, denoted $M \overset{\ell}{\longrightarrow}_r M'$ ($M \overset{\ell}{\longrightarrow}_p M'$), if $M' = \langle S, s', \Sigma, \Delta^r, \Delta^p \rangle$ and $(s^0, \ell, s') \in \Delta^r$ ($(s^0, \ell, s') \in \Delta^p$). If (s^0, ℓ, s') is a maybe transition, i.e. $(s^0, \ell, s') \in \Delta^p \setminus \Delta^r$, we write $M \overset{\ell}{\longrightarrow}_m M'$.

Let $w = w_1 \ldots w_k$ be a word over Σ. Then $M \overset{w}{\longrightarrow}_p M'$ means that there exist $M_0, \ldots, M_k$ such that $M = M_0$, $M' = M_k$, and $M_i \overset{w_{i+1}}{\longrightarrow}_p M_{i+1}$ for $0 \leq i < k$. We write $M \overset{w}{\longrightarrow}_p$ to mean $\exists M' \cdot M \overset{w}{\longrightarrow}_p M'$. The language of an MTS M is defined as $\mathcal{L}(M) = \{w \in \alpha M \mid M \overset{w}{\longrightarrow}_p\}$. Finally we call optimistic implementation of M (M^+) the LTS obtained by making all possible transitions of M required.

Definition 4 (Parallel Composition). *Let $M = \langle S_M, s_M^0, \Sigma, \Delta_M^r, \Delta_M^p \rangle$ and $N = \langle S_N, s_N^0, \Sigma, \Delta_N^r, \Delta_N^p \rangle$ be MTSs. Parallel composition ($\|$) is a symmetric operator and $M \| N$ is the MTS $\langle S_M \times S_N, (s_M^0, s_N^0), \Sigma, \Delta^r, \Delta^p \rangle$ where Δ^r and Δ^p are the smallest relations that satisfy the rules in Figure 1.*

Parallel composition for MTSs with all transitions required (i.e. an LTS) is the same that parallel composition for LTSs [Mil89].

Strong refinement, or simply *refinement*[LT88], of MTSs captures the notion of elaboration of a partial description into a more comprehensive one, in which some knowledge of the maybe behaviour has been gained. It can be seen as being a "more defined than" relation between two partial models. An MTS N refines

$$\frac{M \xrightarrow{\ell}_m M', \; N \xrightarrow{\ell}_m N'}{M \| N \xrightarrow{\ell}_m M' \| N'} \quad \frac{M \xrightarrow{\ell}_m M', \; N \xrightarrow{\ell}_r N'}{M \| N \xrightarrow{\ell}_m M' \| N'} \quad \frac{M \xrightarrow{\ell}_r M', \; N \xrightarrow{\ell}_r N'}{M \| N \xrightarrow{\ell}_r M' \| N'}$$

$$\frac{M \xrightarrow{\ell}_\gamma M', \; \ell \notin \alpha N, \; \gamma \in \{p,r\}}{M \| N \xrightarrow{\ell}_\gamma M' \| N} \quad \frac{\ell \notin \alpha M, \; N \xrightarrow{\ell}_\gamma N', \; \gamma \in \{p,r\}}{M \| N \xrightarrow{\ell}_\gamma M \| N'}$$

Fig. 1. Rules for parallel composition

M if N preserves all of the required and all of the proscribed behaviours of M. Alternatively, an MTS N refines M if N can simulate the required behaviour of M, and M can simulate the possible behaviour of N.

Definition 5. (Refinement) *Let MTSs N and M such that $\alpha M = \alpha N = \Sigma$. N is a* strong refinement *of M, written $M \preceq N$, if (M, N) is contained in some strong refinement relation R, for which the following holds for all $\ell \in Act$ and for all $(M', N') \in R$:*

1. $\forall \ell \in \Sigma, \forall M'' \cdot (M' \xrightarrow{\ell}_r M'' \implies \exists N'' \cdot N' \xrightarrow{\ell}_r N'' \wedge (M'', N'') \in R)$.
2. $\forall \ell \in \Sigma, \forall N'' \cdot (N' \xrightarrow{\ell}_p N'' \implies \exists M'' \cdot M' \xrightarrow{\ell}_p M'' \wedge (M'', N'') \in R)$.

Property 1. Refinement is a precongruence with regards to $\|$ meaning that if $M_i \preceq I_i$ for $i \in [n]$ then $\|_{i \in [n]} M_i \preceq \|_{i \in [n]} I_i$ where $[n] = \{1, \ldots, n\}$.

LTSs that refine an MTS M are complete descriptions of the system behaviour up to the alphabet of M. We refer to them as the *implementations* of M.

Definition 6. (Implementation) *We say that an LTS $I = \langle S_I, i^0, \Sigma, \Delta_I \rangle$ is an implementation of an MTS M, written $M \preceq I$, if $M \preceq M_I$ with $M_I = \langle S_I, i^0, \Sigma, \Delta_I, \Delta_I \rangle$. We also define the set of implementations of M as $\mathcal{I}[M] = \{LTS \; I \mid M \preceq I\}$.*

An MTS can be thought of as a model that represents the set of LTSs that implement it. The diversity of the set results from making different choices on the maybe behaviour of the MTS. As expected, refinement preserves implementations: $M \preceq M'$ then $\mathcal{I}[M] \supseteq \mathcal{I}[M']$.

Given a word $w \in \Sigma^*$ the projection of w onto $\Sigma_i \subseteq \Sigma$ ($w|_{\Sigma_i}$) is obtained by removing from w the actions not in Σ_i.

Let $A \subseteq \Sigma$, $M = \langle S, s^0, \Sigma, \Delta^p, \Delta^r \rangle$ and $s \in S$ then the closure of the state s over A is the set of states reachable from s using only transitions labelled by an action in A. Formally:

$$\mathcal{C}_A(s) = \{s' \mid s \xrightarrow{w}_p s' \wedge w \in A^*\}$$

The projection of an MTS M over an alphabet Σ is an MTS $M|_\Sigma$ obtained from M by replacing the labels in M that are not in Σ by the internal action τ (written tau in the graphic representation of the MTS). Note that for any alphabet Σ in this paper holds that $\tau \notin \Sigma$.

We now discuss distribution of LTS models. Distribution of an LTS is with respect to a specification of component interfaces (the actions each component controls and monitors). Such specification is given by an alphabet distribution.

Given an alphabet Σ we say that $\Gamma = \langle \Sigma_1, \ldots, \Sigma_n \rangle$ is an alphabet distribution over Σ iff $\Sigma = \cup_{i \in [n]} \Sigma_i$ were each Σ_i is the (non-empty) alphabet of the local process i.

Definition 7 (Distributable LTS). *Given I, an LTS over Σ, and $\Gamma = \langle \Sigma_1, \ldots, \Sigma_n \rangle$ an alphabet distribution of Σ, I is* distributable *if there exist component LTSs $I_1, \ldots, I_n$ with $\alpha I_i = \Sigma_i$ such that $\|_{i \in [n]} I_i \sim I$.*

The distributed synthesis problem consists on deciding whether an LTS is distributable and, if so, build the distributed component LTSs. Unfortunately, it is unknown if deciding whether an LTS is distributable is decidable in general [CMT99]. However, it has been solved for weaker equivalence notions such as isomorphism [Mor98, CMT99] and language equivalence [CMT99, Ste06], and for restricted forms of LTS such as deterministic LTS [CMT99].

The following is a formal yet abstract distribution algorithm for determinstic LTS defined in terms of the procedure in [CMT99, Ste06]. The procedure builds the component I_i by projecting I over Σ_i and then determinising (using a subset construction [HU79]) I_i.

Definition 8 (LTS distribution). *Let $I = \langle S, s^0, \Sigma, \Delta \rangle$ be an LTS and Γ an alphabet distribution then the distribution of I over Γ is $\mathcal{DIST}_{\Gamma}^{\mathcal{LTS}}[I] = \{I_1, \ldots, I_n\}$ where $\forall i \in [1, n] \cdot I_i = \langle S_i, s_i^0, \Sigma_i, \Delta_i \rangle$ and:*

- $S_i \in 2^S$ *where S_i is reachable from the initial state following Δ_i.*
- $s_i^0 = \mathcal{C}_{\overline{\Sigma_i}}(s_0)$.
- $(s, t, q) \in \Delta_i \leftrightarrow q = \bigcup_{k \in s} \{k'' \in \mathcal{C}_{\overline{\Sigma_i}}(k') \mid k \xrightarrow{t}_p k'\}$.

When Γ is clear from the context we just write $\mathcal{DIST}^{\mathcal{LTS}}[I]$.

Theorem 1 (LTS Distribution Soundness and Completeness). *[CMT99] Let I be a deterministic LTS, Γ an alphabet distribution and $\mathcal{DIST}_{\Gamma}^{\mathcal{LTS}}[I] = \{I_1, \ldots, I_n\}$ then I is distributable (and in fact $\|_{i \in [n]} I_i \sim I$) iff $\mathcal{L}(I) = \mathcal{L}(\|_{i \in [n]} I_i)$.*

3 MTS Distribution

A distribution of an MTS according to an alphabet distribution Γ is simply a set of component MTSs $\{M_1, \ldots, M_n\}$ such that $\alpha M_i = \Sigma_i$. Of course, a first basic requirement for a distribution of a system MTS into component MTSs is soundness with respect to refinement: any implementation of the component MTSs, when composed in parallel, yields an implementation of the system MTS (i.e. if $M_i \preceq I_i$ for $i \in [n]$ then $M \preceq \|_{i \in [n]} I_i$).

A second desirable requirement is completeness, meaning no distributable implementation is lost: a decomposition of M over Γ into a set of components $\{M_1, \ldots, M_n\}$ such that every distributable implementation of M is captured by the components. In other words, $\forall I$ implementation of M that is distributable over Γ there are I_i with $i \in [n]$ such that $M_i \preceq I_i$ and $\|_{i \in [n]} I_i \sim I$.

As discussed in the background section, multiple definitions of distribution for LTS exist. We restrict to deterministic implementations but take the most general distribution criteria, namely bisimilarity which under determinism is the same as language equivalence. The restriction to deterministic implementations is because as an LTS is also an MTS and MTS refinement applied to LTS is bisimulation, solving sound distribution for non-deterministic MTS would solve distribution for non-deterministic LTS considering bisimulation equivalence. The latter is not known to be decidable [CMT99].

Definition 9 (Deterministic and Distributable Implementations). *Let M be an MTS and Γ a distribution. We define $\mathcal{DDI}_\Gamma[M] = \{I \in \mathcal{I}[M] \mid I$ is deterministic and distributable over $\Gamma\}$.*

Definition 10 (Complete and Sound MTS Distributions). *Given an MTS M and an alphabet distribution Γ, a complete and sound distribution of M over Γ are component MTSs $M_1, \ldots, M_n$ such that $\alpha M_i = \Sigma_i$ and:*

1. *(soundness) for any set of LTSs $\{I_1, \ldots, I_n\}$, if $M_i \preceq I_i$ then $M \preceq \|_{i \in [n]} I_i$.*

2. *(completeness) for every $I \in \mathcal{DDI}_\Gamma[M]$ there are I_i with $i \in [n]$ where $M_i \preceq I_i$ and $\|_{i \in [n]} I_i \sim I$.*

A general result for distribution of MTS is not possible. There are MTS for which all their distributable implementations cannot be captured by a set of component MTSs.

Property 2. In general, a complete and sound distribution does not always exist.

Proof. Let's consider the MTS M in Figure 2(a) and the distribution $\Gamma = \langle \Sigma_1 = \{a, w, y\}, \Sigma_2 = \{b, w, y\}\rangle$. The MTSs in Figures 2(b) and 2(c) refine M. Let J and K be the optimistic implementations of the MTSs in Figures 2(b) and 2(c) respectively. As the MTSs in the aforementioned figures refine M, its implementations are also implementations of M. It is easy to see that J and K are both distributable over Γ. Then, a compact complete distribution of M should capture J and K. We shall show that in order to capture J and K the distribution cannot be sound.

Let M_1, M_2 be a complete distribution of M over Γ with $\alpha M_i = \Sigma_i$. As it is complete and J is distributable, there must be implementations of M_1 and M_2 that composed are bisimilar to J. Analogously, there must be implementations of M_1 and M_2 that composed are bisimilar to K. Let us consider a characteristic that an implementation J_1 of M_1 must have in order to yield J when composed with an implementation J_2 of M_2. As $J \xrightarrow{a}$, $a \in \alpha M_1$ and $a \notin \alpha M_2$, it must be the case that $J_1 \xrightarrow{a}$.

The same reasoning can be applied to an implementation K_2 of M_2: In order to yield K when composed with an implementation K_1 of M_1, as $K \xrightarrow{b}$, $b \in \alpha M_2$ and $b \notin \alpha M_1$, it must be the case that $K_2 \xrightarrow{b}$. Hence, we have an implementation J_1 of M_1 such that $J_1 \xrightarrow{a}$ and an implementation K_2 of M_2 such that $K_2 \xrightarrow{b}$. This entails that $J_1 \| K_2 \xrightarrow{ab}$. As $M \xcancel{\xrightarrow{ab}}$ then $J_1 \| K_2$ is not a refinement of M.

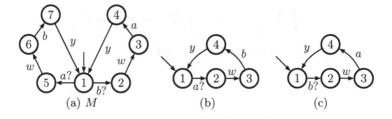

Fig. 2. MTSs used for proof of Property 2

Having assumed that M_1 and M_2 where a complete distribution of M over Γ we have concluded that it is not a sound distribution of M over Γ.   □

This above property is reasonable: not all distributable implementations of an MTS can be achieved by refining independently partial specifications of components. Some decisions (or lack of them) regarding system behaviour captured in the system MTS may require coordinated refinement of component MTSs. In the counter-example described above, the system MTS states that either a or b will occur initially but not both. The decision on which will be provided in the final implementation requires coordinated refinement of the component models: Either J provides a and K does not provide b or the other way round.

3.1   Distribution of a Deterministic MTS

Despite negative result in Property 2 there is a relevant class of MTSs for which a sound and complete distribution is guaranteed to exist and for which an algorithm that produces such distribution can be formulated. The class is that of deterministic MTSs which assign modalities consistently and their optimistic implementation (M^+) is a distributable LTS.

We first give an overview of the distribution algorithm for MTS, then prove soundness of the distributions produced by the algorithm, then define modal consistency of transitions and prove the distributions produced by the algorithm are also complete under modal consistency.

The distribution algorithm requires a deterministic MTS M for which its optimistic implementation M^+ is a distributable LTS. The algorithm builds on the LTS distribution algorithm for deterministic LTS under bisimulation equivalence (see Background). The main difference is that it associates modalities to transitions of component models it produces based on the modalities of the system MTS.

As a running example consider the MTS N in Figure 3 with alphabet $\Sigma = \{a, b, c, d\}$ and the alphabet distribution $\Gamma = \langle \Sigma_1 = \{a, b\}, \Sigma_2 = \{b, c, d\} \rangle$. Conceptually, the algorithm projects N^+ onto the component alphabets and determinises each projection. The modality of a component MTS transition is set to required if and only if at least one of its corresponding transitions in the system MTS is required. The projections of N^+ on Σ_1 and Σ_2 are depicted in Figure 4, the deterministic versions of these projections are depicted in Figure 5, and the

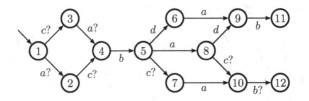

Fig. 3. Running example: N

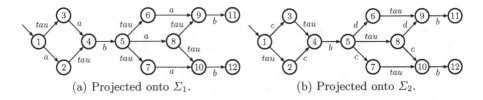

(a) Projected onto Σ_1.   (b) Projected onto Σ_2.

Fig. 4. N^+ projected onto the local alphabets

component MTS resulting from adding modalities to transitions is depicted in Figure 6. Note that the numbers in states of the deterministic MTS in Figures 5 and 6 correspond to the states of N as a result of determinisation.

We now present a formal yet abstract distribution algorithm defined in terms of the subset construction for determinising LTS models [HU79] and the LTS distribution algorithm in [Ste06].

Definition 11 (MTS distribution). *Let $M = \langle S, s^0, \Sigma, \Delta^p, \Delta^r \rangle$ be an MTS and Γ a distribution then the distribution of M over Γ is $\mathcal{DIST}_\Gamma^{MTS}[M] = \{M_1, \ldots, M_n\}$ where $\forall i \in [1, n] M_i = \langle S_i, s_i^0, \Sigma_i, \Delta_i^p, \Delta_i^r \rangle$ and:*

- $S_i \in 2^S$ *where S_i is reachable from the initial state following Δ_i^p.*
- $s_i^0 = C_{\overline{\Sigma_i}}(s_0)$.
- $(s, t, q) \in \Delta_i^p \leftrightarrow q = \bigcup_{k \in s} \{k'' \in C_{\overline{\Sigma_i}}(k') \mid k \xrightarrow{t}_p k'\}$.
- $(s, t, q) \in \Delta_i^r \leftrightarrow (s, t, q) \in \Delta_i^p \wedge \exists k \in s \cdot k \xrightarrow{t}_r$.

When Γ is clear from the context we just write $\mathcal{DIST}^{MTS}[M]$.

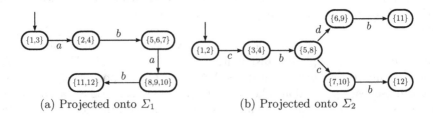

(a) Projected onto Σ_1 (b) Projected onto Σ_2

Fig. 5. N^+ projected onto the local alphabets and determinised

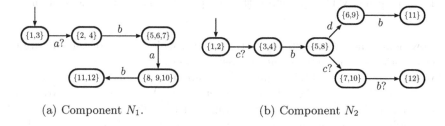

(a) Component N_1.   (b) Component N_2

Fig. 6. Distribution of MTS in Figure 3

Note that in component N_1 of Figure 6 the required b transition from state $\{8, 9, 10\}$ to $\{11, 12\}$ is a consequence of the required b transition from 9 to 11 and the maybe b transition from 10 to 12 in N. Had the transition from $\{8, 9, 10\}$ to $\{11, 12\}$ in N_1 been a maybe rather than required then the distribution would not be sound. Let N_1' be such component. N_1' allows an implementation as in Figure 5(a) but without the last b transition from $\{8, 9, 10\}$ to $\{11, 12\}$. We refer to this implementation as I^1: $I^1 \xrightarrow{aba}_p \overset{b}{\nrightarrow}$. Let I^2 be the LTS in Figure 5(b). I^2 is actually an implementation of N_2. But $I^1 \parallel I^2$ is not an implementation of N as $I^1 \parallel I^2 \xrightarrow{acbad}_p \overset{b}{\nrightarrow}$ and $N \xrightarrow{acbad}_p \overset{b}{\rightarrow}_r$. Hence the need to make the b transition $\{8, 9, 10\}$ to $\{11, 12\}$ required in order to ensure soundness.

We now discuss soundness of MTS distributions as constructed in Definition 11. First, note that Definition 11 when applied to LTS is equivalent to Definition 8, that is the distribution constructed when the MTS is a deterministic LTS is, in effect, a distribution of the LTS. What follows is a sketch of the more general soundness proof.

Theorem 2 (Soundness). *Let M be a deterministic MTS and Γ a distribution such that M^+ is a distributable LTS over Γ, then the MTS distribution (Definition 11) is sound (as defined in Definition 10).*

Proof. We need to prove that for any $I_1, \ldots, I_n$ such that $M_i \preceq I_i$ then $M \preceq \parallel_{i \in [n]} I$. As refinement is a precongruence with regards to $\parallel$ meaning that if $M_i \preceq I_i$ for $i \in [n]$ then $\parallel_{i \in [n]} M_i \preceq \parallel_{i \in [n]} I_i$ we just need to prove $M \preceq \parallel_{i \in [n]} M_i$. Thus $M \preceq \parallel_{i \in [n]} I_i$.

We now prove $M \preceq \parallel_{i \in [n]} M_i$. M^+ is distributable and the component MTSs produced by $\mathcal{DIST}^{\mathcal{MTS}}[M]$ are isomorphic, without considering the transitions' modality, to the component LTSs produced by $\mathcal{DIST}^{\mathcal{LTS}}[M^+]$. So the parallel composition of the component MTSs is isomorphic, again without considering the transitions' modality, to the parallel composition of the component LTSs. When the component MTSs are created if, after the closure, there is a required transition then the component will have a required transition and so the composition may have a required transition where the monolithic MTS had a maybe transition. But any possible behaviour in the composed MTS is also possible in the monolithic MTS. Therefore the composed MTS is a refinement of the monolithic MTS.   □

We now define modal consistency of transitions, which is one of the conditions for Definition 11 to produce complete distributions.

We say that the modalities of an MTS M are inconsistent with respect to an alphabet distribution Γ when there is an action ℓ such that there are two traces w and y leading to two transitions with different modalities on ℓ (i.e. a required and a maybe ℓ-transition) and that for each component alphabet $\Sigma_i \in \Gamma$ where $\ell \in \Sigma_i$, the projection of w and y on Σ_i are the same.

The intuition is that if M is going to be distributed to deterministic partial component models, then some component contributing to the ocurrence of the ℓ after w and y must have reached both points through different paths (i.e. $w|_{\Sigma_i} \neq y|_{\Sigma_i}$). If this is not the case, then the distribution will have to make ℓ after w and y always maybe or always required.

Definition 12 (Alphabet Distribution Modal Consistency). *Let Γ be an alphabet distribution and $M = \langle S, s_0, \Sigma, \Delta^r, \Delta^p \rangle$ an MTS then M is modal consistent with respect to Γ iff $\forall w, y \in \Sigma^*, \ell \in \Sigma \cdot M \xrightarrow{w}_p \xrightarrow{\ell}_r \wedge M \xrightarrow{y}_p \xrightarrow{\ell}_m$ implies $\exists i \in [n] \cdot \ell \in \Sigma_i \wedge w|_{\Sigma_i} \neq y|_{\Sigma_i}$.*

Consider model N from Figure 3. This MTS is modal consistent for $\Gamma = \langle \Sigma_1 = \{a, b\}, \Sigma_2 = \{b, c, d\} \rangle$ as the only w, y and ℓ such that $N \xrightarrow{w}_p \xrightarrow{\ell}_m$ and $N \xrightarrow{y}_p \xrightarrow{\ell}_m$ are $\ell = b$, and w and y sequences leading to states 9 and 10 (for instance $w = cabda$ and $y = acbac$). However, all sequences leading to 9 when projected onto Σ_2 yield cbd while those leading to 10 yield cbc. Hence, consistency is satisfied.

Now consider model P in Figure 7 (a modified version of N but with the following modalities changed: $5 \xrightarrow{a}_m 8$ and $6 \xrightarrow{a}_m 9$). P is not modal consistent with respect to $\Gamma = \langle \Sigma_1 = \{a, b\}, \Sigma_2 = \{b, c, d\} \rangle$: Now there are $w = acb$ and $y = acbc$ such that $P \xrightarrow{w}_p \xrightarrow{a}_m$ and $P \xrightarrow{y}_p \xrightarrow{a}_m$ yet the only Σ_i that includes a is Σ_1 and $w|_{\Sigma_1} = y|_{\Sigma_1} = ab$.

A sound and complete distribution of P would require a deterministic component MTS for $\Sigma_1 = \{a, b\}$ that would either require a after ab or have a maybe a after ab. The former would disallow the implementation I_1 of Figure 8(b) which in turn would make impossible having a component implementation I_2 such that $I_1 \parallel I_2$ yields I of Figure 8(a) which is a deterministic distributable implementation of P. Hence requiring a after ab would lead to an incomplete distribution. Choosing the latter would allow implementation I_1 which would make the distribution unsound: In order to have implementations that when composed yield P^+, an implementation with alphabet $\Sigma_2 = \{b, c, d\}$ bisimilar to Figure 8(c) is needed. However, such an implementation, when composed with I_1 is not a refinement of P.

Theorem 3 (Completeness). *Let M be a deterministic MTS and Γ a distribution such that M^+ is a distributable LTS over Γ, and M is modal consistent*

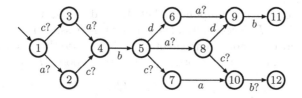

Fig. 7. *P*: Modal Inconsistent MTS

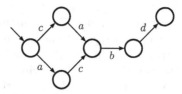

(a) Implementation of Figure 7

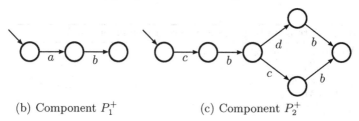

(b) Component P_1^+ (c) Component P_2^+

Fig. 8.

then the MTS distribution (Definition 11) is complete (as defined in Definition 10).

The proof of this theorem uses the following lemmas:

Lemma 1. *Let M, N be deterministic MTSs with $\alpha N = \alpha M$ if $\forall w \in \Sigma^*, t \in \Sigma$*

- *$N \xrightarrow{w}_{\mathrm{p}} \implies M \xrightarrow{w}_{\mathrm{p}}$.*
- *$N \xrightarrow{w}_{\mathrm{p}} \wedge M \xrightarrow{w}_{\mathrm{p}} M' \xrightarrow{t}_{\mathrm{r}} \implies N' \xrightarrow{t}_{\mathrm{r}}$.*

Then $M \preceq N$.

Lemma 2. *Let M be an MTS and $I \in \mathcal{DDI}[M]$. For every $\Sigma_i \in \Gamma$ let M_i and I_i be the components corresponding to Σ_i in $\mathcal{DIST}^{\mathcal{MTS}}[M]$ and $\mathcal{DIST}^{\mathcal{LTS}}[I]$ respectively then $\forall w \in \Sigma_i \cdot I_i \xrightarrow{w}_{\mathrm{p}} \implies M_i \xrightarrow{w}_{\mathrm{p}}$.*

Proof (Theorem 3). Let $\mathcal{DIST}_\Gamma^{\mathcal{MTS}}[M] = \{M_1, \dots, M_n\}$. We need to prove that for every $I \in \mathcal{DDI}_\Gamma[M]$ there are I_i with $i \in [n]$ where $M_i \preceq I_i$ and $\|_{i \in [n]} I_i \sim I$. As I is distributable over Γ then $\mathcal{DIST}_\Gamma^{\mathcal{LTS}}[I] = \{Q_1 \dots Q_n\}$ and $\|_{i \in [n]} Q_i \sim I$.

    Recall that the distribution algorithms produce deterministic components. Therefore we can use Lemma 1 to show that each MTS component is refined by its corresponding LTS component. Let M_i and Q_i be the MTS and LTS components for $\Sigma_i \in \Gamma$. Every possible trace in Q_i is possible in M_i (Lemma 2). Then the only way Q_i is not a refinement of M_i is because there is some required behaviour in M_i that is not present in Q_i. So lets suppose $M_i \not\preceq Q_i$, then

$$\exists z \in \Sigma_i^*, t \in \Sigma_i \text{ such that } M_i \xrightarrow{z}_p T \xrightarrow{t}_r \wedge Q_i \xrightarrow{z}_p Q \xrightarrow{t}\!\!\!\!\not\rightarrow.$$

We now present an algorithm that creates, for every $i \in [n]$, a new component I_i from Q_i by adding the missing required transitions from M_i in order to get $M_i \preceq I_i$. The algorithm iteratively takes a pair (M_i, I_i^j), where I_i^j is the component I_i constructed up to iteration j, such that $M_i \not\preceq I_i^j$ and adds a required transition for a pair mirroring M_i structure. The structure of M_i has to be kept in the resulting I_i in order to avoid trying to add infinite required transitions due to a loop of required transitions in M_i. If the added transitions are part, and complete, a loop in M_i then that same loop will be created in I_i when the algorithm adds the required transitions. Furthermore, the added transitions do not modify the composition (Lemma 3).

Algorithm 1. Extension to each Q_i to get a refinement of M_i

---

Input: $\{(M_1, Q_1), \ldots, (M_n, Q_n)\}$
Output: $\{I_1, \ldots, I_n\}$
  $I_1 = Q_1; \ldots; I_n = Q_n;$
  while $\exists i \in [n] \cdot M_i \not\preceq I_i$ **do**
    take $(M_i, I_i) \cdot M_i \not\preceq I_i;$

    take $z \in \Sigma_i^* \cdot M_i \xrightarrow{z}_p P \xrightarrow{t}_r P' \wedge I_i \xrightarrow{z} Q \xrightarrow{t}\!\!\!\!\not\rightarrow;$
    if $\exists u \in \Sigma_i^* \cdot M_i \xrightarrow{u}_p P' \wedge I_i \xrightarrow{u} Q'$ **then**
      $Q \xrightarrow{t} Q';$
    else
      Add a new state Q' to I_i and then the transition $Q \xrightarrow{t} Q';$
    end if
  end while

As an example of how the algorithm works consider the MTS E in Figure 9(a), that is like N from Figure 3 only that the d transitions are maybe in E instead of required, and $\Gamma = \langle \Sigma_1 = \{a, b\}, \Sigma_2 = \{b, c, d\}\rangle$. Let $\mathcal{DIST}^{MTS}[E] = \{E_1, E_2\}$. E_1 is the same as component N_1 in Figure 6(a). E_2 is like component N_2 in Figure 6(b) only that the d transition from $\{5, 8\}$ to $\{6, 9\}$ is a maybe d transition. I^E in Figure 9(b) is an implementation of E and $\mathcal{DIST}^{LTS}[I^E] = \{Q_1, Q_2\}$ (Figure 10(a) and 10(b)). The algorithm takes $\{(E_1, Q_1), (E_2, Q_2)\}$ and returns components I_1 (I_1 is the same as the LTS in Figure 5(a)) and I_2 (I_2 is in fact Q_2). As $E_2 \preceq Q_2$ then the algorithm will not change Q_2 so $I_2 = Q_2$. $E_1 \not\preceq Q_1$ because $E_1 \xrightarrow{aba}_p \xrightarrow{b}_r$ and $Q_1 \xrightarrow{aba}_p \xrightarrow{b}\!\!\!\!\not\rightarrow$. The algorithm then adds the missing transition to Q_1 and the result is I_1 (I_1 is the same as the LTS in Figure 5(a)). Now $E_1 \preceq I_1$ and the algorithm finishes. See how $I_1 \parallel I_2 \sim Q_1 \parallel Q_2$ as the added b transition to Q_1 in I_1 does not appear in the composition because Q_2 does not provide the needed synchronisation.

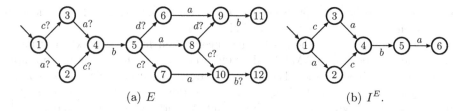

(a) E (b) I^E.

Fig. 9.

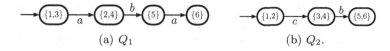

(a) Q_1 (b) Q_2.

Fig. 10.

Finally we prove that the algorithm finishes. As there are finite components it is sufficient to show that $M_i \preceq I_i^m$ with m finite where I_i^j is I_i after doing j additions of required transitions to I_i.

Each iteration adds a missing required t transition to a I_i^j that is present in M_i. If the required transition in M_i goes to P' and there is a $u \in \Sigma_i^*$ from M_i to P' such that u is possible in I_i^j leading to Q' then the new transition goes to Q'. Q' is already present in I_i^{j-1} and the algorithm never modifies possible transitions so any possible behaviour in I_i^{j-1} is possible in M_i and the same stands for I_i^j. On the other hand, if P' is not reachable by a word that is possible in I_i^j then the added required transition goes to a new state. This procedure modifies I_i until all reachable required transitions in M_i not present in I_i are added. As loops of required transitions in M_i that have to be added to I_i are added preserving the loop structure then the iterations for component M_i can not be more than the amount of required transitions present in M_i. And this is done for every pair of components but as they are n the algorithm finishes.   □

The following lemma is used in the proof of Theorem 3. For all $i \in [n]$ I_i refines M_i and the added transitions do not modify the composition. Formally:

Lemma 3. *Let M be a deterministic MTS such that M^+ is distributable over Γ and modal consistent. Let $I \in \mathcal{DDI}[M]$, $\mathcal{DIST}^{\mathcal{LTS}}[I] = \{Q_1, \dots, Q_n\}$, $\mathcal{DIST}^{\mathcal{MTS}}[M_i] = \{M_1, \dots, M_n\}$ and $\{I_1, \dots, I_n\}$ the output of Algorithm 1 for $\{(M_1, Q_1), \dots, (M_n, Q_n)\}$ then:*

- *$\forall i \in [n]$ $M_i \preceq I_i$.*
- *$\|_{i \in [n]} I_i \sim \|_{i \in [n]} Q_i$ (and therefore $\|_{i \in [n]} I_i \sim I$).*

4   Related Work

Distributed implementability and synthesis has been studied for LTS for different equivalences   notion   like   isomorphism,   language   equivalence   and bisimulation [Mor98, CMT99, Ste06, HS05]. The general distributed implementability problem has not been studied for MTS.

A component view of the system has been taken in the context of studies on parallel composition of MTS [BKLS09b], however such view is bottom-up: Given partial behaviour models of components, what is the (partial) behaviour of the system resulting of their parallel composition. The only notable example that takes a top-down approach is [KBEM09] A synthesis procedure is proposed that given system level OCL properties and UML scenarios, component partial behaviour models are automatically constructed such that their composition requires the behaviour required by system level properties and scenarios, and proscribes the behaviour not permitted by the same properties and scenarios.

In [QG08], MTS distribution is studied as a instance of more general contract-based formalism. The notion that corresponds to our definition of complete and sound MTS Distribution (see Definition 10) is called decomposability, Definition 3.8 [QG08]. Decomposability is a strictly stronger notion which requires all implementations of M to be captured by some distribution $\|_{i\in[n]}M_i$. Our definition only requires distributable implementations of M to be refinements of $\|_{i\in[n]}M_i$. In particular Figure 3, with transition from 6 to 9 changed to being only possible, is not distributable according to [QG08] but is according to our definition. Moreover, the distribution algorithm of [QG08] cannot handle examples such as Figure 3.3 in [Ste06] which can be handled by standard LTS distribution algorithms (and ours) by determinising projections.

5   Conclusions

In this paper we provide results that support moving from iterative refinement of a monolithic system models to component-wise iterative refinement. We present a distribution algorithm for partial behaviour system models specified as MTS to component-wise partial behaviour models given as sets of MTSs. We precisely characterise when the decomposition provided is sound and complete, we also discuss why the restrictions to the distribution problem (namely determinism, modal consistency and distributability of M^+) are reasonable, are unlikely to be avoidable for any sound and complete distribution method, and can be seen as a natural extension of the limitations of existing LTS distribution results.

Future work will involve experimenting with case studies to assess the practical limitations imposed by the restrictions introduced to enforce completeness of distributions. We expect insights gained to allow for definition of more generally applicable sound but not complete distribution algorithms and elaboration techniques to support refinement of system models into models for which distribution algorithms exist.

References

[BKLS09a] Beneš, N., Křetínský, J., Larsen, K.G., Srba, J.: Checking Thorough Refinement on Modal Transition Systems Is EXPTIME-Complete. In: Leucker, M., Morgan, C. (eds.) ICTAC 2009. LNCS, vol. 5684, pp. 112–126. Springer, Heidelberg (2009)

[BKLS09b] Beneš, N., Ketínský, J., Larsen, K.G., Srba, J.: On determinism in modal transition systems. Theor. Comput. Sci. 410(41), 4026–4043 (2009)

[CMT99] Castellani, I., Mukund, M., Thiagarajan, P.S.: Synthesizing Distributed Transition Systems from Global Specifications. In: Pandu Rangan, C., Raman, V., Sarukkai, S. (eds.) FST TCS 1999. LNCS, vol. 1738, pp. 219–231. Springer, Heidelberg (1999)

[DFFU07] D'Ippolito, N., Fishbein, D., Foster, H., Uchitel, S.: MTSA: Eclipse support for modal transition systems construction, analysis and elaboration. In: Eclipse 2007: Proceedings of the 2007 OOPSLA Workshop on Eclipse Technology Exchange, pp. 6–10. ACM (2007)

[FBD+11] Fischbein, D., Brunet, G., D'Ippolito, N., Chechik, M., Uchitel, S.: Weak alphabet merging of partial behaviour models. In: TOSEM, pp. 1–49 (2011)

[GP11] Godefroid, P., Piterman, N.: Ltl generalized model checking revisited. STTT 13(6), 571–584 (2011)

[HS05] Heljanko, K., Stefanescu, A.: Complexity results for checking distributed implementability. In: Proc. of the Fifth Int. Conf. on Application of Concurrency to System Design, pp. 78–87. IEEE Computer Society Press (2005)

[HU79] Hopcroft, J.E., Ullman, J.D.: In: Introduction to automata theory, languages, and computation. Addison-Wesley (1979)

[KBEM09] Krka, I., Brun, Y., Edwards, G., Medvidovic, N.: Synthesizing partial component-level behavior models from system specifications. In: ESEC/FSE 2009, pp. 305–314. ACM (2009)

[LT88] Larsen, K.G., Thomsen, B.: A modal process logic. In: LICS 1988, pp. 203–210. IEEE Computer Society (1988)

[Mil89] Milner, R.: Communication and Concurrency. Prentice-Hall, New York (1989)

[MK99] Magee, J., Kramer, J.: Concurrency - State Models and Java Programs. John Wiley (1999)

[Mor98] Morin, R.: Decompositions of Asynchronous Systems. In: Sangiorgi, D., de Simone, R. (eds.) CONCUR 1998. LNCS, vol. 1466, pp. 549–564. Springer, Heidelberg (1998)

[QG08] Quinton, S., Graf, S.: Contract-based verification of hierarchical systems of components. In: SEFM 2008, pp. 377–381 (2008)

[Ste06] Stefanescu, A.: Automatic Synthesis of Distributed Systems. PhD thesis (2006)

[Sto05] Stoll, M.: MoTraS: A Tool for Modal Transition Systems. Master's thesis, Technische Universitat Munchen, Fakultat fur Informatik (August 2005)

[SUB08] Sibay, G., Uchitel, S., Braberman, V.: Existential live sequence charts revisited. In: ICSE 2008, pp. 41–50 (2008)

[UKM04] Uchitel, S., Kramer, J., Magee, J.: Incremental elaboration of scenario-based specifications and behaviour models using implied scenarios. ACM TOSEM 13(1) (2004)

Efficient Malware Detection Using Model-Checking★

Fu Song and Tayssir Touili

LIAFA, CNRS and Univ. Paris Diderot, France
{song,touili}@liafa.jussieu.fr

Abstract. Over the past decade, malware costs more than $10 billion every year and the cost is still increasing. Classical signature-based and emulation-based methods are becoming insufficient, since malware writers can easily obfuscate existing malware such that new variants cannot be detected by these methods. Thus, it is important to have more robust techniques for malware detection. In our previous work [24], we proposed to use model-checking to identify malware. We used pushdown systems (PDSs) to model the program (this allows to keep track of the program's stack behavior), and we defined the SCTPL logic to specify the malicious behaviors, where SCTPL can be seen as an extension of the branching-time temporal logic CTL with variables, quantifiers, and predicates over the stack. Malware detection was then reduced to SCTPL model-checking of PDSs. However, in our previous work [24], the way we used SCTPL to specify malicious behaviors was not very precise. Indeed, we used the *names* of the registers and memory locations instead of their *values*. We show in this work how to sidestep this limitation and use precise SCTPL formulas that consider the *values* of the registers and memory locations to specify malware. Moreover, to make the detection procedure more efficient, we propose an abstraction that reduces drastically the size of the program model, and show that this abstraction preserves all SCTPL\X formulas, where SCTPL\X is a fragment of SCTPL that is sufficient to precisely characterize malware specifications. We implemented our techniques in a tool and applied it to *automatically* detect several malwares. The experimental results are encouraging.

1 Introduction

The number of malwares that produced incidents in 2010 is more than 1.5 billion [11]. A malware may bring serious damage, e.g., the worm MyDoom slowed down global internet access by ten percent in 2004 [9]. Thus, it is crucial to have efficient up-to-date virus detectors. Existing antivirus systems use various detection techniques to identify viruses such as (1) code emulation where the virus is executed in a virtual environment to get detected; or (2) signature detection, where a signature is a pattern of program code that characterizes the virus. A file is declared as a virus if it contains a sequence of binary code instructions that matches one of the known signatures. Each virus variant has its corresponding signature. These techniques have some limitations. Indeed, emulation based techniques can only check the program's behavior in a limited time interval. They cannot check what happens after the timeout. Thus, they might miss the viral behavior if

---

★ Work partially funded by ANR grant ANR-08-SEGI-006.

D. Giannakopoulou and D. Méry (Eds.): FM 2012, LNCS 7436, pp. 418–433, 2012.

it occurs after this time interval. As for signature based systems, it is very easy to virus developers to get around them. It suffices to apply obfuscation techniques to change the structure of the code while keeping the same functionality, so that the new version does not match the known signatures. Obfuscation techniques can consist of inserting dead code, substituting instructions by equivalent ones, etc. Virus writers update their viruses frequently to make them undetectable by these antivirus systems.

Recently, to sidestep these limitations, model-checking techniques have been used for virus detection [5,22,7,8,16,14,17]. Such techniques allow to check the *behavior* (not the syntax) of the program without executing it. These works use finite state graphs as program model. Thus, they cannot accurately represent the program's stack. However, as shown in [20], being able to track the program's stack is very important for malware detection. For example, to check whether a program is malicious, anti-viruses start by identifying the system calls it makes. To evade these virus detectors, malware writers try to obfuscate the system calls by using pushes and jumps. Thus, it is important to be able to track the stack to detect such calls.

To this aim, we proposed in our previous work [24] a new approach for malware detection that consists in (1) Modeling the program using a Pushdown System (PDS). This allows to take into account the behavior of the stack. (2) Introducing a new logic, called SCTPL, to represent the malicious behavior. SCTPL can be seen as an extension of the branching-time temporal logic CTL with variables, quantifiers, and predicates over the stack. (3) And reducing the malware detection problem to the model-checking problem of PDSs against SCTPL formulas. Our techniques were implemented in a tool and applied to detect several viruses.

However, [24] still has some limitations: (1) The PDS corresponding to the program to be analyzed was generated by hand by the user. (2) Due to the high complexity of SCTPL model-checking, we were not able to check several examples (they run out of memory). (3) When specifying malicious behavior using SCTPL, we used formulas where the variables range over the names of the program's registers, not over their values. Thus, the specifications were not precise. To understand this last problem, let us consider the program of Figure 1(a). It corresponds to a critical fragment of the Email-worm Klez that shows the typical behavior of an email worm: it calls the API function *GetModuleFileNameA* with 0 as first parameter and an address a as second parameter[1]. This function will store the file name of the worm's own executable into the memory pointed by a, so that later, the worm can infect other files by copying this executable stored in the memory pointed by a into them.

Using SCTPL, in [24] we specify this malicious behavior by the following formula:

$$\psi = \exists a \exists r_1 \mathbf{EF}\big(xor(r_1, r_1) \wedge \mathbf{EXE}[\neg \exists v\, mov(r_1, v)\mathbf{U}push(r_1) \wedge \mathbf{EXE}[\neg(push(r_1) \vee \exists r'(pop(r')$$
$$\wedge\ r_1\Gamma^*))\mathbf{U}call(GetModuleFileNameA) \wedge r_1 a\Gamma^* \wedge \mathbf{EF}(call(CopyFileA) \wedge a\Gamma^*)]]\big)$$

where $r_1 a\Gamma^*$ (resp. $a\Gamma^*$) is a regular predicate expressing that the topmost symbols of the stack are r_1 and a (resp. a). This SCTPL formula ψ states that there exists a register r_1 that is first assigned 0 ($xor(r_1, r_1)$) and such that it is not assigned any other value later until r_1 is pushed onto the stack. Later, r_1 is never popped from the stack nor

---

[1] Parameters of a function in assembly are passed by pushing them into the stack before calling the function. The callee retrieves these parameters from the stack.

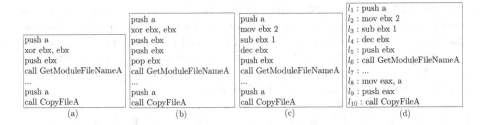

Fig. 1. (a) Worm fragment; (b), (c) and (d) Obfuscated fragments

pushed onto it again until the function *GetModuleFileNameA* is invoked. When this call is made, the topmost symbols of the stack have to be r_1 and a. This ensures that the first parameter of *GetModuleFileNameA* is the value of r_1, i.e. 0, and that the file name of its own executable returned by the function is stored in the memory pointed by a. This specification can detect the fragment in Figure 1(a). However, a virus writer can easily use some obfuscation techniques in order to escape from this specification. For example, if we add a *push ebx* followed by a *pop ebx* as done in Figure 1 (b); or instead of using *xor ebx ebx* to put 0 into *ebx*, let us put the value 2 in *ebx* and then remove 1 twice as done in Figure 1 (c). These two fragments keep the same malicious behavior than the fragment of Figure 1(a), however, they cannot be detected by the formula ψ. A virus writer can also escape from this specification by first assigning the address a to the register *eax* and then pushing the value of *eax* onto the stack as shown in Figure 1 (d) (instead of pushing a directly to the stack). When calling *CopyFileA*, the topmost symbol of the stack is equal to *the value* stored in a, but is different from *the name a*. Thus, this fragment cannot be detected by the above specification ψ.

To overcome this problem, we propose in this work to specify malicious behaviors using SCTPL formulas where the variables range over the values of the program's registers and memory, not over their names. In this way, the malicious behavior of Figures 1 (a), (b), (c) and (d) can be specified as follows:

$$\Omega = \exists m \ \mathbf{EF}(call(GetModuleFileNameA) \wedge \{0\} \ m \ \Gamma^* \wedge \mathbf{EF}(call(CopyFileA) \wedge m\Gamma^*))$$

This expresses that a call to the API function *GetModuleFileNameA* is made with 0 and the *value* of the address m of the memory on top of the stack, followed by a call to the API function *CopyFileA* with the *value* of m on top of the stack. Unlike [24], m represents the *values* of the program's registers and addresses, not their names.

In order to consider such specifications, we need to track the values of the different registers of the program. To do this, we consider an oracle O that gives an overapproximation of the current state at each control point of the program, i.e., an overapproximation of the values of the different registers and memory locations. To implement this oracle, we use Jakstab [18] and IDA Pro [13]. Based on the oracle O, we implement a translator that *automatically* constructs a PDS from the binary program.

To overcome the high complexity problem of SCTPL model-checking, we introduce the *collapsing abstraction*, which is an abstraction that drastically reduces the size of the program model by removing the instructions that do not change the stack (instructions using push or pop are not removed), nor the control flow of the programs (instructions using jump-like operators, e.g., jmp, jz, etc. are not removed); as well as the instructions whose operators do not appear in the considered SCTPL formula. We show that this abstraction preserves all SCTPL\X formulas, where SCTPL\X is a subclass of SCTPL that uses the next time operator X only to specify the return addresses of the callers. We show that this fragment SCTPL\X is sufficient to specify all the malicious behaviors we considered. Our abstraction allowed to apply our techniques to large programs. In our experiments, several examples terminate when we use our abstraction, whereas without it, they run out of memory.

The main contributions of this paper are:

1. We propose to specify malicious behaviors using SCTPL formulas where the variables range over the values of the program's registers, not over their names as done in [24]. Thus, we get more precise malware specifications.
2. We present a new approach to model a binary program as a PDS. Our translation is more precise than the other existing translations from programs to PDSs.
3. We identify the sub-logic SCTPL\X, which is a subclass of SCTPL where the next time operator X is used only to specify the return addresses of the callers. We show that SCTPL\X is sufficient to specify all the malware behaviors we considered, and we proposed the *collapsing abstraction* and show that it preserves SCTPL\X properties. This abstraction reduces drastically the model size, and thus makes the model-checking problem more efficient.
4. We implement our techniques in a tool for malware detection. All the steps are completely automated. Our tool takes as input a binary program and a set of SCTPL\X formulas representing a set of malicious behaviors. It outputs *"Yes, the program may be a malware"* if the program satisfies one of the formulas, and *"NO"* if not. We get encouraging results.

Related Work. These last years, there has been a substantial amount of research to find efficient techniques that can detect viruses. A lot of techniques use signature based or emulation based approaches. As already mentioned in the introduction, such techniques have some limitations. Indeed, signature matching fails if the virus does not use a known signature. As for emulation techniques, they can execute the program only in a given time interval. Thus, they can miss the malicious behaviors if they occur after the timeout.

Model-checking and static analysis techniques have been applied to detect malicious behaviors e.g. in [5,22,7,8,16,14,17]. However, all these works are based on modeling the program as a finite-state system, and thus, they miss the behavior of the stack. As we have seen, being able to track the stack is important for many malicious behaviors. [6,3] use tree automata to represent a set of malicious behaviors. However, these works cannot specify predicates over the stack content.

[20] keeps track of the stack by computing an abstract stack graph which finitely represents the infinite set of all the possible stacks for every control point of the program. Their technique can detect obfuscated calls and obfuscated returns. However, they cannot specify the other malicious behaviors that we are able to detect using our SCTPL specifications.

[19] performs context-sensitive analysis of *call* and *ret* obfuscated binaries. They use abstract interpretation to compute an abstraction of the stack. We believe that our techniques are more precise since we do not abstract the stack. Moreover, the techniques of [19] were only tried on toy examples, they have not been applied for malware detection.

[4] uses pushdown systems for binary program analysis. However, the translation from programs to PDSs in [4] assumes that the program follows a standard compilation model where calls and returns match. As we have shown, several malicious behaviors do not follow this model. Our translation from a control flow graph to a PDS does not make this assumption.

SCTPL can be seen as an extension of CTPL with predicates over the stack content. CTPL was introduced in [16,14,17]. In these works, the authors show how CTPL can be used to succinctly specify malicious behaviors. Our SCTPL logic is more expressive than CTPL. Indeed, CTPL cannot specify predicates over the stack. Thus, SCTPL allows to specify more malicious behaviors than CTPL. Indeed, most of the malicious behaviors we considered cannot be expressed in CTPL.

Outline. In Section 2, we give our formal model. Section 3 recalls the definition of the SCTPL logic and shows how this logic can precisely represent malicious behavior. We give the definition of the fragment SCTPL\X and of the collapsing abstraction in Section 4. Our experiments are described in Section 5. Due to lack of space, proofs are omitted. They can be found in the full version of the paper [23].

2   Binary Code Modeling

In this section, we show how to build a PDS from a binary program. We suppose we are given an oracle O that extracts from the binary program a control flow graph equipped with informations about the values of the registers and the memory locations at each control point of the program. In our implementation, we use Jakstab [18] and IDA Pro [13] to get this oracle. We translate the control flow graph into a pushdown system where the control locations store the control points of the binary program and the stack tracks the stack of the program. This translation takes into account the values of the different registers and memory locations of the program.

2.1   Control Flow Graphs

Let $\mathbf{R}$ be the finite set of registers used in the binary program. Let **States** be the set of functions from $\mathbf{R} \cup \mathbb{Z}$ to $2^{\mathbb{Z}}$ where $\mathbb{Z}$ is the set of integers. Intuitively, let $s \in$ **States**. For every $r \in \mathbf{R}$, $s(r)$ gives the possible values of the register r in the state s, while for every $d \in \mathbb{Z}$, $s(d)$ gives the possible values of the memory at address d in the state s. Let **EXP** be the set of expressions over the registers and the memory locations used in the program. **States** is extended over expressions in **EXP** in the usual way.

A *control flow graph* (CFG) is a tuple $G = (N, I, E)$, where N is a finite set of nodes corresponding to the control points of the program, I is a finite set of assembly instructions used in the program, and $E : N \times I \times N$ is a finite set of edges each of them associated with an assembly instruction of the program. We write $n_1 \xrightarrow{i} n_2$ for every (n_1, i, n_2) in E. Given a binary program, the oracle O computes a corresponding control flow graph G and a function $\varrho : N \longrightarrow$ **States** that associates to each node n an overapproximation of the set of possible states of the program at the control point n.

2.2 Pushdown Systems

A *Pushdown System* (PDS) is a tuple $\mathcal{P} = (P, \Gamma, \Delta)$, where P is a finite set of control locations, Γ is the stack alphabet, $\Delta \subseteq (P \times \Gamma) \times (P \times \Gamma^*)$ is a finite set of transition rules.

A configuration $\langle p, \omega \rangle$ of $\mathcal{P}$ is an element of $P \times \Gamma^*$. We write $\langle p, \gamma \rangle \hookrightarrow \langle q, \omega \rangle$ instead of $((p, \gamma), (q, \omega)) \in \Delta$. The successor relation $\leadsto_{\mathcal{P}} \subseteq (P \times \Gamma^*) \times (P \times \Gamma^*)$ is defined as follows: if $\langle p, \gamma \rangle \hookrightarrow \langle q, \omega \rangle$, then $\langle p, \gamma\omega' \rangle \leadsto_{\mathcal{P}} \langle q, \omega\omega' \rangle$ for every $\omega' \in \Gamma^*$. A *path* of the PDS is a sequence of configurations $c_1, c_2, \ldots$ such that c_{i+1} is an *immediate successor* of the configuration c_i, i.e., $c_i \leadsto_{\mathcal{P}} c_{i+1}$, for every $i \geq 1$.

2.3 From Control Flow Graphs to Pushdown Systems

In this section, we present a novel approach to derive a pushdown system from a control flow graph. Consider a binary program. Let (N, I, E) be the CFG and ϱ be the state function provided by the oracle O. We construct the PDS $\mathcal{P} = (P, \Gamma, \Delta)$ as follows:

- the control locations P are the nodes N;
- Γ is the smallest set of symbols satisfying the following:
  - if $n \xrightarrow{call\ proc} n' \in E$, then $\{n'\} \in \Gamma$ where n' is the return address of the call;
  - if $n \xrightarrow{push\ exp} n' \in E$, where exp is an expression in EXP, then $\varrho(n)(exp) \in \Gamma$ where $\varrho(n)(exp)$ denotes the set of possible values of the expression exp at the control point n (given by the state $\varrho(n)$);
- the set of rules Δ contain transition rules that mimic the instructions of the program: for every edge $e \in E, \gamma \in \Gamma$:
  - if $e = n_1 \xrightarrow{push\ exp} n_2$, we add the transition rule $\langle n_1, \gamma \rangle \hookrightarrow \langle n_2, \gamma'\gamma \rangle$ where $\gamma' = \varrho(n_1)(exp)$. This rule moves the program's control point from n_1 to n_2, and pushes the set of all the possible values of the expression exp at control point n_1 onto the stack;
  - if $e = n_1 \xrightarrow{call\ proc} n_2$, we add the transition rule $\langle n_1, \gamma \rangle \hookrightarrow \langle proc_e, \{n_2\}\gamma \rangle$, for every $proc_e \in \varrho(n_1)(proc)$. This rule moves the program's control point to the entry point of the procedure $proc$, and pushes the return address n_2 onto the stack. Here, we let $proc_e$ be in $\varrho(n_1)(proc)$ because in assembly code, the operand of a call instruction can be any expression including the address of an instruction;
  - if $e = n_1 \xrightarrow{pop\ exp} n_2$, we add the transition rule $\langle n_1, \gamma \rangle \hookrightarrow \langle n_2, \epsilon \rangle$ which moves the program's control point to n_2 and pops the topmost symbol from the stack;
  - if $e = n_1 \xrightarrow{ret} n_2$, we add a transition rule $\langle n_1, \gamma \rangle \hookrightarrow \langle addr, \epsilon \rangle$ for every $addr \in \gamma$. This moves the program's control point to every address $addr$ in γ, and pops the topmost symbol from the stack;

- if $e = n_1 \xrightarrow{cjmp\ e} n_2$ where $cjmp$ denotes a conditional jump instruction (je, jg, etc.). Let $flag$ be the flag register (ZF,CF, etc.) of $cjmp$. Depending on whether the flag register satisfies the condition of $cjmp$ or not (i.e., whether $false \in \varrho(n_1)(flag)$ or not), we add the transition rules $r_1 = \langle n_1, \gamma \rangle \hookrightarrow \langle n_2, \gamma \rangle$ and/or $r_2 = \langle n_1, \gamma \rangle \hookrightarrow \langle addr, \gamma \rangle$ for every $addr \in \varrho(n_1)(e)$. r_1 moves the program's control point to n_2 whereas r_2 moves the programs's control point to the address $addr$ that corresponds to the value of e at point n_1.

- if $e = n_1 \xrightarrow{i} n_2$ is any other transition, we add a transition rule $r_1 = \langle n_1, \gamma \rangle \hookrightarrow \langle n_2, \gamma \rangle$ which moves the program's control point from n_1 to n_2 without changing the stack.

Note that in our modeling, the PDS control locations correspond to the program's control points, and the PDS stack mimics the program's execution stack. The above transition rules allow the PDS to mimic the behavior of the program's stack. This is different from standard program translations to PDSs where the control points of the program are stored in the stack [10,4]. These standard translations assume that the program follows a standard compilation model, where the return addresses are never modified. We do not make such assumptions since behaviors where the return addresses are modified can occur in malicious code. We only make the assumption that pushes and pops can be done only using *push*, *pop*, *call*, and *return* operations, not by manipulating the stack pointer. Our translation is also more precise than the one given in [24]. Indeed, here the stack content is (an over-approximation of) the program's stack, whereas in [24], the stack contains the names of the pushed registers, not their values. For example, in [24], a push instruction of the form $n_1 \xrightarrow{push\ eax} n_2$ is modeled by a push rule where the name of the register eax is pushed onto the stack, whereas in this work, we push the possible values of eax onto the stack.

3   Malicious Behavior Specification

In this section, we recall the definition of the Stack Computation Tree Predicate Logic (SCTPL) [24], and show how we can use it to specify malicious behaviors in a more precise and succinct way than done in [24].

3.1   Environments, Predicates and Regular Variable Expressions

Hereafter, we fix the following notations. Let $X = \{x_1, x_2, ...\}$ be a finite set of variables ranging over a finite domain $\mathcal{D}$. Let $B : X \cup \mathcal{D} \longrightarrow \mathcal{D}$ be an environment function that assigns a value $c \in \mathcal{D}$ to each variable $x \in X$ and such that $B(c) = c$ for every $c \in \mathcal{D}$. $B[x \leftarrow c]$ denotes the environment function such that $B[x \leftarrow c](x) = c$ and $B[x \leftarrow c](y) = B(y)$ for every $y \neq x$. Let $\mathcal{B}$ be the set of all the environment functions.

Let $AP = \{a, b, c, ...\}$ be a finite set of atomic propositions, AP_X be a finite set of atomic predicates in the form of $b(\alpha_1, ..., \alpha_m)$ such that $b \in AP$, $\alpha_i \in X \cup \mathcal{D}$ for every $1 \leq i \leq m$, and $AP_{\mathcal{D}}$ be a finite set of atomic predicates of the form $b(\alpha_1, ..., \alpha_m)$ such that $b \in AP$, $\alpha_i \in \mathcal{D}$ for every $1 \leq i \leq m$.

Given a PDS $\mathcal{P} = (P, \Gamma, \Delta)$, let $\mathcal{R}$ be a finite set of regular variable expressions over $X \cup \Gamma$ given by: $e ::= \emptyset \mid \epsilon \mid a \in X \cup \Gamma \mid e + e \mid e \cdot e \mid e^*$.

The language $L(e)$ of a regular variable expression e is a subset of $P \times \Gamma^* \times \mathcal{B}$ defined inductively as follows: $L(\emptyset) = \emptyset$; $L(\epsilon) = \{(\langle p, \epsilon \rangle, B) \mid p \in P, B \in \mathcal{B}\}$; $L(x)$, where $x \in X$ is the set $\{(\langle p, \gamma \rangle, B) \mid p \in P, \gamma \in \Gamma, B \in \mathcal{B} : B(x) = \gamma\}$; $L(\gamma)$, where $\gamma \in \Gamma$ is the set $\{(\langle p, \gamma \rangle, B) \mid p \in P, B \in \mathcal{B}\}$; $L(e_1 + e_2) = L(e_1) \cup L(e_1)$; $L(e_1 \cdot e_2) = \{(\langle p, \omega_1\omega_2 \rangle, B) \mid (\langle p, \omega_1 \rangle, B) \in L(e_1); (\langle p, \omega_2 \rangle, B) \in L(e_2)\}$; and $L(e^*) = \{(\langle p, \omega \rangle, B) \mid B \in \mathcal{B}$ and $\omega = \omega_1 \cdots \omega_n$, s.t. $\forall i, 1 \leq i \leq n, (\langle p, \omega_i \rangle, B) \in L(e)\}$. E.g., $(\langle p, \gamma_1\gamma_1\gamma_2 \rangle, B)$ is an element of $L(x^*\gamma_2)$ when $B(x) = \gamma_1$.

3.2 Stack Computation Tree Predicate Logic

A SCTPL formula is a CTL formula where predicates and regular variable expressions are used as atomic propositions, and where quantifiers over variables are used. Using regular variable expressions allows to express predicates on the stack content of the PDS. For technical reasons, we suppose w.l.o.g. that formulas are given in positive normal form, i.e., negations are applied only to atomic propositions. More precisely, the set of *SCTPL formulas* is given by (where $x \in X$, $a(x_1, ..., x_n) \in AP_X$ and $e \in \mathcal{R}$):

$$\varphi ::= a(x_1, ..., x_n) \mid \neg a(x_1, ..., x_n) \mid e \mid \neg e \mid \varphi \wedge \varphi \mid \varphi \vee \varphi \mid \forall x\, \varphi$$
$$\mid \exists x\, \varphi \mid AX\varphi \mid EX\varphi \mid A[\varphi U\varphi] \mid E[\varphi U\varphi] \mid A[\varphi R\varphi] \mid E[\varphi R\varphi]$$

Let φ be a SCTPL formula. The closure $cl(\varphi)$ denotes the set of all the subformulas of φ including φ.

Given a PDS $\mathcal{P} = (P, \Gamma, \Delta)$ s.t. $\Gamma \subseteq \mathcal{D}$, Let $\lambda : AP_{\mathcal{D}} \to 2^P$ be a labeling function that assigns a set of control locations to a predicate. Let $c = \langle p, w \rangle$ be a configuration of $\mathcal{P}$. $\mathcal{P}$ satisfies a SCTPL formula ψ in c, denoted by $c \models_\lambda \psi$, iff there exists an environment $B \in \mathcal{B}$ s.t. $c \models_\lambda^B \psi$, where $c \models_\lambda^B \psi$ is defined by induction as follows:

- $c \models_\lambda^B a(x_1, ..., x_n)$ iff $p \in \lambda\big(a(B(x_1), ..., B(x_n))\big)$.
- $c \models_\lambda^B \neg a(x_1, ..., x_n)$ iff $p \notin \lambda\big(a(B(x_1), ..., B(x_n))\big)$.
- $c \models_\lambda^B e$ iff $(c, B) \in L(e)$.
- $c \models_\lambda^B \neg e$ iff $(c, B) \notin L(e)$.
- $c \models_\lambda^B \psi_1 \wedge \psi_2$ iff $c \models_\lambda^B \psi_1$ and $c \models_\lambda^B \psi_2$.
- $c \models_\lambda^B \psi_1 \vee \psi_2$ iff $c \models_\lambda^B \psi_1$ or $c \models_\lambda^B \psi_2$.
- $c \models_\lambda^B \forall x\, \psi$ iff $\forall v \in \mathcal{D}$, $c \models_\lambda^{B[x \leftarrow v]} \psi$.
- $c \models_\lambda^B \exists x\, \psi$ iff $\exists v \in \mathcal{D}$ s.t. $c \models_\lambda^{B[x \leftarrow v]} \psi$.
- $c \models_\lambda^B AX\, \psi$ iff $c' \models_\lambda^B \psi$ for every successor c' of c.
- $c \models_\lambda^B EX\, \psi$ iff there exists a successor c' of c s.t. $c' \models_\lambda^B \psi$.
- $c \models_\lambda^B A[\psi_1 U\psi_2]$ iff for every path $\pi = c_0, c_1, ...,$ of $\mathcal{P}$ with $c_0 = c$, $\exists i \geq 0$ s.t. $c_i \models_\lambda^B \psi_2$ and $\forall 0 \leq j < i : c_j \models_\lambda^B \psi_1$.
- $c \models_\lambda^B E[\psi_1 U\psi_2]$ iff there exists a path $\pi = c_0, c_1, ...,$ of $\mathcal{P}$ with $c_0 = c$ s.t. $\exists i \geq 0$, $c_i \models_\lambda^B \psi_2$ and $\forall 0 \leq j < i, c_j \models_\lambda^B \psi_1$.
- $c \models_\lambda^B A[\psi_1 R\psi_2]$ iff for every path $\pi = c_0, c_1, ...,$ of $\mathcal{P}$ with $c_0 = c$, $\forall i \geq 0$ s.t. $c_i \not\models_\lambda^B \psi_2$, $\exists 0 \leq j < i$ s.t. $c_j \models_\lambda^B \psi_1$.

– $c \models_\lambda^B E[\psi_1 R \psi_2]$ iff there exists a path $\pi = c_0, c_1, ...,$ of $\mathcal{P}$ with $c_0 = c$ s.t. $\forall i \geq 0$ s.t. $c_i \not\models_\lambda^B \psi_2$, $\exists 0 \leq j < i$ s.t. $c_j \models_\lambda^B \psi_1$.

Intuitively, $c \models_\lambda^B \psi$ holds iff the configuration c satisfies the formula ψ under the environment B. Note that a path π satisfies $\psi_1 R \psi_2$ iff either ψ_2 holds everywhere in π, or the first occurrence in the path where ψ_2 does not hold must be preceded by a position where ψ_1 holds.

Theorem 1. *[24] Given a PDS $\mathcal{P} = (P, \Gamma, \Delta)$ and a SCTPL formula ψ, whether a configuration of $\mathcal{P}$ satisfies ψ can be decided.*

3.3   Using SCTPL Formulas in a Precise Manner

In [24], the stack alphabet Γ (which is a subset of the domain $\mathcal{D}$) we considered consists of the set of registers **R** and the set of the return addresses of the different calls. As explained in the introduction, using the names of the registers instead of their values is not robust and is not very precise. To sidestep this problem, we propose in this work to use the values of the registers instead of their names. Hence, in this work, the stack alphabet Γ consists of sets of (over-approximations of) values of registers (elements of $2^{\mathbb{Z}}$), together with the return addresses of the calls.

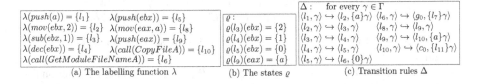

(a) The labelling function λ (b) The states ϱ (c) Transition rules Δ

Fig. 2. (a) The labeling function λ, (b) the states ϱ and (c) Transition rules Δ, where g_0 and c_0 are entry points of the function GetModuleFileNameA and CopyFileA, respectively, and l_{11} is the next location of l_{10}

An Illustrating Example. Let us consider the fragment of Figure 1(d) and the SCTPL formula Ω described in the introduction. Suppose the oracle O provides the function ρ of Figure[2] 2(b). Then, we have:

– $\Gamma = \{ \{a\}, \{0\}, \{l_7\}, \{l_{11}\} \}$ is the stack alphabet, where l_{11} is the location after l_{10};
– $\mathcal{R} = \{\{0\} m \Gamma^*, m\Gamma^*\}$ is the set of regular variable expressions in the formula Ω;
– $AP = \{call, mov, sub, dec, push\}$ is the set of atomic propositions corresponding to the instructions of the program;
– $AP_{\mathcal{D}} = \{push(a), mov(ebx, 2), sub(ebx, 1), dec(ebx), push(ebx), mov(eax, a),$ $push(eax), call(GetModuleFileNameA), call(CopyFileA)\}$ is the set of predicates that appear in the program;
– $\mathcal{D} = \{\{a\}, \{0\}, \{l_7\}, \{l_{11}\}, 1, 2, a, eax, ebx, GetModuleFileNameA, CopyFileA\}$;
– The labeling function λ is shown Figure 2(a).
– The set of transition rules Δ of the PDS modeling this fragment is shown in Figure 2(c), where g_0 is the entry point of the procedure GetModuleFileNameA and c_0 is the entry point of the procedure CopyFileA.

[2] We give only the values of ρ that are needed to compute the transition relation Δ of Figure 2(c).

3.4 Specifying Malicious Behaviors in SCTPL

We show in this section how SCTPL allows to precisely and succinctly specify several malware behaviors.

Data-Stealing Malware. The main purpose of a data-stealing malware is to steal the user's personal confidential data such as username, password, credit card number, etc and send it to another computer (usually the malware writer). The typical behavior of data-stealing malware can be summarized as follows: the malware will first call the API function *ReadFile* in order to load some file of the victim into memory. To do this, it needs to call this function with a file pointer f (i.e., the return value of the calling function *OpenFile*) as the first parameter and a buffer m as the second parameter (m corresponds to the address of a memory location), i.e., with f m on the top of the stack since in assembly, function parameters are passed through the stack. Then, the malware will send its file (whose data is pointed by m) to another computer using the function *send*. It needs to call *send* with a connection c (i.e., the return value of the calling function *socket*) as first parameter and the buffer m as the second parameter, i.e., with c m on the top of the stack. Figure 3 shows a disassembled fragment of a malware corresponding to this typical behavior. Before calling the function *ReadFile*, it pushes the two parameters m and f onto the stack. Later it calls the function *send* after pushing the two parameters m and c onto the stack. (since in assembly, function parameters are passed through the stack.) This behavior can be expressed by the following SCTPL formula Ω_{ds}.

```
push m
push f
call ReadFile
...
push m
push c
call send
```
Fig. 3. Data-stealing malware

$$\Omega_{ds} = \exists m \ \mathbf{EF}\big(call(ReadFile) \wedge \Gamma \ m \ \Gamma^* \wedge \mathbf{AF}(call(send) \wedge \Gamma \ m \ \Gamma^*)\big)$$

where the regular variable expression $\Gamma \ m \ \Gamma^*$ states that the second value of the stack is m (corresponding to the second parameter of the function *ReadFile* and *send*). Ω_{ds} states that there exists an address m which is the second parameter when calling *ReadFile*, and such that later, eventually, *send* will be called with m as its second parameter.

Kernel32.dll Base Address Viruses. Many of Windows viruses use an API to achieve their malicious tasks. The Kernel32.dll file includes several API functions that can be used by the viruses. In order to use these functions, the viruses have to find the entry addresses of these API functions. To do this, they need to determine the Kernel32.dll entry point. They determine first the Kernel32.dll PE header in memory and use this information to locate Kernel32.dll export section and find the entry addresses of the API functions. For this, the virus looks first for the DOS header (the first word of the DOS header is *5A4Dh* in hex (*MZ* in ascii)); and then looks for the PE header (the first two words of the PE header is *4550h* in hex (*PE00* in ascii)). Figure 4 presents a disassembled code fragment performing this malicious behavior. This can be specified in SCTPL as follows:

```
l₁ : cmp [eax], 5A4Dh
jnz l₂
...
cmp [ebx], 4550h
jz l₃
l₂ : ...
jmp l₁
l₃
```
Fig. 4. Virus

$$\psi_{wv} = EG\big(EF(\exists r_1 \ cmp(r_1, 5A4Dh) \wedge EF \ \exists r_2 \ cmp(r_2, 4550h))\big).$$

This SCTPL formula expresses that the program has a loop such that there are two variables r_1 and r_2 such that first, r_1 is compared to *5A4Dh*, and then r_2 is compared to *4550h*. Note that this formula can detect all the class of viruses that have such behavior.

Obfuscated Calls. Virus writers try to obfuscate their code by e.g. hiding the calls to the operating system. For example, a *call* instruction can be replaced by pushes and jumps. Figure 5 shows two equivalent fragments achiev-ing a "call" instruction. Figure 5(a) shows a normal call/ret where the function f consists just of a *return* instruction. When control point f is reached, the *return* instruction moves the control point to l_1 which is the return address of the call instruction (at l_0). As shown in Figure 5(b), the *call* can be equivalently substituted by two other instruc-tions, where *push* l_2' pushes the return address l_2' onto the

l_0 : call f	l_0' : push l_2'
l_1 : ...	l_1' : jmp f
	l_2' : ...
f: ret	
	f: ret
(a)	(b)

Fig. 5. (a) Normal call. (b) Obfusated call

stack, and *jmp f* moves the control point to the entry point of f. These instructions do exactly the same thing than the *call* instruction. When reaching the control point f, the *ret* instruction will pop the stack and thus, move the control point to l_2'. Such obfuscated calls can be described by the following SCTPL formula:

$$\psi_{oc} = \exists\, addr\, \mathbf{E}[\neg(\exists\, proc\, call(proc) \wedge \mathbf{AX}\, addr\Gamma^*)\, \mathbf{U}\, (ret \wedge addr\Gamma^*)]$$

The subformula $(\exists\, proc\, call(proc) \wedge \mathbf{AX}\, addr\Gamma^*)$ means that there exists a procedure call having *addr* as return address, since when a procedure call is made, the program will push its corresponding return address *addr* to the stack, and thus, at the next step, we will have *addr* on the top of the stack (i.e., $addr\Gamma^*$). The subformula $(ret \wedge addr\Gamma^*)$ expresses that we have a return instruction with *addr* on the top of the stack, i.e., a return instruction that will return to *addr*. Thus the formula ψ_{oc} expresses that there exists a return address *addr* such that there exists a path where there is no call to a procedure *proc* having *addr* as return address until a return instruction with *addr* as return address occurs. This formula can then detect a return that does not correspond to a call.

Obfuscated Returns. Virus writers usually obfuscate the returns of their calls in order to make it difficult to manually or automatically analyze their code. Benign programs move the control point to the return address using the *ret* instruction. Viruses may replace the *ret* instruction by other equivalent instructions such as *pop eax, jmp eax,* etc. E.g., the program in Figure 6 is a disassem-bled fragment from the virus Klinge that pops the return address *00401028* from the stack. This phenomenon can be detected by the following specification:

```
00401023: call 004011CE
00401028: ...
...
004011CE: ...
...
0040121A: pop eax
```

Fig. 6. Fragment of the Virus Klinge

$$\psi_{or} = \mathbf{AG}\left(\forall proc \forall addr((call(proc) \wedge \mathbf{AX}\, addr\Gamma^*) \implies \mathbf{AF}(ret \wedge addr\Gamma^*))\right).$$

ψ_{or} expresses that for every procedure *proc*, if *proc* is called with *addr* as the return address of the caller, then there exists a *ret* instruction which will return to *addr*. Indeed, since when an assembly program runs, if an instruction *call proc* is executed, then the return address *addr* of the caller is pushed onto the stack. Thus, in the subformula *call(proc)* $\wedge$ **AX** *addrΓ^**, *addr* refers to the return address of the call, because this subformula expresses that in all the immediate successors of the call, *addr* is on the top of the stack. Moreover, *ret* $\wedge$ *addrΓ^** means that when the return is executed, then the return address *addr* should be on the top of the stack.[3]

Appending Viruses. An appending virus is a virus that inserts a copy of its malicious code at the end of the target file. To do this, the virus has to first calculate its real absolute address in the memory, because the real OFFSET of the virus' variables depends on the size of the infected file. To achieve this, the viruses have to call the routine in Figure 7 (this code is a fragment of the virus Alcaul.b). The instruction *call* l_2 will push the return address l_2 onto the stack. Then, the *pop* instruction will put the value of this address into the register *eax*. In this way, the virus can get its real absolute address in the memory. This malicious behavior can be detected using the specification ψ_{or}, since there does not exist any *return* instruction corresponding to the *call* instruction.

l_1 : call l_2
l_2 : pop eax
...

Fig. 7.

4   SCTPL\X and the Collapsing Abstraction

As discussed in [24], the algorithm underlying Theorem 1 is very expensive. It is exponential on the size of the PDS. Thus, it is important to model binary programs by PDSs with small sizes. For this, we propose in this section to use the *collapsing abstraction* to drastically reduce the size of the PDS model of the program. Moreover, we consider SCTPL\X, a fragment of SCTPL that uses the next time operator X only to specify the return addresses of the callers. All the malicious behaviors that we considered can be specified using SCTPL\X formulas. We show that the collapsing abstraction preserves SCTPL\X formulas.

4.1   SCTPL\X

SCTPL\X is defined by the following, where $a(x_1, ..., x_n) \in AP_X$, *func* is a function, $e \in \mathcal{R}$ and $r \in \Gamma \cup X$:

$$\varphi ::= a(x_1, ..., x_n) \mid \neg a(x_1, ..., x_n) \mid e \mid \neg e \mid \varphi \wedge \varphi \mid \varphi \vee \varphi \mid \forall x\, \varphi \mid \exists x\, \varphi$$
$$\mid call(func) \wedge AX\, r\Gamma^* \mid A[\varphi U\varphi] \mid E[\varphi U\varphi] \mid A[\varphi R\varphi] \mid E[\varphi R\varphi]$$

Intuitively, SCTPL\X is the sub-logic of SCTPL where the next time operator **X** is used only to specify the return addresses of the callers. Indeed, the SCTPL formula *call(func)* $\wedge$ **AX** $r\Gamma^*$ means that r is the return address of the function *func*, since the return address is always pushed onto the stack when a function is called. The subformula **AX** $r\Gamma^*$ ensures that the return address r is the topmost symbol of the stack at the next control point after calling the function *func*.

---

[3] Note that for the case of a procedure that has a possibly infinite loop, this specification can detect a suspected malware. This formula can be changed slightly to avoid this. We do not present this here for the sake of presentation.

SCTPL\X is sufficient to specify malware. Indeed, arbitrary SCTPL formulas of the form $AX\psi$ or $EX\psi$ that cannot be expressed by SCTPL\X should not be used for malware specifications since such formulas are not robust. Indeed, suppose that at some control point n, a piece of malware satisfies a formula $AX\psi$. Then inserting some dead code at control point n will make the formula $AX\psi$ unsatisfiable. Thus, if a specification that involves such formulas can detect a given malware, it cannot detect variants of this malware where dead code is added at some locations. It is then not recommended to use such subformulas for malware specification. Thus, to make these specifications of malicious behaviors more robust, we should specify these behaviors by $AF\psi$ or $EF\psi$.

4.2 The Collapsing Abstraction

Given a program, the collapsing abstraction reduces the size of the program model by removing all the irrelevant instructions of the program, i.e., all the instructions that do not change the stack (instructions using push or pop are not removed), nor the control flow of the program (instructions using jump-like operators, e.g., jmp, jz, etc. are not removed); as well as the instructions whose operators do not appear in the considered SCTPL formula.

More precisely, consider a SCTPL formula ψ and a binary program. Let $G = (N, I, E)$ and ϱ be respectively the CFG and the state function provided by the oracle O. Let $op(b(a_1, ..., a_n))$ denote the operator b for every instruction $b(a_1, ..., a_n) \in I$. Let $I_\psi = \{b \mid \exists b(x_1, ..., x_n) \in cl(\psi)\}$ be the set of operators that appear in the formula ψ, $I_{stack} = \{push, pop, call, ret\}$ be the set of operators that modify the program's stack, and $I_{jump} = \{jmp, jz, je, jnz, jne, js, jns, jo, jno, jp, jnp, jpe, jpo, jc, jb, jnae, jnc, jnb, jae, jbe, jna, jnbe, ja, jl, jnge, jnl, jge, jle, jng, jnle, jg, jcxz\}$ be the set of all the jump instructions. Let $N_{target} = \{n \in N \mid \exists n_1 \xrightarrow{b(e)} n_2 \in E \text{ s.t. } e \in EXP, n \in \varrho(n_1)(e) \wedge b \in I_{jump} \cup \{call\}\}$ be the set of nodes that can be reached by a *call* or a *jump* instruction of the program.

The collapsing abstraction removes from the program all the instructions whose operators are not in $I_\psi \cup I_{stack} \cup I_{jump}$ and whose control points are not in N_{target}. More precisely, we compute a new control flow graph $G_\psi = (N', I', E')$ such that N' is a subset of N, $I' = \{\bot\} \cup \{i \in I \mid op(i) \in I_\psi \cup I_{stack} \cup I_{jump}\}$, E' is defined as follows: $n \xrightarrow{i} n' \in E'$ iff

- $n \xrightarrow{i} n' \in E$ and $i \in I'$;
- or $i = \bot$ is a fake instruction that we add, $n \in N_{target}$, and $\exists n \xrightarrow{i'} n' \in E$ s.t. $i' \notin I'$;
- or $i = \bot$, there exists in G a path of the form $p \xrightarrow{l_1} n \xrightarrow{i_1} n_1 \xrightarrow{i_2} n_2 \cdots n_{k-1} \xrightarrow{i_k} n' \xrightarrow{l_2} p'$ s.t. $p \xrightarrow{l_1} n \in E'$ and $n' \xrightarrow{l_2} p' \in E'$ are two edges in E' meaning that either l_1 and/or l_2 cannot be removed or is $\bot$, whereas for every $1 \leq j \leq k$, the instruction i_j is removed, i.e., the operator $op(i_j)$ of the instruction i_j is not in $I_\psi \cup I_{stack} \cup I_{jump}$ and for every $1 \leq j \leq k - 1$ node n_j is not in N_{target}.

We add the instructions $\bot$ to relate two nodes that are related by a path in G and such that removing the irrelevant instructions could make these nodes disconnected in G'.

Note that we do not remove nodes in N_{target} because they could be reached by different paths.

The control flow graph G_ψ can be computed in linear time:

Lemma 1. *Given a SCTPL formula ψ, and a control flow graph G, G_ψ can be effectively computed in linear time.*

We can show that this abstraction preserves formulas that do not involve properties about the next state. Formulas using the **X** operator in an arbitrary manner are not preserved since this abstraction removes instructions from the program. However, formulas of the form $call(func) \wedge AX\ r\Gamma^*$ are preserved since they express that a call to the function $func$ is made, and r is the return address of this call. Therefore, such a formula is related to the *single* instruction $call(func)$. So, removing the irrelevant instructions as described above will not change the satisfiability of this formula. Thus, we can show that this abstraction preserves SCTPL\X formulas:

Theorem 2. *Let ψ be a SCTPL\X formula. Let $\mathcal{P}$ be the PDS modeling a CFG G w.r.t. a state function ϱ, and let $\mathcal{P}'$ be the PDS modeling the CFG G_ψ w.r.t. the state function ϱ. Then $\mathcal{P}$ satisfies ψ iff $\mathcal{P}'$ satisfies ψ.*

5   Experiments

We implemented our techniques in a tool for malware detection. Our tool gets a binary program as input, and outputs Yes or No, depending on whether the code contains a malicious behavior or not. To implement an oracle O, we use Jakstab [18] and IDA Pro [13]. Jakstab performs static analysis of the binary program and provides a control flow graph and a state function ϱ. However, it does not allow to extract API functions' information and some indirect calls to the API functions. We use IDA Pro to get these

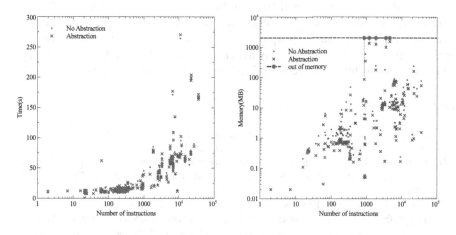

Fig. 8. Time Comparison   **Fig. 9.** Memory Comparison

informations. We use BDDs to represent sets of environments. To perform SCTPL model-checking of PDSs, we implement the algorithms of [24]. All the experiments were run on a Linux platform (Fedora 13) with a 2.4GHz CPU, 2GB of memory. The time limit is fixed to 30 minutes.

We evaluated our tool on 200 malwares taken from VX Heavens [12] and 8 benign programs taken from system32 of Microsoft Windows XP: cmd.exe, find.exe, java.exe, notepad.exe, ping.exe, print.exe, regedt.exe and shutdown.exe. Our tool was able to detect all the 200 malwares. Moreover, it reported that the benign programs that we considered are not malicious, except for java.exe. Our tool detected a malicious behavior in this program. This behavior was introduced by the over-approximation provided by Jakstab [18]. The time and memory consumptions are shown in Figures 8 and 9. These figures show the gain in time and memory consumption when the collapsing abstraction is used. The analysis of several examples (such as Bagle.m, print.exe and notepad.exe e.g.) terminates when using the collapsing abstraction, whereas it runs out of memory without this abstraction.

Table 1. Detection of variants generated by NGVCK and VCL32

Generator	No. of Variants	Our techniques detection rate	Avira detection rate	kaspersky detection rate	Avast antivirus detection rate	Qihoo 360 detection rate
NGVCK	100	**100%**	0%	23%	18%	68%
VCL32	100	**100%**	0%	2%	100%	99%

Furthermore, to compare our techniques with the well-known existing anti-virus tools, and show the robustness of our tool, we automatically generated 200 new malwares using the generators NGVCK and VCL32 available at VX Heavens [12]. We generated 100 malwares using NGVCK, and 100 using VCL32. [25] showed that these systems are the best malware generators, compared to the other generators of VX Heavens [12]. These programs use very sophisticated features such as anti-disassembly, anti-debugging, anti-emulation, and anti-behavior blocking and come equipped with code morphing ability which allows them to produce different-looking viruses. Our results are reported in Table 1. Our techniques were able to detect all these 200 malwares, whereas the four well known and widely used anti-viruses Avira [2], Avast [1], Kaspersky [15] and Qihoo 360 [21] were not able to detect several of these viruses.

References

1. Avast. Free avast antivirus, http://www.avast.com, Version 6.0.1367
2. Avira, http://www.avira.com, Version 12.0.0.849
3. Babić, D., Reynaud, D., Song, D.: Malware Analysis with Tree Automata Inference. In: Gopalakrishnan, G., Qadeer, S. (eds.) CAV 2011. LNCS, vol. 6806, pp. 116–131. Springer, Heidelberg (2011)
4. Balakrishnan, G., Reps, T., Kidd, N., Lal, A., Lim, J., Melski, D., Gruian, R., Yong, S., Chen, C.-H., Teitelbaum, T.: Model Checking x86 Executables with CodeSurfer/x86 and WPDS++. In: Etessami, K., Rajamani, S.K. (eds.) CAV 2005. LNCS, vol. 3576, pp. 158–163. Springer, Heidelberg (2005)

5. Bergeron, J., Debbabi, M., Desharnais, J., Erhioui, M., Lavoie, Y., Tawbi, N.: Static detection of malicious code in executable programs. In: SREIS (2001)
6. Bonfante, G., Kaczmarek, M., Marion, J.-Y.: Architecture of a Morphological Malware Detector. Journal in Computer Virology 5, 263–270 (2009)
7. Christodorescu, M., Jha, S.: Static analysis of executables to detect malicious patterns. In: 12th USENIX Security Symposium, pp. 169–186 (2003)
8. Christodorescu, M., Jha, S., Seshia, S.A., Song, D.X., Bryant, R.E.: Semantics-aware malware detection. In: IEEE Symposium on Security and Privacy, pp. 32–46 (2005)
9. Eric, S.: 10 most destructive computer worms and viruses ever (2010),
   http://wildammo.com/2010/10/12/
   10-most-destructive-computer-worms-and-viruses-ever
10. Esparza, J., Schwoon, S.: A BDD-Based Model Checker for Recursive Programs. In: Berry, G., Comon, H., Finkel, A. (eds.) CAV 2001. LNCS, vol. 2102, pp. 324–336. Springer, Heidelberg (2001)
11. Gostev, A.: Kaspersky security bulletin, malware evolution. Kaspersky Lab ZAO (2010),
   http://www.securelist.com/en/analysis/204792161/
   Kaspersky_Security_Bulletin_Malware_Evolution_2010
12. Heavens, V.: http://vx.netlux.org
13. Hex-Rays. IDAPro (2011)
14. Holzer, A., Kinder, J., Veith, H.: Using Verification Technology to Specify and Detect Malware. In: Moreno Díaz, R., Pichler, F., Quesada Arencibia, A. (eds.) EUROCAST 2007. LNCS, vol. 4739, pp. 497–504. Springer, Heidelberg (2007)
15. Kaspersky, http://www.kaspersky.com, Version 12.0.0.374
16. Kinder, J., Katzenbeisser, S., Schallhart, C., Veith, H.: Detecting Malicious Code by Model Checking. In: Julisch, K., Kruegel, C. (eds.) DIMVA 2005. LNCS, vol. 3548, pp. 174–187. Springer, Heidelberg (2005)
17. Kinder, J., Katzenbeisser, S., Schallhart, C., Veith, H.: Proactive detection of computer worms using model checking. IEEE Trans. on Dependable and Secure Computing 7(4) (2010)
18. Kinder, J., Veith, H.: Jakstab: A Static Analysis Platform for Binaries. In: Gupta, A., Malik, S. (eds.) CAV 2008. LNCS, vol. 5123, pp. 423–427. Springer, Heidelberg (2008)
19. Lakhotia, A., Boccardo, D.R., Singh, A., Manacero, A.: Context-sensitive analysis of obfuscated x86 executables. In: PEPM (2010)
20. Lakhotia, A., Kumar, E.U., Venable, M.: A method for detecting obfuscated calls in malicious binaries. IEEE Trans. Software Eng. 31(11) (2005)
21. Qihoo 360, http://www.360.cn
22. Singh, P.K., Lakhotia, A.: Static verification of worm and virus behavior in binary executables using model checking. In: IAW, pp. 298–300 (2003)
23. Song, F., Touili, T.: Efficient Malware detection using model-checking. Research report (2012),
   http://www.liafa.jussieu.fr/~song/full.pdf
24. Song, F., Touili, T.: Pushdown Model Checking for Malware Detection. In: Flanagan, C., König, B. (eds.) TACAS 2012. LNCS, vol. 7214, pp. 110–125. Springer, Heidelberg (2012)
25. Wong, W.: Analysis and detection of metamorphic computer viruses. Master's thesis, San Jose State University (2006)

Formalization of Incremental Simplex Algorithm by Stepwise Refinement

Mirko Spasić and Filip Marić

Faculty of Mathematics, University of Belgrade*

Abstract. We present an Isabelle/HOL formalization and total correctness proof for the incremental version of the Simplex algorithm which is used in most state-of-the-art SMT solvers. Formalization relies on stepwise program and data refinement, starting from a simple specification, going through a number of fine refinement steps, and ending up in a fully executable functional implementation. Symmetries present in the algorithm are handled with special care.

1 Introduction

Linear arithmetic solvers that decide satisfiability of linear constraint problems have many practical uses (e.g., modeling finite sets, program arithmetic, manipulation of pointers and memory, real-time constraints, physical properties of the environment) and are very important modules of many automated reasoning tools (e.g., theorem provers, SMT solvers). Throughout history, many different algorithms have been developed and, due to their importance, many have been formally verified with machine checkable proofs [7,14,15,16].

The quantifier-free fragment of linear arithmetic is very important for many applications (especially in SMT solving [4]). Most efficient decision procedures for this fragment are based on an *incremental version of the Simplex algorithm* [10,9]. They are specially adapted for use within SMT solvers and used in many industrial applications. The basic procedure is formulated for linear rational arithmetic, but its extensions use branch-and-bound and Gomory cuts techniques [10] and can also handle integer constraints. We are not aware that any Simplex based algorithm has been formally verified within a proof assistant (and literature [9] shows only a sketch of its termination, but no partial correctness).

We present an Isabelle/HOL [18] formalization and total correctness proof of the Simplex-based satisfiability checking procedure for linear rational arithmetic given by Dutertre and de Moura [9,10]. Only the central case of deciding conjunctions of constraints is considered — handling richer propositional structure of the formula is left for future integrations with verified SAT solvers [13].

Our formalization is highly modular and based on the *stepwise program and data refinement* — a well-studied technique due to Dijkstra [8] and Wirth [19],

---

* Supported by the Serbian Ministry of Education and Science grant 174021 and by the SNF grant SCOPES IZ73Z0127979/1.

D. Giannakopoulou and D. Méry (Eds.): FM 2012, LNCS 7436, pp. 434–449, 2012.

and given mathematical rigor by Back [2]. Our formalization exploits several different refinement techniques described for Isabelle/HOL [11,17]. The Simplex algorithm exhibits several symmetric cases that are handled with special care, significantly simplifying the proofs. The importance of treating symmetries carefully has already been suggested in the literature [12,16].

Although unverified SMT solving procedures can be successfully used within theorem provers using the *certificate checking* technique [1,5], we advocate that the formal verification here presented has its own merits.

- The formalization offers clear explanations for subtle procedure details.
- By strictly applying the refinement techniques, the procedure can be analyzed and understood on different levels of abstraction.
- Abstract layers in the formalization allow easy porting of our formalization to other theorem provers and verification systems.
- Executable code can be generated from the formalization and, by means of *reflection* [7,15], the procedure can be used to decide validity of universally quantified linear arithmetic constraints.
- The refinement approach makes this formalization suitable for a case study for teaching formal methods.
- The formalization is a contribution to the growing body of verified theorem proving algorithms.

The paper contains precise specifications (preconditions and effects) for all functions and aims to describe how these are obtained from decisions made during the algorithm development. All proofs are omitted from the presentation. Stepwise refinement is pursued down to several simple functions, that can be easily implemented. Their implementation is omitted from the present text, but is given in the Isabelle/HOL formalization[1] (containing a fully executable code).

Outline. The rest of the paper is structured as follows. In Section 2 we give a brief overview of linear arithmetic and the Simplex algorithm, Isabelle/HOL and techniques for program and data refinement in Isabelle/HOL. In Section 3 we present our formalization of the Simplex-based LRA solver and show all refinement steps. In Section 4 we discuss the related work and give some experimental comparisons. In Section 5 we draw some conclusions and discuss further work.

2   Background

Linear arithmetic. Linear arithmetic is a decidable fragment of arithmetic involving addition and multiplication by constants. Constraints are usually formulated either over reals or rationals (linear rational arithmetic, or *LRA*) or over integers (linear integer arithmetic, or *LIA*). A quantifier-free linear arithmetic formula is a first-order formula with atoms of the form: $a_1x_1 + \ldots + a_nx_n \bowtie c$, where a_i and c are rational numbers, x_i are (rational or integer) variables, and $\bowtie$ is one of the operators $=, \leq, <, >, \geq$, or $\neq$. Most popular methods for deciding satisfiability of LA formulae are the Fourier-Motzkin procedure and the Simplex algorithm.

---

[1] Available online http://argo.matf.bg.ac.rs

Simplex. The Simplex algorithm (invented by George Dantzig in 1947.) is listed among the top 10 algorithms of the 20th century, and it is originally constructed to solve linear programming optimization problem (to maximize an objective function on a convex polytope, specified by a set of linear constraints). The decision procedure for linear arithmetic does not maximize anything, but finds a single feasible solution of input constraints. The variant of Simplex that can be used for this purpose is the *dual Simplex algorithm* which is efficient when constraints are added incrementally.

Isabelle/HOL. Isabelle/HOL[18] is a proof assistant for *Higher-order logic (HOL)*. HOL conforms largely to everyday mathematical notation. Terms are built using function applications (e.g., $f\,x$) and λ-abstractions (e.g., $\lambda x.x$). let $x = t$ in $P\,x$ reduces to $P\,t$. if-then-else and case expressions are also supported. Basic types we use are Booleans (*bool*), naturals (*nat*), and rationals (*rat*). Type variables are denoted by $'a$, $'b$, ... Sets over type $'a$ (denoted by $'a\ set$) follow usual conventions. Lists over type $'a$ (denoted by $'a\ list$) come with the empty list [], the infix constructor #, and standard higher-order functionals *map* and *foldl*. Missing values are modeled by options over type $'a$ (denoted by $'a\ option$) that are either *None* or *Some* $'a$, and *the* is the function such that $the(Some\ x) = x$. Finite mappings from type $'a$ to type $'b$ (denoted by $('a,'b)mapping$) come with a lookup (here denoted by *look*), and update (here denoted by *upd*) operators. Algebraic datatypes (using the keyword **datatype**) and compound types (using the keyword **record**) are supported. For each record field, there is a selector function of the same name (e.g., accessing the field x in record r is denoted by $x\,r$). Equality is polymorphic and is denoted by either $=$, $\equiv$ or $\longleftrightarrow$ (on type *bool*). Object-level implication is represented by $\longrightarrow$, and meta-level implication by $\Longrightarrow$. Functions are defined by both primitive and general recursion. From the specifications, executable code in several functional languages can be generated.

Refinement in Isabelle/HOL. Since Isabelle/HOL is a general proof-assistant, there are many ways to express refinement. Several frameworks for refinement (e.g., by Proteasa and Back or by Lammich) are available at Archive of Formal Proofs (http://afp.sf.net). However, our formalization uses only the following two lightweight approaches.

One approach for data and program refinement, based on code-generation facilities of Isabelle/HOL, is described by Haftmann and Nipkow [11]. To replace one function implementation by another, a proof of their equivalence must be made and the code generator must be instructed to use the desired implementation. No axiomatic specification is used in this case. For data refinement, the first step requires defining an abstract data type representation and functions operating on this representation. Further steps require defining concrete data type representation, defining the conversion from the concrete to the abstract representation, and defining functions that operate on the concrete type. Formalizations should rely only on the abstract representation, while concrete representations are used only during code generation. For more details see [11].

Another approach for program refinement is based on *locales* [3] — Isabelle's version of parametrized theories. A locale is a named context of functions f_1,

..., f_n and assumptions $P_1, \ldots, P_m$ about them that is introduced roughly like **locale** loc = **fixes** $f_1, \ldots, f_n$ **assumes** $P_1, \ldots, P_m$. Locales can be hierarchical as in **locale** loc = $loc_1 + loc_2$ + **fixes** .... In the context of a locale, definitions can be made and theorems can be proved. Locales can be interpreted by concrete instances of $f_1, \ldots, f_n$, and then it must be shown that these satisfy assumptions $P_1, \ldots, P_m$. A locale loc is a *sublocale* of a locale loc' if all functions of loc' can be defined using the functions of loc and all assumptions of loc' can be proved using the assumptions of loc. Then every interpretation for loc can be automatically converted to an interpretation of loc'.

In the context of program refinement, locales are used to define specifications, i.e., abstract interfaces of functions (e.g., **locale** F = **fixes** f **assumes** P). A refinement step can consist of changing the interface by adding stronger premises (e.g., **locale** F' = **fixes** f **assumes** P'). Then a sublocale relation between F and F' must be proved. A slightly more complicated case is when the function f can be implemented using several functions g_i, each specified in its own locale (e.g., **locale** G_i = **fixes** g_i **assumes** Q_i). Then, a joint locale can be defined (e.g., **locale** F' = $G_1 + \ldots + G_k$) and f can be defined in it. To prove the refinement, the sublocale relation between F and F' must be proved. A similar technique is described by Nipkow [17].

3 Formalization

Next, we present our formalization of the incremental Simplex procedure.

3.1 Linear Polynomials and Constraints

Linear polynomials are of the form $a_1 \cdot x_1 + \ldots + a_n \cdot x_n$. Their formalization follows the data-refinement approach of Isabelle/HOL [11]. Abstract representation of polynomials are functions mapping variables to their coefficients, where only finitely many variables have non-zero coefficients. Operations on polynomials are defined as operations on functions. For example, the sum of p_1 and p_2 is defined by $\lambda x.\ p_1\ x + p_2\ x$ and the value of a polynomial p for a valuation v (denoted by $p\{\!\{v\}\!\}$), is defined by $\sum x \in \{x.\ p\ x \neq 0\}.\ p\ x \cdot v\ x$. Executable representations of polynomials use either lists or red-black-tree mappings.

Linear constraints are of the form $p \bowtie c$ or $p_1 \bowtie p_2$, where p, p_1, and p_2, are linear polynomials, c is a rational constant and $\bowtie \in \{<, >, \leq, \geq, =\}$. Their abstract syntax is given by the *constraint* type, and semantics is given by the relation $\models_c$, defined straightforwardly by primitive recursion over the *constraint* type. The list of constraints is satisfied, denoted by $\models_{cs}$, if all constraints are.

datatype *constraint* = *LT linear-poly rat* | *GT linear-poly rat* | ...
$v \models_c LT\ l\ r \longleftrightarrow l\{\!\{v\}\!\} < r \quad v \models_c GT\ l\ r \longleftrightarrow l\{\!\{v\}\!\} > r \quad \ldots$
$v \models_{cs} cs \longleftrightarrow (\forall c \in cs.\ v \models_c c)$

3.2 Procedure Specification

The specification for the satisfiability check procedure is given by:

locale *Solve =*
— Decide if the given list of constraints is satisfiable. Return the satisfiability status and, in the satisfiable case, one satisfying valuation.
fixes *solve :: constraint list* $\Rightarrow$ *bool* $\times$ *rat valuation option*
— If the status *True* is returned, then returned valuation satisfies all constraints.
assumes let $(sat, v) = solve\ cs$ in $sat \longrightarrow the\ v \models_{cs} cs$
— If the status *False* is returned, then constraints are unsatisfiable.
assumes let $(sat, v) = solve\ cs$ in $\neg\ sat \longrightarrow (\nexists\ v.\ v \models_{cs} cs)$

Note that the above specification requires returning a valuation (defined as a HOL function), which is not efficiently executable. In order to enable more efficient data structures for representing valuations, a refinement of this specification is needed and the function *solve* is replaced by the function *solve-exec* returning optional (var, rat) *mapping* instead of $var \Rightarrow rat$ function. This way, efficient data structures for representing mappings can be easily plugged-in during code generation [11]. A conversion from the *mapping* datatype to HOL function is denoted by $\langle - \rangle$ and given by: $\langle v \rangle\ x \equiv$ case *look v x* of *Some y* $\Rightarrow$ *y*.

3.3 Handling Strict Inequalities

The first step of the procedure is removing all equalities and strict inequalities. Equalities can be easily rewritten to non-strict inequalities. Removing strict inequalities can be done by replacing the list of constraints by a new one, formulated over an extension $\mathbb{Q}'$ of the space of rationals $\mathbb{Q}$. $\mathbb{Q}'$ must have a structure of a linearly ordered vector space over $\mathbb{Q}$ (represented by the type class *lrv*) and must guarantee that if some non-strict constraints are satisfied in $\mathbb{Q}'$, then there is a satisfying valuation for the original constraints in $\mathbb{Q}$. Our final implementation uses the $\mathbb{Q}_\delta$ space, defined in [10] (basic idea is to replace $p < c$ by $p \leq c - \delta$ and $p > c$ by $p \geq c + \delta$ for a symbolic parameter δ). So, all constraints are reduced to the form $p \bowtie b$, where p is a linear polynomial (still over $\mathbb{Q}$), b is constant from $\mathbb{Q}'$ and $\bowtie \in \{\leq, \geq\}$. The non-strict constraints are represented by the type $'a$ *ns-constraint*, and their semantics is denoted by $\models_{ns}$ and $\models_{nss}$.

datatype $'a$ *ns-constraint* $= LEQ_{ns}$ *linear-poly* $'a$ $\mid$ GEQ_{ns} *linear-poly* $'a$
$v \models_{ns} LEQ_{ns} l\ r \longleftrightarrow l\{\!\{v\}\!\} \leq r \quad v \models_{ns} GEQ_{ns} l\ r \longleftrightarrow l\{\!\{v\}\!\} \geq r$
$v \models_{nss} cs \longleftrightarrow (\forall c \in cs.\ v \models_{ns} c)$

Specification of reduction of constraints to non-strict form is given by:

locale *To-ns =*
— Convert a constraint list to an equisatisfiable non-strict constraint list.
fixes *to-ns :: constraint list* $\Rightarrow$ $'a::lrv$ *ns-constraint list*
assumes $v \models_{cs} cs \Longrightarrow \exists\ v'.\ v' \models_{nss}$ *to-ns cs*
— Convert the valuation that satisfies all non-strict constraints to the valuation that satisfies all initial constraints.
fixes *from-ns ::* $(var, 'a)$ *mapping* $\Rightarrow$ $'a$ *ns-constraint list* $\Rightarrow$ (var, rat) *mapping*
assumes $\langle v' \rangle \models_{nss}$ *to-ns cs* $\Longrightarrow \langle$ *from-ns v' (to-ns cs)* $\rangle \models_{cs} cs$

After the transformation, the procedure is reduced to solving only the non-strict constraints, implemented in the *solve-exec-ns* function having an analogous specification to the *solve* function. If *to-ns*, *from-ns* and *solve-exec-ns* are available, the *solve-exec* function can be easily defined and it can be easily shown that this definition satisfies its specification (also analogous to *solve*).

$$solve\text{-}exec\ cs \equiv \textsf{let}\ cs' = to\text{-}ns\ cs;\ (sat,\ v) = solve\text{-}exec\text{-}ns\ cs'\ \textsf{in}$$
$$\textsf{if}\ sat\ \textsf{then}\ (\textit{True},\ Some\ (from\text{-}ns\ (the\ v)\ cs'))\ \textsf{else}\ (\textit{False},\ None)$$

3.4 Preprocessing

The next step in the procedure rewrites a list of non-strict constraints into an equisatisfiable form consisting of a list of linear equations (called the *tableau*) and of a list of *atoms* of the form $x_i \bowtie b_i$ where x_i is a variable and b_i is a constant (from the extension field). The transformation is straightforward and introduces auxiliary variables for linear polynomials occurring in the initial formula. For example, $[x_1 + x_2 \le b_1,\ x_1 + x_2 \ge b_2,\ x_2 \ge b_3]$ can be transformed to the tableau $[x_3 = x_1 + x_2]$ and atoms $[x_3 \le b_1,\ x_3 \ge b_2,\ x_2 \ge b_3]$.

Equations are of the form $x = p$, where x is a variable and p is a polynomial, and are represented by the type $eq = var \times linear\text{-}poly$. Semantics of equations is given by $v \models_e (x,\ p) \longleftrightarrow v\ x = p\ \{\!\!\{\ v\ \}\!\!\}$. Tableau is represented as a list of equations, by the type $tableau = eq\ list$. Semantics for a tableau is given by $v \models_t t \longleftrightarrow \forall e \in t.\ v \models_e e$. Functions *lvars* and *rvars* return sets of variables appearing on the left hand side (lhs) and the right hand side (rhs) of a tableau. Lhs variables are called *basic* while rhs variables are called *non-basic* variables. A tableau t is *normalized*, denoted by N t, iff no variable occurs on the lhs of two equations in a tableau and if sets of lhs and rhs variables are disjoint. Tableaux t_1 and t_2 are *equivalent*, denoted by $t_1 \equiv_t t_2$, iff $\forall v.\ v \models_t t_1 \longleftrightarrow v \models_t t_2$.

Elementary atoms are represented by the type $'a\ atom$ and semantics for atoms and sets of atoms is denoted by $\models_a$ and $\models_{as}$ and given by:

datatype $'a\ atom = Leq\ var\ 'a\ \mid\ Geq\ var\ 'a$
$v \models_a Leq\ x\ c \longleftrightarrow v\ x \le c \quad v \models_a Geq\ x\ c \longleftrightarrow v\ x \ge c$
$v \models_{as} as \longleftrightarrow (\forall a \in as.\ v \models_a a)$

The specification of the preprocessing function is given by:

locale *Preprocess* = **fixes** $preprocess::'a::lrv\ ns\text{-}constraint\ list \Rightarrow tableau \times 'a\ atom\ list$
    assumes
    — The returned tableau is always normalized.
    let $(t,\ as) = preprocess\ cs$ **in** N t
    — Tableau and atoms are equisatisfiable with starting non-strict constraints.
    let $(t,\ as) = preprocess\ cs$ **in** $v \models_{as} as \wedge v \models_t t \longrightarrow v \models_{nss} cs$
    let $(t,\ as) = preprocess\ cs$ **in** $v \models_{nss} cs \longrightarrow (\exists v'.\ v' \models_{as} as \wedge v' \models_t t)$

Once the preprocessing is done and tableau and atoms are obtained, their satisfiability is checked by the *assert-all* function. Its precondition is that the starting tableau is normalized, and its specification is analogue to the one for the *solve* function. If *preprocess* and *assert-all* are available, the *solve-exec-ns* can be defined, and it can easily be shown that this definition satisfies the specification.

$$solve\text{-}exec\text{-}ns\ s \equiv \textsf{let}\ (t,\ as) = preprocess\ s\ \textsf{in}\ assert\text{-}all\ t\ as$$

3.5   Incrementally Asserting Atoms

The function *assert-all* can be implemented by iteratively asserting one by one atom from the given list.

Asserted atoms will be stored in a form of *bounds* for a given variable. Bounds are of the form $l_i \leq x_i \leq u_i$, where l_i and u_i and are either scalars or $\pm\infty$. Each time a new atom is asserted, a bound for the corresponding variable is updated (checking for conflict with the previous bounds). Since bounds for a variable can be either finite or $\pm\infty$, they are represented by (partial) maps from variables to values (*'a bounds = var $\rightharpoonup$ 'a*). Upper and lower bounds are represented separately. Infinite bounds map to *None* and this is reflected in the semantics:

$c \geq_{ub} b \longleftrightarrow$ case b of *None* $\Rightarrow$ *False* | *Some* $b' \Rightarrow c \geq b'$

$c \leq_{ub} b \longleftrightarrow$ case b of *None* $\Rightarrow$ *True* | *Some* $b' \Rightarrow c \leq b'$

Strict comparisons, and comparisons with lower bounds are performed similarly.

A valuation satisfies bounds iff the value of each variable respects both its lower and upper bound, i.e, $v \models_b (lb, ub) \longleftrightarrow \forall x.\ v\,x \geq_{lb} lb\,x \wedge v\,x \leq_{ub} ub\,x$. Asserted atoms are precisely encoded by the current bounds in a state (denoted by $\doteq$) if every valuation satisfies them iff it satisfies the bounds, i.e., $as \doteq (lb, ub) \longleftrightarrow (\forall v.\ v \models_{as} as \longleftrightarrow v \models_b (lb, ub))$.

The procedure also keeps track of a valuation that is a candidate solution. Whenever a new atom is asserted, it is checked whether the valuation is still satisfying. If not, the procedure tries to fix that by changing it and the tableau if necessary (but so that it remains equivalent to the initial tableau).

Therefore, the state of the procedure stores the tableau (denoted by $\mathcal{T}$), lower and upper bounds (denoted by $\mathcal{B}_l$ and $\mathcal{B}_u$, and ordered pair of lower and upper bounds denoted by $\mathcal{B}$), candidate solution (denoted by $\mathcal{V}$) and a flag (denoted by $\mathcal{U}$) indicating if unsatisfiability has been detected so far:

record *'a state =*
   $\mathcal{T}$ :: *tableau* $\mathcal{B}_l$ :: *'a bounds* $\mathcal{B}_u$ :: *'a bounds* $\mathcal{V}$ :: *(var, 'a) mapping* $\mathcal{U}$ :: *bool*

To be a solution of the initial problem, a valuation should satisfy the initial tableau and list of atoms. Since tableau is changed only by equivalency preserving transformations and asserted atoms are encoded in the bounds, a valuation is a solution if it satisfies both the tableau and the bounds in the final state (when all atoms have been asserted). So, a valuation v satisfies a state s (denoted by $\models_s$) if it satisfies the tableau and the bounds, i.e., $v \models_s s \longleftrightarrow v \models_b \mathcal{B}\,s \wedge v \models_t \mathcal{T}\,s$. Since $\mathcal{V}$ should be a candidate solution, it should satisfy the state (unless the $\mathcal{U}$ flag is raised). This is denoted by $\models s$ and defined by $\models s \longleftrightarrow \langle \mathcal{V}\,s \rangle \models_s s$. The notation V s will denote that all variables of $\mathcal{T}\,s$ are explicitly valuated in $\mathcal{V}\,s$.

Assuming that the $\mathcal{U}$ flag and the current valuation $\mathcal{V}$ in the final state determine the solution of a problem, the *assert-all* function can be reduced to the *assert-all-state* function that operates on the states:

assert-all t as $\equiv$ let $s = $ *assert-all-state t as* in
   if $(\mathcal{U}\,s)$ then (*False, None*) else (*True, Some* $(\mathcal{V}\,s)$)

Specification for the *assert-all-state* can be directly obtained from the specification of *assert-all*, and it describes the connection between the valuation in the final state and the initial tableau and atoms. However, we will make an additional refinement step and give stronger assumptions about the *assert-all-state* function that describes the connection between the initial tableau and atoms with the tableau and bounds in the final state.

locale *AssertAllState* = **fixes** *assert-all-state::tableau* $\Rightarrow$ *'a::lrv atom list* $\Rightarrow$ *'a state*
   assumes
  — The final and the initial tableau are equivalent.
  N $t \implies$ let $s' = $ *assert-all-state t as* in $t \equiv_t \mathcal{T} s'$
  — If $\mathcal{U}$ is not raised, then the valuation in the final state satisfies its tableau and its bounds (that are, in this case, equivalent to the set of all asserted bounds).
  N $t \implies$ let $s' = $ *assert-all-state t as* in $\neg \mathcal{U} s' \longrightarrow \models s'$
  N $t \implies$ let $s' = $ *assert-all-state t as* in $\neg \mathcal{U} s' \longrightarrow as \doteq \mathcal{B} s'$
  — If $\mathcal{U}$ is raised, then there is no valuation satisfying the tableau and the bounds in the final state (that are, in this case, equivalent to a subset of asserted atoms).
  N $t \implies$ let $s' = $ *assert-all-state t as* in $\mathcal{U} s' \longrightarrow (\nexists\, v.\, v \models_s s')$
  N $t \implies$ let $s' = $ *assert-all-state t as* in $\mathcal{U} s' \longrightarrow (\exists\, as'.\, as' \subseteq as \land as' \doteq \mathcal{B} s')$

The *assert-all-state* function can be implemented by first applying the *init* function that creates an initial state based on the starting tableau, and then by iteratively applying the *assert* function for each atom in the starting atoms list.

   assert-loop as s $\equiv$ *foldl* $(\lambda\, s'\, a.$ if $(\mathcal{U} s')$ then s' else *assert a s'$)$ *s as*
   assert-all-state t as $\equiv$ *assert-loop ats (init t)*

Specification for *init* can be obtained from the specification of *assert-all-state* since all its assumptions must also hold for *init* (when the list of atoms is empty). Also, since *init* is the first step in the *assert-all-state* implementation, the precondition for *init* is the same as for the *assert-all-state*. However, unsatisfiability is never going to be detected during initialization and $\mathcal{U}$ flag is never going to be raised. Also, the tableau in the initial state can just be initialized with the starting tableau. The condition $\{\} \doteq \mathcal{B}$ *(init t)* is equivalent to asking that initial bounds are empty. Therefore, specification for *init* can be refined to:

locale *Init* = **fixes** *init::tableau* $\Rightarrow$ *'a::lrv state*
   assumes
  — Tableau in the initial state for t is t: $\mathcal{T}$ *(init t)* $= t$
  — Since unsatisfiability is not detected, $\mathcal{U}$ flag must not be set: $\neg \mathcal{U}$ *(init t)*
  — The current valuation must satisfy the tableau: $\langle \mathcal{V}$ *(init t)*$\rangle \models_t t$
  — In an initial state no atoms are yet asserted so the bounds must be empty:
   $\mathcal{B}_l$ *(init t)* $= (\lambda\, \text{-}.\ None)$ $\mathcal{B}_u$ *(init t)* $= (\lambda\, \text{-}.\ None)$
  — All tableau vars are valuated: V *(init t)*

The *assert* function asserts a single atom. Since the *init* function does not raise the $\mathcal{U}$ flag, from the definition of *assert-loop*, it is clear that the flag is not raised when the *assert* function is called. Moreover, the assumptions about the *assert-all-state* imply that the loop invariant must be that if the $\mathcal{U}$ flag is not raised, then the current valuation must satisfy the state (i.e., $\models s$). The *assert* function will be more easily implemented if it is always applied to a state with a normalized and valuated tableau, so we make this another loop invariant. Therefore, the precondition for the *assert a s* function call is that $\neg\,\mathcal{U}\ s$, $\models s$, N $(\mathcal{T}\ s)$ and V s hold. The specification for *assert* directly follows from the specification of *assert-all-state* (except that it is additionally required that bounds reflect asserted atoms also when unsatisfiability is detected, and that it is required that *assert* keeps the tableau normalized and valuated).

locale *Assert* = **fixes** *assert*::$'a$::*lrv atom* $\Rightarrow$ $'a$ *state* $\Rightarrow$ $'a$ *state*
   assumes
— Tableau remains equivalent to the previous one and normalized and valuated.
   $[\neg\,\mathcal{U}\ s;\ \models s;\ \text{N}\ (\mathcal{T}\ s);\ \text{V}\ s] \Longrightarrow$ **let** $s' = assert\ a\ s$ **in**
     $\mathcal{T}\ s \equiv_t \mathcal{T}\ s' \wedge \text{N}\ (\mathcal{T}\ s') \wedge \text{V}\ s'$
— If the $\mathcal{U}$ flag is not raised, then the current valuation is updated so that it satisfies the current tableau and the current bounds.
   $[\neg\,\mathcal{U}\ s;\ \models s;\ \text{N}\ (\mathcal{T}\ s);\ \text{V}\ s] \Longrightarrow \neg\,\mathcal{U}\ (assert\ a\ s) \longrightarrow\ \models (assert\ a\ s)$
— The set of asserted atoms remains equivalent to the bounds in the state.
   $[\neg\,\mathcal{U}\ s;\ \models s;\ \text{N}\ (\mathcal{T}\ s);\ \text{V}\ s] \Longrightarrow ats \doteq \mathcal{B}\ s \longrightarrow (ats \cup \{a\}) \doteq \mathcal{B}\ (assert\ a\ s)$
— If the $\mathcal{U}$ flag is raised, then there is no valuation that satisfies both the current tableau and the current bounds.
   $[\neg\,\mathcal{U}\ s;\ \models s;\ \text{N}\ (\mathcal{T}\ s);\ \text{V}\ s] \Longrightarrow \mathcal{U}\ (assert\ a\ s) \longrightarrow (\nexists\ v.\ v \models_s (assert\ a\ s))$

Under these assumptions, it can easily be shown (mainly by induction over *as*) that the given implementation of *assert-all-state* satisfies its specification.

3.6   Asserting Single Atoms

The *assert* function is split in two phases. First, *assert-bound* updates the bounds and checks only for conflicts cheap to detect. Next, *check* performs the full Simplex algorithm. The *assert* function can be implemented as *assert a s.* = *check* (*assert-bound a s*). Note that it is also possible to do the first phase for several asserted atoms, and only then to let the expensive second phase work.

Asserting an atom $x \bowtie b$ begins with the function *assert-bound*. If the atom is subsumed by the current bounds, then no changes are performed. Otherwise, bounds for x are changed to incorporate the atom. If the atom is inconsistent with the previous bounds for x, the $\mathcal{U}$ flag is raised. If x is not a lhs variable in the current tableau and if the value for x in the current valuation violates the new bound b, the value for x can be updated and set to b, meanwhile updating the values for lhs variables of the tableau so that it remains satisfied. Otherwise, no changes to the current valuation are performed.

So, the *assert-bound* function must ensure that the given atom is included in the bounds, that the tableau remains satisfied by the valuation and that all variables except the lhs variables in the tableau are within their bounds. To formalize this, we introduce the notation $v \models_b (lb,\ ub) \parallel S$, and define $v \models_b (lb,\ ub) \parallel S \longleftrightarrow \forall x \in S.\ v\ x \geq_{lb} lb\ x \wedge v\ x \leq_{ub} ub\ x$, and $\models_{nolhs} s \longleftrightarrow \langle V\ s \rangle \models_t \mathcal{T}\ s \wedge \langle V\ s \rangle \models_b \mathcal{B}\ s \parallel - lvars\ (\mathcal{T}\ s)$. The *assert-bound* function raises the $\mathcal{U}$ flag if and only if lower and upper bounds overlap. Otherwise, bounds are *consistent*, denoted by B_c s, and defined by B_c s $\longleftrightarrow$ $\forall x.$ if $\mathcal{B}_l$ s x = *None* $\lor$ $\mathcal{B}_u$ s x = *None* then *True* else *the* $(\mathcal{B}_l$ s $x)$ $\leq$ *the* $(\mathcal{B}_u$ s $x)$.

Since the *assert-bound* is the first step in the *assert* function implementation, the preconditions for *assert-bound* are the same as preconditions for the *assert* function. The specification for the *assert-bound* is:

locale *AssertBound* = **fixes** *assert-bound*::$'a$::*lrv atom* $\Rightarrow$ $'a$ *state* $\Rightarrow$ $'a$ *state*
   assumes
   — The tableau remains unchanged and valuated.
   $[\![\neg\, \mathcal{U}\, s;\, \models s;\, N\, (\mathcal{T}\, s);\, V\, s]\!] \Longrightarrow$ let $s' = $ *assert-bound* a s in $\mathcal{T}$ $s' = \mathcal{T}$ $s \land V$ s'
   — If the $\mathcal{U}$ flag is not set, all but the lhs variables in the tableau remain within their bounds, the new valuation satisfies the tableau, and bounds do not overlap.
   $[\![\neg\, \mathcal{U}\, s;\, \models s;\, N\, (\mathcal{T}\, s);\, V\, s]\!] \Longrightarrow$
     let $s' = $ *assert-bound* a s in $\neg\, \mathcal{U}$ $s' \longrightarrow \models_{nolhs} s' \land B_c$ s'
   — The set of asserted atoms remains equivalent to the bounds in the state.
   $[\![\neg\, \mathcal{U}\, s;\, \models s;\, N\, (\mathcal{T}\, s);\, V\, s]\!] \Longrightarrow ats \doteq \mathcal{B}$ $s \longrightarrow (ats \cup \{a\}) \doteq \mathcal{B}$ (*assert-bound* a s)
   — $\mathcal{U}$ flag is raised, only if the bounds became inconsistent:
   $[\![\neg\, \mathcal{U}\, s;\, \models s;\, N\, (\mathcal{T}\, s);\, V\, s]\!] \Longrightarrow$ let $s' = $ *assert-bound* a s in $\mathcal{U}$ $s' \longrightarrow (\nexists v.\ v \models_s s')$

The second phase of *assert*, the *check* function, is the heart of the Simplex algorithm. It is always called after *assert-bound*, but in two different situations. In the first case *assert-bound* raised the $\mathcal{U}$ flag and then *check* should retain the flag and should not perform any changes. In the second case *assert-bound* did not raise the $\mathcal{U}$ flag, so $\models_{nolhs} s$, B_c s, N $(\mathcal{T}\, s)$, and V s hold.

locale *Check* = **fixes** *check*::$'a$::*lrv state* $\Rightarrow$ $'a$ *state*
   assumes
   — If *check* is called from an inconsistent state, the state is unchanged.
   $[\, \mathcal{U}\, s\,] \Longrightarrow$ *check* $s = s$
   — The tableau remains equivalent to the previous one, normalized and valuated.
   $[\![\neg\, \mathcal{U}\, s;\, \models_{nolhs} s;\, B_c\, s;\, N\, (\mathcal{T}\, s);\, V\, s]\!] \Longrightarrow$
     let $s' = $ *check* s in $\mathcal{T}$ $s \equiv_t \mathcal{T}$ $s' \land N$ $(\mathcal{T}\, s') \land V$ s'
   — The bounds remain unchanged.
   $[\![\neg\, \mathcal{U}\, s;\, \models_{nolhs} s;\, B_c\, s;\, N\, (\mathcal{T}\, s);\, V\, s]\!] \Longrightarrow \mathcal{B}$ (*check* s) $= \mathcal{B}$ s
   — If $\mathcal{U}$ flag is not raised, the current valuation $\mathcal{V}$ satisfies both the tableau and the bounds and if it is raised, there is no valuation that satisfies them.
   $[\![\neg\, \mathcal{U}\, s;\, \models_{nolhs} s;\, B_c\, s;\, N\, (\mathcal{T}\, s);\, V\, s]\!] \Longrightarrow \neg\, \mathcal{U}$ (*check* s) $\longrightarrow\ \models$ (*check* s)
   $[\![\neg\, \mathcal{U}\, s;\, \models_{nolhs} s;\, B_c\, s;\, N\, (\mathcal{T}\, s);\, V\, s]\!] \Longrightarrow \mathcal{U}$ (*check* s) $\longrightarrow (\nexists\ v.\ v \models_s$ (*check* s))

Under these assumptions for *assert-bound* and *check*, it can be easily shown that the implementation of *assert* (previously given) satisfies its specification.

However, for efficiency reasons, we want to allow implementations that delay the *check* function call and call it after several *assert-bound* calls. For example:

   assert-bound-loop ats s $\equiv$ *foldl* $(\lambda s'\ a.$ if $\mathcal{U}$ s' then s' else *assert-bound* a $s')$ s *ats*
   assert-all-state t ats $\equiv$ *check* (*assert-bound-loop ats* (*init t*))

Then, the loop consists only of *assert-bound* calls, so the *assert-bound* postcondition must imply its precondition. This is not the case, since variables on the lhs may be out of their bounds. Therefore, we make a refinement and specify weaker preconditions (replace $\models$ s, by $\models_{nolhs}$ s and B$_c$ s) for *assert-bound*, and show that these preconditions are still good enough to prove the correctness of this alternative *assert-all-state* definition.

3.7 Update and Pivot

Both *assert-bound* and *check* need to update the valuation so that the tableau remains satisfied. If the value for a variable not on the lhs of the tableau is changed, this can be done rather easily (once the value of that variable is changed, one should recalculate and change the values for all lhs variables of the tableau). The *update* function does this, and it is specified by:

locale *Update* = **fixes** *update*::*var* $\Rightarrow$ $'a$::*lrv* $\Rightarrow$ $'a$ *state* $\Rightarrow$ $'a$ *state*
  assumes
  — Tableau, bounds, and the unsatisfiability flag are preserved.
  $[\![\text{N} \ (\mathcal{T} \ s); \text{V} \ s; x \notin lvars \ (\mathcal{T} \ s)]\!] \Longrightarrow$
    let $s' = update \ x \ c \ s$ in $\mathcal{T} \ s' = \mathcal{T} \ s \wedge \mathcal{B} \ s' = \mathcal{B} \ s \wedge \mathcal{U} \ s' = \mathcal{U} \ s$
  — Tableau remains valuated.
  $[\![\text{N} \ (\mathcal{T} \ s); \text{V} \ s; x \notin lvars \ (\mathcal{T} \ s)]\!] \Longrightarrow \text{V} \ (update \ x \ v \ s)$
  — The given variable x in the updated valuation is set to the given value v while all other variables (except those on the lhs of the tableau) are unchanged.
  $[\![\text{N} \ (\mathcal{T} \ s); \text{V} \ s; x \notin lvars \ (\mathcal{T} \ s)]\!] \Longrightarrow x' \notin lvars \ (\mathcal{T} \ s) \longrightarrow$
    $look \ (\mathcal{V} \ (update \ x \ v \ s)) \ x' = (\text{if } x = x' \text{ then } Some \ v \text{ else } look \ (\mathcal{V} \ s) \ x')$
  — Updated valuation continues to satisfy the tableau.
  $[\![\text{N} \ (\mathcal{T} \ s); \text{V} \ s; x \notin lvars \ (\mathcal{T} \ s)]\!] \Longrightarrow \langle \mathcal{V} \ s \rangle \models_t \mathcal{T} \ s \longrightarrow \langle \mathcal{V} \ (update \ x \ c \ s) \rangle \models_t \mathcal{T} \ s$

Given the *update* function, *assert-bound* can be implemented as follows.

assert-bound $(Leq \ x \ c) \ s \equiv$
    if $c \geq_{ub} \mathcal{B}_u \ s \ x$ then s
    else let $s' = s \ (\!\mid \mathcal{B}_u := (\mathcal{B}_u \ s) \ (x := Some \ c) \mid\!)$
        in if $c <_{lb} \mathcal{B}_l \ s \ x$ then $s' \ (\!\mid \mathcal{U} := True \mid\!)$
        else if $x \notin lvars \ (\mathcal{T} \ s') \wedge c < \langle \mathcal{V} \ s \rangle \ x$ then $update \ x \ c \ s'$ else s'

The case of $Geq \ x \ c$ atoms is analogous (a systematic way to avoid symmetries is discussed in Section 3.9). This implementation satisfies both its specifications.

Updating changes the value of x and then updates values of all lhs variables so that the tableau remains satisfied. This can be based on a function that recalculates rhs polynomial values in the changed valuation:

locale *RhsEqVal* = **fixes** *rhs-eq-val*::$(var, 'a$::*lrv*$)$ *mapping* $\Rightarrow$ *var* $\Rightarrow$ $'a$ $\Rightarrow$ *eq* $\Rightarrow$ $'a$
  — *rhs-eq-val* computes the value of the rhs of e in $\langle v \rangle (x := c)$.
  assumes $\langle v \rangle \models_e e \Longrightarrow rhs\text{-}eq\text{-}val \ v \ x \ c \ e = rhs \ e \ \{\!\mid \langle v \rangle \ (x := c) \mid\!\}$

Then, the next implementation of *update* satisfies its specification:

update-eq $v \ x \ c \ v' \ e \equiv upd \ (lhs \ e) \ (rhs\text{-}eq\text{-}val \ v \ x \ c \ e) \ v'$
update $x \ c \ s \equiv s (\!\mid \mathcal{V} := upd \ x \ c \ (foldl \ (update\text{-}eq \ (\mathcal{V} \ s) \ x \ c) \ (\mathcal{V} \ s) \ (\mathcal{T} \ s)) \mid\!)$

To update the valuation for a variable that is on the lhs of the tableau it should first be swapped with some rhs variable of its equation, in an operation called *pivoting*. Pivoting has the precondition that the tableau is normalized and that it is always called for a lhs variable of the tableau, and a rhs variable in the equation with that lhs variable. The set of rhs variables for the given lhs variable is found using the *rvars-of-lvar* function (specified in a very simple locale *EqForLVar*, that we do not print).

locale *Pivot* = *EqForLVar* + **fixes** *pivot::var* $\Rightarrow$ *var* $\Rightarrow$ *'a::lrv state* $\Rightarrow$ *'a state*
assumes
— Valuation, bounds, and the unsatisfiability flag are not changed.
$[\![$N $(\mathcal{T}\ s)$; $x_i \in$ *lvars* $(\mathcal{T}\ s)$; $x_j \in$ *rvars-of-lvar* $(\mathcal{T}\ s)\ x_i]\!] \Longrightarrow$
    let $s' = $ *pivot* $x_i\ x_j\ s$ in $\mathcal{V}\ s' = \mathcal{V}\ s \wedge \mathcal{B}\ s' = \mathcal{B}\ s \wedge \mathcal{U}\ s' = \mathcal{U}\ s$
— The tableau remains equivalent to the previous one and normalized.
$[\![$N $(\mathcal{T}\ s)$; $x_i \in$ *lvars* $(\mathcal{T}\ s)$; $x_j \in$ *rvars-of-lvar* $(\mathcal{T}\ s)\ x_i]\!] \Longrightarrow$
    let $s' = $ *pivot* $x_i\ x_j\ s$ in $\mathcal{T}\ s \equiv_t \mathcal{T}\ s' \wedge$ N $(\mathcal{T}\ s')$
— x_i and x_j are swapped, while the other variables do not change sides.
$[\![$N $(\mathcal{T}\ s)$; $x_i \in$ *lvars* $(\mathcal{T}\ s)$; $x_j \in$ *rvars-of-lvar* $(\mathcal{T}\ s)\ x_i]\!] \Longrightarrow$ let $s' = $ *pivot* $x_i\ x_j\ s$ in
    $rvars(\mathcal{T}\ s') = rvars(\mathcal{T}\ s) - \{x_j\} \cup \{x_i\}\ \wedge\ lvars(\mathcal{T}\ s') = lvars(\mathcal{T}\ s) - \{x_i\} \cup \{x_j\}$

Functions *pivot* and *update* can be used to implement the *check* function. In its context, *pivot* and *update* functions are always called together, so the following definition can be used: *pivot-and-update* $x_i\ x_j\ c\ s = $ *update* $x_i\ c$ (*pivot* $x_i\ x_j$ s). It is possible to make a more efficient implementation of *pivot-and-update* that does not use separate implementations of *pivot* and *update*. To allow this, a separate specification for *pivot-and-update* can be given. It can be easily shown that the *pivot-and-update* definition above satisfies this specification.

Pivoting the tableau can be reduced to pivoting single equations, and substituting variables by polynomials. These operations are specified by:

locale *PivotEq* = **fixes** *pivot-eq::eq* $\Rightarrow$ *var* $\Rightarrow$ *eq*
assumes
— Lhs var of *eq* and x_j are swapped, while the other variables do not change sides.
$[\![x_j \in$ *rvars-eq* *eq*; *lhs* *eq* $\notin$ *rvars-eq* *eq* $]\!] \Longrightarrow$ let *eq'* = *pivot-eq* *eq* x_j in
    lhs *eq'* = $x_j \wedge$ *rvars-eq* *eq'* = $\{$*lhs* *eq*$\} \cup$ (*rvars-eq* *eq* $- \{x_j\}$)
— Pivoting keeps the equation equisatisfiable.
$[\![x_j \in$ *rvars-eq* *eq*; *lhs* *eq* $\notin$ *rvars-eq* *eq* $]\!] \Longrightarrow v \models_e$ *pivot-eq* *eq* $x_j \longleftrightarrow v \models_e$ *eq*
locale *SubstVar* = **fixes** *subst-var::var* $\Rightarrow$ *linear-poly* $\Rightarrow$ *linear-poly* $\Rightarrow$ *linear-poly*
assumes
— Effect of *subst-var* x_j *lp'* *lp* on *lp* variables.
(*vars* *lp* $- \{x_j\}$) $-$ *vars* *lp'* $\subseteq$ *vars* (*subst-var* x_j *lp'* *lp*) $\subseteq$ (*vars* *lp* $- \{x_j\}$) $\cup$ *vars* *lp'*
— Effect of *subst-var* x_j *lp'* *lp* on *lp* value.
$v\ x_j = lp'\ \{\!|v|\!\} \longrightarrow lp\ \{\!|v|\!\} = $ (*subst-var* x_j *lp'* *lp*) $\{\!|v|\!\}$

Then, the next implementation of *pivot* satisfies its specification:

pivot-tableau $x_i\ x_j\ t \equiv$ let *eq* = *eq-for-lvar* *t* x_i; *eq'* = *pivot-eq* *eq* x_j in
    map (λ *e*. if *lhs* *e* = *lhs* *eq* then *eq'* else *subst-var-eq* x_j (*rhs* *eq'*) *e*) *t*
pivot $x_i\ x_j\ s \equiv s(\![\ \mathcal{T} := $ *pivot-tableau* $x_i\ x_j$ $(\mathcal{T}\ s)\ ]\!)$

3.8 Check Implementation

The *check* function is called when all rhs variables are in bounds, and it checks if there is a lhs variable that is not. If there is no such variable, then satisfiability is detected and *check* succeeds. If there is a lhs variable x_i out of its bounds, a rhs variable x_j is sought which allows pivoting with x_i and updating x_i to its violated bound. If x_i is under its lower bound it must be increased, and if x_j has a positive coefficient it must be increased so it must be under its upper bound and if it has a negative coefficient it must be decreased so it must be above its lower bound. The case when x_i is above its upper bound is symmetric (avoiding symmetries is discussed in Section 3.9). If there is no such x_j, unsatisfiability is detected and *check* fails. The procedure is recursively repeated, until it either succeeds or fails. To ensure termination, variables x_i and x_j must be chosen with respect to a fixed variable ordering. For choosing these variables auxiliary functions *min-lvar-not-in-bounds*, *min-rvar-inc* and *min-rvar-dec* are specified (each in its own locale). For, example:

locale *MinLVarNotInBounds* = **fixes** *min-lvar-not-in-bounds*::$'a$::*lrv state* $\Rightarrow$ *var option*
assumes
min-lvar-not-in-bounds s = *None* $\longrightarrow$ ($\forall x \in lvars$ ($\mathcal{T}$ s). *in-bounds* x $\langle \mathcal{V}$ $s \rangle$ ($\mathcal{B}$ s))
min-lvar-not-in-bounds s = *Some* x_i $\longrightarrow$ $x_i \in lvars$ ($\mathcal{T}$ s) $\wedge$ $\neg$*in-bounds* x_i $\langle \mathcal{V}$ $s \rangle$ ($\mathcal{B}$ s)
    $\wedge$ ($\forall x \in lvars$ ($\mathcal{T}$ s). $x < x_i$ $\longrightarrow$ *in-bounds* x $\langle \mathcal{V}$ $s \rangle$ ($\mathcal{B}$ s))

The definition of *check* can be given by:

check s $\equiv$ **if** $\mathcal{U}$ s **then** s
          else let x_i' = *min-lvar-not-in-bounds* s **in**
               case x_i' **of** *None* $\Rightarrow$ s
                    | *Some* x_i $\Rightarrow$ **if** $\langle \mathcal{V}$ $s \rangle$ x_i $<_{lb}$ $\mathcal{B}_l$ s x_i **then** *check* (*check-inc* x_i s)
                          else *check* (*check-dec* x_i s)

check-inc x_i s $\equiv$ **let** l_i = *the* ($\mathcal{B}_l$ s x_i); x_j' = *min-rvar-inc* s x_i **in**
    case x_j' **of** *None* $\Rightarrow$ s ⦇ $\mathcal{U}$:= *True* ⦈ | *Some* x_j $\Rightarrow$ *pivot-and-update* x_i x_j l_i s

The definition of *check-dec* is analogous. It is shown (mainly by induction) that this definition satisfies the *check* specification. Note that this definition uses general recursion, so its termination is non-trivial. It has been shown that it terminates for all states satisfying the check preconditions. The proof is based on the proof outline given in [10]. It is very technically involved, but due to the lack of space we do not discuss it in more details.

3.9   Symmetries

The Simplex algorithm exhibits many symmetric cases. For example, *assert-bound* treats atoms *Leq* x c and *Geq* x c in a symmetric manner, *check-inc* and *check-dec* are symmetric, etc. These symmetric cases differ only in several aspects: order relations between numbers ($<$ vs $>$ and $\leq$ vs $\geq$), the role of lower and upper bounds ($\mathcal{B}_l$ vs $\mathcal{B}_u$) and their updating functions, comparisons with bounds (e.g., $\geq_{ub}$ vs $\leq_{lb}$ or $<_{lb}$ vs $>_{ub}$), and atom constructors (*Leq* and *Geq*). These can be attributed to two different orientations (positive and negative) of the rational axis. To avoid duplicating definitions and proofs, *assert-bound* definition cases for *Leq* and *Geq* are replaced by a call to a newly introduced function parametrized by a *Direction* — a record containing a minimal set of aspects listed above that differ in two definition cases such that other aspects can be derived from them (e.g., only $<$ need to be stored while $\leq$ can be derived from it). Two constants of the type *Direction* are defined: *Positive* (with $<$, $\leq$ orders, $\mathcal{B}_l$ for lower and $\mathcal{B}_u$ for upper bounds and their corresponding updating functions, and *Leq* constructor) and *Negative* (completely opposite from the previous one). Similarly, *check-inc* and *check-dec* are replaced by a new function *check-incdec* parametrized by a *Direction*. All lemmas, previously repeated for each symmetric instance, were replaced by a more abstract one, again parametrized by a *Direction* parameter.

4   Related Work

The literature on decision procedures for linear arithmetic is vast. Regarding the formally verified algorithms, the closest work to ours is done by Chaieb and Nipkow [7,14,15,16]. They have verified a number of quantifier-elimination algorithms for both rational and integer case. They cover arbitrary quantifiers and propositional structure (although by a simple DNF-based approach), but restrict atoms only to $<$ and $=$ relations. Our approach has more limited scope since it covers only the quantifier-free case for rational arithmetic, but our experimental results show that, due to the Simplex procedure, it significantly outperforms Fourier-Motzkin procedure verified by Nipkow [16]. We have tested 90 random generated quantifier-free LRA instances with 2-10 variables and 10-100 constraints. Fourier-Motzkin procedure solved only 8 within a 300s time-limit with average time of 66.40s, while Simplex solved all 90 with average time of 0.44s.

5   Conclusions and Further Work

We have presented a formalization of a functional model for the incremental Simplex procedure [10] used in most state-of-the art SMT solvers and proved its total correctness. Only the central case of deciding conjunctions of constraints was discussed, while other important but simpler questions (e.g., explanations, propagations) are left for further work.

The decision to use a stepwise refinement approach enormously simplified reasoning about the procedure. Initially, we started a formalization by implementing the whole procedure and reasoning about it at once, and our experience shows that this monolith approach required proofs that are several times longer and much harder to make and understand. Stepwise refinement makes the formalization modular and it is much easier to make changes to the procedure.

Another important decision in our formalization was to pay special attention to symmetric cases in the proof. Pen-and-paper termination proof outline [9] deals only with one of four symmetric cases arising in that context and concludes that other cases are handled „similarly". A direct approach would be to copy-paste the case four times and adapt the proof in each case. However, our generalizations made in basic predicate definitions, completly removed the need for case-analysis in the proof text.

The main obstacle for achieving the maximal efficiency is the lack of imperative data-structures in our formalization. This can be improved if the Imperative/HOL framework [6] is used. However, this does not fit well with our stepwise refinement approach. Imperative/HOL would require redefining the whole code using the monadic approach and proving some kind of equivalence with the current purely functional implementation.

References

1. Armand, M., Faure, G., Grégoire, B., Keller, C., Théry, L., Werner, B.: A Modular Integration of SAT/SMT Solvers to Coq through Proof Witnesses. In: Jouannaud, J.-P., Shao, Z. (eds.) CPP 2011. LNCS, vol. 7086, pp. 135–150. Springer, Heidelberg (2011)
2. Back, R.-J.: On the Correctness of Refinement Steps in Program Development. PhD thesis, Åbo Akademi, Helsinki, Finland, Report A–1978–4 (1978)
3. Ballarin, C.: Interpretation of Locales in Isabelle: Theories and Proof Contexts. In: Borwein, J.M., Farmer, W.M. (eds.) MKM 2006. LNCS (LNAI), vol. 4108, pp. 31–43. Springer, Heidelberg (2006)
4. Barrett, C., Sebastiani, R., Seshia, S., Tinelli, C.: Satisfiability Modulo Theories. In: Biere, A., Heule, M., van Maaren, H., Walsh, T. (eds.) Handbook of Satisfiability. IOS Press (2009)
5. Böhme, S., Weber, T.: Fast LCF-Style Proof Reconstruction for Z3. In: Kaufmann, M., Paulson, L.C. (eds.) ITP 2010. LNCS, vol. 6172, pp. 179–194. Springer, Heidelberg (2010)
6. Bulwahn, L., Krauss, A., Haftmann, F., Erkök, L., Matthews, J.: Imperative Functional Programming with Isabelle/HOL. In: Mohamed, O.A., Muñoz, C., Tahar, S. (eds.) TPHOLs 2008. LNCS, vol. 5170, pp. 134–149. Springer, Heidelberg (2008)
7. Chaieb, A., Nipkow, T.: Proof Synthesis and Reflection for Linear Arithmetic. J. Automated Reasoning 41, 33–59 (2008)
8. Dijkstra, E.W.: A Constructive Approach to the Problem of Program Correctness. BIT Numerical Mathematics 8, 174–186 (1968)
9. Dutertre, B., de Moura, L.: Integrating Simplex with DPLL(T). Technical Report SRI-CSL-06-01, SRI International (2006)
10. Dutertre, B., de Moura, L.: A Fast Linear-Arithmetic Solver for DPLL(T). In: Ball, T., Jones, R.B. (eds.) CAV 2006. LNCS, vol. 4144, pp. 81–94. Springer, Heidelberg (2006)
11. Haftmann, F., Nipkow, T.: Code Generation via Higher-Order Rewrite Systems. In: Blume, M., Kobayashi, N., Vidal, G. (eds.) FLOPS 2010. LNCS, vol. 6009, pp. 103–117. Springer, Heidelberg (2010)
12. Harrison, J.: Without Loss of Generality. In: Berghofer, S., Nipkow, T., Urban, C., Wenzel, M. (eds.) TPHOLs 2009. LNCS, vol. 5674, pp. 43–59. Springer, Heidelberg (2009)
13. Marić, F.: Formal Verification of a Modern SAT Solver by Shallow Embedding into Isabelle/HOL. Theor. Comput. Sci. 411(50), 4333–4356 (2010)
14. Nipkow, T.: Linear Quantifier Elimination. In: Armando, A., Baumgartner, P., Dowek, G. (eds.) IJCAR 2008. LNCS (LNAI), vol. 5195, pp. 18–33. Springer, Heidelberg (2008)

15. Nipkow, T.: Reflecting Quantifier Elimination for Linear Arithmetic. In: Formal Logical Methods for System Security and Correctness. IOS Press (2008)
16. Nipkow, T.: Linear Quantifier Elimination. J. Automated Reasoning 45, 189–212 (2010)
17. Nipkow, T.: Verified Efficient Enumeration of Plane Graphs Modulo Isomorphism. In: van Eekelen, M., Geuvers, H., Schmaltz, J., Wiedijk, F. (eds.) ITP 2011. LNCS, vol. 6898, pp. 281–296. Springer, Heidelberg (2011)
18. Nipkow, T., Paulson, L.C., Wenzel, M.T.: Isabelle/HOL. LNCS, vol. 2283. Springer, Heidelberg (2002)
19. Wirth, N.: Program Development by Stepwise Refinement. Commun. ACM 26(1), 70–74 (1983)

VMC: A Tool for Product Variability Analysis

Maurice H. ter Beek, Franco Mazzanti, and Aldi Sulova

Istituto di Scienza e Tecnologie dell'Informazione, ISTI–CNR, Pisa, Italy

Abstract. We present VMC, a tool for the modeling and analysis of variability in product lines. It accepts a product family specified as a modal transition system, possibly with additional variability constraints, after which it can automatically generate all the family's valid products, visualize the family/products as modal/labeled transition systems, and efficiently model check properties expressed in an action- and state-based branching-time temporal logic over products and families alike.

1 Introduction

Product Line Engineering (PLE) is a paradigm for developing a variety of related products from a common product family. Commonality and variability are defined in terms of *features* and managing variability is about identifying variation points in a family design and deciding which combinations are valid products.

In [7], Modal Transition Systems (MTSs) were recognized as a formal method to describe in a compact way the possible operational behavior of all products of a product family. An MTS is a Labeled Transition System (LTS) distinguishing *optional* (may) and *mandatory* (must) transitions. The standard way to derive products (which become LTSs) from an MTS modeling a product family is to include all its (reachable) must transitions and a subset of its (reachable) may transitions; each selection is a product. However, MTSs are incapable of modeling all common variability constraints. The solution chosen in [1,2] is to add a set of constraints to the MTS to define which derivable products are to be considered valid ones. In particular, an appropriate variability and action-based temporal logic to formalize these constraints is defined in [1] and an algorithm to derive only (and possibly all) LTSs describing valid products is defined in [2].

We introduce an experimental tool we developed to implement this solution: the *Variability Model Checker* VMC. We guide the reader through a case study, a family of coffee machines from [1,2] with the following informal requirements:

1. *Initially, a coin must be inserted: either a euro, exclusively for European products, or a dollar, exclusively for Canadian products;*
2. *After inserting a coin, the user has to choose whether (s)he wants sugar, by pressing one of two buttons, after which (s)he may select a beverage;*
3. *The choice of beverage (coffee, tea, cappuccino) varies, but all products must offer coffee while only European products may offer cappuccino;*
4. *Optionally, a ringtone may be rung after delivering a beverage. However, a ringtone must be rung in all products offering cappuccino;*

D. Giannakopoulou and D. Méry (Eds.): FM 2012, LNCS 7436, pp. 450–454, 2012.

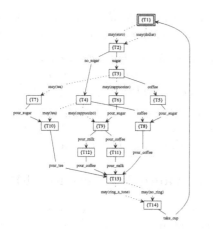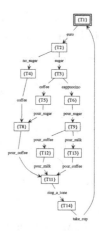

Fig. 1. MTS of coffee machine family (l) and apparently valid European product (r) as generated by VMC; dashed edges labeled may(·) are may transitions, the others must

2   Encoding and Analyzing Product Families in VMC

VMC (http://fmtlab.isti.cnr.it/vmc/), beyond interactively exploring an MTS, model checking properties over an MTS, and visualizing the interactive explanations of a verification result, furthermore allows the generation of valid products (according to the given constraints) of an MTS describing a product family and the verification of properties over each valid product.

VMC takes as input the textual encoding of an MTS and a set of constraints of the form ALTernative, EXCludes, REQuires and IFF (a shorthand for bilateral REQs), thus hiding their logic formalization given in [1]. The distinction among may and must transitions is encoded in the resulting LTS by structuring action labels corresponding to may transitions as may(·) (i.e., typed actions). We model all valid product behavior of the coffee machine family by the MTS of Fig. 1(l), whose textual representation and associated set of constraints are as follows:

```
T1 = may(euro).T2 + may(dollar).T2        T11 = pour_milk.T13
T2 = sugar.T3 + no_sugar.T4               T12 = pour_coffee.T13
T3 = coffee.T5 + may(cappuccino).T6 + may(tea).T7   T13 = may(ring_a_tone).T14
T4 = coffee.T8 + may(cappuccino).T9 + may(tea).T10      + may(no_ring).T14
T5 = pour_sugar.T8                        T14 = take_cup.T1
T6 = pour_sugar.T9                        net SYS = T1
T7 = pour_sugar.T10                       Constraints { euro ALT dollar
T8 = pour_coffee.T13                                    dollar EXC cappuccino
T9 = pour_coffee.T11 + pour_milk.T12                    cappuccino REQ ring_a_tone
T10 = pour_tea.T13                                      ring_a_tone ALT no_ring }
```

The variability logic defined in [1] can be directly encoded in the logic accepted by VMC by considering the typed actions. This latter logic contains the classic box and diamond modal operators $[], \langle\rangle$, the classic existential and universal state operators E, A (quantifying over paths), and action-based versions of the CTL until operators W, U (resulting also in an action-based version of the 'eventually' operator F). Using VMC it is thus possible to specify and verify properties which are definitely preserved in all products by checking them over the family MTS:

(1) *The MTS guarantees that if a euro or dollar action occurs, afterwards for all standardly derivable products it is eventually possible to reach action coffee*: $[may(euro)\ or\ may(dollar)]\ E\ [true\ \{not\ may(*)\}\ U\ \{coffee\}\ true]$

This formula prohibits a path leading to action coffee to contain *any* (i.e. $*$) may transition (beyond the initial one). Asked to check it over the MTS of Fig. 1(l), VMC reports it holds. It moreover offers the possibility to explain the result.

3   Generating and Analyzing Valid Products in VMC

VMC implements the algorithm defined in [2] to generate valid products derivable from an MTS when taking into account an associated set of constraints. The latter can also be used to specify (and analyze) specific subsets of the product set. Beyond generating valid products (LTSs), VMC allows browsing them, verifying whether they satisfy a certain property (logic formula) and investigating why a specific valid product does (not) satisfy the verified property. To do so, VMC allows to open for each product a new window with its textual encoding.

Suppose we generate all valid products in VMC and then check for each one:

(2) *If it is possible to obtain a sugared cappuccino, then also an unsugared one*: $(EF\ \langle sugar \rangle\ \langle cappuccino \rangle\ true)\ implies\ EF\ \langle no\_sugar \rangle\ \langle cappuccino \rangle\ true$

Property 2 does not hold for all valid products, revealing ambiguous constraints: the one of Fig. 1(r) satisfies all constraints but offers cappuccino only with sugar. To resolve such ambiguity, we refine the optional actions cappuccino and tea by explicitly distinguishing sugared and unsugared ones and extend the constraints:

```
Constraints {
    euro ALT dollar                              dollar EXC unsugared_cappuccino
    unsugared_cappuccino IFF sugared_cappuccino  unsugared_cappuccino REQ ring_a_tone
    unsugared_tea IFF sugared_tea                ring_a_tone ALT no_ring }
```

This case study `coffeemodel2.txt` is available in VMC as one of the examples. Next we check if all valid European products now offer both types of cappuccino:

$[euro]\ ((EF\ \langle sugared\_cappuccino \rangle\ true)\ and\ EF\ \langle unsugared\_cappuccino \rangle\ true)$

VMC then produces a table of 10 products (no longer containing that of Fig. 1(r)) listing which optional actions they contain and whether they satisfy the formula.

4   VMC and Related Tools

VMC's core contains a command-line version of the model checker and a product generation procedure, both stand-alone executables in Ada (easy to compile for Windows|Linux|Solaris|Mac) wrapped with CGI scripts handled by a web server, facilitating an html-oriented GUI and integration with graph drawing tools. Its development is ongoing, a prototype for academic purposes is freely usable online (`fmtlab.isti.cnr.it/vmc`) and its executables are available upon request.

The current version of VMC is not targeted to very large systems. Its main limitation, however, lies in generating the model from its input language, while its on-the-fly verification engine and advanced explanation techniques are those of the highly optimized family of on-the-fly model checkers developed at ISTI–CNR over the last decades for verifying formulae in an action- and state-based branching-time temporal logic derived from the CTL family of logics, such as FMC [8], UMC [3] and CMC [6]. Their on-the-fly nature means that in general not the whole state space needs to be generated and explored. This feature improves performance and allows to deal with infinite-state systems.

We are aware of two other tools dealing with verification of product families.

MTSA [5] is a prototype, built on top of the LTS Analyser LTSA, for the analysis of MTSs specified in an extension of the process algebra FSP (Finite State Processes). MTSA allows 3-valued FLTL (Fluent LTL) model checking of MTSs by reducing the verification to two FLTL model-checking runs on LTSs.

SNIP [4] is a model checker for PLs modeled as FTSs (Featured Transition Systems) specified in a language based on that of SPIN. Features must be declared in the Text-based Variability Language TVL and are taken into account by SNIP's explicit-state model-checking algorithm for the verification of properties expressed in fLTL (feature LTL) interpreted over FTSs, e.g. to verify a property over only a subset of a family's valid products. Exhaustive model-checking algorithms (continuing the search after a violation is found) moreover allow to verify all products of a family at once and to output all products violating a property. SNIP treats features as first-class citizens, has built-in support for feature diagrams, and it implements model-checking algorithms tailored for PLs.

Acknowledgment. We thank our colleagues Patrizia Asirelli, Alessandro Fantechi and Stefania Gnesi for their contributions to the research that has led to VMC.

References

1. Asirelli, P., ter Beek, M.H., Fantechi, A., Gnesi, S.: A Logical Framework to Deal with Variability. In: Méry, D., Merz, S. (eds.) IFM 2010. LNCS, vol. 6396, pp. 43–58. Springer, Heidelberg (2010)
2. Asirelli, P., ter Beek, M.H., Fantechi, A., Gnesi, S.: Formal Description of Variability in Product Families. In: SPLC 2011, pp. 130–139. IEEE (2011)
3. ter Beek, M.H., Fantechi, A., Gnesi, S., Mazzanti, F.: A state/event-based model-checking approach for the analysis of abstract system properties. Sci. Comput. Program. 76(2), 119–135 (2011)
4. Classen, A., Cordy, M., Heymans, P., Legay, A., Schobbens, P.-Y.: Model Checking Software Product Lines with SNIP. To appear in Int. J. Softw. Tools Technol. Transfer (2012)
5. D'Ippolito, N., Fischbein, D., Chechik, M., Uchitel, S.: MTSA: The Modal Transition System Analyser. In: ASE 2008, pp. 475–476. IEEE (2008)

6. Fantechi, A., Gnesi, S., Lapadula, A., Mazzanti, F., Pugliese, R., Tiezzi, F.: A Logical Verification Methodology for Service-Oriented Computing. ACM Trans. Softw. Eng. Methodol. 21(3), article 16, 1–46 (2012)
7. Fischbein, D., Uchitel, S., Braberman, V.A.: A foundation for behavioural conformance in software product line architectures. In: ROSATEA 2006, pp. 39–48. ACM (2006)
8. Gnesi, S., Mazzanti, F.: On the Fly Verification of Networks of Automata. In: PDPTA 1999, pp. 1040–1046. CSREA Press (1999)

Specification-Based Test Repair Using a Lightweight Formal Method

Guowei Yang, Sarfraz Khurshid, and Miryung Kim

The University of Texas at Austin
guoweiyang@utexas.edu, {khurshid,miryung}@ece.utexas.edu

Abstract. When a program evolves, its test suite must be modified to reflect changes in requirements or to account for new feature additions. This problem of modifying tests as a program evolves is termed *test repair*. Existing approaches either assume that updated implementation is correct, or assume that most test repairs require simply fixing compilation errors caused by refactoring of previously tested implementation. This paper focuses on the problem of repairing *semantically broken or outdated* tests by leveraging specifications. Our technique, SPECTR, employs a lightweight formal method to perform specification-based repair. Specifically, SPECTR supports the Alloy language for writing specifications and uses its SAT-based analyzer for repairing JUnit tests. Since SPECTR utilizes specifications, it works even when the specification is modified but the change has not yet been implemented in code—in such a case, SPECTR is able to repair tests that previous techniques would not even consider as candidates for test repair. An experimental evaluation using a suite of subject programs with pre-conditions and post-conditions shows SPECTR can effectively repair tests even for programs that perform complex manipulation of dynamically allocated data.

1 Introduction

Testing is the most commonly used technique for validating software quality. While conceptually simple, testing can be expensive and involves much manual effort, specifically in writing test cases and describing expected test outputs. To reduce this cost, regression test suites are commonly used to check behavioral modifications as a program evolves. However, behavioral modifications may render certain existing tests invalid due to new feature additions or bug fixes, which in turn modify the expected test outputs.

Several research projects have addressed this problem of *test repair* [8,6,5]. Existing techniques can fix compilation errors in tests caused by simple refactorings such as method renamings or signature changes, so that the old tests could run as before. Some can modify test assertions to ensure those tests that passed before could still pass. However, all existing techniques perform test updates with respect to implementation changes, assuming that implementation is always correct. If the specification changes, but the implementation has not yet been modified or has been modified incorrectly, existing techniques are not able to repair tests to correctly reflect the updated specifications.

D. Giannakopoulou and D. Méry (Eds.): FM 2012, LNCS 7436, pp. 455–470, 2012.

This paper presents SPECTR, a novel specification-based test repair technique using a lightweight formal method. Given the specifications of a modified program—*pre-conditions* defining expected inputs and *post-conditions* defining expected behavior—and an existing test suite, SPECTR repairs each test that exercises modified behavior. Specifically, it repairs test assertions that check the actual output against the expected output, so that failing tests reflect specification violation and passing tests reflect specification conformance.

As an enabling technology, SPECTR uses the Alloy tool set [13]. Alloy is a first-order declarative language based on relations, and is particularly suitable for expressing structural invariants on graphs, such as class invariants on object-graphs in a Java program. The Alloy tool set includes a fully automatic SAT solver engine that checks Alloy formulas within a given *scope*, i.e., bound on the universe of discourse. The back-end deployment of state-of-the-art SAT solvers makes the Alloy tool set particularly effective for test repair.

Given Alloy specifications, SPECTR uses a SAT solver to compute expected outputs for test assertions using post-conditions. The key insight behind our approach is that because each test case represents a single program execution for deterministic programs, updating a test oracle needs to explore only one execution behavior and does not need enumerate all possible behaviors. Thus SPECTR differs from previous testing and verification techniques using Alloy [21,16,7,9] by avoiding the traditional state-space explosion. Moreover, for manually written tests, SPECTR allows utilizing the tester's intuition behind the design of test inputs, since they directly form a part of the repaired test cases.

SPECTR repairs JUnit [1] tests that have a fairly general structure with three primary components: (1) *initialization*—initializing input values, i.e., the pre-state, for the *sequence* of methods under test, e.g., using explicit object allocations and field assignments, (2) *execution*—invoking the sequence of methods under test on the inputs, and (3) *assertion*—checking the post-state for the sequence using a test assertion, e.g., using the `assertEquals` method in `org.junit.Assert`. To repair a test, SPECTR first uses the initialization component to initialize an Alloy *instance* that represents the pre-state. Next, it uses Alloy to compute an expected post-state subject to the execution component. Finally, it updates affected assertions to reflect behavioral conformance to the updated specification.

SPECTR makes it possible to repair tests even before the implementation is modified to reflect the updated specifications. Thus, SPECTR directly supports test-driven development, a key practice behind the success of Extreme Programming and other agile software development processes. To the best of our knowledge, SPECTR is the first such technique for test repair.

This paper makes the following contributions:

- **Specification-based test repair.** We introduce the idea of repairing tests to reflect modifications to expected behavior as encoded in specifications. Previous techniques for test repair are based on implementation changes, assuming that updated code is always correct. Therefore, they do not handle semantic changes with respect to modified specifications.

- **A lightweight formal method for test repair.** To our knowledge, SPECTR is the first technique for test repair using a lightweight formal method. It leverages the Alloy tool set and presents a non-conventional application of propositional satisfiability solvers for repairing tests.
- **Evaluation.** We perform an experimental evaluation using our prototype embodiment of SPECTR to repair tests for a suite of subject programs. Our experiments show that SPECTR effectively repairs tests, even for programs that perform complex manipulations of dynamically allocated data.

While our approach is based on Alloy specifications, our ideas generalize to programs annotated using different specification languages, such as the Java Modeling Language, which enhances the applicability of our approach. In fact, our approach directly applies to code with Java Modeling Language (JML) annotations: the JForge tool [7] performs Alloy-based static analysis of JML annotated code and provides an enabling technology for our technique.

2   Related Work

Test Repair. The need of test repair is well-recognized in regression testing [19,3] and software evolution [26]. Recent years have seen several frameworks that automate test repair [8,6,5,18]. The key difference between SPECTR and previous work is SPECTR's use of specifications for test repair. Previous techniques for test repair use changes in implementation to repair tests, and hence can only repair tests to reflect actual behavior, which may not be the *intended* behavior. In contrast, SPECTR can repair tests even when the modified implementation is buggy. Indeed, SPECTR does not even require the implementation to be modified before the tests are repaired.

Daniel et al. [6,5] proposed a technique which performs a combined dynamic and static analysis to find test repairs that developers are likely to accept. However, their approach assumes the implementation is correct, and then repairs failing tests by recording its runtime behavior. [18] proposed an approach to repairing test cases for evolving method declarations. It only repairs test case compilation errors that depend on changes in parameters or return values. It assumes that the original functionality is preserved for the given test inputs.

Test repair has also been investigated for GUI-based systems, where it is common for developers to create test scripts using record-and-replay testing tools in GUI testing. The scripts generated in this way are quite fragile and easy to be broken when the system changes. To address this problem, Memon [17] proposed techniques for correcting sequences of test scripts so that they compile with the tested application. More recently, Grechanik et al. [11] presented a technique to identify modified GUI objects and locate test script statements that reference these modified GUI objects, so the test engineers can fix the test scripts.

Debugging. Recent years have seen much progress in automated techniques for removing bugs, i.e., debugging – the process of locating faults, i.e., fault localization [12,4,15] and fixing them, i.e., program repair [27,14,24,10]. Test repair is a special case of program repair where the program to repair is the old test suite. However, existing techniques for program repair are not well suited for test repair since they are ambivalent of the specific structure of test case. In contrast, test repair techniques utilize this structure for enhanced effectiveness.

Alloy. The Alloy tool-set has provided an enabling technology for various analyses for Java programs, including static checking using Jalloy [21], systematic testing using TestEra [16], data structure repair using Tarmeem [25], and most recently for program repair by Gopinath et al [10]. Our work shares insights with previous work and provides a novel use of the Alloy tool-set in test repair. The problem of test repair has similarities with the problem of test generation and the problem of program repair. SPECTR's technical approach is different from TestEra's, which generates inputs at the concrete level using sequences of field assignments and uses the Alloy Analyzer to evaluate Alloy post-conditions as test oracles. In contrast, SPECTR supports method sequences for input creation, enables re-use of existing test inputs, and generates test assertions that directly check correctness criteria. Also, SPECTR's approach is different from Gopinath et al.'s approach for program repair, which repairs faulty object field assignment statements. In contrast, SPECTR repairs JUnit test assertions, which are written using arbitrary Java expressions.

N-version Programming. Our work bears resemblance[1] to N-version programming—a methodology where the same initial specification is used to create $N \geq 2$ functionally equivalent programs to enable fault tolerance [2]. There are three basic differences between our approach and N-version programming. First, we are performing *specification*-based repair where the specification is in a *declarative* language. We do not have two (or more) *imperative* programs implementing the same specification—the central condition for N-version programming. Second, N-version programming does not account for specification evolution, which is the central theme of our work. Third, N-version programming is defined for fault tolerance, not for test repair. However, we could generalize the spirit of N-version programming to view a specification—assuming it is *executable*—itself as one program version that may evolve. Then, after an evolution, the results of specification execution, if feasible, can be used to repair tests. For Alloy specifications, execution is made feasible by Alloy's SAT-based back-end, which is indeed the enabling technology for SPECTR's test repair. It is plausible to optimize solving of Alloy formulas in the specific context of test repair, but that is an open research problem.

3   Illustrative Example

This section presents an example to illustrate SPECTR's test repair process; we describe basic Alloy syntax and semantics as we introduce it; details on Alloy can be found elsewhere [13].

---

[1] We thank an anonymous reviewer for pointing us to N-version programming.

| ① | Code | ```public class List {
    Node header;
    static class Node {int elem; Node next;}
    public int size(){...}
    public void add(int){...}
}``` |
|---|---|---|
| ② | **Old Spec:** acyclic, sorted lists with unique elements | ```pred RepOk(l: List, s: State) {
    all n: l.(header.s).*(next.s) {
    n not in n.^(next.s) // list is acyclic
    // list is sorted with unique elements
    some n.(next.s) => n.(elem.s) < n.(next.s).(elem.s)
    }
}

pred add_pre(l: List, x: Int, s: State) {
    RepOk[l, s]
}

pred add_post(l: List, x: Int, s, s': State) {
    RepOk[l, s']
    l.(header.s').*(next.s').(elem.s')
    = l.(header.s).*(next.s).(elem.s) + x
}

pred size_pre(l: List, s: State) {
    RepOk[l, s]
}

pred size_post(l: List, result: Int, s: State) {
    result = #l.(header.s).*(next.s)
}``` |
| ③ | **New Spec:** acyclic, sorted lists that allow repetitions

Modified Spec: "RepOk", "add_post"

Unchanged Spec: "add_pre", "size_pre", "size_post" | ```pred RepOk(l: List, s: State) {
    all n: l.(header.s).*(next.s) {
    n not in n.^(next.s) // list is acyclic
    // list is sorted, while allowing repetitions
    some n.(next.s) => n.(elem.s) <= n.(next.s).(elem.s)
    }
}

pred add_pre(l: List, x: Int, s: State) {...}

pred add_post(l: List, x: Int, s, s': State) {
    RepOk[l, s']
    all i: Int {
    i != x =>
    #{n: l.(header.s).*(next.s) | n.(elem.s)=i}
    = #{n: l.(header.s').*(next.s') | n.(elem.s')=i}
    else
    #{n: l.(header.s).*(next.s) | n.(elem.s)=i} + 1
    = #{n: l.(header.s').*(next.s') | n.(elem.s')=i}
    }
}

pred size_pre(l: List, s: State) {...}

pred size_post(l: List, result: Int, s: State) {...}``` |
| ④ | **Example Test Repair:** assertion updated | ```@Test public void test() {
    List l = new List();
    l.add(0);
    l.add(0);
    assertEquals(1, l.size());
}```   ```@Test public void test() {
    List l = new List();
    l.add(0);
    l.add(0);
    assertEquals(2, l.size());
}```
(a)   (b) |

Fig. 1. Example program evolution and test repair

SPECTR takes as input an old test and a modified specification and repairs the old test. To illustrate, consider a singly-linked acyclic list data structure that stores integers in sorted order. Fig. 1 illustrates test repair for this example; the figure shows ① a Java declaration for lists; ② an old Alloy specification that defines the list class invariant (RepOk) and methods add and size; ③ a new Alloy specification that defines the modified list class invariant and method add; and ④ an example test repair performed by SPECTR.

The Java code declares that each list has a header node, and each node has an integer elem and has a next node. The method size returns the number of elements in the list. The method add inserts a given integer into the list.

The Alloy specification in Fig. 1-② has five *predicates*; each predicate (pred) defines a parameterized formula. The predicate RepOk states the class invariant and has two parameters: a list l and a state s. This universally quantified (all) formula expresses acyclicity and sortedness of unique elements. The operator '.' represents relational join. An expression o.(f.s) represents dereferencing of field f of object o in state s. '*' represents reflexive transitive closure. For example, header.*next denotes all nodes reachable from header. '^' represents transitive closure. The first sub-formula states directed acyclicity by ensuring that a traversal that starts node x cannot revisit the same node. The second sub-formula ensures that the list is sorted and contains no repetitions. The predicate add_post states the post-condition of method add. States s and s' represent a pre-state and a post-state after invoking add respectively. The first formula states the class invariant holds in the post-state. The second formula states the elements in the list is a union of the elements in the pre-state and an added element x. The predicate size_post states the post-condition of method size. The operator '#' denotes the cardinality of a set. The parameter result represents the return value. Since size is a *pure* method, i.e., the execution of the method does not change the state of its inputs, its predicate does not need a post-state. The predicates add_pre and size_pre state the pre-conditions of add and size respectively; both the predicates state that the class invariant holds in the pre-state s.

An example JUnit test with respect to this specification is shown in Fig. 1-④-(a). The test allocates a new list and makes two invocations of add followed by a correctness check using assertEquals. Since the class invariant does not allow repetitions, the assertion checks that the size of the list after the two add operations is 1. This test passes only if method add correctly avoids repetitions.

To demonstrate SPECTR's test repair process, consider the following modification to the list specification: a list may now contain repeated elements, and must still be acyclic and sorted (Fig. 1-③). Note the comparison operator in RepOk is now '<=' instead of '<'. The post-condition of add is updated correspondingly. This modified post-condition states that the number of times each integer other than x appears in the list in the pre-state is the same as the number of times that they appear in the post-state, whereas the number of times that x appears in the list is increased by 1.

With respect to this modified specification, the JUnit test in Fig. 1-④-(a) is no longer correct, since the list size is expected to be 2 instead of 1. SPECTR transforms the old test to the repaired test shown in Fig. 1-④-(b). The repaired test is now correct with respect to the modified specification in the sense that every test failure now represents a violated specification. We emphasize that SPECTR does not require method implementations to be correct with respect to the modified specification. Moreover, none of the previous test repair techniques [8,6,5,18] can repair the above test since they use the updated code as opposed to the updated specification as a basis for test repair.

4   SPECTR

SPECTR repairs JUnit tests using method-level specifications written in Alloy. SPECTR takes as input an existing test and the modified specifications of the methods invoked by the test, and corrects the test's expected output. Section 4.1 describes our test repair algorithm. Section 4.2 describes how we leverage the Alloy tool set as an enabling technology for automated test repair.

4.1   Algorithm Overview

Given a set of tests that need to be repaired with respect to the modified specifications, SPECTR repairs the tests one at a time. SPECTR assumes that each test case consists of three components in the following style:

```
@Test public void testcase() {
    // 1. initialization: code to create pre-state (inputs)
    ...
    // 2. execution: code to execute sequence of methods under test
    ...
    // 3. assertion: code to check post-state (output)
}
```

In general, JUnit methods can contain arbitrary Java code and may not follow this structure, e.g., have no assertion to check the output. Such non-conforming tests are not handled by SPECTR. However, our approach can, in principle, leverage the JForge framework [7] to handle more general JUnit tests, including those with loops, conditional statements, or even multiple test assertions.

Fig. 2 describes our test repair algorithm. Given an old test to repair (oldTest) and a modified specification (newSpec), it returns a repaired test (newTest) conforming to newSpec. The resulting repaired test must have the same initialization and method execution code as the old version followed by *updated assertion checks*, conforming to modified specifications.

Identification of Expected Test Behavior. SPECTR emulates the execution of a test case by executing corresponding modified specifications using Alloy. The execution of a JUnit test essentially makes several state transitions starting from the initial state and checks certain properties at certain states. Given an initial state, a sequence of method invocations, and the specifications of invoked methods, the Alloy Analyzer generates the pre-states and post-states of those method invocations to identify the expected behavior of the test.

```
1 TestCase repair(TestCase oldTest, Spec newSpec) {
2     // extract the three elements of the given test
3     Code testInit = oldTest.getTestInitCode();
4     Code methodExec = oldTest.getMethodExecution();
5     AssertEquals assertion = oldTest.getAssertEquals();
6
7     TestCase newTest = new Test(); // output
8     newTest.append(testInit);
9     newTest.append(methodExec);
10
11    // compute expected post-state
12    Instance post; // expected post-state w.r.t spec
13    Instance pre = abstract(Java.execute(testInit));
14    post = Alloy.solve(createModel(pre, methodExec, newSpec));
15
16    // synthesize new correctness check(s)
17    Expression actual = assertion.getActual();
18    newTest.append(new AssertEquals(
19      concretize(Alloy.solve(createModel(post, actual, newSpec))), actual);
20    return newTest;
21 }
```

Fig. 2. Test repair algorithm

Consider a sequence of method invocations and state transitions in a test: $\langle \sigma_0 \rangle m_1(); \langle \sigma_1 \rangle m_2(); \langle \sigma_2 \rangle ...; \langle \sigma_{k-1} \rangle m_k(); \langle \sigma_k \rangle$. m_1 is invoked on a pre-state σ_0 (initial state abstracted from test initialization code). If σ_0 satisfies m_1's pre-condition, its expected post-state σ_1 is generated by the Alloy Analyzer using the pre-state σ_0 and m_1's post-condition. For the invocation of m_i, where $1 < i \leq k$, the post-state of m_{i-1}, σ_{i-1} is the pre-state for m_i. Assuming σ_{i-1} satisfies the pre-condition of m_i, the Alloy Analyzer computes a corresponding post-state σ_i based on the post-condition of m_i. If any method's pre-condition is not satisfied by the method invocation's pre-state, it means that the inputs of the method invocation do not meet a pre-condition, and thus the test is broken and cannot be repaired. These tests need to be removed from the test suite.

Replacement of Expected Values in JUnit Assertions. JUnit provides several assert methods to write correctness properties, which can be de-sugared into the `assertEquals` method. Each test is repaired by using the post-state Alloy instance after the invocation of the sequence of methods under test to compute the expected value for the assertion check.

4.2   Using Alloy for Test Repair

The initialization code of the old test is used to generate the pre-state Alloy instance using an abstraction translation [16], which traverses the Java data structures and initializes a corresponding Alloy instance.

Each method of a class has its corresponding specification, i.e., a pre-condition and a post-condition. Consider a method m in class C:

```
class C{T m (T1 p1, T2 p2, ..., Tk pk){...}}
```

The Alloy pre-condition for m has the following declaration:

```
pred m_pre(c:C, p1:T1, p2:T2, ..., pk:Tk, s_pre:State){...}
```

If the return type T is not void, and method m is not a pure method, the post-condition for method m has the following declaration:

```
pred m_post(c:C, p1:T1, p2:T2, ..., pk:Tk, result:T,
     s_pre:State, s_post:State){...}
```

If the return type T is void, then the parameter `result:T` in m_post does not exist. If method m is a pure method, the parameter `s_post:State` does not exist, since the values other than the return value don't change between the pre-state and post-state of the method invocation.

If the method m is static, for both pre-condition and post-condition, the parameter `c:C` does not exist in the parameter list.

To illustrate, in our running example (Section 3), the class `List` has methods `add` and `size`. The method `add` is not pure, its return type is void, and it has an `int` type parameter; while the method `size` is pure, its return type is `int`, and it has no parameters. Their pre-conditions and post-conditions have the following declarations:

```
pred add_pre(l:List, p1:Int, s_pre:State){...}
pred add_post(l:List, p1:Int, s_pre:State, s_post:State){...}
pred size_pre(l:List, s_pre:State){...}
pred size_post(l:List, result:Int, s_pre:State){...}
```

Alloy directly supports primitive integers. Support for other primitive types can be provided through Alloy libraries, e.g., the standard Alloy library includes a model for Boolean.

Given the specifications for each method, the method invocations are translated to an Alloy model using four steps:

1. Model the receiver object and include it as the first parameter for the pre/post-conditions;
2. Model the formal parameters and append them to the parameter list for the pre/post-conditions;
3. For post-condition specification, if there's a return value, create an Alloy signature with the corresponding return type, and append it to the parameter list; and
4. Append the current state to the parameter list. If the list is for the post-condition and the method is not pure, create a new Alloy State and append it to the parameter list, and update the current state to the newly created one.

For example, consider the following method invocation in state S1:

```
l.add(2);
```

This invocation is translated to the following Alloy code:

```
add_pre[l, 2, S1]
add_post[l, 2, S1, S2]
```

and the current state is updated to S2.

Given the specifications for methods invoked, and an initial state abstracted from the execution result of test initialization code, the Alloy Analyzer checks the satisfiability of each method's pre-condition before the invocation of the method, and generates a post-state using the pre-state and post-condition. For example, for the test shown in Fig. 1-④-(a), SPECTR generates the following Alloy code to check whether the pre-state of the first add method invocation (the initial state S0) satisfies the method's pre-condition.

```
one sig S0 extends State {}
one sig l extends List {}
fact {
  no l.(header.S0)
  add_pre[l, 0, S0]
}

pred test() {}
run test
```

If the Alloy Analyzer finds no solution, which means that the pre-condition is not satisfied, SPECTR reports to the users that the inputs in the test are not as expected and that the test cannot be repaired and should be removed from the test suite; otherwise, the pre-condition is satisfied, and SPECTR can generate an expected post-state of the method invocation by constructing the following Alloy code and solving it with the Alloy Analyzer.

```
one sig S0, S1 extends State {}
one sig l extends List {}
fact {
  no l.(header.S0)
  add_pre[l, 0, S0] && add_post[l, 0, S0, S1]
}

pred test() {}
run test
```

The post-state of the method invocation, which is the Alloy instance at S1, is generated using the pre-state, which is the Alloy instance at S0, and the method's post-condition add_post. Similarly, all pre-states of other method invocations can be checked, and all post-states of those invocations can be generated. Thus, each method invocation triggers a state transition from a state to its next state. Except for the initial state S0, all other states are expected states resulting from reasoning on S0 and specifications.

The Alloy instance at the state where the assertion is to be checked is used to compute the expected value. For the actual expression in the assertEquals method, SPECTR uses its corresponding value in the Alloy instance as expected value and replaces the old value with it for the updated test.

For the test example shown in Fig. 1-④-(a), SPECTR generates the following Alloy model and solves it using the Alloy Analyzer.

```
one sig S0, S1, S2 extends State {}
one sig l extends List {}
one sig Result {val: Int}
fact {
  no l.(header.S0)
  add_pre[l, 0, S0] && add_post[l, 0, S0, S1]
  add_pre[l, 0, S1] && add_post[l, 0, S1, S2]
  size_pre[l, S2] && size_post[l, Result.val, S2]
}

pred test() {}
run test
```

Given this Alloy model and a scope, the Alloy Analyzer finds an instance that shows at S2 Result.val is 2, which is the expected value with respect to the

Table 1. Evolution scenarios

Sce.	Subject	Old Spec	Modified Spec	Test Method Executions	Assertion Method
#1	Sorted Singly-Linked List	The comparison among list elements is "<"	The comparison among list elements is "<="	add(0), remove(0), add(1), remove(1)	size()
#2	Binary Heap	Min heap	Max heap	insert(0), insert(1), insert(2), insert(3)	peek()
#3	java.util. LinkedList	Method add(E e) appends e to the end of the list	Method add(E e) inserts e at the beginning of the list	add(0), add(1), add(2), add(3)	getFirst()
#4	java.util. TreeSet	All integer values are allowed in the set	Only positive integer values are allowed in the set	add(-1), add(0), add(1), add(2)	add(E e)

modified specification. SPECTR then replaces the expected value of the assertion with 2 to repair the test.

Our current SPECTR prototype repairs tests by updating primitive values. A more comprehensive tool would allow updating more complex data structures, which can be achieved by concretizing an output from SAT and using the equals method for checking the validity of the output from the program under test.

5 Experiments

This section describes experiments to evaluate test repair performed by our prototype implementation of SPECTR. The goal of our study is to demonstrate SPECTR's ability to repair tests using modified specifications for structurally complex subjects and to demonstrate its feasibility for repairing test suites with a few hundred tests.

5.1 Evolution Scenarios

Table 1 shows the four evolution scenarios used in our study. Each row in the table lists the subjects, specification changes, the methods under test, and the methods used in correctness check. Those subject programs have been previously used to evaluate various approaches in testing and verification [9,7]. **Sorted singly-linked list** represents sorted acyclic lists as described in Section 3. **Binary heap** is a heap data structure based on a binary tree. The tree is a complete binary tree. Heaps can be of two kinds: max-heap and min-heap. In a max-heap, each node is greater than or equal to each of its children. In a min-heap, each node is less than or equal to each of its children. The subjects **java.util.LinkedList** and **java.util.TreeSet** are from the standard Java libraries. The implementations of the subjects remain the same during evolutions. Having the old specifications is not necessary for applying SPECTR; however, if we also have access to the old specifications, we can reduce the number of tests we attempt to repair by identifying a subset of tests that invoke methods with modified specifications.

Test Case Generation Using Java PathFinder. SPECTR assumes a regression test suite exists—developers may have already written test cases for the

Table 2. Test repair by SPECTR

Sce.	Old Tests	Affected Tests	Sucessfully Repaired	Modified Tests	Unchanged Tests	Total (seconds)	Average (seconds)
#1	340	100%	100%	112	228	38	0.11
#2	340	100%	100%	340	0	53	0.16
#3	340	100%	100%	252	88	15	0.04
#4	340	100%	100%	99	241	12	0.03

Table 3. Test repair by ReAssert

Sce.	Old Tests	Passing Tests	Failing Tests	Repaired Tests
#1	340	340	0	0
#2	340	340	0	0
#3	340	340	0	0
#4	340	340	0	0

old program version or generated them using an automated test generation tool. In our evaluation study, we use the Java PathFinder (JPF) model checker [22] to automatically generate a test suite for the old program version following a variant of an earlier approach [23].

We use JPF's non-deterministic choice operator to enumerate JUnit tests, where each test starts with a default constructor call, executes methods under test, and checks a correctness property. Note that the correctness check in each test reflects the actual behavior of the old version, but not the expected behavior according to a given specification. Fig. 4 in Appendix A shows an example test generator for singly-linked lists.

This JPF-based driver generates 340 tests in total for each data structure: 4 tests with one method execution, 16 tests (4*4) with two method executions, 64 tests (4*4*4) with three method executions, and 256 tests (4*4*4*4) with four method executions. Repetition is allowed in each sequence of method execution. Tests for `TreeSet` execute the last add(E e) in the sequence of method executions in the test assertion.

5.2   Test Repair Results

We compiled all our subject programs and JUnit tests using Java version 6 and JUnit 4.4. We used the Alloy Analyzer version 4 as a back-end for solving Alloy specifications. The study was performed on a Dell Desktop running at 2.8 GHz Intel Core i7 CPU with 8 GB of memory and running Windows 7 Professional.

Table 2 shows SPECTR's repairing results. `Old Tests` column indicates the number of tests in the old test suite, and `Affected Tests` column shows the percentage of tests, which invoke some method with a specification change. Column `Successfully Repaired` shows the percentage of tests successfully repaired out of all affected tests. Column `Modified Tests` indicates the number of tests that are modified after the repair, while column `Unchanged Tests` shows the number of tests that are not changed by SPECTR. Column `Total` is the total time taken

```
@Test public void testcase47() {          @Test public void testcase311() {
  LinkedList l = new LinkedList();           LinkedList l = new LinkedList();
  l.add(1);                                  l.add(3);
  l.add(2);                                  l.add(2);
  l.add(3);                                  l.add(0);
- assertEquals(1, l.getFirst());            l.add(3);
+ assertEquals(3, l.getFirst());            assertEquals(3, l.getFirst());
}                                          }
      (a) Modified Test                         (b) Unchanged Test
```

Fig. 3. Two example test repairs performed by SPECTR

to repair all the tests, while column Average is the average time taken for a single test repair.

For all program evolutions considered in this study, all tests are affected, and SPECTR successfully repaired all of them. However, the number of modified tests, unchanged tests, and the time cost vary for different evolution scenarios. For instance, all tests were modified in scenario #2, while only 112 tests, less than one third of the total, were modified in scenario #1. Moreover, 53 seconds were spent on repairing the 340 tests in scenario #2, while only 12 seconds were spent on repairing the same number of tests in scenario #4. The cost of repair depends on the complexity of the modified specification and the length of the test execution.

Note that a test repair technique that does not take into account specifications and is driven purely by implementation would not repair any of the old tests. We applied ReAssert [6], a recent test repair technique, in these four scenarios. ReAssert did not repair or modify any tests since all tests passed and ReAssert only repairs failing tests (Table 3).

To validate repairs made by SPECTR, we manually inspected all repaired tests and found that all of them correctly reflect the modified specifications.

Fig. 3-(a) shows an example of the repair done by SPECTR for scenario #3. In the modified specification, add(E e) inserts e at the beginning instead of appending e to the end, thus the expected result of l.getFirst() in testcase47 is modified from 1 to 3 to reflect the modified specification.

Note that some tests remain unchanged after repair, since the test inputs result in the same outputs according to the old specification as well as the modified specification. Fig. 3-(b) shows such a case for scenario #3, where the first element and the last element added to the list are the same.

We ran the repaired tests against the implementation, and found that all the *modified* tests failed. Those failing tests reflect the errors in implementations which have not yet undergone modifications.

Our study demonstrates that for the subject programs and the selected types of evolution used in the study, SPECTR effectively repairs existing tests to reflect the modified specifications. SPECTR automatically updates the expected test outcomes. *The cost of test repair using SPECTR is reasonable, with a range from 0.03 to 0.16 seconds per test.* Our SPECTR prototype is not optimized, e.g., it uses several file-I/O operations to read each old test and write each modified test. We plan to optimize SPECTR is future work.

6   Conclusions and Future Work

This paper presents SPECTR, a novel specification-based technique for test repair. Given behavioral specifications for the modified program and an existing test suite, SPECTR repairs each test that exercises modified behaviors. It leverages the existing test inputs and updates the test assertions to reflect the modified specification.

The experiments conducted on a suite of subject programs with modified specifications show that SPECTR can effectively repair tests with respect to modified specifications. Moreover, SPECTR is efficient in terms of test repair performance, and the time spent on each repair is less than a half second on average for the subject programs used in our experiments.

SPECTR leverages the Alloy tool-set as an enabling technology and hence requires the use of first-order logic and SAT. While properties of a diverse class of programs can conveniently be expressed in Alloy and checked using SAT, for some programs, e.g., those that perform complex numeric calculations, effective test repair would need an alternative enabling technology. However, our basic approach for test repair would still be applicable, for example, to enable the Pex framework [20] to repair C# tests using Spec# specifications.

As future work, we plan to conduct more extensive evaluation of SPECTR, especially using more complex subjects, such as open source programs.

Acknowledgments.   This work is supported in part by NSF grants under CCF-0845628, CCF-1043810, CCF-1117902, and CCF-1149391, AFOSR grant FA9550-09-1-0351, and 2011 Microsoft SEIF Award.

References

1. JUnit website, http://www.junit.org
2. Chen, L., Avizienis, A.: N-version programming: a fault-tolerance approach to reliability. In: FTCS, vol. 8, pp. 3–9 (1978)
3. Chen, Y.F., Rosenblum, D.S., Vo, K.P.: Testtube: a system for selective regression testing. In: ICSE, pp. 211–220 (1994)
4. Cleve, H., Zeller, A.: Locating causes of program failures. In: ICSE (2005)
5. Daniel, B., Gvero, T., Marinov, D.: On test repair using symbolic execution. In: ISSTA, pp. 207–218 (2010)
6. Daniel, B., Jagannath, V., Dig, D., Marinov, D.: ReAssert: Suggesting repairs for broken unit tests. In: ASE, pp. 433–444 (2009)
7. Dennis, G., Chang, F.S.H., Jackson, D.: Modular verification of code with SAT. In: ISSTA, pp. 109–120 (2006)
8. Deursen, A.V., Moonen, L., Bergh, A., Kok, G.: Refactoring test code. In: XP, pp. 92–95 (2001)
9. Galeotti, J.P., Rosner, N., López Pombo, C.G., Frias, M.F.: Analysis of invariants for efficient bounded verification. In: ISSTA, pp. 25–36 (2010)
10. Gopinath, D., Malik, M.Z., Khurshid, S.: Specification-Based Program Repair Using SAT. In: Abdulla, P.A., Leino, K.R.M. (eds.) TACAS 2011. LNCS, vol. 6605, pp. 173–188. Springer, Heidelberg (2011)

11. Grechanik, M., Xie, Q., Fu, C.: Maintaining and evolving GUI-directed test scripts. In: ICSE, pp. 408–418 (2009)
12. Hangal, S., Lam, M.S.: Tracking down software bugs using automatic anomaly detection. In: ICSE, pp. 291–301 (2002)
13. Jackson, D.: Software Abstractions: Logic, Language, and Analysis. The MIT Press (2006)
14. Jeffrey, D., Feng, M., Gupta, N., Gupta, R.: BugFix: A learning-based tool to assist developers in fixing bugs. In: ICPC, pp. 70–79 (2009)
15. Jiang, L., Su, Z.: Context-aware statistical debugging: from bug predictors to faulty control flow paths. In: ASE, pp. 184–193 (2007)
16. Khurshid, S., Marinov, D.: TestEra: Specification-based testing of Java programs using SAT. In: ASE, vol. 11(4), pp. 403–434 (2004)
17. Memon, A.M.: Automatically repairing event sequence-based GUI test suites for regression testing. TOSEM 18(2), 1–36 (2008)
18. Mirzaaghaei, M., Pastore, F., Pezze, M.: Automatically repairing test cases for evolving method declarations. In: ICSM, pp. 1–5 (2010)
19. Rothermel, G., Harrold, M.J.: A safe, efficient regression test selection technique. TOSEM 6(2), 173–210 (1997)
20. Tillmann, N., de Halleux, J.: Pex–White Box Test Generation for .NET. In: Beckert, B., Hähnle, R. (eds.) TAP 2008. LNCS, vol. 4966, pp. 134–153. Springer, Heidelberg (2008)
21. Vaziri, M.: Finding Bugs Using a Constraint Solver. Ph.D. thesis, CSAIL, MIT (2003)
22. Visser, W., Havelund, K., Brat, G.P., Park, S., Lerda, F.: Model checking programs. In: ASE, vol. 10(2), pp. 203–232 (2003)
23. Visser, W., Păsăreanu, C.S., Khurshid, S.: Test input generation with Java PathFinder. In: ISSTA, pp. 97–107 (2004)
24. Weimer, W., Nguyen, T., Le Goues, C., Forrest, S.: Automatically finding patches using genetic programming. In: ICSE, pp. 364–374 (2009)
25. Nokhbeh Zaeem, R., Khurshid, S.: Contract-Based Data Structure Repair Using Alloy. In: D'Hondt, T. (ed.) ECOOP 2010. LNCS, vol. 6183, pp. 577–598. Springer, Heidelberg (2010)
26. Zaidman, A., Rompaey, B.V., van Deursen, A., Demeyer, S.: Studying the co-evolution of production and test code in open source and industrial developer test processes through repository mining. ESE 16(3), 325–364 (2011)
27. Zeller, A.: Automated debugging: Are we close? Computer 34, 26–31 (2001)

A   JPF-Based Test Generator

Fig. 4 shows an example test generator, which we use for generating singly-linked lists using Java PathFinder in our experiments (Section 5).

```
1 static void testGenerator() {
2   Verify.resetCounter(0); // test ID
3   final int SEQ_LENGTH = Verify.getInt(1, 4);
4   StringBuilder tc = new StringBuilder(); // test case
5   tc.append("    List l = new List();\n");
6   List l = new List();
7   for (int i = 0; i < SEQ_LENGTH; i++) {
8     int arg = Verify.getInt(0, 1);
9     if (Verify.getBoolean()) {
10      tc.append("    l.add(" + arg + ");\n");
11      l.add(arg);
12    } else {
13      tc.append("    l.remove(" + arg + ");\n");
14      l.remove(arg);
15    }
16  }
17  int expected = l.size();
18  tc.append("    assertEquals(" + expected + ", l.size());\n" + "}");
19  tc.insert(0, "@Test public void testcase" + Verify.getCounter(0) + "() {\n");
20  System.out.println(tc + "\n");
21  Verify.incrementCounter(0);
22 }
```

Fig. 4. JPF-based test generator. It generates tests that represent all possible sequences involving one to four method executions on a list l: l.add(0), l.add(1), l.remove(0), and l.remove(1). Line 3 non-deterministically chooses the length of the sequence between 1 to 4. The for-loop from line 7 to 16 non-deterministically chooses one of the four possible method executions. In addition to generating method sequences, JPF also runs them on the old program implementation (Lines 6, 11, 14, and 17) and computes the value of the expressions (l.size()) in assertion checks.

A "Hybrid" Approach for Synthesizing Optimal Controllers of Hybrid Systems: A Case Study of the Oil Pump Industrial Example

Hengjun Zhao[1,2], Naijun Zhan[2], Deepak Kapur[3], and Kim G. Larsen[4,*]

[1] State Key Lab. of Comput. Sci., Institute of Software, CAS, Beijing, China
[2] Graduate University of Chinese Academy of Sciences, Beijing, China
[3] Dept. of Comput. Sci., University of New Mexico, Albuquerque, NM, USA
[4] CISS, CS, Aalborg University, Denmark

Abstract. We propose an approach to reduce the optimal controller synthesis problem of hybrid systems to quantifier elimination; furthermore, we also show how to combine quantifier elimination with numerical computation in order to make it more scalable but at the same time, keep arising errors due to discretization manageable and within bounds. A major advantage of our approach is not only that it avoids errors due to numerical computation, but it also gives a better optimal controller. In order to illustrate our approach, we use the real industrial example of an oil pump provided by the German company HYDAC within the European project *Quasimodo* as a case study throughout this paper, and show that our method improves (up to 7.5%) the results reported in [4] based on game theory and model checking.

Keywords: Hybrid System, Optimal Control, Quantifier Elimination, Numerical Computation.

1 Introduction

Hybrid systems such as physical devices controlled by computer software, are systems that exhibit both continuous and discrete behaviors. Controller synthesis for hybrid systems is an important area of research in both academia and industry. A synthesis problem focuses on designing a controller that ensures the given system will satisfy a safety requirement, a liveness requirement (e.g. reachability to a given set of states), or meet an optimality criterion, or a desired combination of these requirements.

Numerous work have been done on controller synthesis for safety and/or reachability requirements. For example, in [1,28], a general framework for synthesizing controllers based on hybrid automata to meet a given safety requirement was proposed, which relies on *backward reachable set* computation and *fixed point*

* The first and second authors are supported by NSFC projects 91118007 and 60970031; the third author is supported by NSF CCF-0729097 and CNS-0905222; the fourth author is supported by The Danish VKR Center of Excellence MT-LAB and The Sino-Danish Basic Research Center IDEA4CPS.

D. Giannakopoulou and D. Méry (Eds.): FM 2012, LNCS 7436, pp. 471–485, 2012.

iteration; while in [25], a symbolic approach based on templates and constraint solving to the same problem was proposed, and in [26], the symbolic approach is extended to meet both safety and reachability requirements.

However, the optimal controller synthesis problem is more involved, also quite important in the design of hybrid systems. In the literature, few work has been done on the problem. Larsen et al proposed an approach based on energy automata and model-checking [4], while Jha, Seshia and Tiwari gave a solution to the problem using unconstrained numerical optimization and machine learning [15]. However, in [4], allowing control only to be exercised at discrete time points certainly limits the opportunity of synthesizing the optimal controller (though one can get arbitrarily close). Moreover, discretizing could cause an incorrect controller to be synthesized — which therefore requires a posterior analysis (e.g. in [4], PHAVER [10] is used for the purpose). The approach of [15] suffers from imprecision caused by numerical computation, and cannot synthesize a really optimal controller sometimes because the machine learning technique cannot guarantee its completeness.

In this paper, we propose a "hybrid" approach for synthesizing optimal controllers of hybrid systems subject to safety requirements. The basic idea is as follows. Firstly, we reduce optimal controller synthesis subject to safety requirements to quantifier elimination (QE for short). Secondly, in order to make our approach scalable, we discuss how to combine QE with numerical computation, but at the same time, keep arising errors due to discretization manageable and within bounds. A major advantage of our approach is not only that it avoids errors due to numerical computation, but also it gives a better optimal controller.

Application of QE in controller synthesis of hybrid systems is not new. The tool HyTech was the first symbolic model checker that can do parametric analysis [13] for linear hybrid automata, but for the oil pump example it will abort soon due to arithmetic overflow. Recently, verification and synthesis of switched dynamical systems using QE were discussed in [24], where the authors gave principles and heuristics for combining different tools, to solve QE problems that are out of the scope of each component tool.

Our encoding of a MIN-MAX-MIN optimization problem into a QE problem is inspired by the idea in [8]: minimizing a polynomial objective function $f(x_1, x_2, \ldots, x_n)$ can be done by introducing an additional constraint $z \geq f(x_1, x_2, \ldots, x_n)$ and then eliminating variables $x_1, x_2, \ldots, x_n$, where z is a newly introduced variable. Similar ideas can also be found in [5].

The computation of optimal control strategies in this paper is typically a *parametric optimization* problem, a topic researched extensively in both operation research and control communities. Symbolic methods have advantages in addressing parametric optimization problems [29,9,16]. However, we do not find any algorithm suitable for solving a parametric quadratic optimization problem over constraint with complex Boolean structure and hundreds of (or thousands of) atomic formulas as in this paper.

It was shown in [2] that for certain parametric quadratic optimization problems, the closed form solution exists: the optimizer is a piecewise affine function in the parameters, and the optimal value is a piecewise quadratic function in the parameters. Our experiment results confirm this.

In order to illustrate our approach, we use the oil pump industrial example provided by the German company HYDAC within the European project *Quasimodo* as a case study throughout this paper, and show that our method results in a better optimal controller (up to 7.5% improvement) than those reported in [4] based on game theory and model checking. Moreover, we prove that the theoretically optimal controller of the oil pump example can be synthesized and its correctness is also guaranteed with our approach.

Paper Organization: In Section 2 we propose a general framework for optimal controller synthesis of hybrid systems based on QE and numerical computation. We focus on the oil pump case study in Section 3-5: a description of the oil pump control problem is given in Section 3, modeling of the system and safety requirements is shown in Section 4, a "hybrid" approach for performing optimization is presented in Section 5, in which further improvement by increasing activation times of the pump is also discussed. We conclude this paper by Section 6.

2   The Overall Approach

In this section we propose an approach that reduces optimal controller synthesis of hybrid systems subject to safety requirements to QE. Reachable sets of hybrid systems are modeled exactly or approximated using polynomial formulas. Optimality criteria and safety requirements are also modeled in the same way. Existentially quantified formulas can be reduced to a finite set of disjunctions by discretizing the existentially quantified variables over bounded intervals, which often leads to scalability.

Generally, a hybrid system consists of a set of discrete operating modes Q, with each of which a continuous dynamics is associated, specifying the behavior of a set of continuous states $\mathbf{x}$. Discrete jumps between different modes may happen if some *transition conditions* are satisfied by $\mathbf{x}$.

The optimal controller synthesis problem studied in this paper can be stated as follows. Suppose we are given an under-specified hybrid system $\mathcal{H}$, in which the transition conditions are not determined but parameterized by $\mathbf{u}$, a vector of control parameters. Our task is to determine values of $\mathbf{u}$ such that $\mathcal{H}$ can make discrete jumps at desired points, thus guaranteeing that

1) a safety requirement $\mathcal{S}$ is satisfied, that is, $\mathbf{x}$ stays in a designated safe region at any time point; and
2) an optimization goal $\mathcal{G}$, possibly

$$\min_{\mathbf{u}} g(\mathbf{u}), \ \max_{\mathbf{u}_2}\min_{\mathbf{u}_1} g(\mathbf{u}), \text{ or } \min_{\mathbf{u}_3}\max_{\mathbf{u}_2}\min_{\mathbf{u}_1} g(\mathbf{u}),\,^1$$

where $g(\mathbf{u})$ is an objective function in parameters $\mathbf{u}$, is achieved.

---

[1] We assume that $\mathbf{u}$ is chosen from a compact (i.e. bounded closed) set, and the elements of $\mathbf{u}$ are divided into groups $\mathbf{u}_1, \mathbf{u}_2, \mathbf{u}_3, \ldots$ according to their roles in $\mathcal{G}$.

Our approach for solving the synthesis problem can be described as the following steps.

Step 1. *Derive constraint $D(\mathbf{u})$ on $\mathbf{u}$ from the safety requirements of the system.*

If the reachable set R (parameterized by $\mathbf{u}$) of $\mathcal{H}$ can be exactly computed (e.g. for very simple linear hybrid automata), then we just require that R should be contained in the safe region. Otherwise we have to approximate R (with sufficient precision) by automatically generating inductive invariants of $\mathcal{H}$ (e.g. for general linear or nonlinear hybrid systems). The notion of *inductive invariant* is crucial in safety verification of hybrid systems [11,22], and constraint-based approaches have been proposed for automatic generation of inductive invariants [23,11,21,17].

Step 2. *Encode the optimization problem $\mathcal{G}$ over constraint $D(\mathbf{u})$ into a quantified first-order formula $\mathbf{Qu}.\varphi(\mathbf{u}, z)$, where z is a fresh variable.*

Our encoding is based on the following proposition, in which we discuss all the aforementioned optimization functions together.

Proposition 1. *Suppose $g_1(\mathbf{u}_1)$, $g_2(\mathbf{u}_1, \mathbf{u}_2)$, $g_3(\mathbf{u}_1, \mathbf{u}_2, \mathbf{u}_3)$ are polynomials, and $D_1(\mathbf{u}_1)$, $D_2(\mathbf{u}_1, \mathbf{u}_2)$, $D_3(\mathbf{u}_1, \mathbf{u}_2, \mathbf{u}_3)$ are nonempty compact semi-algebraic sets[2]. Then there exist c_1, c_2, $c_3 \in \mathbb{R}$ s.t.*

$$\exists \mathbf{u}_1.(D_1 \wedge g_1 \leq z) \iff z \geq c_1, \tag{1}$$

$$\forall \mathbf{u}_2.\big(\exists \mathbf{u}_1.D_2 \longrightarrow \exists \mathbf{u}_1.(D_2 \wedge g_2 \leq z)\big) \iff z \geq c_2, \tag{2}$$

$$\exists \mathbf{u}_3.\big((\exists \mathbf{u}_1\mathbf{u}_2.D_3) \wedge \forall \mathbf{u}_2.(\exists \mathbf{u}_1.D_3 \longrightarrow \exists \mathbf{u}_1.(D_3 \wedge g_3 \leq z))\big) \iff z \rhd c_3, \tag{3}$$

where $\rhd \in \{>, \geq\}$, and c_1, c_2, c_3 satisfy

$$c_1 = \min_{\mathbf{u}_1} g_1(\mathbf{u}_1) \quad \text{over } D_1(\mathbf{u}_1), \tag{4}$$

$$c_2 = \sup_{\mathbf{u}_2} \min_{\mathbf{u}_1} g_2(\mathbf{u}_1, \mathbf{u}_2) \quad \text{over } D_2(\mathbf{u}_1, \mathbf{u}_2), \tag{5}$$

$$c_3 = \inf_{\mathbf{u}_3} \sup_{\mathbf{u}_2} \min_{\mathbf{u}_1} g_3(\mathbf{u}_1, \mathbf{u}_2, \mathbf{u}_3) \quad \text{over } D_3(\mathbf{u}_1, \mathbf{u}_2, \mathbf{u}_3). \tag{6}$$

We omit the proof of this proposition due to space limitation. All the proofs, as well as the formulas generated by QE, can be found in the full version [30] of the paper.

Step 3. *Eliminate quantifiers in $\mathbf{Qu}.\varphi(\mathbf{u}, z)$ and from the result we can retrieve the optimal value of $\mathcal{G}$ and the corresponding optimal controller $\mathbf{u}$.*

By Proposition 1, the optimal value of a MIN, MAX-MIN or MIN-MAX-MIN[3] problem can be obtained by applying QE to the left hand side (LHS) formulas in (1)-(3) respectively. Although QE for the first-order theory of real closed fields

---

[2] A semi-algebraic set is defined by Boolean combinations of polynomial equations and inequalities.

[3] By Proposition 1, the MIN (MAX) notation can really be INF (SUP) sometimes.

is a complete decision procedure [27], due to the inherent doubly exponential complexity [6], direct QE would fail on big formulas with many alternations of quantifiers, as in LHS of (3). It is then necessary to devise heuristics to do QE more efficiently for such special formulas.

Note that in (3), any instantiation of the outmost quantified variables $\mathbf{u}_3$ would result in a simpler formula, whose quantifier-free equivalence gives an upper bound of c_3. If in some way we know the bounds of $\mathbf{u}_3$, i.e. $l_i \leq \mathbf{u}_3^i \leq u_i$, for $1 \leq i \leq \dim(\mathbf{u}_3)$, then by discretizing $\mathbf{u}_3$ over all $[l_i, u_i]$ with certain granularity Δ, and using the set of discretized values to instantiate the outmost existential quantifiers of (3), we can get a finite set of simplified formulas, each of which produces an upper approximation of c_3. Finally, through an exhaustive search in this set we can select such an approximation that is closest to c_3. Finer granularity yields better approximation of the optimal value, so one can seek for a good balance between timing and optimality by tuning the granularity Δ. Furthermore, the above computation is well suited for parallelization to make full use of available computing resources, because the intervals $[l_i, u_i]$ and corresponding instantiations can be divided into subgroups and allocated to different processes.

3   Description of the Oil Pump Control Problem

The oil pump example [4] was a real industrial case provided by the German company HYDAC ELECTRONICS GMBH, and studied at length within the European research project *Quasimodo*. The whole system, depicted by Fig. 1, consists of a machine, an accumulator, a reservoir and a pump. The machine consumes oil periodically out of the accumulator with a period of $20s$ (second) for one consumption cycle. The profile of consumption rate is shown in Fig. 2. The pump adds oil from the reservoir into the accumulator with power $2.2l/s$ (liter/second).

Control objectives for this system are: by switching on/off the pump at certain time points

$$0 \leq t_1 \leq t_2 \leq \cdots \leq t_n \leq t_{n+1} \leq \cdots, \tag{7}$$

ensuring that

- R_s (*safety*): the system can run arbitrarily long while maintaining $v(t)$ within $[V_{\min}, V_{\max}]$ for any time point t, where $v(t)$ denotes the oil volume in the accumulator at time t, $V_{\min} = 4.9l$ (liter) and $V_{\max} = 25.1l$;

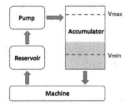

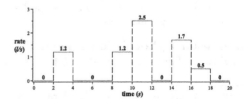

Fig. 1. The oil pump system. (This picture is based on [4].)

Fig. 2. Consumption rate of the machine in one cycle

and considering the energy cost and wear of the system, a second objective:

- R_o (*optimality*): minimizing the average accumulated oil volume in the limit, i.e. minimizing

$$\lim_{T \to \infty} \frac{1}{T} \int_{t=0}^{T} v(t)\mathrm{d}t \ .$$

Both objectives should be achieved under two additional constraints:

- R_{pl} (*pump latency*): there must be a latency of at least $2s$ between any two consecutive operations of the pump; and
- R_r (*robustness*): uncertainty of the system should be taken into account:
  - fluctuation of consumption rate (if it is not 0), up to $f = 0.1l/s$;
  - imprecision in the measurement of oil volume, up to $\epsilon = 0.06l$;
  - imprecision in the measurement of time, up to $\delta = 0.015s$.[4]

In [4], the authors used timed game automata to model the above system, and applied the tool UPPAAL-TIGA to synthesize near-optimal controllers. Due to discretization made in the timed-game model, an incorrect controller might be synthesized. Therefore the correctness and robustness of the synthesized controllers are checked using the tool PHAVER. Through simulations with SIMULINK, it was shown that the controller synthesized by UPPAAL-TIGA provides big improvement (about 40%) over the *Bang-Bang Controller* and *Smart Controller* that are currently used at the HYDAC company. We will show how further improvement can be achieved using our approach.

4   Deriving Constraints from Safety Requirements

Following [4], the determination of control points (7) can be localized by exploiting the periodicity of oil consumption. That is, decisions on when to switch on/off the pump in one cycle can be made *locally* by measuring the initial oil volume v_0 at the beginning of each cycle. Accordingly, the safety requirement R_s in Section 3 can be reformulated as: find an interval $[L, U] \subseteq [V_{\min}, V_{\max}]$ s.t.

- R_{lu} (*constraint for L, U*): for all $v_0 \in [L, U]$, there is a finite sequence of time points $\mathbf{t} = (t_1, t_2, \ldots, t_n)$,[5] where $0 \leq t_1 \leq t_2 \leq \ldots \leq t_n \leq 20$ satisfy R_{pl}, for turning on/off the pump so that the resulting $v(t)$ with $v(0) = v_0$ satisfies
  - R_i (*inductiveness*): $v(20) \in [L, U]$; and
  - R_{ls} (*local safety*): $v(t) \in [V_{\min}, V_{\max}]$ for all $t \in [0, 20]$
  under the constraint R_r.

Definition 1 (Local Controller). *The above $\mathbf{t}$ corresponding to v_0 is called a local controller; the interval $[L, U]$ is called a stable interval.*

---

[4] In [4], δ is assumed to be 0.01. Here we include an extra rounding error of 0.005 due to floating point calculations in the implementation of our control strategy.

[5] The choice of n will be made later (in this paper n can be $0, 2, 4, 6$), but larger n's obviously will have the potential of allowing improved controllers.

Basically, R_{lu} says that there is a stable interval $[L, U]$ and a corresponding family of local control strategies which can be repeated for arbitrarily many cycles and guarantee safety in each cycle.

Modeling Oil Consumption. Let $V_{out}(t)$ with $V_{out}(0) = 0$ denote the amount of oil consumed by time t in one cycle, and modify the consumption rate in Fig. 2 by f in (R_r). Then by simply integrating the lower and upper bounds of the consumption rate over the time interval $[0, 20]$ we can get

$$
C_1 \widehat{=} \begin{array}{l}
(0 \leq t \leq 2 \quad \longrightarrow \quad V_{out}=0) \\
\wedge (2 \leq t \leq 4 \quad \longrightarrow \quad 1.1(t-2) \leq V_{out} \leq 1.3(t-2)) \\
\wedge (4 \leq t \leq 8 \quad \longrightarrow \quad 2.2 \leq V_{out} \leq 2.6) \\
\wedge (8 \leq t \leq 10 \quad \longrightarrow \quad 2.2+1.1(t-8) \leq V_{out} \leq 2.6+1.3(t-8)) \\
\wedge (10 \leq t \leq 12 \quad \longrightarrow \quad 4.4+2.4(t-10) \leq V_{out} \leq 5.2+2.6(t-10)) \\
\wedge (12 \leq t \leq 14 \quad \longrightarrow \quad 9.2 \leq V_{out} \leq 10.4) \\
\wedge (14 \leq t \leq 16 \quad \longrightarrow \quad 9.2+1.6(t-14) \leq V_{out} \leq 10.4+1.8(t-14)) \\
\wedge (16 \leq t \leq 18 \quad \longrightarrow \quad 12.4+0.4(t-16) \leq V_{out} \leq 14+0.6(t-16)) \\
\wedge (18 \leq t \leq 20 \quad \longrightarrow \quad 13.2 \leq V_{out} \leq 15.2)
\end{array} \quad .[6]
$$

Actually, if the machine consuming oil is regarded as a hybrid system $\mathcal{H}$ with state variable V_{out} and continuous dynamics subject to *box* constraints, then C_1 is the exact *reachable set* of $\mathcal{H}$ from initial point $V_{out} = 0$ within 20 time units. Therefore we do not need to approximate the reachable set of $\mathcal{H}$ by generating inductive invariants. This is also the case with the following pump system. However, if the consumption profile is more complicated, say piecewise polynomial, then approximations are indeed necessary.

Modeling Pump. In [4] it is assumed that the number of activations of pump in one cycle is at most 2. We will adopt this assumption at first and increase this number later on. With this assumption, there will be at most four time points to switch the pump on/off in one cycle, denoted by $0 \leq t_1 \leq t_2 \leq t_3 \leq t_4 \leq 20$. If the pump is started only once or zero times, then we just set $t_3 = t_4 = 20$ or $t_1 = t_2 = t_3 = t_4 = 20$ respectively. Then the 2-second latency requirement (R_{pl}) can be modeled by

$$
C_2 \widehat{=} \begin{array}{l}
(t_1 \geq 2 \wedge t_2-t_1 \geq 2 \wedge t_3-t_2 \geq 2 \wedge t_4-t_3 \geq 2 \wedge t_4 \leq 20) \\
\vee (t_1 \geq 2 \wedge t_2-t_1 \geq 2 \wedge t_2 \leq 20 \wedge t_3=20 \wedge t_4=20) \\
\vee (t_1=20 \wedge t_2=20 \wedge t_3=20 \wedge t_4=20)
\end{array} \quad .
$$

Let $V_{in}(t)$ with $V_{in}(0) = 0$ denote the amount of oil introduced into the accumulator by time t in one cycle. Then we have

$$
C_3 \widehat{=} \begin{array}{l}
(0 \leq t \leq t_1 \quad \longrightarrow \quad V_{in}=0) \\
\wedge (t_1 \leq t \leq t_2 \quad \longrightarrow \quad V_{in}=2.2(t-t_1)) \\
\wedge (t_2 \leq t \leq t_3 \quad \longrightarrow \quad V_{in}=2.2(t_2-t_1)) \\
\wedge (t_3 \leq t \leq t_4 \quad \longrightarrow \quad V_{in}=2.2(t_2-t_1)+2.2(t-t_3)) \\
\wedge (t_4 \leq t \leq 20 \quad \longrightarrow \quad V_{in}=2.2(t_2+t_4-t_1-t_3))
\end{array} \quad .
$$

---

[6] In the sequel when a function $\gamma(t)$ appears in a formula, the argument t is dropped and γ is taken as a real-valued variable.

Encoding Safety Requirements. Denote the oil volume in the accumulator at the beginning of one cycle by v_0, and the volume at time t by $v(t)$. Then for any $0 \le t \le 20$ we have:

$$C_4 \widehat{=} v = v_0 + V_{in} - V_{out} .$$

According to (R_r), the measurement of t_i $(1 \le i \le 4)$ and v_0 may deviate from their actual values, so $v(t)$ will deviate from its predicted value as stated in the constraint C_4. Nevertheless, we have the following estimation of the deviation of $v(t)$.

Lemma 1. *Let $\tilde{v}(t)$ denote the actual oil volume in the accumulator at time t. Then for any $0 \le t \le 20$, $|v(t) - \tilde{v}(t)| \le 8.8\,\delta + \epsilon < 0.2$.*

Please refer to [30] for the proof of Lemma 1. By Lemma 1, it is sufficient to rectify the safety bounds in (R_i) and (R_{ls}) by an amount of 0.2. Let

$$C_5 \widehat{=} t = 20 \longrightarrow L + 0.2 \le v \le U - 0.2$$
$$C_6 \widehat{=} 0 \le t \le 20 \longrightarrow V_{\min} + 0.2 \le v \le V_{\max} - 0.2 .$$

Then (R_i) and (R_{ls}) can be expressed as

$$S \widehat{=} \forall t, v, V_{in}, V_{out}.(C_1 \wedge C_3 \wedge C_4 \longrightarrow C_5 \wedge C_6) .$$

Deriving Constraints. To find $[L, U]$ such that for every $v_0 \in [L, U]$ there is a local control strategy satisfying R_i and R_{ls}, let

$$C_7 \widehat{=} L \le v_0 \le U ,$$

and then R_{lu} can be encoded into

$$C_8 \widehat{=} \forall v_0.\Big(C_7 \longrightarrow \exists t_1 t_2 t_3 t_4.(C_2 \wedge S)\Big) .$$

We use the tool Mjollnir [19] to do QE on C_8 and the following result is returned:

$$C_9 \widehat{=} L \ge 5.1 \wedge U \le 24.9 \wedge U - L \ge 2.4 .$$

Then the relation between L, U, v_0 and the corresponding local control strategy $\mathbf{t} = (t_1, t_2, t_3, t_4)$ can be obtained by applying QE to

$$C_{10} \widehat{=} C_2 \wedge C_7 \wedge C_9 \wedge S.$$

The result given by Mjollnir, when converted to DNF, is a disjunction of 92 components:

$$\mathcal{D}(L, U, v_0, t_1, t_2, t_3, t_4) \widehat{=} \bigvee_{i=1}^{92} D_i$$

(denoted by $\mathcal{D}$ for short), with each D_i representing a nonempty closed convex polyhedron.[7]

---

[7] The fact that each D_i is a nonempty closed set can be checked using QE.

5   A "Hybrid" Approach for Optimization

5.1   Encoding of the Optimization Objective

By Definition 1, the optimal average accumulated oil volume in R_o can be redefined as

$$\bullet \; R'_o : \qquad \min_{[L,U]} \; \max_{v_0 \in [L,U]} \; \min_{\mathbf{t}} \; \frac{1}{20} \int_{t=0}^{20} v(t)\mathrm{d}t \; . \qquad (8)$$

The intuitive meaning of (R'_o) is:

- for each admissible $[L,U]$ satisfying C_9 and each $v_0 \in [L,U]$, minimize the average accumulated oil volume in one cycle, i.e. $\frac{1}{20}\int_{t=0}^{20} v(t)\mathrm{d}t$, over all admissible local controllers $\mathbf{t}$;
- fix $[L,U]$ and select the *worst* local minimum by traversing all $v_0 \in [L,U]$;
- then the global minimum is obtained at the interval whose worst local minimum is *minimal*.

Definition 2 (Local Optimal Controller). *Let* $\mathcal{D}_{\mathbf{t}} \stackrel{\frown}{=} \{\mathbf{t} \mid (L, U, v_0, \mathbf{t}) \in \mathcal{D}\}$ *for fixed* L, U, v_0. *Then we call*

$$\min_{\mathbf{t} \in \mathcal{D}_{\mathbf{t}}} \frac{1}{20} \int_{t=0}^{20} v(t)\mathrm{d}t$$

the local optimal average accumulated oil volume corresponding to L, U, v_0, *and the optimizer* $\mathbf{t}$ *is called the local optimal controller.*

Let $g(v_0, t_1, t_2, t_3, t_4) \stackrel{\frown}{=} \frac{1}{20}\int_{t=0}^{20} v(t)\mathrm{d}t$, denoted by g for short. It can be computed from C_1, C_3, C_4 without considering fluctuations of consumption rate that

$$g = \frac{20v_0 + 1.1(t_1^2 - t_2^2 + t_3^2 - t_4^2 - 40t_1 + 40t_2 - 40t_3 + 40t_4) - 132.2}{20} \; .$$

Then by Proposition 1, (R'_o) can be encoded into

$$\exists L, U. \Big(C_9 \wedge \forall v_0. \big(C_7 \longrightarrow \exists t_1 t_2 t_3 t_4. (\mathcal{D} \wedge g \le z) \big) \Big), \qquad (9)$$

which is equivalent to $z \ge z^*$ or $z > z^*$, where z^* equals the value of (8).

5.2   Techniques for Performing QE

The above deduced (9) is a nonlinear formula with hundreds of atomic formulas and two alternations of quantifiers, for which QE tools such as Redlog [7] or QEP-CAD [3] fail. Therefore we have developed specialized heuristics to decompose the QE problem into manageable parts.

Eliminating the Inner Quantifiers. We first eliminate the innermost quantified variables $\exists t_1 t_2 t_3 t_4$ by employing the theory of quadratic programming.

Note that D_i in $\mathcal{D}$ is a closed convex polyhedron for all i and g is a quadratic polynomial function, so minimization of g on D_i is a *quadratic programming* problem. Then the *Karush-Kuhn-Tucker* (KKT) [14] condition

$$\theta_{kkt} \cong \exists \boldsymbol{\mu}. \mathcal{L}(g, D_i), \tag{10}$$

where $\mathcal{L}(g, D_i)$ is a linear formula constructed from g and D_i, and $\boldsymbol{\mu}$ is a vector of new variables, gives a *necessary* condition for a local minimum of g on D_i.

By applying the KKT condition to each D_i and eliminating all $\boldsymbol{\mu}$, we can get a *necessary* condition $\mathcal{D}'$, a disjunction of 580 parts, for the minimum of g on $\mathcal{D}$:

$$\mathcal{D}' = \bigvee_{j=1}^{580} B_j .$$

Furthermore, each B_j has the nice property that for any L, U, v_0, a *unique* $\mathbf{t}_j$ is determined by B_j.[8] For instance, one of the B_j reads:

$$
\begin{aligned}
&t_4 = 20 \wedge 16t_2 + 10L - 349 = 0 \wedge \\
&t_2 - t_3 + 2 = 0 \wedge 22t_1 - 16t_2 - 10v_0 + 107 = 0 \wedge \cdots
\end{aligned} \tag{11}
$$

Since $\mathcal{D}'$ keeps the minimal value point of g on $\mathcal{D}$, the formula obtained by replacing $\mathcal{D}$ by $\mathcal{D}'$ in (9)

$$\exists L, U. \Big(C_9 \wedge \forall v_0. \big(C_7 \longrightarrow \exists t_1 t_2 t_3 t_4. (\mathcal{D}' \wedge g \leq z) \big) \Big) \tag{12}$$

is equivalent to (9). Then according to formulas like (11), $\exists t_1 t_2 t_3 t_4$ in (12) can be eliminated by the distribution of $\exists$ among disjunctions, followed by instantiations of $\mathbf{t}_j$ in each disjunct. Thus (12) can be converted to

$$\exists L, U. \Big(C_9 \wedge \forall v_0. \big(C_7 \longrightarrow \bigvee_{j=1}^{580} (A_j \wedge g_j \leq z) \big) \Big) , \tag{13}$$

where A_j is a constraint on L, U, v_0, and g_j is the instantiation of g using $\mathbf{t}_j$ given by formulas like (11).

Eliminating the Outer Quantifiers. We eliminate the outermost quantifiers $\exists L, U$ in (13) by discretization, as discussed in Section 2.

According to C_9, the interval $[5.1, 24.9]$ is discretized with a granularity of 0.1 (the same granularity adopted in [4]), which gives a set of 199 elements. Then assignments to L, U from this set satisfying C_9 are used to instantiate (13). There are totally 15400 such pairs of L, U, e.g. $(5.1, 7.5)$, $(5.1, 7.6)$ etc, and as many instantiations in the form of

$$\forall v_0. \big(C_7 \longrightarrow \bigvee_{j=1}^{580} (A_j \wedge g_j \leq z) \big) , \tag{14}$$

---

[8] This has been verified by QE.

each of which gives an optimal value corresponding to $[L, U]$. In practice, we start from $L = 5.1, U = 7.5$, and search for the minimal optimal value through all the 15400 cases with L or U incremented by 0.1 every iteration.

Eliminating the Middle Quantifier. We finally eliminate the only quantifier left in (14) by a divide-and-conquer strategy. First, we can show that

Lemma 2. $\bigvee_{j=1}^{580} A_j$ *is equivalent to* C_7 *in (14).*

By this lemma if all A_j are pairwise disjoint then (14) is equivalent to

$$\bigwedge_{j=1}^{580} \forall v_0. \left(v_0 \in A_j \longrightarrow (A_j \wedge g_j \leq z) \right). \tag{15}$$

Since each conjunct in (15) is a small formula with only two variables v_0, z and one universal quantifier, it can be dealt with quite efficiently.

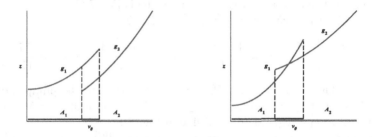

Fig. 3. Region partition

If the set of A_j's are not pairwise disjoint, then we have to partition them into disjoint regions and assign a new cost function g_k' to each region. The idea for performing such partition is simple, which is illustrated by Fig. 3.

Suppose two sets, say A_1, A_2, are chosen arbitrarily from the set of A_j's. If $A_1 \cap A_2 = \emptyset$, then we do nothing. Otherwise check wether $g_1 \leq g_2$ (or $g_2 \leq g_1$) on $A_1 \cap A_2$: if so, assign the smaller one, i.e. $g_1 \leq z$ (or $g_2 \leq z$) to $A_1 \cap A_2$; otherwise we simply assign $(g_1 \leq z) \vee (g_2 \leq z)$ to $A_1 \cap A_2$.

If at the same time of partitioning regions we also make a record of the local control strategy in each region, i.e. $\mathbf{t}_j$, then in the end we can get exactly the family of local optimal controllers corresponding to each v_0.

5.3   Results of QE

Various tools are available for doing QE. In our implementation, the SMT-based tool Mjollnir [20,19] is chosen for QE on linear formulas, while REDLOG [7] implementing *virtual substitution* [18] is chosen for formulas with nonlinear terms.

The computer algebra system REDUCE [12], of which REDLOG is an integral part, allows us to perform some programming tasks, e.g. region partition. Table 1 shows the performance of our approach. All experiments are done on a desktop running Linux with a 2.66 GHz CPU and 3 GB memory.

Table 1. Timing of different QE tasks

formula	C_8	C_{10}	θ_{kkt} (all 92)	all the rest
tool	Mjollnir	Mjollnir	Mjollnir	Redlog/Reduce
time	8m8s	4m13s	31s	<1s

Remark. In Table 1, timing is in minutes (m) and seconds (s); in the last column, the time taken to get the first optimal value[9] is less than 1 second, whereas all 15400 iterations will cost more than 10 hours (using a single computing process). The final results are as follows:

- The interval that produces the optimal value is $[5.1, 7.5]$.
- The local optimal controller for $v_0 \in [5.1, 7.5]$ is

$$t_1 = \frac{10v_0 - 25}{13} \wedge t_2 = \frac{10v_0 + 1}{13} \wedge t_3 = \frac{10v_0 + 153}{22} \wedge t_4 = \frac{157}{11} , \quad (16)$$

which is illustrated by Fig. 4. If $v_0 = 6.5$, then by (16) the pump should be switched on at $t_1 = 40/13$, off at $t_2 = 66/13$, then on at $t_3 = 109/11$, and finally off at $t_4 = 157/11$ (dashed line in Fig. 4).
- The optimal average accumulated oil volume $\frac{215273}{28600} = 7.53$ is obtained (dashed line in Fig. 5), improving by 5% the optimal value 7.95 in [4], which is already a 40% improvement of the controllers from the HYDAC company. The local optimal average accumulated oil volume for $v_0 \in [5.1, 7.5]$ under controller (16), i.e. $V_{aav}(v_0) = \frac{1300v_0^2 + 20420v_0 + 634817}{114400}$, is illustrated by Fig. 5.

5.4   Improvement by Increasing Activation Times

In the controller shown by Fig. 4, we noticed that when v_0 is small and the pump is started on for the second time, it stays on for a period longer than 4 seconds. Based on this observation, we conjectured that if the pump is allowed to be activated three times in one cycle, then each time it could stay on for a shorter period, and the time it is activated for the third time can be postponed. As a result, the accumulated oil volume in one cycle may become less.

To verify the above conjecture, some modifications must be made on the previous model. Firstly, C_2 and C_3 should be replaced by their counterparts with 3 activations respectively; secondly, in C_5 and C_6 the tolerance of noises

---

[9] For the model with 2 activations, this optimal value is only obtained at the 1st iteration, using interval [5.1,7.5].

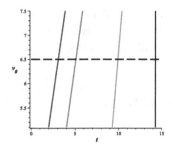

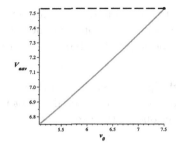

Fig. 4. Optimal controller   **Fig. 5.** Local optimal value for $v_0 \in [5.1, 7.5]$

should be increased to 0.3, because due to the increase of times to operate the pump, the maximal uncertainty caused by imprecision in the measurement of volume and time is now $13.2\delta + \epsilon < 0.3$; thirdly, the objective function g should be recomputed.

For this model, using interval $[5.2, 8.1]$, the optimal average accumulated oil volume $6613/900 = 7.35$ is obtained, which is a 7.5% improvement over the optimum 7.95 in [4]. The explicit form of local optimal controllers like (16) can be found in [30].

Furthermore, the following theorem indicates that the theoretically optimal controller can be obtained using the local control strategy with 3 activations.

Theorem 1. *For each admissible $[L, U]$, each $v_0 \in [L, U]$, and any local control strategy s_4 with at least 4 activations subject to R_{lu}, R_i and R_{ls}, there exists a local control strategy s_3 subject to R_{lu}, R_i and R_{ls} with 3 activations such that $\frac{1}{20} \int_{t=0}^{20} v_{s_3}(t)dt < \frac{1}{20} \int_{t=0}^{20} v_{s_4}(t)dt$, where $v_{s_3}(t)$ (resp. $v_{s_4}(t)$) is the oil volume in the accumulator at t with s_3 (resp. s_4).*

6   Concluding Remarks

We propose a "hybrid" approach for synthesizing optimal controllers of hybrid systems subject to safety requirements by first reducing the problem to QE and then combining symbolic computation and numerical computation for scalability. We illustrate our approach using a real industrial case of an oil pump provided by the HYDAC company.

Compared to the related work, e.g. [4], our approach has the following advantages. 1) Using first-order real arithmetic formulas to model the system, safety requirements as well as optimality objectives uniformly and succinctly, synthesis, verification and optimization are integrated into one elegant framework. The synthesized controllers are guaranteed to be correct. 2) By combining symbolic and numerical computation, we can obtain both high precision and efficiency: for the oil pump example, our approach can synthesize a better optimal controller (up to 7.5% improvement of [4]) in a reasonable amount of time (see Table 1). By Theorem 1, the synthesized controller is even theoretically optimal.

The issues of evaluation and implementation of our controllers are being considered. To make our approach more general with symbolic and numerical components, and apply it to more examples in practice will be our future work.

Acknowledgements. Special thanks go to Mr. Quan Zhao for his kind help in writing an interface between different QE tools, and to Dr. David Monniaux for his instructions on the use of the tool Mjollnir.

References

1. Asarin, E., Bournez, O., Dang, T., Maler, O., Pnueli, A.: Effective synthesis of switching controllers for linear systems. Proc. of the IEEE 88(7), 1011–1025 (2000)
2. Bemporad, A., Morari, M., Dua, V., Pistikopoulos, E.N.: The explicit linear quadratic regulator for constrained systems. Automatica 38(1), 3–20 (2002)
3. Brown, C.W.: QEPCAD B: A program for computing with semi-algebraic sets using CADs. SIGSAM Bulletin 37, 97–108 (2003)
4. Cassez, F., Jessen, J.J., Larsen, K.G., Raskin, J.-F., Reynier, P.-A.: Automatic Synthesis of Robust and Optimal Controllers – An Industrial Case Study. In: Majumdar, R., Tabuada, P. (eds.) HSCC 2009. LNCS, vol. 5469, pp. 90–104. Springer, Heidelberg (2009)
5. Chatterjee, K., de Alfaro, L., Majumdar, R., Raman, V.: Algorithms for game metrics (full version). Logical Methods in Computer Science 6(3) (2010), http://arxiv.org/abs/0809.4326
6. Davenport, J.H., Heintz, J.: Real quantifier elimination is doubly exponential. J. Symb. Comput. 5(1-2), 29–35 (1988)
7. Dolzmann, A., Seidl, A., Sturm, T.: Redlog User Manual, 3.1 edition for redlog Version 3.06 (reduce 3.8) (November 2006), http://redlog.dolzmann.de/downloads/
8. Dolzmann, A., Sturm, T., Weispfenning, V.: Real Quantifier Elimination in Practice. In: Algorithmic Algebra and Number Theory, pp. 221–247. Springer, Heidelberg (1998)
9. Fotiou, I.A., Rostalski, P., Parrilo, P.A., Morari, M.: Parametric optimization and optimal control using algebraic geometry methods. International Journal of Control 79(11), 1340–1358 (2006)
10. Frehse, G.: PHAVer: algorithmic verification of hybrid systems past HyTech. Int. J. Softw. Tools Technol. Transf. 10(3), 263–279 (2008)
11. Gulwani, S., Tiwari, A.: Constraint-based approach for analysis of hybrid systems. In: Gupta, A., Malik, S. (eds.) CAV 2008. LNCS, vol. 5123, pp. 190–203. Springer, Heidelberg (2008)
12. Hearn, A.C.: Reduce User's Manual (February 2004), http://reduce-algebra.com/docs/reduce.pdf, version 3.8
13. Henzinger, T., Ho, P.H., Wong-Toi, H.: HyTech: A Model Checker for Hybrid Systems. In: Grumberg, O. (ed.) CAV 1997. LNCS, vol. 1254, pp. 460–463. Springer, Heidelberg (1997)
14. Jensen, P.A., Bard, J.F.: Operations Research Models and Methods. John Wiley & Sons (October 2002)
15. Jha, S., Seshia, S.A., Tiwari, A.: Synthesis of optimal switching logic for hybrid systems. In: EMSOFT 2011, pp. 107–116. ACM, New York (2011)

16. Kanno, M., Yokoyama, K., Anai, H., Hara, S.: Symbolic optimization of algebraic functions. In: ISSAC 2008, pp. 147–154. ACM, New York (2008)
17. Liu, J., Zhan, N., Zhao, H.: Computing semi-algebraic invariants for polynomial dynamical systems. In: EMSOFT 2011, pp. 97–106. ACM, New York (2011)
18. Loos, R., Weispfenning, V.: Applying linear quantifier elimination. The Computer Journal 36(5), 450–462 (1993)
19. Monniaux, D.: Mjollnir-2009-07-10,
    http://www-verimag.imag.fr/~monniaux/mjollnir.html
20. Monniaux, D.: A Quantifier Elimination Algorithm for Linear Real Arithmetic. In: Cervesato, I., Veith, H., Voronkov, A. (eds.) LPAR 2008. LNCS (LNAI), vol. 5330, pp. 243–257. Springer, Heidelberg (2008)
21. Platzer, A., Clarke, E.M.: Computing Differential Invariants of Hybrid Systems as Fixedpoints. In: Gupta, A., Malik, S. (eds.) CAV 2008. LNCS, vol. 5123, pp. 176–189. Springer, Heidelberg (2008)
22. Platzer, A., Clarke, E.M.: Formal Verification of Curved Flight Collision Avoidance Maneuvers: A Case Study. In: Cavalcanti, A., Dams, D.R. (eds.) FM 2009. LNCS, vol. 5850, pp. 547–562. Springer, Heidelberg (2009)
23. Sankaranarayanan, S., Sipma, H.B., Manna, Z.: Constructing Invariants for Hybrid Systems. In: Alur, R., Pappas, G.J. (eds.) HSCC 2004. LNCS, vol. 2993, pp. 539–554. Springer, Heidelberg (2004)
24. Sturm, T., Tiwari, A.: Verification and synthesis using real quantifier elimination. In: ISSAC 2011, pp. 329–336. ACM, New York (2011)
25. Taly, A., Gulwani, S., Tiwari, A.: Synthesizing Switching Logic Using Constraint Solving. In: Jones, N.D., Müller-Olm, M. (eds.) VMCAI 2009. LNCS, vol. 5403, pp. 305–319. Springer, Heidelberg (2009)
26. Taly, A., Tiwari, A.: Switching logic synthesis for reachability. In: EMSOFT 2010, pp. 19–28. ACM, New York (2010)
27. Tarski, A.: A Decision Method for Elementary Algebra and Geometry. University of California Press, Berkeley (1951)
28. Tomlin, C.J., Lygeros, J., Sastry, S.S.: A game theoretic approach to controller design for hybrid systems. Proc. of the IEEE 88(7), 949–970 (2000)
29. Weispfenning, V.: Parametric linear and quadratic optimization by elimination. Tech. rep., Fakultät für Mathematik und Informatik, Universität Passau (1994)
30. Zhao, H., Zhan, N., Kapur, D., Larsen, K.G.: A "hybrid" approach for synthesizing optimal controllers of hybrid systems: A case study of the oil pump industrial example. CoRR abs/1203.6025 (2012), http://arxiv.org/abs/1203.6025

Author Index